MALTBY -MALTBIE

FAMILY HISTORY

MALTBY -MALTBIE

FAMILY HISTORY

Compiled and Edited

BY

DOROTHY MALTBY VERRILL

KALPAZ

ISBN: 978-93-5128-603-5

First Published in 1916
Indian Reprint in 2017

Published by

Kalpaz Publications
C-30, Satyawati Nagar,
Delhi – 110052
E-mail: kalpaz@hotmail.com
Website: kalpazpublications.com
Ph.: +91-9212142040

Cataloging in Publication Data—DK
Courtesy: D.K. Agencies (P) Ltd. <docinfo@dkagencies.com>

Maltby -Maltbie family history / compiled and edited by Dorothy Maltby Verrill.
pages cm
"First published in 1916"—Title page verso.
ISBN 9789351286035

1. Maltby family. I. Verrill, Dorothy Maltby, 1877-1957, editor.

CS71.M26M35 2017 DDC 929.20973 23

INTRODUCTION

The following pages are the printed records and results of years of painstaking and conscientious work on the part of the author and genealogist, Mrs. Clarence E. Verrill. (See portrait on page 149.)

Few of the readers will appreciate the enormous amount of work required in compiling such information. It is probable that each entry of a line of descent has required at least one personal letter and often many more. The answers to these letters have required checking, further correspondence and final compilation to bring all into the completed and correct tabulation.

All this work has been done by Mrs. Verrill without hope of compensation and at great expense of time, money and vital energy. In fact, a great deal of this work has been done on a sick bed in order to make the publication of the book possible at this time.

Too much credit cannot be given to Mrs. Verrill by the members of the Maltby family and readers of this book for her untiring efforts to bring to a successful completion the records contained herein and.

In behalf of the Maltby family the undersigned wishes to express to Mrs. Verrill his heart-felt appreciation of these years of labor which, though it has been a labor of love, has been none the less arduous.

We also wish to express our appreciation of the generosity and kindness of Mr. B. L. Maltbie, who undertakes the publication of this volume at his own expense and without the hope of ever receiving more than a partial reimbursement of the cost to him.

He has made available the results of the long years of Mrs. Verrill's labor.

Our best wishes and many thanks to both of them.

F. B. MALTBY, *President.*

THE MALTBY ASSOCIATION
611 Chestnut St.,
Philadelphia, Pa.
May 23d, 1916.

PREFACE

It was not the intention of the compiler to write a preface to this book, but upon going over the proof sheets those things I have done, and those left undone, seem very patent. But "what is writ is writ, would that it were worthier."

The records here given to the public are the result of many years of genealogical research work and many of the records are mere fragments which refused to fit in gracefully in any place, but have been included with the hope that they may sometime prove helpful in tracing ancestors.

This work has been carried on far from reference libraries and under adverse conditions, but I have endeavored to give the reference to the source from which every record was taken. There are undoubtedly mistakes, but every effort has been made to keep these down to as few as possible, and it is to be hoped that where errors are discovered it will be called to my attention.

I am indebted to many people for data furnished and wherever possible I have tried to give credit where it was due for material copied from other publications or kindly contributed by individuals —to all of these I am heartily grateful.

It is the sincere wish of the compiler that the records contained in these pages may prove interesting to those who descend from the Maltbys and also helpful to any who seek further information of their ancestors.

DOROTHY MALTBY VERRILL.

CONTENTS

PART ONE

PART TWO

ILLUSTRATIONS

HERALDRY

MALTBY ARMS

During years of genealogical research various references to Maltby Arms have been found, copied and preserved until quite an interesting little collection has been made.

Heraldry is a science in itself, and requires an expert to give accurate explanations, and this article is written by one at the very bottom of the Heraldic ladder, but a word as to the early use of Arms will help toward understanding some of the material which follows.

Rolls of arms are extant in England in the reigns of Henry III. [1216-1272]; Edward I. [1272-1307], and Edward II. [1307-1327].

The Roll of Caerlaverock contains the names and armorial bearings of the knights and barons who attended Edward I. at the siege of the Castle of Caerlaverock, Dumfriesshire, in 1300, and exhibits heraldry already in a developed form.

The use of arms by private persons was prohibited by proclamation in the reign of Henry V. All persons who had not borne arms at Agincourt were prohibited from assuming them unless by hereditary descent or with the sanction of the constituted authorities. Periodical circuits, called visitations, were held afterward by the provincial heralds to take cognizance of the arms, pedigrees and marriages of such as were entitled to the use of armorial bearings. These visitations continued till about the end of the 17th century. The evidence of these records are much sought to establish hereditary right to bear arms. It will be noticed that many of the arms here described are from various visitations.

The earliest Maltby coat-of-arms, so far as has yet been ascertained is that of Sire John Malebis in 1097. The extract is taken from "The Genealogist," New Series, 1896, p. 281. The Parliamentary Roll of Arms:

1097. SIRE JOHN MALEBIS—de argent a iij testes de bis de goul (Vide Yorkshire Parish Reg. Vol I and II). A rough translation of the above I make: "argent, three heads of hinds gules." The above seems to have been a near relative of Hugo de Malebisse, see Pedigree No. I.

The next mention of Maltby arms seems to be in 1339. In the Encyclopedia Britannica, Vol. XI, pp. 686-7 will be found the following: "As the combinations out of which the early coats were formed were limited; it occasionally happened that two persons of the same nation bore the same arms and this gave rise to disputes which, as matters connected with military discipline, came under the jurisdiction of the earl marshall . . . cases . . . were decided between Harding and St. Loo in 1312; Warburton and Gorges in 1321, and Sytsylt and Falsenham in 1333. Hugh Maltby and Harmon Beckwith had a similar dispute in 1339." Another item referring to the same case appears in The Genealogist, in an article "The Right to Bear Arms" by "X," as follows: "The Court of Chivalry (Curia Militaris) sat in 1339 to enquire into a mandate dated 18 Jan., 1339, against Harmon Beckwith by Hugh Lord Maltby, who alleged that Beckwith had assumed his arms. Beckwith proved his right to the satisfaction of the court 14 Oct., 1339." (See Pedigree No. I for Hugh Maltby and Harmon Beckwith).

It was not, however, chance that caused Harmon Beckwith to adopt the Maltby arms. His great grandfather was Sir Hercules Malebisse (Latin form of Maltby) who changed his name to Beckwith on his marriage in 1226 with Lady Dame Beckwith Bruce. Their son, Sir Hercules Beckwith, had a son Nicholas, and it was Harmon, the son of this Nicholas who had the dispute with Hugh Maltby. If one will consult Pedigree No. I it will be seen that William (9) de Malebisse, 1339, died in 1365, and here, with his son, Sir Thomas (10), this line died out. This does not mean that the family died out; simply the failure of male issue of the oldest son. It is very probable, indeed practically certain, that the above Hugh Maltby was nearly related to William (9), probably his uncle. It is rather an odd coincidence that Elizabeth (11) Maltby, daughter and co-heiress of Sir Thomas (10) Maltby married for her second husband, Adam Beckwith of Clint, a great-grandson of Harmon Beckwith, who had the dispute concerning the Maltby arms. It must be borne in mind in the following pages that the Beckwiths are by birth Maltbys and the Beckwith blood is through a maternal ancestress.

Burke's Gen. Armory and Rietstaps Ar. Gen. give: Beckwith. Arms of; Arg. a chev. betw. 3 hinds heads erased gules. Crest: An antelope ppr. in the mouth a branch vert. Motto: Joie en bien." *

Burke also gives: Malbech, Malbesh, Malbish, (Latin form of Maltby) Gu. a chev. or., between 3 hinds heads erased or. Compare these arms with the above Beckwith arms.

* Note the similarity with the arms of Sire John Malebis in 1097. It is very probable that he was an older brother of Hugo (1), Pedigree No. I, and failing male issue his coat of arms was used by the descendants of Hugo (1).

Another item from Burke's Gen. Arm is: Malbys: Ar. a chevron between 3 hinds heads erased gules.

Glover's Visitation of Yorkshire, 1612, edited by Joseph Foster, gives: Beckwith: Arg. a chev between 3 hinds heads.

By consulting Pedigree No. I it will be seen that Margaret Maltby (9) sister of William de Malebisse, married Thomas Fairfax. This will explain the following records:

FAIRFAX (p. 39, Glover's Vist. of Yorks., 1612, edited by Joseph Foster) of Walton and Gilling; one quartering is given as Arg. a chev. between 3 foxes' heads erased gules, for Malbys.

FAIRFAX (p. 96). The same, of Denton, Strelton and Streethorpe.

FAIRFAX (p. 24). In the church of Bolton Percy* you find the arms of Fairfax: Arg. a chev. sa. between 3 hinds' heads, crased gules (sa.)* Also: Arg. a chev. between 3 hinds' heads erased gules for Malbys.

NOTE.—Probably this is an error as to the foxes' heads being *quartered*, as the arms of Malbys. Evidently the arms of Malbys were hinds' heads, which Beckwith adopted and which the Fairfaxes also used after the marriage with Margaret Maltby. The arms of Fairfax as given by Burke's Gen. Armory are: Arg. 3 bars genelles gules, surmounted by a lion rampant, sab.

Burke's Gen. Arm. gives: Malbys as, Arg. a chev. betw. 3 hinds' heads, erased gules.

Burke's Gen. Arm. gives: Malbys: Gules a chev. betw. 3 hinds' heads, erased arg., for Malbech, Malbesh, Malbish.

Maltby and Molzbi, Malbie, Malbysse. Vide Doomsday Book. Burke's Gen. Arm. states: "The Beckwith family of Yorkshire is a very ancient one, which originally bore the name of Malbie or Malbysse, derived from Nicholas Beckwith, son of Hercules de Malbie, by Beckwith, his wife, one of the daughters of Sir William Bruce, Lord of Uglebarby; Sir Roger Beckwith of Aldborough created a baronet, 1681; title extinct in 1741."

Robson's British Herald, pub. 1830, Vol. 2, gives: Malbech, Malbesh or Malbish: gu. a chev. or. betw. 3 hinds' heads, erased or. Also Mawdeby, azure, a cross or.

Burke gives: Malbise: Ar. a chev. betw. 2 closets gu.

In the windows of the York Cathedral in a side aisle of the north part of the transept are these arms: Azure a chevron engrailed with 3 hinds' heads, erased or. Malbyss. (Vide p. 532, "Ebor.")

Since writing the above notes an item proving the theory of the Beckwith arms being hereditary from those of Sir John Male-

* See under date 1668.

bisse, has come to light. The Genealogist, 1888-89, Vol V, has this item: "There is a dead in Betham's Baronetage (Vol. II, app. p. 607) proving the right of Harmon Beckwith, Esq., to the coat armour of John Lord Malebisse" (1339).

From the above notes it is quite clearly shown that the oldest Maltby coat-of-arms is that blazoned with the hinds' heads, and the oldest branch of the family is quite evidently the Yorkshire branch shown in Pedigree No. I.

The next mention found of Maltby arms is in 1373. "Introduction to the Book of Arms" has the following: "All the shields commemorate the descent and alliances of the Pastons and their kinsfolk the Barreys and Mawtebys. . . ."

Margaret, daughter and heiress of John Mawteby, Esquire, the wife of John Paston, about 1440, made her will, 4 February, 1481-2, and thereby directed that many of the shields in this MS. should grace her tomb.

Four scutcheons were to be at the corners of her gravestone, "whereof the first scochen shall be of my husbandes armes and myn departed the ii qte. of Mawtebys arms and Berneys of Redham departed, the iij qte. of Mawtebys arms and Sir Roger Beauchamp departed. And in myddis of seid stoon I will have a scochen sett of Mawtebys' arms alone."

Further impalements are: Mawteby impaled with gules, a fesse and six martlets or., for Beauchamp, Lord of Powilse. Mawteby impaled with gules, billety or and a fess argent for Loveyn (Vide. "The Ancestor," No. 10, pp. 87-9.)

The arms of the family of Mautby [Norfolk] are given in several places in Bloomfield's Hist. of Norfolk as: Azure, a cross or. But in Vol. VIII, p. 407 of Bloomfield they are stated to be: azure, a cross formee or.; and this is the description given in the Visitation of Norfolk. The latter is probably the correct description. (Vide. Bloomfield's, Norfolk, Vol. X, pp. 69-70; Vol. VI, p. 494; Vol. XI, p. 182; Vol. VII, p. 467; Visitation of Norfolk, Edit. by Walter Rye, pp. 64-214). Following are given various records pertaining to the Norfolk branch of the family: (See also Pedigree No. IV.)

Malby (Co. Norfolk) Azure,,a cross formee or.

Mautby (Co. Norfolk, 1373) Az. a cross or.

Malby (Norfolk) Az. a cross formee, coupe, or. (Vide Berry Encylop. Heraldic., and also Burke.)

The Norfolk Maltbys held the Manor of Maltby, Co. Norfolk, from the Crown, prior to 1166. Arms: a cross or. (Vide. Bloomfield Hist. Norf. Vol. X., pp. 69-70; Bloomfield Hist. Norf., Vol. VI., p. 494; Bloomfield Hist. Norf., Vol. XI., p. 182.)

Burke gives arms of Mautebey and Mawedby as Azure, a cross or.

Bloomfield, Vol. VIII., states that " the arms of Paston Mautby, etc., appear in the north window of Gresham Church." (p. 129) "In Oxstraband Church appeared in a window the arms of Mautby-Berney." (p. 146).

The "Herald. and Gen.," Vol. 4, has the following: "On a tomb in Newton Chapel, Bristol Cathedral, is a large escutcheon of 24 quarterings, No. 24 being Azure a cross pattee throughout or. Maultby.

Friar Brackley's Book of Arms, cir. 1440 has: Mawteby: Argent, a chief indented or. (Paston) impaled with azure, a cross or. (Mawteby).

In Vol. XI., of Bloomfield we find: "In the Church of Bacton appear on the steeple window the arms of Paston and Mautby;" (p. 21.) and, "Mautby arms are in the church at Reedham;" (p. 132.) also, "In the Church of St. Peter at Repps, are to be seen the arms of Mautby, az. a cross or." (p. 182.) In Vol VI. we find the following: "The family house of Paston was in Manor Oxmead, Norfolk." In the hall windows were:

ARMS OF MAUTBY

Arms of Mautby and Berney (John Maltby m. Margery Berney.) [Berney quart. az. and gu. a cross engrailed ermine.]

Arms of Mautby impaling Loveine [gu. a fess betw. 14 billets.]

Arms of Mautby impaling Marshall [gu. a bend lozengy or.]

Arms of Mautby impaling Beauchamp [gu. a fess betw. 6 martlets or.]

Arms of Mautby impaling Clifton [Chequer or. and gu., a bend ermine.] (p. 492.)

In the Church of St. Nicholas, Oxnead, a Paston coat-of-arms is to be seen (1597) the 6th quartering being: Azure a cross or. for Mautby (p. 494.)

In Vol. VI. we find: "In the Church of the Virgin or St. Margaret at Calthorpe, Norfolk, in the upper window of the north side appeared with inter . . . the arms of Mautby." (p. 521.)

The arms which follow are quite different from the above and probably belong to a cadet branch of the Norfolk family:

MAWBEY (Mawtby) Co. Norfolk. Or. a cross gules fretty of the field between four eagles displayed azure, each charged on the breast with a bezant.

MAUBEY (Botleys, Co. Surrey, Bart.) Same arms as above. Crest: an eagle displayed azure charged on the breast with a bezant.

MAWBEY (Kemmington, Co. Surrey, granted 1757). Or. a cross gules, fretty of the field. Same as above.

Fairbairn's Book of Crests gives: "Mawby and Mawbrey of Kemmington, Surrey, an eagle displayed azure, charged on the breast with a bezant." Also. Mawbey, Bart. (extinct) of Botleys, Surrey, same crest. Auriga virtutum prudentia. (Vide p. 381, Fairbairn's Crests.) Thomas Robson gives them as also of Vauxhall. Created a baronet, 30 July, 1765.

The British Herald or Cabinet of Armorial Bearings of the Nobility and Gentry of Great Britain and Ireland, from the earliest to the present time, by Thomas Robson, published in 1830, Vol. II. gives the following: Malby [Norfolk] azure a cross formee, coupee, or. Mautby: Az. a cross or.

NOTE.—The arms granted in 1757 were evidently to Sir Joseph Mawbey, b. 1730, see Pedigree No. IV., Joseph (21), and the arms granted in 1765 were probably to his son Joseph (22). For the lineage of Maubey of Botleys, Surrey, consult Burke's English and Dormant Baronetcies. For the union of Paston with Maulby or Mawtby or Mauteby see Paston's General Visitation of Norfolk, 1563, 1589, 1613.

The History of Norfolk gives this item: "There were also in this window, Cat impaling Mawtby." (This was, I believe, in 1462.)

The third Maltby arms to be considered are those of the Maltbys of Cleveland, York. (See Pedigree No. II). The first date found by the compiler connected with these arms is in 1599 and is in The Genealogist, Vol. XXI., p. 120 (Add M.S. 12,225). It reads: Grant of Arms. Maltby . . . of Maltby in Cleveland, Co. York. Patent by Sir W. Segar, Garter (Norry in 1599). Arms: Argent, on a bend Gules, three garbs Or. Crest: A Garb Or, banded *sable*.

If this item is correctly given in The Genealogist it would seem very evident that this was not the first grant to the family, as the original crest was very evidently the garb (sheaf of wheat) banded gules. By consulting Pedigree No. II it will be seen that Christopher Maltby (15), Alderman of York, was born in 1574 and had a daughter Catherine, born in 1599—the year the above arms were granted. The fact that Sir Nicholas Malby was using the wheat sheaves on his arms (with cotises introduced for a difference) in 1576, when he was knighted, would tend to prove that the original Yorkshire arms were much older than 1599.

The following are different references to the arms of this branch of the family:

Parson's Cleveland, York Co.: Maltby, Ar. on a bend gules, 3 garbs or. Crest: Garb.

Edmondson's Heraldry. Fairbairn's Crests, p. 372. Maltby of Maltby, Cleveland, York, a garb or. banded gules. Maltby or Malby: Ar. on a bend gu. 3 garbs or.

Edmondson and Glover assign to Maltby of Maltby in Cleveland, Yorks, Arg. on a bend, 3 garbs or. Glover assigning a crest: Argent, a garb or. banded gules.

Burke's Gen. Armory: Maltby, Cleveland, Co. York, Ar. on a bend gules, 3 garbs or. Crest: a garb or. banded gules (a barley sheaf). Malby arms, same as Maltby (p. 372, Fairbairn's Crests). Crest: an Indian goat passant.

Fairbairn's Crests of England and Ireland (p. 372): Maltby (Essex): Crest, a barley sheaf erect and banded or. Pendant therefrom a bugle horn or.

Note.—This is the crest used by the Maltbys descended from Christopher Maltby of North Allerton. (See Pedigree XIV.) The bugle horn is for a Pennycuick marriage.*

* Since the above was written we have received a copy of the Grant of Arms to Thomas Maltby of Northallerton. (See Pedigree XIV.) The bugle horn is from the Foxton family and not the Pennycuicks.

From Burke's Gen. Arm., 1884 Edit.:

MALBY (Sir Nicholas, Chief Com. of Connaught, knighted at Athlone by Sir Henry Sydney, Lord Dept. of Ireland, 7 Oct., 1576.) Argent on a bend between two cotises gules three garbs or.

NOTE.—This is practically the arms as used by Elizabeth Malby, dau. of Arthur Malby, who m. William Beswick in 1616. The only difference being the cotises were engrailed on her arms, which is simply a zigzag line instead of a straight one, to put it as simply as possible for any who perchance are not familiar with heraldic terms.

The following is a very similar arms: MAWTBY (Granted May, 1612): Ermine on a bend between two cotises engrailed gules, three garbs or.

In the Visitation of Lincolnshire (The Genealogist, Vol. IV., 1880, or 1886?) p. 259, is the following: "Richard Morgan m. Margaret, dau. of —— Maltby."

The Harleian Society Publications, 1903, p. 609, had the pedigree of Morgain of Gainsborough: "Morice Morgan m. Elizabeth, dau. of William Forman of Gainsborough, yeoman, sister of Sir William Forman, the Lord Mayor of London, 1538. Their son, Richard Morgan, of Gainsborough, m. Margaret dau. of —— Maltby. They had a son, William Morgan." In this connection we give an item from an old newspaper: "Sept. 1, 1818, Lady Morgan, an authoress, was visiting her relation, Sir Maltby and Lady Crofton at their country home at Sligo."

Thomas Robson's "British Herald, Vol. II., gives: Malby or Maltby: Argent on a bend gules, three garbs or. Malby: the same arms. Crest: An Indian goat passant or. Maltby (Maltby, Cleveland, Yorks.): Argent on a bend gules, three garbs or. Crest: A garb or, banded gules. Maulby, or Maltby (London): Argent on a bend, between two bendlets engrailed gules, three garbs or.

For a very similar coat-of-arms, see the following: The Visitation of Kent, 1619-1621, has the following: "Will'mus Bseswick de (mar.) Eliza, filia et co— Spilmanden (Spelmaden) in Comm. haer. Arthuri Malbe, Cant'Ar. at vicecocnes ex Urargeria filia comitatus Anno 1616. Rob'ti Couletowe; and under Beswick als' Berwick, one given the arms, with Quarterly 2 and 3, Argent on a bend between 2 cortises engrailed gules, three garbs banded or. (Malby) William Beswicke was a son of Will'mus Beswicke, de, London, alderman, als' dictus Berwick;" he m. Joanna, soror Hen. Harte de Newenham, Co. Cantiji.

Burke's Gen. Armory gives (Edit. 1884): Maltby [Edward, Bishop of Chichester, 1831, and Durham, 1836-1856]: Argent on a bend gules between a lion rampant and a cross pattee of the second, three garbs or.

Fairbairn's Book of Crests, p. 372: Maltby, late Rt. Rev. Edward, D.D., Bishop of Durham, between two branches of olive proper a garb or, charged with a cross pattee gules. Nin sine labore. (For grant of arms, see under article on Bishop Edward Maltby.

The arms generally used in the present day by the Maltbys are the sheaves of wheat on a bend gules. This is the coat-of-arms used by the Maltby Association*. The motto used is: "Virtus sub pondere crescit." The General Isaac (4) Maltby descendants used

* The coat of arms shown in the frontispiece is a modification engraved by Z. U. Maltby, Esq.

"Quod serveus metes." Mr. Brough Maltby has an old seal which has been in his family for generations; the arms are as above and the motto is: "Praesto et Persisto."

Capt. Samuel (2) Maltby had a coat-of-arms, as is shown by the inventory of his estate which mentions "A coat-of-arms, 10 shillings; it also mentions "Seal, 20 shillings." He died in 1751. The Montreal Maltbys, descended from the Maltbys of Leeds, York, also owned a coat-of-arms. It was on a seal ring belonging to their grandfather, but was lost and none of the family recall the device.

The coat-of-arms which has descended in Col. R. L. Maltby's family (descended from the Maltbys of Scarborough) is very interesting. Roughly speaking the arms are quarterly or. and argent. The crest is a Wyren, as nearly as can be ascertained and the motto is "Fear God in Life." There is no questioning the fact that the family believed these arms to be Maltby coat armour, but as a matter of fact they are the arms of the Claverings. These arms were sent to an English correspondent, who knowing nothing of the people, replied: "This is *not* a Maltby arms; evidently someone fancies he descends from the Maultby or Maltby who married a Clavering. If this surmise is correct and he can prove his descent from Miss Clavering you have struck a good find. The Clavering arms being similar; i.e., quart. or. and gules, over all a bend sab. (or a bendlet)."

As a matter of fact the Maltbys owning these arms never heard of any Clavering marriage and it would seem very probable that John Maltby, born at Scarborough in 1712, descended from Sir John Mawtby, Knt., who mar. Elizabeth (or Isabel?) dau. of Robert Clavering, son of Roger, Lord of Clavering, 9 Edward II. (1326). See Pedigree No. IV-A. Paston-Maltby.

The following record from the Visitations of Norfolk, 1563-1613, give: "Sir John Mautby Arms: Quart.. or and gules a bendlet sable." It is quite evident that these arms came into use from the Clavering marriage just mentioned. The compiler can not state positively, indeed feels very doubtful, that the Maltby arms of the Scarborough branch should read or. and arg. A rough sketch of the arms was furnished by a descendant and the dots in the first and fourth quarters of the shield indicated gold. As the second and third quarters were left plain it was assumed they were argent. However, it seems unusual to use two metals in this manner and it would seem very probable that there was originally a color blazoned on the shield.

Foster's Visitations of Yorkshire, p. 298 gives Dynely* of Swillington, Mary Maltby, wife of Christopher Maltby, Alderman of York. On page 194 Morley† of Normaby; Isabel, daughter and heir of William de Maultby, was the first wife of Robert Morley of Normanby, dwelling at Maltby. Index of Arms, 194, Maultby—Maltby, p. 551. II Quarterly, one and four, argent on a bend gules, three garbs or. Maultby, Quartered with Morley arms.

1. Nicholas Morley of Normanby, Co. York, 24 Henry VI. (about 1400 ?) m. Joan, dau. of John Hedlam, Esq., 24 Henry VI.
2. Christopher Morley of Normanby in Cleveland, Esq.
3. Robert Morley of Normanby; he dwelt at Maltby; m. 1st, Isabel, dau. of William Maltby of Maltby; 2nd, Elizabeth, dau. of —— Symonds of Kirklington.
4. James Morley of Maltby, 1584, m. Phillis Thornaby.
4. Michael Warton of Beverly Park, Esq., aetat 42 annos, 15 Sept., 1666, m. Susan, dau. of John Lord Paulet,* of St. George, Somerset. Children:
   5. Sir Miles Warton of Beverly, Kted et supra cumr. 1666; d. —— day of March, 1724-5; buried at ——
   5. Sir Ralf of Beverly, Kted, et supra, living 1668.
   5. Charles Warton of Beverly.
   5. John Warton.
   5. Elizabeth Warton.
   5. Susan Warton, m. Sir John Newton, Kt.
   5. Mary Warton.

See Pedigree No. II., for this Maltby-Morley marriage.

There is one other Maltby coat-of-arms given in Rietstap's Armorial General, viz.: Malbee (Languedoc) D'arg au cerf d'azur. (Silver, a hart [or translation hind] blue.)

The Genealogist, Vol. 77, 1894, p. 215, gives the Arms of Warton as follows: Quart. Or. on a chev. az. a martlet 2 and 3 Maltby on a stump of a tree, couped and sprouting, a squirrell sejeant all proper, holding in his paws a nut, Or. We give the Wharton Pedigree from Le Neves Pedigrees of Knights. Edit. Geo. W. Marshall (1873) Vol. VIII., p. 205. Ebor. Sir Miles Wharton Kted at Whitehall, 3d June, 1666. Sir Ralf Warton of Beverly Kted at Newmarket, 19 March, 1668. (See Sir William Dugdales, Vist. of Yorks, vol. 237). Coat, Crest, Quarterings, etc. Or, on a chevron azure a martlet bet. two Pheons of first. (See Vist. of

* Note.—In Swillington Church (1620) was the following ("North quyer, a plate of brass on the wall") epitaph: "Here lyeth Dame Mary Maltby (married at St. Crux, York, 11 July, 1581) widdow; one of the daughters of Arthur Dyneley of Swillington, gentleman: late wife of Christopher Maltby of the cytty of York: alderman; a man worthy of memory. She departed this world the third of October, 1585."

† Graves Hist. of Cleveland, p. 444, gives this pedigree of Morley.

* Note. Sarah Maltby, dau. of Sir George Maltby, Kt., grandau. of Capt. Henry and great-grandaughter of Sir Nicholas Malby, mar. John Poulett. They had a son and a daughter. There may be a connection here. See Pedigree of Sir Nicholas Malby, No. VI.

York coppied by Sir Philip Constable in my hand. P. Le Neve norroy, page 258, for pedigree and quarterings.

WHARTON

1. Lawrence Warton of Kingston, m. Anne, dau. of —— Radly of Radly, Linc.
2. Sir Michael Warton of Beverly, m. (1) Eliz., dau. and co-heir of Ralf Hansby, Knt.; dyed A. D. 1655.
3. Michael Wharton of Beverly m. Catherine, dau. and co-heir of Xtoper Maltby of Maltby, Ebor. "Michaell Warton of Beverly, Esq., dyed in his father's lifetime, being slayn by a cannon bullet at Scarborough Castle in the time of the late wars, it being then a garrison for the King—23 Oct. 1593 at St. John's, Beverly." (This date evidently refers to his birth, as he was married 1 Oct. 1620 at Cottingham to Catherine Maltby.)

In the British Museum there is an Index to the Pedigrees and Arms contained in the "Heralds Visitations and Other Gen. Mans.." edited by R. Sims. Those marked with a star will be found at the end of these heraldry notes; the ones unmarked have never been found by the compiler, and if any of those who read these pages can furnish copies of these missing pedigrees it would be deeply appreciated.

MALTBY, 2109 fo. 63, Bedfordshire.
MALBY, 1096 (or 1696?) fo. 73; 1504 fo. 97, London.
*MAWTEBY, 1552, fo. 173, Norfolk.
MAWTEBY, 6093, p. 2.
*Malby, of Stoneham, fr. Co. Essex, 1560, fo. 197. b. Suffolk.
MAWTEBY, 1449, fo. 4b, Suffolk.
*MALBEIS, 1487, fo. 254b, Yorkshire.
MALBYE of Cowton, 4630, p. 408, Yorks.
*MALTBY of Maltby and Muston, 1487, ff. 465b, 270b York (This is evidently Pedigree No. II.)

In conclusion we find that the Anglo-Norman Malbys family evidently obtained grants temp. of the Conquest—their arms the Hinds' heads. The name Malesbys appears in Le Land's List amongst others who accompanied William the Conqueror to England. (Vide Hist. of the Conquest of England by Augustin

* Since writing these notes on the Maltby arms there came to my attention another blazon quite new to me, and of very early date. In fact, it seems doubtful if it be a Maltby seal. Under date 1219-4, Henry III we find Robert Mauteby giving to St. Mary of Sibton Priory in Suffolk, all his rent in his salt works. A lion rampant on the Seal. Unfortunately the compiler is not sufficiently versed in heraldry to solve this problem. A gentleman writing of Bishop Edward Maltby's coat-of-arms says: "The Lion rampant represents some marriage with a Beaumont." By consulting the English Notes we find the Sutton and Maltby families closely connected and also note the name Beaumont Sutton. It may be a connecting link. (See Will of John Maltby of E. Retford, 1647-8, believed to be father of the three brothers who emigrated to New England. In this will he makes Beaumont Sutton of E. Retford, gent., overseer of his estate.)

Thierry, translated by William Hazlett, 1891; pub. by Geo. Bell and Co.)

We also learn that the Norfolk Mautbys held the Manor of Maltby, Co. Norfolk, from the crown prior to 1166. Arms: a cross.

It seems to the compiler that the progenitor of the Maltby family was Hugo de Malbisse (Pedigree No. I). The Norfolk branch, tracing to Simon de Mauteby it would seem were closely related to Sir Simon Malebisse, Lord of Crowton in Craven, who married a daughter of Lord Methley (See Pedigree No. I); and the Maltbys of Maltby and Muston, Cleveland, York, were probably nearly related to Sir William de Maltby, who had lands in Cleveland, built the chapel at Ayton, where he was Lord of the Manor before 1200.

In regard to the coat-of-arms of the Cleveland, Yorks., Maltbys, Mr. Rees-Webbe, late captain in the English army, and then a clergyman in the Church of England, told the compiler that the garbs in the arms denoted they held large church lands. Mr. Rees-Webbe had a fine collection of seals and was well posted in heraldy. But this statement has been contradicted by another gentleman who maintains the wheat sheaves are used by so many different families they could hardly all have been holders of considerable church lands. However, it is a fact that the Maltbys did give largely to the church land in their possession and were founders of various abbeys; as Hugo (2) who founded the Priory of Spinney; Sir William (3) who built the Chapel at Ayton: Richard (3) who founded the Monastery of Neubo Abbey, Lincoln, in 1198; John (4) who confirmed grants of Morton Grange to the Abbot Neubo; William (5) who confirmed grants to Byland Abbey in 1247; William (6) gave lands to the Priory of Briddlington, 1267, and various other such records which will be found in the English notes.

The conclusion reached by those most familiar with the records of the Maltby family is, that they *all* descend from the original Hugo de Malebisse, who held lands at the time of the Conquest. This seems a broad statement, but if we refer to the emigrant ancestor of the American branch, we find we can state the same; for although three brothers went to New England the line of John in the male issue failed in the third generation; Robert is not known to have had any descendants, consequently this branch of the family all descend from William (1) and in like manner those bearing the name Maltby, must be descendants of the three youngest sons, namely: Daniel (2), Samuel (2) and Jonathon (2). The following extract from an old letter may be of interest in this connection:

The letter is dated "Taunton, Mass., June 14, 1895," and was from Mrs. Lovering to Mrs. George Ellsworth Maltby.

Mrs. Lovering writes: "The home of the English Maltbys is many, yet notwithstanding I have spent many months in England, the only Maltby I have ever met lived in Brussels. We were attending an international exhibition of arts and sciences in Brussels. Walking slowly past a bench or platform devoted to hand decorated china, my attention was attracted to some pieces more original in design than others. Examining them closely I was surprised to see the paintings signed 'Gertrude Maltby' and 'Eva Maltby.' To be as brief as possible . . . I met Gertrude, who was organizing a choir of children, who were to take part in the festivities that afternoon to do honor to King Leopold's guest, Rudolf of Austria, who had come a-courting the Princess Stephanie.

"Gertrude was a matronly English maiden of about thirty-five. She and her sister Eva were the daughters of the English consul at Brussels, who had been stationed there forty years. She said, 'I wish my father could meet you, he is much interested in the family genealogy and is always mousing around old libraries and record cabinets to glean something new. Durham was once a famous headquarters for our race,' etc. When I hinted that my interest was in the *name*, even though we might not have had a common origin, she answered, 'O, do not say that, my father says we are all descended from Hugo de Maltby, who was in the train of William the Conqueror.'"

It was in 1880 that Rudolf of Austria made this trip to Brussels which terminated so disastrously for the Princess. As Mr. Maltby had been for forty years consul at Brussels, this would place his appointment as consul to Brussels in the year 1840; so he was probably born about 1810 or 1815. Could his descendants be discovered it is extremely likely that many of the records so earnestly desired by present day Maltbys would be found.

MALTBY BOOK PLATES

In the Print Room at the British Museum, Book plates of various members of the Maltby family are to be seen. Whether these are registered in the College of Arms I do not know. (E. C. Harte, Wells, Eng.)

BROUGH GEORGE MALTBY. No. 19572.
Arg. a bend gules charged with 3 wheat sheafs.
Crest. A wheat sheaf.
Motto. Praesto et Persto.

ARTHUR MALTBY. Book Plate No. 19575.
Same Arms and Crest.
(Query: Is this Arthur Maltby IV. 8 of Pedigree XV.?)
Motto. Semper Paratus.

There are two Book Plates of Edward Maltby, evidently the Bishop.

EDWARD MALTBY, D.D., No. 19573.

Arg. 3 wheat sheafs on a bend gules. Quartering Beaumont (az. a lion rampant bet. 8 fleur de lys) and impaling Green (or. on a chief indented gules, 3 crescents).

Crest. A wheat sheaf.

Motto. Nil sin labore.

The other plate is

EDWARD MALTBY, D.D., F.R.S., F.S.A.

Arg. on a bend gu. 3 wheat sheaves, a lion ramp. in sinister chief, and across in base impaling az. 3 harts tripp. or, for Green.

Crest. A wheat sheaf charged with a cross, between 2 branches.

Motto. Nil sin labore.

Note.—"From these I gather that when Edward Maltby became a bishop he had to register his arms at the Heralds' College and the lion represents some marriage with a Beaumont and the cross to note the Bishop, or the cross may have reference to the Arms of Malby of Norfolk, and evidently he had not impaled the correct arms of Green, implying that he married a Miss Green."—E. C. Harte.

Note by D. M. V.—According to the biography of the Bishop (Vide. Dict. Nat. Biog.) his wife was a Miss Harvey. His mother was Mary Fearman; his grandmother, Elizabeth Taylor, and his great-grandmother Jane Brough. So if the Beaumont came from a *Maltby* marriage it was before 1640. Of course, it is likely that it was on the maternal side. But in this connection it is well to note that John Maltby of E. Retford makes Beaumont Sutton, gent., overseer of his estate in 1647-8. This may prove a connecting link with the Bishop's family and that of the New England Maltbys, descending from the above John Maltby of E. Retford.

MISCELLANEOUS ENGLISH MALTBY RECORDS

These notes of the English Maltbys have been gathered from time to time and are simply stray items, mostly unclassified. However, where the compiler has been able to place an individual, a note at the end of the record has been added in order that those who are interested may have some help in placing the members of the various branches of the family.

An effort has been made to keep the notes in chronological order, but in spite of numerous revisions of manuscript this has not always been possible, and in some cases, to make the family connections more clear, the notes have purposely been misplaced as to dates.

The compiler wishes particularly to acknowledge the help given by Edward C. Harte, Esq., of Wells, Somerset, who furnished a large number of the English notes and was of much assistance with the

Heraldry of the Maltbys. To the Maulsby Genealogy, admirably compiled by Miss Ella K. Barnard of Baltimore, I am indebted for the births, marriages and deaths transcribed from the Orston Registers. The bulk of the material, in wills, chancery proceedings and so forth, were furnished by Gerald Fothergill, Esqre. of London, whose efficient genealogical services have made possible the publishing of these records and also has done so much toward proving the ancestry of the American Maltbys of New England.

ENGLISH RECORDS 1066-1915

A. D.

1066. Doomsday Oferdshe—Johanes Mably vicannis de Brodwell.
NOTE.—This may be the progenitor of the Maltbys in England.

1066. "The Battle Abbey Roll," by the Duchess of Cleveland is a list of the Knights, Barons, etc., who accompanied William the Conqueror into England and contains the name "Malebys," evidently a nickname and in its Latinized form is "Malabestia."

1097. "The Genealogist," New Series, Vol. XII., p. 281, has the following: "ces cont les noms e les armes abatues de grand signors, Sire John Malebis, de arg., aiij testes de bis de goul." (Translation: "These are the names and the arms worn by the great gentlemen. Sir John Malebis, argent, three heads of hinds gules.) Vide Parliamentary Roll of Arms. See also Maltby Heraldic Notes. This was probably a near relative of Hugo (1) de Malebis of Pedigree No. I.

1189. From "Yorkshire Nobility," p. 341: Ricus Malbis, 1 fe d. ho. d. Gye (Eye?) Freeman of York. See Ped. I. Richard (2) son of Hugo (1).

[1198] 9 Richard I.: Michael Malherbe in Cantebig.

1201. Malebysse, Richard, Eng. judg. 1201-d. 1209 f. (Prob. Richard (3) Ped. I.) Cal. Patent Rolls.

[1203] John 4-10: Hugo Malebisce and Beatrix, his wife, in Fordham. See Ped. I. Chief Justice Hugo (3), brother of Richard (3), mar. for his second wife, Beatrix, Lady of the Manor of Wykes, Co. Cambridge. Founded Priory of Spinney in the reign of Henry III. [1216-1272].

1203. Eustave (Gustave?) Malbeth, Merchand of Abbeville. Vide Cal. Patent Rolls, p. 20.

1210. Ricardi de Malteby (re S' Mary's Abbey) name appears in a York Charter XII. Kal. Juli, anno Domi MCCX (p. 623, "Eboracum," by Francis Drake) Hist. of York. Probably Richard (3) Pedigree I.

1211. Some Cheshire Deeds. Allostock—Before 1211. "Robert

le Brun, son of Picgot. Grant of Alelostoc with all its appurtenances, to be held of the said Robert le Brun and his heirs at a rent of five shillings. Witnesses: Lydulf, the Sheriff, Patrick de Moberlegh, Henry de Stapleford, Peter, the Earl's clerk; Richard de Maltebi, William, son of Hugh, and Richard de Rodest. Seal of a Knight on horseback, the inscription lost. (Ralphde Mesnilwarin was Justice of Chester before Philip de Orreby, who occurs in 1211.) From the "Ancestor," Number 2, p. 140.

[1219] In 4 Hen. III., Robert son of Robert de Mauteby, Gyles, John, Jeffrey, Matthew and Ralph, his brothers came to an agreement with Robert, son of Walter de Mauteby for three caracates of land which they claimed as the inheritance of Robert, son of Richard their father, which they released to Robert, son of Walter. Robert Mauteby, son of Richard aforementioned, gave to God and St. Mary of Sibton Priory in Suffolk, all his rent in his salt works. A lion rampant on the seal.

NOTE.—The above Matthew de Mauteby is evidently the Matthew de Manuteby who accompanied the Earl of Norfolk to Rome in 1245. pp. 227-226, Vol. XI., Bloomfield's Norfolk. By consulting Pedigree IV. it will be found that Richard, who had a son Robert, who had the six sons mentioned above, was very evidently a brother of Simon de Mauteby.

1227. [12-16 Henry III.] Hugo Maleby sec. . . . Wyk.

NOTE.—This is evidently Hugo, who m. Beatrix, Lady of the Manor of Wykses, Co. Cambridge, or possibly his son. See Pedigree I.

1227. Hugo Malebyse ("Eboracum," Cal. Pat. Rolls, p. 160). See Pedigree I.

1227. Johannes Malebisse (Ebor., p. 207, Cal. Patent Rolls). Perhaps John (4), Richard (3), Pedigree I.

1228. Bloomfield's Norfolk, Vol. XI., p. 166, gives: 13 Hen. III. Walter de Malteby conveyed to Simon, the Prior, a messauge and three caracutes of land in Hemesby and Marcham and the Prior conveyed to Walter all the land he had at Becham except adowson. See Pedigree No. IV.

1229. De Mindimis de Jernemne, Roberto Maltcby; p. 273, Cal. Patent Rolls. See Pedigree II. Possibly Robert (4), son of John (3).

1235. Robert de Mauteby, one of the Wardens to keep the peace at Yarmouth Fair; p. 119 (Norfolk) Cal. Patent Rolls. See Pedigree IV. Probably brother of Sir Walter (4)

1239. [24 Henry III.] Michael Malherbe in Cantebrig. (See date 1198.)

1242. Robert de Mauteby appointed one of the wardens for the Fair of Jernemire, Norfolk; p. 304, Cal Patent Rolls.

1242. Protection to Matthew de Mauthebi as long as he be beyond the seas with the King; p. 295. Cal. Patent Rolls.

1245. Protection to Matthew de Manuteby who accompanied the Earl of Norfolk to Rome on the King's affairs; p. 454. Cal. Patent Rolls. Matthew de Matebie held Essex lands about the time of Henry III. [1216-1272]. Manor in Lincoln held of Robert de Wells.

The above items evidently refer to Matthew, son of Robert. See under the year 1219. See also 1270.

1247. In 32 Henry III., Walter de Mauteby had free warren. (Bloomfield's Norfolk.)

1248. In 33 Henry III., Walter de Malteby conveyed to Simon, Prior of Norwich, a message in town of Martham, Norfolk, and three caracutes of land in Hemerby (p. 169, Bloomfield).

1249. In 34 Henry III., Walter de Mauteby had free warren. See Pedigree IV.

1253. Exemption for life of Walter de Mauteby being put on assizes, juries, etc. (Lincoln) p. 257, Cal Patent Rolls. See Pedigree IV., Sir Walter (5).

1256. In 41 Henry III., Walter de Mauteby, son of Robert, was lord. (Vide Bloomfield.) See Pedigree IV.

1257. Exemption to William Malebisse from being made sheriff; p. 603, Cal. Patent Rolls. Perhaps this is William (5) of Pedigree I.

1258. William Malebisse claims forestry in forest of Gawtrys and Langwath by charter of King Richard, the King's uncle (Co. York, p. 627, Cal. Patent Rolls). Probably this is Sir William (4), Pedigree II. As King Richard only reigned ten years, this grant must have been given between 1189 and 1199.

1270. In 1270 the co-feoffees of Richard de Haringby dec. received of Sir Walter de Mauteby six marks of silver due to said Richard (p. 227, Bloomfield). Pedigree No. 4.

1272-1307. Bloomfield Vol. XI., p. 194, mentions Mautebys Manor in Winterton. Also Vol. VIII., p. 259, "Mauteby's Hall, Lordship of, in Sparham, (Town) Norfolk." In Vol IX., p. 377, Bloomfield mentions "Mauteby's Manor in Burston or Briston (Town). The family of de Bassingham was enfeoffed of this Manor from whom it came to the de Mautebys in reign of Edward I. [1272-1307] and so on to the Pastons, temp. Henry VI. [1422-1461]. Sold by Sir William Paston, Bart. 18 Car I.

NOTE.—Christina de Bassingham m. Sir Walter (2) Mauteby, Pedigree IV

1270. In the 54 Henry III., Ronnewell was held by Matthew de Mauteby. See under dates 1242-1245.

1270. In the 54 Henry III., Norfolk. Aleby (Abby?) held of Sir Walter de Mauteby. See dates 1247-8-9-1253, etc.

1277. Bloomfield states in Vol. VIII., pp. 83-84 "The town of which the Bassingham family became enfeoffed." Sir Piers de Bassingham left three daughters and co-heirs. Christina, the eldest m. Sir Walter de Mauteby. Margaret m. Sir John de Flegg. In 6 Edward I. [1278] William le Fleght or Flegg released all his right in the Manor of West Beckam and Matalate to Walter de Mauteby. The Church of Bassingham was a rectory, temp. Edward I. Sir Robert de Mauteby was Patron, 9 Edward II. [1316]. John de Mauteby, Lord of Bassingham.

NOTE.—Robert (3) Mauteby m. Isabel, dau. of William Flegg, and Margaret Bassingham (sister of Christina who m. Walter (2) Mauteby) m. Sir John de Flegg. See Pedigree IV-A.

1280. Sir Robert de Mauteby, Kt., witnesses a grant by Thomas Abbot of Langely (Cal. Close Rolls, p. 60?). Probably Robert (4), Pedigree IV.

1281. Richard Maltbys held three parts of a fee gr. tuft heses (?). (Cal Close Rolls.)

1281. William de Mauteby held a fee gr. Luft huses (p. 106, Cal. Close Rolls).

1281. Letters for John le Mareschel going beyond seas nominating Robert de Maulteby and Hugh le Cressingham his attorneys in Ireland for two years (p. 422, Cal. Patent Rolls).

NOTE.—Robert Mautby m. Ellen, dau. of William Marshall, the younger (Vide Vist. Norfolk). See Pedigree VIII. This is very evidently one and the same person. Perhaps John le Mareschel was a brother-in-law of Robert de Malteby. Notice that in one record the name is spelled Mautby and in the other Malteby. This is the first record I find connecting the Maltbys in any way with Ireland. See also Pedigree IV-A.

1284. Bloomfield, Vol. VI. The Manor of West Becham (or Beckham). In 1284 Simon, the Prior, granted the Manor (except advouson and Glebe lands) to Walter de Malteby or Mawtby, Lord of Malteby, and his heirs. In 1284 Robert de Mawtby had view of frank pledge and assize of bread and beer. Before this temp. Henry III. [1216] Walter de Mawtby was sued for imposing a new toll in Becham fair. See Pedigree IV. Evidently connected with this family.

1289. Robert de Thornoteley imprisoned at York for the death of Maude de Malteby (Cal. Close Rolls). See Pedigree I. William (5), Matilda and Maud, probably the same person.

1291. She is found, in 1291, to have died of quinsey (p. 163, Cal. Close Rolls).

1291. In 20 Edward I., the jury find that neither the Manor or any lands in Mauteby were partable, but were to descend to Robert de Mauteby, son and heir of Walter. Pedigree IV.

1295. Custody of Maritime parts of City of Norwich and other hundreds to Robert de Malteby (Cal. Patent Rolls, p. 169). Probably Robert (4), Pedigree IV.

1296. Demise of Manor of Chalk, Co. Kent, to Robert de Malteby, burgess of Gipperoiz, and anst from Priory of Bermon and saj. (?) (p. 225, Cal. Patent Rolls).

Query: Is it from him the London Maltbys descend?

1296. William de Malteby, keeper of the park about the sea in Norfolk (p. 74). Probably nearly related to Robert de Malteby who had the custody of the maritime parts of the city of Norwich in 1295. Evidently these Norwich Maltbys are a branch from Pedigree IV. (Cal. Close Rolls).

1297. [25-27 Edward I.] John fil Adam Parva Neglburgham v. Walter Mabely of Whaddon and Elicia, his wife, in Wylburgham. Pava Wylburgham (Cal. Patent Rolls).

1299. Dominus Ricardus Malbys (Ebor.). See Pedigree No. I. Evidently belongs to this family.

1299. Robert de Malteby, Yarmouth, Co. Norfolk. This Robert de Malteby was a Knight (p. 432, Cal Patent Rolls). Perhaps Robert (6) Pedigree IV.

1299. Sir Robert de Malteby settled a moiety of the Manor on Sibill, his daughter, till he portioned her, and in 1316, John Fitz Simons and Sibill released the right to Sir John de Malteby, their brother, who was then lord of the Manor. It remained in this family till Margaret, dau. and heir of John Mawtby, Esq., brought it by marriage to John Paston, Esq. It was later sold by Paston heirs to Lord Yarmouth to Lorn Anson (p. 471, Vol. VI. (?) Bloomfield). See Pedigree IV. Robert (6) and Pedigree IV.-A, Robert (4).

1299. Robert de Malteby, collector of customs, Yarmouth, Co. Norfolk (p. 316, Cal. Close Rolls). See Pedigrees IV and IV-A.

1300. In 1300 Sir Robert de Mauteby, Lord (Bloomfield) (Vide Pedigree IV.).

1301. Richard Maltbys (or Malebyse) held a Knights' fee in Neubo, Co. Lincoln and Acastre, Co. York, (pp. 437-439 Cal. Close Rolls). This is evidently a descendant of Richard (3), Pedigree I, who founded Neubo Abbey in 1198 and was of Acaster, near York. See Richard (7) Pedigree I.

1304. Cal. Patent Rolls: "William, son of John de Maltby and Gilbert, son of John de Maltby," p. 250. See Pedigree II., John (3).

1310. Charter of John Miles of Hoton by Ruddeby in Cleveland of land in Hoton, witnessed by Robert de Malteby (Cal. Char. Rolls, p. 85, Vol III.); evidently a brother of above Gilbert. See Pedigree II., John (3), Robert (4).

1310. Charter of Robert, son of William de Scuderscelf, two borates of land in Hoton, witnessed with alia (?) William de Mauteby (p. 146, Vol III. Cal. of Charter Rolls). See Pedigree II., William (4).

1310. William de Mauteby witnesses charter to the Canons of William, son of Roger de Alcum, ten acres in territory of Staling, till age called ailwinloft (p. 14, Cal. Charter Rolls).

1312. Confirmation of Abbot of Fountain by Richard Malebisse of lands in Queltriz (?) Hoton and other places (p. 434-5, Cal. Charter Rolls). Vide article on Maltby, Yorks. See also Richard (7), Pedigree I.

1307. Bloomfield, Vol. XI, p. 229: In 1307 Sir Robert de Mauteby presented to the Rectory of the church of St. Peter and St. Paul at Mauteby. Probably Robert (8) Pedigree IV.

1312. Confirmation of land to Berolington, Convent land, in Fordon and Armesdale. Witness (?) by William Malebisse (p. 443, Cal. Charter Rolls). Probably William (9) Pedigree I.

1313. Pardon to John Malebys, an adherent of Thomas, Earl of Lancaster, respecting the death of Peter de Gervaston, (p. 21, Cal. Patent Rolls). Perhaps John (8) Pedigree I.

1314. Hugh Malebissa witnesses a charter (p. 97, Cal. Charter Rolls). Probably Pedigree I.

1314. Alan de Malteby witnesses a charter of land near Mer Teyse, York (p. 172, Cal Patent Rolls).

Query: Is this the Alan Maltbys mentioned in Pedigree III.

1314. John de Malteby witnesses a charter of John de Ascelacly, burgess of Jarum, York (p. 172). Also a charter of William de Latymer, Lord of Jarum (p. 172, Cal. Patent Rolls). Probably John (8) Pedigree I.

1314. William de Malteby witnesses a charter of Peter de Brusland in Jarum, York (p. 171, Cal. Patent Rolls). Probably William (9) Pedigree I.

1315. Complaint against John Malbys, late sheriff of York (pp. 324-419, Cal. Patent Rolls). See Pedigree I, John (8).

1313. John de Mauteby to levy for debt on lands of John de Claverying in Co. Norfolk (p. 579, Cal. Close Rolls).

Note.—Sir John (5) Mauteby, Pedigree IV.-A., m. Isabel, or Eliz. Clavering, dau. of Robert Clavering.

1315.-1330.-1336. 9 Edward II. John de Mauteby was lord (Bloomfield). See John (7) Pedigree IV.

1316. John Malebys to levy scutage, Co. York (p. 428, Cal. Patent Rolls). Perhaps John (5) Pedigree II.

1316. Lordship of Mauteby's Hall. Aveline de Mauteby, 9 Edward II. Lady of the Manor. Ref. Bloomfield.

Is this Arelina de Grenon, who m. Sir John (2) Pedigree IV.

1316. Protection to John Malebys (p. 203, Cal. Patent Rolls).

1316. Protection to the Abbot of Egleston and others, including William Malbys (p. 536, Cal. Patent Rolls).

1317. Hugh Mallebille witnesses charter (p. 26, Cal. Patent Rolls).

1318. William Malb' witnesses charter of ——, Earl of Chester (Cal. Patent Rolls).

1319. Adam de Malteby, parson of Duns, diocese of St. Andrews (p. 382, Cal. Patent Rolls).

1319. Petition of John de Malteby at York of having been assaulted at Wyrksop, Co. Nottingham (Cal. State Pap., p. 364. Cal. Patent Rolls).

1319. John de Malteby accused with others of trespassing on a slip at Ravenrshere, York (p. 366, Cal. Patent Rolls).

1320. *Sir John Malbys, Kt.† = Agnes.*

*Sir William Malbys, d. prior to 1320.

Thomas, son of Nicholas de Norfolk, granted 5 marks for repose of his father and mother's souls and those of the Malbys* above who were buried at St. Marys Castle Gate, York (p. 285, Eboracum).

1320. Bloomfield, Vol. VII., p. 477; 1 May, 1320. John de Maltby admitted prior of Mulicourt Priory, parish of Outwell, Co. of Norfolk. He died circ., 1333. This Priory was appropriated, 4 Dec., 1449, by Walter Hart, bishop of Norwich. Possibly Sir John (5), Pedigree IV.-A. See also under date 1336.

1324. "Freemen of York," pub. by Surtees So., Vol I., Edward III., Nich. Fowles, Mayore. Willelmus de Malteby. Perhaps William (9), Pedigree I.

1325. [18-19 Edward II.] ——— vs. John Mabely of Whaddon, chaplain in Abyngton (Cal. Patent Rolls).

1326. Bloomfield, Vol. VIII., pp. 83-84. Sir John de Mauteby, patron of the living (of Bassingham). Evidently Sir John (5), Pedigree IV.

1327. Pardon to John Maltby and ors. (Co. Worcester) (p. 203, Cal. Patent Rolls).

* It may be that the above Sir John Malbys and Sir Willm. Malbys refers to John (3) and Sir William (4) Pedigree II, as it states they were buried at St. Marys Castle Gate, York.

† Note. John Malebys, High Sheriff Co. York, 8 Edw. II, 1314 (p. 352 Eboracum) is evidently the above John Malbys, also spelled Malebisse. See Pedigree No. I. John Malebisse mar. Agnes, d. of Sir Edward Willstrope.

1329. William de Malteby regarding land (2 acres) in Bury St. Edmunds (Suffolk) given by him to Abbot and Convent of St. Edmunds (p. 370, Cal. Patent Rolls).

1326. Pardon to Robert de Malteby (Co. Norfolk ?) (p. 263, Cal. Patent Rolls).

1322. Protection for William Malbys accompanying William de Ros of Hamdatre, going with the King to Scotland (p. 185 Cal. State Pap.).

1322. Alan de Malteby, a monk of Whiteby, York (p. 179, Cal. State Pap.).

1328. William de Malteby of Retford, Co. York, (p. 363, Cal. Close Rolls).

Important note for the American Maltbys. As East Retford is, we believe, the birthplace of our emigrant ancestor, William Maltby, Esq., this item showing Maltbys seated at Retford as early as 1328, should be of particular interest to us. We think of East Retford as in Nottinghamshire, and true it is, but Nottingham was anciently in the diocese of York. The information was kindly given by Harry Speight, Esq., of Yorkshire, the well known author and genealogist.

1330. Writ to John de Mauteby and ors. to array the Knights and ors. capable of bearing arms, Co. Norfolk (p. 574, Cal. Patent Rolls). Probably Sir John (5) Pedigree IV.-A.

1334. William de Malteby, freeman Scarborough, (?) Yorks. (p. 18, Cal. Patent Rolls).

NOTE.—This is the earliest Maltby record I find from Scarborough and it is very probably closely related to the Maltbys of Scarborough. See further. Perhaps he was a near relative of William (9), Pedigree I.

1334. John de Malteby, Knt., accused of breaking a close at Lyng, Co. Norfolk. Also Robert, his son, and Ralph "Sire Tonesporest de Malteby; i. e., his chaplain" (p. 579, Cal State Papers). See Pedigree V., John (1)

1336. John de Malteby, complaint against, by Prior of Gisburn; also against William de Hert (p. 355 Cal. Patent Rolls).

1336. Commission to William Malby's sons (?) for North Riding of Yorkshire (Cal. State Papers, p. 138).

1334. Commission of Oyers terminer to William Malbys and sond (?) to try John, son of Roger Malbys re. scuttling a ship near Fyrele, Co. York (p. 576, Cal. State Papers).

NOTE.—The name Roger appears here for the first time, but at intervals later.

1335. William Malbys, Knt., acknowledges he owes John Malbys £20 (p. 499, Cal. Close Rolls).

1337. Sir Robert de Malteby, Knt., is owed 350 marks. Sir Robert de Maltby, Knt., owes 340 marks to be levied on his lands, etc., in Norfolk (pp. 145-251, Cal. Close Rolls). Probably Sir Robert (6), Pedigree IV.-A.

1337. Walter de Malteby of Kerketon (p. 93, Cal. Close Rolls).
Query: Is this Walter (10), Pedigree I.?

1338. Wm. de forentre holds in Askeby an eighth part of a Knight's fee of Richard Mabelise of the fee of the Earl of Chester (p. 37, Cal. Patent Rolls). Probably nearly related to William (9), Pedigree I.

1338. Commission to William Malebys and ors. North Riding, Co. York (p. 138, Cal. Patent Rolls). Probably William (9), Pedigree I.

1338. John de Malteby presented to Vicarage of Pontefract dio. York (p. 125, Cal. Patent Rolls). This was revoked in 1339 (p. 271, Cal. Patent Rolls).

1339. John de Malteby regarding claims of disseisin; claim of Parson of Ruddeby, Co. York (p. 302, Cal. Pat Rolls). Evidently same case as above.

1339-1340. License to William Malebys to unpark his wood of Holt in Scalton, Co. York (pp. 251-441 Cal. Patent Rolls). Very evidently William (9) Pedigree I., as his son Walter (10) mortgaged Scalton to Wm. Fairfax.

1339. Sir William de Malbys, re. land granted to Fountains Abbey (p. 398, Cal. Patent Rolls).

1340. Commission to Wm. Malbys and ors. regarding custody of temporalities of the See of York (p. 495, Cal. Patent Rolls).

1340. John de Malteby presented to Vicarage of Blythe, Dio. York (p. 529, Cal. Patent Rolls).

1340. Commission Robert de Mauteby and others charged with trespass at Great Chasterford, Essex (p. 97, Cal. Patent Rolls).

1340.-1341. Beatricia de Malteby, 16 Edward III., Freeman of York, 1340-1 Per Patres (Pub. Surtees Co., Vol. I.). Possibly descended from Robert and Beatrix Maltby. See Pedigree III.

1343. Robert de Malteby claim against, regarding goods on ships at Loyestoft, Suffolk (pp. 167-385, Cal. Patent Rolls). See Pedigree III., Robert (4).

1344.-1348. John de Malteby, Vicar Broad Clist, Co. Devon. (pp. 197-377, Cal. Patent Rolls).

1346. Commission to William de Malebys (p. 104, Cal. Patent Rolls).

1347. Sir Robert de Mauteby, Lord of Matlask (Bloomfield).

1347. Commission oyer and to William Malbys and ors. (p. 471, Cal. Patent Rolls).

1347. William Malbys, J. P. North Riding, Co. York (p. 462, Cal. Patent Rolls).

1347. 3 April, Charter to Robert de Mauteby, Kt., in his demesne lands of Mauteby, Sowerton, Salle, Rasyngham, Sparham and Matelesk, Co. Norfolk (Cal. Patent Rolls). This is evidently Sir Robert (8), Pedigree IV.

1347. Bloomfield, Vol. VIII., pp. 83-84: Sir Robert de Mauteby, patron of the living (Matalate, etc.). Same person as above, evidently.

1348. John de Malteby had a messouage at Gisburn (p. 16, Cal. Patent Rolls).

1349. Grant to the King's clerk, John de Malteby, of the free chapel of Staughterford, Co. Wilts (p. 438, Cal. Patent Rolls).

1349. Edward de Maultby was Rector, presented by Sir Robert de Mauteby at Mauteby.

1350. Complaint against Robert de Mauteby, "chivaler," and John, his brother, regarding driving (?) arsay cows at Merkessale and Castyre by Norwich (p. 588, Cal. Patent Rolls).

1351. Exemption to serve in juries, William Malbise, Kt. (p. 38, Cal. Patent Rolls).

1355. Bloomfield: Sir Robert de Mauteby and Alianore, his wife, living. See Pedigree IV., Robert (8).

1356. Benedict de Maldeby and ors. sued by Abbot of Whiteby regarding trespass and lordships of borough of Whiteby, Co. York (p. 29, Cal. Patent Rolls).

1362. Robert de Mauteby held one fee of Earl of Pembroke, 35 Edward III. (Bloomfield).

1362. Bloomfield's Hist. Norfolk, Vol. III., p. 259: Avelina de Mauteby was returned to be lady of it (a lordship called Mautby's Hall in the Parish) in the 9th year of Edward II. and Robert de Mautby was found to hold one fee here of the Earl of Pembroke, in the 35th year of Edward III.

NOTE.—Avelina was evidently the wife of Sir John (7), Pedigree IV.

1366. In 1366 and 40 Edward III. [1365] Sir John de Mauteby was a feoffee for the Manors of Lanwades in Weston and Peekhall in Titleshall in Norfolk and *sealed* with a plain cross (Bloomfield).

1369. Sir John Maultby, Patron of the living (Bloomfield, Vol. VIII., pp. 83-84).

1369. John Mautebv, lord of Matlask (Bloomfield).

1373. Willemus de Malteby, tailliom (Freemen of York).

1374. In 1374. Sir John de Mauteby, son of Sir John, was buried before the Altar of St. Mary in the Parish Church of Fritton

St. Edmund, where he lived (Page's Suffolk Traveller, p. 313). See Pedigree VIII. Also Reg. Haydon fo. 45, p. 227.

1373-1377. John de Mauteby was ——— for Norfolk, 1373-1377. John Wand. The case of Wm. Maltby is referred to in Sherwood's "Memoranda."

1374. Sir John de Mauteby, lord of the Manor. The last male heir of this family, leaving an only daughter and heir, Margaret, who brought it by marriage to John Paston, Esq., of Paston, temp. Henry VI. See Pedigrees IV. and VIII.

1378. John de Malteby, Vicar of Alton, Co. Hants., presented to West dione church dioc. Salisbury (p. 162, Cal. Patent Rolls).

1379. Commission regarding guarding the ports, to John de Mauteby and ors., Co. Norfolk (p. 360, Cal. Patent Rolls). Probably Sir John (9), Pedigree IV.

1381. Ricardo Malebise, 26 Henry VI.; 2 May, 18d from Wm. Malbys in Skeldergate, York (Yorks. Nobility, p. 34).

1381. Constance Malbysse married Sir Robert Roclyff (Will dated 7 May, 1381) of Rocklyff by York (York Wills, Vol. I., p. 118). See Vist. York, edited by Chas. Best Norcliffe (1881), Harl. Socy., Vol. XVI, p. 266.

1382. John de Mauteby, J. P. Co. Norfolk (pp. 141-248-508, Cal. Patent Rolls). This is Sir John de Mauteby, Kt.

1384. Exemption for life for serving on juries to John de Mauteby, Kt., of Norfolk (p. 519, Cal. Patent Rolls).

1390. Robert de Malteby, Citizen, London (p. 282, Cal. Patent Rolls).

Note.—This is the first mention of Maltbys in London as yet found.

1390. Commission to John de Maudeby and ors. to try a salvage claim, ship salved off coast of Norfolk (p. 271, Cal. Patent Rolls).

1392. Henry Malbys, Parson of Wyloughby (p. 110, Cal. Patent Rolls); also referred to as Henry Malbrush, 1389 (pp. 3-38), and as Henry Malbyssh in 1396 (p. 11, Cal. Patent Rolls). Sir Nicholas Malby names his son Henry.

1395. April 14, Malbys, William, bur. St. Olaves, York, April 5, 1395 (Yorkshire Wills).

Note.—This is the oldest recorded Maltby Will yet found.

1396. 29 July. Pardon to John Malteby of Hylderwell [Hinderwall] in Quydbystranide (p. 15, Cal. Patent Rolls).

1395. Walter Malteby, monk (p. 625, Cal. Patent Rolls).

1396. (p. 227, Vol XI., Bloomfield) 5 Ric. II. Sir John de Mauteby lord, and in 1396 Sir John de Mauteby and Agnes, his wife, enfeoffed Sir Adam Clifton in his manors of Mauteby,

Winterton, East Somerton, etc., for the use of his eldest son, John, entail. See Pedigree IV., Sir John (9).

1397. Sir John de Mauteby presented this year (Bloomfield, Vol. XI., p. 229). This refers to the Rector of the Church of St. Peter and St. Paul at Mauteby.

1397. Sir John Maultby, Patron of the living (Bloomfield p. 137, p. 84, Vol. VIII.) Temp. Henry VI. The Manor, etc., of Bassingham went to the Pastons on the marriage of Margaret, dau. and heir of Sir John Mauteby, Kt.; 6 Edward I., Walter de Mauteby, lord of Matlask; 9 Edw. II. John de Mauteby, Lord of Matlask; 20 Henry VI., Margaret, brought it to the Pastons (p. 136-7). See Pedigree IV.

NOTE.—Before beginning the records of the next century it may be well to note that in the items above, nearly every person mentioned can be traced, or placed, to the Yorkshire or Norfolk Maltbys found in Pedigrees I., II. and IV. From the commencement of the 15th century, 1400 to 1499, it is more difficult to identify the persons contained in the records; this, of course, owing to the fact that the younger sons emigrated to new counties, and also to the greatly increased number of descendants. It shows very clearly, however, that every generation further back we are able to trace our ancestry, just so much easier becomes the task, as there were comparatively few of the name living in the first two or three hundred years after the Conquest.

1401. Thomas Maltby, Mayor of Limerick, 1401 (Vide: Ferrar's Hist. of Limerick).

NOTE—This is the second record of a Maltby in Ireland in my possession.*

1401. July, Confirmat. Sellers Patent to William Maltby and Margaret, his wife, and others to found a Chantry for 4 Chaplains in the Church of St. Martin Seyestre (p. 371, Cal. Patent Rolls).

1401-1402. Robert de Malteby, Citizen of London (pp. 81-496. Cal. Patent Rolls).

*1402. Tucy (?) Robert Malteby. Citizen of London, suing for 10 marks, John Sampson, Jr., of Plymouth (Cal. Patent Rolls).

NOTE.—These records are about the earliest of any London Maltbys and they probably were of Yorkshire stock.

1405. Oct. 26. Maltby, Matilda de, Aldwerk, York, fst. St. Thomas de "Herfordensis Epi," 1405 (Vol. 3. 238 folio. Yorkshire Wills).

1406. Robert Maltcby (of London) suing Nicholas Waryn of Co. Essex (p. 135, Cal. Patent Rolls). Evidently the same as in item 1402.

* 1401. This item may be important and prove the connection between the London Maltbys and the Malebisse family of Yorkshire. Pedigree I. William (9) de Malebisse, Miles, 1339; died about 1365; married a daughter of John Sampson, Miles, and here we find in 1402, Robert Malteby, Citizen of London, suing John Sampson, junior, of Plymouth for 10 marks. It would seem that Robert was one of the younger children of William and wife—Sampson Malebisse—and that John Sampson, Jr., was his cousin.

* Is this Thomas (2), Pedigree V.?

1406. Richard Malteby [of Scardeburgh] Scarboro (p. 62, Cal. Patent Rolls).

1407. Richard Malteby of York (p. 353, Cal. Patent Rolls).

1407. In 1407 Robert Mautby presented John Begge (Bloomfield).

1403. 27 Oct. 1403-29 Oct. 1403. Will of Sir John de Mauteby appoints Robert Martham and others exors. Mentions: Robert, son and heir; John, a piece of plate. Late John Mautebys, his uncle Thomas, a piece of plate. Will proved 18 Dec. 1403; d. 30 Oct. 1403; bur. in Chapel of St. Mary in the Church of St. Peter and St. Paul of Mauteby. His wife, Agnes, predeceased him (Bloomfield's Norfolk).

NOTE.—From this it will be seen that John (8), Pedigree IV., had a brother Thomas.

*1413. In 1413, Robert Mauteby, Esq., enfeoffed Sir Miles Stapleton, Sir Simon Feltrigge, Sir William Argentien and others in the Manor of Fritton, Suffolk, with other lordships in Norfolk, to fulfil his will made in the same year. The lordship later became vested in the Sydnor family. See Pedigrees V. and IV.-A., Robert (8); Page's Suffolk Traveller, p. 313. See also Suckling's Suffolk, p. 353. See Pedigree of Stoneham-Aspal-Suffolk.

NOTE.—Also in Clivers Manor, Norf. These feoffees presented to the Rectory in 1425. John Mauteby, his son and heir, m. a dau. of John Berney of Reedham and their dau. Margaret, only dau. and heiress, m. a Paston. Her will, proved Dec. 18, 1484, gives each poor household in the town of Sparham, late her tenants, 6/—.

Bloomfield gives: "Mauteby's Manor in Burston or Briston (Town). The family of de Mauteby." (Vol. IX., p. 377). See Pedigree VIII.

1415. Ricardo Malebise, 1415 (Yorkshire Nobility, p. 82).

1415. Freemen of York, Ricardo Malebise.

1424. Thomas Maltby, Parson of Sewalby (Swabey), dioc. Lincoln, after of Besseby (p. 195, Cal. Patent Rolls).

* 1413. (p. 227). Robert Mauteby, Esq., enfeoffed Sir Miles Stapleton, Sir Simon Felbrigge, etc, in Manors of Mauteby, Sparham, Basingham, Beetham, Matlash, Berstow, Kirke-hall in Salle, Flegg-hall in Winterton, Somerton, etc.; 100s rent in Castre and Merkeshale Freton Manor in Suffolk, to fulfil his will etc. Wife named Eleanor (Alianore). Son John, son and heir. Brother John Ocll (qr. a priest). Daughter Eleanor, a nun at Shouldham. Daughter Agnes. Walter, Edward, Peter, Thomas, sons under age. His widow remarried, 20 Henry VI., Thomas Chambers, lord of Sparham, in her right.

(p. 228). John (son and heir of Robert) married Margaret, dau. of John Berney, Esq., of Reedham, by whom he had Margaret, his only daughter and heiress, who married John Paston, Esq., son and heir of Sir William Paston, the judge, and brought a great estate into that family. Margaret Paston's will is dated 4 Feb., 1481 (she was then a widow) and proved 18 Dec., 1484. She desired to be buried in church at Mauteby and her tomb to be embellished with four scotchyns thereon the 1st Paston and Mauteby; 2nd Mauteby and Burney of Reedham; 3rd Mauteby and the Lord Loveyn; 4th Mauteby and Sir Roger Beauchamp, etc., etc.

1426. Oct. 4. Malbys, Dame Sibilla, relic. of Sir Wm. Malbys, Kt., of Acaster Malbys (Am. Vol. 2, folio 497, Yorkshire Wills). See Pedigree I., which ends, in 1377, with Walter Maltby who went to the Holy Lands; but from the above will it is conclusively proved that this family did not die out, but was perpetuated through younger sons.

1426. Dec. 22, Maltby, John, Whytby (Whitby) (May 25, 1426, completed folio 515, Vol. 2, 503, Yorkshire Wills).

1427. John Nikere of Hardingham, Chaplain, held two messuages and five acres of land in Hardingham from John Gilbert and John Malteby (p. 451, Cal. Patent Rolls).

1429. William Maltby, Citizen and Mercer of London, sues John Colvyll of Normanby, York (p. 516, Cal. Patent Rolls).

1430. Feb. William Mallebise witnesses a charter of William, Earl of Warenne, respecting the taking of timber from Lancaster forest by the Abbey (of Lancaster?) (p. 77, Cal. Pat. Rolls).

1431. William Maltby, Citizen and Mercer, London (p. 98, Cal. Patent Rolls).

1432. Sept. 22, Maltby, John, Rect. of Rither (June 22, 1432, Vol. 2, 617, Yorkshire Wills).

1433. Commission to William Malbys of Miton, (Mitton) Yorks, and others (p. 301, Cal. Pat. Rolls).

1435. Robert Malteby, Esquire, died before this date. He had a share in adrouesons of Evarwartown and the Manor of Evarwartown, Suffolk (p. 500, Cal. Patent Rolls). See Pedigree V.

1438. William Maltby, Citizen and Mercer, London (p. 111, Cal. Patent Rolls).

1438. Thomas Maltby [Kent ?] sues Thomas Grenfeld of Chepsted, Kent (p. 207, Cal. Patent Rolls).

1438. Thomas Maltby, chaplain to Vicarage of Stenyng (Steyning) (p. 220, Cal. Patent Rolls).

1438. John Maltby, the elder, John Maltby, the younger, regarding land at Hardyngham (pp. 135-6, Cal. Patent Rolls).

1438. (Bloomfield's Hist. of Norfolk), Peter Mautby, Esquire., by his will dated Oct., 1438. Oct. 4, 1438. By will of this date, Peter Mauteby, Esq., requires to be buried in the church of Sparham, St. Mary. See Pedigree IV., Peter (11).

1442. (Bloomfield, Vol. VIII., p. 259). Sir Simon Feltrig and Trustees of Robert Mauteby, Esq., settles lordship of Mauteby's Hall on John Paston, Esq., who had married Margaret, dau. and heir of John Mautebv, Esq. (son and heir of said Robert) for his life; remainder to Margaret. See Pedigree IV., Robert (10).

1443. (Bloomfield's Norfolk, Vol. I., p. 243). Roger, son of William de Brown of Manor of Browne Hall, near Norton, Norfolk. [on border of Suffolk] m. Petronell, one of the heiresses of Roger de Somery from whom she inherited this Manor. She died before 1443. This Petronell was a daughter of Sir Robert de Maltaby, Kt., and Olive, his wife. How Petronell became Somery's heiress is not known.

NOTE.—In Pedigree IV., it will be seen that Sir Walter (5) Mauteby m. Petronella ——— and his son, Sir Robert (6), m. Olive ———. It is probable that Petronella ——— was a Somery, hence the inheritance to her granddaughter, Petronell. Also it is worthy of note that Bloomfield spells the name Maltaby in Vol. I., p. 243, proving to skeptics that it is the same name as Mauteby.

1438. William Maltby and Joan, his wife, widow of Nicholas Tournay. Lands in Bucks and Lincoln (Close Rolls, 16 Henry VI.) M. I. D.

NOTE.—This is the earliest Maltby record furnished by Mr. Fothergill.

1445. (The Ancestor, Vol. 10, p. 96). "The obits. of the family of Barrey or Berry and its allied houses." "Obitus Magerie uxoris Johannis Mawdeby anmigeir* et filie Johannis Berney de Redam, ao. dmi. MCCCCXLV.

NOTE.—This is Margaret, w. of John Mawtby, and dau. of John Barney (Berney) of Redham. See Norfolk, Pedigree.

1446. Thomas Maltby, bailiff of Bamburgh (Cal. Patent Rolls).

1448. (Freemen of York, p. 34). "18d from Wm. Malbys in Skeldergate, York, 2 May, 26 Henry VI.

1448. In 1448 John Paston, Esq., presented.

In the north window of the chancel in Mauteby Church is an effigy of a man in complete armour. . . . de Hykeling; also effigy of his wife, Alice or Elizabeth de Hickling, with arms sa. a cross argent. At each end of the church lies a curious antique monument of grey marble, a coffin on pavement; on the coffin is the effigy of a Knight Templar* cross legged in armour, in memory, it is said, of a Knight of the de Mauteby family living according to the style of the monument circ. 1250.

The south aisle, where many Mautbys were buried was rebuilt by Margaret Paston and she was buried there but it was in ruins (in 1810). In the church was the shield of St. Peter

* Query: Does "armigeir" refer to John Maltby being of an armorgenous family or has it to do with one who made armor? We find the same term used in the Marbury Pedigree (VII) where it mentions: Anne Marbury, mar. (2) Armiger Warde. Query: Is this Ward family connected with those mentioned in Pedigree notes. Pedigree V.

* It is probable that the coat-of-arms of the Norfolk family are derived from this early Knight Templar. The silver cross on the blue field would be a fitting emblem of his crusades.

and the arms of Mautby and Loveyn, Mautby and Clifton, Mautby and Beauchamp, Mautby and Berney, Mautby and Marshall (p. 230, Vol. XI., Bloomfield's Norfolk).

Burke Gen. Ar. gives Clifton of Bokenham, Co. Norfolk, chequey or. and gu. a bend ermine. Beauchamp, Bletso, Co. Bedford, descended from Roger de Beauchamp, temp. Edward III. Sent to Parliament, 1363: Gu. a fesse bet. 6 martlets or.

1453. Feb. 13., Malteby, Thomas, Slaynton (Jan. 26, 1453. Vol. II., p. 290, Yorkshire Wills).

1455. Rev. John Maltby, Vicar of Send, 6 June, 1455, M. A. Ref. Manning and Bray's Hist. Surry, Vol. III.

1462. Rev. John Maltby, Rector of Ockham. He was Rector, 6 April, 1462, an official of the archdeaconery of Surrey. Evidently same person as above.

1470. Pardon to John Maltby, yeoman of Edynhall, Co. Cumberland (p. 215, Cal. Patent Rolls).

1477. Henry Maltby of Alverstoke (p. 50, Cal. Patent Rolls).

1477. From Baker's Hist. of Uton, Co. Northampton, Isthlingborough, All Saints, Rectors, John Maltby, 6 June, 1477.

1485. Thorpe Malsor (2½ miles from Kettering) Rector John Maltby, 17 July, 1485. Evidently Rev. John Maltby of above records.

1484. Temp. James I. Sir William Paston held lordship of the Manor of Mauteby's Hall, held of Lord Morley, valued at £15—00—4 per annum.

1484. 18 Dec. Will proved of Margaret Paston (widow of John Paston, Esq.) gives to each poor household in the town of Sparham, late her tenants, 6/ (p. 259, Vol. VIII., Bloomfield).

Bloomfield also gives, on the same page: 1300-1400 Mauteby's Hall, Lordship in Sparham (Town) Norfolk.

1497. (Bloomfield, Vol. IV., p. 338). Will. Mawtby, Esq., interred in church of Blackfriars, Norwich [circ. 1497 ?].

1511. John Maltbye, clk., presented to church of Northleve dioc. Exter. Vol. I., p. 229. To Vesy (?) in June, 1513 (p. 607, Vol. I. Letters and Papers, Foreign and Domestic, Henry VIII., edited by Brewer).

1512. June. John Maltcby presented to church of Wassbrynburgh, dioc. Lincoln (Vol. I., p. 365, Ibid).

1513. 4 March, John Maltbye, clerk, presented to Hemeswell, dioc. Lincoln (Vol. I., pp. 503-539, Ibid).

1514. Sir John Maltby, clk. (i. e., Rev'd John Maltby) (Vol. II, part 2, p. 1464, Ibid.

1522. Feb. 5. Maltby, William, Helmssley, gentleman (Nov. 12, 1522, Vol. IX., p. 351, Yorkshire Wills).

1523. Sir John Maltby, Yorks., name in sheriff's list (p. 1488, Vol. III., part 3); i. e. Sir John Maltby, Knight, elig. for office of Sheriff in Co. York.

NOTE.—Evidently related to family in Pedigree I. This note taken from Letters and Papers, Foreign and Domestic, Henry VIII., edited by Brewer.

1531. 17 May. John Maltby and others make statement on oath respecting "a rate for scavage." (Same ref., Letters, For. and Dom.)

1532. 17 Maye. Abstract of the Will of John Maltby: Mother, Jennet Maltby and the children of Richard Norton, his wife, Elizabeth; my sister, Church of Welton, Church Dunam, Cosyn Katherine Jeffrason, poor of Welton, sons Roger,* John,† Nicholas,‡ and Anthony.§ Money put in trust in hands of the Mercers Comp. Brother Thomas Maltby, Master Hill of the Custom House. Roger Deale, underbutler. Every clerk in the Custom House. Hugh, Dyer, Elys Johnson, Richard Watson and his son, Henry (See Will of Will. Maltby, 1558). Thomas Marbury, Haberdasher, of London and Ric. Marbury, Citz. and Merchants Taylor, to be exors. Mary Hawkins, Margaret, her mother.

NOTE.—Mary Hawkins later m. ——— Hancock.

1530. (Nicholas Topographer and Genealogist, Vol. III., p. 513): "Edmond Gresham was borne uppon saynt Clare day, the vyrgen, the xij day of August Ao diy. XVCXXX, John Malby, John Donstall and Thomas Ippeswell, these were his godffathers."

1530. Richard Maltby held, A. D. 1530, one ox-gang of land in Orston of Sir Richard Bozon, Kt. (Indes 185, Inquisitions Post Mortem, Nottinghamshire, edit. W. P. W. Phillimore). This should be of interest to the Orston Maltbys.

The following from Rutland Wills, found in the Boston Library:

1527-32. Mawbie, Robert, Maseby (Book D., p. 205).

1540-42. Malbie, John, Crick. (Book G., p. 118, P. 35).

* The name Roger is uncommon in the Maltby Family up to this date. Perhaps this Roger is the Roger, Vicar of St. Nicholas. See under date 1563. Also in 1592, at Springthorpe, Roger Maltby had a son John, bapt. 26 Nov., 1592.

† The writer has wondered if this John is John Maltby of Kexby Hall, Will 1557. Presumed to be the ancestor of the American Maltbys of New England, 1667-70.

‡ Is this Sir Nicholas Malby of the Irish notes? The records say: "Sir Nicholas Malby's father died when he was four years old—died about 1534." This is near enough so that it would be possible for this Nicholas to be one and the same as Sir Nicholas.

§ Anthony Maltby. This is a name found amongst the Orston Maltbys and also Anthony Marbury is a very common name in the Marbury family. There seems to be a close connection here between the Maltbys and Marburys. See further under Maltby Heraldry.

1545-46. Malbye, Robert, Slapton (p. 72, Book 1545-46, P. 42).

1560-66. Page 64, Malby, William, Crick. (p. 97, Book P. ?).

1590-1602. Page 91, Mawbie, Lambert (p. 22, B. W. 1590-97-1602). For continuation of these Wills, see under years 1600-1699.

1535. Jan. 31., Maltbye, Wylliam, par. St. Den., York. (June 16, 1535, Vol. II., p. 117, Yorkshire Wills).

1536. Examination of William Hurte and others regarding the Lincolnshire Rebellion, 28 Oct., 28 Henry VIII. That Sir Simon Maltby, Parson of Farforthe was on Saturday before the Insurrection, before D. Reynes, the Bishop of Lincoln at Bollyngebrooke at the court of the valuation of Benefices and returning home reported that their silver chalices were to be given to the King in exchange for tin ones, and that he and other priests had determined to take down the said Chancellor and trusted in the support of their neighbors. The Sunday after the Insurrection, Sir Simon prayed for the Pope and College of Cardinals. (Vide p. 401, Vol. XI., Letters and Papers, Foreign and Domestic, Henry VIII, 1536. See also p. 47, Vol. II., "Henry VIII. and the English Monasteries," by F. A. Casquet, 6th edit., pub. John Hodges, 1902.)

NOTE.—"Sir" here is equivalent to "Mr." It was the prefix of respect placed before clergymen's names and equivalent to "Rev'd." Simon is a name found in Pedigree IV.

1538. July 16. Maltby, William, Hull, Adm. Harthill (Yorkshire Wills).

1539. Grant of possessions of the suppressed Priory of Snelshaw, Bucks., of which William Maltebey was the late Prior (Vol. 14 (I), p. 163, Letters and Papers, Foreign and Domestic, Henry VIII., edit. Brewer).

1539. Walt. Maltby appears in the list of Musters for Lindsey, Co. Lincoln, as belonging to [Beesby ? or Maltby ?] (Vol. 14, I., p. 277, above reference).

1542. One Maulby (or Maltby) of London is interested in Army Contracts (Vol. 17, pp. 402-473, above reference).

1543. Wm. Malbe, John Malbe and Joan, his wife, and ———, their sons, hold tenements in Rugby, Co. Warwick; part of Monastic property granted to Sir John Williams (Vol. 18, I., p. 130, above reference).

1543. License to Sir John Williams of Ricote Olon to alienate tenement and land in Rugbie, Warwick, in tenure of Willm. Malbye, which belonged to Chaccombe Priory (Vol. 18, I., p. 368, above reference).

1541. Christopher Maltby of Hemswell, Co. Lincoln, 27 May, 1541. Wife Johan. (Proved in Arch Stow, 17 April, 1542, folio 117.)

1545. Abstract of Will of Johan Maltbye, mayden sister to William Maltbye of All Hallowes, Greswell, 23 Aug. 1545. Church of Willingham, Repingham and Wettellany. Brother's son and daughter, Thomas Maltbye and Isabell Maltbye. Isabell Sutton. Sir Leonard Calvard and Sir Thomas Wessynne. Brother William Maltby and Isabell Maltby, my sister. (Proved in Arch Stow, 22 Nov. 1545, folio 303.)

NOTE.—Evidently Johan and William Maltby were children of Christopher and Johan of Hemswell. See Will 1541.

1543. Mawbye "is a wise fellow"; i. e., Thomes Maltby or Mawbye, who has a provision to contract for victualling the army (!). The exclamation is added by a contemporary Englishman who furnished the record; before the present war, however. (Vol. 18, II., p. 130; Vol. 18, I., p. 728, same reference.)

1544. Grant to Thomas Melby (Malby) and others of lands in Yorks.; lands belonging lately to Roche Monastery (Vol. 19, Part II., p. 77, above reference). Evidently belonging to the family in Pedigree II.

1544. Maltbie has a contract to purvey cheese (to the troops) (Vol. 19, P. 2, p. 88, above reference). This is evidently Thomas Maltby, alias Mawlbie, alias Maulbie.

NOTE.—This is evidently the first time in recording the name of Maltby in its manifold forms, that we find *Maltbie,* which has come to be so much used since.

1545. Thomas Malby of London, fishmonger, regarding victualling Calais and Boulogne (Vol. XX., Pr. 2, p. 194, above reference). This is evidently the same person as above.

1549. May 9. Maltbie, Christopher, Thorneton in Pikernigelieth, husbandman (Oct. 8, 1548, Vol. XIII., 517, Yorkshire Wills). Was this Christopher (13), Pedigree II.?

1547. Abstract of Will of William Maltby of Ingham, 15 Aug., 1547. Son Robert, daus. Elizabeth and Katherine. Mr. Thomas Burton to be supervisor. Wife, Isabell, and son, John, exors. (Proved in Arch Stow, 3 Feby. 1547-8, folio 477.)

1557. Abstract of Will of John Maltby of Kexby Hall, dated 26 Nov., 1557. Burial at Upton. (This is probably the ancestor of the American Maltbys of New England, 1670.) Daughters Margaret, Izabell. Wife, Margerie, and son, Richard, to be exors. Son, William. Mentions Christopher Maultby as a supervisor. (Proved in ons of Lincoln, 3 Dec., 1557.)

NOTE.—This John Maltby, we believe, was nearly related to the family of Maltby, Pedigree II.

1558. Will of William Maltby of Greatwell, Co. Lincoln, 16 Oct. 1558. Jenytt Maltby (for same name see Will 1532). Son, Thomas Maltby. Henry Watson, one of three witnesses. (See will 1532.) (Proved in Arch Stow, 22 Jany., 1558-9, 301.)

1556. Abstract Will of Robert Maltbye of Willoughton, 20 March, 1556. Wife, son Robert, Kinsman William Maltbie, Thomas Maltby, junior, William Maltby, junior, Nicholas Maltby,* Helene Maltby, Isabell Maltby, Thomas's daughter. John, my brother John's son, and Richard. Son Richard. Sons Thomas, Richard and Robert, exors. (Proved in Arch Stow, April 1556, 179.)

1551. April 17. Maltby, James, fisher, (Nov. 11, 1550, Vol. XIII., folio 718, Yorkshire Wills).

1555. March 10, Maltbye, Robert, Orston (Notts) (Feb. 26, 1553, Vol. XIV., 226, Yorkshire Wills). This item should be of interest to the branch of the family who came from Orston.

1558. Wills proved in Consistory Court of Lincoln. Alice Maltbie, Burgh St. Mary and others.

1562. (Bloomfield Vol. X., p. 407.) John Maltby, Vicar of Catton, Norfolk, 1562, presented by Dean Chapter of Norwich Cathedral.

1563. Roger Maltby, Vicar of Church of St. Nicholas last Dereham, Norfolk, presented by Willm. Mowse, Rector (p. 211, Bloomfield). This may be Roger, in will 1532.

1562. (Cal. St. Pap. Dom., edit. Lemon.) Reprieve for Nicholas Malby (qr. of London ?) to be delivered over to the Earl of Warwick for service abroad. (See q. v. under Maltby Irish Notes.)

1574. Abstract of Will of Richard Maltby of Willoughton, Co. Lincoln, 9 Jany. 1574-5. Thomas Maltby, the elder, to bring up testators son, Nicholas. (Proved in Arch Stow, 27 April, 1575, folio 169.)

1582. Abstract of Will of William Maltbie of Kexbie, Co. Lincoln; husbandman; dated 1 Nov., 1583. Burial at Upton. Children, Dorothy, Richard, William, Thomas, Henry and Margaret. Wife, Grace. One of three supervisors, Richard Maltby. (Proved in Archy Stow, 19 Nov. 1582.)

NOTE.—This is a younger brother of Richard Maltby (2), son of John (1) of Kexby Hall. Item of interest to American Maltbys. From the names of the children we shall probably find that John was a son of a Richard

* Perhaps nearly related to Richard Maltby. See Will 1574-5. He may be the father of this Richard.

or a William Maltby. The wid. Grace Maltby, evidently remarried, as the Upton Registers give: "Grace Maltby m. John Walker, 23 May, 1584. The dau. Dorothy, above, is evidently she who marries at Upton, 18 June, 1593, Thomas Tollen.

1582. John Maltbie and Eliz. Greaves, m. 30 July, 1582, Orston.

1584. Anna Maltbye, dau. of Hugh, bapt. 20 Dec., 1584, at Orston.

1587. Abigail Maltbye, filia Hugoris, bapt. 15 June, 1587, at Orston.

1589. Johannes Maltbye, filius Hugoris, bapt. 28 June, 1589, at Orston.

1592. Petrus Maltbye, filius Hugoris Maltbye, bapt. 15 June, at Orston.

1565. May 10. Maltbye, William, Driapole in Holderness (Feb. 1, 1564, Vol. XVII., 424, Yorkshire Wills).

1572-1634. Visitation of Hertfordshire: "Isabel, daughter and heiress of William Maltby of Throwondby, lux, m. Robert Morley, son of Christopher Morley and Elizabeth." He was a son of John and Jane Morely, and he was a son of Michael, living in 1434. Crest: Cap. of Maintance, gules, turned up, ermine., p. 154. See Pedigree II.

1575. Christ. Maltby, Sheriff of York (p. 365, Eboracum, Hist. of York, by Francis Drake). See Pedigree II.

1580. Dec. 19. Maltbye, Robert, Newe Malton (May 21, 1580, Vol. XXI., folio 515, Yorkshire Wills).

1584. Feb. 28. Maltbie, Christopher, Alderman of York City (Feb. 1, 27 Eliz. Vol. XXII., folio 673, Yorkshire Wills). See Pedigree II., Christopher.

1585. Oct. 14. Maltsbye, Dame Mary, widow of Christopher M——, Alderman of York (Aug. 31, 1585. Vol. XXIII, folio 106, Yorkshire Wills).

NOTE.—This was a second wife Mary, dau. of Arthur Dyneley. Foster's Vist. of Yorks., p. 298, gives: "Dyneley of Swillington, Mary Maltby, w. of Christopher Maltby, Alderman of York. Christopher Maltby, Alderman of York, buried his w., Frances Young, 30 Dec., 1580, at St. Crux (York.) where his son, Christopher, was bapt., 18 March, 1574-5; and m. there Mary, dau. of Arthur Dyneley, 11 July, 1581. His sister, Jane Maltby, buried 12 July, 1604, at All Saints' Pavement, m. Robert Brooke, Alderman and M. P. for York, and was mother of the Rev. Samuel Brooke, D.D., Master of Trinity College, Cambridge, 1622-1631; Christopher Brooke, M. P.; the poet, Jane Brooke, w. of Thomas Hesketh of Heslington, whose heir general is the editor of this work. (Yorkshire Wills, etc.) See Pedigree II.

1586. Nov. 22. Maltbye, Margaret, Swillington, Ainsty. (Yorkshire Wills.)

NOTE.—Possibly a sister of Christopher, Pedigree II.; he had a dau Margaret who d. April 17, 1591.

1585. (Bingley Parish Reg.) Born Oct. 3, 1585, Mychaell, son of Isabel Moberly and Mych. oyts.

1584. (Nichols Topographer and Genealogist, Vol. II., p. 556): "For this will as well as an elaborate pedigree of the Morleys of Normanby and Maltby in Stainton parish, I am indebted to Mr. William Paver of York. Cuthbert Morley of Normanby recorded their pedigree at York Visit., 1584, to which his half brother added his achievement, his mother being heir general of Maltby of Maltby in Stainton."

1585. Inquisition made at York Castle, 25 March, 27 Elizabeth. On death of Christopher Maltby, Alderman of City of York. Seised of Muston and Fylaye, manor of Maltby other lands detailed, Will 1 Feby., 27 Elizabeth, all his lands to Raphe Richardson, Alderman of York, William Dynelay of Swillington, for 11 years. Wife, Mary: son, Christopher,* brother, Richard Maltbie. Maltby is held of heirs of late Lord Conyres, d. 2 Feby. last. That Christopher is his son and aged 10. (Chancery Inq. P. M., Vol. 207, No. 95, Series II.) See Pedigree II.

1586. Abstract of Will of Richard Maltbie of Glentworth, Co. Lincoln, dated 10 May, 1586. Sister's son, John Maultby, dwelling in Norfolk, besides Walsingham, 20/ for a legacy left him by my mother. Daughters Jane, Anna. Wife Alls. Sons Roger and John. (Proved Arch Stow. 4 Jany.. 1586. 338.)

NOTE.—This John Maultby, dwelling in Norfolk, is probably a son of Roger Maltby, Vicar of St. Nicholas, Norfolk in 1563. Does this means Walsingham a place? And is this John the brother of Sir Nicholas, who he mentions in 1580?

1589.(?) (Vist. of Lincolnshire, The Genealogist, Vol. IV., 1880 (or 6) p. 259: "Richard Morgan married Margaret, daughter of ——— Maltby." (See p. 248.) Marbury the same name. Arms: Arg. on a fess engrailed gules, 3 garbs or. The Harleian Soc., pub. 1903, p. 690, gives the pedigree of Morgan of Gainsborough. For another refernce see Maltby Heraldry and the Irish Maltby Notes.

1590. Born, Jan. 24, 1590, John, son of Isabell Moberley and Jo. Husler. (Bingley Parish Reg.) Bur. Aug. 31, Isabell Mouberley. (For further records see 1631, 1600, 1610.)

1593. Bloomfield, Vol. VIII., p. 228, gives this pedigree: 1. John Wysse; 2. Margaret Wysse, m. (1) ——— Mauthy, gent.; m. (2) Clement Hyrne, Kt., Mayor of Norwich, 1593.

1595. From "Old Yorkshire," by Will. Smith, p. 176: Gregory

* This is an important record as it shows that this family (Ped. II) did not fall entirely of male issue. Compare the names in the will of John Maltby of Kexby, 1557.

Creyke, the fifth son, succeeded: bapt. at Bridlington April 21, 1595. He m. Ursula, dau. of Sir John Legard, Kt., of Grantum, by Elizabeth, dau. of Sir William Mallory, Kt., of Studly; Everilda, the only daughter; she m., in 1599, Christopher Maltby of Maltby. She had three daughters.

Foster's Vist. of York., 1584-1612, gives: Creyeke of Cottingham. Arms: Quarterly 1 and 4. Per fesse arg. and sable, a pale countercharged, and 3 birds of the last. Creyke 2 and 3: Paly of 6 or. and gu., in chief argent, 3 lozenges of the 2nd arden. Crest: An eagle sable, standing on a garb fesseways or. 1. Wm. Creyke Esq. of Cottingham, Co. York., m. Frances, dau. of Sir William Babthorpe of Osgodby. 2. Ralph Creyke, twice m., had by Catherine, dau. to Thomas Crathorne of Crathorne. 3. Everild Creyke, w. of Christopher Maltby, Esq.

1595. 4 Dec. Grant of a Canowry and Prebend at St. Stephen's Church, Westminster, to Thomas Goodric, the King's Chaplain. Vice. John Maltby, dec., Vol. VI., p. 651.

1591. April 17, Maltby, George and Margaret, children of Christopher Maltby, Alderman of York, dec. City. Aug. 31, 1585 (Vol. XXIII., folio 106, Yorkshire Wills). See Pedigree II. This is an interesting item, showing that besides Christopher, who m. Everilda Creyke, there were other children.

1593. Feby. ult. Maltby, Agnes, Thormeton (Ridall) widow. Feb. 17, 1593 (Vol. XXV., folio 1513, Yorkshire Wills).

1593. March 1, Maltby, Roger, Thormeton (Ridall) Apri. 6, 1593 (Vol. 251, folio 1513, Yorkshire Wills). Perhaps son of the widow, Agnes Maltby, above.

1594. April 25, Maltby, John, Farnedon, Newark, (Yorkshire Wills).

1596. Sept. 29, Maltbie, John, Robinhoodbaie, Cleveland (Yorkshire Wills).

1596. (?) Forthe Pedigree. Robert Forthe, Sheriff, 1596. Anne Forthe, m. second ——— Mendham; had Annie Ward, who m. Edward Malbye, Esq. (For further records consult years 1617-18. See also Pedigree V.)

1597. April 30, Maltbie, Mary, Dickering (Yorkshire Wills).

1599. Thomas Malby gets a grant (Cal. State Papers, p. 224). Evidencly has been building ships for the Navy.

A stray item, without date, is the following: "John Rivers m. Anne, dau. of Arthur Maltby and sister and co-heir of Thomas Maltby."

1595. Baptized at Orston, Notts. Willmus Maltby, son of Hugh, bapt. 4 Apr.

1599. Buried at Orston. John Maultby, buried 1st March.

1600. Elizabeth Maltby, filia Hugoris Maltby, bapt. at Orston, Notts.

1600. Buried (Bingly Parish Reg), 17 May 1600. Uxor Lawrencii Moberley de Cottingham.

1601. Dec. 17. Maltbie, Robert, Hunmandbie, Derckering (Yorkshire Wills).

1602. Dec. 20. Maltby, Wm. Hundemandby, Oct. 26, 1602, (Vol. XXVIII, folio 824).

1602. Dec. 20. Maltbie, Janet, Hunmandbie, Dickering.

1602. Abstract of Will of Richard Maultbye, the elder, of Kexbie. Son Christopher, son John, son Richard; daughters Ellen Quipp and Margaret Wilkinson. My Lord Willoubie. (Proved in Arch Stow ult. Dec., 1602.)

NOTE.—Ancestor of American branch, Richard (2), John (1).

1603. Abstract of Will of Christopher Maultby of Upton, Lincoln. Husbandman. Dated 3 March, 1602. (Note. This is the oldest son of above Richard, brother to John (3) progenitor of Amerincan Maltbys.) Son Richard, son Thomas under 21, son Christopher under 21, brother Richard, son John under 21, daughter Elizabeth under 21. Wife Elizabeth. Brother John. (Proved Arch Stow, 25 March, 1603.)

NOTE.—Married at Upton, Christopher Maltby and Eliz. Fysher, 27 May, 1593.

1603. Buried at St. James, 5 Sept. 1603. Nicholas, son of Mres. Malbey.

1604. The Yorksire Papists, Harthill-Cottingham, noncommunicant, returned Jane Ashe, servant to Xpofer Maltbie, gentleman, noncommunicant for a year past. "Taken from" A List of Roman Catholics in the County of York in 1604, by Ed. Peacock, F.S.A. (See item dated 1600, Lawrence Moberley of Cottingham.)

1604. Thomas Maltby, filius Hugoris Maultby, bapt. June, 1604, at Orston.

1605. Oct. 3. Maltbie, Richard, Hunmandby, bachelor, Sept. 16, 1605 (Vol. XXIX., 702) son of Richard Malteby of Hunmandby, dec. Tin. Dickering.

1605. Johanis Maltby, hauc vitam reli quit, 5 June, 1605, Orston.

1606. Vol. I., p. 159: "The plague raged in the parish of Buckland in 1606, by which the rector, John Maltbee lost six children in one month."

1610. Abstract of Will of John Maltbie of Springthorpe, Co. Lincoln, yeoman. Dated 20 May.

NOTE.—This is a will pertaining to the American Maltbys, John (3), Richard (2), John (1), and is given entire under another heading. It may be well to give here births and baptisms of his children recorded at Springthorpe.

CHILDREN OF JOHN MALTBIE OF SPRINGTHORPE

1592-3. Richard, son of John, bapt. 24 Feb.
1594. Jane, dau. of John, bapt. 26 Nov.
1594-5. Jane Maltby, buried 23 Jany.
1595. Hellen, dau. of John, bapt. 2 Jany.
1598. Allice, dau. of John, bapt. 28 March.
1599-1600. Elizabeth, dau. of John, bapt. 27 Feb.
1606. William, son of John, bapt. 8 Nov.
1609. Robert, son of John, bapt. 1 Apl.
1609. Alice, dau. of John, buried 10 Feby.
1610. John Maltby, buried 27 May.

NOTE.—It will be seen that the second son, *John*, is not amongst these children; he was probably born at Upton. Neither are the births of his daughters, Margaret and Mary, recorded at Springthorpe. The daughter Ellen, mentioned in his will, was probably the Hellen, bapt. in 1595.

1610. 29 June. Buried *Humfrey Maltby at Upton.

1610. 29 June Admon. of *Humfrey Maltbie of Upton, Co. Lincoln, to Richard Maltbie of Upton, the brother (Arch Stow, 113). Bond of Richard Maltbie, William Kyrke of Hepam, Co. Lincoln, and Richard Maltbie of Kexbie in £20. Inventory £152—16—8. See Pedigree, VII., Humphrey Marbury. He was probably a brother of the Richard Maltbie of Upton, whose will follows: Abstract of Will, 28 Oct., 1617. Son William, land at Stourton, next Stow. Wife Elizabeth.* Daughter Ann Maltbie, daughter Margaret. Wife's daughter Elizabeth Maultby,* who is a daughter of Christopher Maltby. John Maltbie. Brothers William and Thomas. (Proved Arch. Stow, 18 Dec. 1618, 370.)

The Upton Registers give the children of Richard as follows:

1604. John, son of Richard Maltby, bapt. 2 Aug.
1604. Mary, dau. of Richard Maltby, bapt. 18 Nov.
1604. Mary, dau. of Richard Maltby, buried 24 Dec.
1605. William, son of Richard Maltby, bapt. 20 Dec.
1608. Margaret, dau. of Richard Maltby, bapt. 16 Apl.
1609. Richard, son of Richard Maltby, bapt. 22 Feby.
1609. Richard, son of Richard Maltby, buried 24 Feby.
1610. Ann, dau. of Richard Maltby, bapt. 14 Feby.
1611. Ann, dau. of Richard Maltby, bapt. (?) 27 June.
1612. Richard, son of Richard Maltby, bapt.
1612. Mary, dau. of Richard Maltby, bapt. 8 Nov.
1613. Elizabeth, dau. of Richard Maltby, bapt. 10 Oct., 1613.

* Elizabeth Fysher mar. Christopher Maltby in 1593. He died in 1603 and she married Richard Maltby.

1610. Buried, June 15, 1610, Lawrencii Moberley de Cottingham (Bingley Parish Register).

1614. Aug. 5. Maultbie als. Conyers, John, Blawgill par Hawnbie, Nov. 16, 1613, (Vol. XXXIII, folio 224, Yorkshire Wills). See Note 1585 which states that "Maltby is held of heirs of late Lord Conyers, died Feby. last."

1618. Abstract Will Thomas Maultby, the elder, of Willoughton, Co. Lincoln. (Proved Arch. Stow, 4 Feby., 1618-19.)

1619. March, Elizabeth Maltby, Orston, Notts, Oct. 22, 1639 (Yorkshire Wills).

NOTE.—This will should be looked up and abstracted for the Orston Maltbys, as it might throw additional light on the ancestry of their progenitor, William Maltby, gent., b. in 1641.

1619. April 15, Maltby, Christopher, Cottingham, Esq., Harthill (Yorkshire Wills). Probably Christopher, son of Christopher and Everilda Creyke. See Pedigree II. See also dates 1610, 1604, 1600.

1620. Abigail Maltbie, m. Wm. Taber, Oct. 22, 1620, at Orston.

1620. Thomas Maltbie, hauc vitam reliquit Vicessimo, 4 April, 1620, at Orston.

1620. Michael Wharton m. Catharine, dau. and co-heir of Christopher Maltby of Maltby in coun. Ebor. 1 Oct., 1620, at Cottingham.

NOTE.—From the dates 1610 and 1600 it would seem that Lawrence Moberly of Cottingham was nearly related to Christopher of Cottingham.

1619. The York Marriage Licenses read: Sir Michael Warton of Beverley and Evereld Maltby of Cottingham at Beverley or Cottingham, 1619.

NOTE.—Query: Should the previous note read Evereld and not Catharine? And did Evereld marry twice? Still she would have been called widow if the following record applied to her. It is from York Marriage Licenses, 1626, and reads: "Geo. Wentworth, gent., of Wolley and Averil Maltby of Cottingham, 1626, at Royston or Cottingham." The York Marriage Licenses also have "Robert Hemhough of Drax and Thomazine Maltby of Drax, 1612. (The wid. of Sir Nicholas Malby was Thomasine.)

1622. Lincoln Marriage Licenses, 1598-1628. 1622, May 28. Robert Maultby of Gaudly, husbandman, ae. 23 (hence born, 1599) and Alice Howden of Hemmingley, spinster, ae. 22, parents' consent (Gaudbie).

1622. April 29, Maltbie, Katherine, Carwood, Amisty (Yorkshire Wills).

1622-3. Maltby, John, son of John of Buckland, Co. Gloucester, sacred Magdalen Hall, matriculated 31 Jan. 1622-3, aged 15 (hence born in 1607) B. A., 14 Feb., 1625-6; his father, rector of Buckland, 1591-1632.

NOTE.—Refer to date 1606.

1623. Robt. Maltby and Susan Ransome m. last day of July, 1623. From Transcripts of N. Muskham, 1623-1633 and 1638.

1623. London Marriage Licenses: Maultby, John, brewer, and Anne Jenks of St. Aephage, London, wid. of Jonah Jenks, late of same, white, baker, of St. Aephage, aforesaid, 2 Dec. 1623. B. (Also Harleian Soc. Pub. 1887.)

1623. Page 140: Mawbe, Edward Crick, O. 159-1623; page 191, Mabley, J., 139; page 191, Malby, J., 35. W. 64; page 192, Mawbie, E., 140. Eliz. 140 J. 111. (From Rutland Wills.)

1624. May 7, Edw. Sweete of Anderby, yeom., a. 24, and Dorothy Maltby of same, aged 21 (born 1603) a parish near Alford. (Lincoln Marriage Licenses, St. Paul.)

1624. Abstract of Will of Richard Maltbie of Upton, Co. Lincoln, batchelor, 20 Fby., 1623-4. Sisters Margaret, Ann; brothers William, John. Mother Elizabeth. Uncles Robert Fisher and Richard Maltbie. (Proved in Arch Stow, 4 Aug. 1623, 48.)

NOTE.—This is Richard, son of Christopher, Will proved 1603.

1626. 13 June. Thomas Maultby of Sleeford applies for license for Jno. Marsh and Agnes Pike, widow.

1627. Anthonie Maltbie and Phillipe Challand, m. Feb. 21, 1627, Orston.

1627. William Maultby and Isabell Pepper, Apr. 17, 1627, m. Orston.

1625. Abstract of Will of Peter Maltby of S. Olave in Southwarke, Co. Surrey, Cordwayner, dated Aug., 1625. Child unborn, brothers, William, John; Sister Elizabeth. Wife, Joane. Father, Hugh. Cozens, Stephen and Francis Segood, sons of Henry Segood. Uncle, John Maltby. All my apprentices. (Proved in the P. C. C., 30 Aug., 1625, by Hugh Maltby; Jane, the exex. having died. 84 Clarke.)

NOTE.—Unless the child survived this line evidently died out.

1627. Anthonie Maulthie, s. of Anthonie Maulthie, bapt. 28 July, 1627, at Orston.

1627. Anne Maulthie, w. of Anthonie, buried 27 Aug., 1627, Orston.

1627. Anthonie Maulthie, the son of Anthonie Maulthie, buried 7 Feb., 1627, Orston.

1628. Elizabeth Maulthie, dau. of Anthonie Maulthie, bapt. 28 Dec., 1628, Orston.

1628. John Maultby and Elizabeth Blount, m. June 24, 1628, Orston.

1628. William (?) and Eliz. (?) m. Aug. 3, 1628, Orston.

1629. Elizabeth Maltbie and Rich. Challand, m. Nov. 23, 1629, Orston.

1629. Dorothie Maltbie and Henry Worsingcrip (?) m. June 7, 1629, Orston.

1629. William Maultbie, son of John Maultbie, bapt. 5 Sept., 1629, Orston.

1629. Anne Maltbie, wife of John Maltbie, was buried 5 Sept., 1629, Orston.

1629. William Maultbie, son of John Maultbie, was buried 21 Oct., 1629, Orston.

1630. Katherine Maultbie, dau. of Anthonie Maultbie, bapt. 7 Sept. 1630, Orston.

1631. John Maultbie, son of John Maultbie, bapt. 29 Nov., 1631, Orston.

1631. Mawbie, Thomas, B. A. from Magdalen Hall, 10 Dec., 1631.

1632. Thomas Maultbie, son of Anthonie Maultbie, bapt. 10 Feb., 1632, Orston.

1632. Thomas Maultbie buried 14 Feb.

1633. Elizabeth Maultbie, dau. of John Maultbie and Marie, his wife, bapt. 7 Aug., Orston.

1633. Hugh Maultbie buried 9 March, Orston.

1633. Abigail Maultbie, dau. of Anthonie Maultbie and Phillip, his wife, bapt. ye 11th March.

1633. John Maltbie of Bainton m. Elizabeth Ward of Bain.

1634. Anne Maultbie, dau. of John Maultbie and Marie, his wife, bapt. 7 Dec., Orston.

1635. Abstract of Will of Richard Maltby of Kexby, dated 1635. Burial at Upton. Son John, house in Kexby; dau. Elizabeth; sons, Christopher, William, Nicholas (?), Robert, Richard. (Proved in Arch Stow, May, 1635. 2.)

Note.—This is Richard, son of Richard, W. P. 1602, and brother of John (3) from whom the American branch probably descends.

1636. Abstract of Will of John Maultbie of S. Olaves, Southwarke, Co. Surrey, Brewer, dated 14 March, 1634-5. Daughter Elizabeth. Mary Sherwood, my first wife's daughter, and to Jona and Josias Jinks, my second wifes sons; to Elizabeth Martin, my cozen. (Proved in P. C. C., 6 Sept., 1636, by Anne, the relict. 101 Pile.

NOTE.—This is evidently the "brother John" mentioned in the will of Peter Maltby in 1625.

1636. N. B.—The Orston records which follow are in bad shape owing to the register being eaten away, torn and badly damaged. It will be noted that after 1639 the Maltby records cease until 1662. As it was in 1641 that William Maltby, gent., who married Jane Brough, was born, it is very probable that his birth follows that of Mary Maltby in 1639, and that he was a son of John and Mary Maltby.

1636. Hugh Maltbie, son of John (hole); Marie, his wife, bapt. (hole)

1636. (eaten away) Maltbie was buried 24 July.

1636. Henrie Maltbie, son of Anthonie and Phillipp, his wife, bapt. 15 Octbr.

1636. Elizabeth Maultbie was buried ye (——) of (March ?).

1637. Elizabeth Maltbie (——) Maultbie was buried ye (——).

1638. Hugh Maltby (——); his wife, was bapt. (——).

1638. Hugh Maltby, the son of (——); his wife, was buried 19 of June.

1639. Mary (John) Maltby (——) was bapt. (Jan)uary.

1639. Mary, the dau. of John and Mary, his wife, was buried 26 Jan.

NOTE.—The descendants of William Maltby of Orston, b. 1641, should study these records well. Let us look at the names of the children of John and Mary Maltby, viz.:

1633. Elizabeth.
1634. Anne.
1636. Hugh.
1639. Mary; and there was evidently Thomas, as in 1662 we find: "Thomas, son of John Maltby, buried 27 Oct., 1662."

Suppose, for example, William, b. 1641, was a son of the above John and Mary Maltby. He m. Jane, dau. of George Brough. Now let us glance over the names of his children, as follows:

William, named for himself.
Mary, named for his mother.
George, named for his wife's father.
Anne, named for his sister and perhaps his grandmother as well.
Thomas. He evidently had a brother Thomas, and it may have been his grandfather's name.
John, named for his father.
Charles. This is not a Maltby name; perhaps it was a Brough name, or on the maternal side of his family.
Elizabeth. He had a sister Elizabeth.

Surely, if there is anything in the names of children to indicate a family's descent, here is strong evidence. And there certainly is a finger post pointing the way, to be read plainly by any genealogist in the way children were named in the early days.

1638. Abstract of the Will of Richard Maltby of Springthorpe, Co. Lincoln, yeoman, dated 22 April 1638. Son Richard, son William, dau. Sarah, grandchild Sara Parke, dau. Margaret, dau. Mary; mother, Scendle; each man servant; wife Sarai. (Proved in P. C. C. 10 Nov., 1638, by Sarah Maltby, the relict and exex. 147 Lee.)

NOTE.—This is a brother of John (4) from whom the New England Maltbys claim descent.

NOTE.—Eldest daughter Sarah, m. 23 Aug., 1636, Wm. Parke of Springthorpe.

1638. Abstract of Will of Christopher Maltby of Kexby, Co. Lincoln, batchelor; dated 14 Dec., 1638. Eldest brother John, brother William, brother Robert, youngest brother Nicholas; sisters Mary, Prudence and Elizabeth; brother Derby's children, Mary and Ann; brother John's son, Richard; brother Richard's daughter, Elizabeth. (Proved in Arch Stow, 10 Jany. 1638-9, 10.)

See Pedigree of Kexby Maltbys.

1639. Abstract of Will of Robert Maltby of Wilgheton, Lincoln, March 1635. Son Nicholas, land in Kirton; wife Dorothy, son John, son Hammond. (Proved in Arch Stow, 19 April, 1639, 54.)

1639. Abstract of Will of Sir George Maltbie, Kt., dated 6 Dec., 1638. Nephew and niece Paulett; my wife (Anne). (P. C. C., 29 June, 1639.

See under notes of Sir Nicholas Malby.

Inquisition made at Lincoln, 8 Jany. 14 Car. I., after death of Richard Maltby of Springthorpe. Concerning land in Humberston and a messuage in East Retford. William is his son and next heir and aged, at the death of his father, four years. (Miscel. Chancery Inq. P. M. 14 Car. I., pt. 2-86.)

1642. Chancery Proceedings Car. I., M. 9-33. 12 May 1642, Orators Thomas Maltby of Kirton, Co. Lincoln, yeoman, and Ann, his wife.

NOTE.—This Thomas may be nearly related to Robert of Wilgheton, Will 1639, who left land in Kirton to son Nicholas.

1643. Yorkshire Parish Reg. Soc. Burton-Fleming, 1538-1812. Married John Maltbie and Isabel Robinson, 25th Feb., 1643.

1645. Abstract of the Will of Thomas Maultbie of Willoughton, Co. Lincoln, yeoman, dated 16 Oct., 1645. Cozen William, son of my brother Richard (really his nephew); brother William's children, Thomas Southwell's children and his wife Ann; Richard Raw, Thomas Raw; brother Richard's sons, Nicholas and William. Wife Anna's brother William and John Raw to be exors. (Proved in Arch Stow, 30 Nov., 1645, 331.) (The wid. of Sir Nicholas Malby mar. George Rawe.) Note. His wife was evidently Anna Raw.

1646. From Gloucester Notes and Queries, Vol. III., p. 71: Alice Maberly, wid. parish of Baunton.

1647. Will of John Maultby of E. Retford, Co. Nottingham, alderman, dated 6 Oct., 1647. (Supposed father of the New England emigrants, John, William and Robert.) Eldest son, John Maltby, houses in Briggate, E. Retford, Carr Lane, close in Little Gringly in Clarborough. Second son, William, my lands in Springthorpe and Little Corringham, Co. Lincoln. Eldest dau., Jane Maltby, £100, under 21. Brother Robert Maultby of Bawtry. Younger dau., Elizabeth Maltby, £100. Mrs. Anne Mason, godmother of Elizabeth. Child my wife is now with, £50. Wife Mary to hold my house during the nonage of my sons, Jon and William, to have the residue and to be exex. Sister Ellin Chatterton, 10/—. Nephew John Maltby, 10/—. Servant, Alice Moore, 20/—. Poor of Springthorpe, 20/—. Brother Robert friends, Mr. Dickens of Saundley, clk., and Beaumont Sutton of E. Retford, gent., to be overseers. Annie Stounton, Tho Maulby +, Witnesses. Codicil, 28 Dec., 1647: House in Briggate to be sold and £100 to son John at 21, and the residue for my youngest son, lately born. Tho. Biggs, Tho. Maultby, P. C. Y., Apl., 1648. Filed Will.

This Will appears again under the American section of the book, but it will bear considerable study here. From the Retford Baptisms we learn that John Maultbie had a son Richard, bapt. 15 Aug., 1642, and from the Retford Burials that Richard died 7 Aug., 1644. John Maltby, the father, died 4 Jan., 1647-8.

Mrs. Anne Mason, godmother of his daughter Elizabeth, was probably a connection by marriage, as his niece Margaret married William Mason, gent., of E. Retford. His nephew John was a son of his brother Robert of Bautry.

It will be noticed that in his will John Maltby leaves "Eldest son, John Maltby, houses in Briggate, E. Retford, etc." And further: "Wife Mary to hold my houses during the nonage of my sons Jon and William," and still further in the codicil: "House in Briggate to be sold and £100 to son John at 21 and the residue for my youngest son, lately born." This youngest son was Robert. The Retford Baptisms give: "28 Dec., 1647, Robt. son of John Maultby."

Now if we turn to the year 1662 we find William Carr and Dorothy, his wife; John Maltby; George Holmes and Mary, his wife; Robert Maltby; Robert White and Johne, his wife, selling two messuages, two gardens, 25 acres of land, etc., in East Retford, etc.

William Carr and wife Dorothy I fail to place. John Maltby I take to be John, son of John, who had come of age (hence he would have been born in 1641) and was selling the houses in Briggate to secure his £100 and it was probably this money received thai started him in the New World, for it will be remembered that only two years later, 1664, April, we find John Maltby's signature in New England.

George Holmes and Mary, his wife. This I presume to be Mary Maltby, wid. of John Maltby, who had remarried. This would explain why no will of a Mary Maltby could be found by Mr. Fothergill.

Robert White and Johne, his wife. In the will of William, son of Robert Maltby of Bawtry, he mentions: "his cousin, Jane Turnell," always presumed to be Jane, dau. of John Maltby. Possibly she m. first Robert White. Much of this is purely conjecture, but it is plausible and worth keeping in mind.

Inquisition indented made at Swineshead, Lincoln, 2 Jany., 14 James I., on the death of William Maltby of Billinghay, Lincoln. Gave his message in Billinghay to son William, excepting three arable lands to son Robert; if William die without issue, Thomas is to have the message; wife Margery to have messuage until son William is 21. William senior died 5 Feby., 8 James I. The messuage was held by knights, service being a twentieh part of a knight's fee, worth 20/. That John Maltby is the son and next heir and was aged at the time of his father's death, 15 years and 4 months. John Maltby died 28 May, 14 James I., at South Kynne. William is his brother and next heir, aged at the time of his brother's death, 16 or more. The messuage is in the hands of the King by reason of the minority of John, the son. Inquest Post Mortem, 4 James 1 pt. 2, No. 65. Chancery Inquisition, 22 James I., pt. 1, No. 71.

1645. 22 Nov. Maltby V. Sanderson. Orators William Maltby of Willoughton als Willerton, Co. Lincoln, yeoman, and Elizabeth, his wife, and Mary Dales of Willoughton, wid., dau. of Hamond Sutton, dec. That Hamond Sutton had issue by a first wife, Nicholas and Ann (Sutton) and by Margaret, his second wife, formerly the wife of Pickering, your said Oratrixes, Elizabeth and Mary, and the said Margaret had issue by Pickering, Katherine, now wife of John Chapman of Willoughton aforesaid.

Nicholas Sutton, uncle of Hamond Sutton, fifty years ago settled his estate on the marriage of Hamond Sutton and Margaret Pickering. Dispute about the trusts. Defendants: Sir Peregrine Saunderson, now Lord Castleton; Lady Francis, his mother; Lady Jane Saunderson, wid.; John Chapman, Katherine, his wife and William Tomlinson. (Chancery Proceedings, Car. I., M. 35-9.)

NOTE.—The Suttons and Maltbys seem to have been closely connected. The name Hamond Maltby evidently came from the Suttons. The Will of John Maltby, of E. Retford, 1647, mentions for overseer, "Beaumont Sutton, Gent." The Will of Johan Maltbye, 1545, mentions Isabell Sutton. (It has been thought that the name Isabell in the Maltby family was derived from the Suttons.) The Will of Robert Maltby of Wilghcton, 1635, mentions son Hammond. It may also be that the name Nicholas comes from the Sutton family.

1648. Lambe V. Maltby. The answer of Margaret Maltby, relict of Martin Maltby, dec., deft., to complaint of Thomas Lambe, Ric. Lyme and Elizabeth, his wife. Abraham Lambe held land in Stillington holden from Merton College, Oxford. (Chancery Proceedings before 1714, H. 218-17.)

NOTE.—Sir Nicholas Malby's w. was Thomasine Lamb of Leeds, York.

1649. Final agreement made in the Court of our Lord the King, at Westminster, between John Story, plaintiff, and Hugh Maltby and Elizabeth, his wife, deforcients of a messuage, a garden, an orchard, 22 acres of land, 7 of meadow, 2 of pasture in Gotham, Notts. Feet of Fines Hily, 1649.

1650. 24 Sept. Administration of the goods of Thomas Maltby of Gt. Chilton in Merrington, Durham to Anne, the relict. P. C. C., 146.

1653. Robert Maltbie, son of John Maltbie, bapt. (York Par. Reg. Soc.)

1651. Committee for Compounding William Maltby, 4 July, 1651. Begs to compound, not being requestered for going into the King's army in his minority. Has only wearing apparel, value £6. 25 Feb. (or July). Fine at 1/6—£1. (Vide Printed State Papers.)

1654. Letters and Papers relating to the Navy. Aug. 1654. Letter from Comrs. for Sick and Wounded to the Admiralty. In favor of John Maltby, surgeon of Hull, for payment of sums due for his charge of the sick and wounded there in 1655 (3 ?). (Vide. Printed State Papers.)

1651. Abstract of Nuncupative Will of Thomas Malbye, 8 June 1651. Wife and child, Sarah £58 a year out of the Manor of Chakewell; Margaret, dau. of my sister, Mary Frewin, two wodds. Copyhold called Stubrids and the great Fusser Feild to be sold and divided amongst my three sisters, except my eldest sister. (Proved in P. C. C., 14 Oct., 1651, by Sarah Baker, otherwise Malbye, the relict. 192, Grey.)

N. B.—A friend who is a barrister informs me that soldiers, sailors, etc., when dying were allowed to make verbal wills in the presence of witnesses which were legal. The above is such a will.

1654. 18 Nov. Commission issued to Christopher Maultby, uncle and curator of Christopher and Dorcas Maultby, children of Thomas Maultby, late of Miningsey, Co. Lincoln, widdower. (P. C. C. 221.)

1657-8. Abstract of the Will of Richard Maltby of Kexby, dated 2 Feby., 1657-8. Burial at Upton. Eldest daughter Elizabeth, under 21. Son Richard Maltby at 21, the house in occupation of Tho. Crane. Son John at 21, house in occupation of John Lamin. Daughters Ann and Mary at 21. Brother Robert Maltby's four children. Wife Mary. (P. C. C., 30 July 1658, by Maultby the relict and exex. 512 Wotten.)

1658. Robert Maltby of Bawtry, Yorks, admitted to Greys Inn, London, 1658. (Query: Is this Robert Maltby of Bawtry, will made 1660, proved 1663, or is it his son Robert?)

1659. John Mabley and Anne Lake (?) m. 1659 (p. 101) Old Yorkshire.

1659. Final agreement made in the Court of our Lord the King at Westminster between William Wood Clerk, purchaser, and John Maultby, gent., and Anne Aubynne, widdow, vendor of one messuage, 2 cottages, 20 acres of land, 40 of meadow, 80 of pasture in Billinghay, alias Billinghey and North Kynne, Co. Lincoln. Feet of Fines Trinity, 1659.

1659. Between William Maltby, William Bingley, John Bingley, purchaseors and John Maltby and Bridgett, his wife; Thomas Barker and Mary, his wife; George Cartwright and Elizabeth, his wife; vendors of 3 messuages, etc., in Littleburrow and Sturton. Notes of Fines, Notts, Easter, 1659.

Note.—The above I take to be William Maltby, bapt. 20 Dec., 1605, whose father, Richard, Will 1618, left him lands, etc., in Stourton next Stow. He had a brother John, bapt. 1604; a sister Anne, bapt. 1611 (perhaps the wid. Anne Aubynne above); Mary, bapt. 1612, (wife of Thomas Barker ?), and a sister Elizabeth, bapt. 1613 (w. of George Cartwright ?).

1659. Maultby V. Humberston. Orator John Maultby of Sturton in Stowe, Co. Lincoln, gent. Action about right of common. Deft. Robert Humberston. Chanc. Proc. bef. 1714. Mit 518-67.

1659. Abstract of Will of Christopher Maultby of Gosberkirke, Co., Lincoln, husbandman, dated 13 May, 1658. Son-in-law Henry Jefferye, son-in-law Edward Jeffery, son-in-law Thomas Jefferye, daughter-in-law Mary Jefferye, Uncle William Maltby, Aunt Jefferye of Long Sutton, Kinsman Francis Hill. To my brother William Maultby (if he be living). Tho. Jefferye of Long Sutton and Robert Hill of Gosberkirke. (P. C. C., 26 July, 1659.)

1660. Final agreement between John Booth and Thomas Dickenson, purchaseors, and Thomas Maultby and Eliz., his wife; Thomas Clayton and Sara, his wife; Robert Thornton and Elizabeth, his wife, vendors of land in Billinghey and North Kynne, Co. Lincoln. Feet of Fines Hily, 12-13, Car. II., 1660.

1660. From St. Peter's Church: "Hugh Maultby of Hoveringham, Notts, and Mary Gibson of Cossall, Notts. (license) 1 25 Feby., 1660."

1660. Final agreement made between John Smyth, purchaseor, and John Hallifax, clerk; Elizabeth, his wife; William Mason, Margaret, his wife; Robert Farmery and Mary, his wife, and Sarah Maultby, widdow, vendors of third part of a messuage, a barn, a stable, a garden, an orchard, 60 acres of land, 23 of meadow, 20 of pasture and pasture for 17 animals in Humberston, Co. Lincoln. Feet of Fines Hily, 12 and 13, Car. II., 1660. (See Will of Richard Maltby, Will 1638.)

1660. Abstract of the Will of Richard Maltby of Hommanby, Co. York, weaver, dated 6 Sept., 1658. Sons Richard, Thomas, Christopher, Robert, Mathew; daughter Eliz., now wife of Wm. Atkinson. John Mawger of Flambrough. Wife Ann, son John. Codicil, son-in-law, Robert Blackwell. P. C. Y., 1660-1, 43-455. (See Will of Thomas Maltby, 1666-7.)

1660. Abstract of the Will of Robert Maltby of Bawtry, dated 10 Nov., 1660. Eldest son, William Maltby, land I had with his mother in Clarebrough William Morhouse and house in E. Retford. (This William d.s.i. See Will 1665.) Second son, Robert Maltby, the house I now live in, land called Catts. Bethey Moore, land at Springthorp in Lincolnshire and to be exor. (This is the Robert Maltby who sold and mortgaged land about 1670, and who is presumed to be the Robert Maltby, Senior, who was in New Haven in 1671, and "being to return to England"; he was cousin to Robert Maltby, b. 1648, at East Retford, who is presumed to have been the "Robert Maltby, Junior," with him, "strangers" in New Haven.) Son, John Maltby, under 21, £200. (Bapt. at E. Retford, 2 Aug., 1642, John, son of Robert Maultbie.) Cosin John Chattor. (His sister Hellen (or Ellen) m. John Chatterton. He probably refers to a nephew, John Chatterton.) Fourth son, Daniel Maltby, the Crowne. (He was born in 1650, as we learn later, where he is called "aged 17" in 1667.) Daughter, Barbara Maltbie, £200. (She was born in 1648 as she is called "aged 18" in 1668, when she married Richard Thwaytes, gent.) Nephew John Chattor, 20/—. Cousin Ratchell Williamson, 10/—. Sister Mary Long, £5. Newpews, Ro Maltbie, £5; John Maltby. (Supposed to be the emigrants to New England.) Cosins John Chatterton and Robert Hindmarsh to be supervisors. Wife Ann, £100. Tho. Swallow +. Anne Watton +. P. C. Y., 1663-5, 46-66.

1660. Raw V. Maultby. 1 June, 1660. Orators Thomas Raw of Willoughton, Co. Lincoln, yeoman, and Richard Raw, his brother, of Aiseby. That Anne Maltby, late of Willoughton, wid., dec., had a personal estate worth £60 and died in 1657 and admon. was granted to your Orators, they being nephews and next of kinn. One William Maltby of Willoughton, has combined with Henry Pridden and forceably put your Orators out of possession, pretending a will, when in truth she made none. Deft. William Maltby. (Chancery Proceedings before 1714, R. 22-139. See Will of Thomas Maultbie, 1645.)

1662. Buried at Orston, Thomas, son of John, 27 Oct.

1662-65. The Genealogist, Vol. 10, 1894, p. 164: "Thomas Tancred, Esq., of Broughbridge, a Bart. by Charles II., 1662, buried at Aldborough, 19 Aug., 1663; m. Frances, dau. and co-heir of Christopher Maltby, Esq. of Cottingham. She was buried at Aldborough, 27 April, 1655 or 1665 (?). Children: Sir William Tancred and Catherine Tancred." (See Pedigree No. II.)

1662. Maltby V. Andrews. 2 Nov., 1662. Orator John Maltby of Wiborton, Co. Lincoln, yeoman. Two years since your Orator sold 3 acres of land in Boston to Robert Andrews. Orator's wife not of age till Michaelmas next. Relief from a bond. (Chanc. Proc. before 1714, C. 160.)

1663. This is the final agreement made between William Wood, clerk, John Booth and Robert Andrews, purchaseors, and John Maltby, gent., and Mary, his wife; vendors of 2 messuages, 2 cottages, 20 acres of land, 40 acres of pasture, 87 acres of pasture and common of pasture for all animals in Billinghay, alias Billinghey, Northkune, Boston and Kerton in Holland. Feet of

Fines, 15 Car. II., 1663, Mic. Lincoln. (For further record see 1668.)

1662. Final agreement between Peter Booth, John Langfitt, purchaseors, and Sir George Savile, bart., and Dorothy, his wife; Robert Farmery and Mary, his wife; Cecilia Cherbury, widdow; William Mason, gent., and John Maultby, vendors of a messuage, 2 cottages, 2 gardens, 2 orchards, etc., etc., in East Retford, Co. Notts. Feet of Fines, 14-15, Car. II., 1662.

NOTE.—The above are evidently descendants of Richard Maltby, Will proved 1638. Dorothy, w. of Sir George Savile is evidently a dau. of Elizabeth Maltby Hallifax or of her brother, William Maltby. Sarah Maltby m. William Parke and had a dau. Sicely, who is evidently the wid., Cecilia Cherbury. Margaret Maltby m. William Mason, gent., and Mary Maltby m. Robert Farmary. The John Maltby is evidently John, the son of Richard's brother John, or in other words, the John we believe emigrated to New England. His father having died, he evidently was co-heir with his cousins.

The following agreement has previously been mentioned and it is believed to be the sale which furnished the funds for John Maltby to start life in the New World.

1662. Final agreement between John Darell, gent.; John Ward and Elizabeth, his wife; Richard Otter, Anne, his wife, purchaseors, William Carr and Dorothy, his wife; John Maltby, George Holmes, Mary, his wife, Robert Maltby, Robert White and Johne, his wife, vendors of two messuages, two gardens, 25 acres of land, 6 of meadow, 2 of pasture and common of pasture with appurts. in East Retford, West Retford and Babworth in Co. Notts. Feet of Fines Trinity, 14 Car. II., 1662.

NOTE.—The Dorothy Carr I fail to place. John Maltby is evidently the son of John, Will proved 1647-8, and when he became of age the property in Briggate was to be sold and he was to receive £100 and his brother Robert was to have the residue. Consequently John Maltby was evidently b. in 1640-41. Mary Holmes I take to be his widowed mother, who m. George Holmes and Johne (Joan) White may have been his sister Jane.

1665. John Mabley, son of Luke, buried at St. Michael, Cornhill, Sept. 17, 1665 (p. 225) Old Yorkshire.

1664. Indenture made 25 April, 16 Car. II., 1664, betweene Owfeld als Oldfeld of Elsham, Co. Lincoln, Esq., of first part, William Maltby of London, haberdasher of hats, executor of John Julian of St. Dunstons in West of the second part and Jonathain Boole, Vicar of Elsham, Edward Smith, Thomas Smith, William Smith, Junior, William Mumby, Francis Holmes, Alexander Holmes,

John Markham, George Brooke, and Robert Hudson, all inhabitants of Elsham. Trust deed for apprenticeships and bread for the parish of Elsham with money left by John Julian. (Close Roll, 4172).

1665. Abstract of Will of Sarah Maltby of Springthorpe, Co. Lincoln, widdow, dated 6 Jany., 1664. (Widow of Richard, Will proved 1638.) Daughter Margaret Mason, Daughter Elizabeth Hallifax's children. Daughter Mary Farmary's children, which I paid for Robert Farmary, her husband, to one John Atkinson of E. Retford. Sarah, daughter of Robert Farmary. Son-in-law, William Parke, dec., Sicely, his daughter. Nephew Richard Hornby of Springthorpe. Thomas, son of William Hornby. Richard, son of Richard Hornby. Margaret and Elizabeth, sisters of said Richard. Servant, Anthony Smith. Richard Tyler, Brother John Hornby. Son-in-law John Hallifax to be exor. Robert Spicer, Thomas Robinson, William Parks, Witnesses. Proved in Arch of Stow, 17 April, 1665, 237.

1665. Abstract of Will of William Maltby of Bawtry, Co. York, gent., dated 29 June, 1665. (This is the oldest son of Robert of Bawtry, will proved 1663-65.) Brother Daniel Maltby and Sister Barbara Maltby, all my houses, lands in E. Retford, Moregate, Clarkborow, Spitlehill and Welham, Co. Notts, and my house in Bawtry, and after the death of Daniel and Barbara to my cozen, Wm. Stokeham, son of Mr. Wm. Stokeham, late of E. Retford, dec., with remainder to Richard Stookham, halfe brother of said Wm. Brother Robert Maltby £5. Cozen John Maltby £5. (John of E. Retford.) Mrs. Margaret Cordingley £5. Cozen Wm. Maltby £5 (i.e., supposed to be the emigrant to New England.) Cozen Jane Turnell 20/—. (Is this the sister of John and Wm ?) Capt. Benjamin Marchall of Doncaster £5 (Yorks.). Brother John Maltby 20/—. John Thompson 20/—. Aunt Margaret Stoakham 40/— every year. Brother and sister, Daniel and Babara, to be exors. Cozen John Hallifax, clk., 20/—. My mother Maltby one muffe. Wm. Midwinter £5. Cozen Hindmarsh £5. Wm. Midwinter, Robert Hindmarsh. P. C. Y. 1666-7, 48-127.

NOTE.—For some reason unknown William cut his two eldest brothers off with a very small share of his estate. It would appear that his mother was Anne Stoakham from his Will.

1666. 14 Nov. Administration of the goods of William Maltby of S. Dunstan's in West London, to Elizabeth, the relict. (Query: Is this a connection with Sir George Maltby, will proved 1639? See Irish records.)

1667. 10 Dec. Administration of Cuthbert Maultby of All Hallowes, Lombard St., London, to Elizabeth, the relict. P. C. C.

1667. Maltby V. Marshall. 18 May, 1667. Orator Daniel Maltby of Doncaster, Co. York, aged 17, by his guardian, Richard Thwaites, of Arnthorp. Messuage called the Crown in Bawtry. Orator's father was Robert Maltby. Title. Defts. Rowland Cottan, John Noble, Benjamin Marshall. (Chanc. Proc. before 1714, Ham 489.

1666. York Marriage Licenses. Ric. Thwaytes,* gent., als Clarworth or Tickhill of Armthorpe and Barba Maltby, aged 18, of Bawtry, spinster, 1666.

NOTE.—It will be seen that the guardian of Daniel Maltby was his brother-in-law, husband of his sister Barbara. Benjamin Marshall is perhaps the "Capt. Benjamin Marshall of Doncaster" mentioned in the Will of William Maltby, 1665, older brother of Daniel of Doncaster.

1668. Cannon V. Maltby. 22 May, 1668. Orator Richard Cannon of S. Clement Danes, Middlesex, merchant taylor. Leonard Pettie of Luppitt, Devon, owed your Orator money. Nathaniel Burroughs of Bovey Tracey, Devon, and Wm. Maltby of Sherborne, Dorset, Innkeeper, have combined to defraude your Orator and are made defts. (Chancery Proceedings before 1714, C. 46-55.)

1669. Orston Records: Peter Maltby, son of Widdow Maltby, buried 24 Nov., 1669.

1669. John Maltby, buried the (sic) 13 Jan.

1669. Maltby V. Potterell. 5 May, 1669. Answer of Ralph Potterell to complaint of Elizabeth Maultby, widdow. That the compt. is relict and administratrix of William Maultby, Citizen and Haberdasher, of London. Money matters. (Chanc. Proc. before 1714, C. 183.)

1669. Maultby V. Phillipps. 28 Apl., 1669. Oratrix Elizabeth Maultby of S. Olaves, Southwark, wid., relict and administratrix of William Maltby, Citizen and Haberdasher, of London. William in his lifetime four years ago, became bound for Tho. Phillipps and Tho. Sturges. Reliefe from the bond being put in suit. (Chanc. Proceedings, Bridges before 1714, 51-82.

1668. Abstract of Will of John Maltby of Kingston upon Hull, yeo., 11 Sept., 1668. Wife Anne a cottage in Awbrough in Holder-

* It was Isabel Thwaites whom William Fairfax of Steeton carried off from the clutches of the Abbess of Nun Appleton. Isabel Thwaites was a great heiress and Mother Church intended her for its own, but Will Fairfax managed to get her out of the church where she was confined and they were married at Bolton Percy "and there was scarce any end of the riches this stolen bride showered upon the happy thief." The Abbess lived to see the Dissolution and her nunnery was granted to none other than the son of William and Isabel Thwaites Fairfax.

ness. Son Stephen, second son John, third son Joseph, daughter Susanna, daughter Mary. (10 May 1671. Proved in P. C. Y., 52-144.) See Wills 1679-80 and 1680-81.

1666. Abstract of Will of Thomas Maltby of Hunmanby, York, batchelor, dated 21 Aug. 1666. Brothers John, Richard, Mathew. Sister Eliz. Atkinson, her children 5/— each. Brother Robert Maltby, his children 5/— each. Brother Christopher's child. Brother-in-law Robert Blackwell. (P. C. Y., 1666-7, 48-250.)

1668. Final agreement between Helen Webberly and John Maultby and Mary, his wife, Robert Andrew and Elizabeth, his wife, messuage and land in Weberton. (Feet of Fines, 20 Car. II., 1668, Mic. Lincoln.)

1669. Final agreement made between Thomas Wilson, gent., and John Maltby and Thomas Maltby, vendors of 2 messuages, a barn, a stable, a garden, an orchard, 6 acres of land, 52 acres of pasture common of turbary and pasture in Northkyne. (Feet of Fines, 21 Car. II., 1669, Trinity, Lincoln.)

1670. Married at Orston. Ann Maltbie and Thomas Wright, by vicar of Orston in Elton Church, July 6, 1670.

1670-71. Final Agreement between Josuam Maltby and Joseph Claxton, vendor of a message with appurts. in Boston. (Feet of Fines, Lincoln Hil, 22-23 Car. II., Lincoln.)

1670. Final agreement between Richard Willan, gent., purchaseor, and John Willie, gent., and Rebecca, his wife, and Rebecca Maltby, widdow, vendors of 2 messuages, 2 gardens, 2 orchards, 10 acres of land, 20 acres of meadow, 20 acres of pasture in Littlebrough and Sturton, Co. Notts. (Feet of Fines, 22 Car. II., 1670 E. Notts.)

1671. Cotton V. Maltby. 13 Feby., 1657-8. Orator Rowland Cotton of Crake Marsh, Co. Stafford, Esq., son and heir of Wm. Cotton and Ann Cotton. Orator's mother, Ann, was seised of the Crowne Inn in Bawtry, Co. York, and worth £50 per ann. In 1642, your Orator was in ward of the Court of Wards and a fine was set at £450 and £40 rent. By assignments the Crowne became vested in Robert Maltby, who is since dead and the messuage has come to Daniel Maltby, an infant son and heir of said Robert, who with Richard Thwaits, gent., have threatened to

* Arthur H. Norway in "Highways and Byways in Yorkshire" writes: "I have ridden far (on bicycle) and am going into the 'Crown,' that picturesque old hostelry, for some refreshment, over which the proverbial saying about the town warns me not to hurry, lest I be overtaken by the fate of 'the saddler of Bawtry, who was hanged for leaving his liquor.'" The incident follows. This "Crown," where he stopped is very probably the same "Crowne" messuage owned by Daniel Maltby. A note on the Twaite family (Richard Thwaite was brother-in-law of Daniel Maltby) will be found under date 1668.

eject your Orator. Object of suit equity of redemption of the Crowne.* Defts. Daniel Maltby, Richard Thwaites and John Noble. The answer of Daniel Maultby is that it was an absolute purchase, as it appears by deed dated 30 Oct., 1654. This deft. is now 21 years of age, but is willing to reconvey the messuage if paid for it. (Chancery Proceedings before 1714, C. 201.)

1670. Diglyn V. Maltby. Easter 22, Car. II., Orator Ezekiel Diglyn of Orston, Co. Notts, Clerk, Parson of Orston. William Maltby, the elder, of Orston has not paid his tithes for eight years last past . . . says your Orator does nothing for him. Object: to recover £4, the value of the tithes. (Excheq. Proceedings, Notts, Car. II., Notts.)

NOTE.—This is probably William Maltby of Orston, father of William Maltby, b. 1641, who m. Jane Brough.

1671. Abstract of Nuncupative Will of Elizabeth Maltby, dated 9 Jany., 1670-1. Daughter Martha leases in Fleet Street and King Street. My sister Hales. Nephew Josiah Wadsworth, Jonathon and Thomas Reeves. Bother Thomas Wadsworth. Uncle Wadsworth. She cosen Hammond. Cosens Duffil, Manning, Hales. 17 Jan., 1670-1. Administration with will to John Parker, the curator of Martha Maltby, the residuary legatee, a minor. (6 Duke.)

NOTE.—Elizabeth Maltby was evidently born a Wadsworth.

1671. Abstract of Will of William Maltby of Broxholm, Co. Lincoln, Farmer, dated 29 Sept. 1671. Son John, son William, son Richard, daughters Ann, Mary. Brother Robert Maltby's children. Brother Nicholas' child. Wife Mary. (Proved in Arch Stow, 3 Nov. 1671, 70.)

1672. Abstract of the Will of Richard Beare of Bautrey, Co. York. To my daughter, Mary Boare, a house in Bautrey, wherein one Elizabeth Carbonell now dwelleth, lately purchased of Robert Maultby and John Phillips. Dated 6 August, 1672. (Proved in P. C. Y., 18 Sept. 1672, 53-262.)

NOTE.—From this item we find that Robert Maultby of Bawtry sold a house in Bawtry to Richard Beare a short time before 6 August 1672. It It was probably in order to have ready money for his voyage to New England that he sold this house. See under American notes where Robert Maltby, Senior, was a "stranger in New Haven," Dec. 29, 1671.

1672-3. Abstract of Will of Hammon Maltbie of Thonnocke, Co. Lincoln, batchelor, dated 15 March, 1671-2. Brother William's son William. Brothers Thomas, John, Mathew. Sister Mary

Labley. House in Bishops Norton (Proved in Archdeacony Stow, 6 March, 1672, 123.)

1672. Final agreement between John Flamsteed, senior, gent., and Stephen Flamsteed, gent., purchaseors, and Sir John Shore, Kt., Hugh Maultby, Mary, his wife, vendors of three messauges, three gardens, three orchards, 60 acres of land, 20 acres of meadow, 40 acres of pasture in Chilwell, Attenborow and Cassall, Co. Notts. (Feet of Fines, 24 Car. II., 1672, Trinity.)

1673. Abstract of Will of Henry Maltby of Hummanby. Dated 2 April, 1673. Daughters Elizabeth, Ellin, Jane, Grace. Close called Dammes. Son Richard. Wife Katherine. (P. C. Y., 1675, 56-67.)

1674. 15 Aug. Administration of William Maltby of Sherborne, Dorset, to Grace, the relict. (P. C. C.)

1672-3. Maltby V. Maltby. 17 Feby., 1672-3. Orator Daniel Maltby of Doncaster, Co. York, gent. Robert Maltby of Bawtry borrowed £50 from Robert Langley of Bawtry and for security mortgaged three messuages in Bawtry. Langley conveyed his interest in the mortgage to your Orator. Robert Maltby has failed to pay the principal and interest. To recover money and discovery of a deed of agreement. Defts. Robert Maultbie, Cornelius Clarke, Wm. Simpson and Eliz. Partridge. (Chanc. Proc. before 1714, C. 542-206.)

NOTE.—This also bears out the supposition that to raise money to go to New England, Robert Maultbie mortgaged his three messuages in Bawtry. See American notes, where he mentions "ye wrong sustained in coming from England," etc.

1673. Maltby V. Alured. 15 June, 1673. Oratrix Sarah Maltby, spinster, ye only daughter now living of Robert Maltby of Bawtry, Co. York, by the said Robert, her father and guardian. Anne Maltby of Bawtry, ye elder, (her grandmother) was, during her widowhood, seized of a good estate. To recover rents. Ann Maltby, the younger, dec. sister to your Oratrix. The answers of Mary Coulson, Richard Wayne (or Wavnd) and Dorothy, his wife, defts. to bill of Sarah Maltby, an infant, by Robert Maltby, her guardian. Robert Coulston of Cottingham was agent for Ann Maltby, the elder, as collector of rents. Ann directed that any money that should remain more than herselfe should receive should go to the children of one Robert Maltby, which they believe were Ann, who is since dec. and Sarah, the now complt. Ready to perform the trusts. The answer of John Alured, a defendant. Anne Maltby died intestate, Oct. 19, Car. II., (1667-8) and admon. was granted to this deft. as next of kin by the P. C. Y. Estate of Ann Maltby. (Chanc. Proc. before 1714, C. 63.)

NOTE.—It would seem that Ann, w. of Robert Maltby of Bawtry, Will proved 1663-5, was an Alured or possibly John Alured was a sister's son. If she were an Alured, then William Maltby, Will 1666-7, was probably the son by a first wife (perhaps Barbara) Stoakham. It also would seem that Robert Maltby, returning to England and needing funds, tried to collect rents from the estate left his infant daughter by her grandmother. The fact that this Robert of Bawtry was slighted in his brother's will and that he seems to have been in more or less legal difficulties, rather points to the fact that he was personna non grata with his relatives.

1675. Abstract of Will of William Maltby of Speeton, Co. York, yeoman, dated 15 May, 1675. Grandchild Katherine Johnson, my house in Bridlington, remainder to her sister, Elizabeth Johnson. Son-in-law John Hodgsen. Grandchildren Benjamin Johnson and George Hodgson. Eme Maltby, wife of John Lumbard. Brother Robert Maltby's children, living at Flamboro. Brother Robert Norram's two daughters. Son Richard Hardye's children. Son Thomas Vickerman's children. Son-in-law John Vickerman of Bridlington. Grandchild Tho. Preston. (Proved in P. C. Y., 1675, 56-198.)

1678-9. Marriage Licenses, London: Jan. 27, John Ayent (Ayest ?) of St. Magnus, London, Widr. about 35; and Martha Maltby of St. Olaves, Southwark, spinster, 21 or upward, at her own disposal, at St. Thomas in Southwark, or (blank).

NOTE.—This I take to be Martha, dau. of Elizabeth Maltby, Will 1670-1, and that Elizabeth Maltby, who made the Will is the wid. Elizabeth, of S. Olaves, Southwark, relict of William Maltby, haberdasher, of London.

1679. John Maltbie was buried 8 May, 1679 (Yorkshire Parish Reg. Society, Burton-Fleming, 1538-1812).

1679. Abstract of Will of John Maltby of Kexbie, Co. Lincoln, yeoman, dated 4 Oct., 1679. Burial at Upton. Wife Elizabeth, a house and one close called Cooper's Close, an oxgang purchased of William Lambe and £70. Brother Robert and his children. Brother Nicholas and his daughter Sarah. Grandchildren Richard Maltby, Cooper's Close after my wife. Grandchild Elizabeth Maltby. William Darbie's children of Apley. (His sister Elizabeth m. Wm. Derby.) Thomas Johnson of Bransby. John Johnson, dec. Thomas Johnson's children of Bransby. William and John Leary. (Stepchildren, see will 1684.) (Proved in Arch Stow, 19 Dec., 1679, 21 and 24.

From the Upton Parish Register: John Maltby, m. 23 Jany., 1633-34, Prudence Johnson. She evidently died and he married again, Elizabeth, wid. of a Mr. Leary. See her will, 1684.

1679-8. Abstract of Will of William Maltby of Kingston, upon Hull, Marriner, dated 1 Feby., 1679-8. Dorothy Maltby, daughter of my eldest brother James Maltby. Stephen, John, Joseph. Susanna and Mary, sons and daughters of my second brother, John Maltby. Wife Judith. (P. C. Y., 1680, 58-2411.) See Robert Maltby, Will 1680-81.

1679-80. Abstract of Will of William Maltbie of Broxholme, Co. Lincoln, farmer, 1 March, 1679. Daughters Ann, Elizabeth. Mercy Rementon, Ann Fanna. My sisters and brother, Ann, Mary and Richard Maltby. Wife Ann.

1680-1. Abstract of Will of Robert Maltby of Flamborough, Co. York, husbandman. Son-in-law John Meeke. Grandchild Ann Meeke. Son Robert, son Stephen, daughter Ann. Dorothy Norham of Bempton and Isabell, her sister. Son Robert and wife to be exors. (Proved in P. C. Y., 18 Jany., 1680-1, 59-41.)

NOTE.—Probably a brother of William Maltby, Will 1679-80.

1679. Abstract of Will of Mary Maultby of Normanby, in Stowe, Co. Lincoln, widdow, ult. Dec., 1674. Grandchildren William Clarke, Mary Maultby, daughter of Richard of Ingham. Ann and Thomas, son and daughter of John Tompson of Willingham. Richard, son of my son John Maltby. Sons Richard and John. (Proved in Archdeacony Stow, 9 Jany. 1679-80, by exors.)

Maultby V. Humberston. Orator John Maultby of Sturton in Stowe, Co. Lincoln, gent. Action about right of common. Deft. Robert Humberston. (Chance. Proc. before 1714. Mit., 518-67.

1682. William Maltby of Orston, Notts, married Jane Brough of Shelton, Oct. 31, 1682.

1684. Abstract of Will of Elizabeth Maultby of Upton, Co. Lincoln, widdow, 20 April 1684. Youngest son, John Leary. Eldest son, William Leary. (Proved in Arch Stow, 13 June, 1684, 40.)

1685. Abstract of Will of Judith Maultby of Grayingham, Co. Lincoln, widdower, 4 April, 1685. Sister Jane Newill, a cottage. Mother Margaret Newill. Sister Anne Tompkinson. Ann Tompkinson, daughter of John. John Tompkinson, son of John, my nephew. Sister Mary Smith. Thomas Smith, Junior. Sister Sarah Crane. Sister Margaret Newill. Joseph Tompkinson. Poor of Ingham. (Proved in Archy of Stow, 10 April, 1685.)

1686. Abstract of Will of John Maultby of Kingston upon Hull, Co. York, mariner, dated 27 Oct., 1685. Mentions only friends in London. (P. C. C., 1 Nov., 1686, by John Bateman. 151 Lloyd.)

1686. Allegations for Marriage Licenses Issued by the Commissary Court of Surrey. Transcribed by Alfred Ridley Bax, F.S.A.

Note.—The two items from the above work were kindly furnished by the transcriber.

1686. 8th October. William Mawbey of St. Martin in the ffields, bachelor, 24 (hence born 1662) and Martha Farmer of St. Michael, Wood Street, London, single woman, 21 (to be married) at St. Saviours, Southwark. With the consent of Richard Farmer, her father.

1689-90. "Richard Rogers of St. Sepulchre, Lond., bach., 22, and Mary Mallaber of same, spinster, 18, consent of her parents attested by Richard Mallaber—at St. Sep., 3 Jan., 1689-90." B.

1689. Maltby V. Slater. 30 June, 1689. Orators William Maltby and Jane, his wife, ye daughter of Compton, lately dec., by Elizabeth, his wife, who afterwards married one Maltby, yeoman, since also dec. and now the widow of Samuel Slater. (Chance. Proc. before 1714, B. 88, 65-64; Chance Proc. before 174, Whit., 344; Chance. Proc. before 1714, Mit., 547-105.)

1690-1. Feby. 26. Coker V. Maltby. Orator William Coker of Beamister, Dorset, gent., son and heir of Edward Coker of Sherborne, dec., who died 1670. Estate of Edward Coker. One Grace Maltby of Sherborne, relict of Wm. Maltby of Sherborne, was guardian to your Orator. Deft. Grace Maltby. See 1674. (Chancery Proceedings before 1714, C. 315.)

1690-1. Abstract of Will of Wm. Maultby of Sutton upon Trent, Co. Notts, farmer, dated 8 Feby., 1690-1. Brother George Maultby. Brother's children, Mary and Elizabeth. Wife Elizabeth and daughter Mary Maultby. Bond dated 1 Dec., 1702. Inventory £126:5:0. Filed will.

1691. Maltby V. Royston. 2 Dec., 1691. Orator William Maltby of ———, Co. Lincoln, gent., exor. of John Maltby, his father. Money matters. (Chanc. Proc. before 1714, C. 544-44.)

1693. Abstract of Will of William Maultby of Martin in Timberland, Co. Lincoln, weaver, dated 18 Jany., 1693-4. Son George.

daughters Mary, Elizabeth, son William. Wife Elizabeth. (Proved in Cons. of Lincoln, 30 Jany., 1693-4, folio 83.)

1695. Faith Maltbee, wid., d. 1695 (Old York).

1695. Maltby V. Royston. Orator William Maltby of Stow, exor. of his father, John Maltby. Deft. John Royston. Money matters. Chancery Proceedings before 1714, Whit. 353.

1696. Maltby V. Pollard. Orators William Maltby of Crowland, Co. Lincoln, yeoman, and Susanna, his wife, late widow and exex. of William Turlington, etc. Dispute as to right of common. (Chance. Proc. before 1714, C. 544-40.)

1697. America and West Indies, p. 326, Vol. X.: "On Governor Fletcher's arrival Malby applied to him for pay to discharge his debts contracted in the service, while Governor Fletcher refusing, Malby was obliged to leave the country secretly without satisfying his creditors." Board of Trade, New York, Jan. 26, 1697.

Answer (p. 331): "If anything be due Sergeant Malby it is from her (Bradshaw's widow) but Malby did not leave the country, as Mr. Shanke alleges, for he served a considerable time in the country's pay after Governor Fletcher's arrival."

NOTE.—It would be of considerable interest and great value if it could be ascertained just who was this Malby, serving in the army or navy in 1697. Could it have been the emigrant, Robert Maltbye, brother of John and William?

1697-8. Abstract of Will of John Maultby of Broxholme, Co. Lincoln, farmer, dated 7 March, 1697-8. Son-in-law William Quip of Thorp in the Fallowes. Wife Elizabeth. Sister Mary Blakey. Sister Anne Kilne. Brother Richard Maltby. (Proved in Arch Stow, 1697-8, by the exors. 146.)

1698. "There was a Maltby, a freeholder of Newton, in 1698, in Derbyshire and Lincolnshire—the surname also occurs in the last Nottinghamshire."

1698-9. Abstract of Will of Joseph Maultby of S. Paul, Shadwell, Co. Middlesex, marriner, dated 2 Dec., 1695. Mentions no relatives. (Proved in P. C. C., 6 Feby., 1698-9, by Wm. Westall. 27 Pett.)

1698-9. Abstract of Will of Hugh Maultby of Hoveringham, Co. Notts, husbandman, dated 25 March, 1699-1700. Son William, my house. Son Hugh Maultby. Son Richard Maultby. Son John Maultby. Son James Maultby. Daughter Mary. Wife Mary to have the residue. (P. C. Y., 1698-9, 63-302.)

NOTE.—This should be of interest to the Hoveringham Maltbys. We find the same names still appearing in this branch of the family. The fol-

.lowing record from St. Peter's Church evidently refers to the above Hugh and Mary, his wife: "Hugh Maultby of Hoveringham, Notts, and Mary Gibson of Cossall, Notts (license) 25 Feby., 1660.

1698. Abstract of Will of Thomas Maltby of S. Paul, Shadwell, Co. Middlesex, mariner, dated 28 March, 1698. Thomas Maultby of Shadwell to be exor. (Proved in P. C. C. 27 Feby., 1700-1. 25 Dyer.)

1700. Maltby V. Jolland. 23 Jany., 1700. Orator William Maltby of Sturton in Stow, Co. Lincoln, yeoman. Former bill in 1699 against John Willie, etc. Dispute about purchase of lands. Orator's father, John Maltby. John Willie married your Orator's aunt. Defts. Joseph Willie, John Jolland and Rebecca, his wife, and Rebecca Willie. (Chancery Proceedings before 1714, Whit. 257. Further answer in this suit, Whit. 258.) Amended in 1703-4. Orator's (William Maltby) grandmother was Rebecca Maltby. Orator's father, John Maltby, had a sister Rebecca Maltby, who married John Willie. Joseph and Rebecca Willie are children of John and Rebecca Maltby Willie. (Chanc. Proc. before 1714, C. 543-168.)

1701. Maltby V. Hicks. 19 Dec. 1701. Orator Richard Maltby of Righton, Co. Yorke, yeoman, and Dinah, his wife, late widdow and administratrix of John Hewittson of Righton, etc. (Chanc. Proc. before 1714, H. 611.)

1700. Abstract of Will of Mercy Maltby of Grantham, Co. Lincoln, widdow, dated 16 April, 1700. Sons William and Henry. Daughter Mercy Lambe. (Proved in Cons. of Lincoln, 24 April, 1700, folio 107.

1702. Abstract of Will of Thomas Maltby of Shadwell, marriner, dated 22 Aug., 1702. Wife Margaret. (Proved in P. C. C., 26 June, 1710. 125 Smith.)

1704. Abstract of Will of Richard Maltby of Ciam Cloas in Greasley, Co. Notts. Sons John, William, Thomas. Wife Rebecca. Wife and Daniel Maltby to be exors. Inventory, 8 Feby., 1703-4. £18:11:8. Indorsed, 3 May, 1704. Filed will at York.

1706. Reg. St. Mary Le Bow. William Maltby, emg. and Mary Westly (p. 38, London Marriage Licenses).

1710. Married at Orston. John Maltby and Anne Kirk. Feb. 4. 1710.

1711. Abstract of Will of Mary Maltby of Reighton, York, widow, 26 Dec., 1711. Son Richard, son William, son John. (Proved in P. C. Y., 27 May, 1714, 68-61.) See Maltby V. Hicks, 1701.

1714. Orston. William, son of John Maltby, bapt. April 25.

1716. Orston. Eliz., dau. of John Maltby, bapt. Oct. 15.
1717. Orston. Hugh, son of John Maltby, bapt. Feb. 14.
1717. Bloomfield's Norfolk, Vol. IV., p. 501: "In North aisle of St. Saviour's Hospital in Caselany, Norwich, is a monument to Anne, dau. of William and Jane Maultby of Orston, Notts, 1717, 29."

NOTE.—This is Anne, dau. of William and Jane *Brough* Maltby. She d. 25 Aug., 1717, and from the above note, evidently ae. 29, hence b. 1688.

1718. At Orston. William Maltby, gent., Sepult., Oct. ye 4th.

NOTE.—This is quite evidently William Maltby, who m. Jane Brough, though notes furnished by a descendant state that he died Nov. 1st, 1718.

1718-19. Abstract of Will of William Maltby of Orston, Co. Notts, gent., dated 29 March, 1718. Daughter Elizabeth Maltby, £200. Sons and daughters, Wm. Maltby, Mary Parnham, George Maltby, Tho. Maltby, John Maltby and Charles Maltby 21/—. Wife Jane sole exex. Ric. Holder, +; Tho. Cragg, +; Wm. Gaylby, +. (P. C. Y., 1718-19, 73-207.)
1719. 4 July. Administration of the goods of William Maltby of St. Mary le Bow, London, to Mary, the relict. (P. C. C., 116.)
1721. Orston. Anne Maltby, buried March ye 30.
1721. Orston. Catharin Maltby, sepult., 11 Nov.
1724. Orston. Hugh, son of John Maltby, bapt. Sept. 13.
1724. Orston. Mrs. Jane Maltby, sepult., Nov. 6.

NOTE.—This is Jane Brough, wid. of William Maltby.

1725. George, son of John and Mary Maltby, bapt. June 15, Orston.
1725. Orston. Mary, dau. of Peter Maltby, bapt. Jan. 27.
1727. Orston. Stephen, son of Peter Mattby, bapt. Jan. 1.
1728. Orston. Anne, dau. of John Maltby, bapt. 30 of April.
1728. Bloomfield's Norfolk, Vol. III., p. 449: Thomas Maltby, Sheriff of Norwich, 1728.

NOTE.—This is evidently Thomas, son of William and Jane *Brough* Maltby.

1729. Bloomfield's Norfolk, Vol. IV., p. 404: In the nave of the Church of St. Edmund the King of Martyrs, Norwich, is a stone slab—Martha, wife of Charles Malteby, 1729-32 and two of their children. Martha, their daughter 1725-2.

NOTE.—This is evidently the wife of Charles, son of William and Jane *Brough* Maltby. She would have been born in 1697 and was probably about the same age as her husband. The dau. Martha seems to have been born in 1723 and Charles Maltby probably m. about 1720.

1729. Orston. Hugh Maltby, son of John Maltby, sepult., Ap. 18.
1730. Orston. Hugh, son of John Maltby, bapt. Sept. 13.
1732. Orston. Mary, dau. of John Maltby, bapt. July 18.
1732. Orston. Hugh, son of Peter and Avis Maltby, bapt., Nov. 17.
1734. Orston. George, son of John Maltby, bapt., No. 21.
1734. Orston. Mary Maltby, sepult., Nov. 25.
1735. Orston. Catherine, dau. of Peter Maltby, sepult., Nov. 6.
1735. 19 June. Maltby V. Fawcett. Orators Thomas Maltby of Friday Street, London, Mercer and Thomas Newby of S. Johns Wapping, hatmaker. Money matters. (Chancery Proceeding. 1714-58, 1523.)

NOTE.—The year 1735 was as late as Mr. Fothergill searched for Maltby records; this date being twenty-five years after the death of William Maltby, emigrant to New England.

1736. Orston. John, son of Peter and Avice Maultby, bapt. July 18.
1736. Orston. William, son of John and Mary Maultby, bapt. Oct. 14.

NOTE.—From the names of the children of the above John and Mary Maltby it would seem probable that John was John, the son of William and Jane Brough Maltby.

1736. John Maultby and Elizabeth Cook, m. Nov. 18, at Orston.
1737. Bloomfield's Norfolk, Vol. III., p. 450: Charles Maltby, Sheriff of Norwich in 1737.

NOTE.—This is evidently Charles, son of William and Jane Brough Maltby.

1738. Orston. Eliz., dau. of Peter and Avice Maultby, bapt. Aug. 11.
1739. Orston. Mary, dau. of John Maultby, buried June 3.
1740. Orston. Katharin, dau. of Peter and Avice Mautlby, bapt. Feb. 7.
1740. Orston. Katherine Maultby, infant, buried Feb. 17.
1742. Orston. Avis, the wife of Peter Maltby, was buried Oct. ye 5.
1745. Orston. Married, Elizabeth Maltby and George Oldershaw, July 1, 1745.
1746. Orston. William Maultby and Eliz. Hill, m. Aug. 4, 1746.

1744. Dec. 29. Buried, Elizabeth, dau. of Brough Maltby, linen-draper.

1746. April 6. Buried, Ann Maltby, a child.

1748. May 17. Buried, Affiah Maltby, sister to Mr. Maltby, linen-draper.

NOTE.—These three records from St. Mary, Woolworth Burials.

1746. In 1746 a Charles Maltby was committed to York Castle for High Treason.

With the hope that some descendant, either in England or the States may be able to furnish some information concerning the following item we are publishing it in this book. Anyone who can throw any light on this subject is earnestly requested to inform the compiler.

"The History of Massachusetts, from the first settlement in 1628 to 1750 by Thomas Hutchinson, late Governor of Massachusetts, Boston, 1795," page 357.

(In the year 1740.) "At length it being known that Lord Euston's election for Coventry was dubious, one of these gentlemen undertook to the Duke of Grafton to secure the election, provided Mr. Belcher might immediately be removed, and to accomplish his design he represented to Mr. Maltby, a large dealer in Coventry stuffs, and a zealous dissenter, that Mr. Belcher was with the Episcopal clergy, conspiring the ruin of the Congregational interest in New England, and unless he was immediately removed, it would be irrevocably lost; that the Duke of Grafton had promised if Lord Euston's election could be secured it should be done; that letters to his friends in Coventry would infallibly secure it; that he could not better employ his interest than in the cause of God and religion. Maltby swallowed the bait, used all his interest for Lord Euston; the twe gentlemen spent three weeks at Coventry, and having succeeded, agreeable to the Duke's promise, Mr. Belcher was removed a day or two after their return. This account I received from Mr. Maltby himself, who lamented that he had suffered himself to be so easily imposed on."

From the syntax it would seem that the "Mr. Maltby" of whom Governor Hutchinson wrote, resided in the Colony and journeyed to England to labor for the interests of the Congregational Church in New England, and that he returned to New England, where he had an interview with Governor Hutchinson. Who was this "Mr. Maltby?" Was it Captain Samuel (2) Maltby? The Genealogist can think of no other Maltby who would have been of the proper age and educationally fitted for such a mission. If this was Samuel (2) Maltby, did he visit relatives in England at this time, and did he perhaps bring back that "coat-of-arms" which figures in the inventory of his estate some ten years later?

Could some reader look up the above mentioned reference? Doubtless if we had more material copied we should have some clue to the identity of the "Mr. Maltby" mentioned. Possibly there are other references to the Maltbys in this book. It is certainly worth investigating.

1746. Orston. William, son of William and Eliz. Maltby, bapt. Nov. 7.

1747. Orston. Elizabeth, dau. of Peter Maltby was buried March 30.

1747. Orston. Thomas, the son of Peter Maltby, was buried March 30.

NOTE.—The word "Illegit" is added to the above, but in this sense it only denotes that he was baptized by a dissenting minister.

1747. John, son of Wm. and Eliz. Maltby, bapt. Jan. 5.
1747. John, son of Wm. and Eliz. Maltby, buried Jan. 7.
1747. Mary, the dau. of Peter Maltby, buried Feb. 13.
1748. Mary, the dau. of John and Mary Maltby, bapt. May 30.
1748. John, son of William and Eliz. Maltby, bapt. Oct. 29.
1748. Peter Maltby, buried Jan. 27.
1749. Stephen Maltby, a servant, buried Oct. 29.
1750. George, the son of John and Mary Maltby, bapt. Oct. 14.
1753. Ann Maltby and Thomas Weat, m. March 6, 1753.

The above records from Orston, Notts.

1757. Orston. William Maltby and Ellen Drvig, m. Dec. 15, 1757.
1762. [1754-1774] British Officers serving in America:

Name.	Rank.	Regt.	Date of Commission.
Mawby, John	Lieut.	22	13 Feb. 1762
Mawby, John	Lieut.	22	1 Oct. 1762
Mawby, Thomas	Ensign	22	1 Oct. 1762
Mawby, John	Ensign	18	23 Nov. 1768
Mawby, ———	Adjt.	18	11 Feb. 1769
Mawby, ———	Lieut.	18	19 July 1771
Mawby, ———	Capt.	18	19 July 1771

N. B.—There is another list under Maltby, but not available for copying without too much delay.*

1763. From Modern Eng. Biog., Boase, Vol. 2 I. 2: Maltby, Mrs. Harriet, b. 1763; a friend of W. Wilberforce, W. Pitt, Hannah More and other celebrities; a large contributor of the Bath Charities. Died Royal Crescent, Bath, Dec., 1852. (See Orston Maltby Pedigree.)

* The list referred to contains these names:

Name	Rank	Regt.	Date of Commission
Maltby, John	Lieut.	22	1 Oct. 1762
Maltby, Thomas	Ensign	22	1 Oct. 1762

(Ref. N. E. Hist. and Gen. Reg. Vol. XLVIII., October, 1894, p. 424.)

1765. From Allegations for Marriage licenses Issued by the Commissary Court of Surrey. Transcribed by Alferd Ridley Bax, F.S.A. 16 June, 1765, John Mawbey of Lambeth, abode 4 weeks, gentleman, widower, and Ann Fielding of Lambeth, abode 4 weeks, spinster, 21 (to be married) at Lambeth. Sign of J. M.

1768. Orston. Mary Maltby and John Kirk, m. March 23, 1768.

1771. Orston. William Maltby and Sarah Taylor, m. June 4, 1771.

1777. Orston. Catherine Maltby, lic. and Thomas Marshall, Dec. 9, 1777.

1777. Orston. John Maltby and Sarah Pepper, w. Dc. 15, 1777.

1779. Orston. Ann Maltby and William, Beau, m. Apr. 27, 1779.

1783. Orston. John Maltby and Sarah Waun, Feb. 13, 1783.

1788. Musgraves Obituary Records: Maltby, Thomas, Lakenham Grove, Norfolk, 16 March, 1788. (E. M. 232, G. M. 277.)

1791. (Same reference): Maltby, Thomas, of New Court, Swithins Lane, 16 Feb., 1791. (E. M. 239, G. M. 190.)

1791. Orston. Thomas Maltby and Eliz. Breedon, lic., Jnly 2, 1791.

1795. Maltby-Drake. pp. 8, 73, 165, Vol. I., Glos. Notes and Queries: "Sir Frances Henry Drake, baronet of Buckland, Co. Devon, m. Ann Frances, dau. of Thomas Maltby, Esq., of St. Mary-le-bone, or Great Marylebone St., London, m. Nov. 3, 1795.

NOTE.—A letter from Lady Drake to the compiler, dated April, 1905, Nutwell Court, Lympstone, Devon, explains the history of the above person, who, although a Drake by blood, had no right to style himself "Sir Francis." Lady Drake's sympathies seemed to be with the unfortunate Miss Maltby.

1800. In Harwich churchyard: "Mr. Charles, 3rd son of Mr. George Maltby, late of Norwich, merchant, d. on the passage from Hamburg, 26 Oct., 1800, aged 33 (hence born 1767).

NOTE.—This is an older brother of Bishop Edward Maltby. He m. Sarah Sweers at Philadelphia, Pa., Aug. 17, 1796.

Cyrus Hamlin's "My Life and Times," p. 409: "I had a very interesting week in Berlin, with my nephew, William Maltby, professor elect of modern languages in Bowdoin College."

NOTE.—A. B. Seymour writes: "This, I understand, was soon after the Crimean War," (1854).

1804. Orston. William Maltby w. and Eliz. Bagnly (?) w., m. Feb. 20, 1804.

1809. William Maltby, w., and Mary Taylor, w., April 4, 1809.

1814. John Ince Maltby. R. Shelton, Notts, 24 March, 1814. P. C. Sibthorpe and Catham, Notts, 13 Apr., 1837. (See Orston Maltby Pedigree.)

1837. Henry Joseph Maltby, B.A. Vicar Egglingham, Northumberland, 2 June, 1837. (See Orston Maltby Pedigree.)

1872. Orston. Ann Maltby and John Green, 1872.

1871. Charles Maltby, eldest son of Joseph of Ilkestone, Derbyshire, b. in 1848; m. in 1871, Eliza, Long. Address: Dalby House, Ilkestone, R.S.O., Derbyshire.

1878. Thomas Maltby, C. T. E. 1878, Ordinary Companions.

1887. Lt. Gen. Robert Mallaby, served in Afghan war in 1880. T. S. C., Major General, 1887.

1813. Harriet Maltby, dau. of Brough Maltby, Esq., of Skelton, Notts, m., 1813, George Nichols, Esq. Poor Law Commission of London (Burke Landed Gentry, p. 932, Vol. II., 1846).

1879. Emily Maltby d. at Clifton near Bristol, Co. Gloster, 17 March, 1879, aged 73 (hence born 1806). Vide Tombstone in churchyard of Redland Green Church, near the Dwidham Downs, Clifton, near Bristol.

1816. "Barbadoes Mercury." Died, Richard Maltby, Esq., of Bridgetown, Barbadoes, within a few days of Sept. 14, 1816. Mrs. Maltby, his w., d. the morning of March 23, 1813.

1800. "West Indian Deeds on the Close Rolls, London, is one of Butler Claxton, by Thomas Maltby, Henrietta, his w., Nevis, 1800, 7, 13, 14, 15, 16."

NOTE.—This is evidently Thomas Maltby, b. 1752; who m. 1787, Henrietta Crichton. He d. in 1830 and his w. d. 1837. See Pedigree of Maltby of North Allerton, York.

WHO'S WHO 1914

MALTBY, Gerald Rivers, M. V. O. 1902, son of late Rev. Henry Joseph Maltby, Canon of Durham, b. 1851; m. 1876, Hersey, Eliza Cecilia, dau. of late Admiral Sir George Elliot, K. C. B. Entered navy in 1866, retired in 1876; served at Ashanti, 1874 (despatches, promoted, medal and clasp); Asst. Hon. Sec. Gen. Comm. R. N. Exhib. 1891; Hon. Sec. R. N. Fund 1892; Sec. R. N. Scien. Inst. 1893-98; Asst. Sec. Imp. Inst. 1898-92. Address: 54 St. George's Square, S. W. London. Clubs: United Service—Naval and Military. (See Orston Pedigree. Clergy List, 1911.)

MALTBY, Edward Secker, B. A., Keble Coll. Oxford, d. 1886; p. 1887 (Ripon); cur. of Mirfield, York., 1886-9; Thornhill, York., 1889-91; Fardon, Notts, 1891-4; St. Augustine, Haggerston, N. E., 1894-6; St. Philip, Clerkenwell, 1901-4; St. Bartholomew (in ch. of Mary's Mission) Camberwell, S. E. from 1905. Address: 7 Erlam Road, s. Bermondsey, S. E. (See Orston Pedigree.)

MALTBY, Henry Vaughan, d. 1902; p. 1903 (Keewatin) missny. dioc. Keewatin, 1902-3; inc. of Keewatin, 1903-8; R. D. of Rainy River from 1900, and inc. of Fort Francis, Ont., Canada, from 1908. (See Orston Pedigree.)

MALTBY, Jas. Chadwick, M. A., Keble Coll. Oxford; d. 1877; p. 1878 (Linc.) cur. of Gt. Grimsby, Linc., 1877-80. R. D. of Flute from 1904; rect. from 1880 of Aspley-Guise, Woburn, Beds. (See Orston Pedigree.)

MALTBY, Maurice, Chich. d. 1892; p. 1893 (Chich.); cur. St. Paul, Chichester, 1892-7; St. Peter, Coventry, 1897-9; cur. in ch. of St. Leonard, So. Banbury, Ox. 1899-1907; chapl. of Banbury union, 1904, S. vic from 1907 of Cropredy, Leamington.

MALTBY, Robert Walter Scott, B. A., T. C. D., d. 1906 (Arun); p. 1907 (Dorm for Arun) sur. of Armagh, Ireland from 1906; sen cur. from 1907; 4 Beresford Row, Armagh.

MALTBY

Pedigree I.

Acaster Malbisse

"Visitation of Yorkshire," Edited by Foster, 1487, fo. 254, b. Yorks.

Pedigree from Hugo de Malebisse.

N. B.—It is said that this Hugo de Malebisse is the progenitor from whom all the Maltbys descend.

I. HUGO de Malebisse held lands in Yorkshire at the time of William the Conqueror. Some of his children were: Richard (2), Hugo (2) and Gulfrid (2), who was witness to the charter of the foundation of Beverly Abbey, Co. Lincoln, in 1142. Founded by the Earl of Lincold. Richard (2) witness to Charter of Adam de Raineville. (Lib. de Pontefracto, fo. 5.)

II. HUGO (2) m. Emma de Percy, dau. and heiress of Henry de Percy of Acaster. He had: Hugo (3), Chief Justice, m. first, Constance ——; m. second, Beatrix, Lady of the Manor of Wykes, County Cambridge. He founded the Priory of Spinney, time Henry III., 1216. Sir William (3) de Maltby, 1207, held lands in Cleveland, Co. York; built Chapel at Ayton, where he was Lord of the Manor, before 1200; (this Sir William was probably nearly related to the Maltbys of Maltby and Muston. See Pedigree II.) Sir Simon (3), Lord of Cowton in Craven, York., m. a dau. of John, Lord of Methley (see under Beckwith). Matilda (3) m. Richard de Perri, Lord of Tillerton; Richard (3).

III. RICHARD (3) founded the Monastery of Neubo Abbey, Lincolnshire, 1198, Acaster near York; d. in 1209; Chief Justice of Assize. Had Warrennam with Scalton, near York. Lord chief forester, Galtres, Derwent and Wemsdaley. Had large possessions, including Acaster, near York. Children were: Richard (4), 1245; Emma (4) m. first, Robert de Maisnil; m. second, Robert de Streleril. Robertus (4). John (4). Richard (4). Richard (4) was of Benningsburgh. Robertus (4) had a son, Richard (5), of Benningworth, who m. Alicia Skipworth.

IV. JOHN (4), 1213, confirmed grant his father had made from Morton Grange to the Abbot Neubo, 14 John.

V. WILLIAM (5) confirmed grants to Byland Abbey, 1247; m. Matilda, dau. and co-heiress of Ralph Neville.

VI. WILLIAM (6), 29 Henry III., gave lands to Priory of Bridlington, 1267.

VII. RICHARD (7) Miles, 9 Edward III. D. about 1312. Of Acaster Malebis (de Eya).

VIII. JOHN (8), Lord Malebisse-y-Miles, Viscome's Ebor., High Sheriff, Co. York, 1314 (8 Edward II.); d. in 1316. He m. Agnes, dau. of Sir Edward Wilktrope.

IX. WILLIAM (9) de Malebisse, Miles, 1339 (d. about 1365, 12 Edward III.); m. a dau. of John Sampson, Miles. His sister Margaret (9) m. Thomas Fairfax of Walton. They had Clarissa (10) Fairfax, who m. first, William Palmes (q.v.) and second, Sir William Malbis. William (9) Maltby had Sir Thomas (10).

X. WALTER (10), the latter, on going to the Holy Lands mortgaged Scalton to William Fairfax, making latter's son, Richard, his heir if he did not return. His brother, Sir Thomas (10) de Malebisse, had a daughter, Margaret (11) who m. Richard Fairfax (son of William to whom Walter (10) Maltby mortgaged Scalton), who was heir of her uncle Walter (10). Sir Thomas (10) also had a daughter, Elizabeth (11) Maltby, co-heiress with Margaret Maltby Fairfax.

· XI. MARGARET Malebisse Fairfax had a dau. Elizabeth (12) Fairfax, who m. first, John Herringe, and second Adam Beckwith of Clynt, according to one authority; another claims it was Elizabeth (11) Malebisse, co-heiress with Margaret (11), who m. first John Herringe and second Adam Beckwith of Clint. It must be remembered that Adam Beckwith was a Maltby by blood, the Beckwith being a maternal ancestry. See Pedigree of Beckwith.

This family apparently dies out, as it ends in female lines only, but it must be remembered that only the line of one son was carried down, and there must have been many branches from this tree. For proof that this was the case we find: "4 Oct., 1426, the Will of Dame Sibilla, relic. of Sir William Malbys, Kt., of Acaster Malbys. Adm. Vol. II., folio 497.

NOTE—It is probable that Guilfrid (2), who witnessed the charter of the founding of Beverly Abbey, Lincolnshire, was the progenitor of the Lincolnshire Malbys (see Pedigree) and that Sir William (3) de Maltby, 1207, who held lands in Cleveland was the head of the Maltbys of Maltby branch (see Pedigree II.); though as yet this has not been proven.

An item that evidently refers to Walter (10) Maltby of this pedigree, appears in Miss Mary Cholmondeley's "Diana Tempest" and is well worth inserting here. The item is quoted from memory, but relates how, while at church, one of the characters looked up to the window, where the sun streamed through the painted arms of the Maltbys "of the pious, penniless Maltby who sold his lands to his grasping Tempest (?) brother-in-law, that he might go to the Holy Lands." And later two of the characters stand in the window of the tower of the castle and look down at the sill where "Tom Fairfax carved his name in the days of Cromwell." *

From these items it seemed quite evident that Miss Cholmondeley was acquainted with some of the ancient history of the Maltbys, Fairfaxes, etc., and the compiler wrote requesting any further information she might be able to give. Miss Cholmondeley replied in the third person: "Miss Cholmondeley knows nothing of the Maltbys." A note so curt and lacking in the ordinary forms of civility, it needs must leave anything but a fortunate impression of the author of "Red Pottage," etc. Cholmondeley Castle was, and still is, in Cheshire, and the description given of the ancient tower in "Diana Tempest" is evidently a description of the one at Cholmondeley Castle, so perhaps the Maltby arms are also there. For a Maltby residing in Cheshire, see under date 1211, relating to Richard de Maltebi.

Supplementary Notes Pedigree I.

I. Hugo Malebis, to whom Roger de Mobrai (son and heir of Nigel de Albina) granted (inter alia) the fee of lands in Carlton,* Silton, Kepwick, Morton, Dale and Hornby. (Vide York Cop. Papers, Vol. II., p. 950.)

II. One authority states: "Sir William Malebis m. Emma de Percey, dau. of Henry de Percy of Acaster." I am inclined to think this is the correct record, and that Sir William (2) is the same person as William de Maltby (1), Pedigree II., who was in Co. York, 1100 A. D. Note that William (1) of Pedigree II., names a son Henry. Was he not named for Henry de Percy?

III. Sir Richard Malebis (Ricardus Malebyse) of Acaster Malbis, Aug. 28, 1179, Roger de Molbray and Henry de Munford released the capital messuage "et totam medietatem terra de Eton" to Richard Malebisse. (Vide York Cor. Papers, Vol. II., p. 954.)

Note.—Acaster-Malbis: Emma de Percy was evidently either sole, or co-heiress of Henry de Percy of Acaster, hence her son is called "of Acaster Malbis." The name Roger de Molbray (Mobrai) is perhaps that from which

* The quotation may be found on pp. 33-34, Vol. II. of "Diana Tempest" as follows: "The very sun himself smote, not through the gaudy figures of Scripture story, but through the painted arms of the Malbys; of the penniless, pious Malby, who sold his land to his clutching Tempest brother-in-law in order to get out to the Crusades." And on p. 256 of Vol. I. we find: "He rose suddenly and went across to the deep bay window, on the stone sill of which Amyas Tempest, and Tom Fairfax, his friend, who together had held Overleigh against the Roundheads, had cut their names."

* Is Carlton later called Scalton.

descend the Roger Maltbys in later years. It is well to note the reference to the land of Eton, for we find (Pedigree II.) that John (3) de Maltby m. a de Etton. "Gilbert" is a name frequently found in the Etton family; and as John (3) names a son Gilbert, it is very probable that his wife was a du. of Gilbert de Etton. The writer descends from Maltilda de Etton, living about 1399. The Townshend Family says of her " of noble race in the County York." In Pedigree I. we find that Sir William (3) de Maltby, 1207, held lands in Cleveland, Co. York, and built a Chapel at Ayton, where he was lord of the manor before 1200. Query: Is Ayton and Etton not the same name?

IV. 1227. Johannes Malebisse (Ebor., p. 207; Cal Pat. Rolls).

V. 1257. William Malebisse, exemption from being made sheriff, 1258. William Malebisse claims forestry in forest of Gawtrys and Langwath.

VII. Richard: Richard Malbys (or Malebyse) held a knight's fee in Neubo, Co. Lincoln, and Acastre, Co. York, 1312. Confirmation of Abbot of Fountain by Richard Malebisse of lands in Queltbriz and Hoton (now spelled Hooton).

VIII. John de Maltcby, witnesses a Charter in York.

IX. Willelmus de Malteby, Freeman of York, 1324. See also date 1335.*

X. 1337. Walter de Maltby of Kerketon. Perhaps the same Walter. There was a Walter Maltcby about this time who was outlawed for some misdeed and it seems very probable that he was the same person, and that he made a pilgrimage to the Holy Land to expiate for his sin.

BECKWITH

Pedigree I.-A

I. Hugo de Malebisse.

II. Hugo de Malebisse m. Emma de Percy.

III. Sir Simon de Malebisse, Lord of Cowton in Craven, York., m. a dau. of John, Lord of Methley.

IV. Sir Hercules Malebisse, third son of above, changed his name to Beckwith on his marriage in 1226 to Lady Dame Beckwith Bruce, dau. of Sir William Bruce.

V. Sir Hercules Beckwith, m. a dau. of Sir John Ferrers.*

VI. Nicholas Beckwith, m. a dau. of Sir John Chaworth.

* He evidently had a near relative, Hugh, as it was in 1339 that Harmon Beckwith and Hugh, Lord Maltby, have a dispute over their coat-of-arms.

* The Ferrers are a very old Norman family. Robert de Ferrers was created Earl of Derby about 1100.

VII. Harmon Beckwith m. a dau. of Sir Philip Tylney. He took upon him a coat-of-arms of Hugh Maltby in 1339, incident to John Lord Malebisse. (q. v.)

VIII. William Beckwith m. ——— Usfleet.

IX. Thomas Beckwith, 4 Richard III., m. ——— Sawley.

X. Adam Beckwith.

XI. Adam Beckwith of Clint. m. Elizabeth Malebisse, coheiress of Thomas Malebisse, wid. of John Herringe. (Vide Vist. of Yorkshire, edit C. B. Northcliffe; Harl. Soc. Pub., Vol. XVI., p. 117.)

MALTBY

Pedigree II.

Maltby of Maltby and Muston

Arms: Argent, on a bend gules three garbs or.

Maultby, 900, 6070. "Glover's Visitation of Yorkshire," p. 551. Edited by Joseph Foster in 1875.

I. WILLIAM de Maltby in Co. York, 1100.

II. HENRY Maltby of Maltby in Cleveland, Co. York.

Note.—See Sir William (3), Pedigree I., who held lands in Cleveland. These two I believe to have been closely related.

III. JOHN de Maltby m. de Etton, dau. of Gilbert (?). Children: Gilbert (4), Robert (4), Christian (4), Catharine (4), Constance (4), William (4). Catharine m. Robert Waryan and Constance m. Robert Haux (Hoo) or Hauy.

IV. SIR WILLIAM de Maltby, son and heir, 1209, (?); 1309 (?) m. (2) Oristianna ———.

V. JOHN de Maltby, son and heir (1331), m. Alice, dau. of Nicholas Blount of Uphliam, (Upleatham) Cleveland.

Note.—This may be where the name Nichols comes from in the Maltby family. There is an error somewhere in the dates, as it is too long a break between 1209 and 1331. It evidently should read 1309 and 1339 may refer to the death of John. A letter from Mr. Charles Maltby to the compiler mentioned that his father died "aged 101 years, 101 days."

VI. GEORGE Maltby, living about 1364, m. Alice, dau. and heiress of Thomas and Mary —— Seymour, and granddaughter of Richard, Lord Seymour. See St. Maur Pedigree. This may be where the names Thomas and Richard come into the family, as the Seymours were prominent and they would have been apt to keep their names in the family. (Vide. Visit. York., edited by Norcliffe.)*

VII. JOHN de Maltby, son and heir (1406), m. Elizabeth, dau. of Thomas de Marton in Cleveland.

VIII. THOMAS de Maltby, son and heir, 30 Henry VI. (1443), m. Elizabeth ———. (I think she was either a widow or a second wife.)

IX. THOMAS de Maltby 30 Henry IV., 1429, m. Isabel, dau. of John Sayer of Preston, Co. York.

X. MATTHEW de Maltby, A. 2 Richard III., 1485. He had William (11), son and heir; Robert de M., 2nd son (11). Isabella (12), dau. and heiress of William (11), m. Robert Merley or Morleys of Normanby; dwelt at Maltby. They had a son James (13) Morley of Maltby, 1584; m. Phillis Thomaby. A son Cuthbert (13) Morley recorded their pedigree at York Visit., 1584. Robert (11) Maltby, the second son is now taken up.

XI. ROBERT de Maltby, second son.

XII. WILLIAM de Maltby.

XIII. CHRISTOPHER Maltby, Sheriff of York, 1575; alderman of York. (The notes are confusing. It is hard to discover whether there should be another Christopher between William (12) and Christopher above. Christopher seems to be a Morley name.) Christopher Maltby m. first, Frances Young, who d. 30 Dec., 1580. He m. second, July 11, 1581, at St. Crux, York, Mary, dau. of Arthur Dyneley of Swillington. He d. Feb. 28, 1584-5 and his wid. d. Oct. 14, 1585. The children were Christopher (14), bapt. 18 March, 1574-5; George (14) d. April 17, 1591; Margaret (14) d. April 17, 1591. He also had a brother Richard (13) living about 1584-5. (See Will of Christopher, 1585.) Also a sister Jane (13), who m. Robert Brooke, M. P. for York. She was buried July 12, 1604, at All Saints' Pavement. Her son, Rev. Samuel (14) Brooke, D.D., Master of Trinity Coll., Cambridge, 1622-31; his son was Christopher Brooke (15), M. P., the poet; his dau. Jane (16) Brook was the w. of Thomas Hesketh of Heslington, whose heir general is the editor of this work: i.e. Yorkshire Wills. (See photo. Silver Plate.)

XIV. CHRISTOPHER Maltby, bapt. 18 March, 1574-5, at St. Crux, York; Alderman of York; m., in 1599, Everilda, dau. of Ralph Creyke of Cottingham and Marton. See Supplementary Notes. Children:

* See pedigree II-A.

XV. CHRISTOPHER Maltby, d. 1619-1620 (?).

15 Catharine Maltby, b. 1599; m. Michael Warton of Beverly, Esq.

15 Everild Maltby, b. 1605; m., 1626, Sir George Wentworth of Woolsey, Kt.

15 Frances Maltby, b. 1608; m. Ninian Tankred, of Brunton, Esq.

Silver Plate presented to New York City by Christopher Maltby, Alderman of York, 1580.

15. Catharine Maltby, b. 1599; m. Michael Warton of Beverly, who died in the lifetime of his father, Sir Michael Warton of Beverly (d. 1655). His wife was Elizabeth, dau. and co-heiress of Ralp Hawsby. Catharine Maltby Warton had a son Michael (16) Warton of Beverly Park, Esq., ae. abt. 42. anno. 15 Sept., 1666. His w. was Susan, dau. of John, Lord Paulet of Hinton, St. George Somerset. (Vide. le Neves Knights, edit. Geo. W. Marshall, 1873; Vol. VIII., p. 205, Harl. Soc.)

NOTE.—"Susan, dau. of John, Lord Paulet." Here we have the surname of the heiress of Sir George Maltby, his sister, Sarah Maltby having married John Poulett. See under date 1640 in Irish Notes.

The above data states that Catharine Maltby m. Michael Warton, yet the following record is taken from the York Marriage Licenses: "Sir Michael

Warton of Beverly and Evereld Maltby of Cottingham at Beverly or Cottingham (m.) 1619."

The York Marriage Licenses also give: "George Wentworth, gent., of Wolley and Averilla Maltby of Cottingham (mar.) 1636, at Royston or Cottingham."

It would seem that Evereld Maltby who m. Sir Michael Warton in 1619, was Everild, wid. of Christopher Maltby, and that she was also a second wife of Sir Michael Warton, and that their children, who would have been step-brother and sister, m. in 1620.

The Genealogist, Vol. II., (1894) p. 217, states: "Michaell Warton of Beverly, Esq., dyed in his father's lifetime, being slayn by a cannon bullet at Scarborough Castle in the time of the late wars, it being then a garrison for the King [Pap. ?] 23 Oct., 1593, at St. John's, Beverly. He m. Catharine, dau. and co-heiress of Christopher Maltby of Maltby in Coun— Ebor; m. 1 Oct., 1620, at Cottingham." Their children were:

1. Michael Warton, named for himself and father.
2. Sir Ralphe Warton, named for her grandfather, Ralph Creyke; also for his grandfather, Ralph Hawsby.
3. Everill Warton, named for her mother.
4. Catherine Warton, named for herself.
5. Elizabeth Warton, named for his mother, Elizabeth Hawsby.
6. James Warton.
7. Mary Warton, named for her grandmother, Mary Dyneley.
8. Christopher Warton, named for her father.
9. Francis Warton.

15. Everild Maltby, b. 1605; m., in 1626, Sir George Wentworth of Woolsey, Kt. (Vide York Marriage Licenses: "Geo. Wentworth, gent., of Woolley and Averill Maltby of Cottingham, 1626, at Royston or Cottingham.") Under the year 1615, we find an indenture made 1 November, 1615, between Michael Wentworth of Wolley, Co. York, Esquire, and Edward Ward of Mendham, gent. Confirmation of title to the Manor of Mendham Hall granted to Michael Wentworth, Esquire, grandfather of the said Michael, by Sir Richard Freston of Mendham. Signature of Micha Wentworth. Witnesses: Fra. Cleobury, Jo. Whithorne.

In 1617-18 is another indenture made 13 March, 1617-18, between (1) Edward Ward of Mendham, Esquire, and (2) Richard Freston of Mendham, Co. Norfolk, Esquire, and his brother Thomas Freston, gent. Sale of tithes of Mendham, Metfield and Nedham. Signatures of Richard Freston, Thomas Freston. Witnesses: Edward Malby, Thomas Tyte, John Goddard, Anth. Barry, Richard Sparke.

Note.—In the Forthe Pedigree we find Robert Forthe, Sheriff, 1596. His dau. Anne Forthe, m. second, ———, Mendham; they had issue, Anne Ward, who m. Edward Malbye, Esq. From this it will be seen that the second husband of Anne Forthe was probably Edward Ward, and their dau. Anne, m. Edward Malby, who witnesses the above Indenture. See Pedigree V.

1619 Under this date there is a Bond dated 24 April, 1619, of Sir Thomas Hollond of Quidneham, Co. Norfolk, Kt., to Edward Ward, junior, of Mendham, gent., and Hannah, his w. (Delivered into the hands of Edward Ward, the elder, of Mendham, Esquire.) Signature and seal of Thomas Holland. Witnesses: John Hobert, William Dalleson, Francis Vardon.

1623. The following indenture made 26 April, 1623, between (1) Henry Ward of Gray's Inn, Co. Middlesex, gent., and Edward Ward, the younger of Stonham Aspall, gent., and (2) Edward Ward, the elder, of Mendham, Esquire. Conveyance of "Millfield" and "Bush Close" in Mendham, etc. Signatures of Henrie Ward and Edward Warde. Witnesses. Notary Public, ——— ———, Dickens.

There seems to be a close connection with the Wentworths here; also with the Malbys of Stonham Aspall, and in 1633, we find John Maltbie of Bainton marrying Elizabeth Ward of Bain. See also under date 1662, where John Ward and Elizabeth, his wife, sell property in East Retford, etc. Perhaps she was a dau. of John Maltbie and Elizabeth Ward.

The Genealogist, Vol. XXI., p. 120, Dugdale's Visit of Yorkshire, gives the following: "Wentworth Family of Wolley. Arms: Sable a chev. between 3 leopard's faces, or. Michael Wentworth of Wolley, Esq., ob. 1641, m. Frances, dau. and sole heiress of George Downes of Pawnton, Co. Hereford. Their children were: Thomas, Michael and Sir George Wentworth, Kt. of Wolley, ob. 19 Oct., 1660. He was twice married; to Anne, dau. of Lord Fairfax, and to Averell (Everild) dau. of Christopher Maltby, Alderman of York.

15. Frances Maltby, b. 1608; m. Ninian (or Thomas ?) Tancred, Esq., of Broughbridge. The Genealogist, Vol. X., 1894, p. 164, states she m. Thomas Tancred, a Bart. by Charles II., 1662; buried at Aldborough, 19 Aug., 1663. His wid. was buried at Aldborough, 27 April, 1665. Their Children were Sir William Tancred, second Baronet and Catherine Tancred.

NOTE.—Sir Roger Beckwith, descended from Sir Hercules Malbie, was of Aldborough, created a Baronet, 1681. Title extinct in 1741.

The Tancred pedigree is given by Mrs. Clara H. Manning in "The Lore of Ancestry," as follows: "Tancred Arms: Argent, a chevron between three escallops gules. Crest: An olive tree fructed proper.

"About the time of Henry III." (1216-1272) "we find one William Tanckard at Boroughbridge, where he had estates, as well as at Aldborough, Minckip, Rowcliffe and other places in Yorkshire. His son, William (2), m. Anne, dau. of John Paileyene of Killinghall. They had, with other issue,

Thomas (3), who m. Jane, dau. of Bernard Paver of Brampton. Their son, Thomas (4) Tancred of Boroughbridge, m. Anne, dau. of Edward Fitton of Cheshire, and had Sir Thomas (5) Tancred, the first bart. of Boroughbridge, who was created a baronet November 17, 1662, and m. Frances, dau. of Christopher Maltby of Cottingham. Their son, William (6), succeeded his father as second bart. and m. secondly, Elizabeth, dau. of C. Waldegrave of Stanning Hall, Co. Norfolk, by whom he had Thomas (7), third bart., who m. Elizabeth, dau. of William Messenger, of Fountains Abbey, Co. York, and d. in 1744, when he was succeeed as fourth bart. by his son, Thomas (8), who m. Judith, dau. of Peter Dalton of Grenanstown, Co. Tipperary, and d. June, 1759. His son, Thomas (9), became fifth bart. and m., in 1776, Penelope, dau. of Thomas Assheton Smith. Sir Thomas Tancred d. in 1784 and was succeeded by his son, Thomas (10), as sixth bart."—Heraldica.

NOTES PEDIGREE II.

The three silver castors reproduced in this book are part of a collection of silver plate presented to the City of York, and were the gift of Christopher Maltby, Alderman of York. See his will, 1 Feb., 27 Elizabeth, 1585.

It will be seen that the castors have a cross on them in a shield. Query: Does this pertain to some coat-of-arms of the City of York, or is it the arms of the Norfolk Maltbys? An English friend tells me that the plate would be likely to bear the family arms of the donor. If this is true it would be a most interesting piece of evidence in connecting the Yorkshire and Norfolk branches of the family.

Supplementary Notes Pedigree II.

III. John de Maultby (3) had Gilbert (4), Robert (4), Christian (4), Catharine (4), Constance (4), William (4). The Cal. Pat. Rolls mentions: "William, son of John de Maltby, and Gilbert son of John de Malteby." This William is evidently Sir William (4) and gives an indication of the period in which he lived. The date should probably be 1309 and not 1209. Under date 1310, we evidently find a reference to Robert (4), son of John (3).

V. John de Maltby presented to Vicarage of Pontefort, York. Was this John (5)?

X. See under year 1584. Isabella (12), dau. of William (11), m. Robert Morley. A son, Cuthbert (13) Morely recorded their pedigree at York. Visit. in 1584, and his half-brother added his achievement, his mother being heiress general of Maltby of Maltby in Stainton.

XIV. "Old Yorkshire," by Will Smith, p. 176, states: "Gregory Creyke, the fifth son, succeeded, bapt. at Bridlington April 21,

1595.* He m. Ursula, dau. of Sir John Legard, Kt., of Grantum, by Elizabeth, dau. of Sir William Mallory, Kt. of Studley; Everilda, the only dau., m., in 1599, Christopher Maltby of Maltby. She had three daughters."

Pedigree II. A

St. Maur (Seymour)

St. Maur. Arms: Argent, two chevrons gules, in a chief a file of the* (query 3) points azure.

Pedigree

I. Lawrence St. Maure.

II. Nicholas St. Maure, married the daughter and co-heir of Alan Lord Zouch.

III. Nicholas St. Maure, married Muriel, daughter and heiress of James Lovell.

IV. Nicholas St. Maure, married Elener, daughter and co-heir of Alan Lord Zouche of Ashby.

V. Richard, Lord Seymour died in 1401.

VI. Thomas de Seymour married Mary, widow of Robert Boughton.

VII. Alice Seymour, daughter and heiress, married George Maltby, who was living in anno 1364.

(Vide. Glover's Visitation, 1584, p. 551. Harleian Society, Vol. XVI., p. 283.)

MALTBY

Pedigree III.

Malbys of Enderby Malbys

"Lincolnshire Pedigrees," pp. 622-629, Vol. II.; Episcopal Register at Lincoln.

* The date is, of course, wrong and probably the item is not properly transcribed, for the Visit. of York, edited by Foster, gives: 1. Wm. Creyke m. Frances Babthorp; 2. Ralph Creyke m. Catherine Crathorne; 3. Everild Creyke, w. of Christopher Maltby, Esq. As Everild and Christopher Maltby named their daughters: Catherine, for her mother, Catherine Crathorne; Frances, for her grandmother, Frances Babthorp; Everild, for herself; it is very good evidence that the Visitat. of York is the correct line of descent.

* NOTE—Barons of St. Maur by writ of Summons, dated 29 July, 1314, came from Normandy with William the Conqueror. County Somerset, England. The name became corrupted to Seymour. To this family belonged Jane Seymour, the queen of Henry VIII.; Edward VI., their son, and the Lord Protector Seymour and also the Lord Admiral Thomas Seymour, the early suitor for the hand of Queen Elizabeth, and who later became the husband of Queen Catherine Parr.

I. WILLIAM Malbys presented to Rectory of Enderby Malbys in 1219.

II. ROBERT Malbys m. Beatrice, dau. of ———.

III. ALAN Malbys of Enderby Malby, under age in 1272. Lord of the Manor of Enderby Malbys in 1293; m. Matilda, dau. of Gilbert de Ponte. Children: Robert (4), John (4), Richard (4).

IV. RICHARD Malby, 1316, presents to Rectory of Enderby Malbys.

NOTE.—Henry Malbys, Rector of Willoughby-by-Alford, Lincoln, 1396, instituted March, 1365-6, by Sir William de Huntingfield, Kt., was evidently descended from this family. Enderby Malbys is now Maris Enderby. This family was probably a branch of the Maltbys or Malebisses of Pedigrees I. and II. From the spelling, Malby, and the name Henry, in this branch, it may be the branch of Sir Nicholas Malby.

SUPPLEMENTARY NOTES PEDIGREE III.

III. In 1314 we find an Alan de Maltebу witnessing a Charter of land near Mer Teyse, York. It is perhaps more likely that he was a son of Alan (3), Pedigree III. In 1322, we find an Alan de Malteby a Monk of Whiteby (Whitby ?), York.

Query: Is he the same person, who, in 1356, is called Benedict de Maldeby, who was sued by the Abbot of Whiteby?

MAWBEY [MALTBY]

PEDIGREE IV.

Mawbey of Botleys, Surrey

Betham's "Baronetage," Botleys. Surrey; "Bloomfield's Norfolk."

I. SIMON de Mauteby. Simon also evidently had a brother Richard (1), who had a son Robert (2) and he had six sons, Robert (3), Gyles (3), John (3), Jeffrey (3), Matthew (3), Ralph (3). Vide under date 1219. This Robert (2) gave to St. Mary of Sibton Priory, Suffolk, all his rent in his salt works. A lion rampant on the seal.

NOTE.—This name is rather uncommon. Note the name Sir Simon Malbisse (3), Pedigree I.

II. WALTER de Mauteby.

III. ROBERT de Mauteby. Vide under date 1219. (See Pedigree IV.-A.)

IV. Sir WALTER de Mauteby, m. Christiana de Bassingham, dau. of Sir Piers de Bassingham. (See under date 1272-1307.)

V. Sir WALTER m. Petronilla ——— (Somery ?).

VI. Sir WALTER m. Alice (or Olive ?) ———. They had

a dau. Petronilla (7) Maltaby (or Mautby) who m. Roger de Brom of Brom Hall, Norfolk. He was a son of William Brom.

VII. Sir JOHN m. Avelina de Crenon (Lady of Mauteby's Hall, 1362).

VIII. Sir ROBERT m. Elianora ——.

IX. Sir JOHN m. Agnes ——.

X. Sir ROBERT m. Eleanora ——; m. (2) Margaret, d. Beauchamp (?). He had a brother, Sir John, who had a dau. Elianore, who m. Sir William Calthorpe, and from her descended John, Earl of Egmont. His Will 1413. His wid. m. Thomas Chambers, Lord of Sparham in her right, 1442. The children of Robert and Eleanor were:

XI. John Malby, Squier. From him descend the Pastons. Se Pedigree.
11 Walter.
11 Edward.
11 Peter. Will dated 1438. Vide Bloomfield; buried in church at Sparham.
11 Thomas.
11 Eleanor, a nun at Shouldham.
11 Agnes.

See Bloomfield, p. 227.

XI. THOMAS.

XII. WALTER de Mauteby m. Agnes Dawtree.

XIII. RICHARD Mautby m. Mary Baker.

XIV. ROGER Mautby m. Mary Drayton.

XV. RICHARD Mautby m. Margaret Spencer, d. 1598, of S. Kilworth. He had a brother Robert (15). Their children were:

XVI. (1) William, m. 1581, Augusta Carr. He d. 1621.
XVI. (2) Richard, m. Joanna Bird. He d. 1607.
XVI. (3) Robert, bapt. 12 May, 1561; m. Alicia Coleman, July 1, 1582.

XVI. (1) WILLIAM and Augusta Carr had

XVII. (1) John, who m. Agnes Chamberlayne, dau. of William, had Roger (18), Erasmus (18).
XVII. (2) Richard, who m. E. Shudsborough.
XVII. (3) Anne.
XVII. (4) Elizabeth.
XVII. (5) Thomas m. E. Cartwright; had a son William (18). From Thomas, third son, descend the present Mawbeys of S. Kilworth.

XVI. (2) RICHARD m. Joanna Bird and had

XVII. (6) William, had John (18) and William (18).

XVII. (7) John.

XVII. (8) Dorothy m. George Mawbey, her cousin.

XVII. (1) JOHN and Agnes Chamberlayne had Erasmus (17), who in 1643 was killed at Roundway Down. He of South Kilworth.

XVII. (2) RICHARD and E. Shudsborough had
XVIII. Erasmus, b. 1616; only son.
18 Elizabeth, b. 1619.
18 Mary, b. 1626.

XVIII. ERASMUS m. (1) M. Wight and (2) E. Slee, of Shenton, Co. Leicester. Children by first marriage:
XIX. Robert.
19 Richard.
19 Erasmus.
19 Thomas.
19 John.
19 Francis.
19 William m. A. Walker. He died 1733.
19 John.
19 James.
19 Mary.
19 Isaac.
19 Elizabeth.
19 Joseph.
19 Stephen.

XIX. WILLIAM and A. Walker had:

XX. JOHN Mawbey, b. 1693; d. 1754; m. J. Shepherd. He also m. Martha, dau. of Thomas Pratt. Children:
XXI. Francis.
21 Martha.
21 John.
21 Anne.
21 Mary.
21 Elizabeth.
21 Sir JOSEPH, b. 1730; d. 1798; m. E. Pratt. Children:
XXII. Sir JOSEPH, m. C. Henchman.
21 Catherine.
21 Mary.
21 Emily.

MAWBEY-SURREY (See Pedigree IV.)

From "Manning and Bray's Hist. of Surrey," Vol. III.: "In the small church of Ravenstone, in the road between Leicester and Ashby-de-la-Zouch, about two miles from the latter, against the north wall in the Chancel, on a white marble table, is this inscription: 'Mr. John Mawbey, late of this parish died, on 4 Sept., 1754, in the 62d year of his age. Descended from an ancient and genteel family, long settled in the counties of Leicester and Northampton into which latter they came from the County of Norfolk, where formerly they were owners of large possessions. The said John Mawbey m. Martha, dau. of Mr. Thomas Pratt, late of this parish, and by her, who died in 1737 had [4 sons and 4 daughters]. John Mawbey above mentioned was the only son of Mr. William Mawbey of this parish, who died in 1733, seventh son of Erasmus Mawbey of Sherrton in the Co. of Leicester, only son of Richard Mawbey of South Kilworth, whose elder brother John, by Agnes, dau. of William Chamberlayne, Esq., of Leicester, was father of Erasmus Mawbey or Mautbey, who in 1643, joining the regiment of horse commanded by Sir Arthur Haselrigg, bart., with many recruits raised at his own expense, was soon afterwards killed at the battle of Roundway Down, near the Deviges in Wiltshire, valiantly fighting for the liberties of his country. His unfortunate death, his widow's second marriage, and his misfortunes brought on them by the Civil War, were greatly prejudicial to the interests of his family. John and Richard Mawbey were the eldest sons of William Mawbey. From Thomas, the third son, are descended the Mawbeys at this time of South Kilworth. The said William, with his brothers Richard and Robert, the last of whom was bapt. at South Kilworth (as appears by the Register of that parish) on 12 May, 1561, were the sons of Richard Mawbey, Esq., by Margaret, his wife, of South Kilworth, aforesaid, born at Keltering in the Co. of Northampton and *descended from the ancient family of Mawbeys or Mautbeys of the Co. of Norfolk.'* Joseph Mawbey, Esq., of Kennigton and Botleys, in the Co. of Surrey, sheriff, in 1757, for that county and afterwards Member of Parliament for the Borough of Southwark, dedicated this monument in 1764, to the memory of his parents and progenitors."

"Seats of Great Britain," 2nd Series, Vol. I., p. 116. Botleys in the Co. of Surrey: "Sir Joseph Mawbey was descended from a family in Norfolk, where the village of Maltby (originally Maws-by) still marks the dwelling place of his Danish ancestors: and a ruined chapel at East Flegg exhibited at the close of the last century the tomb and effigy of a Knight Templar named De Mauteby. The property of the family being confiscated in the Civil Wars, they removed into Leicestershire. Colonel Mawbey fell at the head of his volunteers in Sir Arthur Hesilrigg's corps at Roundway Down."

"John Dryden wrote an epitaph for Margaret Mawbey Paston."

Supplementary Notes Pedigree IV.

I. It will be seen that Richard (1), brother of Simon de Mauteby, had a son Robert (2), who had six sons, one was John (3). It seems very probable that this John (3) was the Sir John Malbye of Malbye Hall, progenitor of the Malbyes of Stonham Aspall, Suffolk. See Pedigree V., as we see that Robert (2) gave to St. Mary of Sibton Priory, Suffolk. The brother Matthew (3) is very evidently he who accompanied the Earl of Norfolk to Rome in 1245; and with "the King beyond the Seas" in 1242. A Matthew de Matebie held Essex lands about the time of Henry III. [1216-1272]. See Pedigree.

II. Walter de Mauteby. Bloomfield gives under date 1228: "Walter de Malteby conveyed to Simon, the Prior, a messuage, etc., in Hemsby and Marcham; the Prior conveyed to Walter all the land he had at Becham except adowson." Query: Is this Walter (2)?

III. In 1229 the Cal. Pat. Rolls mentions Roberto Malteby and in 1235 and 1242 we find Robert de Mauteby, one of the wardens to keep the peace at Yarmouth Fair. Perhaps Robert (3).

IV. Perhaps the following items pertain to Walter (4): 1247. Walter de Mauteby had free warren (Norfolk). See also under dates 1249, 1253, 1256, 1270, 1272.

IX. Sir John m. Agnes ——. Bloomfield states under date 1396: "Sir John de Mauteby and Agnes, his wife, enfeoffed Sir Adam Clifton in his manors of Mauteby, Winterton, East Somerton, etc., for the use of his eldest son, John, entail." In Pedigree IV-A the record reads: "Sir John Mawtby m. Elianor (Elen) dau. of Adam Clifton de Bokenham." These records are very confusing and quite beyond the compiler to untangle.

MAULTBY

Pedigree IV-A.

Maultby of Norfolk

"Visitation of Norfolk," 1563-89-1613; "Harl. Soc. Pub." 1891, p. 215; Vide "Paston Pedigree," p. 215, edited by Walter Rye, pub. 1891, Vol. XXXII.

Arms: Quart 12. Maultby, Azure, a cross formed throughout or, Mauteby, Mawtby, Maultby.

I. ROBERT Mautby m. Sara, dau. of Robert Mantell.

NOTE.—This is evidently Robert (3), Pedigree IV.

II. WALTER Mautby m. (1) Alice, dau. of Roger Fitz Osborne; m. (2) Christian, dau. of Sir Piers de Bassingham; 6th Edward I., 1278.

III. ROBERT Maltby m. Isabell, dau. of William Flegg.

NOTE.—This would seem to be a younger brother of Sir Walter (5), Pedigree IV.

IV. ROBERT Mawtby m. Ellen, dau. of William Marshall, the younger, 1281; (first cousin to Sir Robert (6), Pedigree IV.)

V. Sir John Mautby, Kt., m. Isabel (or Elizabeth), dau. of Robert Clavering, son of Roger, Lord of Clavering, 9 Edward II. [1326]. Arms: Quart or. and gules, a bendlet sable.

* NOTE—For same arms see Pedigree Maltby of Scarborough, Yorkshire. See Pedigree IV. B.

VI. Sir ROBERT Mawtby, Kt., m. Ellen, dau. and heiress of Thomas Lovayne, Kt., 1347. (Or this may have been Roger (6), who m. Ela, dau. of Thomas Fitz-Matthew de Lovayne.)

VII. Sir JOHN Mawtby, m. Elianor (Elen), dau. of Adam Clifton (de Bokenham).

VIII. ROBERT Mawtby, Squire, m. Margaret, dau. and heiress of Roger de Beauchamp of Blentnesho. His will 1413. See Pedigree IV. C.

IX. JOHN Mawtby, Squire, m. Margaret, dau. of John Barney (Berney), Esq., of Redham.

X. Margaret Mawtby, dau. and heiress; born about 1420 (?); m. John Paston of Paston, Esq., son of Sir William Paston, Judge. She died about 1481-4. Her will 4 Feb., 1481, proved 18 Dec., 1484. From here the notes are a bit confused. Their children seem to have been:

XI. Sir John Paston, b. 1439; d. unm. in 1479.
11 John Paston, living 1466.
11 William Paston, b. 1459.
11 Robert Paston.
11 Edmund Paston, youngest son, had Anne (12) Paston, who m. William Yelverton; Constance (12), Margery (12), Dorothy (12) and Phillipa (12) Paston.

It will be seen that this pedigree and that of Mawbey, Botleys, Surrey, do not agree. For whereas both give the Paston descent, the names of wives, etc., are confused. The following footnotes are confusing:

Suffolk, Edward III., reign [1327-1377]: "Sir Robert Mauteby, lord and patron, succeeded by Sir John de Mauteby, *son* of Sir John de Mauteby, Kt. (1374). See Pedigree VIII. This is evidently Sir John (7), who m. Elianor, dau. of Adam Clifton, and Robert (6) was probably his uncle, who, failing male issue, the estates reverted to John, son of Sir John, Kt." A note also states Margaret Mawtbye "possessed the Manors of Sparham, Gresham. etc."

In this connection we append a short pedigree, taken, I think, from Bloomfield:

I. Simon de Mawbey (Maltby, Co. Norfolk) 1198.

Descended from him were:

Sir John Mawbey, who d. 1403.

Sir John Mawbey, whose dau. Alianore m. Sir William Calthorpe. (This should be Sir John, son of Sir Robert (10), Pedigree IV.)

John de Mawby, whose dau. and heiress, Margaret, m. John Paston, ancestor of Ex. Earl of Yarmouth.

Descended from above: Thomas Mautby, Esq., of Sparham.

Here again is confusion of names in the descent.

Descended from this union was Sir William Paston of Paston, and Oxnead (Created Baronet, 1642) and his son, Sir Robert Paston, who was created Viscount Yarmouth and subsequently Earl of Yarmouth. The Pastons of Paston, Co. Norfolk, settled there soon after the Conquest. Their arms were: Az. 6 fleur de lys az., a chief indented or. (Vide Burke's Gen. Arm., 3rd Edit.)

Margaret Mauteby Paston is the author of the famous "Paston Letters," which are most valuable and instructive, giving clear pictures of times, customs, feelings, etc., of English life in the Fifteenth Century, and should most certainly be of interest to all Maltbys.

Supplementary Notes Pedigree IV.-A

VIII. According to Bloomfield, p. 227, the will of Robert Mauteby, Esq., 1413, mentions wife Eleanor (Alianore), son John, son and heir; his brother John; daughter Eleanor; a nun; daughter Agnes; sons, Walter, Peter, Thomas, underage, and his wid. m. 1442, Thomas Chambers, lord of Sparham in her right.

Supplementary Notes to Pedigree No. IV.

Norfolk Pedigree. (Before Conquest ?)

From Bloomfield's Hist. of Norfolk: "The Manor (or Lordship) of Maltby or Mautby, Co. Norfolk, was in existence before the Conquest. When Wiston the (Saxon ?) tenant was expelled." Further Bloomfield says: "A family *who took their name* from the the town were EARLY ENFEOFFED of it by the Crown. In 1198 Simon de Maudeby had interests in the Manor of Maltby. Also a Walter de Malteby in 1166, had dealings respecting land (Becham Manor) with Simon, the Prior of Norwich. In 1284, a Walter de Mallety or Mautby described as Lord of Maltebv also had dealings respecting Becham Manor lands with the prior of Norwich Monastery." From this I conclude that the name Maltby (of Maltby, Co. Norfolk) was adopted by this family before 1166. I also take "early enfeoffed" to mean that the family were probably enfeoffed by the Crown soon after the Crown took possession of it, say temp. Will. I., or Will. II.—probably Will. I. Contributed Note by Edward Wells Harte, of Wells, England: The Anglo-Norman Malbys family evidently obtained grants temp. Conquest. Arms: Hinds' heads.

Pedigree IV. B
Claveringe

1. Sir Robert Claveringe, founder of Langley, son of Roger Claveringe the First Baron.
2. Sir John Claveringe, Knt, s. and h.
3. Sir Roger Claveringe, 1st son m. Isabel ——.
4. Robert Claveringe, s. and h. m. Margaret, dau. of ye Lord Zouche.
5. Elizabeth Claveringe m. Sir John Mautby.

(Ref. Norfolk Archaeology.)

Pedigree IV. C
Beauchamp

1. Roger Mortimer, the founder of Wiginore.
2. Johane, his dau. mar. Walter Beauchamp, Baron of Elmeley.
3. Will Beauchamp, Earl of Warw. in the right of Isabel his wife, dau. and heiress of Will Mauduit, Earl of Warwick.
4. Walter Beauchamp, son of above, was Lord of Powyke.
5. Roger Beauchamp, Lord of Bletsoe, Chamberlaine to King Edward III., mar. Sibill, dau. and heiress of John de Pateshall. (See Pedigree IV. D.)
6. Roger Beauchampe, of Bletsoe, m. Johane, dau. of William Clopton of Clayton.
7. Margaret Beauchampe m. Robert Mawtby. (See Pedigree IV. A.)

(Ref. p. 23, Vol. IV., Norfolk Archaeology.)

Pedigree IV. D
Pateshull

1. Simon de Pateshull.
2. Walter de Pateshull, son and heir of Simon.
3. Simon de Pateshull, son and heir of Walter.

4. John de Pateshull, son and heir of Symon.
5 Simon de Pateshull, m. Isabel, dau. of —— Strugray.
6. John de Pateshull, son and heir of Simon, m. Maud (?). (See Pedigree IV. E, No. 5.)
7 Sibell, dau. and heiress of John, mar. Roger Beauchamp.
8. Roger Beauchampe mar. Johan Clopton.
9. Margaret Beauchamp mar. Robert Mawtby. (See Pedigree IV. A.)

(Ref. Norfolk Archaeology.)

Pedigree IV. E

Tregos

1. Robert Tregos came with William the Conqueror to England.
2. Robert Tregos mar. Julian, dau. of William Cantelupe.
3. John Tregos mar. Mabel, dau. of Foulke Fitz-Warren.
4. Sibil Tregos mar. Will Grauntson.
5. Mabel, one of the daughters of W. Grauntson, mar. John de Pateshull.
6. Sibil de Pateshull mar. Roger Beauchampe, Lord of Bletsoe.
7. Roger Beauchamp mar. Johane Clopton.
8. Margaret Beauchamp mar. Robert Mawtby.

(Ref. Norfolk Archaeology.)

The pedigrees of Claveringe, Beauchamp, Pateshull and Tregos were kindly contributed by Mr. Douglas B. Thompson of Washington, D. C.

MALTBY-PASTON (Addenda)

Since writing the above a few interesting notes concerning this family were found in a delightful book, "The Norfolk Broads," by W. A. Dutt, and seem well worth quoting in this book. On page 194 is the following: "A by-road branching off southeast from the Ormsby road where it skirts the village green leads to Mautby, a parish bordering the Bure. Here again we come in touch with the Pastons, for Margaret Paston, whose letters are the most delighful in the famous collection, was a daughter of John de Mauteby, who held the manor in the middle of the fifteenth century. Undeniably, it is Margaret Paston who gives life to the Letters, which although invaluable to students who would acquaint themselves with the conditions of life in England during the reigns of the kings of the houses of York and Lancaster, would be somewhat dry reading if it were not for her love for her lord and careful guardianship of his interests. Her fond love for her children, too, is often manifested though there are times when we might think her mercenary if we failed to understand the customs of the age in which she lived. For instance she writes to her 'right worshipful husband' as follows: 'I was at Norwich this week to purvey such things as needeth me this winter; and I was at my mother's, and while I was there, there came in one Wrothe, a kinsman of Elizabeth Clere, and he saw your daughter, and praised her to my mother, and said she was a goodly young woman; and my mother prayed him for to get for her a good marriage if he knew of any; and he said he knew one . . . the which is Sir John Cley's son, that is Chamberlain with my Lady of York, and he is of age eighteen years old. If ye think it to be for to be spoken of, my mother thinketh that it should be got for less money now in this world than it should be hereafter, either that one or some other good marriage.' From this epistle it might be imagined that Dame Margaret considered mutual love an unessential adjunct of matrimonial contracts; but elsewhere she reveals a kindly interest in a love-sick maiden. Writing to her son, Sir John Paston, who was probably with King Edward IV. at Pomfret at the time, she says, 'I would you should speak with Wekis (Wykes, an usher of the King's Chamber), and know his disposition to Jane Walsham. She hath said, since he departed hence, but (unless) she might have him, she would never marry, her heart is so sore set on him, she told me that he said to her that there was no woman in the world he loved so well. I would not he should jape her, for she meaneth good faith.' But, like a careful match-maker, she is anxious that her young friend's matrimonial prospects should not be entirely marred by this usher who loved and rode away, for she adds, "If he will not have her let me know in haste, and I shall purvey for her in otherwise.' Then the careful mother shows herself, for she goes on to say, 'As for your harness and gear that you left here, it is in Daubeney's keeping, it was never removed since your departing, because that he had not the keys, I trow it shall get injured unless it be taken heed to betimes. . . . I sent your grey horse to Ruston to the farrier, and he saith he shall never be nought to ride, neither right good to plow not to cart: he saith he was splayed, and his shoulder rent from the body. I know not what to do with him.' This letter was conveyed to her son by the rector of Filby, as appears from a postscript: 'I would you should make much of the parson of Filby, the bearer hereof, and make him good cheer if you may." Delightful Dame Margaret! Her gentle wraith seems to haunt the meads of her Caister* home. She was buried in Mautby Church, in accordance with the instructions of her will, in which she desires to be interred 'in the aisle of that church at Mawteby, in which aisle rest the bodies of divers of mine ancestors;' and that 'under a scutcheon of arms' should be inscribed the words, 'God is my trust.' Her tomb has vanished with the south aisle in which it stood; but at the south end of the nave is a marble tomb and cross-legged effigy of Sir Walter de Mauteby, one of her ancestors who died in 1248.

"Within the bounds of the parish is a boat ferry on the Bure. It is called Mautby Swim, being one of the spots where cattle used to swim across the river to and from the marshes. . . . At Mautby are some ancient memorials of the Mawteby family, including the earliest existing in Broadland probably. . . ."

* Caister Castle. (Page 196). This castle is one of the oldest brick houses in England, and was built by Sir John Fastolff, who lived there in great state until he died in 1459. At his death the castle came in to possession of John Paston; but Thomas Mowbray, the powerful Duke of Norfolk asserted that "Sir John had given him Caister and that he would have it plainly"; and in 1469 he laid siege to the castle. Its defenders numbered only twenty-eight, but they seem to have made a gallant defence. In the end, however, "from sore lack of victual and gun powder," they were compelled to surrender. Lengthy legal proceedings ensued. Margaret Paston in a letter to her husband, writes: "My Lord of Norwich said to me that he would not have abide the sorrow and trouble that you have 'abyden' to win all Sir John Fastolff's goods." But the Duke retained possession until his death, when the king confirmed John Paston's right to the estate, and until 1599 the castle was the chief seat of the Pastons family. In that year they removed to the fine Hall Clement Paston had built at Oxnead†. . . . In its original state it was a large quadrangular building containing, besides the state apartments, twenty-six large rooms. It was surrounded by two moats, the inner containing the greater part of the buildings of which there are ruins remaining, the outer a college which, though founded by Fastolff, was not erected until the Paston's time. The chief entrance—a square, ornamented gateway—was on the west side. The principal remaining portions on the north and west walls, and a circular tower, about ninety feet high, at the northwest corner of the quadrangel. These ruins are surrounded by the inner moat. Of the outer moat there are no traces; but some walls and a small round tower embodied in a house adjoining the ruins undoubtedly formed part of the castle; and with the college buildings, were contained within the outer moat. . . . Caister Castle is one of the most interesting ruins in Norfolk. Seen as it is against a background of fine trees growing beyond the moat, its tower and walls are strikingly picturesque.

† Again writing of the Pastons says (page 16): "Vanished, too, is that stately hall at Oxnead which Clement Paston, a distinguished naval commander of the reign of Henry VIII, built and in which King Charles II. was sumptuously entertained. . . ." (page 153): "In 1676, when it was occupied by Robert Paston, Viscount Yarmouth, King Charles II., journeyed to it from Norwich and was lavishly entertained, an immense banqueting hall being built specially for the occasion."

MALTBY

Pedigree V.

Malby of Stonham Aspall

"Metcalf's Suffolk."

Arms: Arg. on a bend bet. 2 cotisses engrailed gules 3 garbs ppr. Vide "Suffolk Traveller," pp. 616-617.

I. Sir JOHN Malbye of Malbye Hall, in Lynn, Norfolk; m. and had Thomas, son and heir. See Pedigree IV. Perhaps he was a son of Robert (2), Richard (1).

II. THOMAS Malby of Dovercourt, Co. Essex, son and heir to Sir John; m. Dorothy, dau. of John Nicholls of Brundish, Co. Suffolk, Gent., and had:

3 John, son and heir.
3 Lyonell, ob.
3 Margery, w. of Robert Temes of Thornage in Norfolk.
3 Julian, w. of Thomas Jennings of Holbrook, Co. Suffolk.

III. JOHN Malby of Stoneham Aspall, Co. Suffolk, m. Margaret, dau. and co-heiress of William Smith of Hevengingham, Co. Suffolk and had:

IV. EDWARD, son and heir (1609-10).
4 Thomas.
4 Mary, m. Thomas Jacobs.
4 Anne, m. Sir Joseph Hayes of London, Alderman, Kt., Maior, 1615.

Supplementary Notes Pedigree V.

I. 1334. John de Malteby, Kt., accused of breaking a close at Lyng (Lynn ?), Norfolk; also Robert, his son, and Ralph sire Tonesporest de Malteby (i.e. his chaplain). Another item in 1350 concerning Robert de Mauteby, chivaler and John, his brother, is a complaint against them for driving arsay cows at Merkessale and Castyre, by Norwich.

1374. Sir John de Mauteby, son of Sir John, was buried before the altar of St. Mary in the parish church of Fritton St. Edmund, where he lived, Suffolk.

II. Thomas Malby. Is this the Thomas Malby who was Mayor of Limerick in 1401? And where is the Limerick referred to?

1413. Robert Mauteby, Esq., enfeoffed Sir Miles Stapleton,

Sir Simon Feltrigge, Sir William Argentein and others in the Manor of Fritton, Suffolk, with other lordships in Norfolk, etc. From these notes it would appear that the Malbys of Pedigree V. and of Pedigree IV.-A were nearly related.

1435. Robert Malteby, Esq., d. before this date. He had a share in the Manor of Evarwartown, Suffolk. (Vide p. 500, Cal. Pat. Rolls.)

IV. Edward Malbye, gent., son and heir of John, had a manor in the parish of Stonham Aspal, Suffolk. He d. about 1654. In the church are to be seen the Arms of Malbye as follows: Arms of Malbye—Arg. on a bend between 2 cotises engrailed gules, 3 garbs, ppr. (Vide Supplement to the Suffolk Traveller, pp. 616-617, Compiled by Augustine Page, 1844.)

NOTE.—Compare this coat-of-arms with that of the Mautebys, granted 1612, as follows: Ermine, on a bend gules between 2 cotises engrailed of the second (gules) 3 garbs or. If *Mautebey* came from Maltby, it is not difficult to see Mauteby into Mautebey. Also see Arms Pedigree XIV.

Edward Malby, son and heir of John Malby of Stonham Aspall, was admitted a barrister at law at Lincoln's Inn on 6 Feb., 1609-10. (Vide Lincoln Inn Reg., Vol. I., p. 152; pub. 1896.)

For further and more complete records see Supplementary Notes to Pedigree II., from which we see that the wife of Edward Malby was very evidently Annie Ward, dau. of —— Ward and Anne Forthe; she was presumably a dau. of Robert Forthe, sheriff in 1596.

ADDENDA PEDIGREE V.

MALBY OF STONEHAM ASPALL

A valuable addition to this pedigree has been sent the compiler by Douglas B. Thompson, Esq., a genealogist, of Washington, D. C. Instead of this pedigree ending with Edward Malby, son and heir, we find these names of other children of John Malby, viz.:

Thomas Maltby, second son.

Mary, wife to Thomas Jacob of Creating in Suffolk.

Anne, wife to Sir Joseph Hayes, son of Thomas Hayes of London, Alderman and Kt., maior 1615.

Ref. Visitation of Suffolk made by Hervey, 1561, and Raven, 1567 (Richmond Herald, 1612), Edited by Walter C. Metcalf, 1882.

MALBY

Pedigree VI.

I. ——— Malby, d. "when Sir Nicholas Malby was about 4 years old," probably he d. about the year 1534.

Note.—Could he have been the John Maltby of Lincolnshire, who made his will, 17 May, 1532, and mentions son Nicholas.

II. Sir NICHOLAS Malby, b. about 1530; m. Thomasine, dau. of Robert Lamb of Leeds, York, whose w. was a Castell of the Castells of E. Hatley, Camb. Lady Maltby* m. (2) George Rawe (or Rowe). Sir Nicholas (2) speaks of his "brother John" (2) and the w. of John Maltby, 1532, also mentions "son John." Sir Nicholas was President of Connaught. He was descended from an old Yorkshire family, mentioned in the Plantation of Leix (Ireland) 1556. He was knighted 7 Oct., 1576: 3 July, 1579, Sir Nicholas Maltby of Kilmallock. He d. at Athlone, Ireland, 4 March, 1584. It is worthy of note that his w., Thomasine, was from Leeds, York.

III. Capt. HENRY Malby, b. 1569; son and heir; m. Elizabeth Jobson; (Vist. of Essex states: "Henry Malby m. Persall Jobson"); granddaughter of Sir Francis Jobson, Lt. of the Tower of London. Apparently he was killed in 1602 in Connaught, Ireland, while in the service of the Crowne. His wid. m. Sir Ralph Sedley.

Sir Nicholas (2) had a dau. (3) who m. Thomas Omesby, and they had a son, Maltby (4) Omesby, and he had a son, Maltby (5) Orsby. Another dau. of Sir Nicholas (2) was Ursula Malby (3). She m. Anthony Brabazon and had a son, Malby (4) Brabazon, Esq. of Ballinash, Co. Roscommon. Malby (4) m. Sarah, dau. of Thomas Burke of Inlahery, Co. Galway. He d. 20 My, 1637. Malby (4) had children:

5 Anthony Brabazon, m. Ellice, dau. of John Dillon, turned Papast; pardoned by the Crown in 1652.

5 Ursula Brabazon, m. Bernard Talbot of Rathdown, Co. Wicklow, Gent.

5 Sarah Brabazon.

5 Dorothy Brabazon.

IV. Sir GEORGE Maltby, Kt., son and heir; m. Anne ———. His will date 1638.

*My notes state: "Lady Malby subsequently m. George Rawe." This can hardly be the wife of Sir Nicholas as we find her will, 1596, as "Dame (or Lady) Thomasin Malbie, wid. of Sir Nicholas Malby, Kt. It probably refers to Anne, wid. of Sir George Maltby, Kt.; his will proved in 1639.

SIR NICHOLAS MALBY

The following account of Sir Nicholas Malby is taken from the Dictionary of National Biography, Vol. XXXV., p. 395:

MALBY, Sir Nicholas (1530?-1584) president of Connaught, descended from an old Yorkshire family of that name, was b. probably about 1530. In 1556 his name appears in a list of persons willing to take part in the plantation of Leix, in Ireland. (State Papers, Ireland, Mary I., 21) On 6 August, 1562, he was found guilty of coining, and with three of his associates, was condemned to death (Machyn, Diary, p. 290). He was, however, reprieved on consenting to serve under Ambrose Dudley, Earl of Warwick, in France (State Papers, Dom. Eliz. XXIV., 41). His letters show him to have been a man of education and intelligence, and in April, 1563, he is described as Warwick's secretary (Cal. State Papers, Fr. VIII., 294). He served with credit during the war, and in 1565 was sent to Spain, where he was commended for his judicious conduct by Phayre, the English minister at Madred (Ibid IX., 520). On his return to England he was sent to Ireland, and was shortly after appointed sergeant-major of the army by Sir Henry Sidney (Cal. Fiants Eliz. No. 1191).

After the death of Shane O'Neill in 1567, he was stationed at Carrick-fergus in order to assist Captain Piers in keeping the Scots of the Glynns in check (Ibid No. 1196). He was reproved by the lord justices for distraining Sir Brian MacPhelim O'Neill's and other Irishmen's castles for cess, but his conduct was justified by Sir Henry Sidney (State Papers, Ireland, Eliz. XXII., 28.37).

His position was a difficult one, and he complained that he had to feed his men at the cost of his carcass (Ibid XXIII., 37-39), but he displayed considerable tact in his management of Sorley Boy MacDonnel (q. v.), and Sidney, on visiting the north in October, 1568, found the charge committed to him in very good state (Ibid XXVI. 12).

In July, 1569, he was sent to the assistance of Sir Peter Carew (q v.) against the Butlers (Hooker's "Life of Sir P. Carew, ed. Maclean," p. 92) and in a skirmish near Carlow, he was severely hurt by a fall from his horse. He was warmly commended for his bravery and military skill by Sir W. Fitzwilliam and Sir Edward Fitton, and on 22 March, 1571, he obtained a grant of the office of collector of customs of Strangford, Ardglass and Dundrum (Cal. Fiants., Eliz. No. 1772).

In the spring of 1571 he visited England. He strongly advocated colonizing the north of Ireland with Englishmen as the best means of preventing the growth of a Scottish power in those parts (State Papers, Ireland, Eliz. XXIII., 37). And on 5 Oct., 1571, he obtained a grant of MacCartan's country, corresponding to the modern barony of Kinelarty, in County Down, on condition that he planted it with civil and loyal subjects before 28 March, 1579. On his way back to Ireland in February, 1572, he captured a Spanish ship in the Channel (Ibid XXXV., 22, 23). On 10 April, he received a commission to execute martial law in MacCartan's county, but the indiscretion of Thomas Smith in publishing his scheme for the plantation of the Ardes Upper Clandeboye, by putting the Irish on their guard, placed insuperable obstacles in the way of realizing his plan. He succeeded in reducing Sir Brian O'Neill to temporary submission in October, 1572, and in the following month captured that chieftain's youngest daughter, but, notwithstanding his utmost exertions in conjunction with Smith, and at a later period with Walter Devereaux, Earl of Essex (q. v.) he failed to establish himself permanently in the country assigned to him (Ibid XXXVIII, 26, 38; XXXIX., 45; XLII., 58; XLVIII., 57).

His efforts were, however, warmly appreciated by Essex, and though, as Waterhouse said, a man of few word and an ill courtier, but of great reputation among soldiers (Ibid XLIX., 1) he was chosen by him to report to the privy council on the situation of affairs in the north in December, 1574 (Ibid XLVIII., 66).

He returned to Ireland on 5 May, 1575, with special instructions for the Earl of Essex, and with an order for his own admission to the privy council (Cal. Carew M. S. S. II., 4-7). He had made a good impression on Leicester and Walsingham, who recommended him to the queen for the government of Connaught, but several months elapsed before this recommendation took effect (Collins, Sidney Papers, I., 70). During the summer of that year he took part in Essex's expedition against Sorley Boy, and may possibly have assisted at the massacre of the MacDonnells on the island of Rathlin (Devereaux, Lives of the Earls of Essex, I., p. 108-17).

He accompanied Sir Henry Sidney into Connaught in Sept., 1576, and having been knighted by him on 7 Oct. (cf Cal. Carew M. S. S. II., 149, where 1578 is evidently a mistake for 1576.)

[Note by the Secretary—Shaw's Book of Knights, p. 77, has the following: "Sir Nicholas Malby, chief of the Commissioners of Connaught—Knighted at Athlone (Ireland 7 Oct. 1576."] He was appointed colonel or military governor of that province (Collins, Sidney Papers, I., 129). As soon as he had established himself firmly in his government, Malby proceeded against John and

Ulick Burke, sons of the Earl of Clanricarde. It was in the dead of winter, but for twenty-one days, he harried their countries with fire and sword, sparing neither young nor old (State Papers, Ireland, Eliz. LVII., 40). The vigor he displayed, and the success that attended his efforts, drew from Sidney, who was at first doubtful of his qualifications for the post, unstinted praise (Collins, Sidney Papers, I., 151, 166).

His strict observance of military discipline and his impartial administration of justice gained for him the respect of the soldiers and natives alike (Bagnell, Ireland under the Tudors, II., 339).

On 19 May, 1577, he was placed on the commission for ecclesiastical causes (Cal. Fiants, Eliz. No. 3047). In October, after arranging a feud between O'Conor Don and MacDonough, he, at O'Conor Sligo's request, attacked the castle of Bundrowes and having captured it from O'Donnell, restored it to O'Conor Sligo. But not having much confidence in the loyalty of the latter, he appointed Richard MacSwnie sheriff of the county of Sligo. He had hardly turned his back when O'Donnell invaded the county, slew the sheriff and besieged Bundrowes, compelling him to retrace his steps. He drove O'Donnell out of the county, but was unable to overtake him. (Annals of Loch Ce, LL., 415-19.) At Sligo, on his way back to Roscommon, he came to terms with Brian O'Rourke, but the arrangement did not last long, owing to O'Rourke's refusal to expel certain coiners he maintained. In April, 1578, Malby invaded his country, captured his chief castle, and put the entire garrison to the sword (Collins, Sidney Papers, I., 249). In connection with this episode, and considering his own antecedents, it is curious to find Malby about this time interceding with Walsingham for his friend Thomas Bavand of Liverpool, suspected of coining (State Papers, Ireland, Eliz. LIX., 48).

In the autumn of 1578 he repaired to England, returning to Ireland in May, 1579, with the higher title of president of Connaught (Cal. Carew M. S. S., II., 154). After the failure of Essex's colonization project, his grant of MacCartan's country had been, by Sidney's advice, revoked (Collins, Sidney Papers, I., 76) but in consideration of his recent services, and the losses he had formerly sustained, he on 12 April, 1579, received a grant of the manor and lordship of Roscommon, together with an annual rent of £200 out of the composition paid by the O'Farrells, and certain lands in Longford (Morrin, Cal. Pat. Rolls, II., 17). During his absence in England his officers and soldiers behaved badly, but Connaught remained tranquil (State Papers, Ireland, Eliz. LXVI., 67, 68). So firmly established, indeed, was the peace of the province, that on the outbreak of James Fitzmaurice's rebellion in July, Malby, with six hundred well-furnished troops, marched to Limerick to co-operate with the lord justice, Sir William Drwry (q. v.). Owing to Drwry's illness the task of suppressing the rebellion devolved mainly upon him. He displayed commendable zeal in prosecuting the rebels and on 3 October he defeated Sir John and Sir James of Desmond at Monasteranenagh in county Limerick (Ibid LXIX., 17-52, LXVIII., 45). He strongly suspected the Earl of Desmond of disloyalty, and after several uneffectual efforts (Ibid LXIX., 52; I., IX.) to secure his co-operation, treated him as a rebel, while Desmond, without much reason, complained that Malby's severity was a chief cause of his rebellion (Ibid LXIX., 70; LXXVII., 52).

On the arrival of the Earl of Ormonde in November with a commission to command the army in Munster, Malby returned to his charge in Connaught. He belonged to the Leicester faction, and for this and other more personal reasons bore no good-will to Ormonde, whom he subsequently charged with misrepresenting his services in Munster, and with abetting disorder in Connaught. With the exception of Richard Burke, called Richard of the Iron, or Iron Dick, none of the Connaught chiefs had shown any active sympathy with the Munster rebels.

In February, 1580, Malby invaded his country and drove him to seek safety among the islands in Clew Bay. After suffering the most terrible privations, Richard of the Iron submitted to the garrison at Bunishoole (Ibid LXXII., 39). During the siege of Carrigfoyle, Malby assisted the operations of the lord justice, Sir William Pelham (q. v.) with supplies from Connaught (Cal. Carew M. S. S., II., 238). In August O'Rourke, animated by the expectation of foreign assistance, rebelled and dismantled the castle of Leitrim. Malby immediately took the field against him, repaired and garrisoned the castle, and routed the rebels (Ibid II., 297). Then hastening to Dublin to the assistance of the lord deputy, Arthur, Lord Grey of Wilton (q. v.) against Baltinglas and Fragh MacHugh O'Byrne (q. v.) he witnessed the disastrous defeat of the English forces at Glenmalure (State Papers, Ireland, Eliz. LXXV., 79, 82). But the news that O'Rourke was again in arms compelled him, in spite of ill-health, to return at once to Connaught (Ibid LXXVI., 15; Cal. Carew M. S. S., II., 310). To those who complained that he used the sword too sharply in his government, he replied that if the queen did not use it more sharply she would lose both sword and realm (Ibid II., 314). O'Rourke fled at his approach (State Papers, Ireland, Eliz. LXXVII., 54) but a new danger instantly presented itself in the rebellion of John and Ulick Burke, who, at the instigation of the catholic bishop of Kilmacduagls, had proclaimed a religious war, and were making wild efforts to relieve the Spaniards at Limerick (Ibid LXXVIII., 41).

Even after the capture of Limerick the situation was sufficiently alarming to cause Grey to send reinforcements to Malby (Ibid LXXVIII., 59) but by the end of January, 1581, the latter announced that he had been so far successful against the rebels that they dare not look abroad, but, like wild wolves, keep to the woods and mountains. O'Rourke, as usual, took advantage of the situation, and invaded Roscommon, but Malby sent Captain Brabazon against him, and O'Rourke at once sued for peace (Cal Carew M. S. S., II., 320). Toward the end of February a body of six hundred Scots invaded the province to co-operate with the Burkes, but Malby had timely notice of the arrival and before the latter could join them he attacked them, and after killing a number of them, drove them across the Moy. At Strade Abbey, in the county Mayo, he decided a controversy between Richard of the Iron Burke and Richard MacOliver, allowing the title of MacWilliam to the former, and making the latter the sheriff of the county of Mayo. (See Malby's graphic description of his journey in State Papers, Ireland, Eliz. LXXXI., 421; and also in Colton M. S. S., Titus, B. XIII. ff. 320-5.)

Important as were his services, it was grievous, Grey complained, to see good Sir Nicholas Malby so thanklessly used (State Papers Ireland, Eliz. LXXXII., 48). He was anxious to lay his case before the Queen personally, and in May he agreed to a short peace with the Burkes (Ibid LXXXVIII., 10) but on the outbreak of hostilities between Turlough Linneach O'Neill and Sir Hugh O'Donnell in July, he was ordered to the assistance of the latter. He marched as far as Lifford, and having destroyed the town, effected a junction with the lord deputy (Ibid LXXXV., 47; Annals of Loch Ce LL., 441). Towards the close of November he went to England to report on the general situation of affairs in Ireland. But, so far as he was personally concerned, his visit was not successful. His enemies charged him with violent, tyrannical and corrupt conduct in his administration, and Elizabeth showed a disposition to listen to the charge. He returned to Ireland on 21 May, 1582, and was warmly welcomed by his brother officers. During his absence Connaught, except for some slight disturbance, created by MacWilliam, had remained tranquil. Early in July, however, Con O'Donnell, at the instigation of Turlough Linneach, invaded Sligo. Malby complained that the order forbidding him to raise men by cessing them on the country rendered him powerless to meet this danger. But O'Conor Sligo behaved well, and at Malby's approach O'Donnell decamped in such haste that some of his men were drowned in crossing the Erne (State Papers, Ireland, Eliz. XCIV., 15-20-32).

After this nothing occurred during his lifetime to disturb the peace of his government.

The fear of Malby, wrote Bonraby Gooche to Burghley in March, 1583, keeps all in good order, his "common dalliance" is "veni, vidi, vici." (Ibid C., 14.)

But he was deeply wounded by Elizabeth's neglect. His disgrace and his debts, he declared, would kill him. His constitution, naturally robust, had been undermined by rough service, and on 4 March, 1584, he died at Athlone. (Ibid CIX., 6.) "There came not to Erin in his own time, nor often before, a better gentleman of the Foreigners than he, and he placed all Connaught under bondage . . . and executed many works, especially in the courts of the towns of Athlone and Roscommon." (Annals of Loch Ce, II., 459.) "He was a man learned in the languages and tongues of the islands of the west of Europe, a brave and victorious man in battles." (Annals of the Four Masters, S. A. 1584.) His official letters, remarkable for their vigorous and graphic style, fully confirm this reputation.

Malby married Thomasine, daughter of Robert Lamb of Leeds, whose wife was a Castell of the Castells of East Hatley in Cambridgeshire (State Papers, Ireland, Eliz. XCI., 59). By her he had a son Henry, who succeeded him, and married Elizabeth, granddaughter of Sir Francis Jobson, lieutenant of the tower, and was killed apparently in November 1602, while serving in Connaught. and a daughter, Ursula, who was married to Anthony Brabazon (Irish Pedigrees, Harl. M. S. 1425, f. 157). Lady Malby subsequently married one George Rawe.

Stevenson's Cal. State Papers, For., Vols. VII.-IX.; Hamilton's Cal. State Papers, Ireland, Vols. I.-II.; Cal. Carew M. S. S., Vols. I.-II.; Collins' Sidney Papers; O'Donovan's Annals of the Four Masters; Hennessy's Annals of Loch Ce; Morrins' Cal. of Patent Rolls., Eliz.; Bagwell's Ireland under the Tudors; W. G. Wood-Martin's Hist. of Sligo; C. O. O'Conor's O'Conors of Connaught.)

R. D.

Note.—The "Visitation of Essex" has the following item: "Persall Jobson married, first to Henry Malby of Ross in Ireland." Is this Captain Henry Malby, son of Sir Nicholas Malby, who is said to have married Elizabeth, granddaughter of Sir Francis Jobson?

A descendant writes that some years ago she read in a newspaper under the English correspondence that Dillion, the great Irish leader, was to speak at Great Maltby—suggesting that there were two towns of Maltby. Possibly Great Maltby is in Ireland. Northwest of Limerick the map of Ireland shows Mal Bay. This may have been so named long before Sir Nicholas Malby was born, but it would be interesting to know certainly, as it seems not unlikely the bay was named for Sir Nicholas.

SIR NICHOLAS MALBY

The following account is taken from "Annals of the Four Masters," A. D. 1584:

"Sir Nicholas Malby, governor of the province of Connaught, died in Athlone, about Shrovetide; he was a man learned in languages and the tongues of the islands of Western Europe, a valiant and battle-triumphant man, throughout Ireland, Scotland and France, in the service of his Sovereign and that was a profitable service for him, for he received a suitable payment from the Queen, the Governorship of the Province of Connaught for seven years before his death, with Roscommon and Beal-atha-na-Sleiaigheadh (Ballinasloe in Galway) in perpetuity to himself and his heirs in succession; but, however, it was from the sons of the Earl of Clarvickard he first procured Ballinasloe."

NOTE.—A third account of Sir Nicholas Malby and Malbys connected with Ireland, follows. It is compiled from miscellaneous notes gathered by the author.

SIR NICHOLAS MALBY

YORKSHIRE—IRELAND

Arms: Malby (Sir Nicholas, chief commissioner of Connaught, knighted at Athlone, Ireland, by Sir Henry Sidney, lord deputy of Ireland, 7 October, 1576.) Argent, on a bend between two cotises gules three garbs or. (Burke's General Armory.) See under Maltby Heraldry.

It is quite evident from these arms that Sir Nicholas Malby believed himself to be descended from the Maltbys of Cleveland, Yorkshire. The name of his father is not known. Sir Nicholas wrote that, his father died when he was four years old. The Dict. of Nat. Biog. states: "Malby was born probably about 1530." It has seemed not unlikely to the compiler that he is the Nicholas Malby mentioned in the will of John Maltby, 17 May, 1532. (See under that date.) In any case it is worth noting.

Of his early life we know nothing. The first record found concerning Nicholas Malby is in 1562 (Domestic Papers, p. 206). It reads:

1562. "A list of prisoners in the Tower (of London), 5 Sept., 1562, including Lady Katharine Grey, Earl of Hertfordshire, etc. Sept. 20.—The Queen to the Sheriffs of London. Reprieve for Tho. Borough and Nicholas Malby who are to be delivered over to the Earl of Warwick for service abroad." (Cal. State Papers, Dom., edit. Lemon.)

1573. N. Malbie has Leach in his family.

1576. Knighted at Athlone, by Sir Henry Sidney, 7 Oct., 1576.* (Vide p. 207, Metcalfe's Book of Knights and p. 77, Shaw's Book of Knights.)

1578. July 7. Sir Nicholas Malbie had Roscommon and Athlone. (Vol. XCI., Irish State Papers.)

1575. Sir Nicholas Malby is referred to as Mr. Maltbie by Lord Burghley in 1575. (Vide p. 480, Carew M. S. S., edit. Brewer and Bullen.)

1579. In 1579 Capt or Sir Nicholas Malby returned to Ireland with great presents from the Sovereign. (From the Annals of the Four Masters.)

1579. Extracts from the Heralds' Visitation of London or Middlesix, 1579 (3 July). Sir Nicholas Maltby of Kilmallock. Sir Nicholas Malby Kt., b. circ. 1530. President of Connaught; descended from an old Yorkshire family mentioned in the Plantation of Leix (Ireland, 1556; d. at Athlone, Ireland, 4 March, 1584; and of Roscommon. He m. Thomassine Lamb, dau. of Robert Lamb of Leeds and his w., Miss Castell of East Hatley, Co. Cambs. His wid. m. George Rawe (or Rowe). His son, Capt. Henry Malby m. Elizabeth, granddaughter of Sir Francis Jobson, Lieut. of the Tower of London. Ursula, dau. of Sir Nicholas, m. Anthony Brabazon.

1579. Colonial Papers, East Indies, 1513-1616; 1579, March 20, p. 53-133: Thomas Allen to Sec. Walsyngham. Has received his letters for sale of the ordnance and Gabriel; the ordnance is sold but Mr. Lok's appraisement of £150 for the Gabriel is too much. Frobisher has bid £80 for her, "but I think ready money is out of the way with him." Sir Nicholas Malby may perhaps

* The records read: "Sir Nicholas Malby, chief of the Commissioners of Connaught, Knighted at Athlone, 7 Oct., 1576." (p. 77, Shaw's Book of Knights). And: "Sir Nicholas Malbey, Knighted, 7 Oct., 1578 at Athlone." (p. 207, Metcalfe's, Walter C. Metcalfe, Book of Knights.)

Note.—It will be seen that wo distinct dates are here given. One by Shaw as 1576 and Metcalfe gives 1578. Possibly an error was made in the transcribing.

have her and pay the money. Wishes "these men" were paid; is sore troubled with them. Many things to be sold in Lok's keeping. What Lok can sell he does, but pays no man a penny. All things should be sold out of hand, that Lok might bring in his "rear accounts" and be discharged. One page Indorsed, 20 March, 1579, with abstract. (Domestic Eliz. Vol. CXXX., No. 10. Cal. p. 620.)

NOTE.—Sir Nicholas Malby was evidently in England at this time, as the Dict. Nat. Biog. states that, " in the autumn of 1578 he repaired to England, returning to Ireland in May, 1579, with the higher title of President of Connaught." The Gabriel is, very evidently, a ship; "these men" may have been sailors or soldiers.

1580. Oct. 25. Athlone, Ireland. Sir Nicholas Malbie writes to Walsingham that his brother John may be sent over with charge of soldiers.

NOTE.—See Dict. Nat. Biog. "Even after the capture of Limerick, the situation was sufficiently alarming to cause Grey to send reinforcements to Malby." Query. Does this "brother John" refer to a brother of Sir Nicholas or to a brother of Walsingham's? If, as it would appear, it refers to John, a brother of Sir Nicholas, this would be additional proof that they were sons of the John Maltby who made his will in May, 1532. That Sir Nicholas had a brother we know. See under date May, 1582.

1579. President of Connaught, 1579; Leix in Ireland. (State Papers of Ireland, May, I., 21; Machyn Diary, p. 290; State Papers, Dom., Eliz. XXIV, 41. Lordship of Roscommon. State Papers Ireland, Eliz. XXXI., 42 I.; Colton M. S. S., Titus B., XVII., ff. 320-5; Irish Ped. Har. M. S. 1425, f. 157.)

1582. Aug. Letters from Sir Nicholas Malby (p. 67, p. 278, Cal. State Papers, Dom.).

1582. 15 June. Henry Malby of Ireland equitis fil New Coll. Oxon. matric. 15 June, 1582, ae. 13; one Nicholas Malby knighted, 1575. (Foster's Alumni Oxomensis.)

NOTE.—This is Sir Nicholas' son, Henry, and evidently b. in 1569.

1582. State Papers Ireland, June 21, 1582: Stephen White to Sir Nicholas Malby, "sorrow for" his brother Edward's naughty dealing.

Query: Does this refer to a brother of Sir Nicholas, or to his own brother? Evidently the latter, as he would hardly write expressing sorrow for the misdeeds of Sir Nicholas' brother.

1582. July 12. Sir Hugh O'Connell's joy at Sir Nicholas Malby's safe arrival.

1581. April 6, Dublin. Sir Nicholas Malbie writes his eldest daughter had married Mr. Anthony, son of Sir W. Brabazon. His son lately in hard case.

1582. Vol. XCI., Irish State Papers, anno 1582, April 30, has a paper giving names of certain persons to be examined touching Sir Nicholas Malbie. On this paper is a pedigree of Sir Nicholas Malby by Durgley, showing connection by marriage with Robert Lamb of Leeds and Robert Castell of East Hatley, near Potton in Cambridgeshire.

NOTE.—A copy of this pedigree was made at the British Museum by a friend, and as the ancient handwriting is practically undecipherable by all but an expert, a translation was added; this may not be entirely correct, but is given here as it was transcribed.

Irish State Papers, 1582, April 30th. No. 59.

1. Barnett in ——— m.
2. Barnett in Clidford, m. (1) ——— and (2) (it looks like Endsey of Aylesford in Cat., Kent.)
3. Doroth. Barnett fd. ist Hons? m. Castell of Est. Hatley, near Co. Cantab. (Cambridge.)
4. Tho. Castell, mortgaged Barnett to Brograve. His sister, Frd Castell, m. Robert Lam of Leedes, York.
5. Thomasine Lam m. Sir Nicholas Mallby and according to the pedigree chart, they had two children, Henry and Ursula, as we know.

1582. 7 May. London. Sir Nicholas Malbie writes Walsingham to have Mr. Wade give his brother writings left by Malbie's father, who died when Malbie was four years old.

1583-4. Sir Nicholas Malby died March 4, 1583-4.

NOTE.—Many of these Irish Notes were taken from Vol II., Irish State Papers, By 4, 068, in Yale University Library.

1584. April 14. Dublin. Lady Thomasine Malby writes Walsingham for payment of late husband's reckonings and for favor for her son Henry.

1584. The Will of Sir Nicholas Malby, Kt., Governor of Connaught and Thomond, was proved in Perog. Court of Ireland in 1584.

1585. Feb. 8. Roscommon Castle. Sir R. Byngham asks for wardship of son of Sir Nicholas Malbie . . . Malbie, Brabazon and Waterhouse draw articles against Sir R. Byngham.

1585. April 2. Ross. Perrot writes, "rent received for Lady Malbie in Co. of Longford. Her son has run from school at Oxford and taken order with Mr. Coffner's runaway man, Marrow."

1585. On July 15, 1585, Queen Elizabeth issued commissions to John Marburie, Robert Ffowler and John Brown, gentlemen.

NOTE.—Was this John, brother of Sir Nicholas? See under date 1590. This note is interesting as it contains the names of three well known emigrant families to New England, John Maltby of Milford and New Haven; Francis Brown, John being a family given name, and Robert Fowler of ——. The Fowlers were of Milford, Conn.

1590. Vol. III., Irish State Papers mentions, "Capt. John," evidently brother of Sir Nicholas Malby. May 3, 1590.

1596. The Will of Dame Thomasin Malbie, wid. of Sir Nicholas Malby, Kt., was proved in Perog. Court, Ireland, in 1596.

1596. Dec. Captain Henry Malby, p. 321.

1599. Warrant to pay £200 to Captain Henry Malby for service and losses sustained in wars in Ireland, pp. 219-224.

1603. Feb. "Tyrone Tyrrell and most of the rebels are retired to the north. They have slain Capt. Malby and most of his company." p. 289.

Query: Is this Capt. John, brother of Sir Nicholas, or is it his son, Capt. Henry? Probably his son, as in 1603, a brother of Sir Nicholas would have been very old. This item is from Cal State Papers.

1618. Dec. Council of Ireland ordered Sir Oliver Lambert to pay to John and Sarah Paulet £30 per annum while he held the wardship of Geo. Malby as interest on £300 due by the late Henry Malby to John Paulet (p. 599. See under date 1640.)

1620. Widow of Captain Malby m. Sir Ralph Sedley and claims wardship of Geo. Malby (p. 125 Cal. State Papers).

1625. George Malby knighted in Ireland by Visct. Falkland, 9 June, 1625 (p. 188, Shawe's Book of Knights).

NOTE.—Mr. Harte writes me that this is recognized as an authentic publication.

New settlers in Linconell in Pynnar's Surrey, 1619 A. D., mentions Sir George Marburie.

The following item is obviously under a wrong date. It is from Ms. Gen. et Herald, Vol. II., 1867-8, p. 174, and reads: "Thomas Onsesby, living in 1569, m. a dau. of Henry Malby, son of Sir Nicholas. They had a son Malby Orsby and a great-grandson Malby Orsby.

1638. Abstract of the Will of Sir George Maltbie, Kt., dated 6 Dec. 1638. I confirm the agreement with James Frese concerning the redemption of my estate out of the hands of Lord Ranelage. Burial at S. Dunstan's in the west and £100 to be spent. My debts in the Fleet to be paid. Nephew and niece Paulett, £100. Nurse Catherine Dudley, £8. Residue to my wife. Walter Alleyne, James Palfreyman, Witnesses.

NOTE.—See date 1666. Administration of goods of William Maltby of S. Dunstans in West London, to Elizabeth, the relict. Is this a connection with Sir George?

1639. 29 June. Administration out of P. C. C. to Anne, the relict of Sir George Maltbie, of S. Brides, Fleet Street for that no exor. was nominated. 101 Harvey.

1640. 11 May. Petition of John Poulett and Sarah, his wife, sister and heiress to Sir George Maltby, Kt., dec. to the King. Queen Elizabeth gave to Sir Nicholas Maltby, petitioner's grandfather, in lieu of his services in reducing Connaught, the Manor of Roscommon in the said province. It descended to his son, Captain Henry Maltby, petitioner's father, who was slain in the service of the Crown in 1602; and then to her brother, Sir George Maltby, who mortgaged it to Viscount Ranelagh, with right of redemption; but when Sir George had secured means to redeem it, Lord Ranelagh refused to reconvey the lands; the said Sir George coming to England to sue for relief was unjustly imprisoned by one Luke Nightengale and died in great misery in the Fleet. Lord Ranelagh still refuses endeavors to obtain a grant for his Majesty to establish his possessions by which petitioners will not only be disinherited, but utterly ruinated. They pray that the Lord Lientenant may call Lord Ranelagh before them. Also that Lord Ranelagh grant may be stayed. Reference to the Lord Lieutenant and order for stay of grant. (Printed State Papers, p. 749.)

1649. Samuel Maltby served in Army in Ireland since 1649, in Captain Richard Franklin's Troop of Lord Deputy Fleetwood's Regiment. Since 1649 (to 1662 ?). (p. 657. Cal. State Papers. Ireland, 1660-1662, edit. by Mahaffy.)

This note is of interest, being a Samuel Maltby contemporary with the emigrant William Maltby who named a son Samuel Maltby. Also the connection in Ireland is worthy of note, as he may have been descended from John Malby, brother of Sir Nicholas.

1663-1665. Cal State Papers, Ireland, edit. by Mahaffy, p. 352, says: "Queen Elizabeth by letters dated 2 June, 21st year of her reign [1579] granted to Sir Nicholas Malthby (Maltby) Kt., Manor of Lordship of Roscommon and the late dissolved Monasterie; also the Monastery of Longford. In 13 Jas. I., the Roscommon property was granted to Edmond Middop. The interest of Sir George Malthby and his heirs did not expire until 1639." Repudiated in 1665. (Vide p. 600, Cal. State Papers, Ireland, 1663-65, edit. Mahaffy.)

It would be of great interest to know to just what this reference refers, as 1663-65 is the date at which we first find John Maltby, the emigrant, in New England, leaving a tradition of "confiscated lands, an ancestor (i.e., prob. relative), a captain in wars for and against the crown," the usual mixed up tradition; one being that, "the family were almost royal." It is very evident that the New England Maltbys were not descendants of Sir Nicholas, but it may be that they were distantly related. Could it be that they believed themselves co-heirs to the above estate, even though not closely related.

The Peerage of Ireland by Lodge, Vol. 4. p. 234. says "and left Sir Nicholas Malby, Gov. of Connaught, possessed of the house of Roscommon and Athlone."

O'Hart's Irish Pedigree, Imolments of the Diocese of Innocents, gives "James Malby," no date.

1818, 1 Sept. "Lady Morgan (au authoress) visted her relatives, Sir Maltby and Lady Crofton at their country home in Sligo."

In connection with the above newspaper clipping, it may be well to give the following pedigree from Harleian Soc. Pub., 1903, p. 690. Lincolnshire Visit.:

MORGAN OF GAINSBOROUGH

1 Morice Morgan m. Elizabeth, dau. of Wm. Forman of Gainsborough, yeom., sister of Sir Wm. Forman, the Lord Mayor of London, in 1538.

2 Richard Morgan m. Margaret, dau. of ——— Maltby. Arms: Arg. on a fess engrailed gules, 3 garbs or. (See arms of Sir Nicholas Malby and Marbury of London.)

3 William Morgan.

There is a space of two hundred years between this marriage of Richard Morgan and Margaret Maltby, to Lady Morgan who visited Sir Maltby and Lady Crofton, yet it is of interest as the genealogist finds that of a truth history repeats itself, and where one family intermarries with another in the course of a few generations, another intermarriage occurs between descendants, who are distant cousins.

The following references are of interest in connection with these Irish notes: pp. 690-694, Families in Ireland at the close of the 17th century. Irish Pedigrees by O'Hart, Vol. II., has this statement: "According to the M. S. Vols. F-3, 23; F-3, 27, and F-4, 18, in Trinity College, Dublin, the families mentioned in this section were among the principal families in Ireland at the close of the 17th century. The reader will find in each of these three volumes much information in relation to the genealogies of the Anglo-Irish families who settled in Ireland since the English invasion, which are not given in this work." Then follows the various families by name; that of Malby is given on page 694.

It would be of immense value could the manuscripts referred to be examined, as here might be found a clue to the immediate family of Sir Nicholas Malby.

In Bagwell's Ireland, the Index gives: "MALTBY, Captain, afterwards Sir Nicholas." and on page 129: "Piers and Maltby at Carrick-fergus pleaded that they had neither ships nor men to guard thirty miles of coast night and day"; also page 132. On page 233 we find: "Maltby, a man of ability and discretion." Page 245 states: "great praise is due to Captain Piers and Captain Maltby for their ability and diligence." Again we find, p. 93: "Maltby refused £1,000 for the prisoner's life, and a like sum for that of Tirlogh O'Brien, a noted rebel."

NOTE.—£2,000 was a considerable fortune in the time of Sir Nicholas Malby.

The Brabazon pedigree is here given as it shows the sort of families with whom the Sir Nicholas branch intermarried. The pedigree is from O'Hart's Irish Pedigrees, Vol. II., p. 66:

BRABAZON

Arms: Gu on a bend or. (another authority gives ar.) three mullets az. (or sable).

1 Anthony Brabazon m. Ursula, dau. of Sir Nicholas Malby of Roscommon, Kt., and had:

2 Malby Brabazon, of Ballinasloe, Co. Roscommon, Esq., who d. 20th May, 1637, and was buried in Roscommon. He m. Sarah, dau. of Thomas Burke, of Tulahery, Co. Galway, and had one son and three daughters, viz.:

3 Anthony Brabazon m. Ellice, dau. of John Dillon. (He turned Papist, but was pardoned in 1652.)

NOTE.—Some years ago a newspaper contained an item to the effect that "Dillon, the great Irish leader was to speak at Greater Maltby."

3 Ursula Brabazon m. Bernard Talbot of Raithdown, Co. Wicklow, gent.

3 Sarah Brabazon.
3 Dorothy Brabazon.

NOTE.—The record concerning Sir Nicholas Malby in 1562 has "qr. of London," after his name. I am not sure whether this query was in the original record or if it was added by the friend who sent the copy of the record. Appended are the few stray early notes of Maltbys in any way connected with Ireland.

1281. John le Mareschel going beyond seas nominating Robert de Malteby and Hugh le Cressingham his attorneys in Ireland for two years (Cal. Pat. Rolls, p. 422).

1401. Thomas Malby, Mayor of Limerick, (Vide Ferrar's Hist. of Limerick).

Since these pages were written we have learned of an Irish branch of the family, but there was not sufficient time to obtain records from Ireland, consequently we can only print what data Mr. William H. Maultby had available.

MAULTBY

CORK, IRELAND

Tradition: "Forefathers went to Ireland with Oliver Cromwell's army, 1649-1650." Note—This ancestor may very possibly have been Samuel Maltby, who served in the Army in Ireland since 1649. See under that date.

1. Arthur Warner Maultby resided in Cork, Ireland. He was an inspector of merchandise shipped from the city of Cork. It is an office, or appointment, from the British Crown. After his death, Henry Maultby (a cousin of William H. Maultby who furnished these records) received the appointment and was holding the office a few years ago, and very probably is still doing so.

   Children of Arthur Warner Maultby were: Joseph, William H. (emigrated about 1831-32), John, Peter, Arthur Warner and Henry.

2. William H. Maultby, emigrated to the States about 1831-2. He went first to Vermont (probably to Washington County). Shortly after 1835 he removed to Landsingburg, Rensselear County, N. Y., and later moved to Sheboygan County, Mich. He was prominent in the county, being one of the chief organizers and held the office of County Clerk and also that of Judge of Probate.

   John (2) Maultby, brother of the above, emigrated to the States about 1840. He resided in Landsingburg with his brother, William H., for a while. He died at Waterford, Albany County, N. Y.

Peter (2) Maultby, another brother, emigrated about 1840 (?). Resided at Landsingburg for a time. Removed to Boonville, Mo., about 1842 and married there. Later he went to Kickapoo, Kansas.

2. Arthur Warner (2) Maultby, emigrated to the States about 1834. He resided in Vermont with his brother William H. Maultby, for a short while, then removed to Landsingburg. Rensselear County, N. Y. Here he met an English lady from near Ipswich, Eng., Mary Ann Scace, and married her. Both died some years ago. Their son is:

3. William H. Maultby, b. Aug. 1, 1838, at Landsingburg. About the year 1840 they removed to Highland on the Hudson. Present address is: Grand Valley, Pennsylvania.

(Query: Were John and William Maltby the emigrants mentioned by Senator Malby of New York? See Pedigree XXIII.)

MARBURY

Pedigree VII.

Of London

Arms: Quart. of 9. 1. Sable a cross engrailed between 4 pheons arg. (Marbury) 2. Or. on a fess engrailed az. 3 garbs of the field (Merbury).

Note.—Compare with the arms of Sir Nicholas Malby.

From "Visit. of London, 1568."

I. WILLIAM Merbury, m. Agnes, dau. and co-heiress of Thomas Blount, younger brother of Sir William Blount, and of his wife, the dau. and heiress of John Hawley. Children: Robert Marbury, 1st son; Thomas. (For another Blount item see Pedigree II.)

II. THOMAS Marbury, citizen and haberdasher of London; m. Agnes, dau. of ——— Lyne of Northampton. Children: Christion m. to Francis Withers; Humphrey Marbury, 2nd son, citizen and haberdasher of London, m. Anne, dau. of Alderman Banker of London; Anne m. (1) ——— Bradley, (2) Armiger Warde: Alice, wife of Thomas Marbury.

There is a break here and then follows:

Joh'nes Marbery.

Thomasine m. to Thomas Jennyns.
Elizabeth m. to Richard Ellis.

NOTES TO PEDIGREE VII.

1565. "Humphrey Marbury." In 1565, March 31, p. 250, Domestic Papers, there is a memorandum of institutions, by Humphrey Marbury, addressed to his cousin Mawbury, for purchasing certain quantities of grain in France. (See under date 1610, Humphrey Maltby of Upton.)

1561. On p. 190 there is an account of dispensations and licenses granted in the Court of Faculities, by Barth. Kempe, Deputy to James Marburye. (Probably nearly connected with the above Humphrey.)

1623. Colonial Papers, Vol. 3, p. 138. Matthew Malberry, a nailor (sailor ?) entertained to go into the Indies at 30s per month, Aug. 15, 1623.

1627. Dom. Papers, Vol. VIII., p. 291. Date 17 Jan., 1627. Owner, Anthony Marbery, Ship "St. George," 350 tons; the owner, captain and master. 21 March, 1627, "St. George (prize)" "Gift of God" of London, Capt. Robert Marberie; 80 tons (p. 294). 1 May, 1627, Anthony Marbery and others, "St. George," 300 tons. Capt. Anthony Marbery. Robert Marbery and others, "Gift of God," 100 tons. Robert Marbery.

1628. Colonial Papers, Vol. 4, p. 460. Petition of Lewis Marbury, gentleman, to Privy Council, etc.

1629. 10 Jan. Navy bill "Capt. Marbury."

1610. (p. 203, Dom. Papers). Thos. Marberie, gentleman, usher to the Lord Chancellor, sworn a free brother of the Comp. (East India) Jan. 9-19, 1610.

1615. (p. 378, E. I. Co.): "Mr. Marberie freed from being an adventurer in the eighth voyage." etc. Feb. 10, 1615. (p 385) Thomas Marbury, Feb. 22, 1615, E. I. Co.

1626. State Dom. Papers, 308. 12 April, 1626. Sixty-seven Ministers of business to be submitted to the King, amongst them a commendau for the Bishop of Cloufert and Kilmacough; an order for the East India merchants to transport Sir Robert Sherley, and Sir Dodmore Cotton to Persia; and other matters relating to Robert Mawbery, Arnold Spencer, Mr. Samuel, Sir Henry Crofts, Thos. Baxter, Mr. Levaston, Mr. Robinson and Sir William Bruncher.

1626. p. 425. Sept. 11, 1626-64. Petition of John Malherbe, Master of the "Francis" of St. Maloes, to the Council. His ship bound from St. Maloes to Calais was stayed by a King's ship and brought to Dover, where great part of her cargo had been spoiled by wet; Sir John Hippisley had been directed by the Lord Admiral to discharge the ship, but desired the order of the Council; prays for an order accordingly.

1654. State Papers, Ireland. 20 April, 1654. Assignment by Thomas Maberly of the parish of St. Peter's, Paul's Wharf, London, weaver. See Will of Richard Maltby of Hommanby, York, weaver, 6 Sept. 1658, in which he mentions his son Thomas. Possibly the above. See also Will of Thomas Maltby, 1666-7. The Joseph Maltby, mariner, Will 1698-9 of St. Paul, Shadwell, Co. Middlesex, may have been a descendant of Thomas Maberly, as London is in Middlesex County.

1655. Col. Papers, West Indies, Vol. I., p. 431. Thomas Maundy, merchant to transport to Barbadoes 40 horses, 600 dozen pairs of shoes, 20 cases of pistols, etc. (p. 427) He has a son-in-law in Barbadoes.

This item is given as it is only ten years later we find our American Maltbys, West India merchants, owning ships and later owning some "estate" in Barbadoes.

1665. Vol II., p. 332. (A ship ?) One gun. Capt. Arah. Malabar. Jamaica. Nov.

1670. Vol. III., p. 100. St. Andrew's parish, Jamaica. John Maverley, 130 acres. Richard Mapeley, 28 acres.

MAUTEBY

Pedigree VIII.

"Reg. Hayden," fo. 45. p. 227; Suckling's "Suffolk"; Page's "Suffolk Traveller," p. 313.

I. Sir ROBERT de Mauteby, Lord and patron of Fritton, Co. Suffolk, temp. Edw. III. [1325-1377].

II. JOHN de Mauteby, Kt., Lord of Fritton. (See Pedigree IV. He was evidently a son of Sir John de Mauteby, Kt.) Will 1374. Proved 1 Oct., 1374. Buried at Fritton before the altar of St. Mary in the parish church of Fritton, St. Edmund, where he lived. See under date 1374.

In 1413 Robert Mauteby, Esq., enfeoffed Sir Miles Stapleton, Sir Simon Fellrigge, Sir William Argentein and others, in the Manor of Fritton, Suffolk, with other lands in Norfolk to fulfil his will made same year. (This is Robert (8), Pedigree IV.-A.)

PALMES

Pedigree IX.

Palmes of Naburn, York.

Note.—This pedigree is given on account of the numerous intermarriages with the Maltbys.

I. Nicholas Palmes m., 1372, Elinor Agnes, dau. of Sir Wm. Morebie of Morebie, Kt.

II. William Palmes m. for his second wife, Clarissa, dau. of Thomas Fairfax of Walton, Esq., by Margaret Malbie. She survived and m. second, Sir William Malbis, Kt. (This was Margaret (9), sister of William (9), Pedigree I.)

III. Mary Palmes m. Thomas Malbie of Acaster Malbis.

IV. Isabella Palmes m. John Malbis of Acaster Malbis.

MALTBY OF KEXBIE, LINCOLNSHIRE

The compiler has given no coat-of-arms to this branch of the family, for the reason that no proof has been found of a title to a coat-of-arms. However, it may be as well to state here that in all the various branches of the American descendants the coat-of-arms of the Yorkshire Maltbys has been handed down, and in the Inventory of the estate of Samuel Maltby (2), son of the emigrant William Maltby, is found the mention of a "coat-of-arms." Various mottoes are used: "Virtus sub pondere crescit," being that used by the descendants of Col. Stephen (4) Maltby and the descendants of his older brother, Gen. Isaac (4) use "Quod serveus metes."

MALTBY

Pedigree X.

Maltby of Kexbie, Lincolnshire.

Genealogy of the descendants of John Maltby of Kexbie Hall, Kexbie, Lincoln. Will proved in 1557.

Compiled from vital records of births, marriages and deaths and Probated Wills.

Explanation: Throughout the genealogies in this book, the * opposite a name denotes the person died without issue. The Roman numerals refer to the generation of the person and the

Arabic figures are individual numbers to distinguish each person mentioned.

I. 1. JOHN Maltby,* probably b. early in the 1500s of Kexbie Hall, Kexbie, Co. Lincoln; m. Margerie ——. Buried at Upton. Children mentioned in his will, 1557, were:

II. 2. Richard Maltby. Will proved 1602.
II. 3. William Maltby. Will proved 1582.
II. 4. Margaret Maltby.
II. 5. Izabell Maltby. (An Isabell Maltby was buried at Upton, 20 May, 1586.)

II. 2. RICHARD Maltby of Kexbie, Co. Lincoln. Will proved in 1602, mentions children:

III. 6. Christopher Maltby, Will proved 1603. Bardicke Close.
III. 7. Ellen Maltby m. John Quipp.
III. 8. Margaret Maltby m. Richard Wilkinson.
III. 9. John Maltby, Springthorpe. Will proved 1610.
III. 10. Richard Maltby. Exor. of Will. Have not found his Will; ment. in 1603.

II. 3. WILLIAM Maltby of Kexbie, Lincoln. Will proved 1582. Burial at Upton; left wid. Grace ——. Se evidently m., 23 May, 1584, John Walker. Children:

III. 11. Dorothy Maltby, m., 18 June, 1593, Tho. Tollen, Upton Ch. Rec.
III. 12. Richard Maltby. Will proved 1618, of Upton.
III. 13. William Maltby. Is he the Wm. of Billinghay Inq., 14 James I.
III. 14. Thomas Maltby. Is this Thomas of Willoughton, W. P. 1618-19.
III. 15. Henry Maltby. Think this is Humfrey. W. P. 1610. Not mentioned in brother's Will, 1618.
III. 16. Margaret Maltby. Not mentioned in brother's Will., 1618.

III. 6. CHRISTOPHER Maltby, owned Bardicke Close, Upton. Will proved 1603; m. Elizabeth Fysher, 27 May, 1593. Children:

IV. 17. Richard Maltby.

* Whereas it is not known who were the parents of John Maltby of Kexbie Hall, Kexbie, it seems well to note the will of William Maltby of Ingham, 15 Aug., 1547, in which he makes "Wife Isabel and son John exors." Here we find several of the names mentioned in the Will of John of Kexbie Hall, 1557. Richard, perhaps named for his wife's father. William would be his own father's name. Margaret, named for his wife. Izabell named for his mother. This item is simply inserted as a possible clue in further researches.

IV. 18. Thomas Maltby. Under 21.
IV. 19. Christopher Maltby. Owned Bardicke Close. Under 21.
IV. 20. John Maltby. Under 21.
IV. 21. Elizabeth Maltby. Under 21.

III. 9. JOHN Maltby of Springthorpe, Co. Lincoln. Will proved 1610; m. Margaret Bishop (had a brother Richard Bishop; also Robert Bishop.) Perhaps she m. (2) a Scendeby. Children bapt. as Springthorpe:

IV. 21-A. John Maltby. He was probably not born at Springthorpe.
IV. 22. Richard Maltby, bapt. 24 Feb. 1592-3; elder son, Fisher's Garth.
*IV. 23. Jane Maltby, bapt. 26 Nov., 1594; buried 23 Jan., 1594-5.
IV. 24. Hellen Maltby, bapt. 2 Jan., 1594; m. John Chatterton.
*IV. 25. Allice Maltby, bapt. 28 March, 1598; buried 10 Feb. 1609.
IV. 26. Elizabeth Maltby, bapt. 27 Feb., 1599-1600 (Did she m. ———Hindmarsh?)
IV. 27. William Maltby, bapt. 8 Nov., 1606; cottage in Springthorpe.
IV. 28. Robert Maltby, bapt. 1 April, 1609 of Bawtry.
IV. 28-A. Margaret Maltby.
IV. 28-B. Marie Maltby m. Long. See Will of Robert of Bawtry, 1663.

III. 10. RICHARD Maltby of Kexbie; burial at Upton. Will proved 1635. Children:

IV. 29. John Maltby, house in Kexbie. Will 1679. Buried at Upton.
IV. 30. Elizabeth Maltby, m. Wm. Derby, had Mary and Ann of Apley.
IV. 31. Christopher Maltby, d. s. i. Will proved 1638-9; of Kexbie.
IV. 32. William Maltby, bapt. 17 Dec., 1618, of Broxholm.
IV. 33. Robert Maltby; had children.
IV. 34. Nicholas Maltby, bapt. 3 May, 1629, at Upton. (Had a dau. Sarah.)
IV. 35. Richard Maltby. Will proved 1658; buried at Upton.

III. 12. RICHARD Maltby of Upton, Lincoln. Will proved

1618. He m. Elizabeth Fysher (Fisher), wid. of Christopher Maltby, his first cousin. Children bapt. at Upton.

IV. 39. John Maltby, bapt. 2 Aug., 1604. Evidently m. Bridgett ——.

*IV. 40. Mary Maltby, bapt. 18 Nov., 1604; buried 24 Dec., 1604.

IV. 41. William Maltby, bapt. 20 Dec., 1605; land Stourton next Stow.

IV. 42. Margaret Maltby, bapt. 16 April, 1608. Close called Scoyning.

*IV. 43. Richard Maltby, bapt. 22 Feby., 1609; buried 24 Feby., 1609.

*IV. 44. Ann Maltby, bapt. 14 Feby., 1610.

IV. 45. Ann Maltby, bapt 27 June, 1611. Under 21.

IV. 46. Richard Maltby, bapt. 1612. Will 20 Feb., 1623-4. Not mentioned in father's will.

IV. 47. Mary Maltby, bapt. 8 Nov., 1612. Not mentioned in father's will.

IV. 48. Elizabeth Maltby, bapt. 10 Oct., 1613. Not mentioned in father's will.

See Agreement in 1659. Mary Maltby evidently m. Thomas Barker. Elizabeth Maltby evidently m. George Cartwright. William's w. was probably Rebecca. (See Agreement 1670.) Ann probably m. John Thompson of Willingham and had Ann and Thomas.

IV. 21-A. JOHN Maltby, alderman, Springthorpe and East Retford, Notts. Will proved 1647-8. Married Mary ——. (Did his wid. m. George Holmes. See Agreement 1662.) Children:

V. 49. John Maltby probably b. about 1640. (Sup. N. E. 1664.)

V. 50. Richard Maltby, bapt. 15 Aug., 1642, at Retford, Notts. (Evidently d. young; not in father's will.)

V. 51. Jane Maltby, eldest dau. (Did she m. —— Turnell? or did she m. Robert White?)

V. 52. William Maltby, bapt. 16 March, 1644-45, Retford, Notts. Supposed to be William Maltby, New Eng., 1672.

V. 53. Elizabeth Maltby, younger daughter.

V. 54. Robert Maltby, bapt. 28 Dec., 1647, at Retford, Notts. Supposed to be Robert who witnessed the deed of William Maltby's home and lot at Branford, Conn., in 1673.

IV. 22. RICHARD Maltby, bapt. 1592-3; m. Sarai (Hornby?).

See her will 1665. He owned Fisher's Garth, Springthorpe. Will proved 1638. Children:

V. 55. Richard Maltby, Springthorpe, Sturgate, Little Coisey. (Not mentioned in his mother's will in 1665.)

*V. 56. John Maltby, buried 20 Nov., 1633, at Springthorpe.

*V. 57. Robert Maltby, b. 1631; d. 1633.

V. 58. Elizabeth Maltby m. John Hallifax; children.

V. 59. William Maltby, b. 1634. (Humberstone; next heir to father; only surviving son.)

V. 60. Sarah Maltby m. 23 Aug., 1636, Wm. Parke, Springthorpe; had daus. Sarah and Sicely Parke.

V. 61. Margaret Maltby m. William Mason, gent., East Retford; m. Cherbury. See Agreement 1662.

V. 62. Mary Maltby, m. Robert Farmary; had a dau. Sarah. Children.

IV. 28. ROBERT Maltby, bapt. 1609; m. Ann Stoakham (?) Alured. He of Bawtry, Yorks. Will proved 1663-5. Children:

V. 63. William Maltby, gent., d. s. i. Will proved 1666-7.

V. 64. Robert Maltby of Bawtry. (Supposed to be the Robert Maltbye Sr., in New Haven in 1672.)

V. 65. John Maltby, bapt. 2 Aug., 1642, at E. Retford.

V. 66. Barbara Maltby, b. 1648.

V. 67. Daniel Maltby, b. 1650.

IV. 29. JOHN Maltby, Kexby, Will proved 1679. Buried at Upton. (Think he m. (1) Prudence Johnson, Jan. 23, 1634, at Upton; m. (2) Elizabeth, wid. Leary. Her Will 1682. Cooper's Close. Child:

V. 68. Richard Maltby. (Had Richard and Elizabeth.) Had Sleighsborough Close and Cooper's Close.

IV. 32. WILLIAM Maltby, bapt. 1618; of Broxholm, Linc. Will proved 1671. Wife Mary. Children:

V. 69. John Maltby of Broxholm, W. P. 1697-8; wife Elizabeth; had a dau. who m. Wm. Quip of Thorp in the Fallows.

V. 70. William Maltby of Broxholm, W. P. 1679; had two daughters, Ann and Elizabeth. His wife was Ann ———.

V. 71. Richard Maltby.

V. 72. Ann Maltby, m. ——— Kilne.

V. 73. Mary Maltby, m. ——— Blakey.

IV. 35. RICHARD Maltby, m. Mary ——— of Kexby; burial at Upton. Children:

V. 74. Elizabeth Maltby, under 21.

V. 75. Richard Maltby, house Thomas Crane occupies; under 21.

V. 76. John Maltby, under 21; house John Lamin occupies.

V. 77. Christopher Maltby, bapt. 1650; d. 1650.

V. 78. Ann Maltby, under 21.

V. 79. Mary Maltby, b. 1655; under 21.

V. 49. Supposed to be John Maltby, emigrant to New England. For further records see under American Section of the book.

V. 52. Supposed to be William Maltby of Branford, Conn. For further records see in the section devoted to the American Maltbys.

V. 53. The compiler has often wondered if she could be the Elizabeth Barker who is mentioned with Hannah Maltby, occupying the first seats in the Branford church.

V. 54. ROBERT Maltby. Supposed to be Robert Maltbye of New England.

V. 64. ROBERT Maltby of Bawtry. Supposed to be he who came to New England about 1671-2. He sold a house in Bawtry and he borrowed £50, mortgaged three messuages in Bawtry just about this time, evidently to obtain the ready money with which to take him to New England. He had two daughters, Ann, who d. before 1673 and Sarah.

V. 66. BARBARA Maltby, b. 1648; m. Richard Thwaytes, gent., als. Clarworth or Tickhill of Arnthorpe in 1666.

V. 67. DANIEL Maltby, gent., of Doncaster, York, in 1672-3. (The Genealogist has a theory that Daniel Maltby, son of the emigrant, William Maltby, who was b. in 1679, was named for this cousin.)

V. 69. JOHN Maltby of Broxholm, Lincoln., W. P. 1697-8. Wife Elizabeth. Child, dau., m. William Quip of Thorp in the Fallowes.

NOTE.—The earliest note found of Maltbys at Retford was in 1328, when William de Malteby's name appeared on the Calendar of the Close Rolls.

MALTBY

PEDIGREE XI.

Maltby of Orston

The arms used by this branch of the Maltby family are: Argent, on a bend gules, three garbs or. Motto: "Praesto et Persisto." Mr.

Brough Maltby has a fine old seal bearing the above arms, which has come down to him from many generations of ancestors, Mr. Brough Maltby being the head of his House of Maltby.

While in London some years ago the compiler had the pleasure of meeting Mr. and Mrs. Maltby and their son, Brough Maltby, junior, and seing some fine old ancestral portraits both of the Maltbys and Broughs which hang in his dining room and along the stairway. The portraits of those with Maltby blood are instantly recognizable by the resemblance borne to the Maltbys of this present time.

We give at some length an account of Bishop Edward Maltby, who was of this family and it has seemed fitting to include a short genealogy of this branch of the family. The bulk of the material was compiled by Edwin Mortimer Blake of the University of Arizona, Tucson, Arizona, August 19, 1907, and now of New York City. Mr. Blake's wife is a descendant of William Maltby of Orston. Various items have been added by the present compiler, many of them being records copied from the Shelton Registers by Mr. E. C. Harte. Some have been furnished by descendants or ferrited out personally, and whereas still far from a complete record of the family it is a very valuable record. I have taken the liberty of changing Mr. Blake's lettering of generations, in order to conform as far as possible to the same style used in all the pedigrees given in this book.

MALTBY OF ORSTON, NOTTS.

I. 1. WILLIAM Maltby, gent., b. in 1641; m. at St. Michael and All Saints, Shelton Parish in 1682, Oct. 31, Jane, dau. of Mr. George Brough of Shelton, Nottingham, Eng. (Shelton Record: George Brough, bapt. at Shelton 10 May, 1631, the son of Richard and Jane ——— Brough.) William Maltby d. 1 Nov., 1718, at Orston, Notts, and his wid. d. 3 Nov., 1724. (It is possible that William Maltby, b. 1641, was a son of John and Mary ——— Maltby of Orston. See under date 1639 and observe the names of the children.) In 1670 we find Ezekiel Diglyn, parson of Orston, speaking of "William Maltby, the elder, of Orston." This may mean that he was the father of William, b. 1641, or it may only refer to him as of an older generation.

The record of William Maltby's death reads: "1718, at Orston, William Maltby, gent. Sepult. Oct. ye 4th." We find his Will in the P. C. Y. 1718-19, 73-207. We give an abstract below:

Abstract of Will of William Maltby of Orston, Co. Notts., gent.

Dated 29 March, 1718. Daughter Elizabeth Maltby, £200. Sons and daughters, Wm. Maltby, Mary Parnham, George Maltby, Tho. Maltby, John Maltby and Charles Maltby, 21/—. Wife Jane, sole exex. Her death is recorded at Orston: "1724, Mrs. Jane Maltby, Sepult., Nov. 6." Children:

II. 2. William Maltby, (b. abt. 1683?).
II. 3. Mary Maltby, m. ——— Parnham.
II. 4. George Maltby, b. 1687-8.
*II. 5. Ann Maltby, b. 1688; d. 25 Aug., 1717; buried at St. Saviour's Hospital, Norwich.
II. 6. Thomas Maltby.
II. 7. John Maltby. (Query: Is he the John Maltby who m. Anne Kirk at Orston in 1710?)
II. 8. Charles Maltby.
II. 9. Elizabeth Maltby, unm. in 1718. See her father's Will.

NOTE.—I find no record of their births at Shelton or at Orston.

II. 4 GEORGE Maltby, m. Elizabeth Brough, dau. of Richard and Catharine ——— Brough, bapt., in 1692. 1731, 23 May.—Mrs. Elizabeth Maltby buried at Shelton. Her tombstone at Shelton reads: 1731, 21 May, Mrs. Elizabeth Maltby, w. of Mr. George Maltby, departed this life May 21st, 1731, in the 36th year of her age(hence b. 1694-95). Their children were:

Query: Should this not read 38th year of her age? The Shelton Register has: 1692, 21 April, Elizabeth, dau. of Mr. Richard and Catherine Brough, bapt. Buried at Shelton, 1749, 28 May. George Maltby, ae. 61 yrs. (hence b. 1688).

*III. 10. George Maltby, b. ——; buried 1st March, 1717, at Shelton.
*III. 11. Elizabeth Maltby, b. ——; buried 12 Dec., 1719, at Shelton.
*III. 12. William Maltby, b. ——; buried 15 July, 1720, Shelton Registers.
III. 13. Elizabeth Maltby, b. April 17, 1721, Shelton Registers.
III. 13-A. William Maltby, b. 21 March, 1721-2, Shelton Registers.
III. 14. Thomas Maltby, b. Aug. 20, 1723. Shelton Registers.

III. 15. George Maltby, b. Dec. 27, 1724, Shelton Registers.
III. 16. Samuel Maltby, b. Jan. 17, 1725-6, Shelton Registers.
III. 17. John Maltby, b. Feb. 12 , 1726-7, Shelton Registers.

NOTE.—This "born" means that the family were Dissenters at this period, therefore the children were not baptized.

II. 6. THOMAS Maltby, m. Elizabeth Taylor, Oct. 9, 1716. Evidently Sheriff of Norwich. See under date 1728. Children:

*III. 18. Charles Maltby, b. Oct. 3, 1717; d. Oct. 16, 1717.
*III. 19. Ann Maltby, b. Oct. 7, 1718; d. Nov. 27, 1718.
III. 20. Brough Maltby, b. Oct., 1719.
III. 21. Thomas Maltby, b. March 7, 1722.
*III. 22. Elizabeth Maltby, b. June 6, 1723; d. Nov. 26, 1724.
III. 23. Ann Maltby, b. Oct. 29, 1724.
*III. 24. Affiah Maltby, b. Aug. 3, 1727; d. unm. May 17, 1748; buried St. Mary Woolworth, London.
III. 25. George Maltby, b. Jan. 10, 1730.
III. 26. Jane Maltby, b. Jan. 15, 1731-2.
III. 27. William Maltby, b. Oct. 6, 1733.

II. 8. CHARLES Maltby, m. Martha ———. She d. in 1729, ae. 32. They had a dau. Martha (3) Maltby, who d., ae. 2, in 1725. In the Church of Et. Edmund, the King of Martyrs, Norwich is a stone slab to Martha, w. of Charles Maltby and two of their children. Martha who d. in 1725, the name of a child is not in my copy. A Charles Maltby was Sheriff of Norwich in 1737.

III. 16. SAMUEL Maltby, b. Jan. 17, 1725; m. Elizabeth Langley, Feb. 20, 1749. Issue: three sons and three daughters. "Samuel Maltby, gentleman, was married to Elizabeth Langley of Grantham in Lincolnshire. Lord George Sutton Manner's father gave her away, 20 Feb., 1749; m. at Shelton." Children:

IV. 28. George (4) Langley Maltby, b. and bapt. March 10, 1750-51, at Shelton.
IV. 29. Brough (4) Maltby, b. Dec. 29, 1752; bapt. Dec. 31, 1752, at Shelton.
IV. 30. Ann Maltby, b. and bapt. 5 Jan., 1752-3, at Shelton.
IV. 31. Jane Maltby, b. 25 Dec. and bapt. Dec. 30, 1753.

IV. 32. Samuel Maltby, b. 20 Feb., 1755; bapt. 23 Feb., 1755, at Shelton.

IV. 33. Elizabeth Maltby, b. 17 Jan., bapt. 23 Jan, 1757, at Shelton.

III. 20. BROUGH Maltby, b. Oct. 9, 1719; m. in London, Ann Dyer. Resided in London. He was a wholesale draper of Mansion House St. (Vide Dict. Nat. Biog.) Said to have had seven sons and four daughters. Linendraper. Children:

IV. 34. Thomas (4) Maltby.

IV. 35. Rowland (4) Maltby.

IV. 36. Brough (4) Maltby.

IV. 37. William (4) Maltby, b. 1763; d. 1854.

IV. 38. Elizabeth (4) Maltby, buried Dec. 27, 1744, at St. Mary, Woolworth.

IV. 39. Ann (4) Maltby, a child buried, April 16, 1746, St. Mary, Woolworth burials, London.

IV. 40.

IV. 41.

IV. 42.

IV. 43.

IV. 44.

III. 21. THOMAS (3) Maltby, b. March 7, 1722. Residence, Germans, Buckinghamshire. He m. Elizabeth Rigby, dau. of John Rigby of Oldfield Hall, Co. Chester. Thomas Maltby is given as of Norwich and Germans. (Vide. Burke's Landed Gentry, Supp. Vol. III., p. 85.) Children:

IV. 45. Elizabeth Maltby, b ——.

IV. 46. Harriet Maltby, b. 1763.

III. 25. GEORGE (3) Maltby, b. Jan. 10, 1730; of Norwich; m. 20 April, 1761, Mary Fearman (she b. 1739; d. 1800). He d. in Aug., 1794. See Portrait. Merchant, master weaver and a deacon of the Pres. congregation at the Octagon Chapel, Norwich. (See portrait.) Children:

*IV. 47. George (4) Maltby, b. Jan. 26, 1762; d. May, 1762, ae. 9 months.

IV. 48. Thomas (4) Maltby, b. July 10, 1763.

IV. 49. George (4) Maltby, b. Sept. 26, 1765.

IV. 50. Charles (4) Maltby, b. Jan. 17, 1767.

*IV. 51. William (4) Maltby, b. Feb. 25, 1768; d. May 9, 1770, ae. 2 years.

*IV. 52. Michael (4) Maltby, b. March 19, 1769; d. May 6, 1770, ae. 1 year.

GEORGE MALTBY, ESQUIRE
(Father of Bishop Edward Maltby)

IV. 53. Edward (4) Maltby, b. April 6. 1770, in parish of St. George Tombland, Norwich.
IV. 54. Anna (4) Maria Maltby, b. May 23, 1771.
IV. 55. Henry (4) Maltby, b. June 1, 1772.
*IV. 56. Rachel (4) Maltby, b. June 16, 1773; d. July 2, 1773.
IV. 57. Sophia (4) Maltby, b. Sept. 4, 1774.
*IV. 58. Brough (4) Maltby, b. Oct. 30, 1775; d. April 16, 1776.
*IV. 59. Elizabeth (4) Maltby, b. April 1, 1779; d. July 27, 1779.
IV. 60. Rachel (4) Elizabeth Maltby, b. Aug. 13, 1782.
IV. 61. Maria ? (4) Maltby.

IV. 29. BROUGH (4) Maltby, b. Dec. 29; bapt. Dec. 31, 1752, at Shelton; m. Mary Ince. Children:

V. 62. Mary (5) Ann Maltby, b. Oct. 5; bapt. 10 Oct., 1779. at Shelton.
V. 63. John (5) Ince Maltby, b. and bapt. Dec. 27, 1780, at Shelton.
V. 64. Elizabeth (5) Maltby, b. Nov. 24; bapt. Nov. 26, 1782, at Shelton. (d. 1796?)
V. 65. Charles (5) Langley Maltby, b. and bapt. Jan. 14, 1784, at Shelton.
*V. 66. Brough (5) Maltby, b. and bapt. April 24, 1785, at Shelton; d. Dec. 21, 1788.
V. 67. Harriet (5) Maltby, b. April 10, and bapt. April 14, 1786, at Shelton.
V. 68. Samuel (5) Maltby, b. and bapt. Oct. 28, 1787, at Shelton.
V. 69. Thomas (5) Maltby, b. Jan. 23; bapt. Jan. 25, 1789, at Shelton.

IV. 30 ANN (4) Maltby, b. Jan. 5, 1752, at Shelton; m., June 22, 1790, Richard C. Harrison.

IV. 31. JANE (4) Maltby, b. Dec. 25, 1753, at Shelton; m. March 1, 1790, John S. Godfrey of Newark.

IV. 32. SAMUEL (4) Maltby, b. Feb. 20, 1755, at Shelton; m. (1) ——— ———. The Shelton record reads: "Aug. 9, 1798, Samuel Maltby of Shelton, widower, and Sarah Karr, par. St. Benedict, in town of Huntingdon, wid., license." The name of his first wife is not known to me. Sarah Karr Maltby d. July 3, 1811, ae. 62 (hence b. 1749): buried at Shelton. The records at Shelton read: "July 6, 1811, Sarah, w. of Samuel Maltby, Esq., (d. 3 July) in her 62nd year." And: "Jan. 16, 1812, Samuel Maltby, Esq., d.

13 Jan., ae. 87." (Probably the 87 is really 57 as Samuel was b. in 1755.)

IV. 33. ELIZABETH (4) Maltby, b. Jan. 17, 1757; mar. "2 May 1786 Willm. Ffarmerie of Newark. Lic. at Shelton."

IV. 37. WILLIAM Maltby-Bibliographer. The following account is from the Dictionary of National Biography, Vol. XXXV., p. 442:

IV. 45. ELIZABETH Maltby, b. ——; m. Sir George Pretyman Tomline. For a full account of Sir George see Vol. LVII., p. 14, Nat. Diog. Dict. Sir George Pretyman, b. Oct. 9, 1750; d. Nov. 14, 1827, was the son of George Pretyman of Bury St. Edmunds, and his w., Susan, dau. of John Hubbard. His father was from an old Suffolk family. In 1784, Sir George m. Elizabeth, eldest dau. and co-heiress of Thomas Maltby of Germans, Buckinghamshire. Elizabeth Maltby, w. of Sir George, "was a woman of considerable ability and character, who was informed and consulted by her husband on all important political matters in which he was engaged." There is a portrait of Tomline, by J. Jackson, now in possession of Captain Pretyman of Rigby Hall, Lincolnshire, and an engraving by H. Meyer in the Gentleman's Magazine, 1899. A leter from Captain Pretyman to the compiler states that he has no further Maltby records other than those we already have. He mentions owning an old print which he believes to be a portrait of Miss Maltby, sister of Elizabeth Maltby, who was his great-grandmother. It would be interesting to secure a copy of this old print. The children of Sir George and Elizabeth Maltby were:

V. 70. William (5) Edward Tomline, M. P. for Truro.
V. 71. George (5) Thomas Pretyman, chancellor of Lincoln and prebendary of Winchester.
V. 72. Richard (5) Pretyman, precenter of Lincoln.

NOTE.—Burke's Landed Gentry, supplement, Vol. III., p. 85, is in error when it states that, "Elizabeth Maltby m. Edward Tomline, D.D., Bishop of Lincoln and Winchester," as this was her son.

WILLIAM MALTBY—BIBLIOGRAPHER—1763-1854

"Maltby, William (1763-1854) bibliographer, b. in London, on 17 January, 1763, was the youngest of the ten children of Brough Maltby, a wholesale draper of Mansion House Street. Edward Maltby (q. v.), the Bishop of Durham, was his cousin. He was educated under the Rev. James Pickbourne at Hackney and there formed a life-long acquaintance with Samuel Rogers, a fellow pupil.

He was the youthful companion of Rogers in his assault upon Dr. Johnson's knocker in Bolt Court, and shared his terror stricken flight before the great man's door could be opened. He proceeded to Gouville and Cains College, Cambridge, but being a dissenter did not take a degree.

He practiced law as a solicitor for several years in connection with his elder brother, Rowland Maltby, formerly clerk of the Fishmongers' Company. On 23 June, 1787, he was called to the bar at Gray's Inn. His tastes were, however, literary, and on the death of Professor Porson in 1808, he succeeded him as principal librarian of the London Institution on 1 February, 1809. Here he was the means of making large additions to the library, more especially in the bibliographical department. He had an extraordinary memory, knowledge of books and facility of quotation from classical and English literature. He twice superintended the removal of the books and twice directed their rearrangement, viz., in 1811, from Sir Robert Clayton's house in the Old Jewry to King's Yard, Coleman Street, and in 1818 to 11 Finsbury Circus. He assisted in the compilation of the original catalogue, as well as in the first volume of a new edition. In 1834 he was superannuated from active duty, but was allowed the use of his apartments. He died at the London Institution on 5 January, 1854, and was buried in Norwood cemetery, where a tablet was erected to his memory by his old friend Rogers.

Maltby contributed to "Recollections of the Table Talk of Samuel Rogers," by the Rev. A. Dyee, 1856, an appendix entitled "Porsoniana," pp. 295-334. Times, 11 Jan., 1854, p. 8; Gent. Mag., 1854, pt. I., pp. 209-210; Clayden's Early Life of Samuel Rogers, and Rogers and His Contemporaries.) G. C. B.

IV. 46. HARRIET (4) Maltby, b. 1763. According to Burke's Landed Gentry, Vol. III., p. 85, Harriet Maltby was a sister and co-heiress of Elizabeth (4) and the reference states she "was living at Bath in 1847." This Miss Harriet Maltby is evidently the lady whose portrait Captain Pretyman owns. In "Modern English Biography," Boase, Vol. II., IV., is given the following item: "Maltby, Mrs. Harriet, b. 1763; a friend of W. Wilberforce, W. Pitt, Hannah More and other celebrities; a large contributor to the Bath charities. Died Royal Crescent, Bath, Dec., 1852." It is evident that this item shuld read Miss and not Mrs. Maltby.

IV. 48. THOMAS (4) Maltby, b. July 10, 1763.

NOTE.—The following record I am not sure of. The Thomas (5) Maltby whose record I give, was a *nephew* of Bishop Edward Maltby, and from the names I have placed him as a son of Thomas (4), though it is quite probable that he was a son of one of the other brothers. However we give:

V. 73. William (5) Maltby, older brother.

V. 74. Thomas (5) Colton Maltby, b. Sept. 22, 1814. (Son of above?)

IV. 49. GEORGE (4) Maltby, b. Sept. 26, 1765. He d. Thursday, Sept. 17, 1807, ae. 42, from an accident near Baltimore, Maryland, U. S. A. A stone was erected to his memory. If he left descendants is unknown to the compiler.

IV. 50. CHARLES (4) Maltby, b. Jan. 17, 1767; d. on a passage from Hamburg, Oct. 26, 1800, ae. 33. He was buried at Harwich, Eng. He m. Sarah Sweers (b. Feb. 22, 1771, d. July 31, 1854) at Brooklyn, N. Y. She was a dau. of Cornelius and Hannah Murdoch Sweers. They were married at Philadelphia, Pa., Aug 17, 1796. Children:

*V. 75. A son, ——— (5) Maltby, d. in infancy.

V. 76. Anna (5) Maria Maltby, b. Dec. 13. 1798 at Philadelphia, Pa.

IV. 53. Bishop EDWARD (4) Maltby, b. April 6, 1770 in parish of St. George, Tombland, Norwich; d. July 3, 1859 at 4 Upper Portland Place, London. He m. ——— Harvey. He was a student at Pembroke Hall, Cambridge. In 1831, Bishop of Chichester and of Durham, 1836. For full account and portrait of the Bishop see further in this work. Children:

V. 77. George (5) Maltby.

V. 78. Frederick (5) Maltby.

V. 79. Charles (5) Harvey Maltby.

V. 80. Edward (5) Harvey Maltby. (Eldest son, b. 1798?)

V. 81. Henry (5) Joseph Maltby.

V. 82. Mary (5) Lydia Maltby.

IV. 54. ANNA (4) Maria Maltby, b. May 23, 1771; m. Col. Elliot. Said to have had no descendants.

IV. 55. SOPHIA (4) Maltby, b. Sept. 1774; m. Michael, only son of Thomas Bland of Gurney and Bland, Norwich, Eng. They were married July 15th, 1800. Children:

V. 83. Thomas (5) Bland, b. Dec. 20, 1802; d. Sept. 8, 1825.

*V. 84. Sophia (5) Bland, b. May 25, 1804; d. Dec. 1, 1818.

V. 85. George (5) Bland, b. Dec. 1, 1805; d. 1880. (He m., in 1840, Frances Collinson. No issue.)

V. 86. Edward (5) Bland, b. Dec. 12, 1807; d. March, 1837.

V. 87. Sarah (5) Bland, b. March 16, 1810; d. Sept. 5, 1905.

V. 88. Anna (5) Maria Bland, b. Feb. 17, 1812; d. in 1887; m. Henry Farley. No issue.

V. 89. Frances (5) Lawrence Bland, b. May 24, 1814; d. Jan. 4, 1869.

V. 90. Priscilla (5) Bland, b. Feb. 2, 1816; d. in 1891.

V. 63. Rev. JOHN (5) Ince Maltby, b. Dec. 27, 1780, at Shelton; d. Sept. 30, 1863. Rector of Shelton, Notts., 24 March, 1814; P. C. Sibthorpe and Cotham Notts., 13 April, 1837. (He had a daughter, Mrs. Egglestone of Southvillia, Central Hill, Upper Norwood, London.)

V. 64. ELIZABETH (5) Maltby, b. Nov. 24, 1782 at Shelton; m. Charles Cook.

V. 65. CHARLES (5) Langley Maltby, b. Jan. 14, 1784, at Shelton, Notts.; m. Mary Watson, April 28, 1825, at Hackney Parish Church. Letter received from above, dated Southwell, Nottingham and Notts., Banking, Co. Lin. 13 April, 1905. Manager of the bank. Children:

VI. 91. Brough (6) Maltby, b. Sept. 29, 1826.

VI. 92. Mary (6) Maltby, b. Oct. 2, 1829; d. Dec. 4, 1890.

VI. 93. Elizabeth (6) Maltby, b. Oct. 7, 1830.

VI. 94. Frances (6) Caroline Maltby, b. April 13, 1833; d. May 5, 1904.

VI. 95. Harriet (6) Maltby, b. Nov. 2, 1835; m. James Chadwick. No issue.

V. 67. HARRIET (5) Maltby, b. April 10, 1786; m. in 1813. George Nichols, Esq., Poor Law Commissioner of London. (Vide. Burke's Landed Gentry, p. 932, Val. II., 1846.)

V. 68. Col. SAMUEL (5) Maltby, b. Oct. 28, 1787, at Shelton. He was a colonel in East India Company. The item which follows probably concerns his son, and is copied from a tablet in Shelton church. The tablet is erected to "Samuel Maltby, Surgeon H. E. I. C. S. and Anne, his wife, only child of Lt. Gen. G. W. A. Lloyd, C. B., both massacred in Indian Mutiny 1857. The tablet was erected by his sorrowing parent.

V. 69. THOMAS (5) Maltby, b. Jan. 25, 1789, at Shelton.

V. 73. WILLIAM (5) Maltby, b. ——. He m. an heiress called the "Pocket Venus," she being hardly five feet high. Their children were:

VI. 96. William (6) Maltby.

VI. 97. George (6) Maltby.

VI. 98. Henry (6) Maltby.

VI. 99. Martin (6) Maltby.

VI. 100. John (6) Percy.

VI. 101. Percy (6) Maltby.

V. 74. THOMAS (5) Colton Maltby, b. Sept. 22, 1814; m. at St. Thomas, Stepney, May 3, 1845, Hannah Dale, b. Sept. 13, 1814, d. June 16, 1877. She was a daughter of Henry and Hannah Ridley Dale. Henry Dale was b. in 1782, and d. in 1852. Thomas (5) Colton Maltby was a nephew of Bishop Edward Maltby of Durham. He was Surveyor of Taxes. Both he and his wife died at Hilburn and are buried at Paddington Cemetery. (Records of this branch of the family were kindly furnished by Hylton B. Dale, Esq.) They had three sons and one daughter.

VI. 102. Patrick Drummond Maltby d. unm. He was engaged to a Miss Jeffs. He seems to have gone through a goodly inheritance and died when about 25 years of age. He was named Drummond after his godfather, Mr. Drummond. Mr. Dale informs me this branch of the family is now extinct.

V. 76. ANNA (5) Maria Maltby, b. Dec. 13, 1798, at Philadelphia, Pa., U. S. A.; m. Jean Baptiste Giles Reynaud St. Felix, Dec. 19, 1818, at Philadelphia, Pa. He was b. Oct. 21, 1790, at Aux Cayes, San Domingo, West Indies, and d. Aug. 3, 1854, at Brooklyn, N. Y. His wife d. April 13, 1869, at Brooklyn, N. Y. Their children were:

*VI. 103. Felixine (6) Maria St. Felix, b. Oct. 20, 1819; d. March 10, 1897, at Brooklyn, N. Y., unm.

VI. 104. Mary (6) Antoinette St. Felix, b. July 13, 1821.

*VI. 105. Charles (6) Adeemar St. Felix, b. Sept. 11, 1822; d. Aug. 8, 1845. unm.

V. 106. John (6) Reynaud St. Felix, b. March 14, 1824; d. in action at Cold Harbor, Virginia, June 6, 1864.

*VI. 107. George (6) Edward St. Felix, b. May 22, 1825; d. Dec. 23, 1860 at San Francisco, Cal., unm.

*VI. 108. Victorine (6) Reynaud St. Felix, b. April 12, 1827; unm.

*VI. 109. Estelle (6) Reynaud St. Felix, b. Feb. 9, 1829; d. Sept. 7, 1883. (She m. George Hanaman, Oct. 14, 1856. No issue.)

VI. 110. Julia (6) Reynaud St. Felix, b. Feb. 7, 1831.

*VI. 111. Louis (6) Henry St. Felix, b. Sept. 5, 1832; d. Feb. 21, 1864, unm.

VI. 112. Josephine (6) Julia St. Felix, b. Nov. 4, 1833, at Brooklyn, N. Y.

*VI. 113. Laura (6) Adele St. Felix, b. Oct. 12, 1836; m. Hon. Franklin Chase. No issue.

*VI. 114. Anna (6) Maria St. Felix, b. Jan. 14, 1839, unm.

V. 77., 78., 79. The compiler has no further records of George (5), Frederick (5) and Charles (5) Maltby.

V. 80. EDWARD (5) Harvey Maltby. The following item is from the Lincoln Inn Register, Vol. II., p. 90: "Edward Harvey Maltby (ae. 22), M. A. Pemb. Coll. Camb., eldest son of Rev. Dr. Maltby of Bugden, Hunts, was admitted a Bar.-at-law at Lincoln Inn on 18 Nov., 1820." Hence we learn he was born in 1798.

V. 81. Rev. HENRY (5) Joseph Maltby. He was twice m.; (1) Julia Katherine Bigge. She d. in 1848; a dau. of Charles William Bigge, Esq., J. P. D. L. of Linden. He was Rector of Egglescliff and d. Nov. 28, 1863, Co. Northumberland. He was Vicar of Egglingham, Northumberland, 2 June, 1887. Canon of Durham. He m. (2) Elizabeth M. Bradford. Children:

VI. 115. Julia (6) Alice Maltby.

VI. 116. Edward (6) Charles Maltby.

Second wife?

VI. 117. Elizabeth (6) Annie Maltby.

VI. 118. Henry (6) Charles Bradford Maltby, "died."

VI. 119. Gerald (6) Rivers Maltby, b. 1851.

VI. 120. Ralph (6) Maltby, "died."

V. 89. FRANCIS (5) Lawrence Bland, b. May 24, 1814; m. Agatha Elizabeth Chapman, July 26, 1842. He d. Jan. 4, 1869. Children:

VI. 121. Francis (6) Maltby Bland, b. June 15, 1845.

VI. 122. Agatha (6) Ellen Bland, b. Dec. 9, 1846.

VI. 123. George (6) Edmund Bland, b. June 8, 1848; d. Dec. 11, 1875.

VI. 124. Louisa (6) Mary Bland, b. Feb. 12, 1850; m., Feb. 5, 1884, George Beck.

VI. 125. Edward (6) Michael Bland, b. Aug. 18, 1851; m. (1) Oct. 7, 1873, Marie Augusta Erbs; m. (2) May 19, 1910, Alice Gertrude Stiff.

VI. 126. Elliott (6) Bland, b. Aug. 7, 1853; m. Agnes Isabel Highton.

VI. 127. Arthur (6) Barclay Bland, b. March 12, 1855; m. Katherine S. F. Boyle.

VI. 128. Madckins (6) Bland, b. March 23, 1857.

VI. 129. Margaret (6) Bland, b. July 21, 1858; m. Dec. 26, 1887, Johnson Clench.

VI. 130. Henry (6) Lawrence Bland, b. April 4, 1860.

VI. 131. Frederick (6) Charles Bland, b. June 16, 1861; m. Agnes Hicks.

VI. 132. Anna (6) Sarah Priscilla Bland, b. Nov. 16, 1863; m. July 15, 1897, Webley Hope Gill.

VI. 133. Frances (6) Georgina Bland, b. May 23, 1867; d. Nov. 11, 1904.

VI. 91. Rev. BROUGH (6) Maltby, b. Sept. 29, 1826, in London; m. Isabella Chadwick, dau. of John Chadwick of Oakwood, Rochdale, Oct. 24, 1850. She d. in 1892. He was Archdeacon of Southwell, Nottingham; Canon of St. Mary's, Cruelspool, Lincoln, and Vicar of Farndon, Notts. His wid. (2nd wife) was living in 1910. He died March 30, 1894; buried beside first wife at Farndon. Children:

VII. 134. Brough (7) Maltby, b. May 6, 1852.
VII. 135. James (7) Chadwick Maltby.
VII. 136. Mary (7) Maltby.
VII. 137. Isabella (7) Maltby.
VII. 138. Charles (7) Langley Maltby.
VII. 139. Edward (7) Secker Maltby.
VII. 140. Margaret (7) Maltby.

VI. 91. On Nov. 1, 1910, a beautiful stained glass window in memory of the late Archdeacon Brough Maltby, sometime vicar of Farndon, was dedicated at Southwell Cathedral. There are already three stained glass windows in memory of other members of the family in the North Chapel of the Choir. One to Mary Maltby, who d. Dec. 4, 1890 (See VI., 92); one to Frances Caroline Maltby who d. May 5, 1904; the third is not stated in the "Newark Advertiser," from which we quote. The inscription under the fourth window reads: "Ad Dei gloriam in memory of Brough Maltby, Archidiaconi de Nottingham, Canonici Lincoln, Vicarri de Farndon. Dui obitapod Farndon iii Kal. April A. D., MDCCCXCIV, annos natus LXVIII. Cujus animee propetietur Deus." The dedication service was conducted by the Rev. Canon C. Gray of West Retford. He attended the grammar school at Southwell; was of St. John's Coll., Cambridge. Took holy orders in 1580; his first Nott. cur. was in 1851, at Whatton: then came the Vicarage of Farndon, in 1864. Bishop Wordsworth singled him out for a Canonry at Lincoln in 1871, and in 1878, made him Archdeacon.

VI. 98. HENRY (6) Maltby. His son:

VII. 141. Percy (7) Drummond Maltby is an officer in the British Navy.

VI. 104. MARY (6) Antoinette St. Felix, b. July 13, 1821; m. Francis Bleeker Ellison, U. S. N., Sept. 2, 1841. She d. Oct. 23. 1843. Children:

*VII. 142. John (7) St. Felix Ellison, b. July 1, 1842; d. May 16, 1843.

*VII. 143. John (7) St. Felix Ellison, b. Sept. 22, 1843; d. Feb. 22, 1883, unm.

VI. 110. JULIA (6) Reynaud St. Felix, b. Feb. 7, 1831; d. about 1892, at Portland, Me. She m. William Isaac Thorn of Derry. N. H., Feb. 7, 1853. He d. at Derry, Sept., 1885. Children:

VII. 144. Julia (7) Josephine Thorn, b. April 17, 1854.

*VII. 145. Harriet (7) Eliza Thorn, b. Nov. 20, 1860; d. Nov. 27, 1863.

VI. 112. JOSEPHINE (6) Julia St. Felix, b. Nov. 4, 1833; m. Frederick Adolph Wittichen, at Brooklyn, N. Y., Dec. 31, 1859. She d. Jan. 15, 1899, at Brooklyn. Children:

VII. 146. Anna (7) Charlotte Wittichen, b. Oct. 26, 1860, at Brooklyn, N. Y.

*VII. 147. Charles (7) Adolph Wittichen, b. Oct. 8, 1863; d. May 23, 1867, at Brooklyn, N. Y.

VII. 148. Josephine (7) St. Felix Wittichen, b. May 27, 1868, at Brooklyn, N. Y.

VI. 117. ELIZABETH (6) Annie Maltby, m. Admiral Sir H. Barry. Children:

VII. 149. Ruth (7) Barry.

VII. 150. Ralph (7) Barry.

VI. 119. Lieut. Gerald Rivers Maltby, R. N., b. in 1851; m. Hersey Eliza Cecilia, dau. of late Admiral Sir George Elliot, K. C. B. The following is taken from "Who's Who," 1914: "Maltby, Gerald Rivers, M. V. O., 1902, son of late Rev. Henry Joseph Maltby, Canon of Durham, b. 1851; . . . Entered navy in 1866; retired 1876; served Ashanti, 1874 (dispatches, promoted, medal and clasp); Assist. Hon. Sec. Gen. Com. R. N. Exhib., 1891; Hon. Sec. R. N. Fund, 1892; Sec. R. N. Scien. Inst., 1893-98; Assist. Sec. Imp. Inst., 1888-92. Address 54 St. George's Square, S. W. London. Clubs: United Service, Naval and Military." Children:

VII. 151. Gerald (7) Edward Maltby.

VII. 152. Eileen (7) Maltby.

VII. 153. Mersey (7) Elizabeth Maltby, bapt. Apr. 6, 1879.

VI. 121. FRANCIS (6) Maltby Bland, b. June 15, 1845; m. July 26, 1872, Edith Rickenda Barclay. Children:

VII. 154. Frances (7) Lawrence Bland, b. Sept. 7, 1873.
VII. 155. Hugh (7) Michael Bland, b. Oct. 8, 1874.
VII. 156. Esther (7) Rosamond Bland, b. May 6, 1876.
VII. 157. Edith (7) Rickenda Bland, b. Feb. 15, 1878.
VII. 158. George (7) Nevile Maltby Bland, b. Dec. 6, 1886.

NOTE.—Records of this family kindly furnished by Miss Esther Rosamond Bland.

VII. 134. BROUGH MALTBY, b. May 6, 1852; m. Alice Howorth, only dau. of Thomas Rawston of Norden, Lancashire, at St. Albans Church, Rochdale. Residence, Rochdale and Beddington, Surrey, Eng. Child:

VIII. 159. Brough (8) Maltby, b. Nov. 29, 1878.

VII. 135. Rev. JAMES (7) Chadwick Maltby, Rector of Apsley Guise Rectory Woburn, Co. Beds. The following is from the Clergy List, 1911: "Maltby, James Chadwick, M. A., Keble Coll., Oxford; d. 1877-p. 1878 (Linc.) cur. of Great Grimsby, Linc., 1877-80; R. D. of Fleete from 1904; rect. from 1880 of Apsley Guise, Woburn, Beds." He m. Isabella Basset of Bedfordshire.

VII. 138. CHARLES Langley Maltby, m. Isalie Bronwell of Nottingham. Resides at Southwell, Notts. He supplied much of the data contained in this family record.

VII. 139. Rev. EDWARD Secker Maltby. From the Clergy List of 1911: "Maltby, Edw. Secker, B. A., Keble Coll., Oxford, d. 1886-p. 1887 (Ripon) cur. of Mirfield, York, 1886-9; Thornhill, York, 1889-91; Farndon, Notts, 1891-4; St. Augustine, Haggerston, N. E., 1894-6; St. Philip, Clerkenwell, 1901-4; St. Bartholomew (in ch. of Mary's missn.) Camberwell, S. E. from 1905. Address: 7 Erlam Road, s. Bermondsey, S. E.

NOTE.—I do not know from whence he derived his name of *Secker*, but if we turn to the Brough pedigree we find that Richard and Jane —— Brough had children:

1. Anne Brough, b. 1633.
2. George Brough, b. 1631. (Father of Jane, who m. William Maltby.)
3. Mary Brough.
4. Abigail Brough, bapt. at Shelton 1638; m. (1) Thomas Secker. They had a son Thomas Secker, Bishop of Bristol, 1735; Bishop of Oxford, 1737; Archbishop of Canterbury, 1758. He was b. at Sibthorpe, near Shelton, 1693, and d. in 1768.

VII. 144. JULIA (7) Josephine Thorn, b. April 17, 1854; m. Sidney Warren Thaxter of Portland, Maine, June 7, 1882. Children:

VIII. 160. Sidney (8) St. Felix Thaxter, b. March 4, 1883.
*VIII. 161. Philip (8) Reynaud Thaxter, b. May 19, 1885; d. May 15, 1886.
VIII. 162. Langdon (8) Thorn Thaxter, b. June, 1889.

VII. 148. JOSEPHINE (7) St. Felix Wittichen, b. May 27, 1868; m. Edwin Mortimer Blake at Brooklyn, N. Y., June 20, 1900. He was Professor of Mechanical Engineering at the University of Arizona, Tucson, Arizona. Mr. Blake was the compiler of a type-written document of some five sheets of this family genealogy, from which I have taken much of the records of this branch of the family. Children:

VIII. 163. Charles (8) Henry Blake, b. June 11, 1901, at Berkeley, California.
VIII. 164. Edwina (8) St. Felix Blake, b. Nov. 12, 1903, at Berkeley, California.

VII. 149. RUTH (7) Barry, m. Henry Oliphant. Child:
VIII. 165. Victoria (8) Oliphant. (See below.)

VII. 151. GERALD (7) Edward Maltby, m. A. Mastin. Child:
VIII. 166. Edward (8) Maltby.

VII. 152. EILEEN Maltby. (See below.)

VII. 153. MERSEY Elizabeth Maltby, m. at St. Saviour's, Pimlico, Mr. George Douglas Hugh Pigot, second son of Sir George Pigot, Bart., and Lady Pigot, of Warfield-grove, Bracknell, Berkshire, on Dec. 15, (?) 1910. The following is from the London "Globe" of Dec. 15, 1910: "The bride, who was given away by her father, wore a gown of white satin, draped with old lace, and a Brussels lace veil. There were six bridesmaids—Miss Eileen Maltby, sister of the bride; Miss Norah Pigot, Miss Vera Davison, Miss May Romley, and Miss Sylvia Campbell—wearing dresses of pale pink satin, veiled with grey ninon edged with fur, and large grey hats similarly trimmed. Master Edward Maltby and Miss Victoria Olliphant, nephew and cousin of the bride, acted as train-bearers in pink satin 'Kate Greenaway' costumes. Mr. George A. Clark was best man. A largely attended reception was afterwards held at 54 St. George's Square."

VII. 154. FRANCES (7) Lawrence Bland, b. Sept. 9, 1873; m. Jan. 19, 1899, Mabel Barbara Gooch. Children:

VIII. 160. John (8) Edward Michael Bland, b. Oct. 25, 1899.
VIII. 161. Evelyn (8) Alice Mary Bland, b. Aug. 17, 1901.
VIII. 162. Thomas (8) Maltby Bland, b. June 15, 1906.

VIII. 159. BROUGH (8) Maltby, b. Nov. 29, 1878; m. Isabel Armstrong Birchoff, Feb. 9, 1907. Children:

IX. 163. May (9) Isabel Maltby, b. Dec. 11, 1907.
IX. 164. Alice (9) Brough Maltby, b. June 10, 1908.
IX. 165. Brough (9) Maltby,* b. Oct. 2, 1910.

In concluding these genealogical notes of the Orston Maltbys I wish to acknowledge the help given by Mr. Edward C. Harte, who kindly copied numerous records in order to assist in compiling a fairly complete record of this family.

What few early records we have from Orston are given below:

1530. Richard Maltby held, A. D. 1530,, one ox gang of land in Orston, of Sir Richard Bozon, Kt.
1555. March 10, Robert Maltbye of Orston. Will proved.
1582. John Maltbie m. Elizabeth Greaves.

Hugh Maltby had children:

1584. Anna Maltby.
1587. Abigail Maltby.
1589. Johannes Maltby.
1592. Petrus Maltby.
1595. Willmus Maltby.
1600. Elizabeth Maltby.
1604. Thomas Maltby.

Supplementary Notes Pedigree XI.

In 1670 Ann Maltbie and Thomas Wright were m. at Orston. (Query: Was this a sister of William, who m. Jane Brough in 1682?) It will be noticed that he names a daughter Ann.

Another item under date 1670 speaks of "William Maltby, the elder, of Orston." It is probable that this is the father of William who m. Jane Brough. as he would have been but 29 years of age in 1670, and he could hardly have been the person alluded to as "the elder," though of course it is quite as probable that "the elder" was an uncle, or even his grandfather.

In 1710 John Maltby m. Anne Kirk at Orston. She d 1721. Their children seem to have been:

William Maltby, bapt. April 25, 1714.
Elizabeth Maltby, bapt. Oct. 15, 1716.
Hugh Maltby, bapt. Feb. 14, 1717; d. April 18, 1729.

It would appear that he married (2) Mary ——— and had:

George Maltby, bapt. June 15, 1725.

* This is a long line of Brough Maltbys, his father, grandfather, and great-grandfather all being named Brough Maltby.

Anne Maltby, bapt. April 30, 1728.
Hugh Maltby, bapt. Sept. 13, 1730.
Mary Maltby, bapt. July 18, 1732; buried June 3, 1739.
George Maltby, bapt. Nov. 21, 1734.
William Maltby. bapt. Oct. 14, 1736.

Mr. Charles William Maltby of Orston, Nottingham wrote the compiler, Nov. 7th, 1905, that his father was Thomas Maltby, who d. March 8th, 1881, at the advanced age of 101 years and 101 days. Hence he was born in 1780. He knew nothing further of his ancestry.

Miss Mabel E. Maltby of 66 East Second Street, Corning, N. Y., writes she descends from Christopher Maltby of Lincolnshire; that she had an ancestor who was a Bishop of Durham, and that her father was William Henry Maltby, who emigrated from England in 1890. We hope to learn something further of this branch of the family before long.

Pedigree.

I. Christopher Maltby of Lincolnshire. Descended from him was
II. Henry Vice Maltby.*
III. William Henry Maltby, who emigrated from England in 1890. His daughter is
IV. Mabel E. Maltby of Corning, New York.

EDWARD MALTBY, BISHOP OF DURHAM

Arms: Argent on a bend gules btween a lion rampant in chef purpure and a cross patee in base of the second three garbs or. Crest: On a wreath of the colours between two branches of olive proper a garb or, charger with a cross patee gules. (Vide Grant of Arms, 1829, following this article.)

The following account of the life of Bishop Edward Maltby is taken from the Dictionary of National Biography, Vol. XXXV., p. 440:

Maltby, Edward (1770-1859), bishop of Durham, was b. in the parish of St. George of Tombland, Norwich, on 6 April, 1770, and bapt. on 8 April, by Samuel Bourn (1714-1796) (q.v.). His father,

* Since writing the above we have learned that Henry Vice Maltby was b. Sept. 15, 1811, at Evington, Leicester, and bapt. Oct. 6, 1811, at St. Martin's Church, Leicester. He had a brother John and a sister Eliza, the latter unmarried. Henry V. Maltby mar. about 1835, Sarah Ann Dunkly. He died March 27, 1882, at Aston, Birmingham, and was buried at Boldmere, Warwickshire.

George Maltby (d. Aug., 1794, ae. 64) was a master weaver and deacon of the Pres. congregation at the Octagon chapel. His first cousin, William, is noticed below.

In 1779, Maltby entered the Norwich grammar school, under Samuel Parr (q.v.); he was at the head of the school in 1785, when Parr resigned, and on Parr's advice he was then sent to Winchester, under Joseph Warton. According to Taylor, he was a pupil of William Enfield (q.v.) at Thorpe, near Norwich; if so, it must have been in preparation for Winchester. Bishop Pretyman, afterward Tomline (q.v.) of Lincoln, who had m. a dau. of his uncle, Thomas Maltby, entered him at Pembroke Hall, Cambridge, where he had a distinguished career.

He was Brown's medallist for epigrams in 1790, and for Greek ode in 1790 and 1791. In the latter year he obtained the Craven scholarship after a three weeks' contest. In 1792, he was chancellor's medallist and eighth wrangler. He grad. B. A., 1792; M. A., by royal mandate, 1794; B. D., 1801; D. D., 1806.

Pretyman made him his domestic chaplain and gave him a prebend at Lincoln, in addition to the vicarages of Buckden, Huntingdonshire, Holbeach, Lincolnshire, and Leighton Buzzard, Bedfordshire. A letter (19 July, 1817) from Parr to Canning, recommending him as preacher at Gray's Inn, speaks of his Whig politics and his advocacy of Catholic emancipation, and describes him as "grave, unaffected and very impressive" in the pulpit.

From 1824 to 1833, he was preacher at Lincoln's Inn. In September 1831 he was made Bishop of Chichester and was translated to Durham in 1836. Before his appointment the palatinate jurisdiction of Durham was separated from the episcopal and vested in the crown (21 June, 1836).

Maltby's Greek scholarship is conspicuous in many of his sermons, but is best known by his useful labors in connection with Greek prosody and metre. At Durham he heartily entered into the scheme for the Durham University (charter granted June, 1837), to which he ultimately left his valuable library. He was also a senator of the London University, and a fellow of the Royal and Antiquarian societies.

In politics and in educational matters his views were of the old Whig type. His liberality of action was sometimes misconstrued. In 1838 he was present with Bishop Stanley of Norwich at the meeting of the British Association in Newcastle-on-Thyne. While there, both Maltby and Stanley subscribed to a forthcoming volume of sermons by William Turner (1761-1859, q.v.) a local Unitarian divine. The appearance of the subscription list excited some commotion; public indignation was stirred by a leader in the "Times" and it is said that Maltby was burned in effigy. Both bishops explained the matter as "a personal compliment," Stanley adding that his subscription was private and the use of his name unauthorized. Maltby's explanatory letter, 25 Oct., 1838, expresses his repugnance to Unitarian doctrine, and refers to the existence of neutral ground in topics of practical religion.

Maltby retained the charge of his diocese till his eighty-seventh year, when increasing infirmities made him anxious to be relieved of his duties. In 1856 a special act of parliament (19 and 20 Vict. r. 115) provided for the retirement of the bishops of London (Bloomfield) and Durham, and Maltby immediately resigned on a pension of £4,500 a year. He d. in his ninetieth year, on 3 July, 1859, at 4 Upper Portland Place, London. His portrait painted in 1832, by Sir William Beechy (q.v.) is at Durham. (According to this statement Bishop Maltby was sixty-two years of age when this portrait of him was painted.)

His chief classical publication was "Lexicon Græco-prosodiacum . . . correxit . . . auxit, et Græcis vocibus Latinam versionem subjecit Edw. Maltby," Sc. Cambridge, 1815, 4to; 2nd edit. 1824, 4to. This work was based on Thomas Morell's Thesawrus," Eton, 1762, 4to. An abridgment appeared as "A New and Complete Greek Gradus," Sc. 1830, 8vo; 2nd edit. 1840, 8vo; 3rd edit., edited by John Grabham, 1851, 8vo. Maltby contributed notes on Euripides to Duncan's edition, Glasgow, 1821, 8vo; 9 vols.

Besides single sermons (1806-35), charges (1835-53), and tracts, he published: 1. "Illustrations of the Truth of the Christian Religion," Cambridge, 1802, 8vo; 2nd edit., 1803, 8vo; 3rd edit, 1803, 8vo. 2. "A Letter to the Freeholders of the County of Huntingdon," Ef. 1807, 8vo. 3. "Reflections upon . . . Public Affairs . . . by an Englishman of the Old School," et. 1809, 8vo. 4. "Thoughts on the . . . British and Foreign Bible Society," etc., 1812, 8vo. 5. "Sermons," etc., 1819, 8vo. . . . "Sermons," etc., 1820, 8vo. 7. "Sermons Preached in the Chapel of Lincoln's Inn," etc., 1831, 8vo. 8. 'Two Sermons . . . at Durham before the University," etc., 1843, 8vo. Though not mentioned in Julian's "Hymnology," 1892, he edited two collections, viz., "Psalms and Hymns . . . for the Churches of Buckden and Holbeach," etc., 1815, 12mo. and "Psalms and Hymns," etc., 1824, 16mo. (Biog. Dict. of Living Authors, 1816, pp. 219-441; Norfolk Town, 1829, II., 1311 sq.; Christian Reforms, 1838, pp. 797 sq., 849 sq.; 1859, p. 442; Taylor's

Hist. of Octagon Chapel, 1846, p. 50; Romilly's Graduati Cantabr., 1856; Clerical Directory, 1858, p. 269; Annual Register, 1859, pp. 456 sq.; Haydens Dict. of Dates, 1860, p. 229; Extracts from burial register of St. George in Tombland and from baptismal register of Octagon Chapel, Norwich; Notes and Queries, 13 July, 1861, p. 23.)

A. G.

In the Print Room at the British Museum Book Plates of various members of the Maltby family are to be seen. Whether these are registered in the College of Arms is not known by the writer. There are two Book Plates of Edward Maltby, evidently the Bishop, as follows:

Edward Maltby, D.D., No. 19573.—Arg. 3 wheat sheaves on a bend gules, quartering Beaumont (az. a lion rampant between 8 fleur de lys) and impaling Green (or. on a chief indented gules 3 crescents). Crest: A wheat sheaf. Motto: Nil sine Labore.

The other plate is: Edward Maltby, D.D., F.R.S., F.S.A.—Arg. on a bend gules 3 wheat sheaves; a lion ramp. in sinister chief and a cross in base impaling az. 3 harts tripp; or. for Green. Crest: A wheat sheaf charged with a cross between 2 branches. Motto: Nil sine labore.

An English correspondent who was kind enough to furnish the above data writes: "From these I gather that when Edward Maltby became a bishop he had to register his arms at the Heralds' College and the lion represents some marriage with a Beaumont and the cross to note the bishop—or the cross may have reference to the Arms of Malby of Norfolk—and evidently he had not impaled the correct arms of Green—implying that he married a Miss Green."

According to genealogical data in possession of the secretary Edward Maltby m. a Miss Harvey. He was the son of George and Mary (Fearman) Maltby, grandson of Thomas and Elizabeth (Taylor) Maltby and great-grandson of William and Jane (Brough) Maltby. If we could discover in what way he was related to the Beaumonts and Greens it would be valuable genealogical data.

There is a book in the reference room at the Astor Library which contains a half page of reading matter relative to the above. the substance being that Edward Maltby made application to the Heralds' College, London, in 1829, for grant of arms, and mentions that his family came originally from Yorkshire. He undoubtedly knew the truth of this statement, but very probably could not prove it. Consequently he was allowed to introduce the wheat sheaves of the family from whom he claimed descent, the coat-of-arms being altered to show that the descent was not proved.

Since writing the above sketch of Bishop Maltby, the compiler received the desired extract from the Miscellanea Genealogica et Heraldica. Mr. Edwin M. Blake was so very kind as to visit the Astor Library and transcribe the article, so we could publish it in this book.

Extract from Miscellanea Genealogica et Heroldica, Series II., Vol. I., 1886, p. 81: "Grant of Arms to Rev. Edward Maltby, D.D, 1829. To all and singular to whom these presents shall come, Sir George Mayler, Knight Garter Principal King of Arms, and Ralph Begland, Esquire Clauenceux, King of Arms of the south, east and West parts of England, from the River Trent southwards send greeting: Whereas, the Reverend Edward Maltby, Doctor of Divinity, preacher to the Society of Lincoln's Inn, son of George Maltby, late of the City of Norwich, Esquire, deceased, hath by memorial represented unto the most noble Bernard Edward, Duke of Norfolk, Earl Marshall and Hereditary Marshall of England, that his ancesters were seated for several generations in the county of Nottingham and according to the tradition preserved in his family derived their descent from a branch of the ancient family of Maltby in the county of York, but the memorialists being prevented by the defects of the family evidence from aducing strict proof of such descent and being unwilling to continue the use of the armorial ensigns hitherto borne by him without unquestionable authority. He therefore requested the favor of his Grace's warrant for our granting and assigning such armorial ensigns as may be proper to be borne by him and his descendants and by other descendants of his said late father with due and proper differences according to the Law of Arms. And for as much as the said Earl Marshall did by warrant under his hand and seal bearing date of the fourth day of July instant, authorize and direct Us to grant and assign such armorial ensigns accordingly know ye therefore, that We the said Garter and Clauenceaux in pursuance of his Grace's warrant and by virtue of the Letters Patent of our several offices to each of us respectively granted under the Great Seal of the United Kingdom of Great Britain and Ireland, do by these presents grant and assign unto the said Edward Maltby the Arms following, that is to say, Argent on a bend Gules between a lion rampant in chief purpure and a cross patee in base of the second three garbs or. And for the crest on a wreath of the colours between two branches of olive proper a garb or. charged with a cross patee gules as the same are in the margin hereof more plainly depicted to be borne and used forever hereafter by him, the said Edward Maltby, and his descendants, and by the other descendants of his aforesaid late father, with due and proper differences according to the Laws of Arms.

"In Witness Whereof, we, the said Garter and Clarenceux, Kings of Arms, have to these presents subscribed our names and affixed the seals of our several offices, this ninth day of July in the tenth year in the reign of our Sovereign Lord George, the Fourth, by the Grace of God of the United Kingdom, of Great Britain and Ireland, King, Defender of the Faith, etc., and in the year of our Lord one thousand eight hundred and twenty-nine.

"GEORGE MAYLER,
"Garter Principal King of Arms.

"RALPH BIGLAND,
"Clarenceux King of Arms."

This grant of arms makes it quite plain that the descendants of Bishop Maltby are entitled to bear his arms and also that the descendants of his father, George Maltby, Esq., are entitled to bear similar arms "with a difference," etc.

The coat-of-arms used originally by Bishop Maltby and his father, George Maltby, Esq., was in all probability the sheaves of wheat on a bend gules just as it has come down to this day in the line of Brough Maltby, Esq. Mr. Brough Maltby descends from the oldest son (who had issue) of William and Jane Brough Maltby, and the coat-of-arms has come down in his family for generations.

Bishop Maltby unquestionably knew that they traced back to the Yorkshire family of Maltby and it is our sincere hope that before so very long we may be able to prove the truth of his statement.

MALTBY

Pedigree XII.

Maltby of Orston, Eastwood, and U. S. A.

For a full account of this branch of the family see Miss Ella K. Barnard's very interesting Maulsby Genealogy. Miss Barnard has gone so thoroughly into the history of this family that we here give only the early generations.

I. 1. WILLIAM Moltby of Orston, Notts, m. Mary Roades of Ripley, Derby, 5 m. 9th, 1689. (She, dau. of John and Elizabeth Roades, b. 11 mo. 30, 1662, a second child; her brother, Adam Roades, was b. in 1660.) He was a Quaker. He d. October 14, 1699. Their children were:

II. 2. John Maltby, b. 3 mo. 4, 1690, in Eastwood, Notts.

II. 3. Mary Maltby, b. 7, 1st mo., 1692 in Eastwood, Notts.

II. 4. Elizabeth Maltby, b. 4 d. 3d m., 1694, in Eastwood, Notts.

II. 5. William Maltby, b. 8 mo. 18, 1695, in Eastwood, Notts.

II. 6. Merchant Maltby, b. 7th of 11 mo., 1698-9, at sea on "Bristol Merchant."

II. 7. David Maltby, b. 1 mo. 20, 1699-1700, in Philadelphia, Pa.

The following are a few extracts from the Maulsby Genealogy. It is difficult to figure whether the notes deal with the above William Maltby, Quaker, who was probably b. about 1660, or with William Maltby b. in 1641. The items are:

p. 33. "May 28, 1676, William Maultby, of Orston, for a meeting held at Rowland Dabenney's house."

p. 34. "28 3rd m., 1676, William Maulby of Orston."
"William Maulsby."
"Oct., 1685, Richard Malsby."
"1694. William Maultby of Eastwood, Notts.

p. 35. "Lies body of Elizabeth Maltby, d. Oct. 29, 1754, ae. 29." (hence b. in 1725).
"Body John Maltby, d. May 9, 1762, ae. 80."(hence b. in 1682).
"Elinor Maltby, w. of William Maltby, d. March 5, 1763, ae. 29." (hence b. in 1734).
"Mary Maltby, w. of John Maltby, d. June 24, 1769, ae. 54." (hence b. in 1715).
"John Maltby, d. Aug. 4, 1781, ae. 69." (hence b. in 1712).
"William Maltby, d. Oct. 26, 1783, ae. 68," (hence b. in 1715).
This is probably the William, son of John Maltby, bapt. in 1714.
"George Maltby, d. May 24, 1846, in 96th year." (hence b. 1750).
(Think he was a son of John and Mary Maltby.)

MRS. DOROTHY MALTBY VERRILL

"George Maltby d. March 19, 1868, ae. 48." (hence b. 1820).

*"Clayton, his son, d. Oct. 17, 1880, in his 18th year." (hence b. 1872).

"Charles, son of George and Elizabeth Maltby, b. Sept. 8, 1865; d. Dec. 15, 1900, ae. 35."

p. 36. "Mary Maltby, w. of William Maltby, d. 1706-7-12-6. Buried at Breach."

In 1705 Thomas and Rebecca Maltby, Quakers, had a son, William. b. 1705.

MALTBY

Pedigree XIII.

Maltby of Scarborough, Yorkshire

Arms: Quart. or. and arg. p party per fess indented. Crest: A Wyren. Motto: Fear God in Life.

This coat of arms has been in the family for many generations and was always presumed to be a Maltby coat-of-arms. A correspondent in England writes: "This is not a Maltby coat-of-arms," and goes on to say, "evidently someone fancies he descends from the Maultby or Maltby who married a Clavering. If this surmise is correct and he can prove his descent from Miss Clavering you have struck a good find. The Clavering arms being similar; i.e., quart. or. and gules overall a band (or bendlet) sable."

There is absolutely no question of this branch of the family fancying they descend from any particular person or branch of the family tree, and indeed, were quite unaware of any Clavering intermarriage with a Maltby. They traced their ancestry back to John Maltby, b. Sept. 12, 1712, and the above arms were in the family. Further than this they had not attempted to trace. Through the Maltby Association one generation back has recently been added.

The above arms are extremely interesting as it would in fact seem that this branch of the family descend from Sir John Mautby.

* This name Clayton seems worth noting in connection with the following: "William Maltby left home in New York state, after unmerited punishment. He was finely educated, and often spoke of Rochester, N. Y. At one time he encountered some relatives in a shop in Cincinnati, but he did not make himself known. He had a sister Mary, for when his oldest daughter was born he wished her named for a dear sister. He named his other children Clayton, George, Ellen and Anna. In 1840 Mr. Maltby settled in Madison Ind. He taught school as a young man; was a Pres. and a great abolitionist. He m. in 1850 and d. in 1861." For years we have tried to connect this William Maltby with the New England Maltbys, but it would almost seem he was connected with the above George and Clayton. It may be that Speaker George R. Malby of New York is of this same branch. Any suggestions or data will be most welcome.

Kt., who m. Isabel (or Elizabeth) Clavering, dau. of Robert, and granddaughter of Roger, Lord of Clavering [1326]. See Pedigree IV.-A. The marriage was into a prominent family, and it is quite easy to see how in the course of time this coat-of-arms might have got to be regarded as a Maltby coat.

Pedigree

I. 1. WILLIAM Maltby of Scarborough, Yorkshire; m. before 1712. He had:

II. 2. JOHN Maltby, "bapt. Sept. 5, 1712, John, son to Wm. Maltby." (From a certified record made by Rev. Cecil Cooper, Vicar and Rural Dean of Scarborough). The old family record gives the date as Sept. 12, evidently an error. He m. Mary Dickenson the 7th day of August, 1738, probably at Scarborough as their children were bapt. there. The following copy of the Baptismal Register of the Parish of Scarborough (Baptisms) are transcribed verbatim from the original register by Cecil H. H. Cooper, Vicar and Rural Dean of Scarborough. Children:

III. 3. "1739, Oct. 19, Mary, dau. of John and Mary Maltby, Sept. y 21." (The last date is b. the first bapt.)

III. 4. "1741, Sept. 24, William, son of John and Mary Maltby, b. Sept. y 10th."

III. 5. "1743, Jan. 4. John, son of John Maltby, Dec. y 9th (1742)."

III. 6. "1745, Sept. 21, Dickinson, son of John and Mary Maltby, b. Sept. y 3rd."

III. 7. "1747, June 5. Hugh, son to John and Mary Maltby, May 10th."

III. 8. "1750, Aug. 23, Isabel, dau. of John and Mary Maltby."

III. 3. MARY Maltby, b. Sept. 27, 1739. She evidently m. a John Todd, as the old Bible contains this item: "John Todd, son of John and Mary Todd, was born the 17th November, at 6 o'clock in ye morning, Thursday, 1763." Child:

IV. 9. John Todd.

III. 5. JOHN Maltby, b. Dec. 9, 1742; bapt. Jan. 4, 1743, at Scarborough, Yorks; m. June 3, 1765, at York to Margaret Addison, wid. of George Addison, Esq., of Whitby, Yorks. (She was probably Margaret Dent, as they name a child William Dent.) Children:

IV. 10. Thomas Maltby, b. Oct. 12, 1766.

IV. 11. Margaret Maltby, b. Aug. 30, 1767.

IV. 12. William Dent Maltby, b. Oct. 29, 1769.

John Maltby evidently died between 1769 and 1775, as we find: "Margaret, wid. of John Maltby, m. William Robinson at Scarborough and had children: George Robinson, b. Aug. 17, 1775; Mary Robinson, b. July 2, 1777; Isabella Robinson, b. July 6, 1780.

The following item evidently applies to the above John Maltby and his older brother William, whose line is not carried out: A letter dated July 29th, 1883, from B. Wilkinson of 17 Elmwood Street, Durham Road, Sunderland, to R. L. Maltby, Esq., states: "Our son has a nice old painting of two ships (that I suppose would belong to your great, great-grandfather) sailing from Scarboro, the birthplace of the old, old Maltbys, say 200 years ago; the names of the ships are on the back of the picture. They are bound for the Greenland whale fishery." Mrs. Orr write: "The ships spoken of were owned by a John and William Maltby." (It is worth noting that in the inventory of the estate of Daniel (2) Maltby of New England, there is mention of "One sealskin chair." Daniel Maltby d. in 1731.

This John Maltby moved from Scarborough, Yorkshire to Sunderland, Durham Co., and taught school there for years. Lieut. Col. Richard Leighton Maltby has an account book of his dating from June, 1765, with the names of his pupils and the amounts of their tuition fees.

IV. 10. THOMAS Maltby "was born" the 12th of October, between the hours of 12 and 1 on the Sunday morning in the year of our Lord 1766."

It may be well to state here that these records are practically all taken from Thomas Maltby's Bible. They were copied by Mrs. Percy Browne of Sunderland, England, who is a great, great-granddaughter of the above Thomas Maltby. Mrs. Browne writes: "The spelling is evidently old English and most beautifully written—some pages of the Bible are missing which might have contained other and older dates and names. The old Bibles are very much torn and discolored but I have copied word for word and spelled as it is spelled in the pages I found." Mrs. Orr, to whom Mrs. Browne sent her copy, forwarded it to the compiler.

Mrs. Orr writes: "Thomas Maltby was a master mariner or sea captain who sailed out of Scarboro. This Thomas Maltby was master of a vessel carrying coals up the Baltic during the Napolian wars and was taken as a prisoner of war in the year 1807 while trying to run a blockade. He was in prison seven years and while thus confined, taught navigation to the other prisoners. We have a letter written by him in 1812 to his wife and family who were then living in Sunderland, Durham County, England." Mr. B. Wilkinson also wrote: "We have letters written by your great-grandfather when in a French prison, and I blush for my poor writing when I consider the perfect formation of every letter in the closely written epistles he sent from his prison home."

Thomas Maltby m. Mary ———. (Probably Mary Baker, as they name a son Thomas Baker.) Their children were:

V. 13. Elizabeth Maltby, b. June 22, 1790.
V. 14. Thomas Baker Maltby, b. June 17, 1792.
V. 15. Mary Maltby, b. Dec. 14, 1797.

V. 14. THOMAS Baker Maltby "was born June 17th, 1792, at a quarter before six o'clock of the Sunday morning, in Scarboro, Yorkshire, England." Mrs. Browne writes: "The following is copied from a very old book of exquisite writing which contains texts and beautiful thoughts on religion:: '1817, April 28th, Monday morning, at half past 9 o'clock, Thos. Baker Maltby sailed from Sunderland as an emigrant for Quebec, with his w. Margaret and dau. Mary Ann, ae. one month and two days' (This is crossed out and 'five weeks tomorrow' added). 'Sailed from Sunderland roads, 2nd May at or between 12 and 1 o'clock in the morning.'"

Note by Mrs. Browne: "Probably they waited for a fair wind."

Thomas Baker Maltby m. Margaret Kirton. Their children were:

VI. 16. Mary Ann Maltby, b. in England. (b. 1816?)
VI. 17. Thomas Maltby, b. in 1818, at New Castle, New Brunswick, Canada.
VI. 18. Robert Maltby.
VI. 19. John Maltby.
VI. 20. George Maltby.
VI. 21. Margaret Maltby.

NOTE.—Thomas Baker Maltby with his wife and infant daughter, landed at New Castle, New Brunswick, and resided there until his death.

V. 15. MARY Maltby, b. Dec. 14. 1797, m. Richard Leighton. She d. at Hartlepool, Yorkshire. Child:

VI. 22. Mary Maltby Leighton, b. ——.

VI. 17. THOMAS Maltby was b. at New Castle, New Brunswick in 1818, and d. in 1900. His second w. was Margaret Keymes, and they had the following children:

VI. 23. Charles Maltby, resides at Nelson, B. C.
VI. 23. Hiram Maltby, resides at Lethbridge, Atlanta.

VI. 24. Richard Leighton Maltby, b. in 1856, in New Castle, N. B.

VI. 22. MARY Maltby Leighton, b. ——; m. Bell Wilkinson, whose letters have been quoted in this article. Child:

VII. 25. John Bell Wilkinson, b. ——.

VI. 24. Lieut-Col. RICHARD Leighton Maltby, b. Sept. 8, 1856, in New Castle, N. B.; m. Margaret Weston. Lieut-Col. Richard L. Maltby has been in business at New Castle all his life and is at present police magistrate of that town. He served thirty-four years in the Canadian militia in the field artillery branch and was placed on the artillery reserve ten years ago with the rank of Lieut.-Colonel. (See portrait on another page.) Children:

VII. 26. Mary Ethel Keymes Maltby, b. Nov. 13, 1882.

VII. 27. Hiram Kirton Maltby, b. Jan. 31, 1886.

VII. 25. JOHN Bell Wilkinson m. Louise Lynn. Children:

VIII. 28. Louise Marie Wilkinson, m. Percy Browne, C. E., of Sunderland, England. (The Mrs. Browne who kindly did the copying from the old Bibles.)

VIII. 29. Lynn Bell Wilkinson, m. Barbara Clough.

VII. 26. MARY Ethel Keymes Maltby, b. Nov. 13, 1882; m. Mr. Orr. Mrs. Orr sailed in April, 1915, to join the Army Medical Service Corps, and is now engaged in the splendid work of caring for England's wounded heroes.

NOTE.—The earliest record found of Maltbys at Scarborough is in 1334, when the name of William de Maltby appears in a list of Freemen (p. 18, Cal. Pat. Rolls).

It is with the deepest regret that we have to record the death of Col. Maltby of Newcastle, New Brunswick.

Col. Maltby had been a member of the 12th Newcastle Field Battery for nearly forty years, having risen from the rank of gunner to that of commanding officer. Upon the outbreak of the present European war, Col. Maltby was most anxious to enlist for active service, but being 59 years of age, it was impossible for him to be accepted by the Department of Militia. He was, however, made recruiting officer for the district. It was while in pursuit of his duties, while on a recruiting tour in the northern part of the province that he contracted pneumonia from which he died after a two weeks' illness. The funeral, under the auspices of the Masonic order, of which Col. Maltby was a member, was most impressive, the casket

COL. RICHARD LEIGHTON MALTBY
(See Maltby Pedigree of Scarborough)

being draped with the flag Col. Maltby loved so well, the Union Jack. The body was laid to rest with full military honors.

Col. Maltby leaves a widow, one daughter, Mrs. Orr, now at the front as a Red Cross nurse and one son, Mr. H. M. R. Maltby.

MALTBY

Pedigree XIV.

Maltby of Northallerton, Yorkshire

Arms: Argent on a bend gules three garbs or. Crest: a barley sheaf erect and banded or. Pendant therefrom a bugle horn or. Motto: Sperat infestis. (There is hope in adversity.")

For grant of arms see below.

The above crest is given in Fairbairn's Crests of England and Scotland, under the heading "Maltby—Essex," with the difference that the bugle horn is argent instead of or.

Mr. Ernest Maltby, from whom most of the following notes were obtained, says he is not sure if the bugle horn comes from the Foxton family—one of his forebears having married a Foxton—or from the Pennycuicks whose crest is a demi forester blowing a bugle and whose motto is "Free for a Blast," this being the only homage in the old days the head of the family had to pay when the king came inside the barony near Edinburgh, now the property of Sir George Clark, or his descendants.

Burke's Gen. Armory gives: Pennycook (that Ilk) Ponts' M. S. Argent a bend azure between 3 hunting horns sable stringed gules. Crest: a man winding a horn. Motto: Free for a blast. "Evidently an old Scottish clan," writes an English friend. The Foxtons of Cambridgeshire and London have a similar coat-of-arms, viz.: Arms: A chevron (another engrailed) gules between 3 bugle horns sable; garnished ar. Crest: A rose ar. barbed vert.

Note.—Through the Maltby Association we have been able to trace this branch of the family back a generation further than the records which were furnished by Mr. Maltby.

Pedigree

I. 1. CHRISTOPHER Maltby of Northallerton, Yorkshire, had wife Mary Foxton. The clerk of the church who consulted the register informs me that there were older Maltby records on the registers and he observed the name of Foxton several times while searching for the birth of Thomas (2) Maltby. A small sum of money would probably obtain records of several generations back of those now known. He is called "deceased in July, 1752, when his son Thomas was baptized."

Miss Henrietta Maltby writes of him: "Grandfather must have been an elder or an only son, as the family property was in his hands. (These lands were in the wilds of the North Riding, near Ripon, York.)

NOTE.—Christopher Maltby probably had a younger brother named Thomas, as the clerk informs me that he found the baptism of William, son of Thomas Maltby of the King's First Regiment of Dragoons; he was bapt. March 23, 1777.

How many children Christopher may have had is not known to me. An old diary (a copy of which Mr. Maltby loaned the compiler), written by Henrietta Maltby, b. in 1788; d. 1876, and the memoir written when she was 76 years of age, states that her father, Thomas (2) "was a posthumous child, many brothers and sisters had preceded him, but one alone of them, Christopher, lived within the scope of my memory. He was much older than his brother Thomas and settled in London." She speaks of her grandfather Maltby and states that she "always understood that grandmother was by birth a Foxton, and it is from her we have the bugle horn in our arms." . . . "Tradition speaks of our grandmother as having been very handsome." Further on in the memoir she speaks of one of the last presents Grandmother Maltby gave her son Thomas was a large silver tankard with the Foxton and other arms on it. Alas, she further states it was so large and out of style she gave it away! She further adds: "Grandmother died about 1795."

I am inclined to think that one of the sons of Christopher was Richard, as we find the two following items in the West Indies, viz.:

Nevis, W. I., 1800. "West Indian Deeds on the Close Rolls, London, is one of Butler Claxton by Thomas Maltby, Henrietta, his wife; Nevis, 1800, 7, 13, 14, 15, 16."

The second item reads: "Barbodoes Mercury, W. I. Died, Richard Maltby, Esq., of Bridgetown, Barbadoes within a few days of Sept. 14, 1816. Mrs. Maltby, his w., d. the morning of March 23, 1813."

The first item refers to Thomas, son of Christopher, and it is possible the second item refers to a brother Richard. However, out of "many children" we can record only the two following:

II. 2. Christopher Maltby, b——? Settled in London.

II. 3. Thomas Maltby, bapt. in All Saints' Church, Northallerton, July 26, 1752.

II. 4. Brother d. in 1754, of smallpox.

II. 2. "CHRISTOPHER Maltby," writes his neice, "was much older than his brother Thomas. My impression of him is that he was mild and gentlemanly, with an air of much suffering from illness. His wife and her sister, Lady Bannerman, had in youth been so noted for their beauty as to have been called the Roses of Yorkshire.

II. 3. THOMAS Maltby, bapt. July 26, 1752, at Northallerton, York, m. at St. Swithin's, London, May 17, 1787, Henrietta Crichton, b. in 1770; d. in 1837. He d. in 1830. She was a dau. of Alderman Crichton.

NOTE.—This is very evidently the Thomas Maltby and wife, Henrietta, who sign the Nevis, W. I. deed in 1800.

Henrietta Maltby in her memoirs writes: "I believe father's [Thomas (2)] birthplace was North Allerton, Yorkshire, where it appears his family had been long resident and held the respectable rank of small proprietors, farming their own land.

"That the Maltbys were long ago persons of some consequence in that part of the country may be inferred by an entry in Dugdale's Monastican of a grant of land made to a convent in that locality by a Sir Thomas de Maltby and Dame ———, his wife, in order that prayers should be kept on for the benefit of their sols; and Henry," (her brother?) "when some years ago at the Heralds' office on other business, profited by the opportunity to make inquiries about the Maltbys of North Allerton. The result of his inquiry was his hearing that though not coming under what it is the fashion of our time to call 'the untitled nobility of the country,' the Maltbys were a respectable race of small landed proprietors in Yorkshire—the class, I fancy, whose younger sons formed the ranks of the formidable cross-bowmen of the times of the Plantagenets; and still more redoubtable Ironsides of Cromwell's more recent period. Men who could equip themselves with horses and arms and were ready to follow fame or fortune wherever their proverbial Yorkshire sagacity told them they were most likely to be found.

"Our father's family were decided adherents to the Established Church. . . . Christmas, Easter and all high festivals were dearly prized by him to the end of his days as recalling the Yule log, the family gatherings round it and all his youthful happiness at those joyful seasons, when like the Vicar of Wakefield's neighbors, they cracked nuts, toasted each other in home made wines, and sung jovial carols. . . . Like all families who have been long settled in a neighborhood the Maltby connections from good and bad marriages and other causes must have included persons holding very different positions in its society." Thomas Maltby's widowed mother married the bailiff and Thomas left home for all time when only 14. Mis Henrietta Maltby writes: "In his old age, I have seen him shed tears as when talking of his mother's loving, fondling ways; of her alarm the first time he was seized with a fainting fit, an ill to which, healthy as he was, he was occasionally subject."

In 1807 the family resided at Plaiston Lodge, near Bromley, Kent, a very beautiful place of some hundred acres, requiring a staff of twenty-two servants. They removed to Boulogne and thence to Brussels. There Mr. Maltby d., "and Octavia d. in April, 1830." (Octavia seems to have been her sister.)

NOTE.—This mention of Brussels leads one to the query as to whether the Mr. Maltby who was British Consul at Brussels from 1840 to 1880.

II. 3. Mr. THOMAS Maltby was a very able merchant and private banker of Harley Street, and owned a very fine country seat at Walthanston in Essex. He practically made the house of Walker and also amassed a considerable fortune himself, being credited with having made over £90,000 ($450,000) before he was thirty-two years of age. Later he went into business himself as old Mr. Walker died, and Mr. Maltby not being able to get on with the son, who was then head of the firm. Ill fortune beset him—through no fault of his own, rather a too kindly opinion of the integrity of his associates—and he lost all he had made and died a poor man.

Mr. Maltby had a great friend in Sir Martin Archer Shee, President of the Royal Academy, 1803-5 (I believe), he painted two grand pictures, one of Mr. Maltby, which we reproduce in this book, and one of his wife with their daughter Ellen, then a little girl. Mr. Ernest Maltby says his grandfather was said to have been the seventh son of his father: also that his father was the fifteenth of sixteen children, and a seventh son. I believe Mr. Maltby is buried at Shelton, Notts. He had eight sons and eight daughters.

III. 5. Henrietta Maltby, b. 1788; d. 1876. (Writer of the Memoir when 76 years of age.)

III. 6. Thomas Maltby

III. 7. Mary Anna Maltby
III. 8. Caroline Maltby
III. 9. William Crichton Maltby, b. 1793; d. 1815, unmar.
III. 10. Thomas Maltby, b. 1794; d. 1866.
III. 11. Jane Maltby, m. 1819, W. Robinson and had eight children.
III. 12. Eleanor Maltby
III. 13. Christopher Maltby
III. 14. Frances Maltby
III. 15. Henry Maltby
III. 16. Emily Maltby
III. 17. Henry Maltby
III. 18. Octavia Maltby
III. 19. Edward Maltby, b. 1811.
III. 20. Francis Newcombe Maltby.

III. 10. THOMAS Maltby, b. 1794; mar. Emma Jellicoe. They had children:

IV. 21. Thomas Maltby, m. Eva Seck in New Zealand. They have one son, George Crichton, b. 1886.
IV. 22. Henrietta Maltby of New Zealand.

III. 19. EDWARD Maltby, b. Jan., 1812. He, and others of his brothers, were educated at Winchester College. He entered Winchester in 1826, and went to Haileyburg College (which was in those days the training college for the India Civil Service) in 1829, and in 1832 he went out to India. Mr. Maltby m. Jane Pennycuick at Betchworth, Surrey, on October 12, 1843. She was the eldest dau. of Brigadier-General John Pennycuick, K. H. C. B., who, with his second son, Alick, were the heroes of the disastrous (to the British) battle of Chillianwallah in the Punjaub of India during the Second Sikt War, and who fell gloriously on January 15, 1849, when the famous 24th foot (of which regiment Brig.-Gen. Pennycuick was also Colonel) were literally mowed down in ten minutes, Lord Gough having ordered them at the end of a long march to charge the Sikt guns in position. Mr. Ernest Maltby says: "My grandfather and his hero boy—only seventeen years old—died fighting nobly and their grand deaths drew forth that stirring letter in the 'Times' of London, England, written in his usual violent style by the well known author of the Peninsular War, Sir William Napier, whose brother, Sir Charles Napier, was a great friend of my grandfather's and an old comrade. In appreciation of his services my grandmother was given rooms in Hampton Court Palace which she occupied till she died there on August 24th, 1878, and Lord Mayo erected a cross on their monument on the battlefield 'to record the names of all the brave officers and men who fell on that fatal field.'"

Mr. Edward Maltby had a most serviceable career in the Madras Civil Service, finishing his long term of thirty-two years in 1864, by having occupied for a number of years the highest post in the Service; viz.: Senior Member in Council, and for some months previous to his retirement he was Acting Governor of Madras while Sir William Dennison, the then Governor, was Acting Viceroy of India at Calcutta.

On his retirement Mr. Maltby was offered a knighthood which he declined. He had eleven children, Mr. Ernest Maltby being the youngest and also a seventh son. All but one of the sons were educated at Cheltenham College in Gloucestershire, England. Children:

IV. 23. Edward Maltby
IV. 24. Frank Maltby
IV. 25. Ellen Maltby
IV. 26. Mary Maltby
IV. 27. Alec Maltby
IV. 28. Ernest Maltby of North Vancouver.
IV. 29. Arthur Maltby of Bedford, Eng., who has an interesting miniature of Mrs. Christopher Maltby, nee Foxton.
IV. 30.
IV. 31.
IV. 32.
IV. 33.

(These names are not arranged in order of birth as I have not the dates.)

NOTE.—Two sons are retired Colonels residing in England and two brothers reside in Australia.

III. 20. FRANCIS Newcombe Maltby was given a writership in the East India Co. at the age of 17 and sailed for India in 1830. Mr. Maltby did extremely good work in Madras, where his elder brother had proceeded him and saved the independence of Travancore after the general upset of the mutiny in 1857. His portrait by Eddis hangs in the Rajah of Travancore's palace at Trivandrum. He m. in 1844, Mary Howard Michael, of an ancient Scotch family. In 1862 Mr. Maltby retired and the family lived at Harrow, where the sons were educated. Children were:

IV. 34. Francis Grant Maltby.
IV. 35. Henry Maltby.

IV. 36. Mary Howard Michael Maltby.

IV. 37. Christopher James Maltby.

IV. 28. ERNEST N. Maltby resides at North Vancouver, B. C. He was for some years in the India Civil Service. Mr. and Mrs. Maltby have two children:

V. 38. Ronald Maltby.

V. 39. Marjerie Maltby.

NOTE.—Mr. Ronald Maltby is not yet out of the 'teens, but he is upholding the honor of the name and has enlisted with the 29th Battalion, Vancouver, B. C., and is on his way to the front to serve his country as his ancestors have served before him. That he may return to fight the smaller battles of everyday life will be the sincere hope of all Maltbys.

IV. 34. FRANCIS Grant Maltby's son, Ronner (?) Maltby, is with General Goringe (commander of the British relief army) in Mesopotamia and has been wounded.

IV. 37. CHRISTOPHER James Maltby, b. in 1853, in India, was educated at Harrow, Eng. In early life he was a tea planter in Travancore, having been given a grant of jungle by the Rajah in recognition of his father's services. Later on he entered the Travancore Civil Service, from which he retired with a pension in 1903, and now resides at Harrow. He married in 1884, Jessie Capper. (Mrs. Maltby's brothers, all in the army, are well known. Maj. Gen. Sir Thompson Capper, who led the famous 7th Division at Ypres, was killed last October. Her three other brothers are all serving.) Children are:

V. 40. Mary Dorothy Maltby, b. 1886; m. Sydney R. Wells. They had five sons. Mrs. Wells kindly furnished a copy of the grant of their coat-of-arms, as well as other records of her family for this book.

V. 41. Gladys Maltby, m. Alfred Nayler.

V. 42. Christopher Michael Maltby (called Michael) has been with the fighting forces on the Persian Gulf and is at present on sick leave in India.

V. 43. Capt. Paul Copeland Maltby, 2nd Welch Fusiliers was with the first expeditionary force and went through Mons, the Marne, Aisne, etc. After ten months of trenches near Armentieres he was wounded and on recovering he joined the flying corps and at present is flying "somewhere in France." He was at one time the youngest Captain in the regulars, being captain at the age of twenty-two years.

V. 44. Audrey Newcombe Maltby.

The following is a copy of the grant of arms to this family which we have called "of North Allerton" but from the wording of this document it is evident that Christopher Maltby originally came from Maltby in Cleveland, and only in his later years resided in North Allerton. This is a very important discovery and will be followed up by this branch of the family.

TO ALL AND SINGULAR

To whom these Presents shall come Sir Isaac Heard, Knight Garter Principal King of Arms and Thomas Lock, Esquire, Clauenceux King of Arms of the South, East and West Parts of England from the River Trent Southwards send greeting:

Whereas, Thomas Maltby of Chatham Square in the City of London and of Bleackheath in the Parish of Lewisham in the County of Kent, Esquire, hath represented unto the Most Noble Charles, Duke of Norfolk, Earl Marshall and Hereditary Marshal of England, that he has always understood and believed that his ancestors came from Maltby in Cleveland in the North Riding of the County of York, but being unable to trace a regular descent from the family of that name whose pedigree was entered at the Heralds Visitation of Yorkshire, made in 1613. He therefore requested the favor of His Grace to issue his warrant for one devising, granting and assigning such armorial ensigns as may be proper to be borne by him and his descendants and by the descendants of his late father, Christopher Maltby, formerly of Maltby aforesaid but last of North Allerton in the County of York, deceased.

And forasmuch as the said Earl Marshal did by warrant under his Hand and Seal bearing date the nineteenth day of September instant, authorize and direct us to devise, grant and assign such armorial ensigns accordingly. Know ye therefore that we, the said Garter and Clauenceux in pursuance of the consent of the said Earl Marshal and by virtue of the Letters Patent of our several offices to each of the respectively granted under the Great Seal of Great Britain have decided and do by these Presents grant and assign to the said Thomas Maltby, Esquire, the Arms following: that is to say, Argent on a bend gules between two cotises engrailed of the second a bugle horn stringed of the field between two garbs or a crescent for differenec. And for the Crest on a wreath of the colours, a garb or banded azure and prendant therefrom a bugle horn sable stringed blue differenced as the Arms, as the same are in the margin hereof more plainly depicted to be borne and used forever hereafter by him, the said Thomas Maltby, Esquire and his descendants and by the descendants of his late father, Christopher Maltby with due and proper differences according to the laws of Arms without the let or interruption of any Person or Persons whatsoever.

In witness whereof, We, the said Garter and Clauenceux Kings of Arms, have to these Presents subscribed our Names and affixed the Seals of our several offices, this twenty-third day of September, in the thirty-ninth year of the Reign of our Sovereign Lord George the Third, by the Grace of God, King of Great Britain, France and Ireland, Defender of the Faith, etc., and in the year of Our Lord, one thousand and seven hundred and ninety-nine.

(Signed) THOMAS LOCH,
Clauenceux King of Arms.

(Signed) ISAAC HEARD,
Garter Principal King of Arms.

NOTE—The original motto was: Opes Parit Industria, but Mrs. Wells writes that her family now use the motto: "Industria Parit Opiam." Mr. Ernest Maltby states the original motto was Copia Parit Industria (Industry bringeth forth riches), but his family now use for their motto: Sperat Infestis (There is hope in adversity).

Supplementary Notes Pedigree XIV.

Recent letters from Mrs. Sydney Wells of 12 Linden Road, Bedford, England, give many more items of interest of this branch of the family.

II. 2. Christopher Maltby settled in London when his brother Thomas was but a boy. He m. Miss Sedgwick. They had children, but no information concerning them is available. One of the daughters married an Italian named Gabrielli (London artist probably) and had a large family who lived in much discomfort owing to scanty means.

II. 3. Thomas (2) was but fourteen years old when he started life in London. He was first of all employed in the house of a Mr. Freeling, lead merchant, after which he formed a connection with the firm of Walker. He resided first at Red Bull Wharf, Thames Street, then at Blackheath, having a winter residence at Chatham Place. In 1807, they moved to Plaiston Lodge and afterwards to Walthanston in 1813. In June, 1823 to 1833, they resided at Upper Harley Street.

MALTBY

Pedigree XV.

Maltby—Hoveringham, Mansfield, Nottinghamshire

Mr. Harte of Wells, Somerset, whose wife is Clara Jane Maltby of this pedigree, and to whom I am indebted for data of this branch of the family, writes me that "in all probability the Maltbys of Mansfield descend from Robert Maltby of Orston." Mr. Harte further states: "I understand that some of the Maltbys were buried at Hoveringham early in 1500 and that about thirty-five years ago (1875) was to be seen in Hoveringham Church, or Churchyard, the name of a William (or John?) Maltby, date early 1600. The church has in recent years been restored."

The earliest Hoveringham record at hand is that of the will of Hugh Maultby proved in 1698-9. He had sons, William, Hugh, Richard, John, James, a wife Mary and a daughter Mary. The name Hugh is one frequently found about this time in the Orston branch of the family.

From St. Peter's Church we have the following record which evidently refers to the above Hugh Maltby: "Hugh Maultby of Hoveringham, Notts, and Mary Gibson of Cosall, Notts, m. (license) 25 Feby., 1660." Very possibly he was the Hugh Maltby b. at Orston in 1636, son of John and Mary Maltby.

We begin this Pedigree with:

I. 1. ——— Maltby. He had a son:

I. 2. WILLIAM Maltby of Hoveringham, m. Anne Mowbray, a kinswoman of Lord Mowbray, at Hoveringham, Nov., 1749. Children:

- III. 3. Thomas (3) Maltby.
- III. 4. James (3) Maltby of Westfield.

Note.—These brothers had a cousin, Thomas Maltby, of Hoveringham.

III. 3. THOMAS Maltby of "Moore Maltby and Middlemore." Banker of Nottingham. Children:

- IV. 5. Thomas Maltby, d. ae. 96; buried at Hoveringham.
- IV. 6. Gilbert Maltby.
- IV. 7. William Maltby, M. D. of Birmingham.
- IV. 8. Arthur Maltby.
- *IV. 9. Sarah Maltby, d. unm.
- IV. 10. Frances Maltby, resided at The Park, Nottingham.

IV. 11. Rev. Frederick Maltby, a poet.
*IV. 12. Clara Maltby, resided at Nottingham; d. unm.
*IV. 13. Harriet Maltby, resided at Nottingham; d. unm.
IV. 13-A. John (second son?)
IV. 13-B. Charles

III. 4. JAMES Maltby, of Westfield, Mansfield, Notts. Banker, b. at Hoveringham (about 1770?); m. Feb. 21, 1797, at St. Mary's, Nottingham, Anne, dau. of Col. Elliot of Gedling Hall, near Nottingham. She was a distant relation. He was buried at Hoveringham. They were m. at St. Mary's Church Nottingham. Children:

IV. 14. William Mowbray Maltby, b. in 1800.
*IV. 15 James Maltby, d. unm.

IV. 5. THOMAS Maltby, eldest son, Squire of Hoveringham, latterly lived at Nottingham (Forest Road); m. a Miss Northcote of London. I think he was twice married. Children:

V. 16. Percy Maltby, Squire of Hoveringham, living in 1915.
V. 17. Louisa Maltby, m. Mr. Hyne.
V. 18. Herbert Maltby, a sailor.
V. 18-A. Fanny Maltby.
V. 18-B. Arthur.

IV. 6. GILBERT Maltby of The Park, Nottingham; wine merchant; later of Sherwood Rise: m. a Miss Northcote. Children:

V. 19. Alfred Maltby, a well known actor.
V. 20. Ernest Maltby, a missionary; d. in India.
V. 21. Allen Maltby.
V. 22. Henry Maltby.
V. 23. Carrie Maltby.
V. 24. Kathleen Maltby.
V. 25. Emily Maltby.

IV. 7. WILLIAM MALTBY, M. D., settled and d. at Birmingham. Child:

V. 26. Mowbray Maltby.

IV. 8. ARTHUR Maltby, youngest son, lived opposite the Race Course, Nottingham, and laterly at Forest Hill, London, where he d. He m. (1) ———, and (2) the wid. of a Mr. Doughty, solicitor of Nottingham. (Is this the Arthur Maltby mentioned in the New York Herald in about the year 1906.) It speaks of him as a London author, who addressed the Metropolitan Psychical Society. "I may tell you," he says, "that I have had an absolutely direct communication from the other world. I am what is called an automatic writer, as William T. Stead would say, although I do not believe in it. I should like to have your opinion. I was writing an American story when my hand suddenly seemed as if paralyzed and automatically wrote 'America will conquer the whole world, and all the world will speak its language,' and then followed the signature, 'George Washington.' Again, writing an article on Haldane's territorial scheme, my hand was affected in the same way as before and I wrote, 'England's salvation lies in conscription.' Then followed details in the way in which our army should be reformed. I had a kettle on the hob at the time, as I intended to make a cup of tea. The kettle boiled over. I stopped writing in order to remove it. On my putting pencil to paper again the language was truly military—you understand—for breaking the current of ideas. On my apologizing to the unknown the details were continued and at the close the message was signed 'Wellington.' I laughed. Again the pencil moved and wrote one word, 'Fool.'"

It will be noted that Mr. Maltby does not believe in automatic writing, yet had experiences which led him to ask an opinion of what had occured of the Metropolitan Psychical Society. The above item may not apply to the Arthur Maltby of Forest Hill, London, but it would seem likely. The children of Arthur Maltby (IV. 8) were:

V. 27. Harold Maltby.

V. 28. Katie Maltby, m. ——— of Bradford.

V. 29. Sophie Maltby, m. and had five children.

V. 30. Florence Maltby, m. a Mr. Doughty and had two sons.

V. 31. Ada Maltby, m. Mr. Hamilton of Grantham; bank manager. Issue: One daughter.

IV. 14. Rev. WILLIAM Mowbray Maltby of Mansfield, b. in 1800; m. Oct. 21, 1822, Mary, dau. of Rev. Canon Parsons, Canon of Lincoln, Rector of Syston and Revesby. He d. circ. 1848, and was buried at Hoveringham. At one time of Pleasley, Notts. He was of Westfield, Mansfield. Children:

V. 32. James William Maltby, b. April 4, 1829.

V. 33. Gilbert Maltby.

V. 34. Anne Maltby.

V. 35. Caroline Maltby.

V. 32. Rev. JAMES William Maltby, Rector of Morton, Co. Derby, b. April 4, 1829; m. Sarah or Eliza Hardwick. He d. April 16, 1910. He had a son:

VI. 36. Henry Vaughan Maltby. From the Clergy List of 1911, we learn the following: "Maltby. Hy.

Vaughan, d. 1902, p. 1903 (Keewatin) missny. dioc. Keewatin, 1902-3; inc. of Keewatin, 1903-8, R. D. of Rainy River from 1900, and inc. of Fort Frances, Ontario, Canada from 1908. A letter dated "The Rectory, May 16, 1911," to the compiler furnished some of the above records. He was the youngest child. There are several other children.

V. 33. GILBERT Maltby, b. 1830; bapt. at Mansfield; m. in 1854, at St. Peter's Drogheda, Jane Isabella, dau. of George and Alicia (nee Corry) Riddock of Triton Lodge, Bettys Town, near Droghedd and Doone, Co. Roscommon and Laird of Dunwoodie in Dumfrieshire. Children:

VI. 37. George Mowbray Maltby.

VI. 38. Clara Jane Maltby, m. at Singapore, Edward Harte of Wells, Somerset, who furnished most of the records of this branch of the family.

NOTE.—A letter dated July 12th, 1906, from Morton Rectory, near Alfreton, Devonshire, from Mr. Gilbert Maltby, who was evidently visiting his brother, who was in ill health, states that they have a cousin in Toronto, a Charles Unwin, Esq., O. L. S. City Surveyor, which proves that Rev. William Mowbray Maltby had a sister who married a Mr. Unwin.

ADDENDA.—As this goes to press we have received an interesting photograph from Mr. Edward C. Harte, showing the Mayor of Mansfield (who is "Alderman Maltby," according to a contemporary English paper) welcoming home Corporal Fuller of Mansfield who has won the Victoria Cross. We feel greatly indebted to Mr. Harte for this photograph and the pleasure it gives us to thus meet another English cousin. Mayor Maltby undoubtedly descends from this Hoveringham, Mansfield branch of the family and we hope to ascertain his line of descent.

MALTBY

PEDIGREE XVI.

Maltby—Selston, Notts.

I. 1. WILLIAM Maltby of Notts.

II. 2. WILLIAM Maltby "had his lands confiscated on account of some political opinions strongly held to."

III. 3. WILLIAM Maltby m. Dorinda Green, about 1850. She was a dau. of Col. Green of the English Army, who was one of the last survivors of the battle of Waterloo.

IV. 4. *ADOLPHUS William Maltby, b. in 1859 in Selston, Notts.

V. 5. WILLIAM Randolph Maltby.

MALTBY

Pedigree XVII.

Maltby—Leeds, Yorkshire.

This family owned o coat-of-arms which was on a fine old seal ring belonging to Mr. William Lassey Maltby's father, and which was lost; unfortunately little interest was taken in such things and the present generation is unable to describe the arms, though Mr. Maltby says he is quite sure it was not the sheaves of wheat.

Pedigree

I. 1. SAMUEL Maltby, of Leeds, Yorkshire, master plumber. He seems to have been quite well off, juding from the fact that a piece of property which should have gone to his son Samuel—by the entail not being cut off—was valued at some £8000 sterling, which of course was but a part of his property.

II. 2. SAMUEL Maltby was b. at Leeds, Yorks. Mr. W. L. Maltby says: "I may as well admit that I have an idea that father was somewhat of a dare-devil, and it was probably his reason for leaving Yorkshire and moving to Derby, where I was born. Father had two sisters married, but I was too young to know much about them, as we emigrated to Montreal, Canada, in 1855, when I was thirteen years old. . . . On mother's side there is a legend attached to the name, true or not I do not know. At the battle of Naseby, a child was found on the field; picked up by the soldiers, they began betting upon its sex. The losers to have the privilege of naming it. It was a boy. They swore a good round oath it should be a Lassie anyway, and that is why the name Lassey came to be. They are so proud of it (absurd) that they dub all their children with that name —all our family have got the Lassey tacked on to us. . . . Father was always bragging about his cousin, the Bishop, but I was not born that way and did not care a continental for the past."

* A newspaper clipping before me speaking of the Yerkes method in Chicago, says: "True, there had been champions of public rights in that body before, notably John H. Hamline, a splendid figure of a man, rugged and vehement. Adolphus W. Maltby followed him—a 'solid' business man—insisting on public rights." Mr. Maltby resides at Concord, California.

NOTE.—It is probable that Mr. Maltby descends from Samuel Maltby, bapt. Feb. 23, 1755, at Shelton, Notts. See Pedigree of Maltby of Orston who was a son of Samuel, b. in 1725. The name Samuel seems to come down well in this branch of the family. I think the above Samuel (2) had seven children.

III. 3. WILLIAM Lassey Maltby, b. in 1842 in Derby, England. Emigrated to Montreal, Canada, in 1855. Mr. Maltby has one daughter by his first wife. He has been very successful in business. Resides at 309 St. James Street, Montreal. Child:

IV. Daughter.

III. 4. HERBERT Lassey Maltby of the Eas. Dept. C. P. R. R., Montreal.

III. 5. C. Lassey Maltby of Medland, Ont. Has 10 children.

III. 4. Mr. Herbert L. Maltby wrote, May 13, 1909: "The Yorkshire Maltbys are the fountainhead of that name or family and their descendants. If you would take up the pedigree of Bishop Maltby of London, you would likely get enlightenment as to the branch of our family both in United States and India. . . ." (See V. 68, Col. Samuel Maltby, b. 1787; Col. in E. India Co., Orston Maltby Ped.) "My brother W. L. Maltby, who is nine years older than I am holds the coat-of-arms which you show on your booklet."

NOTE.—Mr. W. L. Maltby states: "I had an old seal ring of my father's, I unfortunately lost it, twenty years ago, but it certainly was not the wheat sheaves."

H. L. Maltby writes: "I had pedigrees, etc., but unfortunately I lost them in a fire."

Mr. Maltby has been twice married and has twenty children. His eldest boy, if living, would be 39 years old. His youngest child was b. in Jan. (?) 1908.

NOTE.—One of Mr. Maltby's sons has been living in Vancouver for the last four years. He enlisted, when war broke out, with the 72nd Seaforth Highlanders of Vancouver and when last heard from was at the front in the 16th Battalion, 3rd Brigade. May he return unharmed when this frightful war is over.

There is little doubt but that this branch of the family connect with the pedigree of the Maltbys of Orston.

MALTBY

PEDIGREE XVIII.

Maltby—Leeds, Yorkshire.

I. 1. JOSEPH Maltby was b. about 1800, in Leeds, England. He m. June 9, 1830, Betsey Goldsmith Chase, in the old Sands Street Church, Brooklyn, New York, by Noah Levings. She was b. Oct., 1805, in Danbury, Conn. In 1832, Joseph Maltby went to Baltimore, Maryland and started to visit a brother William in Tennessee. Mrs. Maltby d. Oct. 16, 1876, in Brooklyn, N. Y. They had:

II. 2. HARRIET Elizabeth Maltby, b. May 23, 1832 in New York.

NOTE.—I think she married a Mr. Thomas, and had a son, William A. E. (3) Thomas, who was of Trinity College, Hartford, Conn., about 1896; who inserted a query of the above people in the N. E. H. & G. Reg. It would seem that he might have been nearly related to the foregoing family of Maltby of Leeds.

MALTBY

PEDIGREE XIX.

I. Maltby.

II. Edward Maltby, only son, 1760.

III. Edward Maltby, only son, 1793.

IV. Edward Maltby, J. P. of Margate, Co. Kent, England. Mayor of Margate, 1896-7. He was b. at Southwell, Co. Notts, and was living in 1910.

MALTBY

PEDIGREE XX.

Maltby of Lincolnshire

The following records are taken from a letter dated "Cropredy Vicarage, Leamington, Oxfordshire, England, Oct. 13th, 1911." from the Rev. Maurice Maltby. From the Clergy List of 1911, we learn that, "Rev. Maurice Maltby, Chich., d. 1892; p. 1893. (Chich.) cur. St. Paul, Chichester, 1892-7; St. Peter's, Coventry, 1897-9; cur.-in-ch. of St. Leonard, So. Banbury, Oxford, 1899-1907; chapl. of Banbury union, 1904; s. vic. from 1907, of Cropredy, Leamington." Mr. Maltby states that, "as far back as I can remember any of our relations, there has always been Williams and Johns. My grandfather and my father were Johns, and I have a Brother William and I had an Uncle William and an Aunt Elizabeth and a Sister Elizabeth. I know my ancestors came from Yorkshire, but when I do not know, as it is some generations since. For three or four generations we have lived in Lincolnshire County." Mr. Maltby closed with a most cordial invitation to a "fine old English vicarage."

Pedigree

I. 1. JOHN Maltby. Children:
- II. 2. John Maltby.
- II. 3. William Maltby.
- II. 4. Elizabeth Maltby.

II. 2. JOHN Maltby had:
- III. 5. Maurice Maltby.
- III. 6. William Maltby.
- III. 7. Elizabeth Maltby.

Note.—At the present writing we have not placed this branch of the family.

MALTBY

Pedigree XXI.

Maltby—Long Eaton, Derbyshire

The fragmentary records of this branch of the family were gleaned from Mr. Joseph Maltby, 2118 Park Building, Long Beach, California in 1906. We have been unable to obtain replies to letters sent others of this family in England.

I. 1. WILLIAM Maltby, Long Eaton, Derbyshire, had sons:
- II. 2. Thomas Maltby.
- II. 3. Joseph Maltby.
- II. 4. Jabez Maltby.

II. 2. THOMAS Maltby had sons:
- III. 5. Jabez Maltby, resides, The Cottage, Church Street, Long Eaton.
- II. 6. Fletcher Maltby, resides, Main Street, No. 33, Long Eaton.
- III. 7. Thomas Maltby.

II. 3. JOSEPH Maltby had:

III. Joseph Maltby of Long Beach, California, U. S. A.

III. Thomas Maltby (eldest son) Boscovel, Pa., U. S. A.

III. Samuel Maltby. Somewhere in Dakota, U. S. A.

NOTE.—Mr. Maltby made a copy of an old tombstone which he read: "Elizabeth (and William?) Maltby, Thrumpton-on-the-Trent." He remembered seeing this stone when a child. There may be, and probably is, a connection here with Charles Maltby, b. in 1848, eldest son of Joseph Maltby of Ilkestone, Derbyshire; he m. in 1871, Eliza Long. Residence "Dalby House," Ilkestone R. S. O. Derbyshire.

MALTBY

PEDIGREE XXII.

Maltby of Hickling, Notts.

I. 1. WILLIAM Maltby of Hickling. He had a sister who m. a Mr. E. Woolly of Hickling.

NOTE.—In 1910 the Maltby Association forwarded a certain sum for the birth certificate of Gov. Frederick Maltby Warner, son of the above William Maltby, and adopted by the Warners. The Rector made an error and sent the birth of a Frederick Maltby, son of Joseph and Eliza Ann Maltby, he a weaver; bapt. by W. H. Walker, Rect., July 27, 1851—fourteen years before Governor Warner was born. We wrote to ask for the correct certificate, but never received any reply. It occurred to the compiler that possibly the "Charles Maltby, eldest son of Joseph of Ilkestone, Derbyshire, b. 1848, m. 1871, Eliza Long, might be nearly related to the above Joseph.

II. 1. FREDERICK Maltby, b. in Hickling, Notts., July, 1865. Came to the United States when a baby and was adopted by the Hon. P. Dean Warner of Farmington, Michigan. Governor Frederick Maltby Warner of Michigan is well known to all Americans, and we hope before long to connect his branch of the family with one of the older pedigrees.

PEDIGREE XXIII.

Speaker George R. Malby of New York.

Frequent inquiries are received as to the branch of the family to which George R. Malby, Esq., who was speaker of the House at Albany, New York, in 1894, belongs. On March 7th, 1894, Mr.

Malby wrote to Mr. George Ellsworth Maltby of New Haven, Connecticut, as follows:

"I have no doubt but that if the matter could be traced back that it would be found that we all belong to the same family. You are spelling your name correctly and as our ancestors spelled it. I am spelling it incorrectly. However, it is a result of the way I was taught when I was a boy and I have always continued to spell it so.

"My ancestors emigrated to this country about 60 years ago; (1834?) coming from Yorkshire, England. They settled in Northern New York. My grandparents died when I was a boy and I know little of the family history. Two brothers came to this country at that time named William and John. . . .

"I am doing what I can in my modest way to keep up the reputation of the family for honesty and integrity."

Signed: "GEO. R. MALBY."

MALLABY (MALHERBE ?)

Pedigree XXIV.

I. FRANCIS Mallaby. His father is supposed to have come from England, but his name is not known. Francis had four sons. He was an old man, and died when Theodore was a child.

II. 1. Theodore Mallaby.
II. 2. Francis Mallaby.
II. 3. Oliver Mallaby.
II. 4. Thomas Mallaby.

II. 1. THEODORE Mallaby m. when past middle age, a Miss Bleecker. (Ancestry traced many generations.) They had a dau., Miss Theodora F. Mallaby of New York City, who kindly furnished this record.

II. 4. Rev. THOMAS Mallaby of Stonington, Conn., m. Mary N. Taylor, of Kingston. They were married by J. D. S. Pardoe and C. H. Bixbey, Feb. 2, 1878. (Vide Vital Rec. of Rhode Island, p. 594.)

Note.—I have not a Maulsby Genealogy at hand, but do not think from the names that the above are a branch of that family. Personally I am inclined to think this family connected with a "N. Malherbe," who signs a petition to Lord Cornby, at New York in 1702. The petition was signed by 346 persons from New York and Provinces (from a Hist. of Erie Co., N. Y.,

Vol. IV., p. 1006). This French form of Malherby would certainly be Anglicized into Mallaby.

A letter from Arthur Lee, Paris, May 22, 1779, to Samuel Adams, concerning Benjamin Franklin has the following: "Please to enclose your letters a Monsieur le Marquis de Malsherbe, Minister d'Etat, a Paris." (Ref. N. Y. Hist. Soc. Papers, 1891, p. 465.) This may be the branch of the family whom descendants claim were French Huguenots and settled somewhere near New Rochelle, New York.

In 1626 (p. 425, State and Domestic Papers, 64. Date Sept. 11, 1626) there is a petition of John Malherbe, Master of the "Francis" of St. Maloes. His ship was bound from St. Maloes to Calais and was stayed by a King's ship and brought to Dover. This French branch is doubtless of the same stock as the English, though possibly one would have to trace back prior to the Norman Conquest to prove it.

MAULTBY

Pedigree XXV.

CORK, IRELAND

Information has recently been received of a branch of the family, who, if tradition is not at fault, have probably long been seated in Ireland.

This branch of the Maltbys are said to have gone to Ireland with Oliver Cromwell, perhaps in Cromwell's army, which would have been about the year 1649 or 1650.

This tradition would indicate that the following record concerns this family intimately. In the Calendar of State Papers for Ireland, 1660-1662, p. 657, edited Mahaffey, is this item: "Samuel Maltby served in the Army of Ireland since 1649, in Capt. Richard Franklin's troop, of Lord Deputy Fleetwood's Regiment." (1649-1662?). It will be recalled that Lieutenant-General Fleetwood was put in command of Cromwell's troops in Ireland, where he resided as Lord Deputy until 1655.

It would seem that the Samuel Maltby above was, in all probability, the progenitor of this Irish branch of the family.

There has not been time to communicate with the Irish connections, and obtain records of the family, consequently we can give but three generations at the present writing, namely:

I. 1. ARTHUR WARNER MAULTBY, resided in Cork, Ireland. He was an inspector of merchandise shipped from the City of Cork—an office, or appointment, from the British Crown. This he held until his death, when his grandson, Henry Maultby,

Esq., received the appointment, and is probably still in office. Arthur Warner Maultby had six sons, as follows:

II. 2. Joseph Maultby.
II. 3. William H. Maultby.
II. 4. John Maultby.
II. 5. Peter Maultby.
II. 6. Arthur Warner Maultby.
II. 7. Henry Maultby.

II. 4. JOHN MAULTBY emigrated to the United States States about 1831-2, and settled in Washington County (?), Vermont. Not long after he removed to Landsingburg, Rensselaer County, N. Y. Later he went to Sheboygan County, Michigan. He was a prominent man in that county, being one of the chief organizers, holding the office of County Clerk, also that of Probate Judge, etc.

II. 3. JOHN MAULTBY emigrated to the United States about 1840 (?). He resided at Landsingburg for a while. He died at Waterford, Albany County, N. Y.

II. 5. PETER MAULTBY emigrated with his brother, John, and for a while resided at Landsingburg. About 1842 he removed to Boonville, Mo., and there married. Later he moved to Kickapoo, Kansas. (Information of his descendants requested.)

II. 6. ARTHUR WARNER MALTBY emigrated to the United States about 1834. He resided in Vermont with his brother, William H., for a short while and with him removed to Landsingburg, N. Y. Here he married Miss Mary Ann Scace, an English lady from near Ipswich, Eng. Both have been some years deceased.

III. 8. WILLIAM H. MAULTBY, of Grand Valley, Pennsylvania, is a son of the above. He was born August 1, 1838, at Landsingburg, and about 1840 moved with his parents to Highland on the Hudson.

MALTBY

PEDIGREE XXVI.

Leeds-Yorkshire

The following item has recently come to our notice and is taken from the "Connecticut Quarterly," Vol. II., No. 4, page 398, as follows: "Maltby, John (clothier) m. Aug. 3, 1790, in Parish Church, Leeds, Eng., Mary Farrer of Leeds. Desired her father's name. Was he the son of William Maltby, who m. Sept. 9, 1754, in the same church to Hannah Sykes? John and Mary (Farrer) Maltby had in Farnley, Leeds, Eng.

1. William, bapt. April 15, 1792; buried Nov. 28. 1795.
2. Joseph, b. Aug. 8, 1795; bapt. Aug. 30, 1795.
3. Catherine, bapt. Feb. 23, 1794; buried Dec. 6, 1795.
4. William, b. April 2, 1798; bapt. April 22, 1798.
5. George, b. Feb. 28, 1801; bapt. April 12, 1801 in Bramley, Leeds, Eng.
6. Hannah, b. Oct. 1, 1803; bapt. Nov. 30, 1803. in Bramley, Leeds.

Joseph m. 1830, Betsey Goldsmith Chase. What became of William, George and Hannah? H. E. M.

MALTBY-MALTBIE

It is fitting that we should know something of the origin and derivation of the name we bear. There are several ways of spelling the name in use at the present time, the most common being Maltby and Maltbie, though one also finds Maltbey and Molby.

Many inquirers ask why Maltby is usually given as the correct spelling when our emigrant ancestor in New England spelled his name Maltbie. First of all, our emigrant ancestors spelled the name both ways, and the recorders added a variety of spellings to these.

A common idea in the family seemed to be that the village of Maltby, Yorkshire, took its name from the family of Maltby, who were believed to have come down from Denmark before the Norman Conquest. This is an error, as will be subsequently shown; also it explains how the name comes to be claimed by so many nations.

Miss Martha J. Maltby, while in Christiana, Norway, saw a stone house, known for years as the "Maltby House." It was a private residence and was once owned by a physician by the name of Maltby.

Miss Maltby was told by a Norwegian traveling acquaintance (of Chicago, but who was born in Christiana) that Maltby was a Norwegian name.

Miss Margaret Maltby was told by a Danish professor of the University of Copenhagen, that Maltby was a Danish name.

While in Stockholm, Miss Maltby was told that it was Swedish and, Miss Maltby adds: "We know it is English!"

In the "Maulsby Genealogy" Miss Ella K. Barnard has given a most able and clear analysis of this subject and we can not do better than to quote from her comprehensive and instructive summing-up.

Page 13, "The Maulsby Genealogy": "Maltby is an old Norse or Saxon name. Saxon, mealt; Swedish and Danish, malt. It is perhaps scarcely necessary to say that malt is barley or other grain steeped in water until it germinates, then dried on a kiln, evolving the saccharine principal. It is used in brewing.

" 'By' is an old English word, with the same spelling in Danish and Swedish. It is a place suffix, equivalent to town; see Grimsby, Whitby, Derby. Maltby therefore means the town which produces malt, or where malt is made."

The present form of the word Maltby seems to indicate Danish origin but the word malt probably antedates the coming of the Danes who settled in that part of England containing the township and parish of Maltby and probably influenced its later spelling. Saxon history contains many such records and leases, as the following:

"Lufe in 832 charged the inheritors and assigns of her lands at Mundlingham with the following yearly payments to Canterbury forever; that is to say, Sixty ambers of malt, one hundred and 50 loaves, 50 white loaves, 120 alms-loaves, one ox, one hog and four wethers, two weys of bacon and cheese, one mitta of honey, ten geese and 20 hens."

And: "20 hides of land were leased by Peterborough to Wulfred for two hoes on condition of his getting its freedom and for the following yearly rental: First to the Monastery—2 tons of bright ale: two oxen fit for slaughter; two mittan or measures of Welsh ale; and six hundred loaves. To the Abbot's Private Estate—One horse and thirty shillings of silver, £½, one night's pasture; fifteen mittan of bright and five of Welsh ale, and fifteen sesters of mild ale."

And so the parts of Yorkshire where the malt was made in great quantities finally became known as Maltby and they are still known to us through the names of (Page 14) Maltby, a chapelry, a township and parish.

"Maltby, a chapelry, in the parish of Raithby, union of Louth, Wold division of the hundred of South-Eske, parts of Lindsey, county of Lincoln, contains 1100 acres, 3 miles (S. W. by S.) from Louth.

"Here was formerly a preceptory of Knights Templars, to which Ranulph, one of the Earls of Chester was the first benefactor; it afterwards belonged to the Hospitallers.

"Maltby, a township in the parish of Stainton, union of Stockton, W. Division of the liberty of Laughbaugh, N. Riding of the county of York; 3½ miles (E. by N.) from Yarm. Contains 171 inhabitants."

Mrs. G. M. Watson, of Maltby House, Cleveland, Stockton-on-Tees, was kind enough to write the compiler something about the village of Maltby, and we append extracts from her letter:

"It is only a small village with a few outlying farms of about one hundred and forty inhabitants, in the township of Stainton. It consists of some nice cottages, and three or four larger houses and the house I occupy is the largest. In referring to the history of Cleveland, we find little in ancient records concerning this place except that at an early period it gave names to a resident family,

A STREET IN MALTBY, ENGLAND

John de Maltby in the reign of Edward I. (1272-1307). This family was in possession for several generations, till by failure of male issue part of the estate passed to others. It is now in the hands of different proprietors."

The History of Cleveland by Rev. John Graves, has the following account:

"The Parish of Stainton consists of the several townships of Stainton, Maltby and others.

"Maltby lies about a mile to the west of Stainton. The village is small, consisting of a few farm houses and cottages situated on the summit of a gently elevated ridge.

"Maltby temp. Doomsday consisted of 3 caracutes ad geldum. . . ." According to Kirkby's Inquest we find (1272-1307) "John de Maltby held 6 caracutes of land here of the fee of Walter de Fancouberge where ten made one knight's fee. This family continued in possession," etc., "till by failure of male issue* a part of their estate passed by marriage to the Morleys of Normanby after alverated to the Pennymans of Ormsby. The other morety of their estate in the reign of Car. I. (1625-1648) came to Sir George Wentworth of Woolley, Kt., by marriage with Averall, daughter of Christopher Maltby, Esq., Alderman of York."

Graves Hist. of Cleveland, p. 444, has the following pedigree:

"Nicholas Morley of Normanby, Co. York, 24 Hen. VI., m. Joan, dau. of John Hedlam, Esq., 24 Hen. VI. Their son, Christopher Morley of Normanby in Cleveland, Esq., had Robert Morley of Normanby, who dwelt at Maltby. He m. first, Isabel, dau. of William Maltby of Maltby. He m. second, Elizabeth, dau. of ——— Symonds of Kirklington. Their son, James Morley, was of Maltby in 1584. He m. Phillis Thornaby."

(Transcribed for the secretary by Edward C. Harte, Esq., of Wells, Somerset. To the courtesy and kindeness of Mr. Harte, whose wife is a Maltby, we owe a vast amount of valuable and interesting material concerning the Maltby family. The help Mr. Harte has given the compiler with heraldry, explanation of old English forms and so on, has been of inestimable value.)

To return to Miss Barnard's comprehensive study of our name: "Maltby (St. Bartholomew's), a Parish, West Riding, of county of York, 830 inhabitants. Parish contains 3919 acres. Church, residence of Earl of Scarborough, etc.

"Maltby-le Maish, a parish in the county of Lincoln, 3m. (N. E.) from Alford, contains 220 inhabitants, 1177 acres and church," etc.

NOTE.—A Geographical Dictionary of England and Wales, by William Cobbett, London, published by Wm. Cobbett, 1832, also gives "Maultby, Co. Norfolk." This book is in the Mass. Hist. Soc. Rooms, Boston, Massachusetts. There was also "Enderby Malbys," but this place is now Mavis Enderby."

"To these sections of England comprised in the old Kingdom of Northumbria and Mercia we have traced the Maltby family, and

* (Graves History of Cleveland, pp. 476-81.) "Failure of Male Issue.—This does not mean a total failure. It only means that the owner of the estate died leaving a daughter (or daughters) only who inherited the estates—but these daughters may (and very probably had) have had uncles (brothers of their father) and first cousins of the name of Maltby."

it seems likely that they took their name from the land on which they dwelt, the common practice at that time.

"At first one name was considered entirely sufficient for an individual, but as the population increased the necessity for some added designation became urgent; and the surname was the result. It came into use in different countries at different times.

"In England surnames came into general use about the time of the Norman Conquest, before which time some added sobriquets or epithets, and perhaps a few heridatary surnames were used, but they were first recorded in the public documents at this time, and became essential for the identification of the individual hereafter."

(p. 15). "Our ancestor took the name of the place Maltby.

"Guffy classifies the name Maltby as English or Welsh, and says it is to be found at present in three counties of England: Derbyshire (7), Lincolnshire (8), Nottingham (24). [The numbers indicate there are about that many in 16,000 inhabitants.]

The following explanation given by Miss Barnard of the term freemen will be found very interesting:

(page 16). "The freeman is he who possesses enough land to feed himself and family. He aided in the government, making, applying and executing the laws, and as a burger was one of the representatives to the national parliament.

"If a freeman became the owner of one hide (from 33 to 120 acres) of arrable land (with which he would be entitled to a proportionate amount of meadow and forest for his horses, cattle and hogs) he was elected a noble or earl by his fellow freemen and then became eligible to be elected priest, judge or king.

"Below the freemen in the social scale were the stranger, the freedman and the serf."

We give one or two more facts concerning the name Maltby and the numerous ways in which it is spelled. "Maulsby Genealogy," p. 349:

"There is at least presumptive evidence that the surname Maltby arose independently in each of the three places, as it is found as De Maltebv on the Rotuli Hundredorumb 1273 in both Norfolk and Lincolnshire, and as De Maltby on the Poll Tax List of the West Riding of Yorkshire in 1379."

Descendants will please note the following—for many of us have been skeptical as to the Mawtby's of Norfolk being of the same name as Maltby.

"The Norfolk Malteby became Maultby and then Mautby and as a surname further deteriorated into Mawbie and Mawby.

"The name Maltby indicates a Danish settlement in which the malster plied his ancient trade.

"The prototheme is Old Norse malt, which is cognate in etymology and identical in meaning with the old Saxon malt; the Old High German, Middle High German and German malz; the Middle Low German molt and malt; the Dutch mout; the Danish and Swedish malt; Anglo Saxon mealt; (p. 350) Middle English malte, mault and malt, and the Scotch-English maut.

"The denterotheme By is our most common Scandinavian suffix in place-names, and is an infallible proof that the Dane was once in the land. It appears in Danish and Swedish as By; in Norwegian as Bo; in Old Norse as Bast and Bry, and was loaned into Anglo-Saxon as By or Bye. It is derived from the old Norse Bua, "to dwell," and originally denoted a "dwelling," then a "farmstead" and later "a village or town." Domesday Book tom. II., fol. 134b."

This very comprehensive philological account of the name Maltby, explains conclusively why the name is claimed as Danish, Swedish, Norwegian and English. It should also settle the question as to the correct way of spelling the name.

In compiling the Maltby Genealogy it has been clearly shown that where members of the same family resided in close proximity an endeavor was made for one family to change the spelling of the name. This is not only true of the English families but is practiced in our own times in the States, where in one instance Maltbey is used as a distinctive mark; another uses Malby and a third Molby, although they unquestionably belong to the same Maltby family.

A few extracts from personal letters to the compiler are appended; they come from Englishmen conversant with genealogical matters, who were kind enough to offer suggestions concerning English research work.

Hylton B. Dale, Esq., writes: "In searching indexes for the name (i. e. Maltby) it is as well to look under 'Mau' as well as 'Mal,' as the name was frequently spelled 'Mauteby.' "

"The name Maltby is rare."—J. Harvey Bloom.

"The Mautebys, Mawtbys or Maultbys were an old Norfolk family."—Reginald C. Duddine.

"There was a good family of the name with a pedigree entered in one of the 16th or 17th Visitations of Yorkshire. In the 19th Century there were families of the name in Lincolnshire, Notts and Derbyshire; but in the last named county it certainly is not an ancient name, for there are no Maltby Wills at Lichfield down to about 1630.

I have never met with the name in Warwickshire or Staffordshire." —William F. Carter.

"Maltby is quite a characteristic surname of the Vale of Belvoir district, and is frequent also in the more central parts of Nottingham. One of their principal 'habitats' was Orston, a village east of the Trent, about twelve or fourteen miles from Nottingham. Here lived a family of that name, of yeoman rank, for several centuries —indeed, there is, I think, still a Maltby farming in that parish. . . . The name Maltby also occurs in the 16th and 17th centuries in the parish registers of several parishes in the district between the river Trent and Southwell."—Thomas M. Blagg.

"All the Maltbys in Notts and Derbyshire are connected. They come from one common stock. The Maltby family is one of the oldest in the midlands . . . Hoveringham branch . . . this branch was related to the Brough Maltbys also the Maltbys of Hickling and others of the name at Bawtry (Yorks). . . ."—Edward C. Harte.

MALTBY CHAPEL

The following poem was cut from the New York "Independent" in 1867 or 1868 by Miss Martha J. Maltby. It was one of the "Sexton's Tales and Other Poems" of the first collected edition of the poems of Theodore Tilton, issued by Sheldon & Co., New York. Maltby Chapel was very evidently what is now the restored church of St. Bartholomew at Maltby.

I.

"Maltby Chapel, as you know,
Fell two hundred years ago.
Hardly now is left a stone;
Save upon the graves alone.
If your feet should chance to pass
Weary through the churchyard grass,
Rest them by a marble tomb,
Crumbling over bride and groom,
Who, when they were hardly wed,
Found the grave their bridal-bed.

II.

"Flowering in the wall on high,
Like a garden in the sky,
Stood a window of the fane
Whence, through many a rosy pane,

Lights of purple, blue and red,
Down through nave and aisle were shed.
Central in the fair design
Hung the Sorrowing Man divine.
Near him, gazing, knelt or stood
Mary's weeping sisterhood;
Next with colors interchanged,
Holy emblems 'round were ranged;
First a light and then a dark:—
Here the lion of St. Mark;
There the eagle of St. John;
Cherub heads with pinions on;
Virgin lilies, white as frost;
Palm and olive branches, crossed.
Picture of Paschal Lamb;
Letters of the great I Am.
Last and topmost, Cross and Crown
And a white Dove flying down.
Such a window, in the light,
Was itself a wondrous sight;
But the eyes that on it gazed
Saw devoutly, as it blazed,
Not the purple panes alone;
Not the sun that through them shone,
But, beyond the lucent wall,
Heaven itself outshining all.

III.

"Up through Maltby's dusty road
Cromwell and his pikemen strode—
Six and twenty hundred strong—
Roaring forth a battle-song;
Who, in marching to the fray,
Passed the chapel on their way;
Never dreaming how, inside,
Knelt a bridegroom and his bride,—
She the daughter of a peer;
He a knight and cavalier.
Quoth the leader: 'Rub the stains
Out of yonder painted panes.'
Glancing at a mark to strike,
Then a pikeman raised his pike,
Drew it back half its length,
Sent it whizzing through the air,
Sped it with a pious prayer,
Winged it with a holy curse,
Barbed it with a Scripture verse;
Heard it crash through pane and sash,
'Till above the tinkling crash,
Loud his shouting mates exclaimed:
'Bravo, Ironsides! Well aimed!

So may every church of sin
Have the light of God let in.'

IV.

"Like the spear that pierced the side
Of the Saviour crucified,
So the weapon that was hurled
Smote the Saviour of the world;
Tearing out the sacred tree
Where he hung for you and me;
Curving downward, flying fast
Where the streaming rays were cast;
Flashing from the shaft each hue
Which it caught in quivering through;
Plunging to the bridal pair,
While they yet were bent in prayer;
Then, like Death's own dart,
Pierced the maiden to the heart.
Back she fell against the floor,
Lying crimson in her gore,
'Till her bloodless face grew pale
Like the whiteness of her veil.

V.

"Years may come and years may go,
Ere a mortal man shall know
Such a more than mortal pain
As the knight felt in his brain.
Long he knelt beside the dead,
Long he kissed her face and head,
Long he clasped her pulseless palm,
He in tempest, she in calm:
Stricken by his anguish dumb,
Neither words nor tears would come;
'Till at last with groan and shriek,
Brokenly he thus did speak:
'O, sweet body, turned to clay—
Since thy soul has fled away,
Let this lingering soul of mine
Lift its wings and fly to thine:—
Wed us in Thy Heavens, O Lord!'
Rose he then, and drew his sword,
Braced his hilt against the wood
Of the altar where he stood;
Leaned his breast against its point,
Stiffened every limb and joint,
Clenched his hands about the blade;
Muttered words as if he prayed,—
Then, with one ecstatic breath,
Cast himself upon his death.

VI.

"Hence the tomb was made so wide
Both could slumber side by side,
But, though lovers fall to dust
As their mortal bodies must,
Still, to souls that interblend,
Love itself can never end.

VII.

"Rupert, flying in defeat,
Checked at Maltby his retreat;
Through the chapel, bullet proof,
Camped his men beneath the roof;
Stood defiant for a day,
Fiery as a stag at bay;
Made a dim defense, but vain,—
Then in darkness and in rain,
Fearful of the morrow's fight,
Stole away at dead of night.
When the Roundheads saw with rage
How the birds had quit the cage,
They, in spite, with blow on blow,
Fought the chapel for a foe.
So it came that tower and bell
Roof and spire, together fell,—
Battered down in name of Heaven,
April, sixteen fifty-seven.

MALTBY—YORKSHIRE

It is a bromidic saying that no two people see the same thing in the same way, and as this is obviously true we are publishing three accounts of visits to the hamlet of Maltby, Yorkshire, feeling confident that all Maltbys will find new viewpoints, different observations in each article, which are of individual interest.

The first article is by Miss Martha J. Maltby, of Columbus, Ohio, who visited Maltby in 1895. This account appeared in Maltby Booklet No. 2 and is reprinted here for the benefit of those who were unable to obtain the booklet owing to the entire sale of the issue shortly after publication.

The second account was contained in a personal letter to the compiler from Miss Marion Davenport Maltbie of Syracuse, a cousin of the late Dr. Maltbie Davenport Babcock, and a lineal descendant from Ormud de Dauneport, who was born in 1086. Miss Maltbie visited Maltby in the summer of 1909.

Our third account of Maltby was written from Rotherham, Yorkshire, by Mrs. Neavando A. Eldvado, to her mother, Mrs. James T. Hoblit and at the request of the compiler. Mrs. Hoblit consented to allow its publication.

RESTORED CHURCH OF ST. BARTHOLOMEW AT MALTBY

A DAY AT MALTBY, WEST RIDING, YORKSHIRE

By Miss Martha J. Maltby

When in York, in 1885, a gentleman remarked upon introduction, "There is a parish in Yorkshire by your name." I was at once all attention, but succeeded only in learning that it was an ordinary English hamlet which he had once visited in the West Riding.

In 1895 a chance meeting with an English bishop brought the second bit of information, for he remarked, upon learning my name, "My first living was the parish of Maltby and I remember it with pleasure." But our ways parted before I could learn much more, or more helpful knowledge as to how to find the place, for no guide book I have seen has it mentioned and I knew of no railway guide with its name on it. So when a fortunate chance found me in Durham and with the opportunity of questioning the learned archaeologist, Canon Greenwell, the president of the British Archaeological Society, and he too referred to the parish in connection with my name, then I learned what I had long wished to ascertain; i. e., how could Maltby be found?

He had visited the hamlet on an archaeological excursion and remembered it had an old church tower and he gave the much desired information concerning the way.

A few days later my friend and traveling companion and I broke our journey southward at Doncaster, took a train westward for a few miles, leaving it at Conisboro for a seven mile drive southward from that station for Maltby.

Let me note in passing that Conisboro is known for its well preserved Norman tower of the castle which Sir Walter Scott makes the scene of the tournament in "Ivanhoe," which Rebecca reports to the knight. The short way for our trap and driver gave us the opportunity to look at the tower.

Unfortunately a drizzling rain set in as we started for Maltby which is situated up a valley from Conisboro and the mist shut from sight some of what must have been a charming view in the heart of north English country, could we have seen it in the distance. The road wound along between stone walks and English hedges and fertile farms, growing wheat, barley and turnips and with pasturage for cattle and sheep, lay on both sides of the way. The farmhouses had the appearance of comfortable prosperity and from their scattered positions we judged the farms were large in acreage. Two or three hamlets lay on the way and one had an ancient stone cross to testify of its age.

The village school had just closed for the day as we drove through Maltby village to the church whose spire we had seen in the distance. To our driver's question of "Where he should take us?" we had responded, "To the church, of course."

Our trip had excited sufficient interest in the school children for some of them to follow us and gather about the two American women, who had left the carriage and were admiring the oaken Lychgate, built in the ancient style and forming a beautiful entrance to the churchyard. They were as ready to answer questions as we to ask them. The sexton was mowing the churchyard and we knew the church was open as we could hear the organ and we soon found our time of visit was auspicious for the organist and some of the leading parishioners were in the church and they too were willing to give information to the strangers.

The church itself is only some fifty years of age and is neat and pleasing in appearance, but the tower onto which it is built, is very interesting and well worth seeing. It shows some four stages in building and must be very old. The lowest part is doubtless Saxon, having the heron-bone stone work about three feet from the ground. Bits of what look like Roman bricks are scattered along promiscuously in the stone wall. High up from the foundation are small windows. A large modern window has been placed in the western side of the tower. The walls are very thick and are strong and well built.

The sexton told us that when removing the old church, they found its walls so firm that the workmen used powder to blow them up. The tower's first story is some thirty or forty feet in height. The second one is only some over a third as high, and has small, narrow windows on three sides. The third is different and its double windows look like Norman work. This story ends with a paneled battlement. A fourteenth century looking stone spire has been built above this. I can give no authority for my opinion that this tower was some centuries in building but judge this is true from illustrations in books on English architecture.

I have often wished I might have seen Canon Greenwell again after the visit to Maltby for I am sure he would have refreshed his memory of his visit there and given me valuable information.

The sexton opened the old chest in the vestry room to allow us to see the old records. The very oldest were written on parchment and were mildewed with age. I thought I could decipher one date as 1609 but I am not sure.

We could not learn that anyone of the name of Maltby was resting in the churchyard, or lived in the parish, within the sexton's memory, nor had he ever heard of the name in the records. On the last subject he would hardly be authority. He showed us some very old carved stones, one of which is supposed to have been the cross of the bishop who consecrated the first of the three churches to stand on the site of the present one.

The headstones in the churchyard did not look old and their dates were not such, while the names they bore were ordinary English names.

We were told that in digging for the foundations of a new house in the south of the village, the workmen found graves and it was thought that the ground belonged to an ancient burial place.

The old market cross testifies to the age of the hamlet. It was surrounded by flower beds and occupied a small plot of ground in the heart of the town.

The houses of the village are simple and plain but comfortable, with the cleanly air so common in England. The streets were narrow but clean. The whole town looked like a conservative old English place, as it is, with trees about its boundaries and in the lawns of the larger houses.

Maltby Hall is an old place with some fine trees about it. We did not enter it as the hour was growing late and we had a train to catch in Conisboro for our return and our journey on to Lincoln that night.

Some weeks later, in the Library of the British Museum I found what I copied there and give with this for your information.

It was nearly dark when we were set down at the railway station and the hour was decidedly late when I finished writing in my diary and turned—a tired, happy woman—to retire. I had seen Maltby parish. Whether there is any connection between it and the Maltby name, who can tell us.

The following is copied from "Kelly Directory of West Riding of Yorkshire, England, 1897," in the Library of the British Museum, by Miss Martha J. Maltby:

"Maltby parish and township in the Doncaster Division of Riding in the Rotherham union and county court district and rural deanery, archdeanery of Sheffield and diocese of York.

"The church of St. Bartholomew is a plain building of stone in Gothic style and was rebuilt with the exception of the tower in 1859 on the site of the former church. It consists of a chancel, nave, aisles, south porch and western tower with spire containing three bells.

"There are several memorial windows, lecturn, organ and lychgate of carved oak and a lychstone which were given by Miss Crossley and Miss Mary Crossley in 1880. The lychgate and stone were given in memory of their mother.

"The register dates from 1678 (See footnote III.) and is in good condition. The living is a vicarage, average tithe rent charge £58, net yearly valuse £90, including 30 acres of glebe with residence is the gift of the Earl of Scarborough. The poor estate produces £28 yearly. In the village stands an ancient stone cross.

"Two miles southeast are the ruins of the once magnificent Abbey of Roche or de Rupe, founded in 1147 by Richard de Busti and Richard Fitz-Tugis for monks of Cistercian order and dedicated to the Blessed Virgin Mary.

"A natural phenomenon heightened by art probably induced the monks to settle in this rocky limestone valley. A fracture in the rocks bearing some resemblance to Our Saviour on the cross was held in great reverence during the whole period of the existence of the abbey. Henry Crandall, the 28th and last abbot surrendered the abbey with seventeen monks and a yearly revenue of £271-11-4 to Dugdale. Henry VIII. granted to Wm. Ramesden and Thomas Valasor the ruin of the once extensive and splendid abbey. The Earl of Scarborough has made some excavations in the ruins.

"Sandbeck Park, two and one-half miles southeast of the village, is the seat of the Earl of Scarborough, Lord Lieutenant of the Riding, and Lord of the Manor and principal landowner. The mansion is a spacious edifice erected about the middle of the last century and a finely timbered park of 350 acres, surrounded by extensive woods well stocked with deer. Attached to the Hall is a private chapel where services are conducted by the Earl's private chaplain.

"The soil is limestone, some parts clay and loam. The sub-soil is limestone. Chief crops are wheat, barley and turnips, with some pasture. Area of township 4096 acres. Rentable value, £4-10-2. Population in 1891, was 709 and in the parish 766.

"People of some importance: Earl of Scarborough, Sandbeck Park and Army and Navy and Carleton Clubs, London, S. W. Miss White of Maltby Hall; Miss Mary Elizabeth White, Ladies' Boarding School, Maltby Hall."

NOTE I.—Maltby is situated on the edge of the famous Sherwood forest.

NOTE II.—The station for Maltby for those going north is Rotherham, which is a little northeast of Sheffield. It is a seven mile drive from Rotherham to Maltby.

NOTE III.—From a list of Yorkshire parish registers we quote the following: Records begin Maltby, 1597; Muston, 1542; Doncaster, 1557; Rotherham, 1556 (Published); Tickhill, 1538.

FIVE DAYS AT MALTBY, YORKSHIRE

Syracuse, New York.

October 20th, 1909.

My dear Mrs. Verrill:—

How I wish you might have been with me this summer while I spent five days in the charming little English village which bears our name. They call it in Yorkshire the "Queen of Villages." It deserves the title! So quaint and interesting, preserving all the characteristics of a typical old-time English story-book town.

First I must tell you that when I was in Chester, the people in the hotel on hearing my name at once said, "There is a Maltby in our long-distance 'phone book," and I had them call them for me, just for fun, at Rhye, down on the west coast of England. Such astonished people as they were to know that a Maltbie from America was on her way to Maltby in England. They were evidently plain people; the man, who is a butcher was not there, but his wife, with whom I spoke was as pleasant as could be but knew very little about the family. They were the only people of the name I heard of in England.

From Chester I went to York and from York back to Rotherham. In the book shops there I found beautiful postcards of Maltby and its surroundings. From there, while I waited for the quaint old lumbering bus, which runs on certain days to my dear little town, I took trams, first to huge and dirty Sheffield. It is like Pittsburgh. Then to Masboro, a pretty little suburb of Rotherham. Rotherham itself has an interesting history. All the country thereabouts has, from Chester and York with their old walls and gates and cathedrals and towers to Scrooby, ten miles or so the other side of Maltby where Elder Brewster was born and the first Pilgrim church organized.

I left my friends in York and went to Maltby alone. It was quite an adventure. If you could have seen that old stage (looked like a "prairie schooner") with seats along the sides and old ladies and baskets and boxes and bundles all crowded in together. One had to go to an old inn yard in Rotherham to wait for the stage driver to "poot oot the horses." I heard real Yorkshire dialect there, driving out. There were five old ladies, one small boy, the driver, piles of luggage and myself. It was so funny when we rattled up the queer old-fashioned street, out of the inn yard where hung the old lamp and the arms—everything seemed unreal—and far from the busy world. The old ladies wore silk mantillas (I think that is it) and bonnets like this.

(We regret we can not here reproduce Miss Maltbie's clever marginal illustration of the type of old ladies.)

They all had volumes to say about Maltby, but had never heard of a person of the name. They wanted to know all about America. When we stopped at other little villages along the seven-mile drive to Maltby, out came from this inn or that, a pretty barmaid (just like Dickens) to take your order for a "wee glass ma'am." The old ladies took something as a matter of course, but I went thirsty, though I did have two or three glasses of English ale in Maltby. The small boy told me all about his home and the chickens he was raising and about the queer piece of American money—a cent—he owned. He and I sat on the box seat and "Jawhnny," the driver, told us about the country places as we went along, in such a broad dialect, I had to listen with all my mind as well as my ears to understand. Fancy how entertained I was with it all and especially when "Jawhnny" informed me that the "American chilled ploo (plough) ware na goot—toorned te ert opp taw mooch."

NOTE.—"Turned the earth up too much." We believe that the English do not plough as deep as we do in the States, as the climate is not so severe and it is not necessary.

You see the "chilled plough" is made here in Syracuse by an old friend of my mother's. I told my Yorkshire friend I'd tell Mr. Chase he didn't like the ploughs.

When we reached Maltby the old ladies vied with one another in suggesting what I should do for a boarding place. Wanted me to stay with them, but I went to the "White Swan Inn." It has been there five hundred years. Mr. and Mrs. Bishop, the landlord and his wife, were so nice and did everything to make my stay pleasant and interesting. Mr. Bishop is an ex-English soldier, invalided home from the Boer War, but pretty well now.

A huge fire in the diningroom fireplace cheered and warmed me, for I was cold that August evening. It was all just a picture. Mrs. Bishop just took care of me. She has Irish blood and consequently the delightful and winning ways that come with it. Though they have a gas plant which lights the larger rooms down stairs, I went to my room with its pretty fireplace by candle light—much nicer. It was a strange sensation and seemed almost like getting home. You see I am doubly Maltbie, because both my father and mother were Maltbies; so if there is anything in the call of the blood I ought to have felt it there—and I did.

If you have ever gone rapidly from place to place for almost three months, seeing daily the most wonderful sights, historical and artistic as well as Nature's own marvelous pictures of peoples and countries, you know how welcome is a halt. I cannot tell you how

MALTBY HALL

glad I was to be far away from trams and trains and busy crowds and just rest and do nothing some of the time there in peaceful little Maltby.

Sunday morning I went to the historic church and listened to a sermon given to a small handful of people. But what I most enjoyed was wandering about the church and churchyard by myself. The sexton, of course, got out all the records in the little tin box Miss Martha Maltby speaks of, and we could make out Latin records back of 1600. However, at that time most of the people were simply spoken of as John de Maltby or Jane de Maltby, no surnames given. It cannot be proved who were Maltby by name or who just so and so of Maltby. After the records began to be in English it was easy to read but in the memory of the oldest inhabitant no Maltby has lived there or been buried there. The church was burned once and many records destroyed, and these old parchment books are not being carefully preserved. In the city of York, duplicates would possibly be found. . . . Miss Maltbie here tells of her trip. she visited ten countries, and found them all "wonderfully interesting, but England was home."

To return to Maltby. Mr. and Mrs. Bishop owned five "blue ribbon" English carts and ponies and they drove me miles (one day twenty-five) over those perfect pavement-like English country roads to Old Cote and Scrooby, where we lunched, then on to Bawtry, two miles from Scrooby. It was Johnathan Maltby of Bawtry whose name I remember seeing in our large Genealogy.

It is an attractive town and so near to Scrooby where Elder Brewster lived and preached that no doubt our ancestors knew those old Scrooby Pilgrimites. They were repairing the old Scrooby Manor, where Elder Brewster was born, and the woman who lives there now gave me a piece of the old oak beam. I treasure it, I assure you.

Back of this very old building (It was originally some five hundred years ago, a Catholic monastery; think of the irony of fate which made it the home of the Pilgrim church) is a little creek which flows into the River Trent, and down that creek and river floated the Pilgrims and thence across the English Channel to Leyden and so to America. We had not time in Bawtry to look up church records for the Maltby name, but the Bishops have promised me they will go and do it some time. Then we went to Canisboro and Tickhill—where are the old castles—and Stone, another village. Another day I walked over to Roche Abbey, over the stone and wooden stiles, along Maltby Crags, through the beautiful Norwoods and back around by the road. A five mile tramp. Some people I met got the "History of Roche Abbey" from the Rotherham safe for me to read. It tells in that, that all that land was held by the Earl of Merton, brother of William the Conqueror; he also held much land in Lincolnshire and there, is a town of Maltby there. Do you suppose there is any connection in these facts?

Maltby is on the direct road from London to York. Dozens of automobiles fly through and scores of cycles, motor and otherwise. Most of them stop at the White Swan for rest or refreshment. Roche Abbey, which Lord Scarborough keeps open on certain days, is an objective point for many parties from Sheffield, Rotherham and Doncaster. Several wealthy people from these cities have summer homes in Maltby. You know, of course, that the stone for the Houses of Parliament in London, was brought from one of the many fine quarries at Maltby. Now they are mining coal on Lord Scarborough's estate and speculators plan to remodel the cunning place. It is a shame, but the "love of money is the root of all evil."

Two railroads are near to Maltby now. One station two miles and another a mile and a half. No passenger trains yet, but there will be in time and our quaint little place will all be changed.

You have no idea how strange it seemed to see my name on the mile posts all over the county of Yorkshire. Just see the length of this letter—and still I could tell you more.

If any of the Maltby family want to see our quaint little Maltby town still unspoiled, let them hurry over to England, for in a year or two many changes are going to take place there and much of the charm will be gone.

I forgot to tell you—I went to the grammar school and the children recited for me. The first hour of the day is given to the study of the catechism. Isn't that English?

Yours most sincerely,

MARION DAVENPORT MALTBIE.

A DRIVE TO MALTBY, YORKSHIRE

Rotherham, 17 June, 1910.

. . . Rotherham is indeed a dull place, but I found that not eight miles distant was the village of Maltby, and a mile further on, Roche Abbey, so I have something besides Durham Palace about which to write. . . .

We arrived in Rotherham Sunday, at 1:30 P. M., and after dinner Neavar suggested a drive, it being a beautiful day. So he rented a horse and trap and we drove to Daltan Village. Here we stopped at a farmhouse and drank some fresh milk and ate some tea cakes. Then, returning to town by a different route, I noticed a signboard which read, "7 miles to Maltby." That settled it! We must go to Maltby; but it was too late to go so far, so we set Thursday for our "excursion" into the past.

Yesterday being the appointed day (and a lovely June day too) we set out for Maltby with the same horse and trap; and what a fine drive, up hill and down, past green meadows with buttercups and through tiny old-fashioned villages. At last we came to Maltby—the prettiest old village of all—the Parish church nestling down in the valley, just like the picture postcard I sent you. I wanted to see the church register and records but the clerk was not in the village, so I left, disappointed in that respect. When you come we shall go together, mother, and hunt it all up. We next went to Maltby Hall, where now resides Lady Violet Smithe. The Smithes, however, were not "in residence," so I saw only the exterior of the Hall—a charming place, in whose gardens I tried to picture Maltbys strolling about.

But, as interested as I was in Maltby, we "tore ourselves away," to drive on a mile further to Roche Abbey. A steep, winding roadway leads down into a valley in which stand the ruins of Roche Abbey. This is the *most beautiful spot in England.* It simply *beggars description.* Such a vale, with rocky, shaded, fern covered banks, and broad green pastures; such myriads of wild flowers, brackets, springs, and waterfalls, shade and sunlight, and in the midst of it all, those grand, gray ruins. Lucky Abbot and monks who discovered such a secluded garden of Eden in which to build their home. Near at hand are a few dear old cottages and in one of these, you and I are going to spend a week, when you come to me, mother.

Enclosed is a bit of ivy I plucked from the abbey walls. Oh, that lovely ravine, with the cattle and sheep grazing peacefully in the meadows and within a few yards, the old abbey mill and stone quarry!

The drive back was a quiet one, as we could think of nothing save the beauties we had seen. . . . I wonder why the Maltbys ever left so lovely a place. . . .

Mrs. Eldorado has resided abroad for some years. In 1909 she returned to London after having made an extended trip to South Africa and through Northern Europe. When the above letter was written she was touring England with her husband. We regret we have not space to print two exceedingly interesting letters written by her about Durham—its cathedral, palace, university and the town.

In "Highways and Byways in Yorkshire," Arthur H. Norways says of Maltby: "Deep below the road a valley runs, closed at length by the shoulder of a hill, on which the red-roofed village of Maltby stands shining pleasantly in the evening sun. It is a pretty spot. The crags are fantastically piled; a few sheep go browsing in and out among them, and from the depths of the valley, coming out of I know not what cool region, there blows a keen and stimulating air, growing sharper as the sun drops lower in the sky. . . ."

An extract from T. Allen's "A New and Complete History of the County of York," London, 1831. Vol. 5, pp. 193-203:

Maltby is a small parish town, situated four miles and a half from Tickhill, and seven and a half from Rotherham. In 1821, the population of this town amounted to six hundred and seventy-nine persons.

Maltby, in common with the great majority of our villages, first presents itself in the pages of Domesday. We there find, that in the time of the Confessor, Elsi had held four carucates in Maltebi and Helgebi, and that now Roger de Busli has five carucates in demesne and thirteen villains, and eighteen borderers, with eighteen ploughs.

The manor of Hooton-Levit consisted of three carucates and six borates, before the conquest; six quaranteens in length and as many broad. Bugo held it. (Query: Should this not be Hugo?) He was superseded by the Norman, who had here in demesne one carucate and there were eight villains and three borderers, who had three carucates. There was a mill, valued at 28d. It is now the property of the Earl of Scarborough.

The constitution of the church of Maltby was peculiar. The patrons presented a rector, but the rector changed his office into a sinecure, being allowed to nominate a perpetual vicar for the performance of parochial duties. A vicarage was ordained under the circumstances on 12 Ral. Feb., 1240, when there was assigned for the support of the vicar, the altarage, tithe of hay and of the mills and four marks per annum, to be paid by the rector.

It is valued in the Liber regis at £4, 13s, 4d; in the parliamentary returns at £30, and is in the patronage of the Earl of Scarborough. The rectory was very valuable. In Pope Nicholas Taxation, it is estimated at £26, 13s, 4d. The presentation of the vicar came, at the dissolution, to the crown.

The church, which is dedicated to St. Bartholomew, comprises a nave, chancel and south aisle, with a tower and spire at the west end. It is a small and mean building, forming a remarkable contrast to the once magnificent church of the Cistertians, who had established themselves in its vicinity.

Note.—The church has been rebuilt and restored since this article was written.

When Dodsworth visited the church these arms were to be seen in the windows:

Clifford. Checkie, or and az. a fess gu. Az. a fess between three hares seiant ar. Or, on a chevron sa. three crescents ar. Dodsworth also transcribed two sepulchral inscriptions which no longer remain.*

Near this village is the pleasant seat of J. Cook, Esq. A school

* Vide South Yorkshire. Vol. I.

was founded here by one of the earls of Castleton, and is repaired by his heirs.

The foundation of the abbey of Sancta Maria de Rupe, or Roche abbey, was the most splendid act of piety of the early lords of Maltby and Hooton. But, though they were accounted the founders, because they gave the site, the monks must have done much for themselves, and had other great benefactors.

No branch of the great Benedictine family took such deep root in England, or flourished as luxuriantly as the Cistertian. It is an undetermined question, which was the first monastery of this order founded in England; but it is no question whether the house of Rievaulx, founded by Walter Espec, was not among the first, or whether it were not the earliest Cistertian foundation north of the Humber. The era of its foundation corresponds with the presidency of Harding, and the reign of Henry I. The same feeling of dissatisfaction with the laxity of the Benedictine rule manifested itself about the same period, in the great abbey of St. Mary, without the walls of York. Some of the monks withdrew from that house for the purpose of submitting themselves to more austere severities, and lived for some time under the shade of a few yew trees which grew on the banks of the Skell. This was in 1132. These were the small beginnings of the house of St. Mary de Fontibus, or Fountains. The first settlers of Kirkstall came from Fountains. Both adopted the Cistertian habit and rule. Many other houses of this popular order were founded in the diocese of York during that century.

The circumstances which were the immediate occasion of the early establishment of a company of Cistertian monks at this place have not been preserved, neither is it known from what house the original society were a colony.

From charters preserved by Dodsworth, it appears that in the reign of Stephen, that is, not long after the settlement of the Cistertians at Rievaulx, a few religious had seated themselves near the spot where afterwards the abbey arose, and like the original settlers at Fountains, who lived for a while under the shade of the yew trees, they appear to have assembled in this place before any buildings were erected to receive them. The expression which occurs in both foundation deeds, "Monachi de Rupe," monks of the rock, can only be interpreted upon the presumption that these sons of an austere devotion had placed themselves in the valley, where they were screened from the bleak winds of the north by a range of limestone rock, and were content to practice their devotions under the open canopy of heaven.*

* Hunter, Vol. I., 266.

A natural phenomena, probably heightened by art, contributed to induce the monks to make choice of this spot. Among the accidental forms which portions of the fractured limestone had assumed, there was discovered something which bore the resemblance of our Saviour upon the cross. This image was held in considerable reverence during the whole period of the existence of this monastery and devotees were accustomed to come in pilgrimage to "Our Saviour of the Roche."

On the arrival of these monks, they were welcomed by the two lords of the soil on which they settled themselves, Richard de Busli,

MALTBY GREEN

the Lord of Maltby, and Richard, the son of Turquis, called also Richard de Wickersley.

To be the founders of a house of religion was a distinction of which even princes were ambitious; and the two lords of Maltby and Hooton doubtless rejoiced in the opportunity which seemed to be afforded them of connecting their names forever with such a foundation.

By the light which the early charters afford, we discern that there was a friendly rivalry between the two families, who should first take the monks into their protection, and give them for their absolute use ground necessary for their holy purposes. It was finally arranged in a manner which must have been highly satisfactory to the monks. The two lords were to convey to them a considerable portion of their territory, in which was included the rock from which they took their designation.

The Lord of Maltby's original donation is thus described: The whole wood as the middle way goes from Eibrichethorpe to Lowthwaite and so as far as the water which divides Maltby and Hooton; also two sarts which were Gamul's, with a great culture adjacent, and common of pasture for a hundred sheep, six score to the hundred, is sochogia de Maltby.

The Lord of Hooton gave the whole land from the borders of the Eibrichethorpe as far as the brow of the hill beyond the rivulet which runs from Fogswell, and so to a heap of stones which lies in the sart of Elsi, and so beyond the road as far as the Wolfpit and so by the head of the culture of Hartshow, to the borders of Slade Hooton. All land and wood within these boundaries he gave, with common of pasture through all his lands, and fifty carectas, perhaps loads of wood in his wood of Wickersley.

The whole of the ground comprehended in these two donations is described in Pope Urban's confirmation A. D. 1186, as locum ipsum in quo abbatia sita est.*

Neither of these deeds has a date. But the year 1147 was assigned as the date of its foundation, by the uniform tradition of the house.

The architecture of the portions of the building which remain may be referred to that era. There is such an exact conformity with the style of Kirkstall, that the church of Roche evidently belongs to the same age, and Mr. Hunter says that it may almost be affirmed that it was built upon a design sketched by the same architect. It is evident, therefore, that the monks, as soon as they received the grant of the soil, set themselves about erecting their church and apartments for their own residence. Their church was built upon an extensive and magnificent scale, and it cannot be supposed that the burden of its erection rested solely on the lords who gave the land, though they would, without doubt, be forward in the pious design. It is indeed one of the great difficulties attending our monastic antiquities, to account for the command of labor, which must have been vested somewhere, directed for the preparation of so many noble houses of religion as arose during the twelfth century, while England was distracted by foreign and intestine war.

* Hunter, Vol. I., 267.

The following is a correct list of the abbots of this house:

Durandus was the first abbot. His presidency extended from June, 1147 to 1159.

Dionysius, 1159 to 1171.

Roger de Tickhell, 1171 to 1179.

Hugh de Wadworth, 1179 to 1184. He appears to have been an active superior as in his time a confirmation from the Pope was obtained.

Osmund had a much longer presidency that any of his predecessors, namely from 1184 to 1223. He had been the cellarer of Fountains abbey. In his time King Richard I. released the house from a debt of 1300 marks to the Jews, perhaps not very honestly.

Reginald, 1223 to 1238.

Richard, 1238 to 1254.

Walter, 1254 to 1268.

Alan, Jordan, Philip.

Thomas confessed canonical obedience to the archbishop, 1286.

Stephen professed canonical obedience 1287.

John, 1300; Robert, 1300; William, 1324.

Adam de Gykelkwyk, 1330 to 1349. In his time the Earl of Warren gave the rectory of Hatfield for the increase of the number of monks.

Simon de Bankewell professed canonical obedience, 1349.

John de Aston, 1358. Robert, 1396.

John Wakefield, 1438. In his time Maud, Countess of Cambridge, made her will at the monastery, and directed that her remains should be interred there.

John Gray, 1465; William Tikel, 1479; Thomas Thurne, 1486; William Burton, 1487; John Morpetti, 1491; John Heslington, 1503.

Henry Cundel, abbot at the time of the dissolution. The date of the surrender is June 23, 1539. Of the seventeen monks who joined him in the surrender, eleven were alive in 1553.

The stock of the abbey at the period of the dissolution consisted in three score oxen, kine and young beasts, five cart horses, two mares, one foal, one stag, sixscore sheep and fourscore quarters of wheat and malt. The plate was very moderate.

The revenues of the house are estimated by Cromwell's visitors at £170 per annum and the debts are said to be £20.

Of the fabric of the abbey only a gateway, placed at the entrance to the precincts on the side towards Maltby, and some beautiful fragments of the transepts of the church remain. The gateway is of later architecture than the church, indeed so late, and standing at such a distance from the monastery, that it might be taken for part of the novum hospitum mentioned in the account of the abbey property and which was doubtless erected by the monks for the convenience of persons resorting to the abbey, and especially of the pilgrims who came in veneration of the image found in the rock. A large mass of stonework at a distance westward from the principal portion which remains of the church, is evidently the base of one side of the great western entrance. This admitted to the nave, flanked by side aisles, the whole of which has disappeared. Advancing eastward, we arrive at the columns which supported the tower that rose at the intersection of the nave, choir and transepts. Much of these remain. The eastern walls of the transepts still exist, and enough of the inner work to show that in each were two small chapels, to which the entrance was from the open part of the transept, and the light admitted from windows looking eastward. In this we perceive a close resemblance in design to the church at Krikstall [sic], as there is also the closest resemblance in some of the minute decorations. The difference is, that at Kirkstall (spelled both ways in author's copy) there are three of these chapels in each transept. We may observe at Roche a remarkable peculiarity respecting the Northern transept. The north wall must have arisen almost in contact with the perpendicular rock, and indeed the whole of the northern side of the church must have been darkened by that rock, which rises as high as the walls of the abbey themselves. Between these side chapels, and extending considerably beyond them, was the principal choir, with lights at the east end and on the north and south. And with this the church appears to have terminated, as there is nothing to indicate that there was here any lady choir or other building beyond.

On the north side of the choir may be discerned some rich tabernacle work a part of which has been painted of a red color.* This has the appearance of having been canopies over seats or possibly over a tomb.

The ponds in which the monks were accustomed to keep their fish, and the mill at which they ground their corn, are still existing.

Close adjoining to the demesnes of Roche Abbey is Sandbeck, which was once a valuable appendage to the monastery and where is now the seat of the noble family to whom the site of the abbey and much other property in this neighborhood belongs.

This place is not mentioned in Domesday. The land was then either lying waste or it is included in the survey of the manor of Maltby. It first occurs in the 6th year of the reign of Henry III.,

* Hunter's South Yorkshire, Vo. I.

1224, when it is mentioned as one of the places in which lay the six fees and a half which Alice, Countess of Eu, released to Robert and Idonea de Vipont.

Arthur H. Norway in "Highways and Byways in Yorkshire," writing of Roche Abbey says: "This path descends in to the valley of a little river by whose bank, half buried in the greenery, stands the stately gatehouse of Roche Abbey, set close beneath the precipice from which the monks, seizing the most striking feature of their valley with that quick sense of picturesqueness which distinguished the Cistercians, named themselves "monachi de rupe,' Monks of the Rock. . . . The warm glow of the afternoon falls into the valley in a flood. The little stream gleams with its reflection as it steals along beneath the trees. In an open glade a trifle higher up a couple of red-roofed cottages stand shining in the sun, and the fowls go to and fro clucking in the short grass. In the abounding stillness one might fancy that all human life had ceased on the departure of those who planned and built the lovely walls which are now a shattered ruin, waiting in some enchanted slumber till their master's hand shall set them up once more in their ancient glory, and the sound of chanting roll again through the hollow and over the short turf on the limestone crags above. I sit down in the shadow of the bank and rest awhile in this, the loveliest spot I shall see today."

MALTBY

Dictionary of English and Welsh Surnames, by Chas W. Bardsley, M. A., 1901 (pub. by Henry Frowde, Amen Corner, London):

Maltby "of Maltby"—parishes in the dioceses of York and Lincoln (p. 509).

Wm. de Malteby, Co. Lincoln, 1273 (A).

Walter de Malteby, Co. Norfolk, 1273 (A). See Pedigree No. IV., Sir Walter (5).

Robert de Malteby, Co. Norfolk, 20 Edw. I. (R). (1292?) See Pedigree IV., Sir Walter (6).

Willemus de Maltby, 1379—P. T. (Poll Tax) Yorks. (50).

Isabella de Maltby, 1379—P. T. (Poll Tax) Yorks. (p. 53).

MALTBY PLACES

1. Maltby, Yorks, 7 m. E. from Rotherham. (p. 744, Rec. Book I.)
2. Maltby, Stainton, Stockton, Yorks. (W. R. 1566, Book I.)
3. Maltby-le-Marsh, Lincoln.
4. Maltby-Raithby (see Raithby), 2 m. from Louth, Pop. 120.

5. Maultby in Norfolk, p. 199.
6. Maulby, 5 m. N.N.W. from Yarmouth.
7. Maltby, Pennsylvania, U. S. A.
8. Maltby, California, U. S. A.
9. Maltby, Washington, U. S. A.

MALTBY, Alford-Lincolnshire

Through the kindness of the Rev. R. E. H. Duke, we have received a photograph of the old church at Maltby, Lincolnshire. In a letter bearing the letterhead "Maltby Rectory," Mr. Duke writes: "The name Maltby is derived from the Danish Commander Malte."

It is probable that the Maltbys who were in England prior to the Norman conquest descend from this Danish officer, while another and quiet distinct branch, derive their descent from the Norman baron, de Malebisse, who accompanied William the Conqueror to England.

Mr. Duke adds: "There are no Maltbys on the Registers of this church."

MALTBY

Leicestershire

I. Henry Vice Maltby was born Sept. 15, 1811, at Evington, Leicestershire and was christened at St. Martin's Church, Leicester, Oct. 6, 1811. He married Sarah Ann Dunkly on the first Sunday in November about 1835; probably at Leicester. He died March 27th, 1882, at Aston, Birmingham, and was buried at Boldmere, Warwickshire.

A LIST OF MALTBY WILLS IN P. C. C. 1650-1719

Those marked with a star have been abstracted by Mr. Fothergill, and abridged wills are contained in Part I.

1650 Malby, Thomas, Mid., 157 Pembroke.
*1650 Maltby, Tho., Durham, 146 ad.
*1651 Malbye, Tho., —? 192 Grey.
1653 Maltbie, John, Notts., 73 Brent.
1653 Maltby, John, Lincoln, Ad cul 3.
*1654 Maultby, Thomas, Lincoln, Ad 221 II.
1657 Maltby, Anne, Lincoln, Ad 102.

*1658 Maltby, Richard (Kexby), 512 Wotton.
*1659 Maultby, Christopher, Lincoln, 483 Pell.
*1666 Maltby, Wm., Ad Nov.
*1666 Maultby, Cuthbert, Ad Dec.
*1671 Maultby, Eliz., Sur, 6 Duke.
*1671 Maltby, Elizabeth, prior grant Jan. last, Test regis, 6 Duke.
*1674 Maltby, Wm., Ad Aug.
*1686 Maultby, John, pt., 151 Lloyd.
1691 Mawby, Wm., pt., Ad Nov.
1693 Maltby, Jane Northton, Ad Jan.
1693 Maltby, Wm., Dorset, Ad Aug.
*1699 Maulby, Joseph, pt., 27 Pett.
*1701 Maltby, Tho., pt., 25 Dyer.
*1710 Maltby, Tho., pt., 125 Smith.
*1719 Maltby, Wm., Lond., Ad July.

1643-4 Maltby, William, Goulceby, 421.
1645-6 Thomas, Boston, 139.
1647-8 Thomas, Kirton, 415.
1649 John, Fleet, 124.
1651 Robtr, Hemingby, 21
1668 William, Lincoln, 346.
1669 William, Fotherby, 506.
1671 Christopher, Hareby, 722.
1672 Christopher, Anderby, 525.
1673 Richard Hemingby, 211.
*1674 John, Surfleet, 215.
*1693-4 William, Martin in Timberland, 83.
*1697-8 John, Broxholme, 146.

Later Mr. Fothergill sent these additional wills from the P. C. C. of an earlier date than the preceding wills:

1532 Maltby, John, 16 Thower.
1625 Peter, Southwarke, 84 Clarke.
1636 Maltbie, John, Southwarke, Surrey, 101 Pile.
1638 Maltby, Sarah, relict, 147 Lee.
1639 Maltbie, Sir George, Kt., 101 Harvey.

PECULIAR OF STOWE

1689 Maltby, John, Sturton.
1690 Rebecca, Sturton.

CONSISTORY OF LINCOLN—1609-1730

1611 Maltby, Jane, Hamworth, Potter, 3.
1612 John Belchford, Hus., 390.
1613 Ralph, Hemingby, 221.
1614 Jane, w. of Robert Billingborough, 52, bk. 1.
Thomas, Frampton Parish, 141 bk. 1.
1615 Robert, Belchford, servant, 247.
1620 alias Neave Francis, Somerby, wid., 91.
Christopher, Anderby, 420.
1612 Henry, Kirkby green, Shepherd, 117.
1622 William, Stickney, 94 bk. 2.
Dorothy, Hemingby, 112 bk. 2.
1624-34 William, Bishop Norton, 42.
1624-25 Thomas, Wintringham, Yeoman, 240.
1626 Robert, Horbling, 450.
Isabel, Eagle, wid., 544.
1631 Humphry, Thimbleby, yeoman.
Andrew, Skendleby, 25.
1639 Ellen Thimbleby, 34.
1640 Richard, Caulkwell, 504.
1642 John, Killinghohne, 335.

ADMONS. 1582-1780

1595 Maltbie, Francis, Fiskerton, 74.
Thomas Greetwell, 77.
*1607-10 Humfrey, Upton, 113.
1624-25 Agnes, Blyboro, 284.
1720 Thomas, Hemswell.
1729 John, Wiloughton.
1721-40 John, Wiloughton.

DEAN AND CHAPTER OF LINCOLN

1671-1716 1704 Maultby, Thomas, Scamblesby.
1582 John, Strubby, 149.
1609 Thomas, Hibberstowe, 242.
1615 Nicholas, Bishop's Norton, 138.
1663-66 Hammond, Bishop's Norton, 38.
1466-71 William, Binbrook, 59.

MARKED A. B. AND C.

1672-76 1675 Maltby, John, Hemingby, A 218.

CHANCELLOR'S WILLS

1690 Maltby, Robert, Stickney.

D. AND C.

1670-80 Maltby, William, Sturton, 144.
Thomas, Kirton, 148.
Chris., Normanby, 432.
1711 Maltby. John, Hemingby.
1715 Elizabeth, Barlings
1719 Mary, Hycham.
1722 Mathew, Willerton.
1723 William, Bardney.
1723 Elizabeth, Willerton.
1726 George, Frampton.
*1557 John, Kexby.
1675-80 Maltbie, Nicholas, Broxhohne, 100.
Nicholas, ———, 76.
*1679-80 Mary Normanby, 19.
*1679-80 John, Kexby, 21 and 24.
*1679-80 William, Broxhohne, 26.
1681-3 Richard, Ingham, 341.
*1684-6 Elizabeth, Upton, 40.
*1684-6 Maultby, Judith, Grayingham, 200.
1687-90 Susan, Ingham, 160.
*1694-99 John, Broxhohne, 146.
1722 Mathew, Willerton.
1723 Elizabeth, Willerton.
1700-4 Richard, Kexby, 135.
Richard, Saxilby, 145.
1711-16 John, Sugham, 110.
Richard, Kexby, 117.
Robert, Willoughton, 119.
1766 Hannah, Saxilby.
* Thomas, Willoughton, 331.
*1660-63 Maltby, William, Willoughton, 233.
Elizabeth, Willoughton, 469.
Nicholas, ———, 509.

*1664-5		Sarah, Springthorpe, 237.
*1672-4		William Broxhohne, 70.
*		Hammond Thornock, 123.
1675	Maultby,	William, Horncastle, 70.
1678		John, Gowerby, 47.
		William, N. Reston, 229.
1680		Thomas, Harrington, 134.
1682		Christopher, Haltham on Baur, 52.
1683		Robert, Langton by Wragby, 121.
1684		Thomas, Frampton, 147.
1685		Robert, Claxby, 56.
		Jane, Halton Holgate, 98.
1683		William, N. Somercotes, 115.
		Robert, Halton Holgate, 223.
1687		William, Langton by Wragby, 74.
		John, Boston, 109.
1688		John, Lusby, 147.
		William, Bratoft, 51.
*1693		William, Martin, 83.
1697-8		John Lusby, 220.
*1700		Mercy, Grantham, 107.
1702		John, N. Hyckam.
1704		John, Wispington.
		William, Crowland.
1705		Robt., Hemingby.

ARCHDEACONRY OF STOW, 1530-1780

Those marked by a star has been abstracted by Mr. Fothergill, and copies, abridged, will be found in Part I. under the correct dates.

*1530-52-53	Maltby,	Christopher, Hemswell, 117.
*1541-42-45		Joan, Greetwell, 303.
*1547		William, Ingham, 476.
1531-56		William, Greetwell, 316.
*1553-67		Robert, Willoughton, 179.
*1558-59		William, Greetwell, 301.
*1572-74		Richard, Willoughton, 169.
*1582-86		William, Kexby, 67.
*1586		Richard, Glentworth, 338.
1587-90		Alice, Glentworth, 67.
1599-1602		Christopher, Lea, 408.
1602		Thomas, Willoughton, 159.

*1603-06 Richard, Kexby, 256.
*1610 Christopher, Upton, 3.
*1616-18 John, Springthorpe, 55.
* Richard, Upton, 370.
* Thomas, Willoughton, 645.
*1624-25 Richard, Upton, 48.
1630 Maultbie. Richard, Blyboro, 232.
*1634-35 Richard, Kexby, 2.
*1638-39 Christopher, Upton, 10.
* Richard, Springthorpe, 35.
* Robert, Willoughton, 54.
*1640-59 Richard, Kexby, 45.

A LIST OF WILLS AT YORKSHIRE, 1636-1700

*1648 Maltbie, John, E. Retford, Alderman, Oct. 6 Cod. Dec. 28.
*1660-61 Maltby, Richard, Hummanby, 455 (43).
*1663-65 Maltby, Robert, Bawtry, 66 (46).
*1666-67 Maultby, William, Bawtry, 127 (45).
* Maltby, Thomas, Hummanby, 250.
*1670-71 Maltby, John, Hull, 144 (52).
*1675 Maltby, Henry, Hummanby, 67 (56).
* William, Speeton, 198.
*1678-80 William, Hull, 241 (58).
*1681-82 Robert, Flambrough, 41 (59).
*1698-99 Maultby, Hugh, Hoveringham, 302 (62).
1699-1705 Gap
1690-98 Gap
*1712-13 Maltby, Mary, Reighton, 61 (68).
*1718-19 Wm., Orston, 207 (73).
Done Prerogative gap 90-98
Dickering Act book.
1694 Maltby, Stephen, Flambrough, probate 2 Apl.
1694 Ann, Flambrough, probate 26 Nov.
Done Harthill
*1704 Maltby, Richard, Greasley, Notts, Test. 3 May.
Newark Deanery
*1702 Maultby, Wm., Sutton in Trent, 1 Dec.
Done Bulmer, Rydall and Cleveland
*1680 Maltby, William, Kingston upon Hull, 58-241.

1627 ADMONS. AT YORK

*1634 Maltby, Hugh, Orston, 91 Notts, 1 May.
1633 Maltby, John, Hummanby, 315 Dick, 3 Oct.
1647 Maltby, Robert, Muskam, Newark, 29 May.
1646 Maltby, Simon, S. Collingham, Newark, 18 March.

FEET OF FINES, YORKSHIRE

1 James I.

Eliz. Dalby v. Chris. Maltbie and others in Buckton, E. 7 Jas. I.
W. Fairbane v. W. Maltbye and others in Tatwicke, T. 7 Jas. I.
Phi Constable v. V. Maltby and athers in Gowsell, E. 9 Jas. I.
Ro Robinson v. Chris. Maltbye in Bempton, H. 11 Jas. I.
Nic. Maltby and others v. W. Smith in Drax, E. 20 Jas. I.
Robt Maltby v. Jo Elwes, gent, and Mowbray, in Bawtry, Mic. 1654.
J. Ohillipps v. R. Maultby in Bawtry, E. 18 Car. II. (1665?).

ADDITIONAL FEET OF FINES RECORDS

*1649 John Story v. Hugh Maltby and wife, Elizabeth, Gotham, Notts. Hily 1649.

*1659 Wm. Maltby and others v. John Maltby and others. Littleburrow and Sturton, Notts. Easter 1659.

*1659 William Wood v. John Maultby and others, Billinghay and North Kynne, Lincoln. Trinity 1659.

*1660 John Booth v. Thomas Maultby and others, Billinghay, North Kynne, Lincoln. Hily 12-13 Car. II.

*1662 Peter Booth v. John Maultby and others, East Retford, Notts. 14-15 Car. II.

*1662 John Darell, gent., v. John Maltby and others. 14 Car. II.

*1663 William Wood v. John Maltby, gent., and Mary, his wife, Billinghey, Northkune, Boston and Kerton in Holland. 15 Car. II. Mic. Lincoln.

*1668 Helen Webberly v. John Maultby, Mary, his wife, etc. Weberton. 20 Car. II. Mic. Lincoln.

*1669 Thomas Wilson, gent., v. John and Thomas Maltby, Northkyne. 21 Car. II., 1669, Trinity, Lincoln.

*1670 Richard Willan, gent., v. Rebecca Maltby, wd., and others. 22 Car. 11, 1670. E. Notts, Littlebrough and Sturton, Co. Notts.

*1672 John Flamsteed, gent., v. Hugh Maultby and others, Chilwell, Attenboro and Cassall, Co. Notts. 24 Car. II., 1672, Trinity.

CHANCERY PROCEEDINGS BEFORE 1714, MITFORD
(Started at Vol. XI. Car. I.)
Bridges

Marby, Ric. v. Marby, Jno., D.D., 1648, York, 9-7.
*Maultby, Eliz. v. Phillip, Thos., 1669, Mid. 54-82.
*Maltby v. Stephens, 1696 r B. 88-64.
*Maltby v. Slater, 1689, R.B. 88-65.
Marby v. Babb, br 223.
Marby v. Walby, r 284-16.
Marby v. Tomlinson, br 311.

FIN NO. 4 BRIDGES III.

Later we received abstracts of the following Chancery Proceedings, also furnished by Mr. Fothergill:
*Cotton v. Maltby (1557-8) C. 201.
*Hopkinson v. Maltby (1623) Lincoln, W. 479-57.
*Maltby v. Sanderson (1645) Lincoln, M. 35-9.
*Lamb v. Maltby (1648), H. 218-17.
*Cotton v. Maltby (1654), C. 201.
*Raw v. Maultby (1660), R. 22-139.
*Maultby v. Humberston, Mit 518-67.
*Maltby v. Andrews (1662), C. 160.
*Cannon v. Maltby (1668), C. 46-55.
*Maltby v. Potterell (1669), C. 183.
*Maltby v. Maltby (1672-3), York C. 542-206.
*Maltby v. Alured (1673), York C. 63.
*Maltby v. Alured, Whit. 122.
*Maltby v. Marshall (1667) York, Ham 489.
*Maltby v. Slater (1689), B. 88-65.
*Maltby v. Stephens (1690), B. 88-64.
*Maltby v. Royston (1691), C. 544-44.
*Maltby v. Slater (1692), Whit. 344.
*Coker v. Maltby (1690-1), C. 315.
*Maltby v. Harvey (1692), Mit. 547-105.
*Maltby v. Royston (1695), Whit. 353.
*Maltby v. Pollard (1696), C. 544-40.
*Maltby v. Jolland (1700), Whit 258.
*Maltby v. Hicks (1701), H. 611.
*Maltby v. Willey (1703-4), C. 543-168.
*Maltby v. Fawcett (1735), 58-1523.

INQUISITIONS POST MORTEM, 1558-1649

1585 Christopher Maltby, Alderman of City of York, Vol. 207, No. 95, Series II.

8 Jany., 14 Car. I., Richard Maltby, Springthorpe, Lincoln, (pt. 2-86, Lay Subsidy Rolls).

No Maltby was assessed at Retford to the Harth Tax of 1663.† (Lay Subsidy Rolls, 160-322).

No Maltby taxed at Bawtry circ. 1671 (Lay Subsidy Rolls, 262-15).

No Maltby in Subsidy 13-15, Car. II. at Corringham, 140-750.
Searched East Retford, 22 Car. II., 1670-1, 254-29.

Widow Maltby taxed on £3 worth of goods at Springthorpe, Car. II., 13 and 15, 1661-1663. (Lay Subsidy Rolls, 140-750). Same Roll, Mary Maltby taxed at Kexby.

NOTE.—This is very evidently John Maltby's widow, and it proves she had not remarried in 1661-3. Supposed to be mother of the American emigrants.

Richard Maltby paid on £3 goods at Springthorpe, 1628 (Lay Subsidy, 139-717).

Mr. John Maultby, 6-0; Mr. Robert Maultby, 8-0, East Retford, 16 Car. I. (Lay Subsidy, 160-303).

Nottingham Bassetlaw (Lay Subsidy, 15 Car. II., 160-322).

No Maltby in Subsidy 15 Car. II., at Corringham, 140-751.

William Maltbie at Broxhohne, £3—8/—8.

John Maltbie at Kexby, £3—8/—8.

Mary Maltbie at Kexby, £3—8/—8.

William Maltby and Joan, his wife, wid. of Nicholas Tournay, Lands in Bucks and Lincoln. (Close Rolls, 16 Hen. VI., M. I. D.)

Indenture, 25 April, 16 Car. II., 1664. William Maltby of London, etc. (Close Rolls, 4172).

EXCHEQUER PROCEEDINGS

Easter 22, Car. II., William Maltby, the elder, of Orston, Notts.

† An important record, as it shows the Maltbys had left Retford before 1663. American Maltbys will find this of interest.

KINSHIP

BY MAUDE TOWNSHEND MALTBY
(Written for the Maltby Association)

The little creatures of the wild—
Everyone—God calls His child,
And yet instills in each small mind
His age-old law of kind with kind.

Who knows but that the sturdy oak,
Though beech surrounded, feels a yoke
Of closer kinship with a tree which wears
In distant woods the leaves it bears?

So as from pine to pine tree tall
Greatings breathe the world around,
Let us send forth the rally call
"Love to our kin wherever found!"

PART II.

MALTBY AMERICAN NOTES

In Part I. we have endeavored to give as much data as possible of the early English Maltbys and all English pedigrees procurable; notes which should be interesting to all those of Maltby descent.

In Part II. we deal almost entirely with the family records of William Maltby, Esq., of Branford, Connecticut, his ancestors and descendants.

As is well known to most of the American branch the English research work has been carried on by The Maltby Association, and most successfully so, owing to the excellent services of Gerald Fothergill, Esq., of London.

There seems to be little room to doubt that the ancestry of William Maltby, Esq., has been found back to John Maltby of Kexby Hall, Kexbie, Lincolnshire, whose will was proved in 1557. (See Pedigree No. 10, Part I.)

The earliest Maltby record in New England yet discovered is on 27 June, 1664, and reads as follows: Town Records 1662-84, page 4 (New Haven, Conn., Records). "I, underwritten, doe acknowledge to have Rec'd of John Maltbie Twenty gall. of Rum which I doe promise to make saile of (at or upon my arrival in Virginia) to his best advantage, and likewise to make him Returns in the ship with Capt. Newton's goods, or by the first ship to Mr. John Rookeby, merchant in Barbadoes, as witness my hand this Twenty-seventh day of June, 1664.

JOHN GORING.

Samuel Hopkins.

This is a true Record of the original Bill, examined and proved soe to be this 26th of ye 12th mo. 1666, per me,

JAMES BISHOP, *Recorder.*

Recorded at ye desire of John Maltbie.

If we turn to Part I. under date 1662, we find John Maltby selling his property in East Retford, West Retford, Babworth, Notts. And it would appear that it was from these sales that he obtained the capital to start him in business in the New World. As his father's will read that the houses in Briggate, E. Retford, etc., to be sold and £100 to son John at 21, and the residue for my youngest son (Robert) "lately born," we can place the birth of John as in 1640-41.

Another early Maltby record is given below (1664-65) Page 61, Derby Records, 1655-1710, page 14:

"This Indenture made the six day of January in the yere of our Lord one thousand six hundred sixty foure; Between Lieutenant Thomas Wheler of Pagaset in the Jurisdiction of Connecticut, on the one Part & Alexander Bryan of Milford within the Jurisdiction of Connecticut Aforesaid on the other Part, wittneseth that the said Lieutenant Thomas Wheler for a consideration of two hundred pounds in hand paid; hath granted, bargained & sould & by these presents doth bargain & sell to & with the afore Said Alexander Bryan one parcell of land & houses where in now he liveth & oc Cupyeth it being as followeth Bounded with Potatuck River South, west Nagatuck River north East & bounded on the Northwest with trees marked by Towtaemoe Sachem. This Land Containing forty acres more or less Scituate & being as aforesaid to have and to hold the aforesaid land with all appurtenances thereunto Belongin to him his heirs forever without any Lawful Eviction, Erection or mollestation from him the aforesaid Lieutenant Thomas Wheler, his heirs, executors, administrators or assignes or any of them or from any Person or Persons clayming Right from, by or under them or any of them War Rending him Both for himself, his heirs, executors, administrators, asigns to save the aforesaid allexander Bryan blameless from all former Seales Suits in law morgages Debt a Reorages or in Cumbernesses A Rising ffrom the premises by any act or acts of his or any of them by or from under him, & the said Lieutenant thomas Wheeler doth further assure the aforesaid Allexander Bryan that he hath lawfull Right & power To Bargain & Sell the aforesaid Premises & allso that the Said Lieutenant Thomas Wheeler Doth give Allexander Bryan full Power to Record the same to himself & to his heirs forever; in witness whereof the afore Said Lieutenant Thomas Wheler hath hereunto sett his hand & Seale the day & yere above written.

"THOM. WHEELLER.

"THOMAS OVIAT,
"I. MALLBIER,
"JOHN WEBB."

NOTE.—The above record was copied from the printed Colonial Records, and it is quite likely the original signature was "Maltbie." The "I" was of course "J" as I and J were interchangeable in the early colonial days. This "I

Mallbier" was, of course, John Maltby. Alexander Bryan was the grandfather of Mary Bryan, who married John Maltby about 1670-71.

The next Maltby record we have is in 1666, as follows: New Haven, Town Records, 1662-1684, p. 100. "Att a Towne meeting held at New Haven, ffeb. 18, 1666. [1666-67].

"Mr. John Maltbie ppounded to ye towne for Admittance as a planter to buy as he shall see cause. It was Left to ye Comittee, formerly appointed by the Towne for admitting of planters. Sometime hearafter makeing aplication to ye sd comittee, upon ye testimony of John Harriman & John Winston was admitted."

In this connection it is well to insert an item which appeared in the Hartford "Times," Sept. 23, 1907, in answer to query 4,300, Maltby-Downing. The answer reads: "Either a New Haven, Branford or Milford name." (i.e. Maltby). "The original Maltby married a daughter of John Harriman, Milford." Signed (Ed.). Again on Dec. 22, 1910, the Hartford "Weekly Times" had under query 6,297: "New Haven genealogist (L. M. C.) quoted from memory of years back; one of my ancestors, John Harriman, who was one of the first innkeepers in New Haven, had twin daughters, and one married a Maltby—given name forgotten. (Noel Little.)"*

Note.—A letter dated "1866" from Ralph D. Smith says: "I think he" (referring to William (1) Maltby) "had two wives—the first, Mary ——. The second who married him certainly was Abigail (Bishop) Maltby." Another letter from a friend who was searching the Branford records for Maltby-Harrison records wrote: "Somewhere I found an item which, as I recall it, gave the name of William Maltby's wife as Mary." It occurred to the compiler that perhaps this information was in a Harriman record and not a Harrison one, as the lady was looking up Harrisons at the time, and might easily have read some Harriman record, mistaking the old writing, under the impression she was glacing over Harrison data. The compiler has long been under the impression from genealogical deductions that the first wife of William Maltby was Mary ——. We have as yet found no proof that she was a Harriman, but the idea is worth investigating. Of course the above references may not refer to the first wife of William (1) Maltby, but may apply to a first wife of John Maltby, for technically speaking, he was the "original" Maltby. So far as is known, however, John Maltby, emigrant, had only the one wife, Mary Bryan, and certainly he had only the two children, John (2), and Mary (2), twins, by her.

Shortly after the above record we find in the Winthrop Papers, 1666-7, Mass. Hist. Collect. Vol. VIII, Fifth Series Winthrop Papers, Part IV., p. 115, a letter from John Winthrop, Jr., to Richard Nicolls.

* This is an error. Since this went to print it has been conclusively proved that John Harriman had no daughter who could have married a Maltby.

"Hartford, Mar. 6, 1666 [7].

"I could never yet heare of arrival of it at Mr. Bryan's to whom it was directed, at the seaside. Last Friday came a letter from Mr. Charles Hill of N. London, who was newly arrived fro Barbadoes. There was a letter for Capt. Delavall—Understanding by Ed. Messinger, by whom I receive yours of Jan. 18, at his return fro N. Yorke, that the report of it (fire) was gone beyond Milford as he came thither, whc could not but be at New York then quickly, Mr. Malbye at that time being on his journey thither."

Letter to Gen. Nicholls, governor of all his Royall Highnesses, the Duke of York, his territories in America at N. York. The Index refers to "Mr. John Maltby (Malbye)."

This letter gives us the information that John Maltby made a trip to New York in the spring of 1666-7 and that he had carried with him news of some fire. (Was this the fire of London or a fire at Barbadoes?)

To again quote from the Winthrop Papers, Vol. VIII., p. 568, a letter from William Leete to John Winthrop, Jr.

"Newhaven, Apr. 13, 1671.

"I have herein inclosed Governor Lovelace his letter but the instructions are with Mr. Eliot for perusall. *Here is no newes with us, but of Mr. Malby's arrival safe at Nevis; that ship he went in being there cast away by herracane after the goodes were landed & he since gone for England.* Goodman Glover of N. H. saith that he heard at Long Island that Capt. Pearce was arrived in England safe. There is also much speech about Commission and ffriggots coming to N. E. Sorry to hear of the grief and damage to your relations at Antego.* Signed William Leete."

From the above letter of William Leete, who at this time was deputy governor of the Colony of Connecticut, we learn that "Mr. Malbye" had arrived safe at Nevis, W. I., prior to April 13, 1671, that the goods were landed, and he had gone on to England. From the foregoing records it is clearly shown, we believe, that John Maltby was engaged in a West India merchant trade, and up to this time we find him the only Maltby in New England. He was very evidently the older brother who sold his property at East Retford, etc., Notts, in 1662, and set himself up in business.

* John Winthrop, Jr., had a brother, Samuel, who resided at Antiguar, of which island he was deputy governor. The idea has sometimes presented itself to the compiler that the first wife of William Maltby may have been a Winthrop, possibly this would explain whence came the name Samuel in the family of William (1) Maltby.

There is a very strong point, discovered by Mr. Fothergill, namely, that no Maltby was assessed at Retford to the Hearth Tax of 1663 (Lay Subsidy Roll, 160-322). This is a most important fact as it establishes that the Maltbys had left Retford at this date, i.e., the year following the sale of John Maltby's property. On this visit to England John Maltby very evidently fetched his two younger brothers and also his cousin, Robert Maltby of Bawtry, as we shall see from both the English and American records.

If we turn to the English records, under date 1662, where John Maltby sold his property we find "George Holmes and Mary, his wife," as part vendors and the idea suggested was that Mary Maltby, the widowed mother, had married George Holmes. Farther on, in 1664, there is an indenture between various people including "William Maltby of London, Haberdasher of Hats," and the names Francis Holmes and Alexander Holmes also appear. The theory presents itself that if the widow, Mary Maltby, did marry George Holmes and moved to London, that William might have gone with her, or already have been in London, possibly, almost probably, with London relations. Hence the tradition that our emigrant ancestor "came from London."

The above is only a theory and as a William Maltby, Haberdasher of London died about 1664-5, this may be one and the same person, and in no way connected with the Retford Maltbys, but in genealogical research, every clue or theory is worth following till it ends in failure.

To return to the New England records: New Haven, Conn., records, p. 165.

"Dec. 29, 1671.

"Mr. Robert Maltbye, Sr., and Robert Maltbye, junior, being present with them in drinking, but noe disorder appearing & they strangers were dismist with a caution for the future.

"Robt Maltby, Sr., was minded of his disorder ye other night before Authorities as being Distempered with drinke. He acknowledge his evill & sd he was fasting and had been drinking wine with a stranger which distempered him. He was sentenced to pay ten shillings fine but pleading his lownes & ye wrong he had sustained in his coming from England & being to return again it was not required of him."

This record requires careful study and it may be well to analyze its contents. First, we find the prefix of respect applied to Robert Maltby, Sr. Secondly we must remember that in Colonial days

"Sr." and "Jr." did not apply to father and son, but was a distinction of age between those of the same name and might apply to uncle and nephew, or to cousins, as it evidently did in this case. Third, we find them called "strangers," so we may be sure they had but recently arrived in the New Haven Colony and what more likely than that they returned with John Maltby, older brother, to Robert Jr. and cousin to Robert Sr., whom we saw en route for England in April 1671, and returned with his relations by Dec. 1671 (see also record following). Next let us consider the "disorder" of Robert, Sr. This may have been a new occurrence with him, but if we turn to the will of his older brother, William Maltby of Bawtry, 1665, we find a lack of confidence in his brother Robert, and he leaves all his houses and lands, etc., to his youngest brother Daniel and his sister Barbara, and after their deaths to his cousin William Stokeham. His bequest to his brother Robert is "£5"—the same sum that he left his "cousin John Maltby"—i.e., the John Maltby who we believe brough Robert Maltby of Bawtry to New England. He also left his "cousin William Maltby, £5." (i.e., William Maltby, brother of John, emigrants) also to his "cousin Jane Turnell." (Query: Was this Jane Maltby, sister of John, William and Robert of Retford? If so, did she marry, first, Robert White? See Agreement, dated 1662.)

To return to the New Haven record. Robert Maltbye, Sr., pleaded "his lowness and ye wrong he had sustained in coming from England & being to return again." I think "his lowness" in this instance refers to the expense he had been to in coming to New England. By the will of his father in 1660, he was to have "the house I now live in" (i.e., at Bawtry) "land called Catts Bethey Moore, land at Springthorpe in Lincolnshire." Now we find that Robert Maltby sold this house in Bawtry about the time he went to New England. This appears in an abstract from the will of one Richard Beare of Bawtry, will dated 1672, and is only of interest to us because he leaves his "daughter Mary Boare a house in Bawtrey wherein one Elizabeth Carbonell now dwelleth, lately purchased of Robert Maultby and John Phillips. Dated 6 August, 1672." No doubt the sale of this house gave him funds for his voyage to New England. His cousin, John Maltby, probably thought that in the "new world" Robert might acquire the good fortune which seemed to elude him at home. But the sale of this house was not his one source of revenue for under Maltby vs. Maltby in 1672-3 (when Robert Maltby had evidently returned to England) we find his brother, Daniel Maltby, stating that "Robert Maltby borrowed £50 from Robert Langley of Bawtry and for security mortgaged three messuages in Bawtry. Langley conveyed his interest in the mortgage to Daniel Maltby and Robert Maltby has failed to pay the principal and interest."

Again we find that the widow, Anne Maltby, mother of Robert Maltby of Bawtry, seems to have left her property to the children of Robert and not to him, which would also indicate that there was lack of confidence in him. And we find, 15 June, 1673, Robert Maltby, guardian, trying to recover rents, he claimed due his infant daughter Sarah. Robert Coulston of Cottingham was agent for Anne Maltby, the elder, as collector of rents and he was "ready to perform the trusts."

We have seen from the above that two Robert Maltbys were in New Haven on Dec. 29, 1671, and that Robert, Sr., was going to return. We shall now see that the name of *William Maltby* appears in New Haven for the first time about this time, and that Robert Maltby, Jr., evidently remained in New England. The record is dated 29 March, 1672, three months later than the preceding record and is as follows: Town Records, New Haven, 1662-1684, p. 18:

Know all men whom it may concern, That I, John Maltbie of Newhaven in New England, merchant (ffor & in consideration of my beloved brother, William Maltbie, now resident in Newhaven in New England, aforesd merchant ingaging with mee in a bond for the payment of thirty five pounds in porke & pease unto Mr. Richard Raymond, Senior, of Saybrook, in New England afsd, marriner, some time in March next as in and by sd bond doth more fully appear) Have and by these presents Doe, by way of mortgage, make over unto my beloved brother, Wm. Maltbie afsd, Vizt.: Three horses,‡ one cropt on both ears called Bonny, one bay horse and one black horse, which sd horses I have wrought with ye last winter, also one horse cart‡ and wheels withall the irons thereunto belonging, also the harness for the afsd horses, also one plow‡ & irons with a Terse of Rape seed, also one mare with what stocke of hers may bee with her at a place called Eaton's neck on long Island,* also one cow,‡ now at home,† and a heifer in the keeping of Thomas Meeker, also four pigges now at home, also one case of pistolls and houlsters and one gun for his securitie in case any Damage shall come to him by ye afsd ingagement upon my ———; And in case

* The fact that John Maltby owned "a mare" which was then at Easton's Neck, on Long Island, would rather indicate that he owned land there.

† "At home." The compiler has never felt sure of where "home" was to John Maltby. The inventory of his estate taken at New Haven in 1676, is very small, amounting to only £58, 5s, 6d. Whereas he seems to have had a good merchant trade, and tradition has it, owned his own ships. We know positively that his brother, William, owned ships.

of faylure of payment on my part (by anything that may fall out) of the aforesd sume of thirty five pounds, that my bloved brother, aforesd, be necessitated thereby to make good the same, then the aforesd horses, horse cart and wheels, harness, plow, rape seed, mare & stocke, cow, heifer, pigges, pistolls and gun shall be ye proper Estate of my sd brother, his heyres or assignes for ever; or so much of them as shall be to his full satisfaction. But in case of payment by mee made or my order according to the said bond without Damage to my sd brother, That then the aforesd Estate mortgaged, to returne to mee, my heyres or assignes or just satisfaction for any part of that may bee made use by my sd brother. In witness hereof I have hereunto sett my hand & seale this twenty-ninth Day of March, Anno Domini, one thousand six hundred and seventy-two.

1672—Signed, sealed and Delivered
In the presence of
James Bishop JOHN MALTBIE.
her
Martha R. Roundketell
mark

This, so far as is known, is the first record of William Maltby at New Haven. Scarcely more than a month later we find on the New Haven register, "Born, Mary, daughter of Mr. William Maltbye," p. 131.

This shows us that William Maltby was of New Haven in May, 1672, that he must have had his two oldest children, John (2) and Jane (2) prior to coming to New Haven. Where these two oldest children were born and the dates of birth are not known, nor is the name of their mother, the first wife of William Maltby. Ralph D. Smith, in a letter dated 1866, states, referring to John (2), son of William (1), "He lived in Saybrook all of his life and died in August, 1727, aged 57," hence born in 1670. Where Mr. Smith found his authority for this statement is not known, but very probably from his tombstone in Saybrook, which has likely been long

‡ The inventory of William Maltby mentions:

	£	s	d
5 grown swine	4	0	0
a black horse	4	0	0
9 smale swine	3	3	0
a mare and colt	2	15	0
a black mare	2	0	0
a cart and irons belonging to it	1	5	0
Plow and plow irons	1	0	0
7 cows	16	0	0

The "case of pistolls and gun," I do not find mentioned in the above inventory.

since destroyed. His sister, Jane (2), may have been a twin sister. She married David Parker at New Haven, 4 March, 1689-90. From these records we deduce that William (1) Maltby was married about 1669.

A year from the time we find the birth of Mary (2) Maltby at New Haven, we have the record of William Maltby purchasing his homestead and land at Branford, Conn., and this deed is witnessed by "Robert Maltbye" under date "April 16, 1673." There seems to be every reason to believe that this Robert Maltbye was William's younger brother, the Robert Maltby, Jr., who was a "stranger" in New Haven, "Dec. 29, 1671," and that he was the Robert Maltby, son of John, of East Retford, Notts., born in 1648; hence he would have been twenty-five years of age when he witnessed the deed, a copy of which we give under the date 1673.

This is the last record discoverable of Robert Maltby. He may have returned to England or removed to some other place. It is possible he may be the "Sergeant Malby" mentioned in 1697, (see "America and West Indies," p. 326, Vol. X.) but this is hardly probably as he would have been nearly fifty years old. There is a record in Vol. VI., p. 366, from Abstracts of records of all grants made in South Carolina in 1682, which seems more likely to refer to the Robert Maltby above. It reads: "Robert Maltey, Town Lot, 23 March, 1682." As this copy was made from the printed abstracts it is very likely that on the original the name Maltey is spelled Malby or Maltby. This would account for the tradition that "there were three Maltby brothers emigrated to New England, one of them going to Virginia." The fact remains that there are early Maltby records in New England which as yet seem impossible to trace to William and John Maltby.

There is little more known of John Maltby, emigrant, and may as well be summarized here. He maried Mary Bryan, daughter of Richard Bryan, she born at Milford in 164.* (It is well to note

* This is an error. W. A. N. of Bayonne, N. J., kindly sent the following notes on the Bryan-Maltbys to the Hartford Weekly Times. Note 12,202: "In the town records, on a loose scrap of paper, I found a note giving the date of Mary Bryan's birth as February 15, 1649. As the first two leaves are missing from this book from 1639 to about 1653, there is no proof that this note is correct as to the time of her birth; but as the town record shows John Maulbie (Maltby) and Mary Bryan, daughter of Richard (merchant), were married February 28, 1666, it certainly seems more likely that she was born in 1649 than 1654. From the church records of Milford, Conn., under baptisms, is the following: 'May 21, 1654, Mary, daughter of Mary, wife of Richard Briant, and Alexander, her son.' 'Sept. 3, 1654, Hannah, daughter of Mary, wife of Richard Briant.' The town record has: 'Hannah Bryant, daughter of Richard Bryan, was born on the last of August 1654.' From the above it seems very evident that Mary Bryan was born in 1649. She would have been seventeen in 1666 when she married, whereas were her birth placed in 1654 she would have been only twelve years old on the date of her marriage."

that her sister, Hannah Bryan, married John Harriman of Elizabethton, Province of New Jersey, as we find on Milford Records, Vol. 3, p. 188, 8 July, 1677, a bequest of "£50 to the sd John Harriman upon the ack. of his wife are from the estate of sd Mr. Richard Bryan, her father.") It will be seen that Mary Bryan was at least thirteen years the junior of John Maltby; most records say she was married "about 1670" but a record taken, I think, from the Baldwin Genealogy, p. 1324-1397, says: "She married (1) John Maltby, Feb'y 28, 1666, of New Haven, Conn., d. about 1671."

This record would make her but twelve or thirteen when married, and John Maltby was not dead in 1671, as the New Haven Records give the birth of his son, John (2), as "Born, John, son of John Maltby, 1 June, 1673." The Strong Genealogy says Mary (2) Maltby was a twin with him, but I did not find her name on the register. He had a sister, Mary (2), however, as is shown in the will of their great-grandfather, Alexander Bryan of Milford. Mr. Bryan made his will before 1679 and mentions: "To grandchildren" (they were in reality great-grandchildren) "John and Mary Maltby, £5." (p. 1321, Baldwin Genealogy). He also deeded property in 1677 to his "granddaughter, Mary, widow of John Maltby." John Maltby was considered to be dead a year previous to this, however, for in Vol. I., p. 175, of New Haven Records, is the following:

"Jno. Maltbye. An inventory of the Estate of Mr. John Maltbye, reported to be lost at sea and apprized by underwriters, 10th 4th, 1676." (The writing was hard to decipher and there may be many mistakes in the following copy.):

	£	s	d
Impr woollen wearing cloathes . . .	2	0	0
a hatt and leather (?) stockings . . .	0	4	0
It. a shirt, drawers, bands and bandstrings	2	5	0
6 payre of sheets	4	0	0
6 pillow covers	2	0	8
It. 24 lb. of flax	1	4	0
3 yds. of tufted holland	0	9	0
table cloaths and towells	1	0	0
1 yd. ½ of cotton	0	5	2
It. Ribbing	0	12	0
3 bibles	0	10	0
5 yds. of girtnad (?)	0	1	3
2 brushes	0	0	3
cotton & linnen yarns	1	13	0

It. Several baskets	0	17	0
Boxes, buttons & manchester	0	9	8
cases with knives	0	4	0
It. one dozen of cushions	1	10	0
chests and trunks	2	12	0
one bushel of rye			
one bush of indyan meal			
It. old —— & tube	1	15	0
1 pagod (?) Cottons iron			
cher— platters & (?)			
Earthern ware	3	2	0
3 glasses & bottles	0	2	6
powder	2	4	3
1 piece of gold	1	0	0
Iron ware	3	2	0
bedsteads, pillows & bolsters	2	10	0
Several books	0	10	0
1 pillion, saddle & furniture	1	10	2
carpets	0	6	2
Wheells (?)	0	9	2
old cases (?) bottles	0	6	0
tin wares can house (?)	0	10	0
brasse ware	1	4	0
2 tables	0	4	0
hogs	2	0	0
casthosope (?)	1	18	0
2 looking glasses and cubbard cloth . .	0	5	0
2 ounces of spices	0	2	8
7 alcumy spoons *	0	2	0
a child's cradle	0	4	0
2 sives	0	2	0
books (?)	3	3	1½
————	0	14	0
1 payre of gloves	0	3	0
A piredosa (?) Map	0	8	0
For debts due to ye Estate	9	5	4½
Total	58	05	06

* The alcumy spoons, of which we quote below, from Alice Morse Earle's "China Collecting in America," p. 43. She mentions how few people possessed spoons and says: "Extremely elegant people had spoons of alchymy or occomy, alcaney, alcamy, acoury, askamy, accamey, as I have seen it spelt, a metal composed of pan brass and arsenicum."

Signed:
William Bradley
John Winston

As has previously been stated, this Inventory would appear to be part only of the property belonging to John Maltby. Where the bulk of his possessions were is a quandry, possibly England, or some place in the West Indies, or mayhap on Long Island, or at Milford. In this inventory we note the "several books," indicating that he cared for the intellectual side of life. Also we may be sure that only gentlemen of a good station in life wore gloves at this period.

Before leaving the subject of John Maltby, it may be of interest to descendants to learn something of his wife's family. The following notes of the Bryan family are from the New Eng. Hist. and Gen. Register.

BRYAN

I. Thomas Bryan, of Aylesbury, England, bapt. there Sept. 29th, 1602. His w. was Anna, only child of Robert and Joane —— Baldwin.

NOTE.—It is not quite clear whether this was the wife of Thomas or his son, Alexander.

II. Alexander Bryan, son of the above, d. in 1679. He was a prominent merchant of Milford, Conn., and with his son, Richard, stood in such high credit at Boston that his note of hand passed current as bank bills in the present day, says Lambert. From 1668 to 1673 he was assistant Governor of the Colony of Connecticut and in Milford was one of the purchase trustees. The Hon. Alexander Bryan was from Ashton Clinton, Bucks., England.

III. Richard Bryan, son of the above, m. Mary, dau. of William and Margaret ——— Peyntree. On his death William Peyntree left a large estate for those days, inventoried, 29 Nov., 1649, at £1001—10—00, part of which went to his "daughter Mary, wife of Richard Bryan of Milford, Conn."

IV. Mary Bryan, b. in 1649, m., first, about 1671, Mr. John Maltby of New Haven. He was reported dead before 1677. About 1680, she m., second, Rev. Joseph Talyor of Southampton, Long Island, who d. 4 April, 1682, aged 31. She m., third, 30 Jany., 1690, John Howell, Jr., of Southampton, L. I., who died 8 March, 1692, aged 44.

Ref. New England Hist. and Gen. Reg. p. 73. Vol. LXIV.; Milford Records, 3 Vol., p. 188; Thompson's Hist of Long Island; Baldwin Gen.; Old M.S. by Rev. Jonathon (4) Maltby.

The only one of the three emigrant brothers known to have left male descendents was William Maltby, Esq., b. in 1644-5, as we know from his tombstone.* Before taking up an account of his life it will be well to compare the family of John and Mary Maltby of East Retford with the New England emigrants and also to note the names of the children of William Maltby. (The full genealogy is given in Part I., Pedigree X.) We find: John Maltby, Springthorpe and East Retford, Notts, Alderman, with wife, Mary ——. His will proved in 1647-8. His children were:

1. John Maltby, probably b. 1640-41.
2. Richard Maltby, bapt. 15 Aug., 1642, at Retford, evidently d. young.
3. Jane Maltby, eldest daughter.
4. William Maltby, bapt. 16 March, 1644-45, at Retford, Notts.
5. Elizabeth Maltby, youngest daughter.
6. Robert Maltby, bapt. 28 Dec., 1647, at Retford, Notts.

The births of John, Jane and Elizabeth are not recorded at Retford, consequently they were probably older than Richard, William and, of course, Robert.

Let us now look at the list of children of William Maltby, emigrant, and his first wife name, unknown (if his second wife, Hannah Hosmer, wid. of Josiah Willard, had children we have not been able to ascertain it) and of his third wife, Abigail, dau. of Deputy Governor James Bishop. Children by first wife:

1. John Maltby, said to have been b. 1670. (We believe named for William's father, John, of East Retford.)
2. Jane Maltby, b. probably about 1670-71. She m. in 1689-90. (Was she named for their sister, Jane?)
3. Mary Maltby, b. May 1, 1672. (We believe named for William's mother, Mary Maltby of Retford, perhaps also for his wife.)
4. William Maltby, b. 1673. (Named for himself.)
5. Elizabeth Maltby,* b. April 30, 1676. (Was this for his sister Elizabeth?)

* NOTE—This statement is ambiguous. It should read that so far as is known Americans by the name of Maltby descend from William, Esq.—for we know of no descendants of Robert, and the line of John (1) soon failed of male issue.

6. Daniel Maltby,* b. May 19, 1679. (Was this not for a favorite cousin, Daniel Maltby, of Doncaster, Gent.)

Children by third wife, Abigail Bishop:

7. Samuel Maltby, b. 1693.
8. Jonathon Maltby, b. 1698. These may have been Bishop family names.

Hannah Hosmer was b. about 1639 and m. March 20, 1657, Josiah Willard of Wethersfield; as he did not die until 1674 his widow could not have been the mother of William Maltby's four children, John, Jane, Mary and William. But she could have been the mother of Elizabeth, b. in 1676, and of Daniel, b. in 1679. The question is, was she? Between the years 1674 and 1685 we find no record of Hannah Hosmer. There can be no questioning the statement that she was William Maltby's wife, for in Mainwaring's Digest of Probate Records in Hartford County, Vol. I., p. 324, is the will of Thomas Hosmer, dated "27 Feb., 1685" and in it he mentions: "I give unto my daughter, Hannah Malby, £18, which is the Reversio due me out of the estate of Josiah Willard of Wethersfield. I give unto my son-in-law, Malby, £5." . . . "If any of my children shall bring up their children to learning so as to make them fit for publique service, to each such gr. child I bequeathe £10 apiece to be paid them at the age of 21 years." . . . "I give my daughter, Hannah Malby, 40 shillings in money and in case she live to be a widow and in want, I do bequeath her £20 more, to be paid her as she needs it.

Signed: Thomas Hosmer.

Proved, 1 Sept., 1687.

Thus we find in 1685 her father mentions her as Hannah Malby; in 1686, Savage Gen. Dict., calls her wife of William Maltby; in 1687-8, we find her name with William Maltby's on the list of church members in Branford, Conn.; in 1689-90, a deed for John Yale is witnessed by "William Maltbie," "Hannah Maltbie."

These are the only references found concerning her. A word as to the Hosmer family into which William Maltby married. Savage Gen. Dict. gives: "Hosmer, Thomas, Cambridge, 1632, then called Newton; brother of the first James, freeman, 6 May, 1635; removed early, with Hooker, to Hartford, where he had a good estate; selectman and representative several times; had an only son, Stephen, b. about 1645; daus. Hannah, b. about 1639, who m., 20

* There is room for question here as to whether Elizabeth and Daniel were children by a first wife or whether they were the offspring of Hannah Hosmer, widow of Josiah Willard.

March, 1657, Josiah Willard of Wethersfield; he d. 1674. They were m. at Concord and had Samuel and Josiah at Hartford where he was schoolmaster and so employed at Wethersfield, where he had Dorothy, Simon, Stephen, Thomas, John and Hannah; freeman 1665; became a trader, d. insolv.; in 1686 his widow was wife of Maltby."

The Hosmers were from Hawkhurst, Co. Kent., where the records of their family go back to 1066. (Vide Note No. 1809-1 by M. H. H. B., Boston Transcript, Sept. 28, 1914.) The earliest record possessed by the compiler is of Stephen Hosmer who was buried at Hawkhurst, Kent, May 24, 1633. His wife, Dorothy, was buried there Feb. 5, 1640, and are buried in the churchyard of the old St. Lawrence Church, built in A. D. 1291. Their son, Thomas Hosmer, was born at Hawkhurst in 1603. Frances, his wife, was born in 1602 (Saybrook, Conn., Record, Vol. I., p. 130, but 1600 according to Boston Transcript). Thomas Hosmer came from London to Cambridge, Mass., in 1635 (Saybrook Record, or 1632, according to the Transcript). He died April 12, 1687 and his wife died Feb. 15, 1675. Their daughter, Hannah, as we have shown, was the second wife of William Maltby.

These Hosmer records are given to show into what class of society our ancestor married, and we find that his third wife was of an equal station in life. Abigail, daughter of Deputy Governor James Bishop, and widow of John Talmadge. She married John Talmadge in 1686. His inventory was taken April 21, 1691. Abigail Bishop was born in 1659. "Mrs. Abigail Maltbei d. Oct. 24, 1710." See tombstone.

Bishop is a name closely associated with the Maltby family of Springthorpe, etc., from whom we claim descent. In fact if this pedigree is correct, as we believe it is, then the emigrant Maltbys had for their grandmother, a Bishop—Margaret Bishop, who had a brother Richard and also a brother Robert. In fact it would appear that the name Robert in the Maltby family came from the Bishops.

We have endeavored to show from the names of William Maltby's children that there was a very close similarity with those of his father's family, taking it for granted that John Maltby of East Retford was his father. The fact that this John Maltby died when his three sons were but very small children, aged respectively about eight, four and a month or two old, would account for the fact that we find no records in New England calling the emigrant Maltbys "sons of ——— Maltby," as was the case with so many of the early settlers. Another very strong proof that the East Retford Maltbys were the ancestors of the emigrants is the fact that out of the vast number of Maltby records found, the only William Maltby born in 1644-45 (which is the year the emigrant William Maltby was born as is proved by his tombstone) is William Maltby, son of John and Mary ——— Maltby, born at East Retford, March 16, 1644-45.

Another strong piece of evidence is the fact that no Maltby was assessed at Retford to the Hearth Tax of 1663. No Maltby was taxed at Bawtry circ. 1671. In fact there is every reason to believe that the John, William and Robert of East Retford, are the John, William and Robert of New England, and thus far nothing can be found to disprove this theory.

Some of the ground covered by Mr. Fothergill in his researches for this Maltby material included: Feet of Fines, Yorkshire, 1603-1666; Feet of Fines, Nottinghamshire, Lincolnshire and Mixed Counties, 1659-1673: Chancery proceedings, 1558-1758, Plaintiff's side only; Inquisitions, Post Mortem, 1558-1649; Lay Subsidy Rolls, Nottinghamshire and Lincolnshire Close Rolls; Prerogative Court of Canterbury, 1604-1719; Exchequer Proceedings, Nottinghamshire; King's Bench Deeds, 1656-1675; Indentures, 1647-1671; Yorkshire Marriage Licenses; Wills at Yorkshire, 1636-1700; Baga de Secretic.

As, to the lay mind, many of the above terms convey no intelligence, a short explanation is appended.

Pedes Finium, or Feet of Fines.—The conveyance of land by Feet of Fines was very often resorted to; they are of first class importance, as the vendor joins with his wife and children or other heirs in order to dock, dower or entail. (For example see under date 1662, Part I.)

Chancery Proceedings.—The pleadings in the Court of Chancery are of the highest importance as sources of genealogical information, some of them giving as many as nine generations of pedigree, and others even give abstracts of all the deeds in the family muniment room for three hundred years. Besides the general value, they are of great help to Americans, as setting out a claim by descent, they frequently account for some missing relative, by stating that he is now in America in parts beyond the seas. These documents are practically a virgin field, never having been worked out suit by suit as Mr. Waters did the wills in the P. C. C.. It will be observed that Mr. Fothergill searched the plaintiff side only. The chancery suits on the defendant side should be searched but it requires much time, as only the plaintiff side is alphabetically arranged and we had not the funds to render this possible.

Inquisitions Post Mortem.—These give information about the larger land owners and are well known as one of the best sources of genealogy. (For example see under date 1585, Part I.)

Lay Subsidy Rolls and Hearth Tax returns are useful, as they serve as a directory, giving a clue to the parish. (Example: "No Maltby in Subsidy, 15 Car. II, 1663-64 at Corringham, 140-751.)

Close Rolls.—To explain this we quote from "Some Special Studies in Genealogy," by Gerald Fothergill, Esq., from whose works all the explanations of terms have been taken.

"It seems probable that, in order to find capital for the start in the New World, the emigrant would sell any land he possessed; or, if he was without land, it is to be expected that his father would, on giving him a portion, re-settle his estate, and the departing son would join in any conveyance in order to cut any rights he might have in possession or expectancy under any entail that existed. Here it should be noted that men of very small estates, even cottagers, would strictly entail and settle property on themselves and wife with reversion to the eldest son and heirs, and failing these, to the second, third and fourth sons, etc., respectively.

"At different periods the English law has known various ways of conveyancing. The statute, 27 Henry VIII., cap. 16, provided an instrument known as a 'deed of bargain and sale,' and it was enacted that an estate should not pass by this means only unless it was by indenture enrolled in one of the Courts of Westchester or in the county where the lands lie. If this provision had not been evaded, we should have had an almost universal register of conveyances of the freehold, but it was soon defeated by the invention of the conveyance of lease and release, which arose from the omission to extend the statute to bargains and sales for terms of years.

Many thousands of the former deeds are enrolled in Chancery on the Close Rolls, the grantors being indexed in the books called 'Indentures,' kept in the Long Room, and the grantees in the Close Rolls index in the Round Room at the Record Office. Others are on the rolls of the King's Bench, Common Pleas, Exchequer, etc.

The great attack on the (English) records should start with the wills, they being the very backbone of all pedigree research. By far and away the most important set of wills are those proved in the prerogative Court of Canterbury (P. C. C.); these commence in 1383, and continue to 1858. The P. C. C. contains the wills from all parts of England during the Commonwealth, 1650 to 1660."

As is shown in Part I., we have received in the neighborhood of a hundred abstracts from Maltby Wills, and as before stated, none of them (except the East Retford family) can be made to fit our needs, whereas the wills, deeds, etc., of the East Retford family do dovetail in every respect with the history of the New England Maltbys.

In Part I. we gave chronologically these wills, but for the benefit of the American Maltbys it has seemed best to give the complete abstracts as Mr. Fothergill sent them here.

First, it may be well to state that the ancestry of John, William and Robert of East Retford, has been traced by wills to John Maltby of Kexbie Hall, Kexbie, Lincolnshire, Will proved 1557, so he was probably born about 1500. Who his father was is not known, possibly William Maltby of Ingham, Will dated 15 Aug., 1547, which mentions son Robert, daughters, Elizabeth and Katherine. Mr. Thomas Burton to be supervisor. Wife Isabell and son John to be exors. John Jackson, John Colson, William Grave, Witnesses. Proved in Arch. Stow, 3 Feby., 1547-8, folio 477.

The only reasons for believing this William Maltby to have been the father of John of Kexbie is the fact that John names a daughter Izabell, perhaps for his mother as his wife was Margerie. However, the proved line of descent is as follows:

I. John Maltby of Kexbie Hall, Kexbie, Lincolnshire. Wife, Margerie ——. Will proved 3 Dec., 1557.

II. Richard Maultbye (son of the above), Kexbie, Lincolnshire. Will proved last December, 1602.

III. John Maltbie of Springthorpe, Lincoln. Wife, Margaret. Will proved 25 June, 1610.

IV. John Maltby of East Retford, Nottingham, Alderman. Wife, Mary. Will proved April, 1648.

V. John, oldest son, b. about 1640; William, second son, b. March 16, 1644-45; Robert, youngest son, b. Dec. 28, 1648. (They had a brother, Richard, b. 15 Aug., 1642; d. 7 Aug. 1647-8; also a sister Jane and a sister Elizabeth.)

The wills which we now give prove this pedigree to be correct:

I. Abstract of Will of JOHN Maltby of Kexbie Hall. Dated 26 Nov., 1557. Burial at Upton. Alice Huggan, Richard Burr, Elizabeth Burr, Izabell Jackson. Daughters, Margaret, Izabell.* Wife Margerie & *son Richard* to be exors. Sons Richard & William. Will Proctor & Christopher† Maultby to be supervisors.

* From the Upton burials we have this record: "Buried at Upton, Isabell Maltby, 20 May, 1586."

† Christopher Maltby was evidently a kinsman, and may have been Christopher Maltby, Alderman of York, as it seems probable that the two families join not far back of this date.

Richard Parke, Richard Watkinson, Myles Proctor, Roger Dunderdale, Witnesses. Proved in Cons. of Lincoln, 3 Dec., 1557, 31.

Wife Margerie of above John Maltby may have been a Burr, as we find the name Richard and Elizabeth Burr. John's son, Richard, may have been named for Richard Burr. This, of course, is only a theory.

II. Abstract of Will of RICHARD Maultbye, the elder,* of Kexbie. 10 Dec., 1602. My children's children. Son Christopher.† Richard Towne, junior. Elizabeth Smith. Mary Greathead. Daughters Ellen Quipp, Margaret Wilkinson. *Son John*, both my cottages in Springthorpe, paying to Christopher, my son, £10. My Lord Willoubie. Christopher, five acres in Bardicke Close. Son Richard to be exor. John Quipp, Richard Wilkinson, John Maultbie, Witnesses. Proved in Arch. Stow, ult., Dec., 1602, 256.

III. Abstract of Will of JOHN Maltby of Springthorpe, Co. Lincoln, yeoman. Dated 20 May. Eldest son, Richard, massuage I dwell in as I had it from my late father, Richard Maltbie, of Kexbie, but my wife, Margaret, shall occupy for ten years. Son

NOTE.—Richard Maltby was bapt. 24 Feb., 1592-3, at Springthorpe.

John, two cottage houses in Springthorpe, now in tenure of Thomas Ellis & Richard Tythwell & one oxgang* of land purchased of Richard Parker of Springthorpe. Son, William, one cottage in

NOTE.—John Maltby was probably quite a few years the junior of Richard, as there were several children that died (not mentioned, of course, in the will) whose births are recorded at Springthorpe, namely, Jane, b. 1594, d. 1594; Alice, b. 1598, d. 1609; Elizabeth, b. 1599-1600.

Springthorpe in tenure of Henry Parish & oxgang purchased of

NOTE.—William Maltby was bapt. in 1606.

Richard Parke. Eldest son, Richard, land called Fisher's Garth. Son Robert, £40, when 21. Son John, £15. Son William, £15.

NOTE.—Robert was bapt. in 1609.

* Richard Maltby, "the elder." This is a similar instance as "Robert Maltbye, Sen., and Robert Maltby, Jun.," in New Haven. Richard Maltby had a nephew, Richard, son of William, of Kexbie. (See Pedigree XV., Part I.)

† Here again we find the name Christopher being handed down.

Daughter Margaret, if she please my wife* and her uncles, Richard Maltbie of Kexbie, and Richard Bishop of Upton, in choice of her husabnd, £60. Daughter Ellen, £40, when 21. Daughter Marie, £40

NOTE.—Hellen Maltby, bapt. 1595.

when 21. Residue to Margaret, my wife & to be exex. John Quipp, John Farmery, Richard Neeson, Richard Wilkinson, Richard Bishop, Richard Maltby, Witnesses. Sons John and William under 21. Proved in Arch Stow, 25 June, 1610, by the exex. Bond of the exex. with Robert Bishop of Sterrton, Co. Notts., yeoman & Richard Bishop of Upton. Folio 55.

IV. Abstract of Will of JOHN Maltby of East Retford, Co. Nottingham, Alderman. Dated 6 Oct., 1647. Eldest son, John Maltby, houses in Briggate, E. Retford, Carr Lane, close in Little Gringley in Clarborough.* Second son, William,† my lands in Springthorpe and Little Corringham, Co. Lincoln. Eldest daughter, Jane Maltby, £100, under 21. Brother, Robert Maultby, of Bawtry. Younger daughter, Elizabeth Maltby, £100. Mrs. Anne Mason, godmother of Elizabeth. Child my wife is now with, £50. Wife, Mary, to hold my houses during the nonage of my sons, Jon and William to have the residue and to be exor. Sister, Ellin Chatterton, 10/—. Nephew, John Maltby, 10/—. Servant, Alice Moore, 20/—. Poor of Springthorpe, 20/—. Brother, Robert, friends, Nic Dickens, of Saundley, clk., and Beaumont Sutton of E. Retford, gent., to be overseers. Anne Stounton, Tho. Maulby,+ Wits. Codicil, 28 Dec., 1647. House in Briggate to be sold and £100 to son, John, at 21, and the residue for my youngest son lately born. Tho. Biggs, Tho. Maltby. P. C. Y., April, 1648. Filed Will.

NOTE.—From the East Retford baptisms we know that this son was Robert, bapt. 28 Dec., 1647. John Maltby also had a child, Richard, bapt. 15 Aug., 1642, d. 7 Aug., 1647. John Maltby d. "4 Jan., 1647-8, East Retford Burials."

The foregoing records show our claim to four generations of Maltby ancestors in England and brings us to the New World and the founding of new ties and homes. How the Maltbys were regarded by their neighbors and posterity may be best shown by quoting from various sources, viz.:

* As the term "oxgang" is old English, we insert Webster's definition of this word. "Oxgang (from ox and gang) old English laws. As much land as an ox can plow in a season; said to be 15 acres, or as others allege, 20 acres."

† John Maltby's wife, Margaret, was very evidently Margaret Bishop, a sister of Richard and Robert Bishop. John Maltby was buried at Springthorpe, 27 May, 1610.

The "Dwight Strong Genealogy," p. 354, states: "John Maltby, Sr., came with his brother, William, both of the rank of 'gentleman,' from Yorkshire, England, to New Haven, about 1670.

The New Haven Hist. Soc. Papers, Vol. III., p. 265 in "Baldwin's Brantford Annals," gives: "Among the men who came to Branford soon after the Newark exodus" (about 1666) "were Eleazer Stent, William Rosewell, William Maltbie and Samuel Pond. They became especially prominent," and on p. 270: "The Wilfords, Mautlbie, Barkers and Johnsons, that are leading names in Brantford at this time, were of the merchant class and apparently wealthy. They became large land holders.

"The society at Branford at this time must have been most select, comprising the governor and others named," etc. Also on page 300: "Large and most substantial houses were erected by the new settlers, some of whom were possessed of considerable property. This was especially true of the Bartholomews, Maltbies, Wilfords, Greys, Stents, Goulds, Bakers," (query, Barkers?) "Barnes and Blackstones. . . . The Hoadley, Maltbie, Rose, Foote and Harrison families present so many names that were prominently identified with the church, town and business during this period, time fails me to speak individually of them."

Rev. Jonathon (4) Maltby, b. in 1759, stated that William and John Maltby came from London, England.

"The History and Antiquities of New England, New York, New Jersey and Pennsylvania," by John Warner Barker, makes the following statement: "The New Haven Adventurers were the most opulent company which came to New England."

It will be observed that William Maltby is generally alluded to with a title of respect, such as "Mr." "Judge," "Esquire," etc.

A word as to the importance of these titles of respect and of their value in the early days will help us to appreciate just how much they meant in colonial days. We quote from a volume of New Haven records under "Preliminary Remarks,": "Mr. and Mrs. anciently indicated rank, and had no reference to condition. Mrs. was often applied to unmarried as to married females. Among the first settlers of New Haven, or any other town, scarcely half a dozen men were honored with the prefix Mr. The common prefix was Goodman and Goodwoman, contracted into Good'n and Good'y. Junior had no reference to father and son but meant simply younger. Marriages were anciently confirmed by magistrates and clergymen seldom performed the ceremony before the year 1700." Another reference to this same subject is from the "Tuttle Family Genealogy": "The title Hon. was entirely unknown in our records until

1685, and subsequently for many years was applied only to the governor, and seldom to him. The next title was that of Esqre., and

NOTE.—In 1703-4, a special court at New Haven gave a license to "ye worshipfull Mr. William Maltbie of Branford."

meant the same as in England, temp. Elizabeth and James I. Mr. Thomas Wells was magistrate for 17 years, deputy governor one year and was chosen governor the second time before he was distinguished with Esq. The next title was Gentleman, but seems to have been soon discarded in Connecticut. The prefix Master (Mr.)

NOTE.—Jonathon (2) Maltby's will calls himself "gentleman."

belonged to all gentlemen, including those designated by the higher modes of rank. Master corresponds very nearly to the English word gentleman. In Connecticut it embraced clergymen and planters of good family and estate who were members of the General Court, those bred at a university and those of sufficient education to manage the general affairs of the colony, civil or ecclesiastical, and who had been sufficiently well born. Comparatively few of the representatives of the town, even though they might be returned year after year, were honored with the title. To be called Mr. or to have one's name recorded by the secretary with that prefix 200 years ago was a more certain index of the rank of the individual as respects birth, education and good moral character than anyone of the high sounding titles with which men of no merit whatever, in our day of swift locomotion are content to cajole others in order that they may be enriched in their turn with the same spurious currency. It may be observed by reference to our colonial records that there were scores of men of good family and in honorable stations who still did not possess the requisite qualities of Master. It was seldom that young men of whatever rank were called Master. Sir was sometimes applied to young gentlemen undergraduates at a college. Mrs. was applied to the wives of Masters and also to unmarried females of the higher class."

"Military titles were considered of a very high order. Previous to 1654, the highest military officer in the colony was captain."—Hollister's Hist. of Conn.

Palfrey, in "Hist. of New England" says: "There was great punctiliousness in the application of both official and conventional titles. Only a small number of persons of the best condition (always including ministers and their wives) had Mr. or Mrs. prefixed to their names. . . . Wm. Bradford, though at the head of the Bridgewater, Mass., proprietor's, a son of the governor, and himself often lieutenant-governor, was not entitled to Mr."

In "Conn. Hist. Society Pub." Vol. III., p. 306, there is a sketch of Brandford; in it is the following item: "The principal gentlemen of this town were Mr. Topping, Esq., John Wilford, Wm. Maltbie, Esq., Edward Barker."

Rocky's "Hist. of New Haven Colony" gives: "Another settler of prominence was Wm. Maltby, who for a long time was one of the justices of the quorum and usually called Judge Maltby. Samuel (2) Maltby graduated from Yale and also became prominent in affairs. Most of this family removed."

In Dexter's "Biog. and Annals of Yale College" William Maltby is referred to as "Captain William Maltby." He may have had this rank, I do not know. Savage in his Gen. Dict. mentions him as "Cornet of New Haven troop," which is correct as will be shown in later records, and which follow chronologically arranged as far as was possible.

Ralph D. Smith in a letter dated "Guilford, Conn., 1866," says of William and John Maltby: "They belonged to the rank of gentleman, and were both engaged in commercial pursuits. John confined his business principally to the sea, William engaged both on the sea and the land."

Henry Rogers of New Haven, aged 84, wrote the compiler: "William Maltby was a justice of the quorum (or judge of the county court) at the time of his death, 1710, and had been for some twelve years before. He was a man of much influence in his day in Branford. . . . He was without question or doubt one of the men that were looked upon as the men that were qualified to be the leaders of the people in the government of the colony . . I noticed his stone at the Branford Cemetery—it looks well."

WILLIAM MALTBY, ESQ.

1644-45. Born. As we know from his tombstone at Branford.

1667. It is claimed that the first signature of William Maltby is to be seen on the Church Covenant at Branford in 1667. (Branford Town records, Vol. I., p. 319. Ecclesiastical Records, Vol. I., p. 17, State Library, Hartford.) This, I think, is a mistake. I have seen the Branford records and they are a bit confusing. William Maltby's signature seemed to me to be after the reorganization of the church and not before. Also from the deed of John Maltby, 1672, in which he calls William Maltbie "now residing in New Haven," it would appear that he was but lately come to New England.*

1672. March 29th. Deed of John Maltby to William Maltby. See under notes concerning John Maltby.

1672. May 1. "Mary, dau. of Mr. William Maltbye, b. at New Haven (p. 131, N. H. Records).

1673. Jan. 9. William, son of Mr. William Maltby. Recorded at Branford.

NOTE.—This is, of course, "old style." The year formerly commenced March 25th. During the period from 1685 to 1690, when efforts began to be made to change the time of the New Year from March 25, to Jan. 1; the time when such was effected was about the year 1750, all dates from Jan. 1, to March 25, were doubly designated. Consequently the above date should read 1673-4 and William would be twenty months the junior of Mary.

1673. April. William Maltby purchases his mansion house and land at Branford, witnessed by Robert Maltbye. (See record.)

1672. May 1.

1672. Sept. 18. "John Harrison sold to Wm. Maltby a black horse, marked," etc. (Branford Rec., Vol. I., p. 376).

1673. May 16. "The court accepts of the list of Troopers presented by Captayn John Nash, and Captayn Thomas Topping, for New Haven County, and doe confirm Captayn Topping to be Captayn and Mr. William Maltby to be Cornet," (i.e. lieutenant) "of the sayd Troope" (Colonial Records of Conn., 1665-1667, p. 199; M.S.S. Printed Records, Vol. 2, p. 199).

1673. June 2. New Haven Colony Rec., p. 83: "Know all men by these presences that I Garry Gratwick of Branford in the county of Newhaven doth alienate (?) and make over to George Page of the aforesaid towne and countye a parcell of land laying in Canon (?) brooke quarter, comonly so called being about nine acres more or less, bounded with Wm. Maltbye's land on the east side and on the west, withe the common on the north, with the River on the south, as also a parcell of meadow being about 2 acres more or less lying in Cannonbrook quarter, bounded with William Maltbye's byland (?) eastward, etc."

* A letter written by Ralph D. Smith, dated "1866" says apropos of this record: "Mr. Wm. Maltby's name appears among the last of the signers of the second Branford Church Covenant of 1667, made after the departure of Rev. Mr. Abraham Pierson and his company from Branford for Newark, N. J., and apparently Mr. Maltby signed it several years after it was originally drawn up, on his coming to Branford, which was certainly late in 1672 or early in 1673. . . . He was evidently a man of business and ability much above the ordinary and he assumed a prominent position among the people of Branford."

NOTE.—It would seem from this record that William Maltby's land must have been in the vicinity of the old burying ground, judging from the boundaries given in George Page's deed.

1673. April 16. Deed. Know all whom it may concern that I, Thomas Blatchley of Branford, in New England, husbandman, for and in consideration of the sum of one hundred pounds of lawful money of New England to me in hand, at and before the ensealing and delivery proof by William Maltbye, resident at New Haven, in New England aforesaid, merchant, well and truly paid the receipt whereof, I, the said Thomas Blachley do hereby acknowledge and myself to be therewith fully satisfied and thereof and of every part and parcel thereof, do clearly acquit and discharge the said William Maltbye, his executors and assigns, by these presents have granted alienated, bargained, sold, ensealed and confirmed and by these presents do grant, alienate, bargain, sell and enseal, confirm unto the said William Maltbye, his heirs and assigns all that my dwelling house, barns, orchards, garden, homestead, with all other buildings and fencings there upon and all singular ways waters, commodities, privileges and appurtenances whatsoever, to the same, doth or hereafter may belong or in any wise appertain with all my other rights and title to several parcels of land and meadow, viz:—Two acres be it more or less adjacent to Mulliners Neck, and my division therein, my land and meadow at the harbors mouth commonly called Scotch Cap, six acres be it more or less at the great plain, my piece of meadow at the point, one piece of upland lying against it containing by affirmation three acres be it more or less, one piece of upland lying on the other side of the river over against Mr. Wilford, his home lot containing by affirmation, three acres be it more or less. One acre of upland and one piece of meadow in the Indian Neck, one little piece of meadow in the corner of Nortons meadow, one piece of meadow in the mill quarter, with all the right of commonage and other divided and undivided lands that doth or hereafter may belong unto the said accommodations being situated and laying within the township and bounds of the town of Branford, in New England aforesaid, to have and to hold the aforesaid house, barns, lands and all and singular other the premises with the appurtenances unto the said William Maltbye, his heirs, executors and assigns forever to the only proper use and behoof of the said William Maltbye his heirs, executors and assigns forever, and I the said Thomas Blachley for myself, my heirs and executors and assigns, and every of them do covenant, grant and agree to and with the said William Maltbye his heirs, excutors and assigns by these presents in the manner following: that is to say, that the said William Maltbye his heirs and assigns shall or lawfully may from this time to time and at all times hereafter peaceably and quietly have, hold, occupy and possess and enjoy the aforesaid house, barns, lands and all and singular other, the premises with the appurtenances without any the lawsuit trouble coercion—ejection, interruption, denial claim or demand whatsoever of or by me the said Thomas Blachley my heirs, executors or assigns or any of them; freed and discharged or by me the said Thomas Blachley my heirs, executors and administrators well and sufficiently saved and kept harmless and indemnified of from and from all, and all manner of former and other bargains, sales and gifts, grants, mortgages, jointures, dowries, title of dower, wills, entails, titles, trouble charges and encumbrances whatsoever have made, committed, done or suffered or to be had made committed, done or suffered by me the said Thomas Blachley, my heirs, executors and assigns or any of them, or any other person or persons lawfully claiming or to claim from by or under me, them, or any of them or by or through mine, their or them or any of their act, means and faults, privilege—consent or procurement.

In witness whereof I have hereunto set my hand and seal this sixteenth day of April Anno Domini one thousand six hundred and seventy-three. 1673.

Signed, sealed and delivered in the presence of
James Bishop, Assistant.
Edward Barker,
Robert Maltbye. Thomas Blachley.

At a town meeting in the month of April, 1673, Susanna, the wife of Thomas Blachley, did freely give her consent to the above written act and deed of sale.

Recorded by me Eleazer Stent, Recorder.

1673. Oct. 20. A Branford record mentions "Wm. Maltbie's pasture" in locating boundary lines. (Branford Rec., Vol. I., p. 255). On page 313 of Vol. I., "Wm. Maltby" is admitted a planter, to possess the house and land which was Thomas Blachlyses's. (See deed witnessed by Robert Maltbye, 1673). On page 365 "William Maltby's mark for his cattell is a crop upon the top of both ears, and a slit in both the crops."

1673. Dec. 5. William Maltby "exchanges a gray horse with Samuel Ward." (Branford Rec. Vol. I., p. 376).

1673. Jan. 5. "Wm. Maltbye branded a brown bay mare colt with a T on the neer shoulder" (Branford Rec., Vol. I., p. 365).

1673-4. Jan. 6. "Wm. Maltby sold to Edward Barker the above horse" (Branford Rec., Vol. I., p. 376).

1674-5. Feb. 2. "William Maltbye branded a brown bay mare, coming two year old, with M. on the neere buttock, being formerly branded with a T. on the neer shoulder. The same day he branded a dusty black mare colt with T on neere buttock, and M. on ye neer shoulder; naturally marked with a brood star on forehead, above ye signe." (Bran. Rec., Vol. I., p. 368).

NOTE.—Possibly the "T" stood for Tottokel, the Indian name for Branford, the "M" was of course for Maltby.

1674. Branf. Rec., p. 144-147: "Wm. Maltbye was chosen constable."

1674-5. March 12. "Mr. Wm. Maltby and Eleazer Stent are chosen collectors." Under the same date mention is made of the location of his new fence, also some portion of his lands, in fixing boundaries (Branf. Rec., Vol. I., p. 177).

1676. April 30. Elizabeth, dau. of Mr. Wm. Maltby, b. at Branford.

1676. Dec. 8. Wm. Maltbye's land is mentioned in boundary lines. (Branf. Rec. Vol. I., pp. 121-123).

1676. Dec. 14. "He is twice appointed to lay out land (Branf. Rec., Vol. I., p. 109).

1676-77. Jan. 17. List of the children: "Mr. William Maltbye, 5 children." This record being old style, includes John, Jane, Mary, William and Elizabeth, the last named being b. April 30, 1676 (Branf. Rec., p. 118).

1676. A list of estates in 1676 gives Mr. Maltbye £103, 00s, 00d. There were thirty planters in the list. Mrs. Cushman writes that none of the estates in the list reached the sum of £200.

1676-7. March 19. William Maltby's name appears as witness of a sale (Branf. Rec., Vol. I., p. 412).

1677-8. Feb. 24. William Maltby was chosen town collector (Branf. Rec., Vol. I., p. 153).

1677. Dec. 21. He was "appointed to lay out land" (Branf. Rec., Vol. I., p. 127).

1678. June 4. "At a towne meeting, June 4, 1678, the towne have appointed Wm. Hoadley and Wm. Maltby to agree with Mr. Jno. Arnold to keep a scholl in ye towne, and they are to give what may be collected in ye towne, from those that have children, for the satisfaction of ye schoolmaster" (Branf. Rec., p. 121-13).

1678. Aug. 1. "The town appoint Wm. Maltbie and two others to give Mr. John Harrison* a call to settle as minister in Branford. (Branf. Rec., Vol. I., p. 131; also Branford Church Manual, p. 12).

1678-9. 25 Feby. Colony Records, p. 114: "At a towne meeting the towne have granted liberty to William Maltbie of Guilford to soujourn in Branford.

NOTE.—This record would indicate that William Maltby was first of Guilford.

1678. Feb. 25. He was "appointed to lay out land" (Bran. Rec., Vol. I., p. 163).

1678. March 8. Appointed with others "to proportion every man's land according to the agreement of 1676." Also as "collector of what shall be expended in laying out the township (Bran. Rec., Vol. I., p. 142. See also New Eng. Hist. and Gen. Reg., Vol. III., p. 154. History of setting off of Branford).

1678. July 8. Appointed with others to view land (Bran. Rec, Vol. I., p. 312).

1678. Dec. 4. His name appears as a witness (Bran. Rec., Vol. I., p. 159).

1679. May 19. Daniel, son of William Maltby was b. at Branford.

1679. Sept. 11. He was appointed one of the "listors" to make up the countey list (Bran. Rec., Vol. I., p. 111).

1679. Nov. 10. Samuel Martin of Wethersfield sold unto Mr. Wm. Maltby of Branford, a graystone horse about 16 years old marked with EO on ye neer shoulder (Bran. Rec., Vol. I., p. 376).

NOTE.—Here we have a mention of Wethersfield, the home of Hannah Hosmer Willard. (The question is, was he already married to her, or did he marry her later?)

* This name should, I feel sure, be Harriman and not Harrison as the copy sent me read. My own copy of this record reads: "Vol. I., p. 131. At a Towne meeting, 1 August, 1678. The towne have unanimously agreed to give Mr. John Harriman an invitation or call to come amongst us to carry on ye work of ye ministry in Branford and ye towne have appointed Captn. Topping, Thomas Harrison and William Maltbie or any two of them to acquaint Mr. Harriman what is ye desire of ye Towne & to treat with him for and on behalf of ye whole towne."

1679. Dec. 11. "William Maltbye was chosen constable for ye year ensueing (Bran. Rec., Vol. I., p. 144).

1679. Dec. 29. "Wm. Maltby" drew "No. 1, for a cow pasture" (Bran. Rec., Vol. I., p. 397). Also lot "No. 4" (Bran. Rec., Vol. I., p. 398).

1679-80. Feb. 13. "Wm. Maltby and John Frisbie are appointed auditors and collectors. He was also one of the committee to hire and pay a carpenter for building a barn for Mr. Mathers, at town expense (Bran. Rec., Vol. I., p. 146).

1680. Dec. 8. He was appointed to see that someone "performs his engagements" (Bran. Rec., Vol. I., p. 162).

1681. March 31. "Wm. Maltbye and others chosen to appoint what houses shall be fortified, when they judge there is occasion for it, and to appoint who shall belong to each house" (Bran. Rec., Vol. I., p. 308).

1681. May 30. Appointed to view two lots of land (Bran. Rec., Vol. I., p. 310).

1681. Sept. 7. New Haven Colony Records, p. 82: "At a towne meeting Septer ye 7, 1681, Mr. Barker, Mr. Maltbye and Thomas Harrison are apointed to sit in the 2ond seat in the meeting house upon Sabath dayes and other publique dayes and those three men are apointed to seat every man and woman in the towne; viz.: to apoint where they shall sit in the meeting house upon those days."

1681-2. Feb. 1. "Mr. Edward Barker, Mr. William Maltbye and Samuel Pond were chosen Townsmen for the year ensuing" (Bran. Rec., Vol. I., p. 92).

1681-2. Feb. 7. "The town have given William Maltbye a small parcell of land, about half an acre, joining to Georg page's house lot, and ranging with his fence. John Frisbie and George Page are appointed to lay it out" (Bran. Rec., Vol. I., p. 94).

1681-2. March 14. Appointed "to view the general fences;" also "to lay out land by George Page's (Bran. Rec., Vol. I., p. 104). On page 106, William Maltby gives his reasons for declining the office of fence viewer. On p. 99, There is a deed of Daniel Swaine which mentions land "Bounded with William Maltbye on ye southeast" and on page 101, a deed of Robert Foote's "with William Maltbye on the east."

1682. March 31. "Wm. Maltby and George Page; their choice of plowland is at the head of Brushy plain, on ye westward side of Connecticut path between the hill and a rundle of water, that runs into ye beaver swamp." Also: "choice of cow pasture" (Bran. Rec., Vol. I., p. 108).

1682. May 16. He was appointed with others "to act in the matter regarding Mr. Fordham of Long Island (Bran. Rec., Vol. I., p. 412).

1682. June 26. William Maltby purchases land from Nathaniel Foot (Bran. Rec., Vol. II., p. 2).

1682. "Mr. William Mawbley and Noah Rogers are presented for Freemen."

NOTE.—The following items from the Branford Records, Vol. II., are copied without date, but immediately follow the above record.

p. 36. "The town gives to Wm. Maltbie, 2 acres on the west side of the way that leads to his field."

p. 58. "A cow pasture is laid out for Wm. Maltbie at pipe staffe hill."

p. 62. The town gives him "3 or 4 acres, part rocky, adjoining his land."

p. 62. "He is chosen among three townsmen for the ensuing year.

p. 36. "Appointed with others to view a parcel of land.

1682. May. "He was proposed for Freeman and in October was admitted a freeman of the colony." (Ralph D. Smith).

1682. Branford Records, p. 106: "At a Towne meeting, March 27, 1682, George Tyler was chosen. Mr. Maltbye having given his reasons for his dissisting his work."

NOTE.—From 1672, when William Maltby's name first appears upon the Colony records, until the above date, March 27, 1682, the name of William Maltby appears upon the records every year. But from 1682 till 1685, I find no mention of it. Would the death of his first wife account for this? or is it possible that he returned to England during this period?

1685. Feb. 27. The will of Thomas Hosmer of Hartford, Conn., mentions his daughter, "Hannah Malby," and further on his "son-in-law, Malby."

1685. May 14. Mr. Wm. Maulby and Lieut. Eli Stint were elected deputies from Branford (Colonial Records of Conn., Vol. III., p. 168).

1686. Savage's Gen. Dict. calls Hannah Hosmer, widow of Josiah Williard, "wife of William Maltby in 1686."

1686. May 13. Re-elected deputy (p. 195).

1686. July 6. Elected Deputy to Special Court (p. 208).

1686. July 28. Member of General Court (p. 211).

1686. Oct. 14. Member of General Court (p. 214).

1686. Oct. 11. On the 11th of October, 1686, the town agreed to apply to the General Court at Hartford for permission to embody into a church estate, such as were suitable subjects.

Wm. Maltbye was chosen one of the delegates and his name is among those appended to the petition. Mrs. J. P. Cushman (who gathered together most of these Branford records) writes: "We saw the original paper, and the autograph of our ancestor, among the Ecclesiastical Records." (Vol. I., pp. 84, 85. See also Colonial Records, p. 216). This petition was granted. They had previously, April 12, 1686, given Mr. Samuel Russell, a son of Rev. John Russell of Hadley, Massachusetts, and a graduate of Harvard, an invitation to settle with them as their minister and he had given an answer in the affirmative on the 12th of September, 1687 (Branford Church Manual, p. 12. Also Gillette's Semi-Centennial, p. 10). "It was in the large south parlor of his dwelling that the convention of ministers met to found Yale College. He was one of the trustees. It was during his pastorate that the town divided into Old and North Branford, and after a time the latter set off a part of its people who formed a third society called Northford." (Gillett's Sermon, pp. 11-12).

The church records begin: "The afternamed embodied in the church Covenant, etc., etc." This is signed

Samuel Russell*	and women	Elizabeth Barker
Wm. Maltby		Hannah Maltby
Eleazar Stent		Sarai Blatchly
Samuel Pond		Miriam Pond
Jnot. Frisbie		Dorcas Taintor
Jno. Taintor		Eliz. Stent
Peter Tyler		Hannah Wheadon

These were the "seven pillars" mentioned by Gillett in his sermon, p. 10, and the same time adjoined:

Danll Swain	Eliz. Pamer
Aaron Blatchly	Hannah Frisbie
Thos Sargent	Deliver c Rose
Samll Betts	Mary Betts
	Ruth Frisby
	Sarai Page
	Sarah Gutsrel
	Jane Tyler

(Gillett's Sermon, p. 10. See also "Contributions to Ecclesiastical History of Connecticut, p. 354).

The first mention of James Bishop is in 1651. He died in 1691. The first mention of his wife, Mary ———(?) Bishop is in 1661. She died in 1664." (Ref. Approximate Catalogue of First Church in New Haven.)

The Branford Church records, March 7, 1687-8, has the following: "Imbodied in the Church Covenant."

Saml. Russell*	and women	Eliz. Barker
Wm. Maltby		Hannah Maltby
Eleazar Stone		Sarah Blac
John Frisbie		——— Pond
Saml. Pond		Dorcas Taintor
John Taintor		
Etc., etc.		

1686-7. Jan. 26. William Maltby was a Member of Special Court (p. 223).

1686-7. March 30. Member of Special Court (p. 227).

1687. March. (Branford Records, Vol. II., p. 36): "The town have given to Mr. Wm. Maltby two acres of land on the west side of the way that leads to his field against John Whitehead's land at Scotch Cap and have appointed Jno. Whitehead and Jhno. Rose to lay it out. . . . The town have appoyntd Mr. Maltbie, Ensign Harrison and Samuel Bradfield to view a parcell of land neer dod's swamp wh. William Hoadley desires the grain of and they are to make report thereof to the town."

William Maltbie, Commissioner and Justice of Peace, performed the following marriages: (New Haven Records).

Year	Page	Number
1692	98	2
1692	99	1
1698	115	1
1702	136	2
1706	144	2
		8

*Samuel Russell was the minister and in consequence had the first pew in the church. After the minister the people of the highest rank were seated. In connection with the church sittings we quote from "Historic Towns of New England," page 136, by George Dimmick Latimer. "On one side" (the church) "sat the men, on the other the women and small children, each in his proper place, determined by wealth or public office."

NOTE.—It was the custom in the early days for marriages to be performed by a Justice of the Peace.

"From this time (1687?) until 1689, I can find no mention of the name of William Maltby," writes Mrs. J. P. Cushman. "In that year it appears twice, May 9 and June 13, as one of the members of the General Court at Hartford." (Colonial Records of Connecticut, Vol. III., p. 195.)

EDITOR'S NOTE.—This fact suggests the thought that William Maltby was away from New England, as it hardly seems probable that a man so active in the public service would suddenly cease to serve his colony and as suddenly resume active public work. Very probably he visited England at this period.

1689-90. Hannah Maltbie and William Maltbie witness a deed of John Yale.

1689. May 26. In the 10 year of King William, Wm. Maltbie, with others, was commissioned Justice of the Peace, etc., by Gov. Winthrop (Records of New Haven County Court, Vol. II., p. 1).

1689. Aug. 29. "Special Court held at Hartford, Aug. 29. 1689. Deputy, Mr. Wm. Maltby, for Branford (Pub. Rec. of Conn., p. 2).

1689. Oct. 10. "A General Court at Hartford. Mr. Wm. Malby, for Branford, Deputy (P. R. of Conn., p. 3).

1690. April 11. "General Court at Hartford. Mr. Wm. Malby, for Branford (P. R. of Conn., p. 15).

1690. May 8. General Court at Hartford. Mr. Wm. Maltby, for Branford (P. R. of Conn., p. 23).

1691. May 14. Court of Election at Hartford. Mr. Wm. Maltby, for Branford (P. R. of Conn., p. 42).

1691. July 9. Special Court at Hartford. Mr. Wm. Maltby, for Branford (P. R. of Conn., p. 54).

1691. October 8. General Court at Hartford. Mr. Wm. Maltby, for Branford (P. R. of Conn., p. 55).

1692. Nov. 25. "The estate of George Page and the estate of Samuel Ward were laid out for Wm. Maltbie" (Branf. Rec., Vol. II., p. 142). "265 acres."

1690. p. 35. "Mr. Wm. Maltby is confirmed Ensigne of Brandford train band, and is to be commissionated accordingly."

1690. April (p. 18). "This Court have upon the desire of Branford, chose Mr. Malbey and Lnt. Stent to be commissionrs for Branford, and they were sworn accordingly."

1690. May (p. 24). "These were made Comrs for the year ensuing, for Branford, Stent and Mr. Maltby."

1691. May (p. 43). "The Court appoynted these for Commissioners in the severall plantations, Mr. Wm. Maltby and Lnt. Eben. Stent for Branford."

1693. May (p. 92). "These were chosen Commissioners for the year ensuing, Mr. Wm. Maultbey and Lnt. Ebenezer Stent, for Branford."

NOTE.—The list of estates for the colony on 6 Oct., 1691, are 321 persons, £15,622, 00s, 00d. "This Court appoynt Captn Niccols, Mr. Maltby, Mr. Eliphalet Hill and Mr. John Chapman to be a committe to perfect the sayd lists that are imperfect and to return them to the Court."

1693. Aug. 7. Samuel, son of Mr. Wm. Maltby, b. at Branford.

1693. Oct. 12. General Court at Hartford, Mr. Wm. Maltby, for Branford (P. R. of Conn., p. 105).

1694. May 10. Court of Election at Hartford, Mr. Wm. Maltby, for Branford (P. R. of Conn., p. 120).

1694. May. "These Commissioners were chosen for the year ensuing, Lnt. Eben. Stent and Mr. Wm. Maltbey, for Branford (p. 121).

1695. Oct. 10. General Court at Hartford, Mr. Wm. Maltby, for Branford (P. R. of Conn., p. 149).

1696. May 14. General Court at Hartford, Mr. Malbie, for Branford (P. R. of Conn., p. 158).

1696 Oct. 8. General Court, Mr. William Malbie, for Brandford (P. R. of Conn., p. 174).

1697. May 13. Commissioners for Branford: Mr. Will Malbie, Capt. Eleazer Stent (P. R. of Conn., I. 197).

1697. Oct. 14. General Assembly, William Malbie, for Branford (P. R. of Conn., p. 221).

1697-8. Jan. 22. General Court, Mr. Will Malbury, for Branford (P. R. of Conn., p. 235).

1697-8. March 14. Elizabeth (2) Maltby was m. by her father to Abraham Hoadley.

1698. May. Justice appointed for the Countie of Newhaven, Mr. Will Malbie, of the Quorum (p. 260).

1698. May 12. Court of Election, Mr. William Malbie, for Branford (P. R. of Conn., p. 244).

1697. Oct. 16. "In answer to the petition of Mr. Samll Haise (?) this Court doth desire and appoint Majr Moses Mansfield, Majr James Fitch, Mr. Will Malbie, Mr. Josiah Rossiter and Captn Thomas Clerk, they or the majr part of them, to be a committee to indevour (?) an accomodation and agreement between the towns of Fairfield and Norwalk, concerning their dividing line, and others maters of controversie, with reference to propertie of lands, etc."

1698. May (p. 253). "This Court made choice of Capt. Samml Mason, Mr. William Pitkin, Mr. John Chester, Mr. John Woolcutt, Mr. Will Malbie, to frame such bills as they shall judge needful, either for emendation of laws formerly made; or for making other laws that are now wanting in the government and to exhibit the same in Court."

1698. Deputy Surveyor and receiver of Excise Custom Master.

1698. Jonathon, son of William Maltby, was born.

1698. July 5. "Wm. Maltbie of Branford was commissioned Deputy Surveyor and receiver of excise for the County of New Haven, with others; also to treat with Mr. Rich and Rosewell, etc." (Records of New Haven County Court, Vol. I., p. 264).

1698. Aug. 2. "Appointed Custom Master for New Haven County" (New Haven Colonial Records, Vol. I., p. 265). He brings suit against Frederick Platts "for retailing Rhum"; he gained the case and received one half of the fine, which was 40 shillings (Vol. I., p. 264, New Haven Colonial Records).

1698. Nov. 21. Appointed with four others, Justice of the Quorum for Court of Probate (N. H. Col. Rec., Vol. II., p. 2).

1699. May 11. General Assembly, Mr. Will Malbye, for Branford (P. R. of Conn., p. 283).

1699. Oct. 12. General Assembly, Mr. Will Malbye, for Branford (P. R. of Conn., p. 296).

1699. Nov. 13. "Liberty is given Mr. Wm. Maltbie of Branford to retail strong drink out of his house, he having obtained ye consent of ye town" (New Haven Colonial Rec., Vol. II., p. 20).

1699-1700. Feb. 28. Samuel Russell deeds a piece of land to Wm. Malthie (Bran. Rec., Vol. II., p. 129).

1699-1700. March 15. "I, John Maltbie of Saybrook, sell to my honored father, Wm. Malthie, of Branford, for the sum of £8. a piece of land, etc. Acknowledged before Wm. Maltbie, Justice of Peace" (New Haven County Court Records, Vol. II., p. 3).

1700. Oct. 10. "General assembly, Mr. Will Malbye, for Branford" (P. R. of Conn., p. 327).

1700. Oct. 18. "Appointed with others, Justice of Quorum for Court of Probate."

1700-1701. William Maltby lost his son, Captain William (2) Maltbie of New Haven. The following record which was accepted at the New Haven County Court, Jan. 26, 1712-13, must refer to a transaction as far back as 1700:

"To all Christian persons to whom this present act and deed shall come, know ye, etc., etc. I, William Maltbie of Branford, Esq., in the Colony of Connecticut, in New England sendeth greeting. Know ye that I, the sd William Maltbie, for and in consideration of a valuable sum in hand, already paid by Jonathon Atwater of New Haven, in New England aforesd, for and towards the building, fitting, apparrelling and completing the good Brigantine, called the Friends Adventure, now riding at anchor in the harbor of sd. New Haven—burthen about sixty-eight tons."* (He sells one-eighth of everything about her.) "Myself the present owner, etc." (New Haven County Court Records, Vol. II., p. 586).

To Ebenezcor Atwater, ¼ part owner. (p. 587.)
To Moses Mansfield 1/6 part owner. (p. 588.)
These three signed in the presence of Jonathon Maltbie and William Maltbie, Jr.

8 Dec., 1699 WILLIAM MALTBIE.
Wm. Maltbie
Stephen Whitehead

To Ebenezer Atwater, ¼ part. Deed witnessed by Wm. Maltbie, Jr., and Jonathon Atwater.

To Moses Mansfield, 1/16 part. (Note.—Not 1/6 as above.) Same witnesses as above.

To Samuel Mansfield, ⅛ part. Same witnesses.

William Maltby's son, William, was captain of this brigantine, "Friends Adventure," as we learn from a New Haven Record, Vol. II., p. 52, under date "3 Dec., 1700. William Maltbie of New Haven, master of ye Brigantine ffriends Adventure." It was shortly after this that William Maltby, junior, lost his life in the West Indies.

Rev. Jonathon (4), in a paper written in 1848, says: "In the inventory of Wm. Maltby are quite a number of vessels.* Bran-

* Rev. Jonathon Maltby very evidently had seen some inventory unknown to us. It may be that it would be amongst the Custom House records of New Haven. Another descendant of the earlier generations wrote: "Our emigrant ancestor owned three vessels, all of them full of cargo at the same time in New Haven harbor." The exact quotation is mislaid, but if memory is not at fault, it came from a grandchild of Samuel (2) Maltby. Addenda. This statement reads: "One of the Maltbys owned three ships with cargoes afloat at the same time."—Selina (6) Maltby, John (5).

* A further search of this record reads, after the word "tons": "have given, granted, bargained, sold, convey, confirmed and firmly made over unto him the said Jonathon Atwater one whole eighth of the Hull or body of the sd Brigantine together with one eighth of ye masts, yards, boom bolt, spret, hatches, scuttles, grateings, boat oars, sails, anchors, ropes, cables, cordage, stores and all other appurtenances to the same belonging."

ford in those days was a thriving seaport, more business was done in Branford said Captain Parish,† an old gentleman, than in New Haven. The merchants, he said, purchased their West India goods in Branford. The farmers in Northford carried all there. It was the market for their wheat, rye, corn, flax, flaxseed, staves, hoops, etc. Flax and flaxseed was a great article. Capt. Josiah Fowler and Jonathon Fowler, Benjamin Maltby (3) and others raised abundance for the market. In my boyhood I went with my father (Benjamin) (3), grandson of the emigrant, William (1) Maltby, when he carried his effects and was well pleased to see the vessels."

1701. May 8. Court of Election, Mr. William Maltbie, for Branford (P. R. of Conn., p. 342).

1701. "May. Justice of the Peace and Quorum appointed for Newhaven Countie, Mr. William Malbie" (p. 347).

1701. April 30. (Vol. II., p. 65): "Att a Court of Probate, held at New Haven, Present William Maltbie, Jeremiah Osborne, John Alling, Esqrs., Justices Quorum."

1701. May 26. (Vol. II., p. 142). "A Town Meeting in Branford. The town have chosen & appointed Mr. Wm. Maltbie, Sergtnt Nath'l Foot and Edward Barker, Jr., a committee to provide a stock of powder and lead for the town as the law requires and the town do engage to repay them what they shall expend the next winter either in money or provisions at money price."

1701. Oct. 9. General Assembly at New Haven, Mr. Willa Malbie, for Branford (P. R. of Conn., p. 358).

1702. May 14. General Assembly at Hartford, Mr. William Malbie, for Branford (P. R. of Conn., p. 372).

1702. May. Justice of Peace & Quorum, Mr. William Malbie (p. 378).

1702. May (p. 390): "This Assembly grants liberty to Mr. William Malbie to buy four acres of land (and no more) of Jeofferie, an Indian belonging to Branford, which four acres of land is within Branford common field at a place called Indian Neck."

1702. 24 June. Deed of Jeofry, the Indian, to Mr. William Maltby.

Branford Deeds, Vol. II., p. 161:

Know all men by these presents, that we, Jeofry, the father,

† "Captain Parish." Abigail (3) Maltby, daughter of Daniel (2), married for her second husband, Ephraim Parish. This "old gentleman, Capt. Parish, may possibly have been her husband. Abigail Maltby was an aunt of Rev. Jonathon (4).

and John, (so-called by the English) the son, both Indians belonging to the town of Branford, in the County of New Haven, in the Conty of Connecticut, being rightful proprietors of lands lying at a place commonly called and known by the name of Indian Neck, within the township of Branford, upon good consideration and for a valuable sum of money, in hand, payed before the ensealing and delivering hereof, have sold, alianated, enseased, confirmed and made over, and do by these presents, sell, Alianate, Ensease, confir and make over to William Maltbie of the aforementioned Branford, one part or parcell of land, lying and being upon the aforesaid Indian Neck, which parcell of land is four acres and is bounded, southerly by the sea, northerly by a highway and westerly by Richard . . . land easterly by our own land, and the four acres of land with all profits and privileges thereon or in any way appertaining, we do own to have sold to the aforementioned William Malthie, to his heirs and assigns, to have and to hold, use, occupy and enjoy from the day of the date of these presents, forever without any let, suit, disturbance, molestation, eviction or ejection, from by or under us, our heirs, executors, administrators or assigns, or by any of us, or by any person or persons lawfully claiming the same by virtue of any right or title derived from us or any of us, or from any Indian or Indians whatsoever, hereby declaring that we have good and lawful right thereunto, and that it is at the ensealing and delivery hereof, free and clear of and from all manner of gifts, grants, sales, mortgages, dowryes, entails, or any manner of entanglement or incumbrance and do for ourselves and successors, hereby engage to warrant and defend the above named William Maltbie, him, his heirs or assigns in his or their peacable possession, set our hands and affix our seals, this four and twentieth day of June, Annoque Domini, one thousand, seven hundred and two, in the first year of the reign of our Sovereign Lady Anne, by the Grace of God of England, Scotland, ffrance, Ireland, Queen Defender of the Faith, etc.

The mark of (+) Jeofry.

The mark of (+) John.

Signed, sealed and delivered
in the presence of
Francis Tyler
Benjamin Harrington

1702. General Assembly at New Haven, Mr. Will Malbie, for Branford (P. R. of Conn., p. 395).

1703. May 13. Court of Election, Hartford, Mr. Will Malbie, for Branford (P. C. of Conn., p. 407).

1703. May Justice of the Peace and Quorum, William Malbie, Esq. (p. 414).

1703. Nov. 7. Letter to Governor Treat, Milford, from Josiah Rosseter, John Alling, Wm. Maltbie and Jer. Osborn.

1702. Oct. 10. A New Haven Court Record, Vol. II., p. 89, gives: "At a Court of Probate, held in New Haven, October, ye 10th day, 1702, Esquire Judge William Maltbie."

p. 162-3. "The Winthrop Papers," 1703. A letter for the Hounrble Robert Treat, D. Governor att his house in Milford, humbly these

N. Hav. Nov. 7, 1703.

Hournble Sr—After our condolence with yor Honr in ye great breach lately made in yor family, these upon, yor Hounrs commands come to offer our opinion in ye case proposed, viz.: that it being manifestly too late to send for Engld for ye divertion of dangers from the present sessions of Parliam't, there seems to be no occation for a General Court as yett; but it may be a good service for ye Colony if the Governrs Hounr with advice of his Council would hasten letters to Sr Henery, requesting a speedy and full account of our affairs, what probabilities there are ye design against ye forreign corporations will be reviv'd and take effect in Parliament, what reasons he can offer for sending an agent, whether that charg be att all likely to do us any service, whether he with the councel he retains may not be capable of serving our interest as well without as with an agent from home?

It seems to us that if we must fall because we are a corporation, no trouble or charge we put orselves upon can save us; if we must fall because criminal, or crimes will doubtless in form of law be laid before us before we be condemned. There may be time enuf to send an agent if there needs. However, if Sr Henery can shew sufficient business for an agent to be sent, next May Court may hasten one unto him.

We have also thought if the Hounble Governr & Council would draw an address to ye Queen's Majestie, therein plainly representing the true state and interest of this Colony how much our fathrs and we have confided in royal grace for the continuance of our privileges, expended both estate, labr and much bloud in settling, subduing and defending this Colony, how low and poor we yett are, having no forreign trade, & how disheartened our people very generally will be if they must loos their present Charter priveledges, whereupon great numbers will doubtless choos to settle in some better climate & safer country, & so the Queen's interest in ye Colony will be left more exposed to dangers and charges; how little chargable we have been to ye Crown, & how careful not to wrong its interests we have been; if these and what else may be proper were putt into a memorial with a suitable address & lodged in our agents hands with instructions under necessary conection to present ye same to her Majestie when yr should be occation, it might perhaps prevent her giving such an act the royal assent, unless harmless Connecticut be exempted. However, this done, what can we do more but commit our cause to Him that is able to deliver us? Indeed, if we should understand we are neer our end, it doubtless would be very requisite to call a General Court, better to secure our titles to land, or town patents being insufficient to settle or 8 counties & to order some other things of great consequence befr we die. These (with our humble service offered to yor Hounr) are submitted to yor correction by yor humble servants.

JOSIAH ROSSETER.
JOHN ALLING.
WM. MALTBIE.
JER. OSBORN.

1703-4. Jan. 4. "At a special court held at New Haven, Lycence is granted by this Court to ye worshipfull Mr. William Maltbie of Branford, to retail strong drink in small parts.

JEREMIAH OSBORNE, Esq., Judge.
WM. MALTBIE,
JOHN ALLING,
ELEAZER STENT,
Esqrs., Justices of the Quorum.

(New Haven County Court Records, Vol. II., p. 147.)

1704. May. Justice of Peace & Quorum, William Malbie (p. 467).

1705. May. Justice of Peace & Quorum, Mr. William Malbie (p. 468).

1705. May 10. General Assembly, Hartford, Mr. William Malbie, for Branford (P. R. of Conn., p. 499).

1705. Oct. 11. Act passed at General Assembly at Hartford, Mr. Will Malbye, for Branford (P. R. of Conn., p. 521).

1706. May. Justice of Peace & Quorum, Mr. William Malbie (p. 532).

1706. May 9. At General Assembly, Hartford, "Mr. William

Malbie (and others) are by this Assembly appointed to be Justices of the Peace and Quorum in the Countie of New Haven.

1706. March 27. Agreement between Wm. Maltbie, Nathaniel Johnson, Nathaniel Payne and Daniel Payne for division of land (Bran. Rec., Vol. II., p. 271).

1706. Aug. 23. E. Haven Reg., p. 30: Branford, 23 Aug., 1706, Wm. Maltbie, Clerk.

1707. May 12. Derby Records, p. 432: May the 12, 1707, Wm. Maltbie, Jus. Pece.

1708. April 2. Land laid out for Wm. Maltbie, among others, the fifth allotment, fourth division (Bran. Rec., Vol. II., p. 333).

1709-10. Jan. 16. Agreement to draw for lots in 5th allotment, 4th division, Wm. Maltbie, Nathaniel Johnson, Samuel Payne (Bran. Rec., Vol. II., p. 337).

1709-10. March 16. At a meeting of the Proprietors of the town Mr. Wm. Maltbie and Mr. Nathaniel Johnson were voted leave to take ten acres of land for the Payne children (Bran. Rec., Vol. III., p. 9).

(No date). Vol. III., p. 8: "Granted to Mr. Wm. Maltbie 2 acres of land, which had failed to be entered and recorded previously."

1710. Sept. 1. DIED. "William Maltbei, Esq." See Tombstone.

The following is an abbreviated table of some of the more important events in the life of our emigrant ancestor:

WILLIAM MALTBY, ESQ.

1645. Born.

1672-3. Moved from New Haven to Branford.

1673. Cornet of New Haven County Troopers. (N. B. or lieutenant.)

1674. Constable.

1674. Collector.

1676. Appointed twice to lay out land.

1677-8. Town collector.

1677-8. To lay out land.

1678. To lay out land.

1678. To view land.

1679. A Listor.

1679. Constable.

1679-80. Auditor and Collector.

1681-82. To view the general fences.
1680. Constable.
1681. Towns man and to fortify the houses.
1681. To view the lands.
1681. To seat the people at church.
1681-2. Townsman.
1682. Made a Freeman of Connecticut Colony.
1685. Deputy or Representative.
1686. Deputy or Representative.
1687. Deputy or Representative.
1689. Deputy or Representative.
1690. Deputy or Representative.
1691. Deputy or Representative.
1693. Deputy or Representative.
1694. Deputy or Representative.
1695. Deputy or Representative.
1696. Deputy or Representative.
1697. Deputy or Representative.
1698. Deputy or Representative.
1699. Deputy or Representative.
1700. Deputy or Representative.
1701. Deputy or Representative.
1702. Deputy or Representative.
1703. Deputy or Representative.
1705. Deputy or Representative.
1706. Deputy or Representative.
1687. Commissioner.
1688. Commissioner.
1690. Commissioner.
1691. Commissioner.
1693. Commissioner.
1694. Commissioner.
1697. Commissioner.
1689. Justice of Peace.
1698. Justice of Peace.
1701. Justice of Peace.
1702. Justice of Peace.
1703. Justice of Peace.
1704. Justice of Peace.
1705. Justice of Peace.
1706. Justice of Peace.
1710. William Maltby, Esq., died.

The following is the will of William Maltby, Esq., of Branford:

I, William Maltby, of Branford, Esq., being this 28th day of August, Anno Dom 1710 in ye ninth year of her majts reign sick and weak in body but through the mercy of God of composed mind and sound memory do make and ordain this my last will and testament in manner and forme following:

Imprnuis I give and bequeath to my soul unto God that gave it and my body to a decent buriall at the discretion of my Executors hereafter named, hopeing only in the merits of Jesus Christ for the pardon of my sins and an interest in the ressurection of the just.

And as for the dispose of that temporal estate which God of his bounty and goodness hath given to me, I give and dispose the same as followeth:

First, I give and bequeath unto my oldest sonn, John Maltby, all that house and land which I bought for him at Saybrook being all the lands I have there with the appurtenentes thereof, of which sd house and land my sd sonn now stands seized and possessed. Also I give and bequeath unto him my sd Sonn John Maltby my allottment of land which I bought of Capt. Meeriman and Thomas Hall in quantity about one hundred acres lying between the bounds of Wallingford and Middletown and an equall share with the rest of my children in my commons and undivided lands within the town of Branford to be to him his heirs and assignes forever together with the severall particulars of personal estate which are mentioned particularly in my book of accounts.

It I give and bequeath unto my Grandson, William Maltby, son and heir of my son, William Maltby, deceased, the sum due to me on ballance of accounts between me and my son, William Maltby, deceased, as it stand in my account book provided my daughter in law, Elizabeth Maltby, nor my sd Grandchild gives any trouble to my Executors or to any other children or heirs of mine respecting accounts depending between me and my sd son, Wm. Maltby, deceased, but if they or either of them gives trouble respecting any accounts or dealings between myself and my sd son that then the sd summe due to ballance yd account between me and my sd sonn shall be paid to my Executors. Also I give and confirm unto my sd Grandson, William Maltby, sixty four acres of land at that place called Tibbs hill in the third division in Branford aforesd with the addition northward adjoining those unto which sd parcell of land with the appurtenances thereof I give unto him my said Grandson his heirs and assigns forever. It I give unto him a horse, colt & a mare colt of two years old to be paid by my Executors.

Item. I give and bequeath unto my loving son, Daniel Maltby, all that house and land that he now stands in possession of in the town of Branford, the homlott being in quantity ten acres be it more or less as also all my land at Mulliners neck and my divition there also. I further give my sd son Daniel all my land on brushy plaine containing thirteen acres be it more or less all which land & appurtenances my will is shall be & remain to him his heirs & assigns forever.

I give and bequeath unto my loving son, Samuel Maltby, my orchard that lieth eastward of my now dwelling house in Branford from the street to the salt meadow to be to him his heirs and assigns forever.

Item I give and bequeath unto my loving son, Jonathon Maltby, my mansion house I now dwell in within the precinct of Branford aforesd with the homlott of land thereto adjoining and belonging together with all housing, buildings, edifices and appurtenances thereunto belonging the before mentioned given to my son, Samuell on the eastward side of it only excepted to be and belong to him his heirs and assigns forever.

Item I give and bequeath all my other lands arrable pasture or meadows not heretofore disposed of by me or devised in this my last will & testament within the precinct of Branford or elsewhere as the same shall appear on record to be equally divided to & between my sonns, Samuel Maltby and Jonathon Maltby and to be and belong to them and their or each of their heirs and assigns forever.

Item I give unto my daughter, Jane Parker, the bed, bedstead hangings and furniture thereof in my hall which wer her mother's.

Item I give and bequeath to my aforesd sonns, John Maltby and Daniel Maltby, the remainder of my fourth division lott beyond Tibbs Hill part of it being sold to Capt. Fowler to be equally divided between them.

Item My will is yt my right of commonage and undivided land within the town of Branford be and shall be equally divided to and among all my children.

Item I give to my daughter, Elizabeth Hoadley my cupboard with four drawers and long table.

Item My will is that if either or both of my sonns, Samuel Maltby or Jonathan Maltby should dye before they arrive to lawful age, to receive their portions given to them that then the part of them or either of them above devised shall be and belong in equall parts to the rest of my surviving children.

Lastly my will is and I do hereby nominate and appoint my dear and loving wife, Abigail Maltby, and my sonn, Samuel Maltby, to be joynt Executors of this my last will and testament and I give unto my sd dear wife the improvement of one third part of my reall estate during her natural life, desiring her to take care to see my just debts duely paid and I also desire my loving brother, Mr. Samuell Bishop, to be overseer and give assistance in the execution of this my last will and testament and do revoke all other wills heretofore by me made.

In witness whereof I have hereunto set my hand and seal in Branford this twenty ninth day of August, Anno Domini 1710, in the ninth year of her majistys reigne.

I the sd Wm. Maltby do also bequeath five pounds to my son, John Maltby's, eldest sonne and five pounds to each of the rest of my eldest grandson now living to be paid at money value by my Executors and also five shillings apiece to each of my grandchildren.

WM. MALTBY. [SEAL].

Signed, sealed and published as the last will and testament by the subscriber in the presence of us

Jeremiah Osborne.
Samuell Pond.
Uzall Wardell.
her
Mirian W. Pond.
mark

Appeared the witnesses to the last will and testament of Wm. Maltby, Esqr., late of Branford, deceased, and made oath that they saw the sd Wm. Maltby Esqr., sign, seal and publish yd will as his last will and testament and that he was of sound mind and understanding when he so did according to the best of their judgment, whereupon the Court accept and allow of said will and order it be entered on record.

Test

JOHN WINSTON, *Clerk.*

STATE OF CONNECTICUT.
County of New Haven.
ss.

I, Timothy F. Callahan, Clerk of the Court of Probate within and for the District of New Haven, in said County of New Haven, and keeper of the Records and Seal thereof, hereby certify that I have examined the within and foregoing copy of the Record of the last will and testament of William Maltby, Esq., late of Branford, formerly in the Probate District of New Haven, deceased, and the the decree of this court approving and allowing the same, and have compared all of the foregoing with the original Record thereof now remaining in this office, and have found the same to be a correct transcript therefrom and of the whole of said original Record.

In Testimony whereof, I have hereunto set my hand affixed the Seal of said Court, on this 14th day
[SEAL] of September, A. D. 1894.

Timothy F. Callahan, *Clerk.*

STATE OF CONNECTICUT,
County of New Haven,
ss.

I, A. Heaton Robertson, sole and presiding Judge of the Court of Probate within and for the District of New Haven, in said County of New Haven, hereby certify that Timothy F. Callahan, whose name is above written and subscribed, is, and was at the date thereof Clerk of the Court of Probate, within and for the District of New Haven, in said New Haven County, and keeper of the Records and Seal thereof, duly commissioned and sworn, that I am well acquainted with his signature, and know the above to be his, and that the above Certificate by him made is in due form to authenticate the records, files and proceedings of said Court.

In Testimony whereof, I have hereunto set my hand this 14th day of September, A. D. 1894.

A. Heaton Robertson, *Judge.*

STATE OF CONNECTICUT,
County of New Haven,
ss.

I, Timothy F. Callahan, Clerk of the Court of Probate, within and for the District of New Haven, in said County of New Haven, hereby certify that A. Heaton Robertson, whose name is within written and subscribed, is, and was at the date thereof, sole and presiding Judge of the Court of Probate within and for the District of New Haven, in said New Haven County, duly commissioned and sworn; that I am well acquainted with his signature, and know the above to be his.

IN TESTIMONY WHEREOF, I have hereunto set my hand and affixed the Seal of said Court, on this 14th day of September, A. D. 1894.

[SEAL]

TIMOTHY F. CALLAHAN, *Clerk.*

The Inventory of the Estate of William Maltby, Esq., of Branford, will be found of much interest to all descendants. That there was another inventory of his ships we can not but believe, as Rev. Jonathon (4) Maltby states: "in his inventory are quite a number of vessels."

An Inventory of the estate of William Maltby, Esq., late of Branford, deceased, taken and appraised by us whose names are underwritten, this 2d day of Novem, 1710.

	£	s	d
Jenyk Emis—His arms & ammunition	4	8	4
Wearing apparel—woolen & linen	23	4	6
2 yk of oxen, £13, 10s; 7 cows, £16	29	10	
5 yearlings, £6; 2 calves, £1, 2s; 3 yr olds, £4	11		
5 grown swine, £4; nine smule swine, £3, 3s	7	3	
A black horse, £4; a mare & colt, £2, 15s	6	15	
A black mare, £2; a bull, £2, 5s	4	5	
House, barne and other buildings with ye part of the homsestead on which the said buildings stand	215		
The home lot east of the house	35		
15 acres of plow land at Scotch Cap	45		
About 8 acres of salt meadow at the same place	32		
About 12 acres of rough land at Scotch Cap	6	12	
9 acres of land at Great plaine	36		
5 acres of land at Indian Neck	20		
3½ acres of land at point lotte	7		
2 acres of meadow at Indian Neck	9		
¾ acre of meadow	3		
3 acres of Salt Meadow at Peters bridg	13	10	
A small parcell of fresh meadow	1		
1 acre of Salt Meadow in the mill quarter	5		
24 acres of Cow pasture	48		
Wheat in the straws, £2, 2s; rye in the straw, £1, 8s	3	10	
Oates, £1, 10s; Peas, £3, 10s; Ind. Corn, £4, 10s	9	10	
Winter Corn upon ye ground	13	8	8
Flax, undressed, £1, 10s; 19 loads of Hay, £11, 10s	13		
100 acres of land lying between the bounds of Wallingford and Middletowne	50		

	£	s	d
70 acres of land at Sea Hill	35		
About 100 acres of land at Sibbes	100		
8 acres of land Cravery Swamp	8		
A negro man, £45; a negro woman, £30	75		
A bed boulster, fringe, covering, curtains, Valany, bedstead & cord	8		
A cupboard with drawers, £2, 5s; another cubpoard £4	6	5	
A great table, 12s; six leather chairs, 24s	1	16	
Six other chairs, £1, 4s; 2 chairs, 8s	1	12	
2 pictures, 10s; a greate looking glass, £1 . . .	1	10	
	889	0	6
6 Sheepskins, 6s; 3 Rakes, 1s, 6d		7	6
A Mill, £1; horse Gears, 5s	1	5	
A Cart & irons belonging to it	1	16	
116 pounds Iron	1	18	
Casks and Cyder, £13, 3s; More old Casks, 8s, 6d .	13	11	6
A cask of Rum, £8, 3s, 6d; Whalebone & tunell, 2s, 8d	8	6	2
An ax, 1s; Old Tubs, 5s; a lump old iron, 5s . .		11	
A Table Cloth, 1s, 6d; Napkins, 6s; Table Cloth, 11s		18	6
Cotton Napkins, 7s, 6d; More Napkins, £1, 9s, 6d .	1	17	
Towels, 5s; Pillow Coats, 4s; Sheets, £2, 7s . . .	2	16	
4 yds Speckled Linnen, 10s, 2d; more fine linen £3, 13s	4	3	2
A Shirt, 4s; Woollen cloth, 7s; more linnen, £1, 2s, 6d	1	13	6
Kentmes 6s; Mosless, £1, 7s; Cotton Cloth, 2s; Silk, £1	2	15	
Mohair, 10s; Fine thred, 5s; a great bible, £3 . . .	3	15	
More Books, £1, 10s; papor, £13; a chest with drawers, £3	5	3	
Another chest, 4s; a little trunk, 8s; a desk, 4s . .		16	
White Sugar, 2s, 6d; more sugar, 9s; Stone jugs and other things, £1	1	11	6
A wheels, 10s; yoke and chains, £1, 6s	1	16	
A pair of andirons, 13s, 4d; 2 pr Tongs, 4s . . .		17	4
A fire shovel, 6s; a gridiron, 3s; a bransell, 4s . .		13	
A toasting iron, 1s, 8d; Candelstick, 7s, 6d; pr shears, 1s 6d		10	8
An hour glass, 1s; Chairs, 16s; Table, 5s; Salt box, 1s	1	3	
A Lanthorne, 1s, 6d; a sadle & bridle, 16s		17	6
A wheel a pro of hair cloth, 4s; 20 lb Tobacco, 6s, 8d;		10	8
8 bushels of Salt, £2, 4s; a syth and Cradle, 5s . .	2	9	
A Fluite, 6d; Ceder Shingles, 4s; Three Sickles, 2s, 6d		7	

Item	£	s	d
A wheel, a pr hair cloth, 4s; 20 lb. Tobacco, 6s, 8d .		10	8
8 bushels of salt, £2, 4s; a syth and cradle, 5s . .	2	9	0
4 Coverlids, a blanket & bedstead	2		
A quilt, £2, 10s; a blanket, 15s; a sheet, 15s; a pillow, 4s	4	4	
A case with knives, 4s; money scales with weights, 6s		10	
A pewter bottle, 2 boxes, 2s, 6d; a basket with linen, 13s, 4d		15	10
Mault, £1, 13s, 4d; tubbs trays and barke, 16s . .	2	9	4
Hops, 14s, 8d; a Churne, 3s; a Chees press, 3s . .	1	0	8
2 Tubbs, 3s; a Chees tubb, 3s; a kneeding trough, 2s		8	
More Tubbs, 9s; three Gulog (?) 3s; driping pan, 1s		13	
2 Cheese Vuets, 1s; a kan paile strainer, 2s . . .		3	
A basket, 4d; Old tub & barrils & Cart Ropes . .		18	4
40 lbs. Tallow, £1; two ladles & 3 dishes, 1s . . .	1	1	
Tin pans, 6s; a tin kettle, 2s; a cullender, 1s, 4d . .		9	4
2 Cream pots, 2s; earthen pans, 2s; a Crys, 6d . .		4	6
A bushel, 1s; a pot, 1s; a frying pan, 3s		5	
Amount brought forward	974	10	4
Tallow & other things, 2s; a box with Candles, 2s .		4	
An iron back, 4s; a pair of bellows, 6s		10	
3 Forks, 2s; wooden ware, 9s; Trenchers, 2s, 8d .		13	8
Spoons, a pan, Choping knife, 4s, 6d; 2 potts, 14s .		18	6
2 Kettles, 15s; old brass, 2s; hair cloth, £1, 10s . .	2	7	
Amount Forward	889	0	6
A glass case & glasses, 14s; a Joynt Stoole, 2s . .		16	
An iron back, 4s; a pair of bellows, 6s		10	
Earthen ware, 12s; a brush and needles, 6s . . .		18	
button, 15s; Pewter, £4, 5s; More Pewter, £2, 17s .	7	17	
Ivory headed Cane, 6s; Silverheaded Cane, 12s . .		18	
A small casket, with other things		1	6
A pair of cards, 5s; a lock, 3s; tin pans, 1s, 6d . .		9	6
Nails, 1s, 6d; Looking glass, 6s; An ax, 2s . . .		9	6
40 Sheep, £12; 82 lb. of ginger, £1, 6s	13	6	
Nails, 4s, 8d; hatchett & other things, 2s, 6d . . .		7	2
A pair Stillyards, 12s; a pr scales & weight, 12s .	1	4	
A Chest, 4s; a bed, bedstead & furniture, £7, 16s .	8		
Another Bed & furniture	6		
Another Bed & furniture	2	15	
10 yds. & ½ of Kersey, £2, 17s, 3d; More Kersey, 7s, 6d	3	4	9

3 yds. & ½ of Kersey, 19s, 9d; 44 lbs. yarne, £2 .	2	19	9
6 pound Coverlid yarne, 8s, 8d; 10 yds. Cotton Cloth, £1, 6s	1	14	8
2 blankets, 2s; two blankets, 12s; Linen Cloth, 19s .	1	13	
10 yds. ticking, £1, 15s; flax, 11s, 8d	2	6	8
2 barke, 1s, 8d; A pillion & cloth, 6s		7	8
A wheel and other things		7	6
9790 of 8d nails, £5, 16s; 51 lbs. of wool, £2, 19s, 6d	8	15	6
Kettles & other things, £2; Iron Mortoe & other things, 10s	2	10	
More Iron, 10s; Hoo's, a hatchet, 12s, 6d	1	2	6
Moore Tools, 7s; Wedges & other things, 1s, 6d . .		8	6
2½bushels a ½ peck, 4s; pailes, 2s		6	
Plow & plow irons & other old iron	1		
A Stone Jugg and other things, 2s, 9d; a Crowbar & acgles, 11s; A brush and Grater, 2s; Baggs, 13s, 6d; a Silver Cup, £2, 10s	3	5	6
Cash	4	9	
	1051	10	1

Amount brought forward	1051	10	1
An old Scow, £2, 10s; dung, 6s; Sealing wax, 6d; ink horn, 6d	2	17	
1 Table, 6s; 1 Chest, 5s; 4½ doz. buttons, 2s, 3d .		13	3
2 old pair Knives, 6d; a Slead, 7s		7	6
16 Sheep	3		
	1058	7	10

Samuell Maltby, Exr., sworne

according to law.

Nathanll Harrison }
Thomas Shepard } apprisers.

In order that descendants may form some idea as to the importance in the early days of the above estate we quote from the N. E. H. & G. R., p. 73, Vol. LXIV: "At William Peyntree's death in Connecticut, he left a large estate inventoried, 29 Nov., 1649, at £1001, 00s, 00d. to his widow Margaret, son John and his daughter Mary, wife of Richard Bryan of Milford, Conn."

NOTE.—Mary Peyntree was the mother of Mary Bryan, wife of John Maltby, Esq.

This inventory was taken some sixty years before that of William Maltby, which makes some difference in the relative value of the two estates, but in 1710, an estate of £1058 was a goodly inheritance and William Maltby was one of the most substantial men in Branford.

After the death of William Maltby there was some litigation over the estate as is shown by a New Haven Probate Record, viz.:

"John Maltbie of Saybrook, one of the legatees of Mr. William Maultby, late of Branford, Dec'd., did offer ye evidence of Samuel and Miriam Pond to shew that through the Neglect of ye Scribe In writing ye will of sd Dec'd, there was an omition of some Particular grants to ye said John Maultbie and his brother Daniell. But insomuch ty none of yet Interests were present nor cited to bee, ye Court do decline acting in ye affair."

Vol. IV., p. 94: "The Testymonie of Samll Pond and Miriam Pond: These Deponents testyfie and say they being with Mr. William Maultby of Branford, Dec'd, when he, sd Maultby made his last will, heard said Maultby say he gave sixty four acres of his land at Sebee hil to his grandson. William Maltby and ye remainder of his said land at Sebee hil he gave to his son John and his son Daniel to be divided between them and farther saith at Guilford, July 23rd, 1712, the above named Samuel Pond and Miriam Pond made solemn oath to ye truth of the above written testymony before Abraham Fowler, Asst. John Maltby of Saybrook, who desires ye above testymonie affirmed to me ye subscriber yt he had notified all ye persons concerned in ye above William Maltby's estate to be present at time and place above said, but none of them present.

Test. Abraham Fowler, Asst.

A second record reads: At a Court of Probate held at New Haven, ye 1st Monday of January, 1710-11.

Present John Alling, Esqrs., Judge.

Mr. William Maltby — Warham Mather } Esq. Abraham Bradley } Just.

Mr. Joseph Tuttle on behalf of John Maltby, Daniel Maltby, David Parker in right of his wife and Abraham Hoadley in right of his wife, some of the heirs of William Maltby, Esq., late of Branford, deceased, decried the Court to grant letters of administration on ye goods and Chattels of ye said deceased. The Court after thor' consideration thereof do not see cause to grant an administration on the goods and chattels of said deceased from this deny all the said John Maltby, Daniel Maltby, David Parker and Abraham Hoadley appeals to the Court of Assistants to be held at Hartford in May next, John Maltby, Daniel Maltby, David Parker and Abraham Hoadley principals, and Matthew Gilbert and Samuel Cooper suretys acknowledge themselves bound jointly and severally in a recognizance of Forty pounds lawful money of the Colony of Conn. to the Court of Probates for ye county of New Haven, to prosecute their said appeale to the offset and answer all damages in case they make not their plea good." (p. 252, Vol. III., New Haven Probate records.)

It would be interesting to know the outcome of this case, but as yet we have found no record of this appeal at Hartford. The record might throw some light on the question of who was the first wife of William Maltby, as possibly they were contending for property which they thought they were entitled to through their mother. It will be noticed that Samuel and Jonathon, children of Abigail Bishop, do not appear in the above plea. It would rather seem to indicate that John, Jane, Elizabeth and Daniel had the same mother.

NOTE.—William, the other brother, died nine years before his father, and William, Sr., had already given him his share and provided for his grandson, William, 3rd.

This work is in no way intended for a genealogy. (A large and comprehensive record of the descendants of William and John Maltby, emigrants, is about completed, in so much as a genealogy is ever completed). At the same time it has been considered advisable to include in this volume a sketch of each of the children of William Maltby, and these biographies now follow.

JOHN MALTBY (2)

John Maltby, oldest son of William Maltby, Esq., was born, according to Mr. Ralph D. Smith, in 1670. Where he was born and the name of his mother are not known.

"Branford Annals," by Baldwin (N. H. Hist. Soc. Papers, Vol. III., p. 269) has this paragraph, referring to him: "March 9, 1687-8, John Rosewell, Samuel Hoadley, Jon. Foote, Josiah Frisbie, William Barker, John Maultbie and Isaac Bartholemew were granted a parcel of land a mile square in the N. W. portion of the town.

They were to divide it among themselves as they could agree. They were young men pushing out to make new homes. They were thus the founders of families that have been prominent in North Branfird since."

Mr. Ralph D. Smith wrote concerning John Maltby: "He was a Cooper, but belonged to the better class in Society. . . . He lived in Saybrook all of his life." I do not think John Maltby went to Saybrook to live until sometime after 1694, when he would have been twenty-four years of age, as we find these records in Branford: 1682. "Land was given by the town to Jno. Maltbye, about 1682.

On page 43 of "Branford Annals" we find the following:

"North Branford. In 1687, March 4, John Maltbie (also spelled Maultbie). He was probably a son of William Maultbie." Also: "March 21, 1700, John Maultbie removes to New London and sells to his father William."

1686. "John Maltbye makes his mark (+) to an agreement that Jno. Rosewell have his land in one piece, March 8, 1686-7. (Bran. Rec., Vol. II., p. 37). Why he should have made his mark at 16 years of age, with his father so fine a penman is a question, unless he were ill at the time.

Rev. Jonathon (4) Maltby wrote of him: "of Yale Coll., but did not graduate for want of health." As Yale College was not founded till 1700, this can hardly be correct, though it is possible that Rev. Jonathon's (4) statement alluded to his son, John (3).

1694. "John Maltbie entered his earmark, which is a hollow crop, on the top of the near ear, and a crop on the off ear, and a slit in the same ear, April 17, 1694. (Bran. Rec., Vol. I., p. 223). Between this date and 1699, his father purchased a place for him in Saybrook, probably at the time of his marriage in 1696.

According to Mr. Ralph Smith and to Mr. Francis Parker of Hartford, John Maltby married Hannah Lord, daughter of Capt. William and Lydia Buckland (Brown) Lord of Saybrook, and granddaughter of Thomas and Dorothy ——— Lord of Hartford. A marriage into a good family, as is well known. The date of the above marriage was Aug. 13, 1696.

1699. In this year we find the following item: "I John Maltbie of Saybrook, sell to my honored father, Wm. Maltbie of Branford, for the sum of £8 a piece of land, etc. March 15, 1699. Acknowledge before

Wm. Maltbie, Justice Peace.

(Bran. Rec., Vol. II., p. 129; also New Haven County Court Rec., Vol. II., p. 3.)

The Branford Records, Vol. II., p. 44, contains this item: "John Maltbie, among others receives 8 acres in Branford and promises to improve it.

1713, Sept. 30. "Henry Cook of Branford deeds to John Maltbie of Saybrook" for good causes and considerations "land in Branford (Bran. Rec., Vol. IV., p. 246).

The will of John Maltby is dated March 11, 1727, recorded and proved Sept. 12, 1727. It mentions wife Hannah, children John, Nathaniel, Hannah, Mary, Jane and Dorothy. He gave each of

NOTE.—William probably died young.

his daughters a share in his mansion house; gave his Coopers tools and shop; Malt house; tub and haircloth, etc. The amount of his property was £459, 17s, 2d. (Probate record, Guilford). Made his wife Hannah executrix. John Maltby, according to Mr. Ralph Smith, "died August — 1727, at the age of 57." His will is witnessed by "Samuel Williard."*

CHILDREN OF JOHN AND HANNAH (LORD) MALTBY

1. John, b. Sept. 10, 1698 (Saybrook Rec., Vol. II., p. 34).
2. Nathaniel, b. Dec. 29, 1700 (Saybrook Rec. Vol. II., p. 34).
*3. William, b. July 6, 1703 (Saybrook Rec., Vol. II., p. 34).
†4. Hannah, b. Sept. 18, 1704 (Saybrook Rec., Vol. II., p. 540).
5. Mary, b. July 18, 1708 (Saybrook Rec., Vol. II., p. 540)
‡6. Jane, b. May, 1710 (Saybrook Rec., Vol. II., p. 540.)
7. Dorothy, b. April 20, 1715 (Saybrook Rec., Vol. II., p. 540).

Hannah, the widow of John Maltby married, Jan. 17, 1730, Abraham Hodgkin. The records of the descendants of the above John and Hannah Lord Maltby will be found in the Maltby Genealogy, now nearing completion.

Additional notes of the children of John (2) Maltby.

John (3) Maltby m. Mehitable Clarke. They had children: Esther, William, supposed to have died unmarried; Mehitable and

* NOTE—A son of John Maltby's stepmother, by her first husband, Josiah Williard. Samuel Willard resided at Saybrook; as, viz., the following record: "Samuel Willard of Saybrook quit claims to Stephen Willard of Wethersfield, his title to the land of his honored father, Josiah Willard, 30 Dec., 1699."

* William evidently died young as he is not mentioned in his father's will.

† The old Maltby Chest, of which we show a photograph, belonged at one time to Hannah Maltby, and possibly to her father, John. Indeed, there is a strong possibility that he built it himself.

‡ This date of birth may be incorrect as the Guilford records read: "Died. Jane Maltbie, from Saybrook, 30, June 12, 1737." This would make her birth year 1707.

Abby. From these records it will be seen that the male line of John (2) died out in this generation.

Nathaniel (3) Maltby m. Deborah Jones, descended from Deputy Governor William Jones. They had one child, Elizabeth.

William (3) Maltby is presumed to have died young.

Hannah (3) Maltby m. Abraham Hodkin and had children: Abraham, Hannah, John, Jane, Samuel and Lydia.

Mary (3) Maltby m. Gershom Lewis of Guilford, and had children: John, Gershom, d. young, Nathaniel, Mary, Elizabeth, d. young, Ozias and Reuben.

Jane (3) Maltby, d. unm.

Dorothy (3) Maltby m. Isaac Johnson, Jr., of Guilford and had children: Phineas, Daniel and Sarah.

YE MALTBY CHEST

YE MALTBY CHEST
I. M.—1726

Quaint heirloom, as alone this day you stand
A relic of the past, what could you tell
Of our ancestors and the home and land
From whence they came, and of that one as well
Who formed you for his own utility,
With somewhat even of skill and artistry,

In red and black and gold traced clearly see
The letters and the date, which seem to give
An index of the owner's family,
As well as time in which the man did live,—
John Maltby, grandson of the one we own
As sire of Maltbys in our lineage known.

This we may gather, but no further clue,
From which to unroll the years between,
That early date and this, is given by you;
Nor may we ever know all you have seen,
Made as you were full half a century
Before this country's Independency.

You know the natives who tried souls of men;
Witnessed privations, loss, disease and death,
And midst those scenes saw the swift rise and gain
Of a new nation—even to Freedom's breath,—
A nation known this day, her treasure sought
By all lands, and we cry, "What has God wrought!"

Yet pride and honor, wealth and fame must pass,
Not even a nation can unchanged remain,
The things we value in an instant flash
Are gone from us, we must new treasure gain;—
But still, with you old chest, to our loved Tree—
The Maltby Genealogy—cling we.

—SERAPH MALTBIE DEAN.

Cambridge, Massachusetts.

NOTE.—The compiler has a copy of a letter written from Falls Village, Connecticut, December 24th, 1867, by Dr. Charles Benjamin Maltbie, father of Mrs. Dean, in which he says: "I have now in my possession a sea-chest, marked I. M. 1726 on the front of it, the old English standing for J as well. This chest was willed to me in a formal manner by one Abram Hodgkin, a descendant of the elder brother in whose possession it had come into by the way of his mother. These facts are mostly derived from him, he says that the elder John had one son, John, and several daughters, that this son, John, had five daughters and no son, etc."

Abraham (4) Hodgkin was born April 9, 1731, and married March 20, 1755, Sarah Stone. He died "about 1852 at an advanced age" according to Dr. C. B. Maltbie. He was the oldest child of Hannah (3) Maltbie, born Sept. 18, 1704, in Saybrook and who married, Jan. 17, 1730, Abraham Hodkin, in Guilford, Connecticut. Hannah (3) was the daughter of John (2) and Hannah (Lord) Maltbie, and the granddaughter of William (1) and Mary ? ——— Maltbie.

According to Mr. Ralph D. Smith, of Guilford, John (2) Maltby died in August, 1727, so we take it for granted that the sea chest was not his, but belonged to his son, John (3), who màrried Nov. 12, 1724, Mehitable Clarke.

The chest evidently reyerted to his sister Hannah.

Of course there is a possibility that the chest belonged to John (2), and when he died in 1726 it went to his oldest daughter, and she may have had the "I. M. 1726" put on. This perhaps is the most natural explanation. Indeed, "What could you tell of our ancestor!" Could we but discover some secret drawer or hiding place in you—with a bit of yellowed paper, telling something of those who brought you over seas—what a happy find that would be!

JANE MALTBY (2)

Jane Maltby's birth date is not known, nor where she was born. She may have been a twin of John, or a year his junior. She joined the Branford Church in March, 1689, and we judge was probably borne about 1671.

Her marriage is recorded at New Haven, Conn., p. 131, as follows: "David Parkor and Jane Malby were maryod the 4 March, 1689-90."

A Branford Deed, Vol. III., p. 280, states that: "David Parker of Say Brook in the County of New London and Colony of Connecticut, with the consent of Jane, my wife, to John Russell of Branford, our whole right, title and interest in the undivided lands in the Township of Branford, being one-seventh part of ye said land which are our right in the estate of our Honrd Father, Mr. William Maltbie, late of Branford, dec'd.

Daniel Maltbie. 17 Jan., 1710-11.
Samuel Maltbie.

David Parker and Jane Maltby very evidently had no children.

Mr. Francis Parker of Hartford, Conn., very kindly furnished the following records: "David Parker, son of William and Margery ——— Parker, was born in Saybrook, the latter end of February, 1657-8." In May 1682 the General Assembly exempted him from the payment of poll taxes because he was "disabled from attending to his business by a wound in the head." No other reference to this injury is found. Presumably it was permanent in its character and debarred him from severe physical exertion. The town of Saybrook granted him five acres of land in 1679, perhaps for services in the Indian wars, but the reason of the grant is not stated. He held the office of lister in 1695 and 1706, and was constable in 1698. He also held many minor town offices.

David and Jane (Maltbie) Parker had no children and David Parker, "yeoman," as he describes himself, died in Jan., 1723, having survived his wife. His will, dated Jan. 11, 1723, was acknowledged before a magistrate Jan. 15, 1723, and probated in Guilford, Jan. 29, 1723. He gave legacies to his brothers, William and Joseph Parker; to nephews, Joseph and Jonathon Parker; to his grand-nephews, Abner, John and Nathaniel Parker, but bequeathed the bulk of his estate to his grand-niece, Deborah Parker, who subsequently married Isaac Jones. He gave a piece of land, a part of his homestead, to Saybrook Church, on condition that a meeting house be built upon it, also another piece of land for the support of "our orthodox dissenting ministery in Saybrook." The church declined to build a meeting house on the first lot, and it reverted to Deborah Parker. His estate inventoried £487—5—4.

Some of the items in his inventory were:

one gold ring, 18s.
one silver spoon, 10s.
three silver buckles, 3s.
two pairs of silver clasps, 5s.
pewter table ware, £3, 4s, 4d.

also "two volums of sermons, three bibles, one palsm book, two old books and two paper books, and several articles of brass and tin ware."

NOTE.—William Parker was one of the original proprietors of Hartford, 1636. It is not known from what English town he came. He removed to Saybrook in 1645. According to Saybrook Records, Vol. I., p. 24, he married "Margery Allen, daughter of William Allen of London, Eng., and afterwards married Elizabeth Pratt, widow of Lieut. Wm. Pratt and daughter of John Clarke, 1st. He was a doctor. He died 21 Dec., 1686. He was the son of John Parker of Dantry, Northamptonshire, Eng., and his mother was a daughter of William Cross."

WILLIAM MALTBY (2)

William Maltby, Jr., was born Jan. 9, 1673-4, at New Haven, Conn., and was a child of a first wife. He resided in New Haven previous to 1700, and from the following record we learn that he resided on the corner of Water and Union streets, the then fashionable part of town, and here, doubtless, he watched the good Brigantine "Friends Adventure" of which he was captain, and his father owner, riding at anchor in the harbor. The Trowbridge Genealogy, p. 52, tells us that "Hezekiah Sabin came to New Haven about 1743. He bought of the heirs of William Maltbie, the house on the corner of Water and Union streets, near the Creek."

William Maltby, Jun., married Elizabeth Morris, daughter of John Morris. He evidently was of Branford in 1690, for in that year he joined the church there. I think he removed to New Haven about the time of his marriage, as we find this record: (New Haven Town Records, Vol. II., pp. 11-12) "John Morris, shipwright, of New Haven, for £110 sells his house and his land to his son-in-law, William Maltbie of New Haven, Mariner, whose wife is Elizabeth Morris Maltby, Jan. 1, 1698-99."

NOTE.—The wife of John Morris was Hannah Bishop, oldest child of Deputy Governor James Bishop. She was the mother of Elizabeth Morris who married William Maltby, Jr. Abigail Bishop, third wife of William Maltby, Sr., was a sister of Hannah (Bishop) Morris, and therefore own aunt to Elizabeth Morris Maltby and step-mother to her husband, William Maltby, Jr.

"William Maltby was a sea captain and died in the West Indies, 1701, aged only 27," writes Mrs. Cushman, while Mr. Ralph D. Smith says, "he was lost at sea, in March, 1701": and another record reads: "he died of yellow fever in the West Indies." From the few records which follow we can see that he left New Haven in December, 1700, as "Master of the Friend's Adventure," and never returned to his wife and infant son.

1700. Dec. 3. "Wm. Maltbie, Master of ye Brigantine ffriend's Adventure, made complaint against Daniell Thomas of said New Haven, for absenting himself from the vessel without leave." (New Haven Records of County Court, Vol. II., p. 52.) And again in Vol. II., p. 53: "Wm. Maltbie of New Haven, Master of ye Brigantine Friend's Adventure, was fined £5 for receiving on board a quantity of hogs head heading and other timber contrary to law."

Capt. William Maltby died without a will.

Vol. II., p. 65, New Haven Records has the following:

"At a Court of Probate held at New Haven, April ye 30th day, 1701.

Present William Maltbie,
Jeremiah Osborne,
John Alling, Esq.,
Justices Quorum.

Administration of ye estate of William Maltbie, Marriner, late of New Haven, deceased in ye West Indies, was granted to Mr. John Morris and Mrs. Elizabeth Maltbie, widow and relict of sd deceased of sd New Haven upon their recognizance of three hundred pounds well and truly paid to administer ye same."

Vol. II., p. 286, Probate records of New Haven, Conn., give: "The inventory of x/m William Maltbie's Estate, deceased, taken by us whose names are underwritten, this 10th day of June, 1701."

	£	s	d
His Clothes, £9, 3s; Hatt, £1, 13s	10	16	
Stockings, Cane & marking Iron	2	10	
An old Chest, 6s; four books, 4s; sailing instruments	3	10	
2 Boxes & Sheepskin, 4s, 6d; bedding & bedstead, £5, 10s	5	14	6
A trunk with foot, 33s; blue linen, 14s; bagg with Wool, 36s	4	3	
Spiker & Lond, 10s; Fire shovel & Tongs, 16s; Flax, 9s, 9d	1	15	9
Sourrale glass* & and earthern dish—Jug . . .		17	
Two Pwtt of Sugar, 18s; Earthern Ware, 2s, 6d .	1	10	6
Bed Cord and Matt., 6s; Coverlid, 20s; Bolts., £2, 4s, 6d	3	10	6
Basketts—Corrills—Trays, 13s 6d; Woolen Yarne, 4s		17	6
A chist of drawers, £6, 10s; Rowcloth, 45s . . .	8	15	
Seven pr. Sheets, £15; Two pr. Sheets, £4; Pillow borrs, 9s	19	9	
Pillow Borrs, pillow boors, pillow boars	1	17	3
Table cloathes, 20s, 6d; Napkins, 2s, 4d; Napkins, 20			
Man Serv't, £16; Negro Boy, £20.			

John Alling,
William Thomson.

Sundry other articles—House and Lot
£100 Cash

* This is evidently a sour ale glass.

359 gallons Rum
104 gallons molases

	£	s	d
Total	231	5	00

Mr. Wm. Maltbie gives one half his division of £50 an allotment at Sibeis Hill, half as first laid out and half the addition of swamp, which is in Branford bounds, appraised at £50 in money.

Debts due ye Estate in Barbadoes:

	£	s	d
Sundry items	35	13	7½
The Estate Dr.			
To Mr. John Morris, for Freight	17	3	
	18	10	7½

Ex. M. Maltbie, Widow.

Sworn to ye pse onbrod (?)

Mr. John Alling — sworne to ye

Mr. William Thomson — April 20th & Novem 14, 1701

This inventory will bear a little study. The "Corrils, Baskets and Trays he evidently had brought home from his West India voyages, also the Rum and Molases which he, of course, sold in New England, purchased commodities for the Island trade and returned with "full cargoes."

"Debts due ye estate in Barbadoes." This is important and certainly looks as though the Maltbys had property there. The molases, sugar, rum, etc., may have been made from their own plantation.

Mr. John Morris, his father-in-law, had evidently transported goods for him and hence he owed him for freight.

Why Elizabeth Morris should have signed 'M. Maltbie, widow," as executrix, is puzzling. There is no question as to who the widow of William, Jr., was—she was Elizabeth Morris and this is proved by all records.

There is a bill of Samuel Coloys of Milford for £6, 16s, 00d.

Mrs. Maltbie, widdow. The name "Elizabeth Maltbie" appears on page 24 of the First Church, New Haven. She was admitted July 27, 1700-1. (shortly after the death of her husband?)

In 1712, the widow, Mrs. Elizabeth (Morris) Maltbie, was engaged in a suit regarding her father's property.

"Court held 2nd Tuesday of Nov. 1712. Josepeth Smith, James Peck, Stephen Howell* and Elizabeth Maultby, heirs to Mr.

* Susanna, wife of Stephen Howell, is mentioned in Supplementary Catalogue of First Church of New Haven, "admitted Nov. 17, 1751, buried 1783."

John Morris, late of New Haven, deceased, plaintiffs, contra Gershom Brown, mariner, and Matthew Row of New Haven, defendants. (New Haven County Court Records, Vol. II., p. 494.)

Until 1712, Mrs. Elizabeth (Morris) Maltbie seems to have lived with her father, or perhaps we should say her father lived with her in New Haven. In 1712 Mr. Morris died, and in 1713. Mrs. Elizabeth Maltby married Rev. John Davenport of Stamford.

NOTE.—She was the mother of the Hon. Abraham Davenport and the Rev. James Davenport.

On Feb. 6, 1715-16, Mrs. Elizabeth Davenport, alias Maltbie, administratrix of Mr. Wm. Maltbie, late of New Haven, deceased, by letter desires the addition of £8 money to be made to his estate. (Probate Records, New Haven, Vol. IV., p. 381.)

Elizabeth Morris (Maltby) Davenport, died Jan. 11, 1758 (Vol. I., p. 131, New Haven Records and Davenport Genealogy by Amzi Davenport).

CHILD OF WILLIAM AND ELIZABETH (MORRIS) MALTBY

1. William, b. May 26, 1700 (Vol. I., p. 131, New Haven Records).

For records of William Maltby, Junior's descendants see Maltby Genealogy, now nearing completion.

NOTE—Capt. William (3) Maltby was the only child of William (2). He married Sarah Davenport, dau. of Rev. John Davenport of Stamford. They had children as follows: William (according to R. D. Smith, but I have no authority for this statement); John, who died unmarried; Mary, died young, and Elizabeth.

ELIZABETH MALTBY (2)

Elizabeth Maltby was born April 30, 1676, at New Haven. She married Abraham, son of William Hoadley, March 14, 1697-8. She died Dec. 14, 1747. He died July 14, 1748, "advanced in years," in Branford, Conn. (Ref. Branford Records and "Descendants of William Hoadley of Branford, Conn.," by Francis B. Trowbridge.)

CHILDREN OF ABRAHAM AND ELIZABETH (MALTBY) HOADLEY

1. Rachel, b. Aug. 31, 1701, bapt. Sept. 1701 (Branford Records).
2. Abel, b. Dec. 24, 1705 (Branford Records).
3. Abraham, b. July 16, 1708 (Branford Records).
4. Jonathon, b. Jan. 16, 1713-4 (Branford Records).

For descendants of Elizabeth Maltby Hoadley see the Maltby Genealogy.

DANIEL MALTBY (2)

Daniel Maltby was born May 19, 1679, according to the Branford Records. He united with the church at Branford in 1700. Esther Moss, who was to become his wife, joined the church at the same time. She was a daughter of John and Mary (Lothrop) Moss and granddaughter of John Moss of New Haven, 1639. On her mother's side she was descended as follows:

LOWTHROP OF LOWTHROPE, YORKS.

1. John Lowthrope of Lowthrope, was living early in the 16th century, in Cherry Burton, a parish about four miles from Lowthrop, where he had an extensive estate. In 1548 he appeared on York subsidy roll.

2. Robert Lowthrop, son of above, married Ellen ———. He died in 1558.

3. Thomas Lothrop, son of above, was first of Cherry Burton, later of Elton, Yorks. His wife was Mary ———, who died at Elton in 1688.

4. Rev. John Lothrop, 12th child of above, was born at Elton, East Riding, Yorks., Dec. 20, 1584; was bred at Oxford; graduated at Queen's College, 1605. He married Hannah Howse of Eastwell, Kent Co. The marriage license was issued in Canterbury, Kent Co., Oct. 10, 1610. She died in 1633.

5. Samuel Lothrop, 6th child of above, New London, Conn., married Elizabeth Scudder, Nov. 28, 1644.

6. Mary Lothrop, daughter of above, married John Moss.

7. Esther Moss, daughter of above, born Jan. 5, 1678, married Daniel Maltby.

Daniel Maltby married Esther Moss (Morse) October 27, 1702 (Branford Records, Vol. Index of Births, etc., 1694).

1703. June 14. "Daniel Maltbie entered his ear mark, which is a crop on the top of both ears, and a hollow crop on the near ear" (Branf. Rec., Vol. I., p. 224).

1705. April 12. "At a meeting of the Proprietors in Branford commencing March 25, and closing April 12, 1705, Daniel

Maltbie desired them to give him about 2 acres of sedgy land, which was granted" (Branf. Rec., Vol. II., p. 249).

1710. Daniel Maltby seems to have been "set up in life" by his father, for in William Maltby's will he gives "to my son Daniel, all that house and land where he now lives."

1710. October. "Daniel Maltby was appointed guardian to Jonathon Maltbie, minor, son of Wm. Maltbie of Branford, deceased" (New Haven Probate Rec., Vol. III., p. 235). This half-brother, Jonathon, was then but twelve years of age and evidently remained the ward of Daniel only a short while, for on page 66 of the New Haven records, we find: "Jonathon Maultbie, Minor, child of Mr. William Maultbie, Late of Branford did appear and made choice of Mr. Edward Barker of Branford for to be his guardian."

1711. October 15. "In staking out lots on Mulliner's Neck D. M. was to stand for Daniel Maltbie" (Branf. Rec., Vol. I., p. 342).

The following items are from the Branford Records: Vol. III., p. 81. Deed to Daniel Maltbie from Allen Ball. In a list of Freemen in Branford, 1714 to 1730 (Branford Records) the name of Daniel Maltby is 18th on the list.

1712-13. Vol. III., p. 151. "Land layed out to the Estate of Wm. Maltbie for Daniel Maltbie. Jan. 23. 1712-13.

Vol. III., p. 219. Deed from Edwin Barker to Daniel Maltby in consideration of £22. 10s.

1714. Vol. III., p. 221. Deed to Daniel Maltbie from Caleb Parmerly, March 26, 1714.

1714. Vol. III., p. 403. Deed to Daniel Maltby by Noah Rogers, April 27, 1714.

1717. Vol. III., p. 514. Land layed out "to the Estate of Wm. Maltbie, Esqre., on the pitch. of Daniel Maltbie. May 2. 1717.

1718. Vol. IV., p. 86. Deed of John Howd* to Daniel Maltbie. of 3 acres of salt meadow and for another piece of salt meadow Aug. 4. 1718.

1718. Vol. IV., p. 87. Deed of John Parrish† to Daniel Maltbie, of a piece of 5th division land, which he had formerly bought of said Maltbie, for £28. July 29. 1718.

1719. It was in this year (Oct. 26) that Samuel (2) and Jonathon (2), half-brothers of Daniel (2), performed the highly commendable but rather rare act of giving Daniel eight acres of

* Martha (3) Maltby, b. Sept. 11, 1720, dau. of Daniel (2), mar. May 9, 1739, Daniel Howd at Branford. Possibly the above John Howd was his father.

† Abigail (3) Maltby, b. March 7, 1714, dau. of Daniel (2), mar. for her second husband Ephrain Parish of Cheshire, July 19, 1744. Possibly he was closely related to the John Parrish from whom Daniel Maltby received land.

land they believed their father, William, intended Daniel to have, although not specified in his will. This was a very fine thing to do, and also, as a descendant of Daniel, it leads one to believe that Daniel's character was gentle and lovable—for we all know that no one is anxious to bestow gifts upon ill-tempered and unamiable persons.

1722. Vol. IV., p. 445. Deed "Jonathon Maltbie of Stamford, cordwainer, for £130 gives his brother, Daniel Maltbie, of Branford, 10 acres of land, being Jonathon's share of the home lot, given him by his father, William, Dec. 7, 1722.

The tombstone of Daniel Maltby lies quite near those of his father and stepmother. "Daniel Maltbie departed this life, Dec. ye 26, A. D. 1731, in the morning." (Branford Records, Vol., 1694.)

His plain and tasteful tombstone reads:

MR. DANIEL MALTBIE
Died Dec. 25, 1731
In 53d year."

At the end of Christmas day, we judge from the above.

His will is probated at Guilford and was copied, with the inventory of his estate, by Miss Scofield.

His widow, Esther (Moss) Maltby, married Deacon Samuel Todd, June 14, 1739 (Connecticut Marriages Branford). Also "Tuttle Family Genealogy, page 325. This states: "June 20th." The New Haven Records read: "Mrs. Esther Maltby of Branford and Mr. Samuel Todd, Jun. (mar) June 10, 1739.

The will of Daniel Maltbie was found on the Guilford Probate Records, Vol. II., p. 436. He calls himself "Yeoman" and makes his will 22 Dec., 1731. His wife, Esther, and son, Joseph, were named as Executors.

The will provides liberally for wife Esther, sons Joseph, Daniel and Benjamin, and to each of his daughters, Esther, Abigail and Martha.

From Daniel's will it would seem that Mary, William and John were all dead when his will was made. Also that Daniel, third child, died as we find the seventh child also named Daniel.

The children of Daniel and Esther Moss Maltby were:

1. Mary, b. Dec. 7, 1703 (Branford Rec., Vol. I., p. 211).
2. William, b. Feb. 17, 1705 (Branford Rec., Vol. I., p. 211).
3. Daniel, b. June 16, 1708 (Branford Rec., Vol. p. 211).
4. Esther, b. Nov., 1709.
5. Joseph, b. May 31, 1712.
6. Abigail, b. March 6, 1713.

7. Daniel, b. Oct. 29, 1715.
8. Benjamin, b. June 20, 1717.
9. Martha, b. Sept. 10, 1720.
10. John, b. April 25, 1722, "at night."

The Will and Inventory of Daniel Maltby follow:

Guilford Probate Records, Vol. II., p. 436:

Esther Maltbie & Joseph Maltbie Executors of the Last Will and Testament of Daniel Maltby, Late of Branford Dec'd, which being proved was approved in Court and ordered to be Recorded and ye Executors accepted ye Trust therein Committed to them.

The Last Will and Testament of Daniel Maltbie of Branford in ye County of New Haven & Colony of Connecticut in New England, Yeoman, made this Twenty Second Day of December Anno Domini, 1731, as follows:

Calling to mind the mortality of my body being at present of Parfect mind and memory but Knowing that it is appointed for all men once to Dye Do therefore make and ordain this my Last Will and Testament that is to Say principally and first of all I Give and Recommend my Soul into ye Hands of God who Gave it and my Body to the Earth to be buried in Decent Christian Burial at ye Discretion of my Executors nothing Doubting but at the General resurrection I Shall receive the Same again by the mighty Power of God and as Touching such Worldly Estate wherewith it hath pleased God to bless me in this Life I Give Demise and Dispose of ye Same in ye following manner and form:

Imp. I Give and Bequeathe unto my Dearly beloved wife Esther one Third part of all my Houseing Lands and Personal Estate after all my Just Debts are Satisfied, the real Estate During Life and the personal forever.

2ndly. I Give and bequeathe unto my three Sons, Joseph, Daniel & Benjamin, all my Houseing & Lands and right of Lands wheresoever and to be equally Divided between them including my Wives third part in each parcel and in Case Providence Should order it that any one of my sd Sons Should Decease before he arrive at the age of twenty one years than the Survivors of my Sons Shall have the Same equally between them and Shall pay to Each of my Daughters in money or equivalent thereto one Sixth part of that part of my Estate which Did by right Belong to the Deceased. And my son Joseph to have his part in my Housing and Homestead.

3rdly. My will is that Each of my Daughters, Esther, Abigail and Martha shall have out of my Parsonal Estate includeing what each of them has already had and by Me Set out to any of them the Sum of one Hundred and thirty pounds apiece and if my Parsonal Estate be not Sufficient to make up the Sum then to be Equally made up to each of them by Each of my Sons Surviveing and in Case any of my Daughters should Decease before She arrive at Lawfull age to Receive her Part in my Estate as above then that part shall be Equally Divided between my Surviveing Children.

4thly. My will is that my Parsonal Estate after my Just Debts and Widows thirds be taken out be more than enough to Satisfie my Daughters Each one her part as above then the remainder shall be equally divided between my Surviveing Daughters.

And Furthermore I hereby ordain my well beloved wife Esther and my Son Joseph to be Executors of this my Last Will and Testament and to take care that all my Just Debts be Justly paid; and Lastly I hereby disallow, revoke and Disanull all and Every former Testament, wills, Bequests and Executors by me in any way before Named, Ratifying and Confirming this and no other to be my Last Will and Testament. In witness whereof I have hereunto Set my hand and Seal the day and year above written.

DANIEL MALTBIE.

Signed, Sealed, published & Declared by ye said Daniel Maltbie as his Last will and Testament in presence of us Subscribers.

Josiah Frisbie,
Uzall Wardell,
Samuel Maltbie.

Branford, January 8th, 1731-2.

Then Personally appeared Capt. Samuel Maltbie, Mr. Uzall Wardell and made Oath that they Saw Mr. Daniel Maltbie, Late of Branford, Dec'd, Signe, Seal and Declare this Instrument to be his Last Will and Testament and that they with Mr. Josiah Frisbie did then Signe thereunto in his presence as witnesses Judging him to be of Sound mind and Clear understanding at ye time thereof.

Before me, Jno. Russell, Jus. Pac.

Guilford Probate Records, Vol. 2, p. 451:

Esther Maltbie Executor of the Last Will and Testament of Daniel Maltbie, Late of Branford Dec'd exhibited an Inventory of the Sd Deceased's Estate which was approved in Court and ordered to be Recorded.

The Inventory of the Estate of Daniel Maltbie Late of Branford, Dec'd, taken and apprised by Samuel Harrington and Samuel Stent, February, ye 4th, 1731-2:

		£	s	d
Imp.	wareing apparrel One Coat, £3, 5s one Do. lined with black, £5, 10s	8	15	0
it	one Draget vest & breeches, £3, 10s one old Coat and Vest, £3, 10s	7	0	0
it	one Old Greaf Coat, £1 two cotton Vest & Breeches, £3, 14s	4	14	0
it	one Old pair of cotton Breeches, 6s one pair of breeches, 10s	0	16	0
it	one Holland Shirt, £1, 6s; one Do. 10s Woolen Shirt, £1	2	16	0
it	four pr of Stockings, £1, 12s; 2 hats, £2, 8s one pr of Gloves, £3 ($15.00!)	6	8	0
it	one musfin Neckcloath, two Stocks & one Checkered Handkerchief	0	16	0
it	one Sasenet Handkerchief, 7s two Silk muslin Do., 8s	0	15	0
it	one belt, 1s; two pr of Shoes and 1 pr of buckles	1	1	0
Item	The Buildings with the Garden and appurtenances to ye house	178	0	0
	two acres of Orchard adjoining to ye buildings	80	0	0
	One acre of Orchard more in ye homestead	40	0	0
	18 acres & ¼ of land in the homestead beside ye Orchard	237	5	0
	27 acres of Land at bushy plain at £12 per acre	324	0	0
	15 acres of pasture Land and 8 acres of Swamp Land	276	0	0
	18 pd right in ye Common and undivided Land	18	0	0
Item	the Stock one pr of oxen, £14; one pr Ditto, £11	25	0	0
	one pr of two year old Steers, £6, 10s; one bull, £3	9	10	0
	one yearling bull	1	10	0
	one old brown cow, £4, 15s; one young brown cow, £4, 15s	9	10	0

		£	s	d
	one black white face cow, £5; one brown Heifer, £2, 10s	7	10	0
	one red white face Heifer, £2, 10s; one pide black cow, £5	7	10	0
	one yallowish cow, £5; one pide heifer, £4 .	9	0	0
	two three year old heifers, £7; one red white face cow, £5	12		
	20 Sheep, £12; one Horse, £8; one Sorril mare, £11	31	0	0
	one mare coult, £4; one horse coult, £3; one coult, £4	11	0	0
	two brindle Calves, £2; two calves more, £3; two more, £2, 15s	7	15	0
	6 piggs, £3, 12s; one old Sow, 10s; nine Geese, 1-2-6	5	4	6
Item	Puter nine puter plates, £1, 7s; three Old Plates, 6s; one bason, 3s	1	16	0
	three poringers, 7s; Six pounds old puter, 9s, 4p; a salt seller, 4s	0	18	4
	one bason, 8s; one Large Tankard, 16s; one small one, 11s	1	15	0
	one old Chamber pot, 2s; platters, £1, 12s; two platters, £1, 8s	3	2	0
	one puter beacor, 3s; one Quart pot, 4s; one pint pot, 2s, 6p	0	9	6
	one Large puter Platter, £1, 12s; four puter spoons, 2s	1	14	0
Item	one set of Flowered Callico Curtains, £4 one set of Streaked Do., £3	7	0	0
	one Trunk, 6s; one box, 2s; one chest, 4s; one chest more, 4s	0	16	0
	one Chest with Drawes, £1; one more floured, £1	2	0	0
	one chest with mouldings lock and key, £1, 5s; one chest, 5s	1	10	0
	one Chest, 4s; one painted, £1; one old box, 1s	1	5	0
	four pictures in fraims, 12s one Looking glass, 12s; one more, 30s . . .	2	14	0
	three small glasses with pictures in them . .	0	5	0
	Ten pr of New Sheets, £15; 2 pr more, £3 .	18	0	0
	three Sheets, £1, 10s three pair and a half about half worn, £2, 16s, 6p	4	2	6
	one sheet, 15s; one Table Cloath, 15s; two			

	more, 5s	1	15	0
	four Towils, 4s; two towils, 3s; Six napkins, 6s; six more	1	5	0
	one Table cloath, 3s; two table cloaths, 3s; two more, 5s	0	11	0
	four pair of pillow Coats, £1, 10s; two pair more, 8s	1	18	0
	one pair more, 5s, 9p; five cushings, 7s; Six black chairs, £2, 14s	3	6	9
	One Great Black Chair, 14s; Six small black chairs, £1, 13s	2	7	0
	One earthen Chamber pot, 5s	0	5	0
Item	one bedstead cord pillows and boulsters and 3 coverlids	13	0	6
	one bed more with its furniture, and 1 silk grass	8	14	0
	one bed more with all its frniture	20	11	3
	30 pds of feathers, £5; 12 pds of feathers more 18s	5	18	0
	a hand saw, 5s; an Iron Goose, 4s; a walking Staff, 5s	0	14	0
	four chairs, 12s; one Sealskin chair, 9s; four chairs, 7s	1	8	0
	one Great Chair, 5s; one Silvar Spoon, 25s; one more, 19s	2	9	0
	one pair of Money Scales and Waights, 6s; five viol glasses, 1s	0	7	0
	two Drinking glasses, 2s; 4p; one glas caze & ye earthen in it, 19s	1	1	4
	Earthen ware on ye mantle Shelf, 13s, 10p; one Lanthorn, 3s	0	16	10
	five Small baskets, 3s, 8p; two more baskets, 3s	0	6	8
	twenty Seven & ½ ds of flax, £1, 2s, 6p; four pds of 50e, 1s, 8p	1	4	2
	3½ pds of course wool, 5s; right in a puter Still, £1, 6p	1	5	6
	Sundry Small books, 9s, 6p; ten glass bottles, 8s, 4p; nd mr, 1s 4p	0	19	2
	one Two Quart bottle, 2s, 6p; an old spade & Shovel Iron, 6s	0	8	6
Item	Iron Horse Geers, 12s; two yokes and their Irons, 7s, 6p	0	19	6

Item	£	s	d
one half bushel Iron, 4s; one iron Shod shovel, 5s	0	9	0
one broad shovel, 2s; one old shovel, 6p; two hose, 11s	0	13	6
one old hoe, 9p; four axes, £1, 5s; three sickels, 7s	1	12	9
five pounds of old Iron, 4s; three Syths and Tackling	1	19	0
one Syth & Cradle, 8s; plow irons and plated, £1, 4s	1	12	0
one old fork tines bettle rings hammer and iron Shackel	0	6	0
one Sid Saddle, £1, 10s; one saddle, £4; one more, £2, 10s	8	0	0
three old bridles, 18s; one gun and sword, £2, 15s	3	13	0
one pair of Handirons, £1, 13s, 9p; one pr of tongs, 4s, 6p	1	18	3
two trammils, 19s, 6p; one pair of Handirons, Tongs and Shovel	2	19	6
one old fire shovel, 4s; one pair of Stilliards, 12s	0	16	0
one pair of wooden Scales and one brass weight, 1s 6p	0	1	6
one Iron Pott, £1, 5s; one pot more, 8s; one Iron Kittle, 11s	2	4	0
one brass Skillit, 8s; one Iron Skillit, 4s, 6p	0	12	6
one flesh fork Choping knife & Skimer, 3s	0	3	0
one brass Kittle, £3; one brass Kittle, £7	10	0	0
one box Iron and Heeters, 7s; one Crevet, 1s	0	8	0
one brass candlestick, 4s; one Iron candlestick, 2s	0	6	0
one wooden Screw Candlestick, 2s; a warming pan, 16s	0	18	0
it two water pails, 6s; a lignum vitee Morter petil, 7s	0	13	0
" one wooden morter, 1s; a Hetchet, 14s; three milk pails, 5s, 6p	1	0	6
" one hogg Pail, 3s; trays, 5s, 4p; bowls, 8s	0	17	10
" a Marthing tubb & brew tubb, 5s, 6p; four Hogsheads, £1, 12s	1	17	6
" two barrils, 6s; one ½ barril, 2s; tunnel, 1s, 6p; one Small tubb, 1s, 6p	0	11	0

"	one butter tubb, 3s; vinegar cask, 1s, 6p; one half barril, 3s	0	17	6
"	two powdering tubbs, 3s, 6p; a churn, 7s; two flat tubbs, 5s	0	15	6
"	two Hogsheads, 12s; one half Hogshead, 2s, 6p; two wash tubbs, 2s	0	16	6
"	a Meal Trough, 8s; one meal tray, 1s; an old cask in the garret, 13s	1	2	0
"	an old bail, 4s; cart rope, 12s; two great Wheels, 11s	1	7	0
"	two small wheels, 10s; one pair of cards, 1s, 6p; one cubbard, £4	4	11	6
"	one cubbard with bannisters on it £1; one great table, 16s	1	16	0
"	three knot dishes, 4s; two whitewood dishes, 1s; one table, 10s	0	15	0
"	one frying pan, 5s; three Gimblits, 2s; one hammer, 1s	0	8	0
"	earthen ware, 8s, 8p; one cart & Wheels, 14s; one chain, 16s	5	8	2
"	one chain, 16s; one chain more, 14s . . .	1	10	0
"	one stool, 1s, 6p; one old table, 4s; twelve Trenchers, 2s	0	7	6
it	one small pitchfork, 3s; two old Chairs, 9s; one bred sive, 1s	0	13	0
"	one old bedstead & cord, 6s; a Loom Jions and a reed, £1	1	6	0
"	One old Wheel Spindle Spools & Swift, 17s; a pillion and Cloath, 33s	2	10	0
"	one pair of flannel blankets, £2, 10s; one Iron Hayhook, 1s, 6p	2	11	6
"	one Glass Bottle, 10p; two earthen pots, 2s; a wooden bottle, 3s	0	5	10
"	one Small box, 1s; one bagg, 4s	0	5	0
"	a parcel of Household Stuff prepared for Abigail	41	14	2
"	one pound of Coverlid yarn	0	3	0
"	one Iron Candlestick	0	1	0
	Sum Totl . . . . Lbs.	1560	7	6

Esther Maltbie, Executrix.

Sworn in Court — Test Samuel Hill, Clerk.

Samuel Stent }
Samuel Harrington } Appriser.

This inventory shows one much, I believe, of this many times "great" grandfather. One sees all his livestock; can hear him talk about that "old yallowish cow," and see the great number of farm tools (for that he owned a great number is clearly shown by his inventory) stacked about in the barns and sheds; the wheels which spun, the churns which made the butter, and tubs that held the vinegar—"a few old books"—treasured gifts most probably from his father, and sure sign of birth and breeding. Were they not eagerly pored over, read and re-read, perhaps read aloud by the then oldest son, Joseph,* in the long evenings, preparatory to his leaving the farm to be educated at Yale (then King's College) so he might be fitted to occupy his proper place in life.

There had been no college nearer than Harvard when Daniel was young to which he could go and when the college at New Haven was started it was too late to be of use to him, he was married and settled down to the life of a farmer, hence in his will, though equally entitled to the "Gentleman" or "Esqre" of his fathers, he says, "I Daniel Maltbie, Yeoman."

Grandly simple, unassuming words they seem to his descendant who writes this sketch. His father, in making his will, says, "I William Maltby, Esqre." One brother is called "Captain" and another "Gentleman" and this is as it should be, but we who follow after him are fond of this simple-hearted country gentleman living upon his broad acres in this new country, the wholesome, honorable life of an upright land-owner.

Such a one earns what he has by persistence and care; his gain is not taking the life-giving food from another; the money thus gained is not blood-money or got by graft, and so we who descend from this long departed ancestor give thanks for any strain of heredity which teaches us the patience of toil, the homiliness of the big fireside and the joys of life in the open.

* So many subscribers to this book descend from Captain Joseph Maltby that a word or two concerning him is inserted. Until very recently the name of his wife was unknown, but this has now been discovered by Miss Ethel Lord Scofield of East Haven, Conn. She was Elizabeth Pratt. Her ancestry has been very kindly conrtibuted by Mr. Douglas B. Thompson of Washington, D. C., as follows: "Elizabeth Pratt was a daughter of Jonathon and Elizabeth —— Pratt of Hartford, Conn., and granddaughter of John and Hepsiah —— Pratt, and great granddaughter of John and Elizabeth —— Pratt, who died at Hartford, July 15, 1655." The "Descendants of John Pratt," published in 1844, states that "Elizabeth Pratt married William Moulbe and nothing further has been ascertained of her." This is evidently an error, for we find Noah (4) Maltby, son of Capt. Joseph (3) "chooses his uncle Moses Pratt of Hartford, Guardian." In old manuscripts it is claimed that Joseph (3) Maltby entered Yale College, but did not graduate on account of ill health. Rev. Jonathan (4) Maltby states: "He was a ship Master and followed the seas."

This short article is written to the honored memory of her great, great, great, great-grandfather, Daniel Maltby by the compiler of this book.

ADDITIONAL NOTES OF THE DESCENDANTS OF DANIEL (2) MALTBY

Mary (3) Maltby married a Mr. Goodrich. (Further records requested.)

William (3) Maltby, not mentioned in his father's will.

Esther (3) Maltby m. Amos Harrison and had children: Esther (called "Lowly"), Amos, Mary, Lois, Ann and Edward.

Capt. Joseph (3) Maltby married Elizabeth Pratt and had children: Elizabeth, Joseph, Hannah, William, Noah, Jonathon and Martha.

Abigail (3) Maltby, m. (1) John Hall of Cheshire; (2) Ephraim Parish of Cheshire. (Records of descendants desired.)

Capt. Daniel (3) Maltby m. Mary Harrison and had children: Esther, Daniel, Mary, Hannah, Lucretia, Benjamin, Zaccheus, Sabra, Thankful, Lydia and Sarah.

Capt. Benjamin (3) Maltby m. (2) Elizabeth Fowler and had children: Elihu, died young; Benjamin, Thaddeus, Jonathon, Elizabeth, Sarah, Isaac, Stephen.

Martha (3) Maltby m. Daniel Howd at Branford (Descendants are requested to contribute records.)

John (3) Maltby not mentioned in his father's will.

SAMUEL MALTBY (2)

A pen picture of Samuel Maltby was written for the first Reunion of the Maltby family, at Branford, by Mrs. J. P. Cushman, a great, great, great, great-granddaughter, and we consider it the fitting and best of introductions to this long deceased ancestor.

MRS. CUSHMAN'S ADDRESS ON SAMUEL MALTBY (2)

It seems hardly appropriate for a descendant of Samuel (2) to occupy a moment of our precious Reunion afternoon, we are so hopelessly in the minority of members. Have you counted the printed list in our fourth annual report? Seven only from Samuel, eight from Jonathon, and ninety-five from Daniel! One is tempted to ask, "Who would not be a Daniel?" rather than stand so conspicuously alone.

However, as one purpose of our Association is to collect and preserve memorials of those who have passed into the land of silence, let me give a few gleanings made from records and traditions concerning Samuel (2), seventh child of William, our emigrant ancestor, by whose grave we are to stand this afternoon.

For one, I am deeply grateful that English Research work, the past year, has furnished four generations of Maltbys to fill in the background for any sketch of our American forbears. We can now see John (1) and Margerie of five hundred years ago with their four children: Richard (2) and his three: John (3) and Margaret with seven; John (4) and Mary with five—three of whom came to this New World about 1670, viz: John, William and Robert.

It is as the descendants of William that we are gathered at Branford to commemorate the two hundredth anniversary of his death. From our Genealogist we know he was a man of wealth and high position, a "gentleman" of his time, thrice married and the father of eight children. No one has learned the name of his first wife, the mother of two sons and two daughters. The second wife, Hannah Hosmer was undoubtedly the mother of Elizabeth and the Daniel whose descendants make so good a showing on our roll of members. A third wife, Abigail Bishop, was the mother of Samuel and Jonathon. It is this Samuel, of the second generation in America, who is the subject of our thought for a few moments.

His mother, Abigail Bishop, was the daughter of Dept. Gov. James Bishop of New Haven, and was born at that place Oct. 30, 1659. I have found no date of her marriage, but her first son, Samuel (2), was born Aug. 7, 1693, in Branford. It must have been a home of comparative luxury, for the inventory of his father's estate mentions many chairs, looking glasses, forks, spoons, tablecloths and napkins and two negro slaves. It is pleasant to have seen the record of his birth in his father's handwriting. (Branford records, Vol. II.)

The state records show the father was a member of the General Court at Hartford in October of that year. The baby Samuel was baptized before he was a month old as I read in the Branford Church records in manuscript.

These precious church records, Mar. 7, 1687-8, I was permitted to see many years ago at the home of Rev. Mr. Gillet, the Pastor, just a week before his sudden death. They were always kept, carefully wrapped, on a little table near his bed, that in case of fire they might at once be taken up and carried to a place of safety. The church had begun to appreciate their value and voted that, "no one remove them from their present custody except by special permission, granted at a formal business meeting." Is it known where they are now? Of course they should have been transcribed long ago.

Who made up the family circle to which little Samuel was added more than two centuries ago? His half sister Jane had married David Parker three years before. John had not yet married and moved to Saybrook. Mary probably died. William loved the sea, married and moved to New Haven, became Captain of "ye good Brigantine, the 'Friend's Adventure,'" and was lost at sea when only twenty-seven years old. Elizabeth was seventeen, and Daniel fourteen.

When Samuel was less than 3 years old, a little brother, Jonathan, made his advent in the Maltby household. The boyhood of these two own brothers we may picture for ourselves without a line of history. I found no record of Samuel's uniting with the Branford church, and no hint of his preparatory studies. He must have had advantages, however, for he graduated from Yale in 1712, before he was nineteen, in a class of two, the other being young Russel, son of the Branford pastor, Rev. Samuel Russell, in whose house Yale College was founded. During his college course Samuel was bereaved by the death of his father, Sept. 1, 1710, and being a minor became the ward of his uncle, Samuel Bishop. Though only seventeen years old he was named with his mother as executor of his father's will, with this same uncle Samuel Bishop (for whom he may have been named) as advisor and assistant. But the dear mother followed her husband in less than two months, Oct. 24, 1710, and was buried by his side.

By his father's will, Jonathon, the youngest son, received the "mansion house" in Branford and Samuel had the "Orchard" various sections of land in and around Branford with one half of any individual portion. So he was probably well equipped to begin life in his own name. In the list of "Freemen of Branford from 1715 his name accurs as the fifty-first.

December 18, 1715, he married Elizabeth Barker, daughter of William and Elizabeth Barker, who was born in Branford, December, 1691, and so was a year and a half older than her husband. The ceremony was performed by Nathan Harrison, justice of the peace, as was the custom of that time. The graves of her parents, William and Elizabeth Barker, lie very near those of her husband's parents, William and Agigail Maltby.

I found a curious record among the church manuscripts in Rev. Mr. Gillete's possession. It was written by the first pastor, Rev. Samuel Russel, in the church book, and then the pen was drawn across it twice, as if it had been put in the wrong place. I could not decipher every word.

"Agreed with Sl. Maltbie to keep school for the full . . . one year, commencing from the first of January, 1719 (?), and have engaged him thirty pounds passable money . . . his labor.

"Paid to S. Maltbie for the quarter . . . kept school, seven pounds and forty shillings toward payment of the present year."

So Samuel (2) was a school teacher four years after his marriage.

The following item from Vol. IV. of Branford Records was very gratifying: "Deed. Oct. 26, 1719. Samuel & Jonathon Maltbie of Branford, being fully persuaded it was ye mind and will of our Honrd. Father Willm. Maltbie that our brother Daniel Maltbie should have all his right and interest in Beaver Swamp, although not specified in ye last will of our Honrd. Father, have therefore given—&— all our rights in ye above swamp, 8 acres—etc."

The brother Jonathon moved to Stamford and sold out to Samuel some of the Branford lands. To these Samuel added "three several parcels of land in the Crotch of Bantam or Mill River, in Litchfield, for £220 and later three sixty acre lots and a 100-acre lot in the Crotch of Bantam Swamp, so called, for £560." These items I found in Litchfield Records, Vols. I. and II. Had the spirit of speculation already descended upon the earliest colonists of that section!

Samuel was town clerk in Branford from December, 1721, to November 22d, 1746, a period of twenty-five years. The records are in his handwriting from Vol. IV., page 384 to Vol. VI., page 602.

It is a find round hand, easily read, and pleasant to the eyes of his great, great, great, great-granddaughter!

In January, 1724-5, a license was granted him to keep a tavern in his now dwelling house until County Court in April, 1726. Bond of £20. This was renewed to "Capt. Samuel Maltbie" till 1728. How this title of Captain was secured I do not know, but it clung to him from 1727 to his death, and is found on his tombstone. [He was Saptain of Militia, according to Yale Class Histories.]

In the manuscript records at the State House, Hartford, "Vol. III. Ecclesiastical," I found Samuel Maltbie's name signed to a petition, May 12, 1726. Its nature I have not recorded.

The latest date thus far has been 1746, the close of his quarter-century as town clerk. Next comes his will, four years later—January 4th, 1750-1, made nearly a year before his death. "Being very sick and broke in body" he signed it only with a mark! This was found among the Probate Records of Guilford. The estate was valued at £7425.45. Lands amounted to more than £5000. A negro boy, silver spoons, clock, ring, seal and coat-of-arms are mentioned in the personal property. How I should like to recover from the past all—not the African.

This life which we have been tracing was closed on earth December 2, 1751, after fifty-eight and a half years. The burial was in Northford and it is probable Captain Samuel had moved from Branford Center to Northford—a part of Branford—where he owned land, and his son, Samuel (3), Jr., had settled. A picture of the tombstone is given in Booklet No. 2, page 70, also on page 68 the house built by his son, Samuel (3), and in which perhaps Captain Samuel died, as did five generations of his direct descendants. Is not this the oldest Maltby house in existence? It has been suggested that the Association purchase it for a Repository and Rallying place!

The children of Captain Samuel (2) were Abigail, James and Rebecca, who died before their father; Samuel (3) Jr., Mary and Sarah, who outlived him.

This son, Samuel (3), Jr., was father of the third Samuel (4). Then followed John (5), Rev. John (6) and another Samuel (7) my brother. So the line has been:—

1. William, the emigrant
2. Capt. Samuel
3. Samuel
4. Samuel
5. John
6. Rev. John

7. Samuel—seven generations with the very remarkable record that all sleep in the Northford "God's Acre" with the exception of the first, our common ancestor.

The following records were largely furnished by Mrs. Cushman and arranged and added to by the compiler.

CAPTAIN SAMUEL MALTBY (2) "A.B."

Samuel Maltby is called Captain and Squire. He was born at Branford, Aug. 7, 1693, and the record of his birth is there to be seen in the handwriting of his father. He was baptized the same month. (Branf. Ch. Rec., in M.S.)

1712. He was graduated at Yale College in the class of 1712 with the degree of A.B., at the age of 19 (Yale Triennial Catalogue). His father's death occurred during his college course, and on Jan. 13, 1712-13, we find, at a Court held this date, "Samuel Maultby, minor, of Branford, by Samuel Bishop, his overseer and next friend, and William Maultby, of New Haven, minor, by Elizabeth Maultby, his mother and next friend, plaintiffs contra Henry Cook of Branford, yeoman and defendant."

1715. Samuel Maltby married Elizabeth Barker, Dec. 8, 1715. (She was born in Branford, Dec., 1691, Bran. Rec., Vol. II.) The ceremony was performed by Nathan Harrison, Justice of the Peace, as was the custom of the day, but he was very probably a near relative, as Elizabeth Barker was the daughter of William and Elizabeth Harrison Barker. Elizabeth Harrison was born in 1667 and was the daughter of Sergt. Thomas Harrison, who was born in England in 1630 and married March 29, 1665-6, the widow Elizabeth Stent. He died in Branford in 1704. According to Branford Burial Elizabeth Harrison Barker died Jan. 22, 1741, and her husband, William Barker, died Feb. 1, 1741. (For the Harrison data I am indebted to (Mrs.) Frances Harrison Corbin of New Haven.)

1715-1730. Freeman of Branford, No. 51, "Samuel Maltbie."

1717. The following is a Deed witnessed by Samuel Maltbie during the period he was Town Clerk at Branford.

Vol. IV., p. 751. Eleazer Stent and Martha Stent, my wife, of Branford, for £4, 10 shillings to our brother, Samuel Ives, of New Haven, 1 acre of meadow at a place called Mr. Yale's farm. Bounded East by a ditch, North by meadow of our brother Ebenezar Ives, West by the upland and South by meadow of our brother, Samuel Ives.

Witnesses:	Eleazer Stent.
Uzal Wardell	Martha Stent.
Samuel Maltbie	4 April, 1717.

1719, Oct. 26. Jonathon and Samuel divide the land given them by their father (Branf. Rec., Vol. IV., p. 399).

1722, April 16. Jonathon Maltbie of Stamford, cordwainer, sells Samuel Maltbie of Branford, 2 acres and 3 rods of land in Branford, for £100 (Branf. Rec., Vol. IV., p. 426).

1723, March 25. Jonathon Maltbie of Stamford, gentleman, for £38, 10s, gives to his brother, Samuel Maltbie of Branford his interest in Cow pasture, 16½ acres (Branf. Rec., Vol. IV., p. 478).

1723, Nov. Samuel Maltbie of Branford, and William Maltbie* of Stamford, plaintiffs—about 7 acres of land (Vol. III., pp 171-176).

1724-5. License granted to Mr. Samuel Maltbie of Branford to keep a tavern, at his now dwelling house in Branford until County Court in April, 1726. Bond of £20 (Vol. III., p. 192). License renewed till 1727 (Bran. Rec., Vol. III., p. 215).

1726. Plaintiff about 20 acres of land (Vol. III., p. 229). Same case later (Vol. III., p. 234). "Capt. Samuel Maltbie of Branford renews license for tavern keeping till April, 1728. Bond £20 (Vol. III., p. 236).

1727. Same case again, surety for Wheadon. Bond of £300 to prosecute the case (Vol. III., p. 239). A further record states: Surety for Capt. John Wheadon against William Maltbie of New Haven, regarding 79 acres of land. Bond £20 (p. 222); also p. 239: Case of debt. Won the case (Vol. IV., p. 34).

1728. Vol. I., Litchfield Town Records, p. 372. Deed dated Nov. 18, 1728, from "Henry Cook to Capt. Samuel Malby of the town of Branford, in the County of New Haven. Consideration £60."

1730. Also: "Capt. Malbie's deed from Goodrich, July 5, 1730. Deed of land in Litchfield, from William Goodrich Oopotonnock in ye province of Massachusetts Bay, in New England, yeoman, lately of Litchfield, etc., to Samuel Maltbie of Branford, of 3 several parcels of land in the Crotch of Bantam or Mill River, for the consideration of £220" (Litchfield Rec., Vol. I., p. 536).

1732, Dec. 25. He was in two law suits as plaintiff (Vol. III., p. 362). Plaintiff for £80. Won the case (Vol. III., p. 468).

1735. Deed from Samuel Maltbie of ye County of New Haven, to John Lutley, for £560 of the three sixty acre lots in the Crotch of Bantam Swamp, so called, and 1 hundred acre lot. Ye 1st sixty acre lot I bought of Henry Cook and the hundred acre lot of Wm. Goodrich. Dated Apr. 17, 1735 (Litchfield Rec., Vol. II., p. 374).

* This is William (3), son of Capt. William (2). He went to Stamford to reside when his mather married Rev. John Davenport.

1736-7. Feb. 3. Plaintiff for £400. Granted (Vol. III., p. 473).

1743. Case of debt (Vol. IV., p. 191).

1744. Case of debt (Vol. IV., p. 224).

1740. In connection with Capt. Samuel Maltby it would perhaps be well to turn to Part I. under date 1740, and read the article copied from Thomas Hutchinson's History of Massachusetts, which refers to "Mr. Maltby, a large dealer in Coventry Stuffs and a zealous dissenter" and who seems to have spent "three weeks at Coventry," using all his influence. Did he visit relatives in England, and perhaps bring back with him the coat-of-arms mentioned in his inventory?

1743. We insert a deed, dated 1743. The question arises as to whether it pertains to Samuel Maltby, son of William, Esq. We know of no other Samuel Maltby living at this date. Of course it might be that the following record concerns a descendant of Robert Maltby, the emigrant. It is an unsolved problem at present.

"Springfield Deeds, Vol. N., 207. Normand Morrison of Hartford, etc., £1000 to Samuel Maltby of Boston in the Co. of Suffolk and province of Mass. Bay, Merchant, two parcells of land lying in the town of Bedford in the Co. of Hampshire, 1238 acres.

"20 April, 1743."

The compiler believes this refers to Samuel (3), son of Capt. Samuel (2). He was born in 1718, hence would have been 25 years of age in 1743. There is another Boston record in 1739, which reads: "Samuel Maltby married Ann Dyer at Boston, April 30, 1739." This is evidently the same Samuel as of Deed dated 1743.

Information of the above people requested.

1751. "Died at Northford, 1751. Deac. Capt. Sam'l Maltbie, 59. His widow died 1752.

CHILDREN OF CAPT. SAMUEL AND ELIZABETH (BARKER) MALTBY

(From Vol. II., Branford Records):

1. Abigail, b. Oct. 29, 1716.
2. Samuel, b. Oct. 21, 1718.
3. James, b. June 2, 1721.
4. Elizabeth, b. July 8, 1723.
5. Mary, b. Feb. 28, 1725-6.
6. Sarah, b. Nov. 10, 1729.
7. Rebecca, b. July 28, 1732.

1752. From Branford Deeds, Vol. VII., p. 232, we learn that. "Elizabeth Maltbie of Branford, Widow and Relict of Capt. Sampel Maltbie, late of Branford, dec'd, William Gould, Jr., and Mary,* his wife, and Sarah Maltbie, all of Branford, to John Factor of the same town, a parcell of land in the township of Branford at a place called Pipestone Hill, containing about 20 acres, known by the name of Maltbie's Pasture." 17 Feb., 1752.

The following Land Record from Branford, Vol. VI., dated Jan. 7, 1758, is worth inserting here:

"We, Edward Barker of Branford, John Barker of Wallingford, Jonathon Russell and Eunice Russell of Branford. (Probably she was Eunice Barker.) and John Tully and Mary Tully* of Saybrook, quit claim unto Jonathon Rose and Abigail Rose, his wife, John Frisbie and Anna Frisbie, his wife, Huldah Frisbie, William Barker, Samuel Maltbie, Wm. Gould and Mary Gould,† his wife, Edward Russell and Sarah Russell,‡ his wife, James Harrison and Abigail Harrison his wife, L—— Foote and Huldah Foot, all of Branford, all the estate rights that we have ever had unto the 4th, 5th, 6th and 7th division of land laid out to the estate of Mr. Edward Barker the first of Branford.

The following is the Will of Captain Samuel Maltby:

At a Court of Probate held in Guilford, December ye 18th, 1751.

Samuel Hill, Esq., Judge.
Nathaniel Hill, Clerk.

Nathaniel Harrison of Branford one of the Executors of the Last Will and Testament of Capt. Samuel Maltbie Late of Branford Dec'd Exhibited ye Will which being proved was approved in Court and ordered to be recorded and the said Executor accepted the Trust therein Committed to him and Samuel Maltby, son of ye Dec'd an other Executor Signified by writing as on file that he accepted the Trust by ye Will committed to him.

In the Name of God Amen the Twenty fourth Day of January, 1750-51, I Samuel Maltbie of Branford in the County of Newhaven and Colony of Connecticutt in New England being very Sick and weak in Body but of perfect Mind and Memory Thanks be

* John Tully married second, the widow of John Russell whose maiden name was Mary Barker. She died Oct. 11, 1757.

† William Gould's wife was Mary Maultby, daughter of Capt. Samuel (2).

‡ Edward Russel's wife was Mary Maltby, daughter of Capt. Samuel (2).

Note.—All the above are evidently the heirs of Mr. Edward Barker. The children, Samuel, Mary and Sarah, then living of Elizabeth Barker Maltby, inheriting their share through their grandfather William Barker.

given unto God Therefore Calling unto Mind the Mortality of my Body and knowing that it is appointed for all men once to Die Do Make and ordain this my Last Will and Testament that is to say Principally and first of all I Give and Recommend my Soul into the hands of God that gave it and my Body I Recommend to the Earth to be buried in a Decent Christian Burial at ye discretion of my Executors nothing Doubting but at the General Resurrection I Shall Receive the Same again by the Mighty power of God and as Touching Such worldly Estate wherewith it hath pleased God to bless me in this Life (after my Just Debts and Funeral Charges are fully paid and Sattisfied) I Give Demise and Dispose of the Same in the following manner and form:

Imprimis. I give and bequeathe to Elizabeth, my wife, one Third of my Estate, both Real and personal that is to say one Third of my Real Estate During Life the Improvement of which Shall be one Third of Each particular piece of my Land and buildings until her Decease and one Third of my Personal Estate forever to be at her own Dispose.

I Give and bequeathe to my Son Samuel Maltbie all my Land at Northford to wit all my Sixth and Seventh Division Lands and 4 acres Right from the Proprietors to Benjamin Tyler not yet laid out. Also my Right of Propriety and Highways in Branford also my meadow land in the Great Quarter (so called) also all my wareing apparrel also all my Books also my Gun my Cane my Ring my Seal 3 silver Spoons yt was my Hon'rd Fathers my Seal also my Desk my Case of Bottles and my Chest also my Clock and all my Husbandry Tools also my Negro boy upon this condition yet my Son pay all that is due from me to the School Committee of Branford.

I Give and bequeathe to Two Daughters, Mary and Sarah Maltbie all the Remainder of my Estate both Real and personal to be equally Divided betwixt them both.

Lastly I constitute Make and ordain my Son Samuel Maltbie and Nathaniel Harrison of Branford my Joint Executors of this my Last Will and Testament and I do hereby utterly Disalow, Revoke and Disannul all my and every other former Testaments Wills Legacies bequests and Executors by me in any way named willed and beqeauthed Ratifying and Confirming this and no other to be my Last Will and Testament. In witness whereof I have hereunto Set my hand and Seal the Day and year above sd.

his
SAMUEL (+) MALTBIE.
mark

Signed Sealed Published & Declared
by the sd Samuel Maltbie as his Last
Will & Testament in presence of us

Joseph Tyler
Jonathon Harrison, Jr.
Samuel Tyler

Branford, December 11th, 1751.

Then personally appeared Mr. Joseph Tyler, Samuel Tyler and Jonathon Harrison, Jr., and Made Oath that they Saw Capt. Samuel Maltbie Late of Branford Dec'd Sign, Seal and Declare this Instrument to be his Last Will and Testament and that they then Judged him to be of Sound Disposing and did in his presence subscribe thereunto as witnesses.

Nathaniel Harrison, Esq., Executor of the Last Will and Testament of Capt. Samuel Maltbie Late of Branford Dec'd Exhibited an Inventory of the Estate of sd Dec'd which was approved in Court and ordered to be recorded.

Inventory of ye Estate of Capt. Samuel Maltbie, Dec'd as apprised by the Subscribers being first sworn Branford Dec. 23, A. D. 1751.

House Barn & Home Lot about 6 acres . .	Lbs.	2700	0	0
Pasture at Pipestone Hill about 15 acres . . .		375	0	0
Land at Great Plain		1000	0	0
Right of Propriety		10	0	0
4 acres undivided Land		4	0	0
Salt Meadow in ye Great Quarter 7½ acres . .		350	0	0
Land at Northford Society 39 acres		1500	0	0
1 old cow, 18 lbs.; 1 white pide Do., 21 lbs. . .		39	0	0
——, 40 lbs.; Heifer, 18 lbs.; 5 sheep, 11 lbs . .		69	0	0
Wareing Apparrel		72	5	0
Books, ——; Ring, 3 lbs.; Seal, 20s		26	7	6
3 silver Spoons, 14 lbs. 5s; 8 Do., 12 lbs. . . .		56	5	0
Ditto, 4 lbs. 15s; 1 ditto, 2 lbs. 15s		7	10	0
6 Dishes; ———— old Bedstead		25	13	6
6 plates, 14s; 18 ditto, 10s; 7 ditto, 8s		16	0	0
3 pewter measures, 3 lbs. 10s; 2 cups and one bottle, 5s		4	5	0
2 pots, 2 tankards, 2 Spoons and 2 porringers . .		2	14	0
1 gun, 10 lbs.; 1 cane, 5 lbs.; 1 desk, 10 lbs. . .		25	0	0

1 Case of Bottles, 5 lbs.; 1 Clock, 5 lbs. . . .	55	0	0
Husbandry Tools, 20 lbs.; 1 Negro boy, 400 lbs. .	420	0	0
1 Brass Kettle ——— ———	39	8	0
1 small ditto, 40s; 1 Brass Kettle, 40s	4	0	0
1 Iron Kettle, 17 lbs. 2s; 6 Iron pots, 18½ lbs. 2s 6p	4	9	4
1 large ditto 32¾ lbs. 2s 6p; 1 Hand ditto, 40s .	6	1	8
1 frying pan, 17s, 3p; 1 Iron Skillet, 23s . . .	2	3	0
1 Small Brass Skillet, 15s; 1 pr Steelyards, 55s .	3	10	0
1 Cullender, 10s; 1 Skimmer and fork, 24s . .	1	14	0
1 ——— 5s; 1 Tunnel and Cover, 6s	0	11	0
1 Lignum vita Morter, 35s, 4p; Glass bottles, 12s	2	7	0
Sundrey Glasses and Earthen ware	4	12	0
1 Earthen bottle, 4s, 2p; 2 mugs, 3s, 1p; sauce-pan, 20s	1	20	0
1 pr of pinchers, 6s; 1 pr of Skales, 35s; 1 pr of old ditto, 5s	2	6	0
———, 3s, 6p; 6 knives and 13 forks, 28s . . .	2	13	9
3 Earthen Dishes, 12s, 6p; Table and frame, 30s .	2	2	6
1 table, 15s; 1 ditto, 8s; 1 cupboard, 20s . . .	2	3	0
A Lanthorn, 20s; 11 plain chairs, lbs. 8, 5s . .	9	5	0
6 Candlesticks, 8s; 1 ditto, 5s; 2 brass ditto, 30s .	5	13	0
A Great Chair & Cushen, 20s; A candle box, 10s .	1	10	0
2 pails and piggen, 25s; a basket, 5s	1	10	0
A Coat of Arms, 10s; 1 corn basket, 4s, 3p; ———, 7s, 6p	1	1	6
A pr of Tongs and Peals, 40s; 2 Trammels, 30s; 1 pr of Bellows, 5s	7	5	0
1 ovel Table, 4 lbs.; 1 Cherry tree ditto, 5 lbs. .	9	0	0
1 warming pan, 50s; 6 cane chairs, 60s . . .	2	10	0
1 Looking Glass, 25 lbs.; 2 small pictures at 5s .	25	10	0
1 case of Drawers, 25 lbs.; 1 mold table, 15s . .	25	15	0
1 old chest and trunk, 20s; a large form, 5s . .	1	5	0
A Trundle Bedstead and cord, 20s; A Great Spinning Wheel, 50s			
A Chest of Drawers, 10 lbs.; 7 Black Chairs, 11 lbs. 3s	21	3	0
1 flood Gate box Iron, 35s; 1 pr of Andirons, 10s	3	15	0
1 Small trunk, 3 lbs.; 1 ditto, 5 lbs.; 1 large box, 5s	8	5	0
1 Looking Glass, 15s, 1p; Lanscrip and Brazor, 4s	2	1	0
a prospret glass, 10s; a pair of spectacles and cap 10s	1	0	0
1 round box, 18s; fish hook line and lead, 30s . .	1	11	6
1 Buknife, 4s; Powder horn and flint, 5s . . .	0	9	0

——— Coin Silver	3	6	0
1 Damask blanket, 10 lbs.: Calico ditto, 3 lbs. .	13	0	0
22 pr of sheets, 110 lbs.; 6 napkins at 12s 6p . .	115	8	0
6 ditto at 5s; 1 Diaper Table Cloath, 50s . . .	4	0	0
1 Diaper Towell, 24s; 8 pr pillow Capes . . .	9	1	0
2 ditto at 3 lbs.; 10 Towels at 2 lbs. 16s . . .	5	16	0
1 bed 36 lbs; and furniture, 21 lbs.	57	0	0
1 Old Bed and furniture, 10 lbs.	10	0	0
furniture for another bed, 12 lbs. and pillows, 5 lbs. 5s	17	5	0
1 Bed 26 lbs.; furniture, 15 lbs.	41	0	0
1 ditto and furniture, 45 lbs.: 1 Seale, 30s . . .	46	10	0
13 vials, 1 ink bottle and 1 pr of andirons, 45s . .	3	10	0
88 pds of old iron, 6 lbs. 15s; a Dutch wheele, 50s	9	5	0
8 Old casks, 20s; a Meal Trough, 10s	1	10	0
2 Sives at 6s; 1 earthen pot, 4s			
3 bushels of meal at 30s and 3 bags at 8s			
1 Churn, 20s; 1 earthen pot, 4s	1	4	0
4 old Hhds at 20s; 1 Mashing Tub, 30s . . .	5	10	0
old Casks, 12s; 29 Beaf, 37 Tallow, 47 Hide .	20	15	9
——— Pork, 16 lbs.; 4 Swine, 10 lbs.	26	0	0
2 Towels at 5s; 1 chamber pot at 10s; 1 old iron pot	1	15	0
1 wooden Bottle	0	15	0
	7425	9	3

Samuel Barker }
Orchard Guy } Apprisers.

Nathaniel Harrison, Esq., Executor.
Sworn in Court

Test. Nathaniel Hill, Clerk.

It is a matter for sincere regret that the coat-of-arms mentioned in this inventory has been lost to posterity. It might prove the strongest possible evidence in making the connection with some ancient English pedigree.

For a full account of the descendants of Capt. Samuel Maltby see Maltby Genealogy.

Additional Notes of the Descendants of Samuel (2) Maltby

Samuel (3) Maltby m. (1) Abigail Wilford, and (2) Rebecca Foote. Child by first wife was Abigail. By second wife: Samuel, James, Jonathon and Rebecca.

Elizabeth (3) Maltby, believed to have died unmarried.

Mary (3) Maltby m. William Gould, Jr. She had a son, Samuel Gould. There may have been other children.

Sarah (3) Maltby m. Edward Russell of Branford. Children were John, Sarah, Mary, Abigail and Abigail.

CAPT. JONATHON MALTBIE (2), Gentleman

Jonathon Maltbie, the eighth child of William Maltby and the second child of his third wife, Abigail Bishop, was born at Branford, Conn., July 26, 1698, and his birth is so recorded in the handwriting of his father. (Branf. Rec., Vol. II.) He was baptized the same month. (Branf. Ch. Records, in M.S.)

In March, 1715, at the age of seventeen he united with the church at Branford (Branf. Ch. Man. p. 21). In Oct., 1710, Daniel Maltbie, his half-brother, was "appointed guardian to Jonathon Maltbie, minor, son of Wm. Maltbie of Branford, deceased" (New Haven Probate Rec., Vol. III., p. 235). Jonathon at this time was twelve years old. But Daniel was guardian for not more than two years, as then we find "Jonathon Maultbie, Minor, choose Mr. Edward Barker of Branford to be his guardian." (New Haven Probate Rec., p. 66, Vol. I. ?)

1718-19, Jan. License was granted to Jonathon Maltbie of Branford to practice the art and mystery of a tanner" (County Court Rec. of New Haven, Vol. III., p. 101).

1719. Jonathon Maltbie married, Sept. 25, 1719, Mrs. Sarah Potter at Stamford, Conn. They were married by the Rev. John Davenport.

1719, Oct. 26. Jonathon and Samuel Maltbie divide the land given them by their father (Branf. Rec., Vol. IV., p. 399).

1719, Oct. 26. Deed. "Samuel and Jonathon Maltbie of Branford being fully persuaded it was ye mind and will of our Honrd Father, Wm. Maltbie, that our brother Daniel Maltbie should have all his right and interest in Beacon Swamp, although not specified in ye last will of our Honrd Father, have therefore given, etc., all our right in ye above swamp—8 acres" (Vol. IV., p. 197. Branford Records).

This is an act of generosity and "square-dealing" that may well cause a feeling of just pride and respect in all descendants.

Jonathon Maltby evidently resided at Branford in the family homestead which became his by his father's will, 1710, until about 1720, when he evidently removed to Stamford, Conn., for the next record we find is:

1722, Dec. 7. "Deed, Jonathon Maltbie of Stamford, gentleman, gives land to Edward Barker in Branford" (Branf. Rec., Vol. IV., p. 446).

1722, April 16. "Jonathon Maltbie of Stamford, cordwainer, sells Samuel Maltbie of Branford, 2 acres and 3 rods of land in Branford, for £10" (Branf. Rec., Vol. IV., p. 426).

NOTE.—Here we find him called "cordwainer," while in a previous record he is licensed to be a tanner." Evidently he was proficient at both "arts."

1722, Dec. 7. "Deed. Jonathon Maltbie of Stamford, cordwainer, for £130 gives his brother, Daniel Maltbie, of Branford, 10 acres of land, being Jonathon's share of the home lot, given him by his father, William" (Branf. Rec., Vol. IV., p. 445).

1723, March 25. "Jonathon Maltbie of Stamford, gentleman, for £38—10 gives to his brother, Samuel Maltbie, of Branford, his interest in Cow pasture, 16½ acres" (Branf. Rec., Vol. IV., p. 478).

The History of Stamford says the first mention of Jonathon Maltbie is made among those who came in between 1643 and the Revolution.

Jonathon Maltbie represented the town of Stamford in the Legislature from 1735 to 1756 inclusive. He was also Captain of Company Two and on his resignation Ebenezer Weed was chosen Captain, about the year 1755. Begining in 1728 he servered as townsman, or selectman for twenty years and at this time was called Major Maltbie.

N. B.—The spelling is as that in the item sent me. Taken from Huntington's Hist. of Stamford.

Rev. E. B. Huutington also says that Jonathon Maltby was Captain of Company 2 in the French and Indian war.

In the records of the First Church, begun Jan. 1, 1747, is the name of "Jonathon Maltbie, Esqre."

Quoting again from Huntington: "Among the town notables of that day, 1746, were Col. Jonathon Hoyt, Captain Jonathon Maltbie and Mr. Abraham Davenport."

THE CHILDREN OF JONATHON AND MRS. SARAH (POTTER) MALTBIE

1. Jonathon, b. June 29, 1720.
2. Abigail, b. Aug. 26, 1725, at Stamford.
3. David, b. Feb. 7, 1727.
4. Sarah, b. July 5, 1731, at Stamford.
5. Mary, b. March 14, 1733, at Stamford.
6. Hannah, b. Oct. 30, 1741, at Stamford.
7. David, b. May 14, 1748. (This should probably be James).

NOTE.—The births that have "at Stamford" after them were copied from the Stamford records by Rev. R. B. Thurston, in a letter dated "Stamford, Jan. 17, 1866" and written to Mrs. John P. Cushman. There is evidently a mistake in the name of the last child given, as he could not have been born in 1748, and married in 1749. There is confusion in the records somewhere. One authority gives "Davide Maltbie married Sarah Holly, Sept. 28, 1749," while another claims their son Jonathon was born Sept. 28, 1749. Personally I believe that the name of the last born child of Jonathon (2) Maltby was James, and for proof would give the will of his mother. For records of the descendants of Jonathon Maltby (2) see Maltby Genealogy.

The Compiler is indebted to Mrs. Aaron T. Bailey and Miss Emily A. Lynes, descendants of Jonathon (2) for much of the data contained in this sketch. Mrs. Bailey and Miss Lynes endeavored to locate the grave of Capt. Jonathon Maltby and his old homestead, but unsuccessfully.

For the following wills of Jonathon and Mrs. Sarah Potter Maltby we are indebted to Miss Ethel Lord Scofield of New Haven and regret that time prohibited the copying of his inventory.

The Will of Captain Jonathon (2) Maltbie of Stamford (Stamford Probate Records, Vol. III., p. 291):

In the name of God Amen.

I, Jonathon Maltbie of Stamford in Fairfield County and Connecticut Colony in New England in America, being of Sound mind & memory for which God Almighty be thanked yet being advanced in years Laboring under Bodily Infirmities and Disorders Knowing it is appointed for all men once to Die not knowing how Soon my Change may Come Do now Declare my mind in This my Last will and testament as followeth: viz., I give my Soul to God my great Creator and the Lord Jesus Christ my all-sufficient Redeemer The Holy Spirit my Blessed Sanctifyer & Comforter and my Body to the Earth to be Buried in a Decent Christian manner according to the Discretion of my Executrix hereafter named having Hope in the Resurrection of the Just and touching Sad worldly Goods & Lands as it hath Pleased the Divine Bounty to Bless me with is that my Just Debts & funeral Charges Shall be first paid and to Enable my Executrix hereinafter named to pay them I do hereby authorize and Impower her to make Sale of my Lands as she Shall find Occasion and the Remainder of my Estate I Give & Dispose of in the following manner, viz.:

Imprimis. I Give & Bequeath unto my Loving Grandson, Jonathon Maltbie, the Son of my Dec'd Son Jonathon Maltbie of my Estate to the value of Thirty-five pounds Lawful money to be paid to him by my Executrix Hereafter named & to Enable her to pay it Do hereby authorise & Impower her to make Sale of So much of my Land as Shall be needful for that purpose.

Item. The Remainder of my Estate both Real & personal after my Just Debts and funeral Charges & the above Legacy to my Grandson are paid I Give Bequeath & Devise unto my Loving and Beloved wife, Sarah Maltbie, to be unto her and to her heirs & assigns forever. Further the Reason why I Do not in this my will give any of my Estate to any of my Children or to the Children of my Dec'd Son David is not because I have forgot them or have not a Suitable Regard for them but the Reason is this:

I have already advanced for my sd Dec'd Son & my Children which are Living & Given to them as Portion as much of my Estate as the Circumstances thereof will admit of & if my Said wife Shall not have occasion to Improve & Spend all that is above given her (She being the mother of all my children) I Leave it with her to Dispose of it among them as She Shall think Proper.

Finally. I Do nominate Constitute & appoint my said Loving wife, Sarah Maltbie Sole Executrix of this my Last Will & Testament hereby Revoking and Disanulling all and every other and former will and testament by me made & Ratifying & Confirming this & no other to be my Last Will & testament. In Witness whereof I have hereunto Set my hand & Seal the 19th Day of Sept., A. D. 1767.

JONATHON MALTBIE.

Signed Sealed published pronounced & Declared by Jonth Maltbie, Esq., the testator to be his Last will and testament in the presence of

Abrm Davenport
Peter Demill
Daniel Loder.

The will of Sarah Maltbie, widow of Jonathon (2) Maltbie, Esq. (Stamford Probate Records, Vol. III., p. 408):

In the name of God Amen.

I, Sarah Maltbie of Stamford in Fairfield County & Connecticut Colony in New England being of Sound mind & memory for which God Almighty be Thanked yet being advanced in years & Labouring Under bodily Sickness and knowing that it is appointed for all Men once to die and not knowing how soon my Change may come do now make my Last Will & Testament as followeth, viz.:

First of all I Give my soul to God who gave it me, hoping in his mercy thro' the merits of the Lord Jesus Christ for the pardon of all my sins & my body to the Earth to be buried in a decent Christian Manner according to the Discretion of my Executor hereafter named having hope in the Resurrection of the Just & touching such worldly Estate as it hath pleased the Divine Bounty to Bless me with while in this life my Will is that first my Just Debts & funeral charges shall be paid, the Remainder I Give Devise & Bequeath in the following manner & form, viz.:

Imprimis. My wearing apparel I Give & Bequeath unto my three Daughters, viz.: Abigail Squire, Mary Waterbery & Hannah* Buckley to be equally Divided among them & to their own absolutely & forever.

Item. The Remainder & Residue of my Estate I Give Devise & Bequeath unto my two loving Daughters, viz.: Abigail Squire & Mary Waterbury to be equally Divided between them and to be unto them the sd Abigail & Mary and to their Heirs & Assigns forever.

Further. The Reason why I do not give my Daughter Hannah an equal share with her Sisters is not for want of an equal affection to her but because my Dec'd Son James hath given her such a Legacy that I have not enough to make her Sister's equal with her & the Reason why I do not give some part of my Estate to the children of my Dear Son David Maltbie is not for want of a Suitable affection for them but because my Dec'd Husband gave to their Dec'd Father more than an equal share of his Estate.

Lastly I do nominate, constitute & appoint my Loving and Trusting Son-in-law Major David Waterbury Sole Executor of this my Last Will & Testament & I hereby give him full power & authority to sell of my Real Estate what shall be needful to pay my Debts & the Debts of my Dec'd Husband hereby Revoking & Disanulling all and every other former Will & Testament by me made and

Ratifying & Confirming this and no other to be my last Will & Testament in witness whereof I have hereunto set my hand and seal the 24th day of April, A. D. 1770.

her
SARAH (+) MALTBIE.
mark

Peter Demill
Ann Demill
Joseph Demill

NOTE.—Mrs. Maltbie was aged and feeble when she made her will, hence the "mark"; this does not in any way indicate that she was unable to write, as witness the will of Samuel (2) Maltbie, who signed his will with a "mark" although he wrote an unusually fine hand.

* MALTBIE-BULKLEY

Still standing in Fairfield, Connecticut, is the Bulkley House, now 137 years old. This house, which antedates the Revolutionary War, was the home of Peter Ebenezer Bulkley and his wife, Hannah (3) Maltbie. The Bridgeport Daily Standard, March 11, 1916, publishes a photograph of this old Colonial home and also an interesting article on the history of the Bulkleys, by Helen Harrison, from which we quote the most important items.

"The Bulkley family is sufficiently interesting to sketch its early history. Thomas Bulkley was the second son of Rev. Peter Bulkley, who was the tenth in line from Lord Robert Bulkeley, of "Bulkeley" manor, or as it was spelled in ancient days, "Buclough." He lived at the manor during the reign of King John, who died in 1216.

Peter Bulkley was born at Woodhill, Bedfordshire, England, in 1583. He succeeded his father, the Rev. Edward Bulkley, D.D., in the ministry of his native town. . . . He emigrated to New England about 1635, in the "Susan and Ellen."

Peter Ebenezer Bulkley lived in the house at the time the British sailed up the Sound to make an attack on Fairfield. (The view of the house given in Miss Harrison's article, presents the side open to the fire of the British guns.)

It is said that one of the old shingles on the house at that time is preserved as a relic by a Bridgeport family and shows the bullet hole.

As the British fleet was sighted, the men of the town, among them the head of the Bulkley house, hastened to the fort on Grovers Hill witht Lieutenant Jarvis.† Mr. Bulkley's wife, Hannah, a daughter of Major Jonathon (2) Maltbie, hurried the eldest son, Eben(ezer), 12 years of age, out to the yard for the oxen, hitched out front. The cart was hastily loaded with a few of the most necessary household effects and the five children were bundled on top, the house abndoned and the family set out for a place of safety back in the country." (These children were Ebenezer, aged 12; Hannah, 10; Maltbie, 8; Sarah, 5, and Mary, 3. This hurried flight in 1778 may account for the fact that the records show that the sixth child, John, born Oct. 28, 1778, died shortly after. In 1781 Abigail was born and the last child, George, was born in 1784.) "They had trundled along for five miles, up towards Plattsville, before a place of refuge was found, with some hospitable farmers by the name of Wilson.

The possible arrival of the British at the town of Fairfield had been anticipated and to guard against an unprepared attack, the family had taken the precaution to hide its more valuable possessions. Some of the lovely old blue china, brought by the trading vessels from the famous potteries of China and other far eastern ports, was hidden in a hole in the garden. Some delicate crystal bearing an ornamental tracing in delicate lines, was also carefully buried. The simple pewter plates and platters, beautiful in shape, were among the treasures consigned to the hiding place in the ground until the enemy should have departed. Some of these interesting relics of the Bulkley family, which were afterwards unearthed and given their place of honor again in the corner cupboard, are now in the possession of Mrs. F. W. Bolande, a daughter of Mr. and Mrs. John H. Beach and also a great-great-granddaughter of Maltbie Bulkley, who was born in 1770, and was one of the children to make his escape on the family oxcart." (Mr. F. C. Morehouse, a member of the Maltby Association, owns an old powder horn which belonged to this Maltbie Bulkley.) "Maltbie Bulkley's daughter, Ruth, born in 1800, made one of the elaborate bed spreads, with a design in French knots, all the work of the hand looms and of her nimble fingers. This, too, is a treasured possession of Mrs. Bolande.

† This Lieut. Jarvis we believe to be Lieut. Isaac Jarvis, born Jan. 20, 1756. He married Abigail Squire, who was a daughter of Samuel and Abigail (3) (Maltbie) Squire. She was a daughter of Jonathon (2) Maltbie.

After the family had safely got away, the British made a landing in spite of the fire from the fort, and of the bold front maintained by the little group of defenders. As they made their march up Beach lane, one of the first houses to be encountered was the Bulkley's, from which the family had so recently fled. They put the torch to it and passed on in spite of the fact that Tryon had promised that this and the other houses near it should be saved because of the aid given him by the brother of Mrs. Jonathon Bulkley, who lived opposite. A scout followed in the trail of the invaders to put out the fires, if possible.

The little family, who had fled, had left the washtubs filled with water in their haste. Before the flames had gained much headway with the hard and large timbers with which the house was constructed, the scout dashed the water on the flames and quickly had them extinguished. * * *

The motto of the Bulkley family, translated, means, "Neither rashly nor timidly," and the records of the little red salt-box house during the troublesome times of the Revolution showed that the motto was a fitting one.

We append a short note concerning the children of Jonathon (2) Maltbie.

Jonathon (3) Maltbie mar. Abigail Holmes of Greenwich, Conn., and had an only child, Jonathon (4), b. Dec. 7, 1744. He became Captain Maltbie. See his biography.

Abigail (3) Maltbie mar. Samuel Squire of Fairfield, Conn., and had children: Samuel, Sarah, John, David, Abigail, George and William.

David (3) Maltbie, mar. Sarah Holly. They had children: Sarah, Hannah (who died young), David (also died young), Abigail, David and Hannah. From the above Sarah (4) Maltbie, who married Stephen Newman, descend Mr. Henry Brown Dayton, Mrs. Samuel Bradlee Doggett, and Mrs. William Davis Patterson, whose names will be found on the membership list.

Mary (3) Maltbie mar. Major David Waterbury, of Stamford, Conn.

Hannah (3) Maltbie mar. Ebenezer Bulkley.

THE SPARTAN MOTHER

By Maude Townshend Maltby

(Written for Maltby Family First Reunion at Branford)

"A Spartan mother!" do they say
Who sees New England's coasts of gray?
"A Spartan mother!" they exclaim,
And hasten back to whence they came.

So to the child of warmer birth
May seem this rugged bit of earth;
Unsmiling, stern, forbidding,—yea,
Repellant, with its skies of gray.

But We, who know and love to trace
Each line upon our Mother's face,
We know, as loving children should,
Her every phase and trait and mood.

We know her iron-bound coasts that ring
To Ocean's age-old buffeting;
Unconquerable, squared to "face the front,"
And take—of what may come—the brunt.

We know her gentle inland hills;
The merry topaz brook which fills
Our leafy cup as we lie and dream
Long hours away beside its stream,

We know her deep pine woods whose trees
Murmur and breathe in the keen salt breeze
While out from the pine needles' sheltering,
The scent of the Mayflower tells of spring.

We know the harvest fields, and the moon
Which tells of a winter coming soon.
We know the ice fringed marsh and shore—
These things we know, and far, far more.

We know the children our Mother has reared—
World-wide respected, and honored and feared.
Where'er has been danger, or work to be done,
There has been, and shall be, a New England son.

Saints, soldiers and statesmen, where'er there is need,
Some child of New England stands ready to lead,
For the right; for the faith, for the weak against strong.
Glad to die, if in dying they vanquish some wrong.

"A Spartan mother!" Yes, and we
Accept the title reverently,
Rejoicing in her qualities
Wholesome and keen as an ocean breeze.

And so from North and South and West
Home we come at last to rest,
To the land we love beyond all other
To our New England—Spartan mother!

BIOGRAPHIES

REV. JONATHON MALTBY (4)

Rev. Jonathon Maltby was a great-grandson of the emigrant ancestor, William Maltby, Esq., of Branford, and to him we owe much of the genealogical data contained in the present Maltby Genealogy, particularly of the early generations.

Through the kindness of Mrs. Samuel E. Shipp, a descendant of his, we are able to reproduce here a copy of an oil painting made some years ago by Mrs. Shipp of the homestead of her great-grandfather. The old homestead was called "Maltby Place" and was delightfully situated on the bank of the river, alas, for posterity, it was too near the river! For when the two elderly maiden ladies, daughters of Rev. Jonathon (4), died, someone, we know not who, "got rid of the stuff" by throwing the contents of the attic into the river. And in this attic were all sorts and countless numbers of old things, now so prized by lovers of the antique, and chests of old letters and manuscripts there were without end.

The compiler is fortunate in the possession of two old plates which belong to Rev. Jonathon Maltby and possibly to his father,

Benjamin, though this is not certain. A "coffin handled" table spoon, however, came from his mother and bears the mark E. M. for Elizabeth (Fowler) Maltby. This spoon descended to a daughter of Jonathon (4) and is marked also with her initials. The writer remembers well what a delightful air of the past this old homestead used to have about it.

To Mrs. Theodore Clark we are indebted for a copy of a love letter written a few days prior to his marriage to his betrothed, Submit Taintor, by Rev. Jonathon Maltby. While calling on Mrs.

REV. JONATHON MALTBY HOMESTEAD

Stevens in Fair Haven, Conn., the compiler had the pleasure of seeing the charmingly simple but elegant wedding dress of this old-time bride. Made in the Empire style with low neck and short sleeves, of a heavy white silk with a fine blue stripe and an indistinct pale yellow figure in it. An old manuscript written by Rev. Jonathon dealing with the Maltby Genealogy and tied with bits of silk like this wedding gown, was given me by Mrs. Stevens and is a highly valued treasure.

The following is a copy of the letter:

New Haven, June 5th, 1787.

My dearest friend:—

I depend upon being at Northford Sabbath after next extraordinaries excepted. On the evening of that day I expect to hear of the Bride and Bridegroom. It will be the most joyful! The most interesting hour of my life!

I expect on that portentious moment to surrender myself at discretion—a voluntary captive to sweet smiling Hymen, a Devotee to Beauty and to Virtue—to be, not my own, but another's; to give my hand and my heart, and to receive in return the fair hand and the affectionate heart of my Other Self.

I will be thine—entirely thine—and thou shalt be mine, entirely mine, with all thy engaging and unfading charms. Happy! Happy Union! which harmonizes Two in One!!

'Tis Hymen lights the torch of love,
And beams benignant as the sun;
The daw, the rook, and gentle dove
Are ne'er content till two are one.

Innocence and Virtue are inseparably allied; emblematical of their purity is the pure white of this half sheet, which excites the following allusion:

Thou art the dear Maiden innocently sweet,
Who art fair white paper, an unsullied sheet,
I am the happy man, whom Heaven ordains
To write fair my name and take thee for my pains

Has Revd. sufficient health to tie the lovely bands? Or will it be expedient to invite my Revd. friend, Mr. Holmes, to ride out with me, and perform the gentle office?

With the finest sensibilities and the purest emotions, I am waiting to be completely yours.

Jonathon Maltby.

In booklet number one, issued by the Maltby association we published an article written by Rev. Jonathon Maltby and which proves he was "under fire" in the Revolutionary War, which seems of sufficient importance to warrant reprinting here.

Maltby Place, April 21, 1848.

Birthday of my 90th year.

At war with sin, heart from the world full-riven, aged and weary, the soul longs for heaven.

With one or two exceptions I have out-lived all my contemporaries, relatives and friends. Joseph Darling, Esqr., of the class of 1777 and classmate, Hon. Elizur Goodrich, D.D.L., are now living in this city. (NOTE I). I am oldest of the three. The former Treasurer of dear Yale, the venerable Deacon Beers, is several years my senior.

More than three score years ago, three brothers, in good health, were daily looking and expecting to see me sink into the grave. I was struggling with a violent cough and disordered lungs. But, I remain a monument of mercy. "A Wonder to Many! A Wonder To Myself!"

In my 90th year, 63rd year of wedded life. Read and write more than in any former time without aid of glasses. I am the only survivor of my father's numerous family. Mrs. M. is the only one living of her father's (NOTE II.) family, and is closing her 85th year.

My connection with college was in 1775. In the days that "tried men's souls," in time of the Revolution. A war spirit prevailed in the old 13—Patriotism warmed the hearts of the free born sons of Yale. Fired with the news of the death of their countrymen at Lexington, 100 of her sons, marshaled for fight, rush to Boston and I see an old gentleman point his cane and hear him say: "What do you think Gage (Gen. Gage) will say when he knows that a hundred men from Yale College are come to fight him?"

The upper classes, in the interval of studies, are on the lower green (NOTE III.) with their music, practicing, marching, maneuvering. . . . Soon after my acquaintance with alma mater, Col. Ira Allen from Vermont, brought the good news of the capture of the fort of the St. John's—a thrill of joy pervades the city and the college. Cannon are ordered out, 13 thunders, one for each state, tell the heartfelt joy. At the last fire, the Col., soldier-like, leaped on the cannon, swung his hat and cried aloud, "God save the Continental Congress! Three Cheers!" Oh, they were given to the life!

The war occupied too much of the student mind and such was the exposed state of college, while at N. Haven, that it was dispersed into several towns in interior of the state for two or three years, to the great disadvantage of the students. Classes (1776, 1777, '78, '79) had no public commencement.

In the summer time of '78, College returned. President Stiles was inducted into office and took charge of the seminary. July,

1779, Tryan and Traitor Arnold with three or four thousand British troops enter N. H. Night before at 9 o'clock an alarm was fired, again at 1, which put the town in the utmost consternation. That night and next day exhibiting such excruciating distress among the women and children as I hope and pray I may never again witness.

The students request the Selectmen of the town to furnish them with arms to meet the enemy—but are not able. Three of my class obtain arms and go out with Capt. Hillhouse and the Guards. David Austin and Elizur Goodrich are wounded, Austin brings in a prisoner (After Revd. D. Austin). Hon. Elizur Goodrich was a captive and Dr. Nesbitt pronounces his wound mortal. After being one night in town they cross next morning to East Haven. While in town they burn buildings, destroy house furniture, merchants' goods and groceries, and do all the damage that they could well do. The distress they made I will not attempt to describe. On Tuesday, I was one of a reconnoitering party on East Haven Heights where balls were whistling constantly, but no "music for me." A cannon ball took off all upper part of a Mr. Pardee's head and several were wounded. We have the pleasure to witness this 16th of Aug., that the wound of the Hon'l Elizur Goodrich was not mortal—with heartfelt joy we behold him one of the happy alumni. (Here follows a short genealogical sketch.)

J. MALTBY.

NOTE. I.—New Haven, Conn.

NOTE. II.—Mr. Nathaniel Taintor of Northford.

NOTE. III.—Old Green.

Rev. Jonathon (4) Maltby was a son of Benjamin (3), grandson of Daniel (2) and great-grandson of William (1).

GENERAL ISAAC MALTBY

General Isaac Maltby was born Nov. 10, 1767 at Northford, Conn. He was graduated at Yale College in 1786. He was a son of Benjamin and Elizabeth Fowler Maltby, his wife, and a grandson of Daniel (2). He was a student of divinity with Dr. Smalley of New Britain, Conn., and was admitted to the church there July 12, 1789, and licensed to preach the same year by New Haven, East. He married, Nov. 10, 1790, at Hatfield, Mass., Lucinda Murray, the only child of Seth Murray, who was a Brigadier-General in the Hampshire Militia in the time of the Revolutionary War, and he was persuaded by his father-in-law to settle in Hatfield. General Isaac and his wife resided most of their lives in her paternal mansion and their twelve children were all born in the same house where their mother was born. The house still stands on the Main Street at the turn of the Northampton road. (See photograph.) Gen. Isaac Maltby served throughout the War of 1812 and was a distinguished soldier and scholar. His commissions are in the possession of his granddaughter, Mrs. Frederick E. Foster.

General Isaac Maltby served as representative from Hatfield in the Massachusetts Legislature in 1809-10. He was the author

GEN. SETH MURRAY HOMESTEAD AT NORTHFIELD, MASS.
(Here Gen. Isaac Maltby Married and Resided)

of three books on military science, viz.: "Elements of War," "Military Tactics" and "Court Martial."

In 1803 he was appointed major in the militia. He took an active part in proceedings that were instituted vs. Gen'l Benj. Lincoln when he was collector of the port of Boston. In 1812 he was chosen Presidential Elector at a period in American History when the Electoral College was composed of notable men and when it was intended to select deliberately the President of the United States. In 1813 he was made Brigadier-General of Mass. Militia with headquarters in Boston, his son, Seth Murray Maltby, being paymaster in the same brigade with the rank of major. In 1816 he was again elected to the legislature and in 1818 he removed to Waterloo, Seneca County, New York, where he died the following year (1819).

The New Eng. Hist. and Gen. Reg. (1865), Vol. XIX., p. 338, has an article headed: "Reminiscences Connected with the War of 1812." It commences as follows: "In the summer of 1814 many portions of the militia of Massachusetts were called into actual service for the defence of the seaboard, especially in and near Boston. . . . Another brigade of the volunteer militia, organized and placed under the command of Brigadier-General Isaac Maltby, of Hatfield. . . ." (p. 339). "The regiment went into camp at Cambridge for a few days, but was soon removed to a place called Commercial Point, Dorchester, where were better accommodations.

"At Commercial Point, the regiment was drilled daily in the manual exercise, marching, wheeling, etc. It was reviewed twice at a place called Cedar Point, and on Boston Common by Governor Strong, Adjutant General Brooks, Generals Cobb, Mattoon, Whiton, Maltby, Blair and others, General Cobb remarking, 'That regiment knows enough and ought to go home and let the ignorant come and learn.'" A remark which must have been satisfying, as a well earned tribute, to Gen. Isaac Maltby.

His brother, Rev. Jonathon Maltby, speaks of him "as an eminent teacher of music."

Note.—It was the good fortune of the compiler to see a passport through the lines signed by Gen. Isaac Maltby, a document among many Maltby papers which have become the property of a dealer in antiques.

A letter from Rev. Jonathon Maltby to his brother, General Isaac Maltby, of Hatfield, Mass., dated "New Haven, June 20, 1812," is of sufficient interest to descendants to publish in abstract form:

"Dear Brother—

"You will remember that on the 12th of July, 1796, I announced to you the affecting death of our much hond Father—you are now daily expecting to hear of the death of his aged consort, our dear mother. But, Sir, the ways of unerring God are not the ways of erring man . . . it is not the hoary headed mother, but her youngest child, our dear Brother Stephen!

"On Monday evening, 22d Inst., at 12 o'clock the lamp of life was extinguished—after a week's illness. . . . A mother, a wife and her fatherless children, three Brothers and an only Sister mourn with heartfelt sorrow the sudden death," etc.

N. B.—This was Col. Stephen Maltby, great, great-grandfather of the compiler, who, by the kindness of Mrs. Higby, owns this ancient letter.

General Isaac (4) descended from Benjamin (3), Daniel (2), William (1).

The letter which follows was contributed by Mrs. F. E. Foster and is well worthy of insertion in these pages.
Copy of letter from the

Honl. George Thatcher, of Supreme Court,
to
J. Hill, Esq.

Biddeford, 11th Feb'y 1810.

My Dear Sir,

I have just read Genl Maltby's Report Published in the Palladium on our Foreign Relations & the Conduct of our National Administration in relation to the *famous pretended insult.* The Report I fully approve: & to reject it or in anything to weaken it would be treason against good sense & sound policy, & it would be more criminal than to have pardoned Luke Day in the time of Shyes insurrection. Therefore I tell you now, as I told you at that time "do anything but pardon Luke Day." If you reject those Resolutions, you must not return to Biddeford.

Who is this Genl Maltby? His Report argues good. If I am not mistaken he made a very energetic Report & Speech on some great national question last Winter.* I like him. If you have any acquaintance with him make my respects to him & tell him he is right in his notions. Encourage his heart & strengthen his hands to fight the Lord's battles. We have no news here. Everybody that possesses common sense here gives over all expectations of finding Robert Smith's *insult.* They say it is all a matter of juggling to impose a little while on the credulity of Republicans, but the spell is wearing off. Keep up a good tone in your proceedings. There is nothing gained by giving way to the Devil. Yield an inch and he will take an ell.

George Thatcher.

To Jonathan Hill, Esq.

* Refers to the proceedings against Smith.

An account of General Isaac Maltby would be incomplete were some mention not made of a few of his descendants who are, or should be, well known to the public today.

The fourth child of General Isaac Maltby was Maria Maltby, who married Thomas Cutting Love of New York. Their oldest daughter, Madame Cary (Julia Love) has recently died at her home in Buffalo, New York. Madame Cary was a remarkable woman of rare individuality and charm. The following extracts concerning her life are taken from the Buffalo Courier and the Buffalo News, of October 9th and 10th, 1915: "In the passing of Mme. Cary (Julia Love), Buffalo loses a beautiful woman—beautiful in the highest sense of the term—one with all the graces of mind and heart and femininity, a typical gentlewoman, whose loveliness was compelling. Devoted to home, she was always the center of a large family circle, who gave her unmeasured love and attention.

But outside of her kinspeople there were many to whom Mme. Cary was known, for in her younger days she was the acknowledged leader of Buffalo society, and still with the passing of the years, this fine gentlewoman held sway, even though Buffalo society is made of many circles. No charity ball, the climax of each season's gaiety, has seemed complete without the presence of Mme. Cary, the grande dame in her shimmering ivory satins and rare laces, and her advent was always marked by a hum of interest and a steady stream of friends to pay court to her in her box. And a rarely lovely picture she made in her sweet dignity, product of the elegant training of past generations, with a spirit of unquenched youth. Though old in years, as they are counted, Mme. Cary was as young as the youngest and loved to be surrounded by youth and beauty, and to youth and beauty she was ever a stately queen, to whom it was a happiness to pay court.

Every afternoon at 3 o'clock Mme. Cary was wont to take her daily drive, and, in the parks, her passing was always marked with interest by those who knew her, and by those who saw only a lovely old lady, just stepped from a bower of lavender and flowers to enjoy an outing in the sunlight.

"It is given to few women to stand out alone, with no double, no rival, in a city of half a million, and it is thus Mme. Cary has stood for more than half a century. Her death yesterday leaves a vacancy none may hope to fill, because of her enormous individuality and her consistent expression of the same. * * * "She had just returned, with her sister, Miss Love, from an extended trip to Panama, to the San Diego and San Francisco expositions, where she was honored by everyone, many special attentions being paid her in San Francisco where she had many friends."

The return trip was made over the Canadian Pacific route and to her every mile of the trip was a delight * * * and friends made her progress home by easy stages a journey de luxe." "So much was the journey enjoyed by her, that she even talked of extending it to Honolulu and Japan."

Madame Cary was eighty-eight years of age. Five sons and the husband of her only daughter acted as bearers at her funeral, while two grandsons and a great grandson attended the services at the family lot at Forest Lawn."

The above notices refer to Mme. Cary's only daughter, who is Mrs. Lawrence Dana Rumsey. Her son, Charles Cary Rumsey, had many beautiful pieces of sculpture at the San Francisco exposition, and his Pizzaro was one of the four great pieces at the Fair.

Mrs. Rumsey's youngest son, Lawrence, deserves special mention in these pages. He comes from a long line of "fighting ancestors." Since 1630 his ancestors on the Maltby and White side of the house have been fighters. French-Indian wars, Revolutionary War, the War of 1812 and our own Civil War have found his forebears ready to fight, and if need be, die for their country. We have not forgotten that in the black days of our own struggle for Liberty, France came to our aid—certainly Mr. Rumsey has remembered, for now "somewhere in France" his aeroplane hovers over the battlefields.

Shortly after war broke out Mr. Rumsey went to Dunkirk and served ten months in the American Ambulance Corps, carrying the sick and wounded from the station to hospitals about the town and countryside, at times chased by German Taubes dropping shells *at the line of Red Cross ambulances* as close as 50 yards! At the front trenches near Ypres he took his turn relieving the exhausted chauffeurs. *Six* days was all a strong man could endure at a time. (While at Ypres he walked over to "The Cloth House Tower" and picked a yellow rose which he sent his mother.) Later Mr. Rumsey joined The Foreign Legion to become an aviator. His quickness of action acquired from polo, hockey and football have doubtless been a great help in preparing him for this stupendous game of war. Four months' study and thrilling practice at Paris, France, won his "brevet" (commission) as "Pilot;" although he had hoped to obtain a "chasseur"—a plane that is used to chase off and fight to the death the Zeppelins, but it happens that these require men long in the service, who do not even *think* of their machines! Mr. Rumsey's letters are concise and brief—and he failed to speak of his escape from an accident and splintered plane, until his family wrote for particulars, having seen the report in a newspaper.

Mr. Rumsey was practicing his "test for a triangle" at an altitude of 3,600 feet; he had reached his second side when the engine went dead, and the plane, *upside down,* fell 2,400 feet, he pulling and jerking to start the engine. 1,200 feet from the ground he was able to right himself and engine, but had to land as best he could, having no time to "pick the spot!"

The next flight he was lost four hours in the clouds with no compass. Then at last he saw snow covered mountains, and put for them as he realized he was over Spain and to land would mean "internment for the war." As his gasoline was low he was obliged to land again without reaching the hangar; but on the mountain side.

He is "somewhere at the front" pilotting "map-takers" or "bomb-throwers." The papers tell us frequently that "a squadron of French planes hovered over the battle fields," and that is all the news one gets, for the mails lately have brought no news to the anxious hearts at home. To this brave and gallant officer our hearts must go out in sympathy with his work, and honor him as all such brave men should be honored, and when the time comes that our own country has need of such men and service, may we find the Spirit of '76 still living in the hearts of those Americans, who like Mr. Rumsey, come from a long line of ancestors, who freely offered their lives to protect their homes, and their country.

Another descendant of Gen. Isaac Maltby is Major Reginald Love Foster. Major Foster has kept up the military traditions of his family. He was in the class of '91, Yale University. Now after twenty-two years of service he is a major in the 12th Infantry, U. G., N. Y., and aide de camp on the staff of Gov. Whitman. He also served in a similar capacity with Gov. Hughes, Gov. Sulzer, Gov. White and Gov. Glynn. Major Foster is a veteran of the Spanish-American war, and at present is a newspaper man on the New York World.

MRS. LUCINDA MALTBY

wife of Gen. Isaac Maltby

OBITUARY

Died at Buffalo, N. Y., on June 9th, 1844, aged 73 years, relict of Gen. Isaac Maltby, who, in 1818, emigrated from Hatfield, Mass., to Waterloo, N. Y., where he died in the following year.

It may be wondered at that a life so quiet and unobstrusive as Mrs. Maltby's should find more than the common brief record of its close, and, especially, that it should call public attention in a part of the country where she was never much known and from which she had been absent so many years. She had no ambition for posthumous renown. By none would it have been less expected than by her who was not emulous of distinction while among the living. She was too earnestly bent on duty to care much for fame. Her desire was to find favor in the sight of God: and, surely, if in his sight "a meek and quiet spirit is of great price," hers is among the richest treasures gathered from the dust of the world.

Mrs. Maltby was the daughter and, we believe, the only child of Col. Seth Murray, of Hatfield, and was bred in the most intelligent, refined and virtuous society with which her native town and its vicinity were favored. But she reckoned not quality by descent nor searched for her virtues in the family record. Se was a "lady" in the most honorable meaning of that misunderstood word—in those accomplishments which are of far more difficult attainment and of unspeakably more worth than all the affluence of fortune set off with the skill of politeness and the costly array of fashion. Not negligent of the proprieties of outward appearance and demeanor, the grace she most studied and was most adorned by, was of the hidden person of the heart. Good sense and great virtue were the worthy elements which made up her character—elements few as those of the air we breathe, and, like them, forming the transparent vital sustenance of being. Simplicity and godly sincerity a stranger would at once read in her countenance, and an acquaintance always admire in her life. Her benevolence was a matter of deep principle and active habit. It was not with her, as with too many, visible only in the sunshine and on the tranquil sea of life, but, like the humble yet sacred bird of the mariner, most sure to appear in the darkness and peril of the storm. The faults of others she had no willingness to search out, and therefore no special gift to find or to suspect; and, if their obvious presence could not escape her notice, she was more ready to pity and forgive than to inflict censure.

however much deserved. The performance of her duties was a concern of every day and of all their hours. She was not of those who lived abroad, and run to and fro after piety. Her own house was her home, and her religion burned bright and cheerful at her own fireside. Neither was her welfare mainly sought in schemes and efforts for securing distant or imagined good, but her happiness was never nearer being complete than in promoting the joy of those around her. Nevertheless, the law of kindness in her heart was exceeding broad, and, while it shed a blessed influence on her own family and neighborhood, it spread over the largest circle of human need. The rites of hospitality she performed as if she were her own guest, except as she never seemed quite so happy as in blessing others, whether kindred or strangers. Her piety was of the quick conscience rather than of the nimble tongue and of a simple rather than of subtle faith. Equally remote from the exclusiveness of bigotry and the blindness of indiscriminate charity, she thought well of all whose lives exhibited the principles of her blessed Lord and Redeemer. She did not exact from others duties which she was backward to perform herself; but as a wife and mother, as a friend and neighbor, as a disciple and a professed follower of Christ, she was a pattern whom all in these relations might profitably imitate.

Of her own goodness she was neither boastful nor seemed conscious, and well could her lips afford to be silent when her life was so constant a repetition of praise. But with all of her excellent qualities, she was humble for defects not discerned by others, and prayerful for forgiveness of sins and for grace that in nothing she might offend. If meekness and gentleness, if undissembled good will, if not to be weary in well doing, if patience in tribulation, if communion with God, if an humble but cheerful hope in her Redeemer are evidence of Christian character and of a title to the Christian's reward, her inheritance is now with the saints in light.

Blessed spirit! Thou hast indeed entered into thy rest. Thou hast forsaken the cares, the sorrows, and all the infirmities of this sinful and troublous world. They shall never again approach thee, for thou hast ascended to heaven and put on immortality! Thy bright example is yet with us. Happy shall they be who have the wisdom to imitate it. The glory which thou hast shall be theirs also.

Reader, she who is the subject of this heartfelt tribute was to you personally unknown, and, perhaps, the present is the first time you have learned even that she lived. But, if to such virtues as adorned her life yours is not a stranger, this imperfect memorial will not be deemed unworthy of your regard. You will understand that the record of true goodness, wherever and whenever it has lived, though not even the name of its possessor were written, is grateful in every tongue of every clime.

(Signed) G. A.

Worcester, Mass., July 2d, 1844.

MARTHA CHURCH MALTBY

(Mrs. Harlow Swain Love)

For this sketch of Mrs. Harlow Swain Love we are indebted to her daughter, Mrs. Frederick E. Foster. Mrs. Love was a daughter of General Isaac Maltby (See Biography.)

Martha Church Maltby was the youngest of the ten children of Gen. Isaac Maltby and Lucinda Murray, his wife, who was the daughter of Gen. Seth Murray, an officer during the entire war of the Revolution and who participated in nearly all of the early engagements and was present at the Battle of Bennington, and also at the surrender of Burgoyne. She was born in Hatfield, Mass.; later her parents removed to Waterloo, N. Y., when she was but two years of age, and upon her marriage to Mr. Harlow S. Love, their home was established in Buffalo, N. Y., where all of her five children were born. Prior to 1860 the family made several trips to California by way of Panama, and in that year they located permanently in San Francisco, where Mr. Love, until his death in 1866, was a prominent member of the legal profession, and where, later, their son John became Attorney-General of the State of California and subsequently the city and county attorney of San Francisco.

Mrs. Love was a person of great intellectuality, refinement and cultivation and of a lovely and graceful presence. She was endowed in an eminent degree with all those tender attributes which endear a woman to the circle of her familiar friends and possessed that gentleness and benevolence of character which purifies and softens the social atmosphere of her surroundings. To these qualities were united an unostentatious charity and helpfulness which all of her intimates have reason to remember with affectionate gratitude. Her literary attainments were of a high order; and for many years she contributed to the public prints articles on various subjects, which were widely read and favorably received. She also devoted much labor and attention to genealogical research, and was instrumental in tracing and rescuing from oblivion the lines of her descent from Colonial and Revolutionary ancestors, all of whom were of distinguished stock.

Mrs. Love crossed the Pacific Ocean numerous times, visiting Hong Kong, China, on the occasion of the marriage of her daughter, Leila, to William Hammond Foster, Jr. (a member of the celebrated American house of Russell and Co., China) and some years later making her home with the youngest daughter, Martha, the wife of Frederick E. Foster, successively in Yokohama, Japan, and Hong Kong, China, where Mr. Foster represented, as General Agent, the trans-Pacific lines of steamers plying between those ports and San Francisco. Mrs. Love and her husband are interred in Lone Mountain Cemetery, San Francisco, California, and are survived (in 1908) only by their daughter, Martha (Mrs. F. E. Foster) now residing in Mount Vernon, N. Y.*

NOTE.—Mr. Maximilian Foster, the well known author, is a son of Leila Love who married William Hammond Foster, Jr., a grandson of Martha Maltby Love, and great-grandson of General Isaac Maltby.

Major Seth Murray Maltby, son of General Isaac, was the father of Mr. George Beecher Maltby, Mr. John Whitehouse Maltby and Mrs. Albert T. Higby (Mary Maltby), whose pictures will be found on the opposite page. George Beecher and John Whitehouse are the two oldest "Maltby twins" known to the compiler and are seventy-two years of age.

From left to right, seated on the bench are Mr. George Beecher Maltby, Mary Maltby Higby, and Mr. John Whitehouse Maltby. Standing are Mrs. George Beecher Maltby, who kindly furnished the photograph and Mr. Albert T. Higby. This photograph was taken in the summer of 1910, and we regret to record that shortly after Mr. John Whitehouse Maltby's death occurred.

It will be sad news to many of the Maltbys to learn that shortly after photograph of "the Maltby Twins" was taken, Mr. John Whitehouse Maltby began to fail rapidly in health. On June 17th, 1911, he passed away at the home of his twin brother, Mr. George Beecher Maltby, in Aurora, Indiana, a hardening of the arteries being the cause of his death.

* Mrs. Love took great interest in her Maltby ancestors and was indefatigable in her efforts to obtain family records and old documents. This work is always a labor of love and in her time was doubtless unappreciated and undervalued, but posterity can not fail to be grateful for the careful work done by her, and must honor her for her persistency in carrying on labors which met with little encouragement or response.

Mr. Maltby, accompanied by his son, made the sad journey east to the old home in Rochester, New York, and there on June 20th, buried his brother beside his wife, who had died on Oct. 20th, 1908, and whose loss had caused a breaking down in health from which the bereaved husband never recovered.

Mr. George Beecher Maltby died April 22, 1915.

CAPTAIN JONATHON MALTBIE, 3d

The following sketch was written by Miss Lynes:

My great-grandfather, Jonathon Maltbie, 3d, was the only child of Jonathon, Jr., and Abigail Holmes Maltbie; born at Stamford, Conn., December 17, 1744. He removed to Fairfield, Conn., and married Elizabeth, the daughter of David and Sarah Gold Allen Oct. 23d, 1768. He was a sea captain in the East India trade and lived in one of the historical houses given in the "History of Fairfield County" as "Colonial No. 4." This house was built in 1766 by Isaac Tucker, who sold it to Captain Maltbie, who owned and occupied it during Revolutionary times, and was one of the few houses left standing at the burning of Fairfield. Mr. Henry Rowland, a grandson, in writing some reminiscences, states that "grandfather Maltbie's (house) was reserved for a cook house. After the conflagration the inhabitants returned (when the British had gone aboard their ships). Grandfather Maltbie on returning to his house found all their valuable china scooped off the shelves on to the floor and broken into pieces and everything upside down. In the kitchen in the fireplace hung a large brass kettle filled with their hams, but they dare not eat them, fearing that they were poisoned (so they started anew with provisions)."

Captain Maltbie's son, William, inherited this place and sold it to Justin Hobart. The house is still standing today in good condition. Jonathon Maltbie was 1st Lieutenant of the "Trumbull," one of the first cruisers built for the Continental navy; Dudley Saltonstall, Commander. She went into service about April, 1780, carrying 28 guns and her crew numbered 200. Her first engagement under Captain Nicholson, occurred June 2nd of the same year, with the "Watt," (Query: Wasp?) an English letter-of-marque, under Captain Colehart. She carried 34 guns and 250 men. The "Watt" was a private vessel with a cargo of great value and was especially equipped to fight her way. This was the first action of any moment that occurred in 1780 and had the reputation of being the most obstinate and sanguinary naval battle during the Revolution. The "Trumbull," being badly disabled, failed to capture the "Watt," although she defeated her.

The next summer, 1781, she left the Delaware, still under Captain Nicholson, having been thoroughly equipped as convoy to 28 sail of merchant craft bound for Cape Francois, West Indies. Off the capes, the "Trumbull" met three British cruisers astern. Two of them, one being a frigate, stood for the "Trumbull," which

CAPTAIN JONATHON MALTBIE HOMESTEAD AT FAIRFIELD, CONN., PURCHASED AUG. 13, 1773

ship, by hauling up gained the wind of them. While standing on in this manner, hoping everything from the darkenss which was fast approaching, a gale carried away the "Trumbull's" foretop mast, which, in falling, brought down the main gallant mast. She was otherwise disabled and night coming on was unable to clear up the wreck. At 10 o'clock the "Iris," 32 guns, one of the vessels in chase, closed with her and forced her to combat. In the midst of rain and tempestuous winds, Captain Nicholson found himself obliged to go to quarters or to strike without resistance. He preferred to do the first, but the English volunteers on board his ship, instead of obeying orders, went below, extinguished lights and secreted themselves. Near half the remaining men followed their example and Captain Nicholson could not muster fifty of even the diminished crew he had at the guns. The battle that followed might almost be said to have been fought by the officers. These brave men sustained by a party of petty officers and seamen managed a few of the guns for more than an hour, when the "General Monk," 18 guns, coming up and joining in the fire of the "Iris," the "Trumbull" submitted. The "Trumbull," after her capture, was towed into New York harbor and condemned. Though unsuccessful in her battles, she still fought two of the most famous fights that took place on the ocean during the exciting times of the Revolution.

Jonathon Maltby was afterwards appointed Master of the "Argus," a cutter in the service of the United States for the protection of the revenue. He died Feb. 11th, 1798, while in command of this vessel, and was buried in the old cemetery at Fairfield, Conn. The date of Jonathon Maltbie's commission as 1st Lieutenant is Oct. 12th, 1776. Date of commission as Captain by George Washington, March 21st, 1791.

Through the kindness of Mr. Frank Pentecost of Lawrenceville, Georgia, we have received a copy of the commission of Jonathon (4) Maltbie, signed by George Washington. Mr. Pentecost tried to obtain a photograph of the document for us, but the photographers said it would be impossible as the type has become too indistinct.

Mr. Pentecost is a great-grandson of Captain Jonathon (4) Maltbie, descending from William (5) Maltbie who went south, and from William's daughter, Mary (6) Maltbie. The Commission:
George Washington, President of the United States of America.
To all who shall see these Presents Greeting:

Know ye, That reposing special Trust and confidence in the Integrity Diligence and good Conduct of Jonathon Maltbie of Connecticut I do appoint him Master of a Cutter in the service of the United States, for the protection of the Revenue and do authorize and empower him to execute and fulfil the Duties of that Office according to law and to have and to hold said office, with all the rights and Emoluments thereunto legally appertaining unto him the said Jonathon Maltbie during the pleasure of the President of the United States for the Time being.

In testimony whereof I have caused these Letters to be made Patent and the Seal of the United States to be hereunto affixed. Given under my Hand, at the City of Philadelphia, the 21st day of March in the year of our Lord one thousand seven hundred and ninety-one and of the Independence of the United States of America the Fifteenth.

Signed G. WASHINGTON.

By the President,

Thos. Jefferson.

A few records obtained by the compiler are appended:

In Dec., 1775, we find the following record: "Continental Fleet. in which were many Rhode Island officers, as well as from the other colonies, under command of Commodore Esek Hopkins of Providence. Ship Alfred, one of the fleet, Dec., 1775, Capt. Dudley Saltonstall, 1st Lieut. John Paul Jones. Among three other Lieutenants was Lieut. Jonathon Maltbie." (Ref. Civil and Military List of Rhode Island, 1800-1850, by Smith, p. 704.)

1776. His commission as lieutenant is dated October 12, 1776, and signed by John Hancock.

1778. Frigate "Trumbull," Capt. Dudley Saltonstall, was launched. Jonathon Maltby, 1st Lieutenant. Capt. J. Nicholson of Pa., afterwards, Capt. Saltonstall being transferred to the "Warren." "Trumbull" captured off the Delaware Cape by the British ships "Iris" and "General Monk," after a gallant resistance of more than one hour, during which she was completely dismantled and lost five killed and eleven wounded (Ref. Navy of the United States, by Lieutenant Emmons, p. 3).

1791. Commission as Captain dated March 21, 1791, signed by Gen. George Washington.

In Collections, Conn. Hist. Soc. is a letter from Col. Gurdon Saltonstall, dated "New London, Jan. 23, 1776," to Silas Deane, Delegate to the 1st and 2nd Congress at Philadelphia. It mentions "Second Lieut. Maltbie's crew," Vol. II., p. 353.

Mr. John H. Beach of Bridgeport writes that several years ago Mrs. Florence Isham Cross read a very interesting paper at a meeting of the Mary Silliman Chapter, D. A. R., on Lieut. Jonathon Maltbie, in which she describes him as "having red hair and a quick temper." It would be interesting to know how Mrs. Cross obtained this information, whether from written documents or if perchance from a portrait which has been lost to the family.

ZACHEUS MALTBIE

Zacheus (5) Maltbie, whose photograph we show on this page, was born August 19th, 1774, and baptized September 18, 1774, at Norfolk Connecticut.

He was the fifth child of Daniel (4) and Margaret Munson Maltbie. [Daniel (3), Daniel (2), William (1).]

According to the record given in an old family Bible, he married Reunah Burchard, April 5, 1797: she born May 22, 1777. Possibly they were married at New Marlborough, Massachusetts, as Burchard seems to be the name of a resident family in this town.

/.

ZACHEUS MALTBIE

Miss Lucy Ann Morton writes that Reunah Burchard was the daughter of David and Mercy Burchard and that she had two brothers, Ezra and Amos Burchard. David Burchard's name appears in the New Marlborough list, census of 1790—"7 in family."

March 1, 1808, Amos Burchard of New Marlborough, hatter, purchased land of Zacheus Maltby situated in Lee. Shortly after the marriage of Zacheus Maltbie to Reunah Burchard we find them at Lee, Mass., where their first child, Ezra Burchard, was born, April 1, 1798. Their second child, Mercy Burchard, was born Feb. 8, 1800, at Lee, Mass.

On March 1, 1802, Zacheus Maltbie was appointed a fence viewer at Lee, and elected constable and collector in 1805 and 1806. November 30, 1807, the town appointed a committee to settle with him, and chose a collector to succeed him, from which it would apear he had left town about that time. In May, 1808, his "cattle mark" was recorded for another person.

Daniel and Lester Maltbie do not seem to have been born at Lee, for their births are not recorded here.

Miss Lucy Ann Morton, whose mother was the Mercy Maltby born at Lee in 1800, remembers her grandfather and grandmother

REUNAH BURCHARD (MRS. ZACHEUS MALTBIE)

and says "they came overland from Lee, Mass., to Groton City, N. Y., and had to clear the land to build as it was all wooded land at that time. Mother (Mercy Maltby) was seven years old when they came from Massachusetts." Consequently we may suppose the trip was undertaken the last of 1807 or early in 1808.

Zacheus Maltbie settled at Summer Hill, Cayuga County, N. Y., and built himself a house that was quite complete for those days. Miss McGeer tried to obtain a photograph of this old homestead but could not, consequently we must depend upon her description. "The house, of which only a part of the original, is still standing. Formerly there was quite a building in the rear but it has either blown or been torn down. It is one and a half stories high.

"Some of the wall decorations are still to be seen; trees, birds and pictures painted on the walls." (All are painted not papered, you understand.) "Last summer the great big fireplace was boarded up, but I remember the old-fashioned brick oven, and what was called a 'recess' built off the living room. My mother, Margaret Ann Maltby was born here."

Miss McGeer's father also remembers Zacheus Maltby and says: "He was a hatter and used to trap for mink and muskrat which he made into fur hats by the old 'hand process'—people came from Auburn and other places to have him make their hats."

Melville Barry Smith, prior to his death, wrote: "Grandfather Zacheus Maltby was a hat maker. I can just remember his showing me some hats he took from a shelf and telling me he made them."

Sylvester Daniel Maltbie wrote: "Father, Ezra B., served in the war of 1812 for grandfather Zacheus—father being only fourteen or fifteen when he enlisted."

James M. Maltbie wrote: "Grandfather was known and called by nearly everybody 'Uncle Zack.' I have forgotten his father's name. I have heard him say that his parents lived in or near Lee, Mass. He moved into this state when my father was very young, locating in the town of Groton, Tompkins Co., but finally removing to Summer Hill, Cayuga Co., where he died. He was a hatter by trade, and my father worked with him. He used to hunt and trap for furs and was also a noted fisherman. He was a good singer genial and a good story-teller, so the young people all delighted to get Uncle Zack to telling stories. He had six children, Ezra, Mercy, Daniel, Lester, Alanson and Margaret.

"My father, Daniel, married Desire Howland and her sister, Mary Howland, married a cousin of my father's. James Maltby and he had a brother, Seth Maltby, who resided in Syracuse and I think was a banker. He had two daughters.

NOTE.—Allen, Seth, Bridsey and James Maltbie were children of Jehiel and Phoebe Maltbie and Jehiel was the oldest brother of Zacheus, consequently James and Seth were first cousins of Mr. James Maltbie's father, as stated.

Mr. James R. Maltbie also writes: "Grandfather had a younger brother named Daniel, who came into this state with him. He studied medicine for a while but became ill and settled on a small farm in Groton and lived a hermit life there for forty years, but finally came to my father's and spent his last days with us. I think Seth Maltbie of Syracuse removed to Oswego before he died."

Mercy (6) Burchard Maltbie
(Mrs. Abel Knapp)

Daniel (6) Maltbie

Margaret (6) Ann Maltbie
(Mrs. John Camden Wilson)

Ezra (6) Burchard Maltbie

The children of Daniel (4) and Margaret Munson Maltby were:

Anne (or Anna), b. 1765, at Goshen, Conn.
Jehiel Merriman, b. at Goshen, Conn.
Daniel Munson, b. 1770, at Norfolk, Conn.
Sally, b. 1772, at Norfolk. Records wanted.
Zacheus, b. 1774, at Norfolk, Conn.
Hannah, b. 1776, at Norfolk, Conn.; d. Oct. 14, 1777.

Anne married Samuel Stevens of New Marlboro. Descendants wanted.

The children of Zacheus (5) and Reunah Burchard Maltbie were:

1. Ezra Burchard, b. April 1, 1798, at Lee, Mass.
2. Mercy Burchard, b. Feb. 8, 1800, at Lee, Mass.
3. Daniel, b. May 22, 1802.
4. Lester, b. Oct. 5, 1806.
5. Thomas Alanson, b. Jan. 21, 1809. (See below.)
6. Margaret Ann, b. Oct. 8, 1817.

Zacheus Maltbie died July 10, 1856, and his wife, Reunah Burchard Maltby died March 15, 1864, in Summer Hill, Cayuga County, New York.

The photographs which accompany this article were kindly furnished by Miss Clara E. McGeer and are:

1. Zacheus Maltby, b. 1775; d. 1856.
2. Reunah Burchard (his wife), b. 1777; d. 1864.
3. Ezra Burchard Maltby, b. April 1, 1778.
4. Margaret Ann Maltby Wilson, b. Oct. 8, 1817.
5. Daniel Maltby, b. May 22, 1802.
6. Mercy B. Maltby Morton-Knapp, b. Feb. 8, 1800.

The photograph of the Maltby heirlooms shows the walking stick which belonged to Zacheus Maltby. It is a hickory stick mounted in ivory and has the initials "Z. M." on the top.

The cover on the stand was woven by Reunah Burchard Maltby and is a yellow and white check-linen. The candlestick also belonged to Mrs. Zacheus Maltby. The cherry stand with glass knobs and the chair (of maple or birch) with a woven cord seat (woven like split bottom and probably replaces a split bottom one) were both the property of Margaret Maltby Wilson.

The second son of Thomas Alanson Maltby was Corydon Oscar Maltby, born in Homer, Genesee Co., N. Y., May 15, 1838. In early life he moved with his parents to Kenosha, Wis., and later

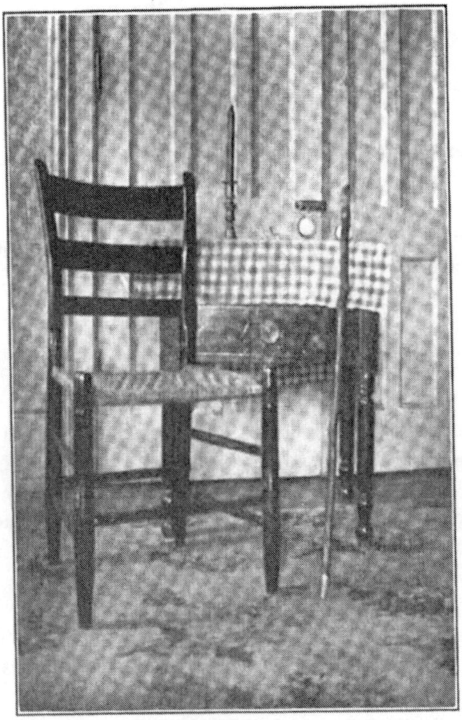

Zacheus Maltbie heirlooms.

See description page 334.

to Lake Co., Illinois. On the 22nd of May, 1859, was married to Mary R. Gilbert. At the outbreak of the Civil War Mr. Maltby enlisted as a private in Co. F, 37th Illinois Infantry. He was engaged with his regiment in many of the important campaigns of the western army and was honorably discharged Sept. 22, 1864. After the war he moved to Allamakee Co., Iowa, and later to Winneshiek Co., where he lived till his death.

He was for many years one of the prosperous agriculturists of the county until his retiring from active life, since which time he made his home with his children.

For many years he took an active part in the politics of the county, ably serving the people for several years as assessor and as a member of the Board of Supervisors. He was also a valued member of the G. A. R., keeping in close touch with his comrades, who will feel the loss of their comrade.

He died Aug. 11, 1915, at the home of his daughter, Mrs. Fannie Whitney.

SARAH KEYES MALTBY

This interesting silhouette was very kindly sent us by Mrs. J. A. Thompson of Owosso, Michigan, a granddaughter of Jacob (5) Maltby and his wife, Sally Keyes. Jacob Maltby was born in 1776, and married Sally Keyes January 3, 1803. He went from Norfolk, Connecticut, and settled on the Western reserve near Unionville, Ohio, called "New Connecticut."

Mrs. Tyler, a granddaughter, has furnished us with some information concerning Sally Maltby. She writes: "Grandmother was lame, a spare built, very prim person. She was a very fine needle woman and taught me to sew and knit. She was born in Litchfield, Connecticut. My grandparents came to Ohio sometime in 1820 or 1821. My grandfather, Jacob, was a very quaint old man. When I look back to my childhood days I see him in the play house he built for my sister and myself, playing with us, entering into all our sports like a little one with us. My mother was his idol and favorite daughter-in-law. My father's family were very proud and men of splendid habits. The old stock of Maltbys, as far as I know, were men of the very best of habits."

It is just such bits of personal data that we desire for our genealogy—little things which bring back more closely to us those who have gone.

Such items are difficult to obtain. Few of us could write much about our grandparents if asked and as for great-grandparents, we should know nothing.

We feel very grateful to Mrs. Tyler for bringing back to us a glimpse of the grandfather who delighted in giving happiness to his grandchildren, and the grandmother who taught the little fingers the art of fine sewing.

John (5) Maltby, Esqre., (see portrait) was born October 22, 1778, in Lenox, Mass. He was the son of William (4) and his second wife, Catherine (Lee) Maltby. Catherine Lee, b. 1755, at Lenox, Mass., was the daughter of Stephen and Catherine (Forbes) Lee; granddaughter of Dr. Isaac and Hary (Hubbard) Lee; great granddaughter of Dr. Stephen and Elizabeth (Royce) Lee; and great, great granddaughter of John and Mary (Hart) Lee of Hartford and Farmington, Conn.

John Maltby married in 1805-6 Lucy Cox, daughter of William and Mary (Sawin) Cox, of Watertown, Mass.

He was in the Revolutionary War and is buried in West Fairlee, Vermont. Upon his tombstone is this inscription: "HE HELPED STEEP THE TEA IN THE ATLANTIC."

Some of the ancestors of Lucy (Cox) Maltby were: Matthew Cox, 1756; John Sawin, 1690; William Russell, 1661; John Coolridge, 1691; Edward Winship, 1613-1688; Simon Stone, 1585-1665; Mary Belcher, d. 1691; Rebecca Barsham, b. 1656; Elizabeth Rouse of Ludbury; George Munning, b. 1597; Sarah Bass; Elias Barron, d. 1676; and Joan Clark, b. 1597.

The children of John and Lucy (Cox) Maltby were:

Milk Maltby, b. Oct. 13, 1807.

Mary Maltby, b. 1810.

Norman Maltby, b. Apr. 15, 1814.

Mrs. John Maltby died Nov. 12, 1844, in Andook, N. Y., and her husband died May 4, 1856, in Footville, Wisconsin.

The following is an abstract from an obituary:

"John Maltby, died in Footville, Wisconsin, May 14th, 1856, aged 79. He was born in Lenox, Mass., and removed to Vernon, N. Y., forty years since. About the same time he experienced the renewal of his heart by the Holy Spirit, and, it is believed, ever after both enjoyed and even exemplified the religion of Christ. He was greatly endeared to the church in this place (Vernon) and when he removed to Footville, his farewell address was full of

JOHN MALTBY

Born October 22, 1778, in Lenox, Mass. Died May 14, 1856, in Footville, Wis. Married 1805-6, Lucy Cox, born 1786; died November 12, 1844, in Andover, N. Y.

kindly admonitions and counsels, we all wept; for in his bending frame and broken voice we read the evidence that we should see his face no more, the world had few better men than father Maltby.

He died as he had lived happy in the prospect of eternal life."

Signed: E. P. WILLIAMS.

MR. NORMAN MALTBY

"Mr. Norman Maltby, whose portrait we publish, was born on his father's farm near Vernon Centre, Oneida County, New York, April 15, 1814; when he was about eighteen years of age it was recommended that he take a sea voyage on account of his health, so he went on a sailing vessel to England. During the voyage an incident occurred which he often related, the ship had been becalmed for several days, and on the day the first breeze came up he was standing on the deck with a companion who asked him, 'When did the Captain say we should reach land?' He replied: 'In about six days.' A sailor standing near remarked: 'The ship may, but you will go over the side before that.' His companion, who was really a robust man but imagined he had every kind of disease, burst into tears and said, 'What will become of *me*, I certainly will die before you do.' To which Mr. Maltby answered: 'What does an old ignoramus of a sailor know about whether I shall live or die, I am going to England on this ship and not only that but I am going back to America.' The sailor looked him over and said: 'Well, when a man looks as you do, has that much grit and nerve it wouldn't surprise me if he did.'

This spirit of never-give-up carried him through many trials in after life.

On his return to America he went to Westmorland where he became a clerk in a general merchandise store; one of the first instructions he had from his employer was 'Obey orders if you break owners.' and, 'If you sell anything that is to be charged, if the store is on fire make the charge, then save the books and anything else you can.' Later he went to Verona and entered into partnership in the general merchandise business with William S. Armitage, under the firm name of Maltby and Armitage. In 1861 he removed to Cleveland, N. Y., and from there in 1863 to Rome, N. Y., where he, in connection with Samuel Wardwell organized the firm of Wardwell and Company, dealers in hardware, at 54 Dominick Street. In 1865 he went to Missouri in farming and sheep

NORMAN MALTBY

Born April 15, 1814, in the town of Vernon, Oneida County, New York. Died November 20, 1886, in Sedalia, Pettis County, Missouri.

raising in Henry county. In 1868 he removed to Sedalia, Mo., and engaged in mercantile business, in which he continued until his death in 1876. While he was never a politician he was elected in 1875 Mayor of Sedalia. He was a States Rights Democrat, was opposed to the war, was a delegate to the peace convention at Charleston, was for many years a member of the Methodist Church, but left it in 1863 as he said 'He could hear all the politics and war talk he wanted to hear during the week, and did not want to hear it from the pulpit.' He soon after became a member of the Episcopal Church at Rome, and was vestryman and warden of the church at Sedalia, being senior warden at the time of his death. He was a conscientious Christian, a man noted for many sterling qualities of head and heart, and for his honesty and integrity.

Mr. Norman Maltby married Sept. 16, 1841, Lovina Maria Wright, daughter of William and Susanna (Sessions) Wright. Mrs. Maltby descended from a great many prominent families, some of them being: John Wales of Idle, Eng.; John Greenaway, Dorchester, Mass.; Thomas Stevens, London, England; Major Simon Willard; Thomas Brigham, b. 1603; Ralph Wheelock; William Ward; John Pope; William Blake, b. 1594; Thomas Axtell; John Corbin; the Spoffords; Alexander Sessions; Edward Wright, etc.

The children of Norman and Lovina (Wright) Maltby were:

1. Lucy Jane Maltby (Mrs. Edward Payson Powell).
2. Helen Lovina Maltby (Mrs. William Taylor Thornton, widow of Ex-Gov. Thornton of New Mexico).
3. Mary Persis Maltby (Mrs. John P. Victory of Santa Fe, New Mexico).
4. William John Maltby.
5. Arthur Norman Maltby, of Kansas City, Mo., who very kindly furnished this record.

REV. MALTBY GELSTON

Rev. Maltby Gelston is a descendant of the emigrant ancestor, Mr. John Maltby, who married Mary Bryan. They had two children, twins, John and Mary, born at New Haven, Conn., June 1, 1673.

John Maltby, Jr., married Susannah Clark and removed to Southampton, Long Island, where he died June 27, 1706. His tombstone is said to be still standing and should be photographed before it is too late. The Maltby name died out in the line of descent from Mr. John Maltby, as John (2) had only one child who married, namely, Mary (3) Maltby, who became the wife of Judge Hugh Gelston. Hugh (4) Gelston was their tenth child, and his only child was the Rev. Maltby (5) Gelston, born July 17, 1766. He was ordained April 26, 1797, and for forty-five years he was settled in the ministry at Sherman, Conn., where he died Dec. 15, 1856, aged 90.

The compiler has one of his sermons written in a beautiful clear handwriting which contrasts vividly to many an "educated hand" of modern times.

ELON MALTBIE, ESQRE.

Elon Maltbie (see portrait) was the seventh child of Benjamin (4) and Abigail (Munger) Maltbie. He was born (probably at Northford, Conn.) March 8, 1783. When but three years old he removed with his father to Norfolk, Conn. He married, April 22, 1807, Hannah Osborne of Colebrook, Conn. She was born June 11, 1786; d. Sept. 10, 1873, aged 87. (See tombstone at Norfolk.) He died Oct. 18, 1865, aged 83. The children were:

1. Elizur Maltbie.
2. Milo Harrison Maltbie.
3. Laura Ann Maltbie.
4. Jesse Alonzo Maltbie.
5. William Henry Maltbie.
6. Charles Benjamin Maltbie.
7. Rhoda Julia Maltbie.
8. Mary Elizabeth Maltbie.

ELON MALTBIE

Son of Benjamin (4). Born near New Haven, Conn., March 8, 1783. Died in Norfolk, Conn., Oct. 18th, 1865. He was one of twelve children and removed to Norfolk with his father when three years old.

CHARLES BENJAMIN MALTBIE, SON OF ELON MALTBIE

TIMOTHY MALTBY, ESQ., AND HIS SIX SONS

We are indebted to Mrs. Albertus Dye for this interesting photograph of Timothy Maltby, Esq., and his six sons, Hiram, John, Charles, Rollin, Col. Ralph Robinson and Chauncey Smith Maltby.

Timothy (6) Maltby was born March 15, 1794 in Paris, New York. He married, first, Beulah Harmon, March 22, 1815, in Richland, Oswego County, New York. He was in the war of 1812. The dates of his sons' births were as follows: Hiram, born in 1817; John, born in 1822; Charles Rollin, born in 1824; Ralph Robinson, born in 1830, and Chauncey Smith, born in 1833.

NATHANIEL HARRISON MALTBY

Nathaniel Harrison (5) Maltby was born in Norfolk, Connecticut, March 31, 1786. He married, first, October 16, 1811, Betsey Patchen in Groton, Thompkins County, New York. He was in the war of 1812, enlisting from New York. He removed to Bristol, Trumbull County, Ohio, and died there in 1855, and with his second wife, Sally Mason, was buried in the Maltby Burial Ground in Southington, Ohio.

The following article contributed by a descendant will be found of interest to members of this branch of the family:

MR. AND MRS. HARRISON MALTBY CELEBRATED GOLDEN WEDDING

("Evening Independent," Ashtabula, Ohio, August 24, 1910.)

A notable event in the history of the Maltby family of Ashtabula County and Saybrook, was the golden wedding celebrated yesterday, August 23, by the family and friends of Mr. and Mrs. Harrison Maltby.

Mr. Maltby is one of the oldest well known residents of this section and is hale and hearty at eighty years of age. He married Miss Emily Hough of Rooktown, Ohio, who has been to him a helpmeet in the founding of a home remarkable for its ideals.

Mr. Maltby, as were his ancestors before him, is a farmer. He is of that sturdy American stock which has wrested a living from the wilderness for as far back as one hundred years before the Revolution. He was born in a log cabin in 1830, at Southing-

TIMOTHY MALTBIE, ESQ., AND HIS SIX SONS

ton, Ohio, and knew well the hardships, the early settlers endured. In him are typified the Maltby characteristics of strong home love, honesty and firm religious principle.

The is the second golden wedding in the House of Maltby. In 1868 under the same hospitable rooftree that sheltered yesterday's event, Mr. Maltby's father, Deacon Daniel Maltby, and his wife, Esther Tapping, gathered about them a company of ninety to rejoice with them in attaining the fiftieth milestone in their married life. Everyone of the thirteen children were present and a host of grandchildren. Deacon Maltby was one of the earliest pioneers of the Western Reserve, journeying with his wife to Ohio in an ox cart in 1820, from New York State.

The occasion of his son's anniversary yesterday was most delightful in every way. At noon bounteous tables were spread in the orchard of the old homestead for the large company of sons, daughters, grandchildren and friends and neighbors present. Rev. Collins of the Congregational church gave the invocation. At the close of the feast, the toastmaster, T. J. Osborne, presided over a short program. Telegrams and letters of congratulation from those unable to be present were read. Some old familiar songs were sung. Toasts were responded to briefly by Mr. H. A. Beckett, Mrs. Clark Throope and Dr. M. C. Scott, pastor of the M. E. church. Rev. W. E. Rix of Wisconsin, pronounced the benediction.

In the evening fifty of the Saybrook friends and neighbors surprised Mr. and Mrs. Maltby by walking in on them to further congratulate and wish them many happy returns of the day. They brought with them substantial refreshments which were served later in the evening, and a token of regard in a gift of gold pieces, Rev. Collins making the presentation speech. Mr. Maltby in a voice broken with emotion, responded.

Various gifts in gold and other suitable presents had been received earlier in the day.

Of the sons and daughters living there were present Mr. and Mrs. T. J. Osborne of Berea, Ky.; Mr. and Mrs. H. A. Beckett and Mr. and Mrs. L. C. Hinman of Lakewood, Ohio, and Miss Ruth Maltby. Other out-of-town guests were: Mr. and Mrs. Clark Throope of Ashtabula, Rev. and Mrs. W. E. Rix of Lake Nebagamon, Wis., Mrs. Mary Beckett of Lakewood.

Two sons, Albert Maltby of Hastings, Fla., and Benjamin Maltby of Long Beach, Cal., and their families were unable to be present.

SKETCH OF THE LIFE OF ESTHER TAPPING MALTBY

Samokov, Bulgaria.

Dear Kindred and Friends:—

I received, by kindness of Mrs. C. S. Verrill, the first two numbers of the Maltby Booklet and found them very interesting indeed.

My life has been so full of work and my field of labor so far away from my family and friends that I have had little time and opportunity to cultivate the acquaintance of even near relatives.

It was with much hesitancy that I undertake, at the request of Mrs. Verrill and my cousin, Miss Martha J. Maltby of Columbus, Ohio, to write a sketch of my life, for I have had very little chance to develop the little literary gift I have. Still, with the hope that some account of my past, on the great battlefield of life, may be of some interest to those of kindred blood, I send this manuscript.

It is vacation time and sitting under the pines at this beautiful wooded mountain resort. I have written this review of a very busy life of service. I am very glad I have had the privilege of laboring so many years for the girls of this young and progressive country of Bulgaria.

Sincerely Yours in the bonds of Kindred.

Esther Tapping Maltbie.

August, 1910.

A LONG LIFE SPINS A LONG YARN

In a large farmhouse in Southington, in the state of Ohio, on the last day of April, 1836, a mother looked into the face of her eleventh child and a patriarchal father thanked God for another little girl to love and cherish. The mother did not shrink from the added burden of care and anxiety when with almost its first breath the little one showed signs of the whooping-cough, but courageously nourished the feeble life that many times seemed to have taken flight until the solicitous father saw his little Esther, the mother's namesake, a happy, joyous child upon his knee at morning and evening family devotions.

Childhood glided swiftly by amid the innocent pleasures of a large group of wide-awake children and the busy scenes of farm-life. A lasting impression was made upon Esther's young mind when her father speaking to a family friend of her baby illness

MISS ESTHER TOPPING MALTBIE

that so many times threatened the life of his favorite, turned and laying his hand upon her head, as she stood near him, said solemnly, "My dear child, God has not spared your life for nothing. He has a work for you to do."

The parents resolved to give their large family of children all the educational advantages in their power, so the older ones, besides the district school, were sent to the Academy in an adjacent town. Dissatisfied with the superficial teaching of the ordinary district school, their oldest daughter was finally installed teacher of the young children. It was in this family school at the age of ten that Esther's mind received an impetus toward higher intellectual development and she entered with great zest into the study of mathematics and nature study. "Dick's Works," of which two great volumes were in her father's small library awakened much wonder and thought, especially his theory of the universe.

Previously she had settled in her own mind her doubts in reference to the existence of God from the effects produced by the invisible powers of nature. If matter could be invisible why not being unembodied? At this time also her spiritual nature opened up to the Light of Truth and she began to realize the deep meaning of an endless life and turned to the Saviour of the world for forgiveness and strength.

Before she had an opportunity to go away from home to school she did considerable reading. Hume's History of England was read before the family rose in the morning. "Plutarch's Lives" interested her much and she devoured nearly all of the books in her father's library.

She commenced the study of Greek and Latin in preparation for college under a French professor at the age of fifteen, when going away to school for the first time. Her class consisted of two young boys and herself. She will always be grateful for the fatherly interest that old gentleman took in his class, whom he addressed as, "doctor, lawyer and professor." The boys fulfilled his prediction and the other life has been spent in teaching.

When Esther consulted her father in reference to going to college, he replied, "If my daughter wishes to live for herself only, the less she knows the better, for her influence will be less for evil; but if she desires to live for others, to help others, the more knowledge she acquires the better, for 'knowledge is power.'" After six months of teaching in a district school she entered the preparatory department of Oberlin College, Ohio, and commenced the hard struggle to obtain an education. To help defray her expenses she taught in the long vacations and graduated with four other girls from the Classical Course in 1862, which was an unpopular thing to do for at that time it was thought unnecessary for girls to study the Classics. During all the years of preparation an inward consciousness of the truth of her father's words abode with her; whispering, "God has something for you to do," and the cry of the millions, sitting in darkness, for light echoed and re-echoed within her heart.

During the Civil War she was a missionary of the American Missionary Association to the Freedmen in Virginia and afterwards taught in Wilberforce University, an institution for colored students, which was burned down on the evening of President Lincoln's assassination, April 14th, 1865. After this she taught for two years near her own home and lastly in Genesee, Illinois in the High School.

Overcoming, by the grace of God, her reluctance to leaving parents, friends and home she made her second application to the American Board—the first was rejected because there was no money to send young ladies to the field. She met the secretary of the A. B. C. F. M. in Chicago the last of May and sailed for Bulgaria in Turkey, the eighth day of September, 1870. Her father said, when she informed him of her purpose, "We hoped you would be the strong staff upon which your parents might lean in their old age; but we gave you to God in baptism and if He call you, go." The mother said, "You have been my care until now; you will be too far away for my help to reach you. I give you up to God. I shall never see your face again on earth, but you are His." Her last words when she bid her daughter farewell were, "At God's call go cheerfully." The daughter remembered how, often in childhood she had heard her enjoin cheerful obedience on her children, for said she, "Obedience that is not cheerful is not obedience."

For three years encouraging, cheering messages came to the exiled daughter from the mother, then six weeks of anxious waiting, then silence. Her last message was, "I am going Home, tell Etta, when she comes, to bring many sheaves with her."

When the father bade his little daughter, as he fondly called her, "Good Bye," he said, "I think I shall see you again," and after six years he clasped her to his heart, and at the age of 82, he made long journeys with her visiting all his children in their distant homes.

It was a bright September day in the year 1870, that the good steamship sailed out of New York harbor with twenty missionaries on board. Fourteen days later the wide ocean had separated them

THOMAS MALTBY, ESQ.

Borne 1793. Died 1815. Photo by Worlds from very beautiful miniature done on ivory. Kindly loaned by Ernest Maltby, Esq. of North Vancouver, B. C.

from the land of their fathers. A five hours' railroad ride through "Eden"-like England brought them to the wonderfully interesting old city of London and a week amid its interesting sights and scenes gave zest and refreshment to the weary travellers. Soon after arriving in Constantinople the startling news came to the new missionary that Miss Norcross, with whom she was to be associated, had suddenly sickened and died, that the school without a head was waiting for her to fill the vacancy. Words fail to express the disappointment of that hour. Good Dr. Riggs and Mrs. Riggs by their sympathy helped and encouraged the inexperienced missionary to realize that the "Strength" of her life would not fail her.

Mr. Bond came from Bulgaria to accompany her to her field of labor. At that time Bulgaria was a country very little known and her subjected people almost unheard of. Much in the beautifully situated city of Constantinople seemed strange and weird but on nearing her destination everything put on a new interest for her.

A night on the choppy waves of the Black Sea brought the travelers to the port of Borgas in Bulgaria. A rude boat received the passengers and a dangerous climb up a ladder some twenty or thirty feet landed them on a platform filled with queer looking people, in dress and manner, who gazed at the foreigners as though they thought them arrivals from some other planet. There is now a fine harbor in the place of that rude landing.

The missionary was hastened through the crowd to the tehan, where a floorless room opened to them, furnitureless, except for a stool and a straw mat in a corner. The curious villagers not satisfied with their inspection of the stranger on the street, filled the door and one paneless window with their eager faces. The first evening amid the jargon of a strange language and an almost sleepless night upon the straw matting will not soon be effaced from her memory. The morning found her seated in a springless, seatless wagon drawn by one horse. Mr. Bond rode upon his own horse and after a long day's ride, they came to a city where they were to spend the night and there she met a mother with her bright-faced daughter who had been in the mission school and received from them a cordial welcome in an unknown tongue. This made the stranger feel at home and gave her a very favorable impression of the down-trodden and oppressed people whom she had come to teach. The evening of the third day they reached Eski Zaghra, the home of the mission school at that time. The missionary carriage with the teachers of the school and girls on foot met them outside the city and gave the new teacher a very cordial welcome and a Thanksgiving dinner awaited them in the missionary home—a touch of American life in the far off land.

Before she was aware of it, Esther became fully absorbed in the work of the bereaved school and gradually, with the help of Miss Elenka H. Evonova, the Bulgarian teacher, who had acquired a good knowledge of English, was able to relieve the over-burdened missionaries of much of the care of the school.

There were twenty-six or seven Bulgarian girls gathered in Dr. Haskell's house and the accommodations were exceedingly limited. The missionary teacher and the famly occupied the second floor and the school-room and a dormitory were on the first small out-buildings in the yard served for dining-room and kitchen while the cook and remaining girls slept in the dining room and over the horse stable, and the landlady who rented them, lived over the street gate.

Of course there was much sickness in the school and much of the new missionary's time was spent in the care of the sick. The pupils were mostly from the wealthiest and most intelligent families of the city. Bright and eager to learn, they made rapid progress. It was the first gymnasium, or high school, for girls in Bulgaria though there then (in 1870) were some for boys. The small children of the more intelligent citizens were gathered in the cloisters of the churches and taught to read and write and a little science by the nuns and priests, but there were no schools for young girls and their time was spent in preparation for married life. Turkish officials of the city were present during the examinations and closing exercises of the school and expressed much surprise that girls could learn as well as boys, which fact was clearly shown by their examinations and compositions. It was not thought needful for girls to study mathematics and science as they were unnecessary for housekeeping.

The city of Eskizagora was one of the most advanced in the country in civilization and intelligence, but it was not long before the bigoted and fanatical priests raised bitter opposition to the school and incited the mob to stone the house, breaking windows and endangering life so that the missionaries were obliged to appeal to the Governor for protection. Some lovely Christian characters were developed during the first few years of this school. Six months after my arrival, the school was removed to Samokov, nearer the center of the missionary field. The people here were so ignorant and prejudicial against foreigners that not a Bulgarian would sell a house to the missionaries and they were obliged to buy of the Turks next to the Bulgarian quarter, and then the Bulgarian neighbor sold to them because he would not live next to the despised foreigner, and as the next neighbor was of the same mind it was possible to get all the lots the Mission required. An addition to the missionary house was hastily built and a schoolroom and temporary meeting house for the first Evangelical church organized here in our field of missionary endeavor. Girls from Macedonia and Bulgarian villages came to our school and gradually the numbers increased until a hundred and twenty were enrolled in all departments.

The school has passed through many vicissitudes and encountered many difficulties during the thirty-eight years I have had the charge of it. Marvelous changes have taken place in this country during the short period of freedom from the Turkish yoke and now it has taken its place among the governments that must be reckoned with, even by the great powers of Europe.

In place of the simple customs of Turkish times the cities, and some of the villages, have introduced European manners and dress and many of the modern improvements, steam and electric roads, automobiles, paved streets, modern hotels and many of the conveniences of modern life are to be found here. This school has had its share in the development of the nation.

The hundred and thirty-five or forty girls who have graduated from the school have had a wide influence as wives of prominent leading men. Those educated here are found in all grades of society and are leaders wherever found. Without doubt the thousand or more girls who have come under the influence of this school have, during this formative period of Bulgarian history, exerted a healthful influence, moral and religious.

A retrospect of the forty years spent in this land endowed with so much of natural beauty and occupied by a progressive people, brings to mind experiences of intense interest. The friendships formed here are of no ordinary type. Miss Maltbie will always be thankful that she was called to be a missionary teacher of the Gospel of Christ in this land of promise.

NOTE.—"In 1908, the cares of the head of the 'School for Girls' (for this is the name by which the school has been known since its removal to Samokov) was resigned by Miss Maltbie but she has retained a position as teacher in the school."—Martha J. Maltby.

A few weeks ago the secretary receive a letter from Miss Esther T. Maltbie and it seems to us fitting that a few extracts should be given to the Maltby cousins. Miss Maltbie writes upon her return from a couple of tours: "Living has become very much more expensive, taxes exhorbitant and productiveness not increased to a great extent so there is much suffering and need.

The "Holy Synod" is trying to get a law passed in the National Assembly to crush out Protestantism. One of the Articles is, that there can be no Evangelical service in any place where there are not seventy-five Protestant families and all the rest of the law in the same spirit.

We have a very full school and greatly need a new building. We have 112 pupils beside the kindergarten and we have not suitable accommodations for half that number—62 are boarders and the rest are day scholars. Will not some of my relatives interest themselves in this good work and help us to stand firmly against this spirit of persecution. . . . I hope we shall soon see another of the Maltby Booklets for they are very interesting. I am surprised that the money needed is not forthcoming. The next time I write I will send the membership money." etc.

Samokov, December 7th, 1910.

To those of us who are interested in foreign missions, we would call attention to Miss Maltby's request for aid. If one would know that one's contribution to such work went where it was greatly needed, here is an opportunity to help such a cause directly and to have the satisfaction of knowing just how the donation was spent.

Miss Maltbie's work has not been unknown or unappreciated, as the following incidents show. Miss Martha J. Maltby writes: "This cousin, Esther, is a modest, self-retiring soul and her life has been spent for others. I wish I could write how great her influence has been through this school for girls in Bulgaria, but I am not equal to the task. There has been no 'trumpet blowing' about her work but it shows in the lives of her pupils.

"At the Columbian Exposition in Chicago, in 1893, I met the Bulgarian who had charge of the exhibit of that country there and I gave him my card, saying, 'I've a cousin in your country.' Immediately he said, 'Miss Esther Maltbie! I know her. My wife was one of her pupils.' Later he said, 'Miss Maltbie is known all over Bulgaria.' "

Another letter, received last winter from John Maltby Conkling, has the following item: "Last evening I listened to Miss Ellen M. Stone tell her experiences with the Turkish bandits. She was an associate with Aunt Esther for a period in Samokov, Bulgaria, and in her lecture paid Aunt Esther a high tribute."

Something in the way of a little sketch of the ancestry of Miss Esther Maltbie will be interesting to the cousins, we believe, and consequently give the following condensed notes:

Esther Tapping Maltbie is the daughter of Daniel (5) and Esther Tapping Maltbie. Daniel Maltbie went to Ohio in 1819 with his father, Benjamin (4) Maltby (Rev. War). Benjamin (4) Maltbie was born May 11, 1750, in Northford, Connecticut, and married Abigail Munger. (Her ancestry was published in our fourth annual report). He was the son of Daniel (3) and Mary Harrison Maltby, the grandson of Daniel (2) and Esther Moss Maltby and great-grandson of William (1) and ——— Maltby, the emigrant ancestor.

As a large number of our members descend from Daniel (3) and Mary Harrison Maltby, we are printing her ancestry for their benefit.

Mary Harrison was the daughter of Nathaniel and Thankful Wilkinson Harrison, granddaughter of Captain Nathaniel and Hannah Frisbie Harrison; great-granddaughter of Thomas Harrison and his first wife, widow Ellen Thompson (widow of John Thompson). Her great, great-grandfather was Richard Harrison of West Kirby, Cheshire, England. He took the oath of allegiance in New Haven, August 5, 1644. He removed to Branford and died there October 25, 1653.

The Tapping ancestry we give also:—

Esther Tapping (or Topping as the name originally appears) was the daughter of Silas and Mary Gilbert Topping; and granddaughter of Elnathan Topping; great-granddaughter of Captain Stephen and second wife, Elizabeth (widow Matthews of East Hampton) Topping; great, great-granddaughter of Captain Elnathan and Mary ——— Topping and great, great, great-granddaughter of Captain Thomas Topping of Wethersfield, later of Milford, Connecticut. His wife was Emma ———.

The following Colonial record will be of interest to this branch of the family: "1673, May 16th. The court accepts of the list of Troopers presented by Captain John Nash, and Captayn Thomas Topping for New Haven County and doe confirm Captayn Topping to be Captayne and Mr. William Maltby to be Cornet of the sayd Troope." (Colonial Records of Connecticut, 1665 to 1667, p. 199 M.S.S.; Vol. II., p. 199, Printed Records.)

In a letter dated August 1, 1915, Miss Martha J. Maltby informs me that owing to ill health Miss Esther T. Maltbie returned to the States and is now living with her nephew, Mr. John Maltby Conklin. Miss Maltby adds: "I have such an interesting account of the parting reception given her in Sophia, Bulgaria, when she left that country in 1912 which should go with her biography."

DEACON WILLIAM MALTBY

Deacon William Maltby of Northford, Conn., was the first child of Henry and Ruth Hart Maltby, and was born March 19, 1825. He married Esther Hall, daughter of Dr. Pierce and Esther (Hall) Hall of Wallingford.

We give a short extract from a sketch of Mr. Maltby's life, which appeared in a local newspaper at the time of his death:

"In the death of Deacon William Maltby the town loses one of its oldest and best citizens. In his younger days he was a school teacher and taught school in Wallingford and other towns. Later, he settled on the farm. He represented his town in the state legislature in 1881. He was a member of the school board for thirty-five years, and for over forty years was a deacon in the Congregational Church."

Deacon Maltby died May 31, 1908, aged 83 years. He was a member of the Maltby Association. He descended from Henry (5), James (4), Samuel (3), Samuel (2), William (1).

MR. GEORGE ERASTUS MALTBY

Mr. George E. Maltby was the first President of the Maltby Association, of which he was president when his death occurred July 31, 1909, at the age of 78 years.

He was the second child of Lucius and Sarah J. (Parks) Maltby and was born February 18th, 1830, in Fair Haven (now a part of New Haven) Connecticut. As a boy, Mr. Maltby lived at home, going to school and helping his father with the farm. Later he became clerk in Dr. Parker's drug store, being at the time eighteen years of age.

Three years later Mr. Maltby went into the drug business for himself. In May, 1852, he married Elizabeth Broughton Maguire. They had two children, Edward Parks, and Mary Louise Maltby. Shortly after the above children were born, the war broke out and Mr. Maltby disposed of his drug business and went South where for sometime he supplied General Grant's army with provisions.

Mr. Maltby established an oyster business in Norfolk, Virginia, and was the first to ship opened oysters in bulk to New York, for a long time averaging five hundred gallons a day.

In 1864, Mr. Maltby lost his wife and for seven years was a widower. In 1871, he married Ruth Atwater Bostwick, and to them were born Margaret Atwater, George Erastus and Lucius Upson Maltby.

In 1878, Mr. Maltby and his family left Virginia and went to New York to live, where the northern branch of the oyster business was supervised by him. Mrs. Maltby died in May, 1898, and soon after Mr. Maltby gave up active business and divided his time between his older daughter, Mrs. Frederick S. Smith of Chester, Conn, and his younger daughter, Mrs. William M. Bernard of New York City, at whose residence he died, in Ardsley, N. Y. The interment was at Trinity Cemetery, New York.

It will be a pleasure to the members of the Maltby Association to know that Mr. Maltby was very proud of his office as our President, and at times during his last illness his near relatives called him "President," which seemed to please him. Many of us never had the pleasure of knowing Mr. Maltby personally, but it is a source of gratitude that we have his photograph and the fine character which was his cannot fail to endear his memory to us, one and all. Mr. Maltby's descent was Lucius (5), Rev. Jonathon (4), Benjamin (3), Daniel (2), William (1).

REV. CLARK ORLANDO MALTBY

Mr. Maltby was born at South Rutland, New York, July 19th, 1836. He is a son of Rev. Sherman and Maria Thomas Maltby.

In June, 1857, he gradutéd from the State Normal School at Albany, New York. After graduation Mr. Maltby taught for one year in the Collegiate and Polytechnic Institute at Brooklyn, New York. In September, 1859, he married Miss Fannie E. Clark and settled in business at Watertown, New York. He remained there for fifteen years, active in church work and served as Deacon, Clerk, Chorister and Treasurer. He also was interested in the Sunday school in which he taught and served as superintendent.

At length, in the winter of 1872, he gave expression to a long felt desire to enter the ministry and the following year began a three years' course of study in the Rochester Theological Seminary. After his graduation in 1877, he assumed the duties of the pastor-

REV. CLARK O. MALTBY

ate of the Baptist Church at Madison, Wisconsin, in response to a call which had been previously extended to him.

In 1881, he made a tour of Europe, visiting many important cities and places of interest. His relations with the church at Madison were very harmonious and when in 1883, he offered his resignation ,it was not accepted, instead, the church offered to give him a year's leave of absence, but the substitute was not accepted by him.

After spending a few months in California, he returned to the vicinity of Chicago, and afterward settled in Philadelphia, where during a successful pastorate, a new house of worship was erected.

His next charge was at Paterson, New Jersey, where after seven years of service, a church building was completed and dedicated. His last pastorate was at Newtown, Pennsylvania, where also a church building was erected.

His aim has always been to build up, not to pull down, consequently he has many friends in the churches where he has served.

Mr. Maltby has written a number of songs which have been appreciated by his friends.

Now, though no longer able to serve as pastor, he finds congenial employment in visiting the sick of the city hospital and in doing good as he has opportunity; and with the companion of his youth still spared to him, he looks back over the years that have fled and rejoices that his labors have not been in vain.

SETH WALDO MALTBIE

Seth Waldo Maltbie, the youngest of thirteen children of Deacon Daniel and Esther (Tappin) Maltbie, was born May 19th, 1840, Southington, Trumbull County, Ohio. After attending the public schools he attended school in the preparatory department of Oberlin College in 1858, and entered that college in 1860. At the outbreak of the war he enlisted and was enrolled in the second company organized among the students of the college. The quota being more than full, his company was disbanded and he continued his studies through the college year when he entered the army as private in Co. D., 87th Regiment, Ohio Volunteer Infantry. He was appointed corporal and then sergeant in his company and the following year he was commissioned captain of Co. E., 4th Regt. U. S. C. T.

At the close of the war he continued his college course at Amherst, Mass., and graduated in 1867. Received the appointment as disciplinarian of the military academy at Cheshire, Conn. The following year was superintendent of the public schools of Princeton, Ill. Then for several years occupied a similar position in the public schools of Genesee, Ill. Then was for two years principal of the Oshkosh High School, Oshkosh, Wis. Health failing, moved to Tama County, Iowa, and engaged in the insurance business and taught a few terms in the public schools. Being informed in mining engineering he was sent to the mountains and employed by various mining companies and worked in Montana, Wyoming, Utah, California and New Mexico. For the past eight years he has been engaged in mining as local manager, where he, and his wife still reside.

He was married in 1867, to Rizpah Stetson Boltwood of Amherst, Mass. They have had five children, Ralph Waldo, Edith Brayton, Gertrude, Guy Southworth and Mildred Noble.

Ralph Waldo Maltbie was born July 1, 1868, at Saybrook, Trumbull County, Ohio. educated in the public schools and Iowa College, Grennell, Iowa, began teaching in the public schools in Iowa; went to Chicago and taught as principal of suburban schools for thirteen years. Health failing, he gave up teaching and engaged in railroading in various capacities, principally as clerk in the general offices. Went to California and began teaching in the public schools of Los Angeles, and is now principal of schools at Chatsworth, Cal. He married Nettie May Webster of Barrington, Ill. They have two sons, Leonard and Robert.

The third and fourth children of Seth Waldo and Rizpah Stetson (Boltwood) Maltbie named Gertrude and Guy Southworth, died in infancy.

The fifth, Edith Brayton, born at Genesee, Ill., Oct. 15th, 1871. In her early childhood she was remarkable for early development of mental and moral qualities and showed wonderful talent in public elocutionary ability and while in the primary department on account of her age and in the high school in one or more studies she was chosen to represent the high school in the state oratorical contest and though only 8 years of age, she was marked third by the judges of the contest. The youngest of all the other contestants was twice her age. She took a course of study at Drake University, Des Moines, Iowa. In Aug., 1891, she married the Rev. A. W. Davis and died Feby. 12th, 1894, leaving a son, Lloyd Shilton Davis, then sixteen months old. This boy is now 17 and has taken high standing in the public schools of Kansas City, Mo., where he now resides.

Mildred Noble, the fifth child of Seth Waldo and Rizpah Stetson (Boltwood) Maltbie, was born May 7th, 1891 at Montown, Tama County, Iowa. After thorough training in the public schools, Iowa College and normal studies she engaged in kindergarten work and taught in the public schools. She married in 1903, Joshua Baldwin Clarke. She has two children, Theodore William and Geraldine Maltby. The family reside at Gronegen, Minn.

MR. GEORGE W. MALTBY

Mr. George W. Maltby was one of the original members of the Maltby Association, and his check for annual dues for ten members of his family was the first ray of light to encourage the little embryo into being. When Mr. Maltby died on July 1st, 1908, we lost one of our strongest supporters.

The following obituary is taken from the "Buffalo Evening News" of July 1, 1908:

BUSINESS MAN OF NATIONAL FAME PASSES AWAY

George W. Maltby died this morning at his home in this city. "He was one of the old type of businessmen, with whom if you had a contract, you wouldn't need to put it in writing," was the remark evoked from a prominent business man by the announcement of the death of George W. Maltby at his home at 3:30 o'clock this morning. Among the tributes to his memory by legions of friends, no encomium will ring truer than this. But it is conceded by all who knew him that business honesty was only an incidental characteristic and one that was regarded as a matter of course by Mr. Maltby. That was the rough stone of his character—"Square-hewn and polished for a grand and sterilng character. . . ."

Mr. Maltby was born in West Henrietta, Monroe County, N. Y., in 1845. When not seventeen he enlisted as a private in Company H of the 108th New York Volunteer Infantry and served with Gen. Winfield Scott at Antietam, Gettysburg and Spottsylvania Court House

He was all day on the battlefield of Antietam, "the bloodiest day of the whole war," and though wounded he stuck to his regiment. At Gettysburg he was hit by splinters of a shell, and in the death carnival at Spottsylvania, his left hand was so shattered by a bullet he could no longer carry a musket. This injury disabled him from active service and he was confined in the Satterlee Military Hospital at Philadelphia until his discharge in November, 1864. For months he ministered with his one hand to his sick and dying comrades in the long wards of Satterlee Hospital, finally becoming head nurse.

Returning from the army, 19 years old at this time, Mr. Maltby decided to continue his studies, and took a course in a business college at Rochester. In 1865 he entered the firm of Whitmore, Carson & Co., Rochester, dealers in cut stone. In 1880 Mr. Maltby came to Buffalo, entering partnership with Gilbert Brady of Rochester, under the name of Brady and Maltby. The partnership was continued until the death of Mr. Brady in 1896. Mr. Maltby was in business alone until 1904, when he took his two sons, James C. and William Maltby, into partnership, under the name of George W. Maltby and Sons.

Memorials of Mr. Maltby's life work exist in monuments of cut stone all over the country. He furnished and dressed the stone for the McKinley Monument in Niagara Square, also for the McKinley National Memorial at Canton, including the interior work and sarcophagus; the Historical Society's Building; the Albright Art Gallery; the bridge over Park Lake, Gate's Circle; the entrance of Forest Lawn, the First Presbyterian Church, the new addition to the Buffalo Club and the Ontario Power Company's building at Niagara Falls.

Mr. Maltby was a member of Bidwell-Wilkeson Post, G. A. R., the Union Veteran League, and Queen City Lodge, F. & A. M. He was a trustee of the Blocher Home, former president of the Builders' Exchange and a member of the Chamber of Commerce. He was also a member of the Plymouth M. E. Church.

On Aug. 27, 1865, Mr. Maltby married Miss Mary J. Pierce, daughter of Caleb Pierce of Rochester. His widow, a daughter, Mrs. D. J. Perry, and two sons, James C. and William C. Maltby, survive him.

(The above extracts are taken in part from the "Christian Advocate.")

MR. ALBERT E. MALTBY

The following is taken from Herringshaw's Encyclopedia of American Biog., p. 613:

Maltby, Albert E.—Educator—born Oct. 27, 1850, in Pulaski, N. Y. Received his education at Fayetteville Academy and at Cornell University. As a teacher in Ury School of Philadelphia and in 1878 he was appointed engineer on survey of boundary line between Guatemala and Mexico. In 1880 he filled chair of mathematics and astronomy in St. Lawrence University, N. Y. In 1884 professor of natural science in the State normal school of Indiana, Penn.; and since 1890 Dr. Maltby has been principal of State Normal School of Slippery Rock, Pa. He is a successful writer on the theoretical and practical in school methods."

Mr. Albert E. Maltby descends from John (7), Timothy (6), Timothy (5), Samuel (4), Samuel (3), Samuel (2), William (1).

GEORGE ELLSWORTH MALTBY.

George (7) Ellsworth Maltby, Esquire, was born in New Haven, Connecticut, February ninth, eighteen fifty-two. He was the fourth child of George (6) Williams and Sarah *Bogert* Maltby.

Those who knew him in childhood speak of him as "a beautiful child"—not only in looks but in character. The beautiful character of his childhood developed and strengthened with youth and manhood, and all who ever came in contact with him, either in business or socially, must have been impressed by his upright, honorable life. When Right was on his side he was absolutely fearless and determined to stand firm, no matter what the consequences or what the powers used against him.

He had many friends among the poor—for his charity was not the sort accompanied by loud proclamation, but done quietly and out of the sympathy he had for those less fortunate than himself.

His education was obtained at the Public and High schools, and his standing was always high.

His father offered him the opportunity to enter Yale University, but he decided for a business career and he very shortly entered the employ of H. W. Benedict and Company, coal dealers, with whom he remained until he was about seventeen years of age. About this time Mr. Benedict's son, Mr. H. H. Benedict, and Mr. Frank W. Pardee formed a partnership to handle coal entirely by wholesale and Mr. Maltby was asked to enter their office. This firm was very successful and soon became one of the leading wholesale coal establishments in New England.

Mr. Maltby's advancement was rapid and while still twenty-one years of age he was taken into partnership and the firm name changed to Benedict, Pardee and Company.

His business ability was of the best, and to those who knew him, knew the large things accomplished by him, and his success, any words of the writer would be superfluous.

At the age of twenty Mr. Maltby married Miss Georgia Lord Morehouse, youngest daughter of Louis Peck and Harriett *Brown* Morehouse, of New Haven, Connecticut. Miss Morehouse was just eighteen at the time of their marriage. They were scarcely more than children, but it proved to be one of those fortunate marriages which one sees once in a lifetime.

Mr.Maltby used frequently to tell his children that all that he was he owed to his wife—to her courage, love, devotion and helpfulness.

Mr. and Mrs. Maltby had two children, Maude Townshend, and Dorothy Lord, Maltby.

Mr. Maltby was a strong supporter of the Calvary Baptist Church of New Haven and for years was chairman of the music committee, and during his office this church had the finest choir in the state. Mr. Maltby contributed liberally toward the maintaining of this choir. He was intensely fond of music and had a fine natural baritone voice.

Mrs. Maltby's voice was far above the ordinary singer's—with remarkable range and sweetness, and showed thorough cultivation and training.

Many of the Maltbys were musical and we know that Mr. Maltby's great grandfather, Col. Stephen (4) Maltby, had been quite prominent in a musical way.

In appearance Mr. Maltby was a typical Maltby, with dark brown hair, large brown eyes, set well apart and rather deep, heavy eyebrows, a firm mouth, with light brown moustache and a Maltby dimple in his chin. His height was five feet ten, and he was quite muscular, though taking little exercise.

He had a great love for athletics and was fond of keeping good driving horses.

He was social and genial, and a member of several clubs—the Quinnipiac, the Republican League, and the Ansantawae; and also a member of the Chamber of Commerce. In politics he was a Republican, and had earnest convictions on such subjects.

Mr. Maltby had a strong feeling of reverence for his ancestors and of kinship for his relations.

In the last year of his life he used frequently to remark, "I should like to meet every one of my relatives and shake each one by the hand."

Shortly before his death Mr. and Mrs. Maltby spent much time and large sums of money tracing the Maltby Genealogy. Mrs. Maltby did the compiling and arranging of the material, and together they travelled to old burying grounds, court houses, churches, etc., gathering the invaluable data, part of which is contained in the Maltby-Morehouse Family printed at Mr. Maltby's expense and which he intended to give away. Mr. Maltby also was employing an English genealogist to work upon the connection with our English family. All this great work was cut short by his sudden death.

The best blood of New England flowed in his veins—no better stock than that from which he came existed. The following are a few of the men from whom he descended on the paternal side of the family:

Deputy Governor George Bartlett, of Connecticut.
Governor William Brenton, of Rhode Island.
Rev. John Davenport, founder of New Haven.
Rev. John Eliot, "Apostle to the Indians."
Rev. Joseph Eliot, Guilford, Conn.
Hon. Major Nathan Gold.
Hon. John Hall.
Rev. Samuel Hall, Patriot.
Governor Jonathan Law, of Connecticut.
Rev. John Lowthrop, Scituate, Mass.
Rev. Richard Mather.
Rev. Eleazer Mather.
Rev. Abraham Pierson.
Elder John Strong.
Thomas Townshend, Esq.
Rev. John Williams, the Redeemed Captive.
Rev. Stephen Williams, the Redeemed Captive.
Rev. Warham Williams.

On the maternal side Mr. Maltby's ancestry was entirely Dutch and French Huguenot. He was eligible to practically all the patriotic societies, and in response to an invitation to join the Colonial Wars his papers had been made out and were to be handed in the day he died.

Mr. Maltby had always been strong and vigorous, but while on a pleasure trip to Annapolis, Maryland, where he had gone accompanied by his family to attend some of the festivities at the Naval Academy, he was taken with a supposedly slight attack of influenza. After a couple of days in bed he was sufficiently recovered to go on to Washington, D. C., where it was planned to spend a few days before returning to New Haven. There, after a pleasant evening spent with his family and friends he was stricken with heart failure and died almost instantly.

His death occurred January 28th, 1895, at the Arlington Hotel, Washington, D. C., when he was but forty-two years of age.

Mr. Maltby was a 32nd degree Mason, belonging to the New Haven Commandery, No. 2, K. T., New Haven, Conn.; to Pyramid Temple, A. A. A. N. M. S., Bridgeport, Conn., and La Fayette Sov. Consistory, S. P. R. S., Bridgeport, Conn.

The above sketch of a useful and beautiful life is written in loving memory by his daughter, Dorothy Maltby Verrill.

DR. MALTBIE DAVENPORT BABCOCK.

Rev. Maltbie Davenport Babcock, D. D., was born at Syracuse, N. Y., August 3d, 1858. He was the eldest son of Henry Babcock and Emily Maria Maltbie. Her father was the Rev. Ebenezer Davenport Maltbie, son of David Maltbie and his wife Nancy Davenport of Stamford, Conn., who was the lineal descendant of Rev. John Davenport of New Haven, Conn. Emily Maria Maltbie's mother was Mary Ann Davis, daughter of Rev. Henry Davis, D. D., and Hannah Phoenix Tredwell.

There were many generations of the most prominent, refined and cultivated men and women behind Dr. Babcock and he went forth to his life work from an ideal home. His maternal great grandfather and his grandfather were both Presbyterian clergymen. He was the eldest of seven children, and his mother's widespread religious influence, and her beautiful life still speak in many of the influential circles of his native city. Here he was educated, taking his classical course at Syracuse University, and his theological course at Auburn Seminary. In both of these institutions he won highest honors and hosts of friends.

Dr. Babcock received immediate recognition in the front rank of his denomination, his first settlement being at Lockport, N. Y. It was not only his brilliant intellect and his stirring oratorical powers that commanded admiration, for his ministry was ideal and no pastor in the land was more beloved. The man was everywhere regarded as a personal friend, so cordial, so frank, so cheerful was he always and so thoroughly unselfish. His influence became in the best sense national. His theology was like his vocal delivery, simple and direct. It was one soul speaking to another. His prayers voiced the cry of a man who wanted help from his Father.

Dr. Babcock could not do anything just as anyone else would. "To divide burdens and centralize responsibility is the ark of accomplishment." This was his rule in doing his varied work, and it gave him his almost supreme executive ability. Perhaps there was no greater tribute to his power and consecration than the fact that he was invariably turned to, as a sort of last resort in the attempt to bring a wandering soul to Christ. Often men said, "Let us get him under Dr. Babcock's influence; he can surely reach him." Dr. Babcock was a very versatile man; exceedingly attractive in physique, pleasant in manner, with a soul that reflected God.

Dr. Babcock was a clear thinker, and a fluent speaker. He was noted for his broad and impartial charity and his vast array of friends among the young men of his country. He reached the people in so many ways. His personal magnetism was marvelous. Those who heard him were entranced and he was called to speak at all great religious gatherings, from one end of the country to the other and crowds, young and old, hung upon his lips. Taught of the Spirit, he revealed to them the open door to heaven and the message of the Jehovah.

Dr. Babcock never published a book. He lived or sang his thoughts. He was a great lover of music, played many instruments extremely well, improvised delightfully and also wrote many songs and hymns which have been published and have won instant recognition as splendid work. But the watchword of his life was: "This one thing I do," to honor his Master and to save souls. His poems are of unquestioned excellence and have been said to resemble those of Emerson. They have been published in connection with a memorial volume of extracts from sermons and addresses gathered by his grief stricken widow, entitled "Thoughts for Every Day Living." His foreign letters, written while last abroad, to the men of the Brick Church in New York City, were also published.

What Dr. Babcock's work was in Baltimore it is simply impossible to estimate in an article as brief as this or to speak of the breadth and reach of that wonderful pastorate in New York. His acquaintance was cosmopolitan, and it knew no denominational bond, and was met by a distinguished hospitality to which his wife, the daughter of a prominent Poughkeepsie lawyer, added both beauty and charm. What Dr. Babcock was in his home only those who lived with him and loved him, upon whom his devotion was showered can tell. At the time of his death, at Naples, Italy, May 18, 1901, in his forty-third year, the papers, both religious and secular, teemed with statements proving in every way his remarkable power.

One who knew Dr. Babcock intimately said: "The only relief in the mystery of his untimely death it seemed to me, was in the fact that his character and work were of such potency that they must reproduce themselves in the living.

MR. FRANK BIERCE MALTBY, C.E.

(President of the Maltby Association.)

Mr. Frank B. Maltby, the second president of the Maltby Association, was graduated from the University of Illinois in 1882, and in 1907 was given an honorary degree. After matriculating, Mr. Maltby followed the engineering profession and has been connected with railroad construction and work under the government on the Mississippi and Missouri Rivers. From 1902 to 1905, Mr. Maltby was in charge of all dredging operations on the Mississippi River below Cairo and at this time had under his direction the largest dredge plant in the world.

In 1905 Mr. Maltby went to Panama as a dredging expert in charge of all dredging operations and was afterwards made Division Engineer and then Principal Assistant Engineer under Mr. Jno. F. Stevens, Chief Engineer of the Isthmian Canal Commission.

While in the service of the canal commission, Mr. Maltby designed and built the dredges now in use in constructing the canal. This plant cost about a million and a half dollars.

Mr. Maltby's work also included the construction of wharves and docks and beginning the construction of the great Gatun lock and dam. He also built a cold storage plant, laundry and a bakery on the Isthmus.

After the canal construction was turned over to the army engineers Mr. Maltby resigned and was chief engineer for the firm of Dodge and Day of Philadelphia.

In 1908, Dodge and Day had the contract for the erection of the largest cableway plant in the world for handling material at Gatun. Later Mr. Maltby became associated with James Stewart & Company of New York, general contractors. At this time Mr. Maltby was in charge of a large contract on the New York State barge canal, as well as of work in Buffalo and Lorain, Ohio. In 1911, Mr. Maltby became a partner with a firm of Contractors and Engineers in New York City, Galwens and Dodge.

The latest work of Mr. Maltby's has been the Cape Cod Canal, recently finished. As a hydraulic engineer and an expert on all classes of dredging operations, Mr. Maltby has made a name for himself of which he well might be proud, but being of a most retiring disposition, it remains for his kinsmen to feel a just satisfaction in the place he has made for himself in the highest ranks of his profession.

Mr. Maltby's line of descent is given below:

1. William Maltby m. (1st or 2nd wife?).
2. Daniel Maltby m. Esther Moss.
3. Daniel Maltby m. Mary Harrison.
4. Benjamin Maltby (R.W.) m. Abigail Munger.
5. Nathaniel Harrison Maltby m. Betsy Patchin.
6. Warren Maltby m. Chlo Elizabeth Bierce.
7. Frank Bierce Maltby m. Margaret Ellen McNavy.

Mr. Maltby has two daughters: Ruth McNavy, and Marion Elizabeth, Maltby. Mr. Maltby married, second, on Feb. 1, 1908. Miss Josephine Hedges of New York City.

BIRDSEY LUCIUS MALTBIE, ESQ.

It is a pleasure to be able to publish the photograph of Mr. Birdsey L. Maltbie, to whom we are indebted for this book. Had it not been for Mr. Maltbie's great generosity in privately financing the publication of these records, they would have been unavailable to the public and doubtless would ultimately have become lost to posterity.

The expense of publishing such a book is great and we can best express our gratitude and appreciation of Mr. Maltbie's kindness by showing our copies to any relations who have not yet subscribed for one.

It must be understood that under the best of conditions as to the sale of the book, etc., there is not one cent of pecuniary gain for Mr. Maltbie, as a result of his philanthropy. He generously declares that should he more than cover the cost of the book, any surplus will go to the compiler as a mark of appreciation of the work of years. This would be very nice, but it should be thoroughly understood by purchasers that neither Mr. Maltbie or Mrs. Verrill went into the editing or publishing with the faintest idea of deriving any personal benefit from their efforts. If the Maltby descendants find the book of interest to such an extent that Mr. B. L. Maltbie

BIRDSEY LUCIUS MALTBIE, ESQ.

may feel no regret for his kindness, then indeed may all those concerned feel well satisfied and amply repaid.

Mr. B. L. Maltbie was born at Cattaraugus, N. Y., September 19th, 1864. At an early age he began his life's work in a drug store, was graduated from the Albany College of Pharmacy, class of 1885, with highest honors (he was elected president of the College Alumni in 1915). In 1888 he started in the drug business in a small way, for himself, and later in partnership with his brother, Ralph H. Maltbie, started in the manufacture of pharmaceutical preparations, which business was later incorporated as The Maltbie Chemical Company, and which is now a thriving organization with laboratories in Newark, N. J.

Mr. Maltbie is the author of "Maltbie's Practical Pharmacy" and editor of several other publications. In 1915 he was elected president of The American Association of Pharmaceutical Chemists.

He was married in 1897 to Emma D. Bancroft in Buffalo, New York. They have one daughter, Harriet B. Maltbie. They reside in East Orange, N. J., except during the winter which time is spent at Altamonte Springs, Florida, where they have a winter home."

MISS MARGARET E. MALTBY

Some years ago a correspondent wrote of Miss Margaret E. Maltby, "she is the only woman professor at Columbia University." If this is still the case is not known to the compiler, but that Miss Maltby is a very brilliant woman, exceedingly clever and a fascinating conversationalist is well known to those who have been so fortunate as to make her acquaintance. The following are a list of degrees conferred upon her: Oberlin, Ohio, A.B. (1882); A.M. (1891); Mass. Institute of Technology, S.B. (1891): Gottinger University (Germany) Ph.D. (1895). Miss Maltby has held the following fellowships: Foreign Scholarship (or Fellowship) from Mass. Institute of Technology, two years while at Gottinger, '93-'95. The foreign fellowship of the Association of Collegiate Alumni, '95-'96.

Miss Maltby is a fellow of the American Association for the Advancement of Science and was private research assistant to President Kohlbrausch of the Physikalisch Technische Reichsaustalt, '98-'99.

In 1899-1900 Miss Maltby studied at Clark University with Professor Webster; for four years and a half she taught at Wellesley College; one year at Lake Erie College and eight years at Barnard.

In 1909 Miss Maltby was Adjunct Professor in charge of the Department of Physics of Barnard University which post she held since the summer of 1903. She is a first cousin of Mr. Frank B. Maltby, C.E. (see sketch) and her line of descent in the Maltby family is: Edmund (6), Nathaniel Harrison (5), Benjamin (4), Daniel (3), Daniel (2), William (1).

MR. WILLIAM HENRY MALTBIE

(First Vice-President of the Maltby Association)

The following sketch of Mr. William H. Maltbie is taken from 'Who's Who in America," 1908-9:

"William Henry Maltbie, professor of mathematics at the Woman's College of Baltimore, Maryland, was born at Toledo, Ohio, Aug. 26, 1867. He is a son of Silas Benjamin and Angie Van Deman Maltbie. He graduated from Ohio Wesleyan University in 1890; A.M., 1892; fellow Johns Hopkins, 1894-5; Ph.D., same, 1895; married, Dec. 19, 1904, Kate A. S. McCurley. Professor of Mathematics, Hedding College, Illinois, 1890-1; instr. Feb.-Sept., 1895; associate professor, 1895; professor, 1899. Woman's College of Baltimore. Member of Phi Beta Kappa, Am. Math. Soc." (For address see Membership Roll.) His line of descent is Silas Benjamin (7), Harrison (6), Benjamin (5), Benjamin (4), Daniel (3), Daniel (2), William (1).

MR. MILO ROY MALTBIE

The following account is taken from "Who's Who," 1908-9:

"Maltbie, Milo Roy—Member Public Utilities Commission, N. Y., since June, 1907; Secretary Art Commission, N. Y., May, 1902, to July, 1907; born at Hinckley, Ill., April 3, 1871; son of Henry M. and Harriet Delano Maltbie; graduated from Upper Iowa University, 1892; Ph.B., Northwestern, 1893; Ph.D., Columbia, 1897; took Dewey prize, $100, and Cushing prize, $100, Northwestern University, 1893; married, July 11, 1901, Lucia McCosh; Prof. Economics and Mathematics, Mt. Morris College, Ill., 1893-5; fellow in administrative law, Columbia, 1895-7; Sec'y Reform Club Commission on City Affairs, 1897-1902; traveled in Europe in the summer of 1899, investigating municipal problems for reform club, and in 1903 civic art; prize lectures on municipal government, Columbia, 1900; editor of Municipal Affair, 1897-1903; conducted investigation in Great Britain into relative merits of municipal and private management of public utilities, 1906; member American Economic Association, Reform Club, Society for Checking Abuses of Public Advertising (London), Municipal Art Soc.; Am. Polit. Science Association, National Civic Federation, Commission on Municipal Ownership and Operation. Author: English Local Government of Today, a Study of the Relations of Central and Local Government, 1897; Municipal Functions, 1898; Street Railways of Chicago, 1901. Contributor to Economic journalism." Mr. Maltbie's line of descent is: Henry Munson (7), Milo Harrison (6), Elon (5), Benjamin (4), Daniel (3), Daniel (2), William (1).

MOLBY GENEALOGY

Recently we have discovered a branch of the Maltby family spelling their name Molby. This branch we believe should connect with parent tree at Jonathon Maltby (4), born Oct. 21, 1751, and said by Rev. Jonathon (4) to have married a Miss Culver, and went to Lenox, Mass. From here he probably went up to Vermont, as Culver was a prominent name in Vermont in Revolutionary Days. As yet this descent has not been proved. What records we have of this family begin with one Jonathon Maltby who went from Salem, Mass., in 1800, to New York State. Now it is tradition that he was from Salem, and tradition is evidently wrong as the Town Clerk assures us the name Maltby is not on the records.

Jonathon Maltby had the following children: Chester Molby, b. Dec. 8, 1788; Jacob Maltby; William Maltby, went west when young, perhaps to Michigan; Isaac Molby, went west when young.

Chester Molby m. Sally Wigent; they named their children Samuel, John, Benjamin, Susanna, Harriet, Polly, Lydia, Loanna, Jane and Daniel.

Jacob Maltby, brother of Chester, named his children William, Minor, Henry, John and Lucy. Further records of this branch requested.

WAR RECORDS

The lists of Maltbys-Maltbies, who have served their country in the various wars our country has been involved in since its infancy should prove of interest to all Maltbys.

These records are far from complete but they have been collected wherever possible and it is the hope of the compiler that they will act as an impetus to kinsmen to send in further data concerning those Maltbys they may know of who in like manner served their country.

These lists would be far more fragmentary were it not for the kindness of Miss Achsah Adelia Maltby of Seattle who very kindly copied all printed lists obtainable there at the library.

The first list contains the names of Maltbys who held military rank, but owing to age, were not available for any actual war, some being born too late or too soon or having died prior to the outbreak of war.

MISCELLANEOUS MILITARY RECORDS

1. William (1) Maltby, Ensign of Train Band.
2. Samuel (2) Maltby, Captain. (Whence his title is not known.)
3. Jonathon (2) Maltby, Major.

Col. Stephen (4) Maltby, [Benjamin (3), Daniel (2), William (1)] born in 1769, too late to serve in the Revolutionary War. He had much military spirit, but it was his misfortune to die just at the beginning of the War of 1812, in which his brother, General Isaac, distinguished himself.

Lieut. John Maltby (5) [Samuel (4), Samuel (3), Samuel (2), William (1)]. A descendant, Dr. Hubbard of Alamedia, Calif., writes of him as "Lieut." He was born in 1768. Query: Was he in the War of 1812?

FRENCH AND INDIAN WARS

Muster Roll of New York Provincial Troops, 1759:

"WILLIAM MALTBY, April 19, age 28, Seabrook (Saybrook) Conn. Capt. Strong's Company Militia. (From a Muster Roll of the men raised and passed muster in the County of Suffolk, 1759, Gilbert Potter, Capt.; Jesse Platt, Joseph Brewster, Lieutenants.)

NOTE.—This is an unplaced Maltby. Does the following record refer to the same person?

Conn. Hist. Soc., Vol. IX., p. 193:

MALTBY, WM. Campaign of 1757; Col. Lyman's Regiment, 13th Co., Capt. Preston. Time of enlisting, March 26. Time of return, Nov. 9. French-Indian War Rolls, 1755-57.

NOTE.—The General Assembly in Feb., 1757, resolved to raise 1400 men for the next campaign, to be formed into one Regiment of 14 companies to act in conjunction with the regular troops under command of Earl of London. In October the Assembly ordered the enlisting of three companies of 94 men each, officers included, out of the troops already in service, to remain in service throughout the winter. An alarm in August at the time of the capture of Fort Wm. Henry called out many of the militia.

From French and Indian War Rolls, Vol. I.; Conn. Hist. Soc. Vol. IX., p. 224; Campaign of 1757; Lieut. Maltbie's Company.

DANIEL Maltbie (of Northford in Branford), Lieut. The Colony of Connecticut to Lieut. Daniel Maltbie, Lieut. of the company under his command in ye 2nd Regiment under Col. Newton, for their service att ye time of the Alarm for the Relief of Fort Wm. Henry, and parts adjacent, August, 1757. Days in service: Daniel Maltbie, Lieut, 8 to 23—15 days.

NOTE.—This was Daniel (3), Daniel (2), William (1).*

"Jonathon Maltbie, Capt. Co. 2, French and Indian Wars." This note was, we believe, taken from a History of Stamford, Conn., by Rev. E. Huntington.

REVOLUTIONARY WAR

Capt. BENJAMIN Maltbie (3), Daniel (2), Wm. (1). There is only one record to show that Benjamin Maltby had the title of "Captain." It is doubtful if he went to "the front," as he was about 60 years of age at the time of the Revolution, but doubtless was captain of a company for "home defense." The record is from the Northford Church records, page 127 and reads: "Apr. 2, 1778. This church make choice of Capt. Benjamin Maltbie and Phineas Baldwin to be their Deacons who accepted this office.* Test. Warham Williams, Pastor.

* Is this a reference to the same person? "Dan'el Maltbie Enl. May 27. Discharged Oct. 31, Ninth Comp., Capt. Wadsworth, 2nd Regiment, 1758."

* Mr. Gillete of Branford states: "The people of North and South societies (Northford and Old Branford) entered with ardor into the war of the Revolution and furnished a full quota of men by voluntary enlistment, both for land and sea service. Benjamin Maltby was captain of trained band."

Col. Jonathon Maltbie (3), Jonathon (2), William (1). History of Stamford by Rev. E. B. Huntington, says of him: "He was born in 1720, and attained the rank of Colonel in military life.

WILLIAM Maltby (4), Joseph (3), Daniel (2), William (1). William M. Olin, Secretary of the Commonwealth of Massachusetts, sent the following certificate of service: "William Maltby, residence not given, as serving in a company commanded by Captain Oliver Belding of Lenox, Colonel John Brown's regiment in 1777." Enlisted Sept. 21, 1777. Discharged Oct. 14, 1777. Service: 24 days at Northward, p. 152.

NOAH Maltby. He enlisted in the Revolutionary War from Goshen, Conn. "Malbye, Noah, private, Goshen, 17th Rev. Conn., Col. Sheldon," (Ref. p. 562, "Conn. in Rev.") "for defence of coast and forests, until 1st March, 1780."

NOTE.—Noah (4) Maltby was a son of Joseph (3), Daniel (2), William (1).

JONATHON Maltby. Wm. Olin, Secretary of the Commonwealth of Massachusetts, sent the following certificate of his service: "Jonathon Maltby, residence not given, as serving as a private in a company commanded by Capt. Josiah Yale, of Lee or Lenox, in 1781, on an alarm at Stillwater." Enlisted Oct. 10, 1781, discharged Oct. 20, 1781. Service: 12 days. Company marched from Lee and Lenox to Stillwater by order of Brig.-Gen. Rosseter on an alarm. (Ref. Mass. Sold. and Sailors in Rev. War., Vol. X.) Joseph (3), Daniel (2), William (1).

BENJAMIN (4) Maltby, Daniel (3), Daniel (2), William (1), served as a private in the Revolutionary War. He was in two different regiments and was in the battles of Long Island and Saratoga. (Ref. "Old Northwest Quarterly," Vol. IX., No. 4, Oct., 1906).

ZACHEUS (4) Maltbie, Daniel (3), Daniel (2), William (1), was a soldier in the Revolutionary War. First Regiment, General Wooster, 1775. Recruited in New Haven, Conn. Raised on first call for troops by Gen. in April-May, 1775. Marched to New York latter part of June and encamped at Harlem. Took part in operations above Lake George and Champlain. Assisted in the reduction of St. John's in October. Stationed at Montreal. Adopted as Continental, 6th Company, 1st Regiment, Captain William Douglass of Northford. (Enlistment Roll is missing.) Discharge Roll,

Zacheus Maltbie discharged in Northern Department, November 28, 1775. (Ref. Conn. Hist. Soc., Vol. VIII., Rev. Rolls and Lists.)

THADDEUS Maltby. Rev. Jonathon (4) Maltby, his brother, [Benjamin (3), Daniel (2), William (1)] wrote of him: "He was brought home sick from the Northern Army and died December, 1776."

NOTE.—The Society of the Children of the American Revolution have a chapter named for this patriot, called "The Thaddeus Maltby Society." It was organized in St. Paul, Minn., March, 1896, by Mrs. Ferederick E. Foster, a descendant of Gen. Isaac (4), brother of Thaddeus (4) Maltby. In an address Mrs. Foster give a brief sketch of this young Revolutionary Ware hero, who gave his life for his country, and from this we quote. "He enlisted at the breaking out of the war, being then but eighteen years of age. For gallant conduct he was soon made Corporal of his company. He lived to see some victories, but unused to the hardship and privations he fell fatally ill from exposure at Ticonderoga and was sent home to die. Of his brothers, one was a student at Yale," [Jonathon (4)] "another was in the army" (Query: Was this Benjamin?) "and of the youngest none was large enough to undertake to bring home the dying soldier. A young cousin* was therefore sent for him" (Who was this "cousin"?) "and from the Northern Army to Northford, Connecticut, the long journey was performed slowly and painfully, both boys riding the same horse. Thaddeus leaning forward on his cousin's shoulders for support. Exhausted and spent he reached the pleasant home from which he had departed but a few months before strong and brave, dying shortly after his return and leaving no descendants to tell of his heroic sacrifice. This brief story of a short life was learned from a bundle of old family letters and the facts since verified from printed records in the State Library." Elizabeth Fowler Maltby, mother of Thaddeus said when she lost her baby she thought it terrible but when a grown up son died in the army "the loss of the baby was nothing in comparison."

WILLIAM Maltby. From Papers of the First Council of Safety of the Revolutionary Party in South Carolina, June-November, 1775. William Maltby, 8 (St. Helena, 26 October). Unplaced in Maltby Genealogy. Information desired.

WM. Malaby. State Records of N. Carolina, Vol. XVI., p 1117, 1782-83. "Wm. Malaby, Pt., Co. Bradley's. Date enlistment July 20, 1778; 9 months service, 10 reg. Abraham Shepard, Colonal." Unplaced in Maltby Genealogy. Information desired.

* One descendant writes: "I have always heard that a brother of Thaddeus, who was also in the army, brought him home." If this statement is correct, it must have been Benjamin. Can some authority for this statement be produced? An item of interest concerning this branch of the family was recently received from Mrs. Shipp. She writes: "I know that Rev. Jonathon (4) was one of the students at Yale who carried the valuable books and records up to West Rock when New Haven was alarmed by the enemy."

WM. Malby, private, Capt. Charles Dibbel's Co., Col. Rosseter's (13th Bershire Co.) regt. Enlisted Oct. 18, 1780; service: 4 days, on the alarm at the Northward of Oct. 18, 1780. (Ref. Mass. Soldiers and Sailors of Rev. War., Vol. X., p. 152.) Query: Is this William (4), Joseph (3), Daniel (2), William (1)?

Rev., JONATHON (4) Maltby, Benjamin (3), Daniel (2), William (1). He was one of a reconnoitering party on East Haven Heights in July, 1777, and was under fire. See under biography of Rev. Jonathon (4).

JONATHON (4) Maltby, Samuel (3), Samuel (2), William (1). According to Rev. Jonathon (4) Maltby he was a soldier in the Revolutionary War. "He and Sol'm Talmage were detached from the troop under Capt. Treat of Milford and were with him at the capture of Bygoih."

Capt. JONATHON (4) Maltbie. 1st Lieut. of Continental cruiser "Trumbull." His commission as lieutenant is dated Oct. 12, 1776, and signed by John Hancock. His commission as Captain is dated March 21, 1791, and signed by General George Washington. (For copy see biography of Capt. Jonathon Maltbie.) In Dec., 1775, Lieut. Jonathon Maltbie was on the "Alfred," Capt. Dudley Saltonstall, and 1st Lieut. John Paul Jones. (Vide Civil and Military List of Rhode Island, 1800-1850, by Smith, p. 704.) Descended from Jonathon (3), Jonathon (2), William (1).

DAVID (4) Maltbie, soldier in the Revolutionary War. "Capt. Jonathon Whitney's Company. David Maltbie, discharged Jan. 8, 1777. Served 1 month, 21 days, 9th Regiment Militia under General Wooster. In 1776-77 marched to Westchester border. The 9th Regiment had but lately returned from New York." After the battle of White Plains, Oct. 28, 1776, the Assembly ordered the 9th, 10th and 16th Militia Regiments to march to Westchester border and place themselves under General Wooster's command. The 9th had but lately returned from New York. Captain Jonathon Whitney's Company, Canaan, Fairfield County, David Maltbie, private, discharged Jan. 23, 1777; one month, five days' service. (Vide p. 485, Rev. War. Records.) He was a descendant of David (3), Jonathon (2), William (1).

ROB'T Mabey (Va.) 2nd Lieut., 15th Virginia, 25 Nov., 1776, 1st Lieut. 19 March, 1777; reg. designated 11th Virginia, 14th Sept., 1778. Capt.-Lt., 14th Sept., 1779, and served to (was in service in 1780). (Name also spelled Mawbrey and Mabries.) The compiler has a theory this was a descendant of Robert Maltby, emigrant, said to have "gone South."

These records of Maltbys who served in the Revolutionary War may be far from complete, as the author has no reference library to consult. At the same time we find that practically all the Maltbys of a suitable age to serve their country did so upon the break with England. Meanwhile, their English cousins were serving their country and a list of British officers serving in America will be found in the N. E. H. & Gen. Reg., about the year 1907. This list contains the names of several Maltbys. (See below.)

According to Mass. Hist. Soc. Proceedings, 1864-1865, there was a Captain Maltby on the British ship "Glasgow." The record is not to his credit, however. It is a court martial record, dated "January 13, 1775, which continued two days this week on board the 'Somerset.'" The account is in a letter of John Andrews, Esq., of Boston.

BRITISH OFFICERS SERVING IN AMERICA

Name.	Rank.	Regiment.	Date of Commission.
Maltby, John	Lieut.	22	1 Oct. 1762
Maltby, Thomas	Ensign	22	1 Oct. 1762
Mawby, John	Lieut.	18	13 Feb. 1762
	Capt.	18	19 July 1771
Mawby, John	Ensign	18	23 Nov. 1768
	Adj.	18	4 Feb. 1769
	Lieut.	18	19 July 1771

Reference. Page 434, New Eng. Hist. & Gen. Reg., Vol. XLVIII, Oct., 1894.

REVOLUTIONARY WAR NOTE

The descendants of Benjamin and Elizabeth Fowler Maltby will be interested to know that this ancestor was an officer in the Revolutionary War, though 60 years of age at the outbreak of hostilities. The Rev. Mr. Gillette said in his Branford address: "The people of North and South societies (Northford and Old Branford) entered with ardor into the war of the Revolution, and furnished a full quota of men by voluntary enlistment, both for land and sea service. Benjamin Maltby was Captain of trained band." He resided near his older brother Daniel (3), "both of them commanded trained bands, as then called, whence his title of Capt."

(Ref. Statement of his son, Rev. Jonathan (4) Maltby) as Capt. Daniel (3) Maltby did not die till late in October, 1776, it is possible that descendants would be eligible through him to any Revolutionary War society.

The Northford Church Records, p. 127, has the following: "Apr. 2, 1778. This church makes choice of Capt. Benjamin Maltbie and Phineas Baldwin to be their Deacons who accepted their office. Test. Warham Williams, Pastor."

Further proof that this Capt. Benjamin is none other than the one claimed is found in a Bond owned by Mrs. F. E. Foster, in which "Benjamin Maltby, Junr., Jonathan Maltby, Isaac Maltby and Stephen Maltby, promise to pay their Honoured Mother Elizabeth Maltby the sum of Twenty pounds lawfull Money within one year from the decease of our Honoured Father, Capt. Benjamin Maltby, in case she survive him," etc. "Dated Branford 20 day Febru'y, 1792."

This Bond, with many other valuable papers, was carefully preserved by Martha Church Maltby, daughter of General Isaac Maltby, (v. v.) and it is to her that we owe the very complete records now existing of this branch of the family. There are no words of praise too high for the work she accomplished, and against the difficulties which frequently beset the path of the genealogist.

WAR OF 1812

General ISAAC (4) Maltby, Benjamin (3), Daniel (2), William (1). Born in 1767, was too young to have been in the Revolutionary War. He served throughout the War of 1812 and was a distinguished soldier and scholar. His commissions are in the possession of his granddaughter, Mrs. Frederick E. Foster. For full account see under Biography of Gen. Isaac Maltby.

NATHANIEL HARRISON (5) Maltby, Benjamin (4), Daniel (3), Daniel (2), William (1). "He was in the War of 1812, a soldier in a New York Regiment."

BENJAMIN Maltby, Ohio, 1st Lieut., 26 infantry, 7 Aug., 1813. Resd 9 May, 1814. (Ref. Hist. Reg. and Dict. of U. S. Army, 187-1903, Heitman, Vol. I., p. 686.)

B. Maltbie, 7 Aug., 1813, 1st Lt. of 26 inf. (List of Officers of U. S. Army, 1776-1900, by Col. Powell. List 1813, p. 91.)

Elizur (or Belizur) Maltby. Query: Was he in the War of 1812? He was born May 1, 1791, and was on the U. S. Ship

"Epiver," for the Mediterranean, a dispatch ship, I believe. He was never after heard from.

Major Gen. SETH MURRAY Maltby was in the War of 1812.

TIMOTHY Maltby served in the War of 1812.

EZRA Burchard Maltby served in the War of 1812 "for grandfather, Zacheus Maltby, he being only fourteen or fifteen when he enlisted."

MILO (6) Maltby, "a soldier in the War of 1812."

MEXICAN WAR

Maltby, CHARLES, 2nd Lt., 4 Ill. Inf. (Ref. War with Mexico, Vol. II., p. 61, Hist. Reg.)

Maltby, JASPER ADALMORN. Served as private and was severely wounded at Chapultepec. (Vide Appleton's Encyclopedia, Vol. IV., p. 185.)

Maltby, THEODORE DWIGHT, born about 1816; married Mary Baylor in 1848 at New Orleans or Texas. Died at New Orleans about 1870. While residing in Boise, Idaho, the compiler knew Captain and Mrs. Ralph Bledsoe, the Captain was an old gentleman and is since deceased. He knew intimately Theodore Dwight Maltby, a grand uncle of the compiler, and served with him in the Mexican War. Capt Bledsoe always spoke of him as "Major Maltby" and recounted many interesting war experiences, and if I remember rightly they were in the battle of Chapultepec. After the war, Major Maltby was for a time in partnership with Capt. Bledsoe and owned one of the first freighting outfits operating in that section of Idaho. Major Maltby often stopped at the Bledsoe's, who kept "open house," and was, according to them, remarkably handsome, well educated, a brilliant conversationalist and of a pleasing personality.

CIVIL WAR

Maltby, JASPER ADALMORN. The following account is from Appleton's Encyclopedia, Vol. IV., p. 185: "Jasper A. Maltby, soldier. Born in Kingsville, Ashtabula Co., Ohio, Nov. 3, 1826;

died in Vicksburg, Miss., Dec. 12, 1867. Served during the Mexican War as private, and was severely wounded at Chapultepec. After his discharge he established himself in mercantile business at Galena, Ill. In 1861, he entered volunteer service as Lieut.-Col. of 45th Illinois infantry; was wounded at Fort Donelson, and after being promoted Col. on 29 Nov., 1862, received a severe wound at Vicksburg. Was commissioned as brig.-gen'l of volunteers on Aug. 4, 1863; served through the subsequent campaigns of the Army of Tennessee, and was mustered out on Jan. 15, 1866. Appointed by Military Commander of the district, Major of Vicksburg on Sept. 3, 1867. Died while in the discharge of duties of that office." Another reference follows:

Maltby, JASPER ADALMORN, Ohio, Ill., Lt.-Col., 45 Ill infantry, 26 Dec., 1861; Col., 5 March, 1863; Brig-Gen'l vols., 4 Aug., 1863; hon. must. out, 15 Jan., 1866. D. 20 March, 1868. (Vide Hist. Reg. and Dict. of U. S. Army, 1789-1903, Heitman, Vol. I., p. 686, also War of Rebellion, Vol. II., Hist. p. 127).

Maltbie, ELIZUR was in the Civil War. He was given a military funeral at Norfolk, Conn. Mustered in Sept. 11, 1862; d. wound at Cold Harbor, June 1, 1864 (leg amputated).

Maltbie, JOHN VAN BUREN; died Sept. 18, 1864, in camp at Elmira, N. Y.

Maltbie, SETH WALDO. At the outbreak of the war enlisted and was enrolled in the second company organized among the students of Oberlin College. The quota being more than full, the company disbanded. Entered the army as private in Co. D., 87th Regt. Ohio Vol. Inf. Appointed corporal, then sergeant. Following year commissioned Capt. of Co. E., 4th Regt., U. S. C. T.

Maltby, RICHARD.

Maltby, ALBERT R., died in the War, March, 1865.

Maltby, MILO BENJAMIN. Private Co. C., 64th O. V. I. and Co. C., 175th O. V. I., discharged July 3, 1865.

Maltby, GEORGE W. A. 16, enlisted Co. H., 108th New York Vol. Infantry and served with Gen. Winfield Scott at Antietam, Gettysburg and Spottsylvania Court House. War Records read: "age 18, M. Aug. 4, 1862. Enlisted at Rochester, N. Y., by Capt. Eugene P. Fuller for 3 years. Bounty $25. Premium $200 in 108th Reg. N. Y. S. V."

Maltby, CHAUNCY SMITH, "in Union Army for a long time."

Maltby, ALBERT ALEXANDER, age 20 (1864) Civil War Enl. Aug. 24, 1864, Disch. June 29, 1865.

Maltby, ULRIC Z. Civil War; Union Army. Enlisted aged 15 years, 7 months. His regiment was at Harrison's Landing, Va. Disch. June 29, 1865 at City Point, Va.

Maltby, Col. RALPH ROBINSON. Enl. Oct., 1861, at Washington, Mason Co., Kentucky, for three years or for the war, under Col. Charles A. Marshall. Had the rank of Adjutant but virtually he performed the duties of Colonel himself. After a year of service he raised a regiment of Cavalry, the 10th Volunteer Regt. of Kentucky Cavalry. He advertised for volunteers the 20th of Aug., 1862 and eight hundred men responded the very next day. (Vide War of Rebellion, Vol. II., Hist., p. 127.)

Mallbie, JOHN WINN. Was evidently in the Civil War. "He died during the war somewhere in Virginia, we never knew the date or place," writes a relative.

Maltby, SAVILION J. Rank, Landsman, No. 1540. Enrolled, Aug. 26, 1862. Mustered in Aug. 26, '62. Period one year. Mustered out July 27, 1863. U. S. Frigate "Sabine." (Vide Rec. of Officers and Men of New Jersey in Civil War, 1861-65, p. 1654).

Mallaby, THEODORE, Jr. N. Y. 2nd Lt. sig. corps, 3 Mar., 1863; hon. mustered out 1 Feb., 1866. D. 29 Mar., 1884. (Ref. Hist. Reg. and Dict. of U. S. Army, 1789-1903, Heitman, Vol. I., p. 686.)

NOTE.—This is evidently a descendant of Rev. Thomas Mallaby of Stonington, Conn. See Biographies.

Maltby, WILLIAM S., soldier from Sanquoit, N. Y., age 21, Sept. 24, 1861, muster roll. Private in company of Thomas H. Bates, Reg. N. Y. Art. Comd'd by Col Bailey.

Maltby, MARCUS, aged 24, in 1862, from Cohicton, M. Roll of Capt. E. H. Pinney. Enl. for 3 years. Commander Col. D. P. De Witt, Co. F., 143rd Reg.

Maltby, DARWIN P., age 21. Enl. May 27, 1861, at Elmira, N. Y., by Curtis C. Gardiner for 2 years in Co. I., 27 Reg. N. Y. -——foot. Comd'd by Col. H. W. Slocum.

Maltby, ALEX. P., age 44. Enrolled Nov. 1, 1861, by W. Lansing, M. by Lieut. Hammond at Saratoga, N. Y., Co. I., 77 Regt. foot. Vol. for the war. Capt. Frank Norton.

Maltby, EDWARD, private, age 21. Mustered 1865, Jan. 30, at Malone, N. Y., by S. C. Thorndike for one year. He came from Oswegatchi, St. Lawrence Co. Co. I., 26 Regt. Cav. N. Y. S. Vol.

Maltby, LEONARD, Co. A., 25 Reg'mt. Cav. N. Y. S. V. Private, age 19. Mustered Dec. 26, 1863, at Hancock (Del. Co.) by Col. Henry Leibenan for 3 years on the Muster Roll of Capt. Sam M. McPherson.

Maltby, CHARLES, private. Enl. at N. Y. C., age 40, 1862; for 3 years. Co. G., 162nd N. Y. S. V. under Capt. Waters.

Maltby, MILTON H., private, age 27. M. Aug. 1, 1862 at Frankfort, N. Y., by Capt. John D. Fish for 3 years. Comp. D., 121st Regt. N. Y. S. V.

Maltby, HORATIO S., private, age 20. M. Aug., 1862, at Edwards, N. Y., by Capt. Alex. Bingham in Col. S. F. Judd's Co. K., 106th Regt. N. Y. S. Vol. His station was at Ogdensburgh, N. Y. Killed at battle of Winchester.

Maltbie, JULIUS B., Capt., age 39. Enrolled at Otto, N. Y., Sept. 16, 1861. Co. C., 64th Reg., N. Y. S. Vol. infantry by Col. Parker for war 3 years at Elmira station.

Maulsby, WM. P. Col., I Potomac Home Brig. Md. inf. He was evidently a West Point Graduate as Col Powell's List of Officers of the U. S. Army, 1776-1900 gives, on page 457: "Maulsby, Wm. P. Mil. Storekeeper, Ord; I. Nov., 1847. Resigned 30 June, 1849. Col. 1st Potomac Home Brig. Md. vols., 29 Nov., 1861. Resigned 25 Aug., 1864."

This list is very incomplete as to showing how many of the Maltby name served their country in this war, but the compiler has not had access to the printed lists and these records are in the most part contributed by relatives of those who served in the war.

Maltby, WARREN, age 19. Enl. 1862. On the muster roll of Capt. Ed. P. Webb's A. A. Died at the defense of Washington, D. C., about 1863, and was brought home to South Rutland, N. Y., for burial.

Maltby, DEXTER JAY. "He saw four years of active service in the Civil War. He was a member of 94th New York Vol.

Inf., and was once captured by the Confederates and confined in Saulsbury Prison."

Maltby, WILLIAM HENDERSON, "was Captain of the Artillery of Texas during the rebellion," writes his sister.

Maltby, HORACE JOHN belonged to Company C., 148th Reg. P. V. I.

Maltby, THEODORE AUGUSTUS, from Conn.

Maltby, JAMES DOWNING. Served four years in the war.

Maltby, APPLETON NOAH. Served three years, with Sherman.

Maltby, SYLVESTER DANIEL. Served during the last nine months of the war in a New York regiment.

Maltby, JAMES M., private, age 19. M. Aug. 11, 1862, for 3 years at Auburn, N. Y., by Capt. Edward A. Thomas in Comp. C., 111th N. Y. S. V.

Maltby, CORYDON OSCAR, enlisted on the outbreak of the war as a private in Co. F., 37th Illinois Infantry. He was engaged with his regiment in many of the important campaigns of the western army and was honorably discharged Sept. 22nd, 1864.

SPANISH-AMERICAN WAR

War with Spain, 1898, Vol. II., Hist:

Maltbie, CHARLES, C. 1st Lt. 5th Ohio Infantry.

Maltby, CHARLES STEVENS. 1st Lt. 16th Ind. Infantry.

Maltbie, JAMES W. 2nd Lt. 5th Ohio Infantry.

Maltbie, PERCY G. Capt. 2nd Wash. Infantry.

EUROPEAN WAR

Maltby ——, Private, 16th battalion, 3rd brigand, 72nd Seaforth Highlanders, 1st Canadian Expeditionary Force, Vancouver.

Maltby, EDWARD, 2nd Lieut. Calgary C. E. F. Seriously injured at Shorncliffe. Address: Royal Victoria Hospital, Folkestone, Kent.

Maltby, MICHAEL, with the fighting forces on the Persian Gulf, now on sick leave in India. British Army.

Maltby, PAUL, 2nd Welch Fusiliers (Regular Army), was with the first British Expeditionary Force, went through Mons, the Marne, Aisne, etc. After ten months of life in the trenches near Armentieres he was wounded. On recovering he joined the Flying Corps and is now flying "somewhere in France." He was at one time the youngest Captain in the regulars, being captain at 22.

Maltby, RONALD, Private, 29th battalion, "Tobius Tigers," Vancouver, B. C., 2nd C. E. F. Fighting "somewhere in France."

Maltby, RONNER (?), is with Gen. Gorringe (of the relief army) in Mesopotamia, and has been wounded.

YALE COLLEGE

1. Samuel Maltby, A.B., Class 1712.
2. Rev. John Maltby, D.D., Class 1747.*

* NOTE—He was to have succeeded President Wheelock as President of Dartmouth, but died suddenly.

3. Rev. Jonathon Maltby, Class 1779. (His diploma owned by the compiler.)
4. Genl. Isaac Maltby, Class 1786.
5. Rev. Erastus Maltby, Class 1821.
6. Dr. Albert Sylvester Maltbie. Yale Med. School.

BRANFORD

By SERAPH MALTBIE DEAN

Lying secure amidst the isles,
And rocky headlands of the Sound,
Was a wild tract with harbor near,
More deep and wide than bays around.

Held by a race wild as this tract,
It caught the eye of pioneers
Seeking a place where merchandise
Might be transported without fears.

The harbor with its smiling grace,
The Stony Creek, the Thimble Isles,
All made a picture to enchant.
And lure one with its magic wiles.

Totoket, had the place been called,
Before our fathers changed the name
To Branford, for the English town
Of Brentford, whence some doubtless came.

For seventy dollars this bold site,
In 1638 was bought
By forty men, and soon became
Noted for shipping craft there wrought.

In that remote ancestral day
A rugged race in Branford stood,
Held fast by creeds and rules severe,
Yet laboring for the general good.

Whoever called the town his home,
Must all the rigid laws obey,
Attend the church, yea, keep awake,
Or heavy fine was his to pay.

A Whipping Post stood on the hill,
To frighten children of the flock
Who naughty were, and Curfew bade
Folk in their bed by ten o'clock.

In center of the town the Green
Was situate with rocky spires,
And round about were houses built
For Sabbath use, with open fires,

Where families gathered at mid-day
To lunch and rest—but dare we think
Our ancestors were frail as we,
Who love to gossip, eat and drink?

'Twas here, in 1700, dwelt
The one whose birth we celebrate,
A man the Public Records show
Identified with Church and State.

Here, too, he died, and here would we,
A loving tribute gladly pay
To William Maltby, honored sire
Of our great family this day.

From homes so widely separate,
We cannot often here return
To solemnize on sacred ground,
The ancestral fires that now we burn.

Yet may we hold fast to the faith
Our fathers held in Church and State,
And write their inscription on our shields—
"Virtue increases under weight."

And then some glad Reunion day,
In Land that knows no pain nor sin,
Meet, a united family,
With sainted host of Maltby kin.

(Written for the First Reunion of the Maltby Family at Branford.)

BRANFORD, CONNECTICUT

In Part I. we gave several pen pictures of Maltby, Yorkshire, the home of some of the English Maltbys and it seems fitting that a short account of the home of our emigrant ancestor should also have a place in this work.

We can hardly do better than quote from an essay written by Miss Olive Hall Pond of Branford, as it gives a very comprehensive idea of the Branford our early ancestors knew.

"Branford was purchased from the Indians in the year 1638 for the sum of $70, and settled six years late (1644) by forty men and their families, who came from Wethersfield. . . .

"At first the chief occupation was farming but the people soon found that the land was not remarkable for its fertility. Branford harbor was then much deeper than it is at the present time and furnished excellent facilities for ships engaging in trade with the West Indies. Consequently, merchandise from foreign ports was brought to Branford and was then carried over the hills to New Haven, which at that time did not have a good harbor.

"Trading necessitated the building of ships. Vessels suitable to transport merchandise to all parts of the world were built where the swimming pool at Mill Plains is now located. . . .

"It is interesting to picture the town as we find it in the year 1700." (Ten years prior to the death of William Maltby.) "The green was then, as now, the center of the town. Large rocks, boulders and tall grass completely covered it. There was but one church, which stood where the town hall does today. This was called the new meeting house, the first having been built on the site of the cemetery* and surrounded by a high stockade, as a protection from hostile Indians.

"Scattered around the green were the 'Sabbath Day Houses.' They were used by families who came from a long distance. They afforded the people places to rest and warm themselves during the noon hour, for the church services there lasted nearly all day.

"Two other conspicuous structures on the green were the Blacksmith shop and the whipping post. The shop stood in the hollow back of the church, the whipping post and public stocks on the hill where the Baptist church now stands.

"There were but few public highways, the chief of which led from New Haven through the town of Branford to Guilford. Montowese street, named from the Indians, ran as now from the center to the river. Here it turned, following the present course of the railroad, thence back to the green. A street upon which the minister and several officials of the town lived, led from Montowese street, east to the river, somewhat similar to Averill avenue. This was called 'Pig Lane.'

"The first postoffice, with public store combined, stood on the site of the Lock works. This hollow formed the principal business section of Branford.

"The kindergarten, grammar and high school combined, consisted of one building, the academy, which now stands, the only remaining relic of former days.

"It is most amusing to notice some of the customs and restrictions of that time. Chief among these were the church laws. Sunday morning a drum was beaten to call the members to church. Every person who did not attend, arrive on time, and stay until the service was over, was heavily fined. Besides this, a man was hired to go among the congregation during the service and prevent them from going to sleep. This he accomplished by means of a long pole. Any weary mortal who chanced to close his eyes for a moment's rest would receive a vigorous poke of the pole, with a command to wake up and listen to the words of the Gospel.

"On this day the Green was transformed into a lively scene. The farmers and their entire families drove into town in their large open wagons; one man coming all the way from Northford, regularly attended with his wife and 26 children.

* The first wife of William Maltby was probably buried near this first meeting house.

"Another law of special importance, the fines for the violation of which would make Branford of today very wealthy, if the law were enforced, was what was known in England as the curfew law. This stated that the streets must be vacated, fires banked and every man in his home at 10 o'clock.

Additional items of interest pertaining to Branford and the Maltbys will be found in the following article which is copied from a Ms. sent by Mrs. John P. Cushman and is here given verbatim:

BRANFORD.

"As Branford may be considered our family home I copy quite an extended account of its early history (see also Mass. Hist. Coll., Vol. 6, p. 319) from the semi-centennial discourse (Morehouse and Taylor, Pub.) of Rev. Timothy P. Gillett (pastor of the church) preached July 7, 1858. 'The tract of land, which for almost two centuries constituted the town of Branford, was purchased of the town of New Haven in the year 1644, by colonists or immigrants from Wethersfield with William Swain at their head. The settlers in New Haven had purchased it of the Indian Sachems in 1638. (Sept. 1, 1640) Totoket, or Branford, was granted to Rev. Samuel Eaton, brother of Theophilus Eaton, Gov. of New Haven Colony, provided he obtained a sufficient number of his friends to settle it. He went to England for that purpose, but was persuaded to remain and preach at Durbenfield and Stockport, in England. As he failed of fulfilling his engagement, Branford was sold to Wm. Swain and others of Wethersfield. Totoket, the original name, seems to have been given by the Aborigines, to a range of mountains running through the northern part of the town, and from them applied to the whole tract. Its present name is said to have been derived from Brentford or Burntford, a village in England, near London.' (Author's note: "Brentford, Middlesex, their friends distinguished themselves on the side of Parliament there in 1642.")

'Probably some of the first settlers came from that place, who, after residing temporarily in other places finally fixed their residence here. It does not appear that there were among them any persons of great wealth, or superior rank. But they were men of strict Puritan principles,—men of stern integrity and zealous for religious liberty, so far as its principles were then understood. The doctrines of their creed were Calvanistic, or those which were embodied shortly after, in the Cambridge and Westminster Confession of Faith. In church policy they were Congregationalists. In common with other colonists of that age, they acted on the scheme of carrying the gospel and its ordinances, education and its advantages, with them, and having the church, the minister and the school, coeval with their settlement. . . . There are no records known to exist showing when a church was organized here, but as early as October, 1644, the salary of Mr. John Sherman as a preacher began, and the records show he was remaining here in 1646, though probably not as a settled minister. (See Barber's Hist. Coll. for further notice of Mr. Sherman.)

The first regular pastor was Abraham Pierson, whose name appears on the town records in 1647. He was born in Yorkshire, Eng., graduated at Cambridge in 1632, preached some years in his own country, came to New England in 1639, joined the church in Boston, soon moved to Lynn, and the next year settled in Southampton, L. I., probably in 1641. In 1647 he removed to Branford, and was pastor of the church here about twenty years. The union of New Haven Colony with that of Connecticut so displeased Mr. Pierson, that he, with many of his people, left Branford about June, 1667, and settled in Newark, N. J., where he died Aug. 9, 1678. He probably carried away the church records, and they are supposed to be lost. The town records were not removed. Branford was without an organized church and settled minister for about twenty years." (Author's note: The descendants of Col. Stephen Maltby (4) have the above Rev. Abraham Pierson for an ancestor, through his daughter Abigail, who married John Davenport.)

"The first church edifice was erected within the old burying ground, and tradition says it was enclosed by a stockade to protect its worshippers from the Indians. Four others have succeeded it, built where the present house now stands. The centre burying ground was the only one in town, for about eighty years after its settlement. There lie the remains of all the pastors and their wives, except Mr. Pierson, and there sleep the first settlers with many of their descendants. . . .

"Formerly the shipping business and the West India trade from Branford were greater than from New Haven. The harbor here was better and safer. The Dutch, sagacious and enterprising, had discovered this long before Daniel" (Compiler's query, William?) "Swain, of Wethersfield, and his company bought Totoket. They had also established a trading house here, and opened a lucrative traffic with the Indians. Their location is still known as Dutch House Point and Dutch House Quarter. But the people of Branford met with great reverses, in the old French wars. Their ships were captured or lost, their spirit of enterprise broken, and the improvements made in New Haven harbor removed the shipping business to that place.

"There is no record or tradition that the Branford Indians made war on our people, or offered any violence to them. Their lands were bought and paid for, besides the price paid to New Haven for the township, and the town passed laws protecting them in all their rights, and prohibiting individuals from purchasing their reservations, lest fraud should be practised."

THE MALTBY ASSOCIATION

OFFICERS

MR. FRANK BIERCE MALTBY.......................... President
MR. WILLIAM HENRY MALTBIE............... 1st Vice President
MRS. JOHN P. VICTORY........................ 2nd Vice President
MRS. JAMES WILLEY TODD.......................... Treasurer
MRS. CLARENCE VERRILL.............. Secretary and Genealogist

STATE SECRETARIES

MRS. A. M. BECKWITH.............................. Colorado
MRS. WILLIAM AUSTIN.............................. Connecticut
MISS MAUDE TOWNSHEND MALTBY...................... Idaho
MRS. JOHN P. CUSHMAN.............................. Maine
MRS. ARTHUR BLISS SEYMOUR...................... Massachusetts
MRS. FREDERICK CRUM.............................. New Jersey
MRS. JOHN P. VICTORY.............................. New Mexico
MISS CLARA E. MCGEER }
MR. UBRIC Z. MALTBY } .... New York
MISS MARTHA J. MALTBY............................. Ohio
MISS ACHSAH MALTBIE.............................. Washington

In February, 1906, a few Maltby descendants formed a Maltby Association, and as it was not intended to confine it to any particular country, but to truly make it a Maltby Association of Maltbys wherever found, there was only one rule adopted as to eligibility, namely that the applicant must descend from a Maltby; the one exception being that widows of Maltbys should be entitled to join providing it was distinctly stated on all membership rolls that they "represented their husband."

In order that no cousin should be deterred from joining owing to prohibitive dues, these were made as low as possible, and the purely nominal sum of $1.00 a year for each member is asked. The fact that the dues are so low makes it absolutely necessary for the success of the Association that descendants will do all in their power to interest other Maltbys and be as prompt as possible in the payment of dues. It must be thoroughly understood that all money received from members is applied to work on the particular branch of the family from which they descend—to try and establish a more complete line of descent.

In the case of the American Maltbys the money paid by them is used for various purposes: some being—the care and restoration of our early ancestors' tombstones; the photographing of ancient Maltby tombstones, portraits, homesteads and heirlooms; the copying of old wills, inventories, family letters and documents of special interest,—these being fees to Town Clerks—the search of early records to prove the connection with our emigrant ancestors to some heretofore unplaced Maltby family; and also to cover the regular running expenses, such as stamps, stationery, letter heads, printed receipt cards for dues, etc.; these in themselves making quite an item. And last, but perhaps most important of all, when we can get sufficient surplus to cover current expenses, we have employed Mr. Gerald Fothergill, the eminent genealogist, of London, England, to work upon establishing the link with our English ancestors. In this work we were materially aided by contributions from individuals, twenty-four members contributing sums ranging from fifty cents to five dollars, giving a total of $51.50. That this money was well invested and that Mr. Fothergill more than gave us full value, must be evident to all those who have read Part I of this book.

Mr. Fothergill visited York in July, 1910, and read all the wills 'round Retford for about fifteen years—no matter what the testator's name, in the hope of getting a mention of Maltby, but only obtained one. This used one ten pound note. The second ten pounds he used in going around Retford. He personally saw the record of William Maltby's baptism—"16 March 1644-45." Mr. Fothergill wrote: "This corresponds with the age on his tomb. I also found the baptism of Robert Maltby in 1647. I hope you will be pleased with this evidence. I had to visit Retford and Springthorpe twice as the Vicar had gone away and had the keys with him. I suspect John" (i. e., brother of William the emigrant) "to have been born at Bawtry. The Bawtry registers ought to be searched as well as Kexbie."

There is every reason to believe that our ancestry is established back to John Maltby of Kexby Hall, Kexby, who made his will in 1557, but this should not satisfy us, and it seems such a very short step from here to a connection with an old English pedigree, such a one as Pedigree No. II—also such a descent would give us a right to use a coat-of-arms, and certainly there is a just satisfaction in knowing that one is entitled to coat-armour, long since justly won by some ancestor.

We need money to carry on this work, £10 ($50.00) is about the smallest sum one can send, and if some of the members who have not already contributed to this good work would care to assist in subscribing to this fund it would be greatly appreciated.

The Association has another object to accomplish, namely to promote a feeling of good-will and kinship to all of our kind wherever found, and to further this end it was planned to hold a Family Reunion at least once every five years. The first reunion was held at Branford in September, 1910 (see account which follows), and this year of 1915 should find a second reunion planned, but owing to an unfortunate chain of circumstances it was not deemed practicable this year.

The Maltby Association have expected to publish annually the reports of the secretary and treasurer, and to date we have issued four publications, viz.: in 1907, a short report, afterwards included in Booklet I, issued in 1908 through the courtesy of Mr. Jay Hayes Maltby of Forman, North Dakota. In February, 1909, Mr. Jay H. Maltby, at his own expense, issued Booklet II, a volume of 150 pages very nicely got up, the sale of which we understand just covered the actual cost of the illustrations and printing. In February, 1910, the Fourth Annual Report of the Secretary and Treasurer was published and sent, gratis, to all members. The autumn following the First Reunion was held which stimulated an interest in the Association, many new members joined, and all seemed anxious to procure copies of the next Maltby book which was promised for the spring of 1911. The Secretary fulfilled her contract and had the MS. ready the last of February. The book was to have been printed at private expense by a Maltby who expected to cover the costs from the sale of the publication. Then came the hitch—it is too long a story and far too unfortunate an incident to go into at length. The printing stopped, all communication ceased, it was impossible to obtain the manuscript; meanwhile members wrote asking when they would receive their books; as time wore on the interest taken in the Association began to lag, dues did not come in and the Secretary, who had labored untiringly since the founding of our little clan, saw the work of years undone, and only the few dying embers left of what had been a well built house.

However, before the last spark was extinguished, one to whom we are greatly indebted, saw that the manuscript reached us, and Fate was indeed kind, when she led Mr. Birdsey L. Maltbie to make his fine offer to print our book at his own expense, trusting to the Maltby descendants' interest in such a production to subscribe sufficiently to cover the very high costs of producing such a book. We earnestly request all those owning copies to tell their relations of the book, as only in this way can Mr. Maltbie be reimbursed for the great expense to which he has been put. The entire book of nearly nine hundred pages has been rewritten, revised and added to by the secretary in the last few months. There is room for much improvement as to literary style, arrangement and so forth, but it has been work done as a "rush order" and with all the imperfections it must seek its own place among you. We hope it will be a successful venture, for if so we shall hope later to publish the large Maltby Genealogy upon which the genealogist has worked for years, and which will include a very complete record of the descendants of the emigrant ancestors, John and William Maltby. Again we urge all those who have not already done so, to send in as full a record as possible of their own family as far as known, also old portraits of ancestors, giving when possible military and official records, names of universities attended, full dates of births, marriages and deaths—in fact any items of particular interest in your family and which you should like to have preserved to posterity, so that when you receive a printed copy you will feel satisfied with the accounts given and find the book says "just what I wanted said."

As the present book is intended for a permanent publication, much of a personal nature was cut out, and all that was stable in our previous publications was included in order that descendants might have the complete printed records in one substantial book.

The list of members which completes this book is made from the last roll taken, and we sincerely hope that all will remain with us for many years, giving us courage to work on, by their help and co-operation.

It may interest the Maltby descendants of William Maltby to know that the head of our house of Maltby is Mr. Charles Eli Maltby. This is the oldest son of an oldest son to have male issue and his line is: William (1), Daniel (2), the third son, but oldest having male issue; Capt. Joseph (3), Joseph (4), Rev. Joseph (5), Milo (6), Chauncy (7), Charles Eli (8), and his oldest son is Chauncy H. (9) Maltby, b. July 29, 1886.

The last report of the Treasurer, Feb. 1, 1911, follows. On this date we had but $33.28 in the bank. Few dues have been received since, and the expenses of stationery and stamps has gone steadily on so that at the present there is practically no money in the treasury. It is intended to issue notices of dues twice a year, on January first and July first, and we trust that all the old members will respond as promptly as possible as we are sadly in need of funds.

TREASURER'S REPORT

Balance on hand Feb. 1, 1910	$70.26
Received in dues to Feb. 1, 1911	99.00
Total	$169.26
Expenses 1910	135.98
Balance on hand Feb. 1, 1911	$33.28

YEAR'S EXPENSES—1910.

Check for Mr. Fothergill	$48.00
Fee for same	.70
Printed reports ($50.00, at half cost)	25.00
500 Envelopes	1.50
500 Letter Heads	3.50
Printed circulars and reunion cards	2.00
Reunion expenses	12.00
Postage	18.73
Express on reunion register	.40
Express on 4th annual reports	6.90
Stationery	4.79
Envelopes	1.74
Pads	.35
Registering valuable documents	.64
Photographs	.92
Hickling certificate	2.55
Post-cards	.10
Miss Scofield	4.00
Query in International Genealogical Directory	2.05
P. O. Money Order	.16
Exchange on American check	.10
	$135.94

From the Treasurer's report it will be seen that ninety-nine members only paid dues while our membership roll shows a list of one hundred and forty-five names. Subtracting the eight honorary memberships of Mr. Jay Hayes Maltby and his family, the dues of Miss Esther Tapping Maltby, which she speaks of sending; $1.00 enclosed by a member which was lost in the mail, and two members' names who joined after February first, (consequently their dues are not included in the year of 1910), we find a total of twelve. This twelve added to ninety-nine paid memberships accounts for one hundred and eleven members. Consequently there remain thirty-four members who have not as yet sent in their dues.

We make an especial appeal to the members and ask that they will try and pay their dues as promptly as convenient after receiving their notifications from the Treasurer. This will save the Treasurer and Secretary a vast amount of time and trouble and also expense. The dues are so small that out of the dollar paid by each member we make not more than eighty or ninety cents profit during the year, as the postage used for each member during the year costs the Association at least ten or twenty cents.

We also wish to notify members that a formal note of resignation will be required if one wishes to resign. Also, where dues are not paid within one year, the member's name will be crossed off the books and will not appear in the membership roll till all dues are paid.

We hope all the members will endeavor to assist the Treasurer and Secretary in the work they are doing for the Association by acquiescing in the above request.

The thirty-four dollars due, with what we have received from private sources, would enable us to continue the English research which now is at a standstill, owing to the very small surplus in the Treasury.

It has not previously been stated that all the officers of the Association pay their annual dues as well as the members, but this fact should, we think, be known. Every cent paid in to the Treasurer is spent in furthering the general good of our large family, and we trust that all may feel satisfied with the work done.

KEY TO REUNION PHOTOGRAPH

(Left to right—beginning at the top of the picture.)

FIRST ROW

Mr. Frederick Crum. Miss Scofield. Mrs. Charles Lewis. Mrs. McChesney. Mrs. Austin. Mrs. F. S. Smith. Mrs. S. E. Shipp. Mr. E. Maltby Shipp. Charles Eli Maltby.

SECOND ROW

Miss Grace Maltby. Rev. Clark O. Maltby. Mrs. James W. Todd. Mr. W. Hubbell. Mrs. Hubbell. Mr. Wilburt S. Maltby. Miss Margaret Stevens. Mrs. Stevens. Mrs. Edwards. Mrs. Clark O. Maltby.

THIRD ROW

Mrs. Dean. Mrs. Haskin. Dr. Mary Cushman, M. D. Miss Anna F. Maltby. Mr. Monroe E. Maltby.

FOURTH ROW

Miss Dean. Mrs. F. H. Crum. Mrs. Haven. Mrs. Cushman. Mrs. Monroe E. Maltby.

FIFTH ROW

Little Miss McChesney. Little Miss McChesney. Master Crum. Miss Margaret Maltby Maltby. Kenneth Maltby.

Those who could not remain until the photograph was taken were:—Mr. and Mrs. J. Elner Beach, Mr. Harry Dean, Miss Mary J. Maltby, Mr. Yale and Mr. Charles Yale.

REUNION PHOTOGRAPH

THE FIRST REUNION OF THE MALTBY FAMILY

The first Maltby Family Reunion was held at Branford and Indian Neck, Connecticut, on September first, 1910—exactly two hundred years from the date of death of our ancestor, William Maltby, Esq.

Those attending assembled at the New Haven Public Library wearing a knot of red and gold, the Maltby colors, as a badge of identification. These were improved upon by buttons which were soon passed to all, having the Maltby coat-of-arms done in heraldic colors—the generous gift of Mr. Wilburt S. Maltby of Plainfield, New Jersey. At quarter to eleven an open trolley was taken for the hour's ride to Branford, and alas, in a downpour of rain. The company went direct to the Montowese House at Indian Neck, where our ancestor owned much land, and held an informal meeting opened by Rev. Clark O. Maltby, which included the recitation of poems, written for the occasion; addresses, letters from absent members, and the singing of appropriate songs. An enjoyable luncheon was served at two o'clock. The place cards were the gift of Mrs. Lee Parker Dean and her son Mr. Henry Dean. The latter engraved the plate and Mrs. Dean personally met all expenses connected with getting the cards out, then they were colored by hand by Mrs. Brown of Toledo, Ohio, Mrs. Hubbell, and Miss Marion Davenport Maltbie, to all of whom the Association is most grateful.

A nicely bound volume was provided for all descendants and guests to register in, and at the close of luncheon the group photograph which appears on the opposite page was taken. The rain having nearly ceased the party took a car to Branford, where the cemetery was visited and two handsome sprays of roses provided by the Association were placed upon the graves of William Maltby, and on that of his wife Abigail. Mrs. Cushman, a descendant of this third wife, Abigail Bishop, laid the white roses upon her grave, and Rev. Clark O. Maltby placed a lovely spray of red roses upon the grave of William Maltby, speaking a few words of dedication. From the cemetery the little company visited the Town Hall, examining the old original documents in the handwriting of our emigrant ancestor.

Thus the eventful day drew to a close. We cannot but appreciate the loyalty of those who were prompted to do honor to the day despite the inclement weather. Forty-one people were expected and forty-one came, although some of these had not signed cards and some of those who had did not come. Had it been pleasant the Reunion would surely have numbered over fifty.

Of the forty-one present, thirty-four were of Maltby blood. One of the tangible results of the Reunion was the addition of thirteen new members to our roll.

The following is a list of those present. First is the list of descendants of William Maltby.

DESCENDANTS

Rev. Clark O. Maltby, Paterson, New Jersey.
Mrs. Lee Parker Dean, Cambridge, Massachusetts.
Mrs. William R. Hubbell, Falls Village, Connecticut.
Mrs. Frederic H. Crum, River Edge, New Jersey.
Miss Mary J. Maltby, Northford, Connecticut.
Mrs. David Stevens, Wallingford, Connecticut.
Mrs. Elmer J. Beach, Northford, Connecticut.
Mrs. Richard Hankin, Passaic, New Jersey.
Mrs. Samuel E. Shipp, Newburgh-on-Hudson, New York.
Mrs. John P. Cushman, Farmington, Maine.
Dr. Mary F. Cushman, M. D., Farmington, Maine.
Mrs. Haven, Needham, Massachusetts.
Miss Olive E. Dean, Cambridge, Massachusetts.
Mr. Henry C. Dean, Cambridge, Massachusetts.
Miss Marguerite Stevens, Wallingford, Connecticut.
Miss Margaret Maltby Maltby, Plainfield, New Jersey.
Mr. E. Maltby Shipp, Newburgh-on-Hudson, New York.
Mrs. Charles Lewis, South Rutland, New York.
Mr. Kenneth Maltby, South Rutland, New York.
Mrs. McChesney and two children, Avon, Connecticut.
Mr. Yale, Wallingford, Connecticut.
Mr. Charles Yale, Wallingford, Connecticut.
Mr. Monroe E. Maltby, Adams Center, New York.
Miss Anna F. Maltby, Adams Center, New York.
Mr. Charles Eli Maltby, South Rutland, New York.
Mrs. Frederick Smith, Chester, Connecticut.
Mr. Wilburt S. Maltby, Plainfield, New Jersey.
Mrs. William Austin, Avon, Connecticut.
Miss Grace Tryon Maltby, New Haven, Connecticut.
Mrs. James Willey Todd, New Haven, Connecticut.

GUESTS

Mrs. Clark O. Maltby, Paterson, New Jersey.
Mrs. M. E. Edwards, New Haven, Connecticut.
Mr. Elmer J. Beach, Northford, Connecticut.
Mr. F. H. Crum, River Edge, New Jersey.
Mrs. Monroe E. Maltby, Adams Center, New York.
Miss Ethel Lord Scofield, New Haven, Connecticut.

DEATHS OF MEMBERS

1. Mrs. Richard Long (Emma Jessie Maltby) (8), George W. (7), Chandler (6), Chandler (5), Joseph (4), Capt. Joseph (3), Daniel (2), William (1). Died Jan. 3, 1906, aged 32 years.

2. Mr. Henry Ernest Maltby (7), Oliver Ellsworth (6), Lucius (5), Rev. Jonathan (4), Benjamin (3), Daniel (2), William (1). Died Feb. 24, 1907, aged 50 years.

3. Mrs. Justin W. Meacham (Elizabeth A. Morehouse) (6), Andrew Morehouse (5), Sarah *Bulkley* (4), Hannah Maltbie (3), Jonathan (2), William (1). Died Sept. 12, 1907, aged 64 years.

4. Mr. Douglass Fowler Maltby, Yale ex '44 (6), Julius (5), Rev. Jonathan (4), Benjamin (3), Daniel (2), William (1). Died May 16, 1907, in Waterbury, Conn., aged 87 years.

5. Mr. Oliver Ellsworth Maltby (6), Lucius (5), Rev. Jonathan (4), Benjamin (3), Daniel (2), William (1). Died Nov. 5, 1907, aged 80 years.

6. Deacon William Maltby (6), Henry (5), James (4), Samuel (3), Samuel (2), William (1). Died May 31, 1908, aged 83 years.

7. Mr. George W. Maltby (7), Chandler (6), Chandler (5), Joseph (4), Capt. Joseph (3), Daniel (2), William (1). Died July 1, 1908, aged 63 years.

8. Mr. Silas Benjamin Maltbie (7), Harrison (6), Benjamin (5), Benjamin (4), Daniel (3), Daniel (2), William (1). Died Nov. 7, 1908, aged 73 years.

9. Mrs. William A. Butler (Frances Isabel Maltbie) (7), James Wills (6), William Davenport (5), David (4), David (3), Jonathan (2), William (1). Died July 15, 1909, aged 67 years.

10. Mr. George Erastus Maltby (6), Lucius (5), Rev. Jonathan (4), Benjamin (3), Daniel (2), William (1). Died July 31, 1909, aged 78 years.

11. Mrs. Edward Payson Powell [Lucy (7) Maltby], Norman (6), John (5), William (4), Capt. Joseph (3), Daniel (2), William (1). Died 1910.

12. Mrs. Henry Hobart Benedict [Eleanor Augusta (7) Maltby]. George Williams (6), Augustus Williams (5), Col. Stephen (4), Benjamin (3), Daniel (2), William (1). Died Nov. 17 (?), 1913, aged 63 years.

13. Mrs. Joshua B. Clark.

14. Mrs. Theodore Clark.

15. Mrs. Charles P. Crosby.

16. Mrs. Otis Loring Hamilton.

17. Mr. Appleton Noah Maltby.

18. Rev. Clark O. Maltby.

19. Mr. George Beecher Maltby.

20. Miss Mary J. Maltby.

21. Lt.-Col. Richard Leighton Maltby.

22. Mr. Williams Rogers Murray.

23. Mrs. Henry J. Stevens.

24. Mrs. Joshua Thompson.

MEMBERSHIP LIST

Name of Member	Line of Descent
1. Mrs. William Henry Austin (Alta Jane Maltby) Pulaski, New York	Charles Rollin Maltby (7) Timothy Maltby (1812) (6) Timothy Maltby (5) Samuel Maltby (4) Samuel Maltby (3) Samuel Maltby (2) William Maltby (1)
2. Mrs. Aaron Turner Bailey (Katharin Gemmel Lynes) Address: 158 West 75th Street, New York City, N. Y.	Banjamin Lynes (6) Hannah Maltbie (5) Capt. Jonathon Maltbie (R.W.) (4) Jonathan Maltbie (3) Jonathan Maltbie (2) William Maltbie (1)
3. Mrs. Myron A. Baldwin (Sarah Hale Murray) Address: 423 13th Street, South Fargo, North Dakota	William Rogers Murray (7) Harriet Maltby (6) Chandler Maltby (5) Joseph Maltby (4) Capt. Joseph Maltby (3) Daniel Maltby (2) William Maltby (1)
4. Mr. John Edwin Barker Address: 1118 Widener Building, Philadelphia, Pennsylvania	Jason A. Barber (8) Lydia Elizabeth Maltby (7) David Maltby (6) William Maltby (5) William Maltby (R.W.) (4) Capt. Joseph Maltby (3) Daniel Maltby (2) William Maltby (1)
5. Mrs. Bayard Barnes (Helen Davenport Benedict) Address: 77 Edgehill Road, New Haven, Connecticut	Eleanor Augusta Maltby (7) George Williams Maltby (6) Augustus Williams Maltby (5) Col. Stephen Maltby (4) Benjamin Maltby (R.W.) (3) Daniel Maltby (2) William Maltby (1)
6 Miss Esther Elberta Barnes Address: 607 Clarence Street Lake Charles, Louisiana	Catharine Maltby (6) Daniel Maltby (5) Benjamin Maltby (R.W.) (4) Daniel Maltby (3) Daniel Maltby (2) William Maltby (1)
7. Mrs. Elmer Jaynes Beach (Ophelia Hall Maltby) Address: Northford, Connecticut	Deacon William Maltby (6) Henry Maltby (5) James Maltby (4) Samuel Maltby (3) Samuel Maltby (2) William Maltby (1)

Name of Member	Line of Descent
8. Mrs. A. M. Beckwith (Alice Asenath Maltbie) Address: 1532 Ninth Avenue, Greeley, Colorado	Noah Maltbie (6) Noah Maltbie (5) Noah Maltbie (R.W.) (4) Capt. Joseph Maltbie (3) Daniel Maltbie (2) William Maltbie (1)
9. Mr. Earl Maltby Benson Care English High School, Boston, Massachusetts	Celia Salina Maltby (7) Timothy Maltby (1812) (6) Timothy Maltby (5) Samuel Maltby (4) Samuel Maltby (3) Samuel Maltby (2) William Maltby (1)
10. Mrs. William M. Bernard (Margaretta Attwater Maltby) Address: 381 Central Park West, New York City, N. Y.	George Erastus Maltby (6) Lucius Maltby (5) Rev. Jonathon Maltby (4) Benjamin Maltby (R.W.) (3) Daniel Maltby (2) William Maltby (1)
11. Mrs. Edwin Mortimer Blake (Josephine St. Felix Wittichen) Address: R. 1406, 1 Liberty Street, New York City, N. Y.	Josephine J. St. Felix (6) Anna Maria Maltby (5) Charles Maltby (4) George Maltby (3) Thomas Maltby (2) William Maltby (1) of Orston, Notts.
12. Mrs. George T. Boles (Loraine Maltby) Address: St. Davids, Pennsylvania	Lucius Upson Maltby (6) Lucius Maltby (5) Rev. Jonathon Maltby (R.W.) (4) Benjamin Maltby (R.W.) (3) Daniel Maltby (2) William Maltby (1)
13. Miss Alice M. Boynton Address: Care Royal Bank of Canada, Nassau, Bahamas	Mary Elizabeth Maltbie (6) Elon Maltbie (5) Benjamin Maltbie (R.W.) (4) Daniel Maltbie (3) Daniel Maltbie (2) William Maltbie (1)
14. Mrs. Robert Maitland Brereton (Alice Fairchild) Address: 525 Everett Street, Portland, Oregon.	Isaac Maltby Fairchild (6) Aurelia Maltby (5) Gen. Isaac Maltby (1812) (4) Benjamin Maltby (R.W.) (3) Daniel Maltby (2) William Maltby (1)
15. Mrs. Fred Austin Bright (Mellie Jane Maltby) Address: 665 Orchard Avenue, Bellevue, Pittsburgh, Pa.	Newell Maltby (6) Nathaniel Harrison Maltby (5) Benjamin Maltby (R.W.) (4) Daniel Maltby (3) Daniel Maltby (2) William Maltby (1)

Name of Member	Line of Descent
16. Mrs. Willard L. Brown (Mary Alice Maltbie) Address: 17 Bronson Place, Toledo, Ohio	Charles Benjamin Maltbie (6) Elon Maltbie (5) Benjamin Maltbie (R.W.) (4) Daniel Maltbie (3) Daniel Maltbie (2) William Maltbie (1)
17. Mr. Walter I. Brush Address: Sterling, Colorado	Ada May Maltbie (7) Noah Maltbie (6) Noah Maltbie (5) Noah Maltbie (R.W.) (4) Capt. Joseph Maltbie (3) Daniel Maltbie (2) William Maltbie (1)
18. Mrs. Thomas H. Burton (Grace G. Maltby) Address: Batavia, Ill.	Albert A. Maltby (8) Hiram Maltby (7) Timothy Maltby (1812) (6) Timothy Maltby (5) Samuel Maltby (4) Samuel Maltby (3) Samuel Maltby (2) William Maltby (1)
19. Mrs. Henry W. Carey (Amelia Blackmond) Address: Oxford, Oakland Co., Michigan	Maria Maltby (6) Chandler Maltby (5) Joseph Maltby (4) Capt. Joseph Maltby (3) Daniel Maltby (2) William Maltby (1)
20. Mr. Maltby Carter Address: 1320 Broadway, Bay City, Michigan	Sabra Maltby (6) Chandler Maltby (5) Joseph Maltby (4) Capt. Joseph Maltby (3) Daniel Maltby (2) William Maltby (1)
21. Mr. Mortimer Carter (C. W.) Address: Flint, Michigan R. F. D. No. 5	Sabra Maltby (6) Chandler Maltby (5) Joseph Maltby (4) Capt. Joseph Maltby (3) Daniel Maltby (2) William Maltby (1)
22. Mr. Oscar Carter Address: West Bay City, Michigan	Sabra Maltby (6) Chandler Maltby (5) Joseph Maltby (4) Capt. Joseph Maltby (3) Daniel Maltby (2) William Maltby (1)
23. Mrs. Ebenezer Cary (Elizabeth Murray Love) Address: 184 Delaware Avenue, Buffalo, N. Y.	Maria Maltby (5) Gen. Isaac Maltby (1812) (4) Benjamin Maltby (R.W.) (3) Daniel Maltby (2) William Maltby (1)

Name of Member	Line of Descent
24. Mrs. Horace Greeley Clark (Ruth Luella Maltbie) Address: 1530 Marion Street, Denver, Colorado	Noah Maltbie (6) Noah Maltbie (5) Noah Maltbie (R.W.) (4) Capt. Joseph Maltbie (3) Daniel Maltbie (2) William Maltbie (1)
* 25. Mrs. Joshua B. Clark (Mildred Noble Maltbie) Address: Gronnigen, Pine County, Minn.	Seth Waldo Maltbie (C.W.) (6) Daniel Maltbie (5) Benjamin Maltbie (R.W.) (4) Daniel Maltbie (3) Daniel Maltbie (2) William Maltbie (1)
26. Mr. Paul Maltby Clark Address: 1530 Marion Street, Denver, Colorado	Ruth Maltby (7) Noah Maltbie (6) Noah Maltbie (5) Noah Maltbie (R.W.) (4) Capt. Joseph Maltbie (3) Daniel Maltbie (2) William Maltbie (1)
* 27. Mrs. Theodore Clark (Grace Amoret Maltby) Address: Ocean Park, California	Lucius Maltby (5) Rev. Jonathon Maltby (R.W.) (4) Benjamin Maltby (3) Daniel Maltby (2) William Maltby (1)
28. Mrs. Ernest Vernon Claypool (Nellie Cornelia Maltby) Address: 516 Pine Street, Michigan City, Indiana	Lauren Baldwin Maltby (6) Jesse Maltby (5) Benjamin Maltby (R.W.) (4) Daniel Maltby (3) Daniel Maltby (2) William Maltby (1)
29. Mrs. James Porter Collins (Theodora Edna Maltbie) Address: Cosmopolis, Washington	Albert Lyman Maltbie (8) James Downing Maltbie (C.W.) (7) Noah Maltbie (6) Noah Maltbie (5) Noah Maltbie (R.W.) (4) Capt. Joseph Maltbie (3) Daniel Maltbie (2) William Maltbie (1)
30. Mr. John Maltby Conkling Address: 221-223 E. Commercial St., Springfield, Missouri	Mary Maltby (6) Daniel Maltby (5) Benjamin Maltby (R.W.) (4) Daniel Maltby (3) Daniel Maltby (2) William Maltby (1)
31. Mrs. E. H. Cope (Cynthia Ann Murray) Address: Mitchell, South Dakota	Harriet Maltby (6) Chandler Maltby (5) Joseph Maltby (4) Capt. Joseph Maltby (3) Daniel Maltby (2) William Maltby (1)

* Deceased.

Name of Member	Line of Descent
32. Mrs. Levi P. Crawford (Helen Mary Maltby) Address: 185 North Euclid Avenue, Pasadena, California	Harrison Maltby (6) Jesse Maltby (5) Jonathon Maltby (R.W.) (4) Capt. Joseph Maltby (3) Daniel Maltby (2) William Maltby (1)
* 33. Mrs. Charles P. Crosby (Frances Jane Maltby) Address: 511 West 111th Street, New York City, N. Y. * Deceased.	De Salvo Maltby (7) Anson Maltby (6) Timothy Maltby (1812) (5) Samuel Maltby (4) Samuel Maltby (3) Samuel Maltby (2) William Maltby (1)
34. Mrs. Charles W. Crouter (Mabel R. Hill) Address: Wheatland, Wyoming	Adelia Mariah Maltbie (7) Noah Maltbie (6) Noah Maltbie (5) Noah Maltbie (R.W.) (4) Capt. Joseph Maltbie (3) Daniel Maltbie (2) William Maltbie (1)
35. Mrs. Frederick H. Crum (Louise Maltbie) Address: River Edge, New Jersey	William Edward Maltbie (7) William Davenport Maltbie (6) William Davenport Maltbie (5) David Maltbie (R.W.) (4) David Maltbie (3) Jonathon Maltbie (2) William Maltbie (1)
36. Mrs. John Paine Cushman (Henrietta Caroline Maltby) Address: Farmington, Maine	Rev. John Maltby (6) John Maltby (5) Samuel Maltby (4) Samuel Maltby (3) Samuel Maltby (2) William Maltby (1)
37. Dr. Mary Floyd Cushman, M.D. Address: Farmington, Maine	Henrietta Caroline Maltby (7) Rev. John Maltby (6) John Maltby (5) Samuel Maltby (4) Samuel Maltby (3) Samuel Maltby (2) William Maltby (1)
38. Mrs. Edward Julius Daniels (Grace Tryon Maltby) Address: 75 Heights Road, Ridgewood, New Jersey	Theodore Augustus Maltby (C.W.) (7) George Williams Maltby (6) Augustus Williams Maltby (5) Col. Stephen Maltby (4) Benjamin Maltby (R.W.) (3) Daniel Maltby (2) William Maltby (1)

* Deceased.

Name of Member	Line of Descent
39. Mr. Lloyd Chilton Davis Care Prof. Ralph Waldo Maltbie, Sierra Madre, California	Edith Brayton Maltbie (7) Seth Waldo Maltbie (C.W.) (6) Daniel Maltbie (5) Benjamin Maltbie (R.W.) (4) Daniel Maltbie (3) Daniel Maltbie (2) William Maltbie (1)
40. Mr. Henry Brown Dayton Address: Stamford, Connecticut	Julia Adelaide Brown (7) Sarah Louise Newman (6) Stephen Newman (5) Sarah Maltby (4) David Maltbie (3) Jonathon Maltbie (2) William Maltbie (1)
41. Mrs. Lee Parker Dean (Seraph Elizabeth Maltbie) Address: Burton Halls, 10 Dana St., Cambridge, Massachusetts	Charles Benjamin Maltbie (6) Elon Maltbie (5) Benjamin Maltbie (R.W.) (4) Daniel Maltbie (3) Daniel Maltbie (2) William Maltbie (1)
42. Mrs. Samuel B. Doggett (Grace H. D) Address: 2018 Commonwealth Ave., Boston, Massachusetts	Julia Adelaide Brown (7) Sarah Louise Newman (6) Stephen Newman (5) Sarah Maltby (4) David Maltbie (3) Jonathon Maltbie (2) William Maltbie (1)
43. Mrs. John William Dickman (Adella Goodrich Maltbie) Address: Fayette, Iowa	Henry Munson Maltbie (7) Milo Harrison Maltbie (6) Elon Maltbie (5) Benjamin Maltbie (R.W.) (4) Daniel Maltbie (3) Daniel Maltbie (2) William Maltbie (1)
44. Mr. John Holmes Drury Address: First National Bank, Troy, Ohio	Harriet Elizabeth Maltby (6) Jonathon Maltby (5) Rev. Jonathon Maltby (R.W.) (4) Benjamin Maltby (3) Daniel Maltby (2) William Maltby (1)
45. Major Reginald Love Foster Address: 732 West End Avenue, New York City, N. Y.	Lelia Love (6) Martha Church Maltby (5) Gen. Isaac Maltby (1812) (4) Benjamin Maltby (R.W.) (3) Daniel Maltby (2) William Maltby (1)
46. Miss Mary C. Gelston Address: 12 Geddes Heights, Ann Arbor, Michigan	Mills Bordwell Gelston (6) Rev. Maltby Gelston (5) Hugh Gelston (4) Mary Maltby (3) John Maltby (2) John Maltby (1)

Name of Member	Line of Descent
47. Mrs. David C. Graham (Marion Ella Maltby) Address: Decorah, Iowa	Alanson Thomas Maltby (6) Zacheus Maltby (5) Daniel Maltby (4) Daniel Maltby (3) Daniel Maltby (2) William Maltby (1)
48. Mrs. Bristol Gram (Mabel Hibbard) Address: Enderlin, North Dakota	Beulah Ann Morris Maltby (7) Timothy Maltby (1812) (6) Timothy Maltby (5) Samuel Maltby (4) Samuel Maltby (3) Samuel Maltby (2) William Maltby (1)
49. Miss Edith Maltby Green Address: 40 Boyden Street, East Orange, New Jersey	Edith Rebecca Maltby (8) Theodore Augustus Maltby (R.W.) (7) George Williams Maltby (6) Augustus Williams Maltby (5) Col. Stephen Maltby (4) Benjamin Maltby (3) Daniel Maltby (2) William Maltby (1)
50. Mrs. William Greene (Jessie Maltby) Address: 607 West 139th Street, New York City, N. Y.	Hiram Maltby (7) Timothy Maltby (1812) (6) Timothy Maltby (5) Samuel Maltby (4) Samuel Maltby (3) Samuel Maltby (2) William Maltby (1)
51. Mrs. Herbert Hallenberg (Marjory Marsh) Address: Carson, Morton County, North Dakota	Phebe Adaline Maltby (7) Thomas Alanson Maltby (6) Zacheus Maltby (5) Daniel Maltby (4) Daniel Maltby (3) Daniel Maltby (2) William Maltby (1)
52. Mrs. James William Hamilton (Julia R. Maltby) Pulaski, New York	Albert Alexander Maltby (C.W.) (8) Hiram Maltby (7) Timothy Maltby (1812) (6) Timothy Maltby (5) Samuel Maltby (4) Samuel Maltby (3) Samuel Maltby (2) William Maltby (1)
* 53. Mrs. Otis Loring Hamilton (Harriet Mirander Murray) Address: P. O. Box 396, Santa Monica, California	Harriet Maltby (6) Chandler Maltby (5) Joseph Maltby (4) Capt. Joseph Maltby (3) Daniel Maltby (2) William Maltby (1)

* Deceased.

Name of Member	Line of Descent
54. Miss Grace Estelle Hankin Address: 38 Franklin Avenue, Passaic, New Jersey	Nina Maltby (9) Albert Alexander Maltby (C.W.) (8) Hiram Maltby (7) Timothy Maltby (1812) (6) Timothy Maltby (5) Samuel Maltby (4) Samuel Maltby (3) Samuel Maltby (2) William Maltby (1)
55. Miss Mildred Maltby Hankin Address: 38 Franklin Avenue, Passaic, New Jersey	Nina Maltby (9) Albert Alexander Maltby (C.W.) (8) Hiram Maltby (7) Timothy Maltby (1812) (6) Timothy Maltby (5) Samuel Maltby (4) Samuel Maltby (3) Samuel Maltby (2) William Maltby (1)
56. Mrs. Richard Hankin (Nina Maltby) Address: 38 Franklin Avenue, Passaic, New Jersey	Albert A. Maltby (C.W.) (8) Hiram Maltby (7) Timothy Maltby (1812) (6) Timothy Maltby (5) Samuel Maltby (4) Samuel Maltby (3) Samuel Maltby (2) William Maltby (1)
57. Mrs. George B. Haven (Margaret Jackson Cushman) Address: Needham, Massachusetts	Henrietta Caroline Maltby (7) Rev. John Maltby (6) John Maltby (5) Samuel Maltby (4) Samuel Maltby (3) Samuel Maltby (2) William Maltby (1)
58. Mrs. Albert Tracy Higby (Mary Love Maltby) Address: Summerfield, Marion County, Florida	Maj. Seth Murray Maltby (1812) (5) Gen. Isaac Maltby (1812) (5) Benjamin Maltby (R.W.) (3) Daniel Maltby (2) William Maltby (1)
59. Mr. Frederic Maltby Hoblit Address: Springfield, Illinois	Louise Maltby (7) Harrison Maltby (6) Jesse Maltby (5) Jonathon Maltby (R.W.) (4) Capt. Joseph Maltby (3) Daniel Maltby (2) William Maltby (1)
60. Mrs. James T. Hoblit (Louise Maltby) Address: Bates Apartment, 128 South Logan Street, Lincoln, Illinois	Harrison Maltby (6) Jesse Maltby (5) Jonathon Maltby (R.W.) (4) Capt. Joseph Maltby (3) Daniel Maltby (2) William Maltby (1)

Name of Member	Line of Descent
61. Mrs. Eugene E. Holroyd (Fannie Maltby) Care Young Women's Christian Association, 255 Hill Street, Los Angeles, California	Lauren Baldwin Maltby (6) Jesse Maltby (5) Benjamin Maltby (R.W.) (4) Daniel Maltby (3) Daniel Maltby (2) William Maltby (1)
62. Mrs. William C. Horworth (Laura Leota Cope) Address: 107 West 5th Street, Mitchell, South Dakota	Cynthia Ann Murray (7) Harriet Maltby (6) Chandler Maltby (5) Joseph Maltby (4) Capt. Joseph Maltby (3) Daniel Maltby (2) William Maltby (1)
63. Mrs. William Houser (Amelia Maltby) Address: 309 Tremont Street, Lincoln, Illinois	Harrison Maltby (6) Jesse Maltby (5) Jonathon Maltby (R.W.) (4) Capt. Joseph Maltby (3) Daniel Maltby (2) William Maltby (1)
64. Mrs. Alfred A. Howard (Lydia Jane Maltbie) Address: Greeley, Colorado	Noah Maltbie (6) Noah Maltbie (5) Noah Maltbie (R.W.) (4) Capt. Joseph Maltbie (3) Daniel Maltby (2) William Maltbie (1)
65. Mrs. William R. Hubbell (Carril Belle Maltbie) Address: Falls Village Connecticut	Charles Benjamin Maltbie (6) Elon Maltbie (5) Benjamin Maltbie (R.W.) (4) Daniel Maltbie (3) Daniel Maltbie (2) William Maltbie (1)
66. Mrs. Ralph U. Kent (Janet Norton) Address: 252 Crescent Avenue, San Francisco, California	Edward Norton (6) Julia Ann Maltby (5) Gen. Isaac Maltby (1812) (4) Benjamin Maltby (R.W.) (3) Daniel Maltby (2) William Maltby (1)
67. Mr. Maltby Gelston Leach Address: Sherman, Connecticut	Betsy Gelston (7) Hugh Gelston (6) Rev. Maltby Gelston (5) Hugh Gelston (4) Mary Maltby (3) John Maltby (2) William Maltby (1)
68. Mrs. Charles E. Lester (Edna May Brush) Address: Lester Hotel, Estes Park, Colorado	Ada May Maltbie (7) Noah Maltbie (6) Noah Maltbie (5) Noah Maltbie (R.W.) (4) Capt. Joseph Maltbie (3) Daniel Maltbie (2) William Maltbie (1)

Name of Member	Line of Descent
69. Mrs. Charles Lewis (Mary L. Maltby) Address: c/o Charles Eli Maltby, Esq. South Rutland, New York.	Chauncy Maltby (7) Milo Maltby (6) Rev. Joseph Maltby (5) Joseph Maltby (4) Capt. Joseph Maltby (3) Daniel Maltby (2) William Maltby (1)
70. Capt. Ray Keyes Linsley (S. A. W.) Address: 22 High Street, Bristol, Connecticut	Rev. Harvey Linsley (6) John Stephen Linsley (5) Sarah Maltby (4) Benjamin Maltby (R.W.) (3) Daniel Maltby (2) William Maltby (1)
71. Miss Maria Maltby Love Address: 184 Delaware Avenue, Buffalo, New York	Maria Maltby (5) Gen. Isaac Maltby (1812) (4) Benjamin Maltby (R.W.) (3) Daniel Maltby (2) William Maltby (1)
72. Mr. Alfred Maltbie Lynes Address: 1628 Garden Street, Santa Barbara, California	Stephen Coley Lynes (6) Hannah Maltbie (5) Cajt. Jonathon Maltbie (R.W.) (4) Jonathon Maltbie (3) Jonathon Maltbie (2) William Maltbie (1)
73. Mr. Edward Hoffman Lynes Address: 249 Warren Street, Hudson, New York	Edward Lynes (6) Hannah Maltbie (5) Capt. Jonathon Maltbie (R.W.) (4) Jonathon Maltbie (3) Jonathon Maltbie (2) William Maltbie (1)
74. Miss Emily Augusta Lynes Address: 38 West Avenue, Norwalk, Connecticut	Dr. Samuel Lynes (6) Hannah Maltbie (5) Capt. Jonathon Maltbie (4) (R.W.) Jonathon Maltbie (3) Jonathon Maltbie (2) William Maltbie (1)
75. Miss Grace Elizabeth Lynes Address: 158 West 75th Street, New York City, N. Y.	Benjamin Lynes (6) Hannah Maltbie (5) Capt. Jonathon Maltbie (4) (R.W.) Jonathon Maltbie (3) Jonathon Maltbie (2) William Maltbie (1)
76. Mr. Samuel Lynes Address: 38 West Avenue, Norwalk, Connecticut	Dr. Samuel Lynes (6) Hannah Maltbie (5) Capt. Jonathon Maltbie (R.W.) (4) Jonathon Maltbie, Jr. (3) Jonathon Maltbie (2) William Maltbie (1)

Name of Member	Line of Descent
77. Mr. Albert Edward Maltby Address: 400 South Lansdowne Ave. Lansdowne, Pennsylvania	Ulric Z. Maltby (C.W.) (8) Hiram Maltby (7) Timothy Maltby (1812) (6) Timothy Maltby (5) Samuel Maltby (4) Samuel Maltby (3) Samuel Maltby (2) William Maltby (1)
78. Mr. Albert Elias Maltby Address: Slippery Rock, Pennsylvania	John Maltby (7) Timothy Maltby (1812) (6) Timothy Maltby (5) Samuel Maltby (4) Samuel Maltby (3) Samuel Maltby (2) William Maltby (1)
79. Mr. Albert Lyman Maltbie Address: Waterville, Washington	James Downing Maltbie (C.W.) (7) Noah Maltbie (6) Noah Maltbie (5) Noah Maltbie (R.W.) (4) Capt. Joseph Maltbie (3) Daniel Maltbie (2) William Maltbie (1)
80. Miss Alice Barnet Maltby Address: 5423 Julian Avenue, Indianapolis, Indiana	Charles Stevens Maltby (S.A.W.) (7) George Beecher Maltby (6) Gen. Seth Murray Maltby (1812) (5) Gen. Isaac Maltby (1812) (4) Benjamin Maltby (R.W.) (3) Daniel Maltby (2) William Maltby (1)
81. Mr. Allan Jay Maltby Address: Forman, North Dakota	Jay Hayes Maltby (8) Dr. Dexter J. Maltby (C.W.) (7) Calvin Maltby (6) Rev. Joseph Maltby (5) Joseph Maltby (4) Capt. Joseph Maltby (3) Daniel Maltby (2) William Maltby (1)
82. Mr. Andrew B. Maltby Address: Corning, New York	Jerome B. Maltby (7) Curtis White Maltby (6) Erastus Maltby (5) Joseph Maltby (4) Capt. Joseph Maltby (3) Daniel Maltby (2) William Maltby (1)
83. Miss Anne Goggin Maltby Address: Washington, Mason County, Kentucky	Lucian Goggin Maltby (8) Col. Ralph Robinson Maltby (C.W.) (7) Timothy Maltby (1812) (6) Timothy Maltby (5) Samuel Maltby (4) Samuel Maltby (3) Samuel Maltby (2) William Maltby (1)

Name of Member	Line of Descent
84. Miss Anna Fay Maltby Address: Adams Center, Jefferson County, New York	Monroe E. Maltby (7) (C.W.) Calvin Maltby (6) Rev. Joseph Maltby (5) Joseph Maltby (4) Capt. Joseph Maltby (3) Daniel Maltby (2) William Maltby (1)
85. Miss Anna Louise Maltby Address: Forman, North Dakota	Jay Hayes Maltby (8) Dr. Dexter J. Maltby (C.W.) (7) Calvin Maltby (6) Rev. Joseph Maltby (5) Joseph Maltby (4) Capt. Joseph Maltby (3) Daniel Maltby (2) William Maltby (1)
86. Mr. Appleton Noah Maltby (C.W.) Address: Oakdale, Wisconsin	Noah Maltbie (6) Noah Maltbie (5) Noah Maltbie (R.W.) (4) Capt. Joseph Maltbie (3) Daniel Maltby (2) William Maltbie (1)
* 87. Mrs. Armstrong Maltbie (Annie Catherine Maltbie) Address: 213 James Street, Syracuse, New York	Ebenezer Davenport Maltbie (5) David Maltbie (R.W.) (4) David Maltbie (3) Jonathon Maltbie (2) William Maltbie (1)
88. Mr. Arthur Norman Maltby Address: 619 Dwight Building, Kansas City, Missouri	Norman Maltby (6) John Maltby (5) William Maltby (R.W.) (4) Capt. Joseph Maltby (3) Daniel Maltby (2) William Maltby (1)
89. Miss Belva A. Maltby Address: Forman, North Dakota	Jay Hayes Maltby (8) Dr. Dexter J. Maltby (C.W.) (7) Calvin Maltby (6) Rev. Joseph Maltby (5) Joseph Maltby (4) Capt. Joseph Maltby (3) Daniel Maltby (2) William Maltby (1)
90. Dr. Benjamin Thomas Maltby Address: Long Beach, California	Harrison Maltby (6) Daniel Maltbie (5) Benjamin Maltby (R.W.) (4) Daniel Maltby (3) Daniel Maltby (2) William Maltby (1)

* Deceased.

Name of Member	Line of Descent
91. Mr. Birdsey Lucius Maltbie Address: East Orange, New Jersey	Lucius Harvey Maltbie (7) Birdsey Maltbie (6) Jekiel Maltbie (5) Daniel Maltbie (4) Daniel Maltbie (3) Daniel Maltbie (2) William Maltbie (1) Lucius Harvey Maltbie (7) Molly Rose Maltbie (5) Charlotte Tucker (6) Zacheus Maltbie (4) Daniel Maltbie (3) Daniel Maltbie (2) William Maltbie (1)
92. Brough Maltby, Esq. Address: Beddington Lane, Near West Croydon, Surrey, England	Brough Maltby (6) Charles Langley Maltby (5) Brough Maltby (4) Samuel Maltby (3) George Maltby (2) William Maltby (1) of Orston, Notts.
93. Mr. Brough Maltby, Jr. Address: Atlanta, Kings County, Nova Scotia, Canada	Brough Maltby (7) Brough Maltby (6) Charles Langley Maltby (5) Brough Maltby (4) Samuel Maltby (3) George Maltby (2) William Maltby (1) of Orston, Notts
94. Mr. Byron Wilbur Maltby Address: R. F. D. No. 4, Trail Post Office, Oregon	William Maltby (6) Rev. Joseph Maltby (5) Joseph Maltby (4) Capt. Joseph Maltby (3) Daniel Maltby (2) William Maltby (1)
95. Mr. Charles Eli Maltby Address: South Rutland, New York	Chauncy Maltby (7) Milo Maltby (6) Rev. Joseph Maltby (5) Joseph Maltby (4) Capt. Joseph Maltby (3) Daniel Maltby (2) William Maltby (1)
96. Mr. Charles Stevens Maltby (S. A. W.) Address: 5423 Julian Avenue, Indianapolis, Indiana	George Beecher Maltby (6) Gen. Seth Murray Maltby (1812) (5) Gen. Isaac Maltby (1812) (4) Benjamin Maltby (R.W.) (3) Daniel Maltby (2) William Maltby (1)
97. Mr. Charles Sumner Maltbie Address: 6014 Hough Avenue, Cleveland, Ohio	Lauren Maltbie (6) Daniel Maltbie (5) Benjamin Maltbie (R.W.) (4) Daniel Maltbie (3) Daniel Maltbie (2) William Maltbie (1)

Name of Member	Line of Descent
98. Christopher James Maltby, Esq. Address: Harrow, Middlesex, England	Francis Newcombe Maltby (3) Thomas Maltby (2) Christopher Maltby (1) of Maltby in Cleveland, later of Northallerton, Yorks.
* 99. Rev. Clark O. Maltby Address: 730 East 26th Street, Paterson, New Jersey	Rev. Sherman Maltby (6) Rev. Joseph Maltby (5) Joseph Maltby (4) Capt. Joseph Maltby (3) Daniel Maltby (2) William Maltbie (1)
100. Mr. Clayton L. Maltby Address: Minnesota Avenue, Kansas City, Kansas	William Maltby, born about 1819 near Rochester, N. Y. Left home. Ancestry wanted.
101. Mr. Dexter Jay Maltby Address: Unknown	Mabel Maltby (8) Dr. Dexter Jay Maltby (C.W.) (7) Calvin Maltby (6) Rev. Joseph Maltby (5) Joseph Maltby (4) Capt. Joseph Maltby (3) Daniel Maltby (2) William Maltby (1)
102. Mrs. Douglas Fowler Maltby (Representing her husband) Address: Waterbury, Connecticut	Julius Maltby (5) Deacon Benjamin Maltby (4) Benjamin Maltby (R.W.) (3) Daniel Maltby (2) William Maltby (1)
103. Mr. Earl Orrin Maltby Address: Clio, Michigan	Grove Benjamin Maltby (7) Orrin Maltby (6) Chandler Maltby (5) Joseph Maltby (4) Capt. Joseph Maltby (3) Daniel Maltby (2) William Maltby (1)
104. Mr. Erwin Horace Maltby Address: Chardon, Ohio R. F. D. No. 3	Allen Maltby (6) Jehiel Merriman Maltby (5) Daniel Maltby (4) Daniel Maltby (3) Daniel Maltby (2) William Maltby (1)
105. Miss Esther Tapping Maltbie Address: 2101 N. Grant Street, Springfield, Missouri	Daniel Maltby (5) Benjamin Maltby (R.W.) (4) Daniel Maltby (3) Daniel Maltbie (2) William Maltby (1)

* Deceased.

Name of Member	Line of Descent
106. Miss Ethel Harriet Maltby Address: 66 East Second Street, Corning, New York	William Henry Maltby (2) Henry Vice Maltby (1) Descended from Christopher Maltby of Lincolnshire. Said to be nearly related to Bishop Maltby.
107. Miss Floy A. Maltby Address: Forman, North Dakota	Jay Hayes Maltby (8) Dr. Dexter Jay Maltby (C.W.) (7) Calvin Maltby (6) Rev. Joseph Maltby (5) Joseph Maltby (4) Capt. Joseph Maltby (3) Daniel Maltby (2) William Maltby (1)
108. Miss Frances Nelson Maltby Address: Washington, Mason County, Kentucky	Lucian Goggin Maltby (8) Col. Ralph Robinson Maltby (C.W.) (7) Timothy Maltby (1812) (6) Timothy Maltby (5) Samuel Maltby (4) Samuel Maltby (3) Samuel Maltby (2) William Maltby (1)
109. Mr. Francis Vail Maltby Address: Forman, North Dakota	Jay Hayes Maltby (8) Dr. Dexter Jay Maltby (C.W.) (7) Calvin Maltby (6) Rev. Joseph Maltby (5) Joseph Maltby (4) Capt. Joseph Maltby (3) Daniel Maltby (2) William Maltby (1)
110. Mr. Frank Maltby Address: Madisonville, Ohio	Grandson of James Maltby of Belloit, Wisconsin. Ancestry never sent to secretary.
111. Mr. Frank Bierce Maltby Address: 611 Chestnut Street, Philadelphia, Pennsylvania	Warren Maltby (6) Nathaniel Harrison Maltby (5) Benjamin Maltby (R.W.) (4) Daniel Maltby (3) Daniel Maltby (2) William Maltby (1)
112. Mr. Frank Calvin Maltby Address: 1153 Market Street, Williamsport, Pennsylvania	Franklin Calvin Maltby (7) Rev. Horace Maltby (6) Rev. Joseph Maltby (5) Joseph Maltby (4) Capt. Joseph Maltby (3) Daniel Maltby (2) William Maltby (1)
113. Mr. Frank Gilbert Maltby Address: Prosper, Minnesota	Corydon Oscar Maltby (C.W.) (7) Alanson Thomas Maltby (6) Zacheus Maltby (5) Daniel Maltby (4) Daniel Maltby (3) Daniel Maltby (2) William Maltby (1)

Name of Member	Line of Descent
* 114. Mr. George Beecher Maltby Address: 65 Fourth Street, Aurora, Indiana	Maj. Seth Murray Maltby (1812) (5) Gen. Isaac Maltby (1812) (4) Benjamin Maltby (R.W.) (3) Daniel Maltby (2) William Maltby (1)
115. Mr. George Beecher Maltby, 2nd Address: 1931 East 101st Street, Cleveland, Ohio	John Whitehouse Maltby (6) Maj. Seth Murray Maltby (1812) (5) Gen. Isaac Maltby (1812) (4) Benjamin Maltby (R.W.) (3) Daniel Maltby (2) William Maltby (1)
116. Mr. George Dewey Maltby Address: Forman, North Dakota	Jay Hayes Maltby (8) Dr. Dexter Jay Maltby (C.W.) (7) Calvin Maltby (6) Rev. Joseph Maltby (5) Joseph Maltby (4) Capt. Joseph Maltby (3) Daniel Maltby (2) William Maltby (1)
117. Mr. George Edward Maltby Address: Jamestown, New York	George Washington Maltby (6) William Maltby (5) William Maltby (R.W.) (4) Capt. Joseph Maltby (3) Daniel Maltby (2) William Maltby (1)
118. Mrs. George Ellsworth Maltby (Representing her husband) Address: 910 The Boulevard, North Vancouver, B. C., Canada	George Williams Maltby (6) Augustus Williams Maltby (5) Col. Stephen Maltby (4) Benjamin Maltby (R.W.) (3) Daniel Maltby (2) William Maltby (1)
119. Miss Grace Maltby Address: 65 Fourth Street, Aurora, Indiana	George Beecher Maltby (6) Maj. Seth Murray Maltby (1812) (5) Gen. Isaac Maltby (1812) (4) Benjamin Maltby (R.W.) (3) Daniel Maltby (2) William Maltby (1)
120. Mr. Grove B. Maltby Address: Clio, Michigan	Orrin Maltby (6) Chandler Maltby (5) Joseph Maltby (4) Capt. Joseph Maltby (3) Daniel Maltby (2) William Maltby (1) Betsey Cook (7) Jernstra Hosmer (6) Mary Maltby (5) Joseph Maltby (4) Capt. Joseph Maltby (3) Daniel Maltby (2) William Maltby (1)

* Deceased.

Name of Member	Line of Descent
121. Mr. Harold Maltby Address: Sedalia, Missouri	William John Maltby (7) Norman Maltby (6) John Maltby (5) William Maltby (R.W.) (4) Capt. Joseph Maltby (3) Daniel Maltby (2) William Maltby (1)
122. Mr. Henry F. Maltby Address: Oakwood Stock Farm, Brighton, Michigan	Almon Maltby (6) Grove Maltby (5) Joseph Maltby (4) Capt. Joseph Maltby (3) Daniel Maltby (2) William Maltby (1)
123. Mr. Howard Scott Maltby Address: 115 South West Fifth St., Richmond, Indiana	George Beecher Maltby (6) Maj. Seth Murray Maltby (1812) (5) Gen. Isaac Maltby (1812) (4) Benjamin Maltby (R.W.) (3) Daniel Maltby (2) William Maltby (1)
124. Miss Jane Maltby Address: 66 East Second Street, Corning, New York	William Henry Maltby (2) Henry Vice Maltby (1) Descended from Christopher Maltby of Lincolnshire. Said to be nearly related to Bishop Maltby.
125. Mr. Jay Hayes Maltby Address: Forman, North Dakota	Dr. Dexter Jay Maltby (C.W.) (7) Calvin Maltby (6) Rev. Joseph Maltby (5) Joseph Maltby (4) Capt. Joseph Maltby (3) Daniel Maltby (2) William Maltby (1)
126. Mr. Julius Maltby Address: Waterbury, Connecticut	Douglas Fowler Maltby (6) Julius Maltby (5) Deacon Benjamin Maltby (4) Benjamin Maltby (R.W.) (3) Daniel Maltby (2) William Maltby (1)
127. Mr. Lucien Goggin Maltby Address: Washington, Mason County, Kentucky	Col. Ralph Robinson Maltby (C.W.) (7) Timothy Maltby (1812) (6) Timothy Maltby (5) Samuel Maltby (4) Samuel Maltby (3) Samuel Maltby (2) William Maltby (1)
128. Mr. Lucius Upson Maltby Address: St. Davids, Pennsylvania	Lucius Maltby (5) Rev. Jonathon Maltby (R.W.) (4) Benjamin Maltby (R.W.) (3) Daniel Maltby (2) William Maltby (1)

Name of Member	Line of Descent
129. Miss Mabel E. Maltby Address: 66 East Second Street, Corning, N. Y.	William Henry Maltby (2) Henry Vice Maltby (1) Descended from Christopher Maltby of Lincolnshire. Said to be nearly related to Bishop Maltby.
130. Miss Mabel Elizabeth Maltby Address: 1931 East 101st Street, Cleveland, Ohio	George Beecher Maltby, 2d (7) John Whitehouse Maltby (6) Maj. Seth Murray Maltby (1812) (5) Gen. Isaac Maltby (1812) (4) Benjamin Maltby (R.W.) (3) Daniel Maltby (2) William Maltby (1)
131. Miss Margaret E. Maltby Address: Barnard College, Columbia University, New York City, N. Y.	Edmund Maltby (6) Nathaniel Harrison Maltby (5) Benjamin Maltby (R.W.) (4) Daniel Maltby (3) Daniel Maltby (2) William Maltby (1)
132. Miss Margaret McCurley Maltbie Address: Care W. H. Maltbie, Esq., 2730 N. Charles Street, Baltimore, Maryland	William Henry Maltbie (8) Silas Benjamin Maltbie (7) Harrison Maltbie (6) Benjamin Maltbie (5) Benjamin Maltbie (R.W.) (4) Daniel Maltbie (3) Daniel Maltbie (2) William Maltbie (1)
133. Miss Martha J. Maltby Address: 112 Hamilton Street, Columbus, Ohio	Edmund Maltby (6) Nathanial Harrison Maltby (5) Benjamin Maltby (R.W.) (4) Daniel Maltby (3) Daniel Maltby (2) William Maltby (1)
* 134. Miss Mary J. Maltby Address: Northford, Connecticut	Deacon William Maltby (6) Henry Maltby (5) James Maltby (4) Samuel Maltby (3) Samuel Maltby (2) William Maltby (1)
135. Miss Mary Page Maltby Address: Washington, Mason County, Kentucky	Lucian Goggin Maltby (8) Col. Ralph Robinson Maltby (C.W.) (7) Timothy Maltby (1812) (6) Timothy Maltby (5) Samuel Maltby (4) Samuel Maltby (3) Samuel Maltby (2) William Maltby (1)

* Deceased.

Name of Member	Line of Descent
136. Miss Maude Townshend Maltby Address: 910 The Boulevard North Vancouver, B. C., Canada	George Ellsworth Maltby (7) George Williams Maltby (6) Augustus Williams Maltby (5) Col Stephen Maltby (4) Benjamin Maltby (3) (R.W.) Daniel Maltby (2) William Maltby (1)
137. Miss Mildred Nelson Maltby Address: 1931 East 101st Street, Cleveland, Ohio	George Beecher Maltby, 2d (7) John Whitehouse Maltby (6) Maj. Seth Murray Maltby (1812) (5) Gen. Isaac Maltby (1812) (4) Benjamin Maltby (R.W.) (3) Daniel Maltby (2) William Maltby (1)
138. Mr. Milo Roy Maltbie Address: 593 Riverside Drive, New York City, N. Y.	Henry Munson Maltbie (7) Milo Harrison Maltbie (6) Elon Maltbie (5) Benjamin Maltbie (R.W.) (4) Daniel Maltbie (3) Daniel Maltbie (2) William Maltbie (1)
139. Mr. Monroe E. Maltby (C. W.) Address: P. O. Box 88, Adams Center, Jefferson County, New York	Calvin Maltby (6) Rev. Joseph Maltby (5) Joseph Maltby (4) Capt. Joseph Maltby (3) Daniel Maltby (2) William Maltby (1)
140. Miss Nettie Grace Maltby Address: Medora, Kansas	Albert Paxton Maltby (7) Lauren Baldwin Maltby (6) Jesse Maltby (5) Benjamin Maltby (R.W.) (4) Daniel Maltby (3) Daniel Maltby (2) William Maltby (1)
141. Mr. Ralph Maltby Address: Lyeth Avenue, Gates, Monroe County, N. Y. Care Lincoln Park P. O.	Henry Maltby (6) Maj. Seth Murray Maltby (1812) (5) Gen. Isaac Maltby (1812) (4) Benjamin Maltby (R.W.) (3) Daniel Maltby (2) William Maltby (1)
142. Mr. Ralph Benjamin Maltby Address: 12047 Lake Avenue, Lakewood, Ohio	Benjamin Maltby (6) Nathaniel Harrison Maltby (5) Benjamin Maltby (R.W.) (4) Daniel Maltby (3) Daniel Maltby (2) William Maltby (1)
143. Col. Ralph Robinson Maltby (C.W.) Address: Washington, Mason County, Kentucky	Timothy Maltby (1812) (6) Timothy Maltby (5) Samuel Maltby (4) Samuel Maltby (3) Samuel Maltby (2) William Maltby (1)

Name of Member	Line of Descent
144. Prof. Ralph Waldo Maltbie Address: Sierra Madre, California	Seth Waldo Maltbie (C.W.) (6) Daniel Maltbie (5) Benjamin Maltbie (R.W.) (4) Daniel Maltbie (3) Daniel Maltbie (2) William Maltbie (1)
* 145. Lieut-Col. Richard Leighton Maltby Address: Newcastle, New Brunswick, Canada	Thomas Maltby (5) Thomas Baker Maltby (4) Thomas Maltby (3) John Maltby (2) William Maltby (1) of Scarborough, Yorkshire.
146. Captain Seth Waldo Maltbie (C. W.) Address: Care Prof. R. W. Maltbie, Sierra Madre, California	Daniel Maltbie (5) Benjamin Maltbie (R.W.) (4) Daniel Maltbie (3) Daniel Maltbie (2) William Maltbie (1)
147. Mr. Ulric Z. Maltby (C.W.) Address: 3 West Mohawk Street, Oswego, New York	Hiram Maltby (7) Timothy Maltby (1812) (6) Timothy Maltby (5) Samuel Maltby (4) Samuel Maltby (3) Samuel Maltby (2) William Maltby (1)
148. Miss Violet Maltby Address: Forman, North Dakota	Jay Hayes Maltby (8) Dr. Dexter Jay Maltby (C.W.) (7) Calvin Maltby (6) Rev. Joseph Maltby (5) Joseph Maltby (4) Capt. Joseph Maltby (3) Daniel Maltby (2) William Maltby (1)
149. Miss Winona N. Maltby Address: 7320 44th Ave., S. W. Seattle, Washington	Arthur Ives Maltby (7) Epaphras Chapman Maltby (6) Julius Maltby (5) Deacon Benjamin Maltby (4) Benjamin Maltby (R.W.) (3) Daniel Maltby (2) William Maltby (1)
150. Mr. Wilburt Stevens Maltby Address: 1203 Putnam Avenue, Plainfield, New Jersey	Epaphras Chapman Maltby (6) Julius Maltby (5) Benjamin Maltby (4) Benjamin Maltby (R.W.) (3) Daniel Maltby (2) William Maltby (1)
151. Mr. William Davenport Maltbie, 3rd Address unknown	Armstrong Maltbie (7) William Davenport Maltbie (6) William Davenport Maltbie (5) David Maltbie (R.W.) (4) David Maltbie (3) Jonathon Maltbie (2) William Maltbie (1)

* Deceased.

Name of Member	Line of Descent
152. Mr. William Henry Maltbie Address: 728 Equitable Building, Baltimore, Maryland	Silas Benjamin Maltbie (7) Harrison Maltbie (6) Benjamin Maltbie (5) Benjamin Maltbie (R.W.) (4) Daniel Maltbie (3) Daniel Maltbie (2) William Maltbie (1)
153. Mr. William Lassie Maltby Address: 309 St. James Street, Montreal, Canada	Samuel Maltby (2) Samuel Maltby 1) of Leeds, Yorkshire, England.
154. Mrs. Martin S. Mayhew (Betsey Patchin Maltby) Address: Cortland, Trumbull County, Ohio	Edmund Maltby (6) Nathaniel Harrison Maltby (5) Benjamin Maltby (R.W.) (4) Daniel Maltby (3) Daniel Maltby (2) William Maltby (1)
155. Mrs. Frank Earle McChesney (Ruth Maltby Austin) Address: Pulaski, New York	Alta Jane Maltby (8) Charles Rollin Maltby (7) Timothy Maltby (1812) (6) Timothy Maltby (5) Samuel Maltby (4) Samuel Maltby (3) Samuel Maltby (2) William Maltby (1)
156. Miss Clara Elizabeth McGeer Address: 1 Court Street, Auburn, New York	Arietta Montgomery Wilson (7) Margaret Ann Maltby (6) Zacheus Maltby (5) Daniel Maltby (4) Daniel Maltby (3) Daniel Maltby (2) William Maltby (1)
157. Mr. Frederic Cook Morehouse Address: 484 Milwaukee Street, Milwaukee, Wisconsin	Linden Husted Morehouse (6) Andrew Morehouse (5) Sarah Bulkley Morehouse (4) Hannah Maltbie (3) Jonathon Maltbie (2) William Maltbie (1)
158. Mrs. Oliver P. Morton (Anna Agnes Maltby) Address: R. F. D. No. 3, Excelsior, Minnesota	Dr. Dexter Jay Maltby (C.W.) (7) Calvin Maltby (6) Rev. Joseph Maltby (5) Joseph Maltby (4) Capt. Joseph Maltby (3) Daniel Maltby (2) William Maltby (1)
* 159. Mr. Williams Rogers Murray Address: 1148 Fourth Street, Santa Monica, California	Harriet Maltby (6) Chandler Maltby (5) Joseph Maltby (4) Capt. Joseph Maltby (3) Daniel Maltby (2) William Maltby (1)

* Deceased.

Name of Member	Line of Descent
160. Mr. Francis Tracy Norton Address: Care Mrs. R. N. Kent, 252 Crescent Avenue, San Francisco, California	Edward Norton (6) Julia Ann Maltby (5) Gen. Isaac Maltby (1812) (4) Benjamin Maltby (R.W.) (3) Daniel Maltby (2) William Maltby (1)
161. Mrs. Perry Oaks (Harriet Malvina Carter) Address: 517 Fifth Street, Flint, Michigan	Sabra Maltby (6) Chandler Maltby (5) Joseph Maltby (4) Capt. Joseph Maltby (3) Daniel Maltby (2) William Maltby (1)
162. Mrs. Robert Oglesby (Lucile Hoblit) Address: 1434 Boulder Avenue, Tulsa, Oklahoma	Louise Maltby (7) Harrison Maltby (6) Jesse Maltby (5) Jonathon Maltby (R.W.) (4) Capt. Joseph Maltby (3) Daniel Maltby. (2) William Maltby (1)
163. Mrs. Anton Frank Overman (Etta Marian French) Address: 877 Cleveland Avenue, Portland, Oregon	Florence Isabella Maltby (7) Daniel Maltby (6) William Maltby (5) William Maltby (R.W.) (4) Capt. Joseph Maltby (3) Daniel Maltby (2) William Maltby (1)
164. Mr. John Orville Parrish Address: R. D. Route, No. 24, Plymouth, Wisconsin	Jane Maltby (7) Timothy Maltby (1812) (6) Timothy Maltby (5) Samuel Maltby (4) Samuel Maltby (3) Samuel Maltby (2) William Maltby (1)
165. Mrs. William Davis Patterson (Louise Marguerite Dayton) Address: High School, Wiscasset, Maine	Julia Adelaide Brown (7) Sarah Louise Newman (6) Stephen Newman (5) Sarah Maltby (4) David Maltbie (3) Jonathon Maltbie (2) William Maltbie (1)
166. Mrs. Sereno Payne (Flouretta Gertrude Knapp) Address: 11 James Street, Auburn, New York.	Oscar Fitzland Knapp (7) Mercy Burchard Maltby (6) Zacheus Maltby (5) Daniel Maltby (4) Daniel Maltby (3) Daniel Maltby (2) William Maltby (1)

Name of Member	Line of Descent
167. Rev. Dryden William Phelps Address: Hotel Duncan, New Haven, Conn.	I. Sophia Emilia Linsley (6) Rev. James Harvey Linsley (5) Sarah Maltby (4) Benjamin Maltby (R.W.) (3) Daniel Maltby (2) William Maltby (1) II. Sophia Emilia Linsley (7) Sophia Brainerd Lyon (6) William Lyon (5) Elizabeth Maltby (4) Nathaniel Maltby (3) John Maltby (2) William Maltby (1)
168. Mrs. Albert L. Potter (Hannah E. Hall) Address: Box 130, Philip, South Dakota	Lois Maltby (6) Rev. Joseph Maltby (5) Joseph Maltby (4) Capt. Joseph Maltby (3) Daniel Maltby (2) William Maltby (1)
169. Mrs. Milton Granger Rawlings (Achsah Adelia Maltbie) Address: Athol, Idaho	Albert Lyman Maltbie (8) James Downing Maltbie (C.W.) (7) Noah Maltbie (6) Noah Maltbie (5) Noah Maltbie (R.W.) (4) Capt. Joseph Maltbie (3) Daniel Maltbie (2) William Maltbie (1)
170. Mrs. Frederick Daniel Rugg (Cora May Maltby) Address: 507 W. University Avenue, Champaign, Illinois	Warren Maltby (6) Nathaniel Harrison Maltby (5) Benjamin Maltby (R.W.) (4) Daniel Maltby (3) Daniel Maltby (2) William Maltby (1)
171. Mrs. Frederick G. Schleswiger (Marcia De Salvo Maltby) Address: 500 West 143rd Street, New York City, New York	De Salvo Maltby (7) Anson Maltby (6) Timothy Maltby (5) Samuel Maltby (4) Samuel Maltby (3) Samuel Maltby (2) William Maltby (1)
172. Mrs. Truman Senear (Clara Ordilla Roberts) Address: 913 Mississippi Avenue, Beuridji, Minnesota	Cynthia Maltby (7) Milo Maltby (6) Rev. Joseph Maltby (5) Joseph Maltby (4) Capt. Joseph Maltby (3) Daniel Maltby (2) William Maltby (1)

Name of Member	Line of Descent
173. Mrs. Arthur Bliss Seymour (Anna Julia Conkling) Address: Waverly, Massachusetts	Mary Maltby (6) Daniel Maltby (5) Benjamin Maltby (R.W.) (4) Daniel Maltby (3) Daniel Maltby (2) William Maltby (1)
174. Mrs. Samuel E. Shipp (Nellie Maltby) Address: Newburgh, New York	Oliver Ellsworth Maltby (6) Lucius Maltby (5) Rev. Jonathon Maltby (R.W.) (4) Benjamin Maltby (R.W.) (3) Daniel Maltby (2) William Maltby (1)
175. Mr. Ernest C. Maltby Simpson Address: Gary, Indiana	Lydia Maltby (7) Daniel Maltby (6) William Maltby (5) William Maltby (R.W.) (4) Capt. Joseph Maltby (3) Daniel Maltby (2) William Maltby (1)
176. Mrs. Franklin Townsend Simpson (Lydia Maltby) Address: 513 South Second Street, Elkhart, Indiana	Daniel Maltby (6) William Maltby (5) William Maltby (R.W.) (4) Capt. Joseph Maltby (3) Daniel Maltby (2) William Maltby (1)
177. Mr. Louis Maltby Simpson Address: Elkhart, Indiana	Lydia Maltby (7) Daniel Maltby (6) William Maltby (5) William Maltby (R.W.) (4) Capt. Joseph Maltby (3) Daniel Maltby (2) William Maltby (1)
178. Mrs. Archer Jerome Smith (Susan Bronson Maltby) Address: 191 Prospect Street, Waterbury, Connecticut	Douglas Fowler Maltby (6) Julius Maltby (5) Deacon Benjamin Maltby (4) Benjamin Maltby (R.W.) (3) Daniel Maltby (2) William Maltby (1)
179. Mrs. Fred Sumner Smith (Louise Maltby) Address: Drawer D, Chester, Connecticut	George Erastus Maltby (6) Lucius Maltby (5) Rev. Jonathon Maltby (R.W.) (4) Benjamin Maltby (R.W.) (3) Daniel Maltby (2) William Maltby (1)
180. Mrs. David S. Stevens (Clara M. Maltby) Address: 5602 California Avenue, Seattle, Washington	Epaphras Chapman Maltby (6) Julius Maltby (5) Benjamin Maltby (4) Benjamin Maltby (R.W.) (3) Daniel Maltby (2) William Maltby (1)

Name of Member	Line of Descent
* 181. Mrs. Henry J. Stevens (Jane Almira Maltby) Address: 90 Grand Avenue, New Haven, Connecticut	Lucius Maltby (5) Rev. Jonathon Maltby (R.W.) (4) Benjamin Maltby (R.W.) (3) Daniel Maltby (2) William Maltby (1)
182. Mrs. John H. Taylor (Olive Elizabeth Dean) Address: 709 West 170th Street, New York City, New York	Seraph Elizabeth Maltbie (7) Charles Benjamin Maltbie (6) Elon Maltbie (5) Benjamin Maltbie (R.W.) (4) Daniel Maltbie (3) Daniel Maltbie (2) William Maltbie (1)
183. Mrs. Joshua Thompson (Juliette A. Cranston) Address: 408 Park Street, Owosso, Michigan	Almira Maltby (6) Jacob Maltby (5) Benjamin Maltby (R.W.) (4) Daniel Maltby (3) Daniel Maltby (2) William Maltby (1)
184. Mrs. William Taylor Thornton (Helen Maltby) Address: Care Mrs. John P. Victory, 129 Garcia Street, Santa Fe, New Mexico	Norman Maltby (6) John Maltby (5) William Maltby (R.W.) (4) Capt. Joseph Maltby (3) Daniel Maltby (2) William Maltby (1)
185. Mr. Eliot Winslow Todd Address: 703 George Street, New Haven, Connecticut	Eleanor Pierson Alling (8) Emily Williams Maltby (7) George Williams Maltby (6) Augustus Williams Maltby (5) Col. Stephen Maltby (4) Benjamin Maltby (3) (R.W.) Daniel Maltby (2) William Maltby (1)
186. Mrs. James Willey Todd (Eleanor Pierson Alling) Address: 703 George Street, New Haven, Connecticut	Emily Williams Maltby (7) George Williams Maltby (6) Augustus Williams Maltby (5) Col. Stephen Maltby (4) Benjamin Maltby (R.W.) (3) Daniel Maltby (2) William Maltby (1)
187. Mrs. Peter Vandarwarka (Hannah Dyantha Maltby) Address: Harrison, Alberta, Canada	Horace Maltby (6) Rev. Joseph Maltby (5) Joseph Maltby (4) Capt. Joseph Maltby (3) Daniel Maltby (2) William Maltby (1)

* Deceased.

Name of Member	Line of Descent
188. Mrs. Clarence Verrill (Dorothy Lord Maltby) Address: 518 Eighth Street, East, North Vancouver, British Columbia, Canada	George Ellsworth Maltby (7) George Williams Maltby (6) Augustus Williams Maltby (5) Col. Stephen Maltby (4) Benjamin Maltby (R.W.) (3) Daniel Maltby (2) William Maltby (1)
189. Miss Rae Maltby Verrill Address: 518 Eighth Street, East, North Vancouver, British Columbia, Canada	Dorothy Lord Maltby (8) George Ellsworth Maltby (7) George Williams Maltby (6) Augustus Williams Maltby (5) Col. Stephen Maltby (4) Benjamin Maltby (R.W.) (3) Daniel Maltby (2) William Maltby (1)
190. Mrs. John P. Victory (Mary Maltby) Address: 129 Garcia Street, Santa Fe, New Mexico	Norman Maltby (6) John Maltby (5) William Maltby (R.W.) (4) Capt. Joseph Maltby (3) Joseph Maltby (2) William Maltby (1)
191. Gov. Fred Maltby Warner Address: Farmington, Michigan	Governor Warner is a son of William Maltby of Hickling, Notts, Eng. His parents dying, he was adopted when two years of age by the Hon. P. Dean Warner of Farmington, Mich. We expect to connect his branch with the parent tree at no late date.
192. Mrs. Sydney R. Wells (Dorothy Maltby) Address: 12, Linden Road, Bedford, England	Christopher James Maltby (4) Francis Newcombe Maltby (3) Thomas Maltby (2) Christopher Maltby (1) of Northallerton, Yorkshire, England
193. Mrs. John N. Welsby (Leah Maltby) Address: Stevens Point, Wisconsin	Appleton Noah Maltby (7) Noah Maltby (6) Noah Maltby (5) Noah Maltby (R.W.) (4) Capt. Joseph Maltby (3) Daniel Maltby (2) William Maltby (1)
194. Mrs. Milton D. Whitney (Fanny R. Maltby) Address: R. F. D., Prosper, Minnesota	Corydon Oscar Maltby (C.W.) (7) Alanson Thomas Maltby (6) Zacheus Maltby (5) Daniel Maltby (4) Daniel Maltby (3) Daniel Maltby (2) William Maltby (1)

Name of Member	Line of Descent
195. Mrs. Charles E. Winter (Alice R. Maltby) Address: 839 South Walcott Street, Casper, Wyoming	Sylvester Daniel Maltby (C.W.) (7) Ezra Burchard Maltby (1812) (6) Zacheus Maltby (5) Daniel Maltby (4) Daniel Maltby (3) Daniel Maltby (2) William Maltby (1)
196. Mr. William Maltbie Wortendyke Address: River Edge, New Jersey	Louise Maltbie (8) William Edward Maltbie (7) William Davenport Maltbie (6) William Davenport Maltbie (5) David Maltbie (R.W.) (4) David Maltbie (3) Jonathon Maltbie (2) William Maltbie (1)

NOTE.—From the above list it will be seen that our members are scattered from Maine to California, residing in twenty-five different states, namely: California, Colorado, Connecticut, Florida, Illinois, Indiana, Kansas, Kentucky, Massachusetts, Maine, Maryland, Michigan, Minnesota, Missouri, New Jersey, New York, New Mexico, North Dakota, Oklahoma, Ohio, Oregon, Pennsylvania, South Dakota, Washington and Wisconsin. In Canada four provinces are represented, British Columbia, New Brunswick, Nova Scotia and Quebec, while we have one member in Bulgaria and another in England.

It will also be seen that our members are of the sixth, seventh, eighth and ninth generations. I do not think there is now living any Maltby of the fifth generation, and those of our members of the ninth generation are children, but there are living Maltby of the tenth and even the eleventh generation.